How Parliament Wor

Written by expert insiders, *How Parliament Works* is a straightforward and readable analysis of one of the country's most complex – and often misunderstood – institutions.

Covering every aspect of the work, membership and structures of both Houses, this key text provides a unique insight into the work and daily life of Parliament. It explains not only what happens but also why, and analyses the institution's strengths and weaknesses, as well as opportunities for Parliament to be more effective.

The seventh edition has been substantially revised to take account of recent changes in both Houses and to cover all the key issues affecting Parliament and politics, such as:

- the Fixed Term Parliaments Act;
- the implications of coalition politics;
- recent developments in Lords reform;
- the Independent Parliamentary Standards Authority's role in pay and expenses;
- advances in scrutiny techniques;
- changes in parliamentary cycles of business and finance;
- member conduct and interests;
- reform and modernisation.

It also covers the latest developments in the legislative process, party discipline and rebellion, the procedure of both Houses, select committee work, and the relationship between Parliament and the European Union. All statistics and examples have been fully updated.

How Parliament Works is essential reading for anyone who has anything to do with the Westminster Parliament: journalists, civil servants, lawyers, lobbyists, business and trade associations, diplomats, overseas parliaments and international bodies – and, indeed, members of both Houses.

Robert Rogers and **Rhodri Walters** retired from the service of the House of Commons and the House of Lords respectively, in 2014. Their careers covered every aspect of the work of both Houses and between them they amassed more than 80 years' experience of Parliament.

This really is how Parliament works. It is an expert, authoritative and unique insiders' view, and essential reading for everyone who wants to know about this complex institution. A truly indispensable book.

Betty Boothroyd (Baroness Boothroyd), Speaker of the House of Commons 1992–2000

Bang up to date, crystal clear and as insightful as ever – *How Parliament Works* is the essential guide to exactly what it says on the cover.

Nick Robinson, Political Editor, BBC

Always erudite, but never dull, it should be on the shelves of every Parliamentarian, and of everyone who really cares about Parliament. As indispensable as *Erskine May*, it is a masterpiece.

Patrick Cormack (Lord Cormack) Member of the House of Commons 1970–2010

Anyone wanting to know what really happens in Parliament – as opposed to the widely peddled myths – should read this latest edition of *How Parliament Works*. From a lifetime of experience at Westminster, the authors explain the procedures, powers and role – as well as, crucially, the culture and habits – in a readable way. No-one should put themselves up as a parliamentary candidate, or become a political journalist, or a senior civil servant, without reading this book.

Peter Riddell, Director, Institute for Government

This is the best introduction known to me and required reading for anyone who wishes to understand the working of Parliament. It is clear, thorough and authoritative.

Vernon Bogdanor, Professor of Government, King's College, London

How Parliament Works

Seventh edition

Robert Rogers and
Rhodri Walters

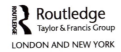
Routledge
Taylor & Francis Group

LONDON AND NEW YORK

First published 1987 by Pearson Education Limited
Sixth edition published 2006 by Pearson Education Limited

Seventh edition published 2015
by Routledge
2 Park Square, Milton Park, Abingdon, Oxon OX14 4RN

and by Routledge
711 Third Avenue, New York, NY 10017

Routledge is an imprint of the Taylor & Francis Group, an informa business

© 2015 Robert Rogers and Rhodri Walters

The right of Robert Rogers and Rhodri Walters to be identified as authors of this work has been asserted by them in accordance with sections 77 and 78 of the Copyright, Designs and Patents Act 1988.

British Library Cataloguing in Publication Data
A catalogue record for this book is available from the British Library

Library of Congress Cataloging in Publication Data
A catalog record for this book has been requested

ISBN: 978-1-138-84377-6 (hbk)
ISBN: 978-0-273-79037-2 (pbk)
ISBN: 978-1-315-73087-5 (ebk)

Typeset in Galliard and Frutiger
by Florence Production Ltd, Stoodleigh, Devon, UK

To those who believe that
Parliament matters

Contents

Foreword

IN THIS SEVENTH EDITION OF *How Parliament Works* our aims remain the same: to explain a complex, and constantly evolving, national institution in straightforward language; to give an insider's feel for how and why things happen; to analyse strengths and weaknesses; and to examine ways in which Parliament might develop. Parliament's ancient functions of legislating, controlling expenditure, representing the citizen and calling government to account have never been more important; and the more effective Parliament is, the better it will serve its real owners – the people of the United Kingdom.

We hope that our readers will include those who have anything to do with Parliament in their daily lives: journalists, lawyers, civil servants, lobbyists, academics, researchers, students and teachers, and, indeed, parliamentary candidates and members of both Houses; and those who simply want to find out how their Parliament works, and what it can do for them.

Eight years have passed since the publication of the previous edition. A great deal has happened at Westminster: the expenses scandal in 2009; a general election resulting in the first peacetime coalition government for 80 years; a frustrated attempt at reforming the House of Lords; and a bewildering amount of political and procedural change in both Houses. Some 40 per cent of this new edition has been updated or, indeed, completely rewritten to keep pace. Previous editions of this book surveyed the devolved Parliament and Assemblies, and their relations with Westminster. Time has moved on, they have matured and developed, and so they are not covered in this edition.

We retired from the service of the Commons and Lords in 2014 with a total of 80 years in the service of Parliament. With an eye to the future, the preparation of this edition has been more widely collaborative. We are hugely grateful to the expert and enthusiastic colleagues who have helped with this edition, and our special thanks go to: Nicolas Besly, Paul Bowers, Sarah Davies, Mark Egan, Tom Goldsmith, Luke Hussey, Tracey Jessup, Richard Kelly, Colin Lee, Ed Little, Simon Patrick, Ed Potton, Crispin Poyser, Fergus Reid, Eve Samson, Isobel White and Huw Yardley.

We are also most grateful to James Bowyer, Paul Bristow, Alexander Brocklehurst, Christopher Clarke, Mark Cooper, Mark Davies, Paul Evans, Anna Murphy, Danielle Nash, Arnold Ridout, Duncan Sagar, Jonathan Smith, Joey Topping, Jake Vaughan, Ben Williams, Anthony Willott and Tom Wilson. The responsibility for any error or omission is of course our own.

We acknowledge with warm thanks and some relief the technical help Caroline Nicholls has given us in preparing the final text; the help and support of our agent, Charlotte Howard; and that of Andrew Taylor and Charlotte Endersby at Taylor & Francis. Special thanks go to Thomas Docherty MP for his championing of the book and for keeping us up to the mark in preparing a new edition.

The reputation of Parliament suffered a grievous blow in 2009 with the expenses scandal. To those of us who have devoted much of our professional careers to making Parliament better understood and valued, it was a sad time. But the 2010 general election produced profound change. The Commons had 227 new members, who were determined to make a difference, and did. Coalition politics produced not only novelty but an element of uncertainty. As we show in this book, the 2010 House of Commons has been at its most rebellious in modern times, and the Lords have been attending and voting in unprecedented numbers. There has been more independence, self-confidence and challenge in both Houses in the last three or four years than we have seen in the length of our careers. Against this background, the degree of disconnection between Parliament and public is frustrating, as well as worrying, and must be addressed. Parliament will be better valued, and engaged with, if it is better understood; and in this endeavour we hope that *How Parliament Works* will continue to play its part.

Robert Rogers
Rhodri Walters

Acknowledgements

We are grateful to both Houses and the Controller of HMSO; the Government Chief Whip's Office; photographers Terry Moore, Roger Harris, Deryc R. Sands, Catherine Bebbington and Annabelle Moller; and graphic designers Jonathan Rix and Nick Battley for assistance and permissions enabling the reproduction of copyright material (as specified in relation to each image).

We are also grateful to Paul Evans and Vacher Dod Publishing Ltd for permission to include material adapted from 'House of Commons Procedure' (3rd edition, 2002) on the annual parliamentary cycle.

Parliament: its home and origins

Mid-Victorian masterpiece: Parliament in its setting

The Palace of Westminster, that magnificent range of Victorian Gothic buildings along the banks of the Thames, is probably the United Kingdom's most famous landmark. The Elizabeth Tower at the north end of the palace and the striking of Big Ben, the hour bell of the Great Clock, are known throughout the world. The palace is one of the greatest achievements of nineteenth-century architecture and art, and even those who work there every day remain awed by its power and confidence.

If the Palace of Westminster were empty, it would still be one of the great tourist attractions of Europe. But this Grade I listed building, part of the World Heritage site that includes Westminster Abbey, as well as the palace, contains a parliament that is one of the biggest and busiest in the world. This is a source of many tensions. Whatever its working methods, and however effective it may be, it is very difficult for a parliament housed in a heritage icon to *look* modern and efficient. And the constraints of conserving and caring for such a building mean that any structural change for parliamentary purposes – from new door locks to constructing an education centre – must run the gauntlet of English Heritage, the planners of Westminster City Council, and countless others who love the building for its art and history. The building is expensive to maintain precisely because everything must be done to the highest standards for the benefit of future generations. Finally, the palace is a perfect example of how buildings shape the activity within them. As we shall see, the nature of the buildings of Parliament has a powerful influence on how business is conducted and the way that members of both Houses work.

The King's palace

It may seem odd that a parliament should meet in a palace; but the Palace of Westminster has been a royal palace for well over 1,000 years. Before the Norman Conquest it was the residence of Edward the Confessor, and it continued to be used by the monarch until the reign of Henry VIII, who bought Whitehall from Cardinal Wolsey in 1529 and then built St James's Palace in 1532. Although Westminster was thereafter no longer a royal residence, it continued to be a royal palace. Property in what is now London SW1 was clearly as much in demand in the sixteenth century as it is now, and the buildings huddled around the great bulk of Westminster Hall were rapidly taken up for use by the two Houses, the law courts (which remained at Westminster until they moved to the Strand in 1882), courtiers, placemen and shopkeepers – and others plying less reputable trades.

The King's summons

Although parliaments have met at Westminster for some 750 years, there is no requirement to do so. Parliament has met, and could meet elsewhere, and still conduct its business with constitutional and legal propriety. Second World War bomb damage forced the two Houses from their own Chambers; and were the modern spectre of global terrorism to make it necessary, Parliament could meet elsewhere with the minimum of infrastructure – and, indeed, has plans to do so.

The word 'parliament', from the French *parler*, to speak or talk, was first used in England in the thirteenth century, when it meant an enlarged meeting of the King's council, attended by barons, bishops and courtiers, to advise the King on law-making, administration and judicial decisions. The origin of the modern institution can be traced back to the parliament summoned on Henry III's behalf by Simon de Montfort in 1265, when representatives from the towns were present for the first time. Parliaments still meet in response to a royal summons; the parliament that met after the 2010 general election was summoned by a proclamation from the Queen, which in part said:

> *And We being desirous and resolved, as soon as may be, to meet Our people and have their advice in Parliament, do hereby make known unto all Our loving Subjects Our Royal Will and Pleasure to call a new Parliament.*

Those words may fall strangely upon a modern ear, but the purport of Elizabeth II's proclamation was the same as those issued during the reigns of 34 of her predecessors.

The development of the two Houses

By the middle of the fourteenth century, the King's Parliaments were attended by knights of the shire and burgesses from the cities and boroughs (the Commons), the magnates (the Lords Temporal) and the bishops and abbots (the Lords Spiritual). At this time, the reign of Edward III, the Commons began to claim that their agreement was required for any taxation by the monarch, in particular the tax on wool. By now the Commons and Lords had emerged as two distinct houses. Once settled at Westminster, the Commons met in the Painted Chamber or in the refectory or the chapter house of Westminster Abbey, and they moved to St Stephen's Chapel in 1547. The Lords settled in the White Chamber of the old palace, moving to the larger White or Lesser Hall in 1801 when the Union with Ireland introduced extra members into the House. After the fire of 1834, they moved to the re-roofed Painted Chamber until they were able to move into their present accommodation in 1847.

The fire

The night of 16 October 1834 was fine, with some high cloud. By seven o'clock that evening the London sky was lit by flames. Two workmen had been told to dispose of large quantities of Exchequer tallies – notched hazel sticks used from early mediaeval times to show what each taxpayer owed; the stick could be split to provide both a record and a receipt. The workmen burned the tallies in the furnaces that heated the flues under the floor of the House of Lords, and their enthusiasm, or possibly their impatience, led to the destruction of the mediaeval palace and the meeting places of both Houses. Thousands watched. One contemporary observer wrote:

> *An immense multitude of spectators assembled at Westminster to witness the ravages of the fire, the lurid glare of which was visible for many miles around the metropolis. Even the river Thames . . . was covered with boats and barges . . . and the reflections of the wavering flames upon the water, on the neighbouring shores and on the many thousands thus congregated, composed a spectacle most strikingly picturesque and impressive.*

The winning design

The destruction of a large part of the old palace and of much of its contents, including irreplaceable manuscripts, paintings and tapestries, was a great loss. Westminster Hall survived, as did other parts of the building that today would undoubtedly have been preserved or restored. But the authorities of the day saw the fire as an opportunity to start afresh. A competition was held for the design of a completely new parliamentary building, which resulted in an extraordinary architectural and artistic partnership. The scheme produced by the architect Sir Charles Barry and the interior designer Augustus Welby Pugin was chosen from among 97 designs submitted, and the foundation stone was laid on 27 April 1840. The Palace that was built over the next 20 years is huge. It covers 8 acres (3.24 hectares), and has 1,100 rooms, 100 staircases and three miles (4.8 km) of passages.

A Victorian Parliament

The Barry and Pugin palace had, apart from its visual merits, one great advantage: it was a purpose-built parliamentary building. As well as the two Chambers, it provided residences for the principal officers and officials, dining rooms, smoking rooms, writing rooms, committee rooms, libraries and all the paraphernalia of a grand country house and London club combined.

This was all a mid-Victorian Parliament needed. There were 658 members of the Commons, and some 500 members of the Lords, no more than 350 of whom turned up to speak in any session; but an MP or peer wrote his correspondence in longhand, and if he wanted to find something out, he went and looked it up, just as he would have done in his library or study at home. Members of the Commons were careful to keep on the right side of local political magnates, but modern constituency pressures were unknown. Indeed, illuminated addresses survive that were presented to the local MP 'on his visit (sometimes *annual* visit!) to the Constituency'.

The New Palace today

Sadly, the ever-present threat of terrorism has meant that public access to the Palace of Westminster has to be closely controlled. During term time, the parties of constituents and other visitors who tour the principal parts of the palace must be sponsored by an MP or peer, although visitors may pay to take a guided tour of the palace (in English, French, German, Italian, Spanish, Russian or Mandarin, or a tactile tour for blind and partially sighted visitors) during the commercial opening on Saturdays, for most of the summer recess and on non-sitting days at other times of the year (see page 411).

Those who come to see the Palace of Westminster begin by following the Queen's route at the State Opening of Parliament, and in the part of the palace still devoted to the monarch. With the exception of the Commons Chamber, much of what they see has changed little and would have been familiar to Gladstone or Disraeli. A plan of the palace is shown on page 6.

The Robing Room and Royal Gallery

When the Queen opens Parliament, her state coach drives under the great archway of the Victoria Tower, the 323-foot (98.5-metre) tower at the south end of the palace that houses the parliamentary archives. She then ascends the Royal Staircase and passes through the Norman Porch (so called because it was intended to place statues of the Norman kings there, but somehow Victorian prime ministers supplanted them) to the Robing Room, where she puts on the state robes and Imperial State Crown before walking in procession through the 110-foot (33.5 m) long Royal Gallery, into the Prince's Chamber and then into the Chamber of the House of Lords.

This southern end of the palace is magnificent and ornate – deliberately conceived as a backdrop to state ceremonial. The perfect proportions of Barry's rooms are complemented by the sumptuousness of Pugin's decoration. His themes of portcullis, rose, lily and lion, together with Queen Victoria's VR cipher, run throughout the palace's decoration, with its Gothic features and linenfold panelling, but his 'graceful fancy' is nowhere more evident than at the south end of the building – the Robing Room and the Royal Gallery.

Although the chief purpose of these two great rooms was to impress, they can also be used for other purposes. Following the destruction of the Commons Chamber by enemy bombing the House of Lords sat in the Robing Room between 1941 and 1949 to enable the Commons to use the Lords Chamber. Both rooms are used when a visiting head of state – or occasionally head of government – addresses members of both Houses of Parliament. As there is no concept of joint sittings of the two Houses, the Royal Gallery and Robing Room provide a convenient place for such events. When the House of Lords hosted the Association of European Senates in 2013, the Robing Room and Royal Gallery provided a wonderful setting for the meeting.

The Chamber of the House of Lords

The visitor then moves to the Chamber of the House of Lords, which is fitted out in the same rich style. At one end, the throne faces north under a gilded canopy and Cloth of Estate. In front of it is the Woolsack, on which sits the Lord Speaker as presiding officer of the House of Lords. The Woolsack is a seat stuffed with wool from the different countries of the Commonwealth. Stuffed sacks or cushions were a standard form of mediaeval furniture but tradition has it that Edward III decided that a sack of wool would be a useful reminder to their lordships of the pastoral basis of the country's economy – and the chief source of his revenue – and the practice has persisted. In front of the Woolsack are the two judges' woolsacks. These remind us that the Court of Appeal and High Court judges still receive Writs of Assistance to attend the House. Nowadays they attend only in a representative capacity on the day of the State Opening. To the left and right of the Woolsack are four rows of red benches for peers, divided into three sections. In the centre of the floor is the Table of the House, and on the far side of the table from the Woolsack there are three further benches.

Looking from the throne, the right of the House is known as the spiritual side, because the bishops sit there, in the front two rows of the section nearest the throne. The left is called the *temporal side*, while beyond the Table are the crossbenches. As well as the bishops, government supporters sit on the *spiritual side*, with ministers who are peers in the front row of the central section. Opposition parties sit on the temporal side. Peers who do not belong to a party sit on the crossbenches. A labelled view of the Chamber and a photograph of the House in session taken in October 2014 are on pages 7 and 8.

Beyond the Lords Chamber, the visitor passes through Peers' Lobby to the Central Lobby, a large octagonal room at the very centre of the palace, beneath the third-largest of the palace's towers. Almost all visitors on business come to the Central Lobby; it is the place where constituents who wish to lobby an MP come to fill in a green card requesting an interview. It lies directly between the two Chambers; and when on State Opening day all the doors are thrown open, the Queen sitting on the throne in the Lords can see the Speaker presiding over the House of Commons more than a hundred yards (91m) away.

PALACE OF WESTMINSTER
PRINCIPAL FLOOR PLAN

The Palace of Westminster – principal floor

Source: Copyright House of Commons, 2014. Artwork by Jonathan Rix

Members' Lobby and the Chamber of the House of Commons

Moving towards the Commons Chamber, the visitor passes into the Members' Lobby. This is a much larger space than Peers' Lobby. When the House is busy, especially before and after votes, it is thronged with MPs and is the haunt of 'lobby' journalists; and it is then a clearing-house of opinion, news and rumour. It contains a message board with a slot for each member's messages (less used in these days of mobiles and pagers), pigeonholes for members' select committee papers (although many committees have gone paperless), a counter where members can get a wide range of parliamentary and government papers, and a post office that deals with some 50,000 items every sitting day. The whips' offices of the major parties (see page 81) adjoin the Members' Lobby.

The Commons Chamber was destroyed in an air raid on the night of 10 May 1941. Even Barry's original Chamber was less ornate than that of the Lords; and the rebuilt Commons Chamber, designed by Sir Giles Gilbert Scott, is austere by comparison with that of the Lords. A labelled view of the Chamber and one of the House in session are shown on pages 9 and 10. From the public gallery one now looks down through a massive 7-tonne glass screen, installed in September 2005 on security advice. Below, the Speaker's canopied Chair is the focal point. During Question Time and ministerial statements, the Speaker's Secretary stands to the right

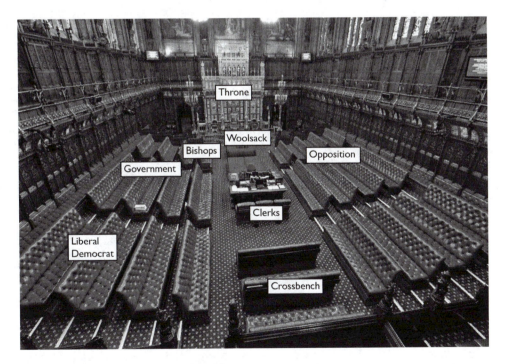

The Chamber of the House of Lords

Source: Copyright House of Lords, 2014. Photography by Terry Moore

The House of Lords in session

Source: Copyright House of Lords, 2014. Photography by Roger Harris

of the Chair (as seen from the gallery) helping the Speaker to identify members and keeping a record of those he has called. To the left of the Chair, against the far wall, is the officials' box for civil servants advising ministers. In front of the Chair is the Table of the House, at which sit the Clerks at the Table, who advise the Speaker and his deputies, Whips and any other member, on the conduct of proceedings, and who also compile the legal record of the House's decisions.

On each side of the Chamber are five rows of green benches, divided by a gangway into two sections. On the left, as seen from the gallery, are the benches occupied by the government party (in the 2010 Parliament, the two coalition parties, with the Liberal Democrats 'below the gangway', further from the Chair). On the right, as seen from the gallery, are the opposition parties, with the smaller parties sitting on the third and fourth benches below the gangway. Ministers sit on the front bench by the Table, and the main opposition party's spokesmen and women (or shadow ministers) sit opposite them. Ministers and their shadows are thus known as frontbenchers; all other MPs are backbenchers.

On each side of the Table are the despatch boxes at which ministers and their counterparts from the main opposition party speak; and at the near end of the Table is the Mace, which symbolises the authority of the House.

At our observer's eye level, above the Speaker's Chair, is the Press Gallery, with seats in the centre for the *Hansard* reporters who compile the record of what is said. Other galleries are for members of the House of Lords and distinguished visitors, as well as for the general public. Two galleries are reserved for MPs and are technically

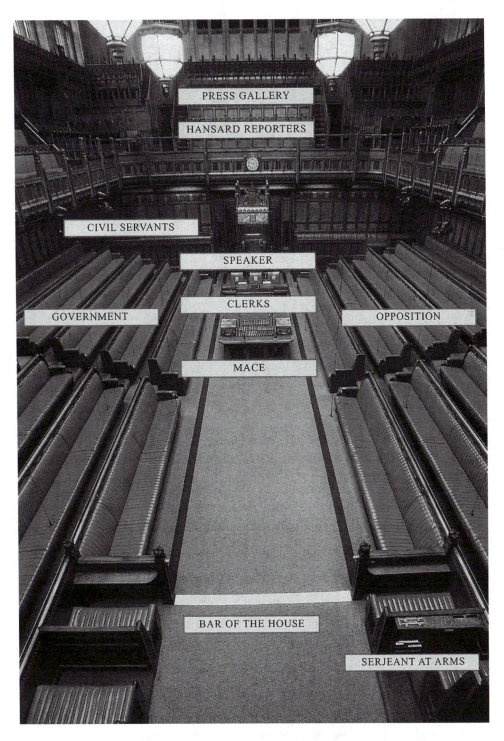

The Chamber of the House of Commons, looking down from the public gallery

Source: Copyright House of Commons, 2014. Photography by Deryc R. Sands

The House of Commons in session

Source: Copyright House of Commons, 2013. Photography by Catherine Bebbington

part of the floor of the House, although Speakers have indicated that they will not call members to speak from there (and there are no microphones). Down below, but not visible except from the front of the gallery, sits the Serjeant at Arms, responsible for order around the House and in the galleries. There, too, are the crossbenches; but as there are, apart from the occupants of the Chair, few members with no party allegiance (one in the 1997 and 2001 parliaments, two in 2005 and in 2010 three (all of whom had previously been elected for parties), these are in practice extensions of the seating for government and opposition members (although MPs may not speak from them).

Westminster Hall

This brief description of the Palace of Westminster would be incomplete without reference to what is one of the finest rooms in Europe – Westminster Hall, the great hall of the mediaeval palace and, along with the crypt Chapel of St Mary Undercroft, the only part of the original building to remain. The hall has been much restored over the years, but at its core it remains an eleventh-century building with a late fourteenth-century hammerbeam roof. It is used today for ceremonial occasions. The Lying in State of The Queen Mother took place in Westminster Hall in April 2002; and The Queen received the Humble Addresses of the two Houses of Parliament there on the occasion of her Diamond Jubilee in 2012. The Hall is sometimes also used instead of the Royal Gallery to hear addresses from visiting Heads of State – Pope Benedict in 2010 and President Obama in 2011 – or other figures, such as Aung San Suu Kyi in 2012. The regular sittings of the House of Commons 'in Westminster Hall' (see page 259) take place not in the Hall itself, but in the Grand Committee Room at the north end.

The palace and parliamentary vocabulary

The layout of the Chambers, derived from earlier meeting rooms of the two Houses, is reflected in the vocabulary of Parliament, which in many cases has passed into general everyday use, as well as around the world with the Westminster model of parliamentary government.

The *opposition* parties sit physically opposite the government party (as well as opposing it). A meeting of the House is a *sitting*, at the end of which the House *rises*. Matters considered by either House are debated *on the floor*. If a member changes parties, he or she is said to have *crossed the floor*. When MPs and peers hand in questions, amendments to bills or notices of motions, or when ministers place documents formally before either House, they are said to have *tabled* them, even if they do not place them on the massive Table of either House. If a bill has its committee stage in a Commons standing committee, it is said to be taken *upstairs* because the palace's committee rooms are on the first floor. When either House votes, it is said to *divide*, because those voting divide physically into two groups ('ayes' and 'noes' in the Commons, 'contents' and 'not contents' in the Lords) and walk through separate lobbies on either side of both Chambers to be counted. Securing something *on the nod* – that is, without debate or division – may derive from a member's brief bow to the Chair when moving a motion formally.

Some supposed parliamentary derivations are bogus. *In the bag* stems not from the petition bag on the back of the Speaker's Chair but from the much older idea of a game bag. It is just as fanciful as the myth that the red lines on the floor of the Commons Chamber are two sword lengths apart, although there is, indeed, a rule that a member speaking from the front row of benches (above or below the gangway) should not step over the lines. And *toe the line* has nothing at all to do with these lines; it comes from the Royal Navy of Nelson's time, when barefooted seamen lined up for inspection on the seams, or lines, in the deck planking. A more frequent error is the description of Westminster as 'the mother of parliaments'. When John Bright coined the phrase in 1865 he was referring to *England* as the mother of parliaments; but, given the immense influence Westminster has had on the development of parliaments around the world, perhaps the mistake is understandable.

'We shape our buildings, and afterwards our buildings shape us'

From the start, the clublike rooms and common spaces of Barry's palace have encouraged members of both Houses to congregate and meet informally. In the

Commons, the Smoking Room (as in the whole of the palace, a no-smoking area since the passing of the Health Act 2006), the Tea Room and the Members' Lobby after a big vote (as well as the division lobbies themselves during it) are places where opinions are formed and exchanged, support is canvassed and tactics planned. This informality and personal contact also produces volatility: rumours travel quickly, even through so large a membership; views – and perhaps backbench rebellions – can gather momentum with surprising speed.

A first-time visitor almost always finds the Commons Chamber smaller than expected; and, for an assembly of 650 members, it is surprisingly intimate – its floor area is not much more than that of a tennis court. Its seating capacity (together with the galleries reserved for members) is usually said to be 427; but as there are no individual seats and members inevitably take up varying amounts of the green leather, this is an approximation.

There are no individual places, so also no desks, telephones or computer terminals; and members speak from their places, not from a podium. When the House is full, perhaps towards the end of a major debate or during Prime Minister's Questions, the atmosphere is made tense by the crush of MPs, and one can appreciate the way in which the House can become great political theatre. The small size of the Chamber also means that, even when only a few MPs are present for some abstruse debate, the feeling of speaking to empty space, which is a problem in many foreign parliaments, is minimised.

It is likely that the rows of benches facing each other derive from the use by the Commons of St Stephen's Chapel in the old palace. The clergy faced each other in choir stalls on each side of the altar, and the arrangement was unchanged when the Tudor House of Commons took over the chapel. Some feel that this encourages adversarial politics (and even, perhaps fancifully, a two-party system). The Commons, unlike the Lords, has no crossbenches spanning the width of the Chamber. It may be significant that standing committee rooms, where legislation is debated in the same way as in the House, are laid out as in the Chamber; but for select committees, where there is a more consensual approach, members sit around horseshoe tables, and MPs and peers do not necessarily sit on party lines.

Certainly, the idea of replacing the Chamber with a hemicycle, of the sort found in many continental parliaments and also in the European Parliament, has its supporters, especially among those who shun confrontational politics. A hemicycle would almost certainly bring with it individual desks and seats, but accommodating a Chamber of that size in Barry's palace would be next to impossible. The House of Commons had a chance to make the change after the old Chamber was destroyed in 1941. However, neither a hemicycle nor a larger traditional Chamber found favour. Churchill represented the majority view in the House when he said in the debate on the rebuilding:

> *if the House is big enough to contain all its Members, nine-tenths of*
> *the debates will be conducted in the depressing atmosphere of an almost empty or*
> *half-empty chamber . . . We wish to see our Parliament as a strong, easy, flexible*

*instrument of free debate. For this purpose a small chamber and a sense of
intimacy are indispensable . . . The conversational style requires a fairly small
space, and there should be on great occasions a sense of crowd and urgency . . .
We shape our buildings, and afterwards our buildings shape us.*

Time and space

In an echo of metaphysics, the way any parliament operates is dictated by time and
space. *Time*: to allow full scrutiny of government, examination of draft legislation,
airing of concerns affecting constituencies and constituents, and the political causes
pursued by political parties and individual members. *Space* is almost as important:
space to provide meeting rooms for committees, political parties and lobby groups;
space for library and research facilities; adequate office accommodation for MPs and
their staff to provide the service that their constituents expect, and for members of
both Houses to support their parliamentary duties.

Add to that the space that is needed for the infrastructure of Parliament: support
for the work of the two Chambers and of legislative and investigative committees;
provision of IT, security, catering, housekeeping, maintenance, and administration
of pay, allowances and personnel. Then there are those who are in Parliament but
not of it: TV, radio and print journalists, and civil servants supporting ministers.
Last, but emphatically not least, are the owners of Parliament: constituents and
taxpayers and their families, who may want to bring problems to their local MP, or
have a cause taken up by a member of either House, or who may simply want to see
Parliament at work.

Neither are these demands constant. Parliament must react to expectations of it,
as well as to events. The creation of a new government department will need a new
select committee to shadow it in the Commons; some major issue of the day may
lead to the establishment of a new select committee in the Lords. More draft bills
will need more select committee consideration, and in turn space for the staff to
support the process; and decisions of the Independent Parliamentary Standards
Authority (see page 62) may have a dramatic effect on the numbers of MPs' own
staff. We consider below the ways in which the two modern Houses have tried to
cope with the constant pressure on their accommodation.

The shoe pinches

The new Palace of Westminster was largely completed by 1852, although it was not
finally finished until 1860. The Lords occupied their Chamber on 15 April 1847;
the Commons first sat in theirs on 30 May 1850 but did not move in permanently
until 3 February 1852. In 1854, Sir Charles Barry produced plans to build additional
offices surrounding New Palace Yard, but these were never pursued. By 1867, a select
committee was examining how the size of the Commons Chamber could be increased
and, in 1894, another Commons select committee was looking at the adequacy of
accommodation more generally.

The pressures

The shortage of accommodation was a recurring theme over the next 100 years. In the Commons, it became particularly acute during the last 20 or 30 years of the last century with the increasing burdens of constituency work, the need to house larger numbers of MPs' own staff, and the growth in select committee work and in research facilities. The administration and support of the House became more professional and better resourced, needing more staff and office accommodation. Every new facility, however desirable in itself, has imposed new strains, from the introduction of broadcasting (with its need for control rooms and archive space) to the establishment of information offices for the public, and educational facilities.

A visitor following the route from the Victoria Tower to the Commons Chamber has an impression of lofty ceilings and spacious rooms, but on the floors above and below (except along the Committee Corridor on the river front) the story is rather different and includes subdivided rooms, mezzanine floors and even temporary huts on flat roofs.

For many years in the Commons, members were prepared, however reluctantly, to share offices – even with nine or ten of their colleagues – or to do much of their constituency work around the House, writing letters in the library or dictating to their secretaries in the Committee Corridor while waiting to vote. That this did not lead to changes may have been partly because of the 'never did me any harm' principle, but also because the scope for change was limited.

New building

The only realistic possibilities lay to the north of the palace, across Bridge Street towards Whitehall. Various schemes blossomed, were rejected and withered. Between 1984 and 1991, however, the buildings in 1 Parliament Street, at the end of Whitehall, were converted to provide some ninety offices for MPs, together with library, catering and meeting facilities. Nearby, the old Scotland Yard police headquarters (the Norman Shaw buildings) were taken over and the next-door Canon Row buildings adapted for office accommodation. And at the other end of the palace, Westminster House at 7 Millbank contains most of the staff of Commons select committees, together with finance, HR and IT staff.

Portcullis House

However, if MPs and their staff were to have proper modern office accommodation that would allow them to give a proper service to their constituents, the key site was that overlooking the river. Here, between 1998 and 2000, Portcullis House was constructed to provide offices for 210 MPs and 400 of their staff, together with a variety of meeting rooms. Designed by Michael Hopkins and Partners (now Hopkins Architects), from the outside the building appears austere, even forbidding, but inside, from the airy atrium to state-of-the-art committee rooms and offices, it shows a confident and innovative style that has won a string of awards.

The £234 million price tag was controversial even for a building designed to complement a world-famous site and to outlast any conventional office accommodation – though the project came in under budget and almost exactly on schedule. The House of Commons Commission, responsible for the House's administration and for the construction of the building, said of it:

> *The building is often described as one purely for Members of Parliament and their staff. This is indeed an important function, and good working conditions play their part in the service which Members give their constituents. But more important are the outstanding facilities for public hearings of select committees, and for meetings of groups of all kinds. This access of the people to the political process is an essential part of the working of a modern Parliament.*

It is safe to say that those who commissioned the new palace after the fire of 1834 would not have recognised any part of this description of the uses of a parliamentary building.

Lords accommodation

As with the Commons, the House of Lords has outgrown the 40 per cent of the original palace that it occupies and, rather late in the day compared with the House of Commons, has started to acquire office space for staff and members in nearby streets. In 1994, 7 Old Palace Yard – an elegant Georgian house opposite the west front of the palace – was returned by the Commons to Lords use; in 2001, Millbank House was leased from the Church Commissioners for mixed office and member use; and, in 2002, Fielden House, an office building in Little College Street, was bought for £13 million and occupied in 2005. Most recently, in March 2005, the House purchased from the Church Commissioners the whole of the Millbank island site comprising Millbank House (already leased to the Lords), 1 Millbank, and 5 Great College Street. The cost was £76 million. 1 Millbank was refitted and better integrated with 2 Millbank, opening in 2011. The property at 5 Great College Street is planned to receive similar treatment in 2015–17. This requirement for space reflects the increased level of activity of the Lords. As we shall see in the Chapter 2, average daily attendance is now higher than ever before. In addition, members' expectations of desk space, IT facilities, research and information, and procedural support are always rising. Unsurprisingly, as in the Commons, this scattering of staff and members' offices has made the Lords seem less of a homogeneous organisation.

Parliament or building site

There has been very little modernisation of the Palace of Westminster over the 150 years of its existence. As, over a century and a half, new requirements and new technologies have emerged, they have been accommodated somehow, but with no strategic plan; and the fabric of the Palace is showing its age. Although the visitor to the main or Principal Floor of the Palace would not guess it, the services in the basement and in the 98 'risers' between floors (water, air-conditioning, steam, sewage, electricity, communications, IT), carried by many miles of pipes and wires, are in poor condition, and the possibility of a catastrophic failure, which could make it impossible for either House to sit is increasing. Over the years, the fabric has deteriorated, and roofs and stonework need attention. In 2013, following a preliminary study by officials, an independent options appraisal was commissioned from a team of consultants led by Deloitte Real Estate to assess the state of the building and its and services, and to consider how to set about a programme of restoration and renewal. Two options were ruled out from the beginning: doing nothing; and constructing a new parliamentary building. Three options remain: first, tackling the problems while the business of both Houses continues, which might mean decades of work; second, 'decanting' first one House, its members and staff to another building acquired for the purpose; and third, decanting both Houses and all the occupants of the Palace for five or six years. Any one of the options will involve huge cost and disruption; but a bold decision will be needed to preserve this iconic building for future generations. The two Houses will have to face up to this soon after the 2015 general election. Meanwhile, major programmes to re-roof the Palace, to clean the stonework of Westminster Hall, to support the mechanical and electrical services, and to replace the thousands of worn and damaged encaustic floor tiles continue.

The parliamentary estate

Today's parliamentary estate is akin to a small town. It covers 206,532 square metres in 14 buildings housing well over 5,000 people – and this population is more than doubled by those from outside Westminster who have business in Parliament each day. A plan of the parliamentary estate appears opposite.

We now move on to consider the institution housed in those buildings.

THE PARLIAMENTARY ESTATE

KEY TO BUILDINGS
1. PALACE OF WESTMINSTER.
2. NORMAN SHAW NORTH.
3. No. 1 DERBY GATE.
4. No. 1 PARLIAMENT STREET.
5. No. 1 CANON ROW.
6. NORMAN SHAW SOUTH.
7. PORTCULLIS HOUSE.
8. No.53 PARLIAMENT STREET.
9. BROAD SANCTUARY
   (LIBRARY STORAGE).
10. No. 6/7 OLD PALACE YARD.
11. FIELDEN HOUSE.
12. MILLBANK HOUSE.
13. No.7 MILLBANK.
14. No.14 TOTHILL STREET.
15. EDUCATION CENTRE
    (UNDER CONSTRUCTION)

HOUSES OF PARLIAMENT Parliamentary Estates Directorate

REVISION K - 14.11.14

The Parliamentary Estate and its surroundings

Source: Copyright House of Commons, 2014. Artwork by Jonathan Rix

2

Who is in Parliament?

The Commons

The size of the Commons

Even in the early fifteenth century, there were more than 250 members of the Commons – two knights from each of 37 counties, two citizens or burgesses from each of the 80 or so cities and boroughs, and 14 members from the Cinque Ports. More were steadily added by statute and royal charter, and by 1673 the membership of the House – at that time only from England and Wales – stood at 513. Union with Scotland in 1707 added 45 members, and a further 100 came from Ireland with the Union of 1801, making 658.

The House grew to 670 members in 1885, and to 707 – the most at any stage – in 1918. Irish independence reduced the numbers to 615 by 1922. The upward trend during the rest of the twentieth century produced a House of 659 members by 1997; but the post-devolution reduction in Scottish seats at Westminster from 72 to 59 meant that there were 646 members of the Commons in 2005. This was increased to 650 by the boundary review that took effect at the 2010 general election. The number sitting for constituencies in England is now 533: 59 in Scotland, 40 in Wales and 18 in Northern Ireland. There is thus one MP for every 98,615 people (or for every 70,984 people entitled to vote).

Too big?

Even for a population of some 64.1 million, this is a large House. By comparison, the Italian Camera dei Deputati has 630 members, or one for every 96,046 people, the French Assemblée nationale has 577 members (one for every 109,586 people) and the Spanish Congreso de los Diputados has 350 members (one for every 131,949 people). A comparison with the US House of Representatives is even more striking

(435 members, one for every 717,809 people) but of course in the USA representation at state level also has to be taken into account.

A big House of Commons has some disadvantages – at least from the point of view of the individual member. Parliamentary time is at a premium. The backbencher must compete with colleagues to ask questions or to be called in debate, and the individual's share of both influence and parliamentary resources is less than in a smaller House.

However, from the point of view of the electorate, a large House means that an individual MP represents a relatively small number of people. An MP's focus on the constituency is very sharp, not only because it is a power base, and he or she must woo the electors to be re-elected, but also because most constituencies are small enough to be fairly homogeneous in terms of character, population and economic activity. Your chances of engaging an MP's attention on an issue are very much greater if it is something that directly affects his or her constituency. And the close and valued relationship between a single MP and a single constituency has undoubtedly been a factor in opposition to some forms of proportional representation.

In addition, the historically large numbers of MPs have led to a large number of ministers; in 2014, 94 (the maximum number of salaried ministers allowed by law is 95) sat in the Commons out of a total of 121 in both Houses. This means that many individual members get ministerial experience (although the proportion – 14 per cent – might well be the same in a smaller House). A large House provides more back-benchers to undertake the scrutiny of government through select committee work; in the 2012–13 session, some 392 MPs were members of investigative or scrutiny select committees. (Even so, the number of such select committees means that some MPs are members of more than one, which blunts effectiveness).

The coalition government sought to reduce the size of the House of Commons to 600 members. All three main political parties had promised 'to reduce the cost of politics' following the expenses scandal of 2009, but a reduction of only 50 seats (less than 8 per cent of the House) was seen by many as marginal – and, indeed, illogical in view of the apparently inexorable increase in the membership of the House of Lords. However, the sixth boundary review, which would have made the change, was abandoned in January 2013. The next boundary review has been postponed until 2018.

The new government in 2015 will have to decide whether to allow the boundary review to restart using the current Rules for Redistribution which require the House of Commons to be 600 members, or whether the Rules should be changed again.

The constituencies

Four Boundary Commissions, one for each part of the UK, keep under review the size, boundaries and numbers of parliamentary constituencies. Following the commitment in 2010 to create fewer and more equal sized constituencies, the Commissions are now formally required to ensure in their recommendations that the House of Commons has 600 members and that the electorate of each constituency is within

5 per cent of the electoral quota for the UK (although these changes have not yet been given effect). Four island constituencies (Orkney and Shetland, Western Isles, and two seats on the Isle of Wight) are exempt from this parity rule. The electoral quota (which had previously been calculated separately for each country of the UK) now applies to the whole of the UK and is currently 76,641. At the 2010 election, the largest constituency was the Isle of Wight at 109,922 electors (where the sitting MP fought a rearguard action against Boundary Commission proposals to divide the island into two constituencies), and the smallest was Na h-Eileanan an Iar (the Western Isles of Scotland) at 21,780 (where the identity of the islands is so distinct that combination with a mainland constituency is not an option). It is huge disparities in the size of constituencies such as these that encouraged changes to the electoral quota per constituency.

The boundary review that was not implemented would have changed the constituency boundaries much more than previous reviews; in the fifth review, implemented at the 2010 general election, only 77 of the 533 constituencies in England were changed by 50 per cent or more; in the sixth review, 203 constituencies would have changed to this extent.

The time-lag between population change and constituency change has in the past benefited the Labour Party. In 2010, the average size of the electorate in Labour seats was 68,487, compared with 72,418 in Conservative seats. The changes to the Rules in 2011 were also seen as a means of addressing this inbuilt bias as part of the review process. (A recent academic study has calculated that if the Commissions' provisional recommendations had been in place in 2010, the Conservative lead over Labour would have been 68, only 2 short of an overall majority.)

The candidates

Anyone may stand for election to the Commons if he or she is a British subject or citizen of the Republic of Ireland, is aged 18 or over, and is not disqualified. Those disqualified include those subject to bankruptcy restrictions orders (or, in Scotland, those against whom sequestration of estates is awarded), people sentenced to more than one year's imprisonment, members of the House of Lords (but hereditary peers not sitting in the Lords are eligible; one, Viscount Thurso, was elected to the Commons in 2001, and two who left the Commons in 2010, Douglas Hogg and Michael Ancram, succeeded to peerages while MPs but did not lose their seats) and holders of offices listed in the House of Commons Disqualification Act 1975. These last, often described as those 'holding an office of profit under the Crown', include civil servants, judges, members of the regular armed forces and police, some local government officers and some members of public bodies.

Independent candidates are occasionally elected. The first for many years was Martin Bell as the 'anti-sleaze' candidate in Tatton in 1997, followed by Richard Taylor in Wyre Forest in 2001 on a platform of saving Kidderminster Hospital (beating a sitting member, who was also a minister, by the large majority of 17,630). Remarkably, Taylor held the seat in 2005, although with a reduced majority of 5,250, but lost in

2010 to the Conservatives. But these results are very much the exception. Bell was a respected former TV journalist, Taylor a local doctor, and each had a clear-cut campaign issue with striking local relevance.

Two other candidates caused upsets in the 2005 general election. Peter Law stood as an independent in Blaenau Gwent after the imposition of an all-women short-list prevented him standing as a Labour candidate, and won with a majority of 9,121; and in Bethnal Green and Bow, the maverick former Labour MP George Galloway, who had founded his own 'Respect' party but was in effect an independent, beat the sitting Labour MP Oona King by 823 votes. Galloway lost his seat at the 2010 general election but returned to the Commons at a by-election in Bradford West in 2012, standing as a Respect candidate. In 2010, shortly before the general election, Sylvia Hermon (Lady Hermon) left the Ulster Unionist Party but retained her North Down seat in the election as an Independent.

Normally, you need to be the adopted candidate of a major political party to have a realistic chance of election to the House of Commons. In the 2010 general election, there were 4,150 candidates altogether; 1,893 of these were from the three major UK-wide parties (one each in every seat in Great Britain, except the Speaker's seat).

For the first time, a Green Party candidate was elected to the House of Commons in 2010 when Caroline Lucas won the Brighton Pavilion seat. The Green Party fielded 335 candidates at the election.

Candidates are chosen by the party organisations in the constituency concerned, although there has been increasing involvement of the central party organisation in the process, especially at high-profile by-elections. In the Labour and Conservative parties, a committee of the local party will draw up a short-list of five or six candidates from as many as one hundred names, who will usually also be on the party's 'approved' list, although it is possible for the central organisation to impose its own short-list. The Labour Party uses all-women short-lists for some seats in an attempt to increase the number of women in the Commons. Candidates are interviewed at a meeting of local party members and then selected by eliminating ballot. The Liberal Democrats draw up panels of suitable candidates in England, Wales and Scotland, and the local party must advertise a vacancy to the people on the relevant list. The local party then prepares a short-list (which must include men and women and pay due regard to the representation of ethnic minorities) and all party members in the relevant constituency may vote to select their candidate.

The selection of candidates is thus subject to local control, although no procedure as elaborate as the primary system in the United States of America has evolved; interestingly, the Conservative Party held primaries for candidate selection in a number of seats before the 2010 general election. However, unlike the USA, it is not necessary for a would-be MP to have considerable personal means. The election deposit required is £500 and is forfeited only if the candidate receives less than 5 per cent of the votes cast. In any case, it is found by the party, as are most of the candidate's expenses (see page 24). Once elected to the Commons, an MP can usually expect to remain the party's candidate at the next election. The Labour Party has a system of mandatory reselection; that is, the sitting member must undergo the selection process before being adopted by the constituency party. Robert Wareing (Labour) in Liverpool, West Derby, was deselected before the 2010 general election. Anne McIntosh (Conservative, Thirsk and Malton) and Tim Yeo (Conservative, South Suffolk) were deselected for 2015; after their local associations' executives refused to endorse them, all association members voted on whether they should be reselected.

Elections: when?

General elections used to be held after Parliament had been dissolved, either by royal proclamation on the advice of the Prime Minister or because the maximum life of a parliament – five years – had expired. Between 1945 and 2010, no parliament ran its full term, although the 1992–97 parliament came within a fortnight of doing so. The average length of parliaments between 1945 and 2010 has been a little over three years and seven months. This contrasted with the fixed terms of the US Congress or the practice in countries such as Belgium or Germany, where parliaments are dissolved early only in exceptional circumstances. The ending of a parliament by royal proclamation – in effect, by decision of the Prime Minister, gave him or her a tactical advantage in the timing of the election, although this did not profit the party in government in June 1970 or February 1974. The coalition government introduced fixed-term Parliaments in 2011 and this ended the prerogative power of dissolution. The next scheduled general election will be on 7 May 2015 and at five-year intervals thereafter, unless a new government legislates to change this.

During its passage, the Fixed-term Parliaments Bill was subject to considerable criticism. MPs argued that such important constitutional legislation should have been subject to more lengthy scrutiny. There was also criticism that the main motivation for the legislation was to sustain the Coalition government for a full parliamentary term and that the proper length of term should be four years, not five. We examine the Fixed-term Parliaments Act 2011 in more detail in Chapter 5 (page 119). Although elections are held only for the Commons (elections for any part of the Lords may still be a long way off), a dissolution covers both Houses: the Queen's proclamation says that she dissolves 'the said Parliament accordingly; And the Lords Spiritual and Temporal, and the Members of the House of Commons, are discharged from further attendance thereat'.

A by-election takes place when a seat becomes vacant because the MP dies or is otherwise no longer eligible to sit (see *the candidates*, page 20). A by-election is not required if an MP changes party, although such a requirement is often canvassed, and might be a reason for a recall process if one were introduced (see page 369). An MP cannot, in terms, resign from the House but, in effect, does so by accepting one of the 'offices of profit' of steward or bailiff of Her Majesty's three Chiltern Hundreds of Stoke, Desborough and Burnham, or of the manor of Northstead, which are in the gift of the Chancellor of the Exchequer. These are not real jobs but purely symbolic offices used to allow an MP to stand down. Unusually, in 2011 Sinn Fein's Gerry Adams sought to resign by writing to the Speaker. Adams was made steward and bailiff of the Manor of Northstead without his having requested the post or, indeed, having accepted it. He wished to leave the Commons, and so was content with the disqualification that flowed from his 'appointment', but denied that he had, in fact, accepted an office of profit under the Crown.

By convention, a by-election normally takes place within three months of the vacancy occurring and the process ('moving the writ') is initiated by the Chief Whip of the party which had the seat (although any MP may move a writ). Until a new MP is elected, constituency matters are normally handled by a neighbouring MP of the same party.

Elections: who can vote?

The United Kingdom has a wider franchise than many for its parliamentary elections. There is no property qualification, since 1928 no sex discrimination, and there are voting rights for Britons who live abroad and choose to register. Commonwealth and Irish citizens resident in Britain are entitled to vote, and the only main categories excluded are those under 18, convicted offenders still in prison, people detained under mental health legislation for criminal activity, and anyone with a seat in the House of Lords. European Union citizens living in the UK who are not Irish or Commonwealth nationals may not vote in parliamentary elections. You do not have to have an address in order to vote; homeless people may make a 'declaration of local connection'. However, you must be on the register of parliamentary electors in a constituency. A new system of individual electoral registration (IER) was introduced in 2014; instead of being registered as part of a household, voters will now be registered individually. The new system was introduced to ensure greater integrity of the register after some high profile electoral fraud cases that involved false registration. Voters' personal details will be verified by cross-checking against the Department of Work and Pensions database. Critics of the new system have argued that more effort should be made to try to increase registration rates among the groups least likely to register; these include the young and those in privately rented accommodation who move frequently. The Electoral Commission estimates that there are some 6 million people who should be on the electoral register but who are not registered: the equivalent of about 85 constituencies.

Elections: the timetable

The parliamentary election timetable was lengthened in 2013 from 17 days to 25 days. The timetable is set out in the Representation of the People Act 1983, as amended by the Electoral Registration and Administration Act 2013. In part, this was in response to the increasing practice of combining parliamentary with local elections which already had a timetable of 25 days, but a longer timetable allows more time for late registration of voters and to apply for and receive and return postal votes.

In 2015, dissolution will need to take place on Monday 30 March to allow polling day to be on Thursday 7 May 2015, the date fixed for the next general election by the Fixed-term Parliaments Act 2011. In the past, the date of the general election was decided by the Prime Minister and, although the timetable for the election was much shorter, at 17 days, Parliament was frequently prorogued before dissolution.

In 2010, the Prime Minister announced the general election on 6 April 2010, and thereafter the timetable ran as follows:

Thursday 8 April 2010	Parliament was prorogued
Monday 12 April 2010	Parliament was dissolved by Royal Proclamation
Thursday 6 May 2010	Polling day
Tuesday 18 May 2010	Parliament met to swear in members and, in the Commons, to elect a Speaker
Tuesday 25 May 2010	State Opening of Parliament and Queen's Speech

Election expenses

We have seen that personal wealth is not a prerequisite for standing for Parliament. Indeed, however well-off a candidate or party may be, the law limits what may be spent in each constituency during an election. The general election limits were last raised in 2005 to £7,150 plus 7p per elector in a county constituency (that is, one which is partly rural) and £7,150 plus 5p per elector in a borough constituency. These rates are likely to be changed for the 2015 general election. For a by-election, the overall limit is £100,000.

The total of a party's campaign expenditure over the 365 days before a general election is £30,000 times the number of constituencies that party is contesting: a maximum of £19.5 million, if all 650 constituencies are contested. A general election also involves public expenditure; the cost of administering the 2010 election for the 573 constituencies in England and Wales was £99 million.

In 2014, new limits were introduced on third-party campaigning at general elections, and a wider range of activities was counted under the limits. The level at which third parties must register with the Electoral Commission, providing accounts and so on, will be £20,000 in England, or £10,000 in Scotland, Wales and Northern Ireland. The maximum expenditure by non-party campaigners at UK general elections will be £319,800 in England, £55,400 in Scotland, £44,000 in Wales, and £30,800 in Northern Ireland.

Is the Commons politically representative?

Electoral law on the timing of campaigns is clear, the franchise is wide and elections are frequent. But whether an election result is representative and properly reflects the views of the voters depends on the voting system. The British system is based on the relative majority method, usually called first-past-the-post. The voter marks a ballot paper with one X against the name of his or her favoured candidate – hedging bets with two Xs will mean that the ballot paper is spoiled and will not be counted – and the candidate with the most votes wins. In this system there are no prizes for coming second; and it also means that the proportions of MPs of each party are not the same as the parties' shares of the votes cast across the nation as a whole. It has the merit of creating clear winners and losers, and giving the elected MP a decisive link with the local electorate. The system is, in essence, descended from the historical composition of the Commons as a set of local representatives.

In the 2010 general election, 27,765,000 votes were cast for parties that won seats in the House of Commons (leaving out votes cast for the Speaker); 26,146,400 of these, or 88 per cent, were for one of the three main UK-wide parties.

These parties share the vote with nationalist parties in Scotland and Wales, and with a variety of smaller parties across the UK, some attempting to break through into the mainstream, some concerned with single issues, some extremist, some colourful or eccentric. The three main UK parties do not stand in Northern Ireland, although the Labour Party enjoys a close relationship with the SDLP, whose MPs informally accept the Labour whip, and the Conservative Party has close ties to the UUP, including having fielded joint candidates in 2010.

Shares of that total, and the number of seats that each party won in the House of Commons, are shown in Table 2.1.

But Table 2.1 also shows the seats that each party would have won had the numbers of MPs corresponded exactly to the votes cast. The Conservatives would be the largest party while their coalition partners, the Liberal Democrats, would gain considerably. UKIP and the BNP, who won no seats in 2010, would have a parliamentary presence for the first time with 20 and 12 seats, respectively.

Table 2.1 Voting patterns in the 2010 general election

Party	Votes received	Percent-age of all votes	Seats won (and percentage of all seats)		Seats in proportion to votes received
Labour	8,606,517	29.0	258	(40)	189
Conservative	10,703,654	36.1	306	(47)	235
Liberal Democrat	6,836,248	23.0	57	(9)	150
UK Independence Party (UKIP)	919,471	3.1	0	(0)	20
Scottish National Party	491,396	1.7	6	(0.9)	11
Green	285,612	1.0	1	(0.2)	7
Democratic Unionist Party	168,216	0.6	8	(1.2)	4
British National Party (BNP)	564,321	1.9	0	(0)	12
Plaid Cymru	165,394	0.6	3	(0.5)	4
Sinn Féin	171,942	0.6	5	(0.8)	4
Ulster Unionist	102,361	0.3	0	(0)	2
SDLP	110,970	0.4	3	(0.5)	3

Note: Figures are rounded to one decimal point; seats do not sum to 650 because of votes cast for independent candidates, and for parties not in the table.

The other side of the story is what is sometimes known as the 'wasted vote'. For example, in 2010 all three major parties must have seen the constituency of Norwich South as winnable. The result was:

Liberal Democrat	13,960
Labour	13,650
Conservative	10,902
Green	7,095
UK Independence Party	1,145
BNP	697
Workers Revolutionary Party	102

Simon Wright won the seat for the Liberal Democrats with only 29.4 per cent of the votes cast; 33,591 people voted for other parties, but their votes were not reflected in the result. However, the *potential* power of each voter in Norwich South (by switching parties as a 'floating voter') was much greater than that of a voter in Liverpool Walton who did not wish to vote for the Labour candidate. There Steve Rotherham won the safest Labour seat in the country with 72.0 per cent of the vote, 24,709 votes compared with his closest rival, the Liberal Democrat, with 4,891 votes. In the country as a whole, the different effect of votes cast for the three main parties was striking. It took 119,900 votes to elect a Liberal Democrat MP, but only 35,000 to elect a Conservative MP and 33,400 to elect a Labour MP.

The 2005 general election showed some of the effects of the first-past-the-post system in an extreme form. The Labour Party remained in power with a reduced, but still very comfortable, majority (commentators who talked up Tony Blair's 'slashed' majority seemed to forget how many Prime Ministers would have delighted in such luxury; the margin of 66 was higher than in 9 of the 18 Parliaments since 1945). More important, Labour's 35.2 per cent of the poll was the lowest ever share of the vote for a winning party. The low turnout magnified the effect: the government was elected on the votes of less than one-quarter of the electorate – 21.6 per cent – again a record for a winning party.

Proponents of the first-past-the-post system usually make three main points in its favour. It is a simple system – no preferences, or second and third choices – and it is easily understood by voters. It usually produces clear results, with one party having a strong mandate to govern. And it avoids 'smoke-filled rooms', shorthand for the situation where political choices are made by negotiation between parties after an election, where deals are made and policies agreed that have not been put before the electorate.

Nevertheless, the 2010 general election created exactly that outcome: the Liberal Democrats returned to government for the first time since the wartime coalition by means of an agreement with the Conservative Party, which was the largest party but did not command an absolute majority. The policy platform that was eventually unveiled in the form of a Coalition Agreement and Programme for Government was thus not a manifesto that had been endorsed by the electorate, but a subsequent deal by politicians. This feature became pointed when the Coalition's first notable act was to create a fixed parliamentary term, all but guaranteeing itself five years in power.

Critics of the system reply that voters are more sophisticated and canny than many pundits might think; that strong governments may be overbearing and insensitive, and actually the last thing the voters want; that, once in office, governments produce policies that have never been put before the electorate anyway; and that most voters would prefer consensus to adversarial politics.

In 2010 the Liberal Democrats made it a condition of entering into the Coalition government that there should be a referendum on a proportional electoral system: the Alternative Vote method, also known as Ranked Choice Voting. Under it, the voter ranks the candidates in order of preference; a candidate with more than half the first preferences is elected outright, but otherwise in successive rounds of counting the lowest-scoring candidates are eliminated and their preferences redistributed among the surviving candidates. The referendum was held on 5 May 2011 when voters rejected a move to AV by a decisive 67.9 per cent to 32.1 per cent. The No vote was in the majority in every UK region and was above 70 per cent in five of the nine English regions: the North-East, the West Midlands, the East Midlands, the East of England and the South-East and, out of 440 vote counting areas, the No vote was in the majority in 430. Of the ten areas that had a majority of Yes votes, six were in London. Ironically, forms of proportional representation are already in widespread use in the UK. The Scottish Parliament has 73 constituency members (elected using the first-past-the-post system) and 56 additional regional members drawn from party lists. Similar systems are used for the National Assembly for Wales (40 and 20) and for the Greater London Assembly (14 and 11). The 108 members of the Northern Ireland Assembly are elected using the single transferable vote (STV) system, and the 73 UK MEPs are elected using a 'closed-list' system in large multi-member regional constituencies.

Are the members of the Commons representative?

Despite a local democratic element in the choice of candidates, the MPs who sit in the Commons are not a microcosm of the electorate as a whole.

Age

The House of Commons is overwhelmingly middle-aged. The average age of MPs elected to the House in 2010 is almost exactly 50, a year younger than at the 2005 election. In the House elected in 2010, 411 MPs were aged between 40 and 60 (63 per cent of the total compared with 28 per cent of the population of the UK as a whole). Fifteen MPs were younger than 30 when elected in 2010, only 3 in 2005, 4 in 2001 and 11 in 1997. The average age of the House is perhaps not surprising. Few young aspiring politicians are lucky enough to be selected for a winnable seat; constituency parties often prefer candidates with some experience outside politics. Nevertheless, although the average age of the population as a whole is rising, the age profile of the Commons may be a factor in distancing younger voters from the political process.

Occupation and education

In the 2010 parliament, 35 per cent of MPs in the three main parties had a professional background: 8 per cent had been school or university teachers, and 14 per cent were solicitors or barristers; 25 per cent had a business background, and 14 per cent cent had previously been a politician or political organiser (compared with 5 per cent in 1987). Just over one-quarter of the UK population has a degree level qualification or equivalent, but 70 per cent of MPs from the three main parties have had a university education (26 per cent at Oxford or Cambridge).

There are many reasons why certain occupations produce a disproportionate number of MPs while others – for example, manual work (4 per cent in the House), nursing and engineering – are less well represented. MPs do not have secure jobs in Parliament and often want to retain part-time work in their old professions – something criticised by those who believe that election as an MP with a salary of just over £67,000 demands full-time attention. Some jobs are communicative and more likely to appeal to those who want to enter politics. In some jobs it is impossible to devote large amounts of time to politics – normally essential if one intends to stand for Parliament. And despite the fact that an MP's pay is almost than two-and-a-half times the national median wage (the level below which 50 per cent of employees fall) of £27,000 (April 2013), some who might consider standing would have to take a substantial pay cut.

Nevertheless, in the past, the picture was more mixed. The impact of the two World Wars meant that many mid-twentieth century MPs had extensive military experience. In addition, there were greater numbers of professionals and of manual workers around that time. Since 1979 there has been a relative decline in legal professionals entering the Commons, and a big decline in former manual workers being elected. There has been a significant increase in MPs from non-professional white collar backgrounds, including in particular those whose career was in other political work.

Women in Parliament

After decades of campaigning, culminating in the suffragette movement, the bill to allow women to stand for Parliament was passed on the day that Parliament was dissolved for the 1918 general election. Paradoxically, it allowed women to be candidates at the age of 21, although women did not then have the right to vote until the age of 30 (reduced to the same age as men, then 21, in 1928).

The first woman elected to the Commons, Countess Markievicz, was elected in 1918 for the St Patrick's division of Dublin as a Sinn Féin member but, in protest against British policy on Ireland, never took her seat. It was ironic that the first woman to do so, Viscountess Astor, who was elected at a by-election on 15 November 1919, had never campaigned for women's rights. Since 1918, 369 women have been elected as members of the House of Commons, some 8 per cent of all MPs over the period. The numbers of women MPs remained very low for 70 years, only passing 5 per cent at the 1987 general election, rising to 9.2 per cent in 1992 and sharply to 18.2 per cent in 1997. The 143 women elected in the 2010 general election was the most ever, 22 per cent of all MPs, but still a very low proportion as women make up more than 51 per cent of the population. The devolved parliaments do much better than Westminster; just over one-third (35 per cent) of members in the Scottish Parliament are women, and 40 per cent of members of National Assembly for Wales are female.

Data from the Inter-Parliamentary Union shows the proportion of women in the lower (or single) House of different countries' legislatures following the most recent elections. The UK is ranked 74th. Rwanda is ranked first, followed by Andorra, Cuba and Sweden. Four countries in the ranking have no women in their lower or single House, while 39 have fewer than 10 per cent women, including two European countries (Hungary and Ukraine).

In the 2010 general election, 21 per cent of the candidates (874) were women, and 79 per cent (3,276) were men, equivalent to 1.3 women and 5.0 men per seat. In 2005, 20.3 per cent of candidates were women, and in 2001 the figure was 19.3 per cent. Of the main parties, Labour had the highest number and percentage of female candidates. In terms of votes and seats won per candidate, Conservative women candidates were less successful than their male counterparts. The reverse was true of female candidates standing for Labour. The Liberal Democrats' female candidates on average won a similar number of votes to the party's male candidates, but won a smaller percentage of seats.

The first three Muslim female MPs were elected in 2010; Shabana Mahmood in Birmingham Ladywood; Rushanara Ali in Bethnal Green and Bow, and Yasmin Qureshi in Bolton South East.

Ethnic minorities

There have been non-white members of the House of Commons in the past (a Liberal, a Conservative and a Communist, who each sat for brief periods between 1892 and 1929) but, despite the substantial immigration into the United Kingdom from its former colonies in the West Indies and from the former Indian Empire in the 1950s and later, no representative of these communities was elected to Parliament until 1987 (although several had been created life peers). There is still no representative of the substantial ethnic Chinese community of around half a million. Efforts have been made in all parties to nominate ethnic minority candidates, but not with great success. In the 1992 parliament there were six MPs who described themselves as being from an ethnic minority. This increased to nine in the 1997 parliament, to twelve, or 1.8 per cent, in the 2001 parliament and to fifteen, or 2.3 per cent of MPs, in 2005. After the 2010 general election there were 27 minority ethnic MPs in the House of Commons; 4.2 per cent of the total. The UK population is becoming increasingly diverse in terms of ethnicity and the 2011 Census showed 18 per cent of the UK population reporting a non-white background, compared with 8 per cent ten years earlier. However, despite an increase of 15 minority ethnic MPs between the 2001 and 2010 general election, the diversity of MPs remains disproportionate to the population as a whole. If the non-white population were represented proportionally in the House of Commons, there would be around 117 minority ethnic MPs.

Does it matter?

In one sense, it can be argued that it matters very little that the make-up of the membership of the House of Commons does not reflect the population as a whole. Every MP is there to represent all the people in a constituency, whether they voted for the MP, or one of the other candidates, or did not vote at all. A man, or a woman, or someone from an ethnic minority, or a single parent, may perhaps be thought to have a better understanding of the outlook of men, of women, of ethnic minorities, or of single parents. Nevertheless, the MP's job is to represent the diversity of the people in the constituency in a conscientious and professional way. Understanding your constituents is part of doing the job well, whether or not you have a particular affinity with one group or another. However, recognising that the House of Commons needed to examine whether the diversity of its membership could be increased, in 2007 Gordon Brown as Prime Minister proposed a Speaker's Conference on parliamentary representation.

The Speaker's Conference on Parliamentary Representation

The Conference was established at the end of 2008 'to consider and make recommendations for rectifying the disparity between the representation of women and ethnic minorities in the House of Commons and their representation in the UK population at large; and to consider such other matters as might, by agreement, be referred to for consideration.' In its final report in January 2010 the Conference made recommendations in four areas. Changes in the administration of the House of Commons were recommended, including establishing a nursery for the children of staff and members and promoting educational visits. The government was called upon to legislate to allow political parties to operate quotas in favour of BME candidates and to allow parties to use all-women shortlists until 2030. Changes in parliamentary business were recommended, including family friendly sitting times and an end to hostile behaviour in the Chamber. Parties were urged to promote candidates from under-represented groups.

The reputation of parliament

Another factor is how the House of Commons is seen by the people it represents. There are many factors that affect the standing of Parliament. In past parliaments, a powerful executive and a large parliamentary majority for one party have conditioned the perception of Parliament's powers and what it can do for the citizen. The politics of coalition, and a much greater independence of mind among MPs, are giving a different impression of the role and effectiveness of Parliament, but this is taking time to work through to the public.

The expenses scandal of 2009 dealt a savage blow to the reputation of Parliament, but most insiders saw the 2010 election as a turning point. There were 227 new MPs elected – some 35 per cent of the House. They knew what they were getting into, and came to Westminster with an evident determination to do things differently. Unfortunately it is much quicker and easier to damage a reputation than to restore it. The behaviour, and thus the standing, of individual MPs is another factor; and, although they may be a tiny minority, MPs who misbehave do disproportionate damage to confidence in Parliament as an institution.

Despite increasing direct access to Parliament and its work, through Parliament's own outreach programme and through the BBC Parliament channel, webcasting on www.parliamentlive.tv and the Parliament website www.parliament.uk, most people hear about Parliament through the media. *Political* reporting in the UK is of a generally high standard, but *parliamentary* reporting, requiring a knowledge of the institution and the way it works, is less so – although improving.

A useful barometer of public perceptions of Parliament is the Hansard Society's *Audit of Political Engagement*, which has tracked opinion over the last 11 years. The 2014 *Audit* showed high scores for Parliament being 'essential to our democracy' (67 per cent of those polled) and that it 'debates and makes decision about issues that matter to me' (51 per cent). However, only 23 per cent agreed that Parliament 'encourages public involvement in politics' and rather worryingly, only 34 per cent saw Parliament as holding government to account. 50 per cent said they were 'very' or 'fairly' interested in politics and 48 per cent thought they had at least 'a fair amount' of knowledge of Parliament (48 per cent of those polled). It was discouraging that only 49 per cent said that they were certain to vote in a general election, with 11 per cent saying that they were absolutely certain not to vote. Turnout is not the only measure of public engagement with parliamentary politics, but it is probably the single most significant one.

Turnout: reconnecting parliament with the people

In the general election of 1992, nearly 78 per cent of those registered to vote did so. The turnout fell to 71.5 per cent in 1997, perhaps because so many people assumed that Labour would win. Even though the result of the 2001 election might also have been easily predicted, the fall in the turnout – to just over 59 per cent – was dramatic. It was lower than at any election since the introduction of the universal franchise, and it was of concern for two reasons. First, a government with an overwhelming Commons majority, and apparent carte blanche to do as it wished, had been elected with the support of only one in four people entitled to vote. Perhaps more seriously, the low turnout seemed to signal a loss of interest in the country's central democratic institution. Subsequently, in the 2005 general election turnout went up slightly to 61.5 per cent, though the government elected with a comfortable majority was now supported by only one in five of the electorate. Turnout rose modestly again in the 2010 general election, to 65.1 per cent.

Many factors have been blamed for historically low levels of general election turnout. Does an adversarial style of politics put the voters off? Or, equally, do people see the less polarised relationship of the two major parties as offering less choice than before? The rise in support for the UK Independence Party (UKIP) could be read as an indication of the latter. Or does the electorate see Parliament as unable to control an over-mighty executive – the 'it won't make any difference' syndrome? No doubt, in the 2015 general election, perspectives of coalition government, and the compromises it requires, will be a factor.

If there has been no agreement on the cause, there is certainly no agreement on the cure. A change in the electoral system? No, because the 2011 referendum on the introduction of AV for parliamentary elections showed that the public had little enthusiasm for ditching the first-past-the-post system. More access to the political process, through online consultations, draft bills and the work of select committees? Fostering a wider understanding of what Parliament does and how it works? We will have a closer look at the possibilities in Chapter 12.

The Lords

Unlike the House of Commons, the House of Lords has never been representative. From its earliest times it was a chamber of individuals. Originally, members of the House were mainly the rich and powerful landed magnates on whom the King relied for his support and whose retainers would turn out to assist him (or when things went wrong, oppose him!) on the battlefield. From the late seventeenth century, the House came to include members whose influence lay elsewhere, in money, commerce and political patronage. During the twentieth century this changed as new members were increasingly drawn from the ranks of former MPs and others without landed or moneyed connection – such as trade unionists, academics, former public servants, local politicians and so forth. But members continued to have one thing in common throughout the ages: they represented no one but themselves.

Current membership

Membership of the House at the beginning of the 2014–15 session was 778, exclusive of those members who were on leave of absence – that is to say, they had been granted leave of the House not to attend in response to their writs of summons to Parliament – and those who were disqualified or suspended. The categories of membership were as follows:

Archbishops and bishops	26
Life peers under the Appellate Jurisdiction Act 1876	12
Life peers under the Life Peerages Act 1958	652
Hereditary peers under the House of Lords Act 1999	88
Total	778

Let us now take a closer look at these different categories. Who are they and how are they selected?

Archbishops and bishops

The Anglican Archbishops of Canterbury and York, the Bishops of Durham, London and Winchester and the 21 senior diocesan bishops from other dioceses of the Church of England sit in the House as 'Lords Spiritual'. All the other Lords are known as 'Lords Temporal'. In the mediaeval Parliament the Lords Spiritual (bishops and mitred abbots) made up about half the membership. Currently they represent about one in 30. Only the Church of England is represented. The other established church, the Church of Scotland, has no nominees; nor do other religious denominations, non-Christian religions or the Anglican churches outside England. When the then Chief Rabbi, Lord Sacks, was made a peer in 2009, it was personal to him. When a bishop retires, he loses his seat in the Lords, though it has been the practice to give life peerages to retiring Archbishops

Life peers under the Life Peerages Act 1958

Most members of the House of Lords are life peers, appointed to the House under the Life Peerages Act 1958. Under this legislation men and women are created peers for life and the titles they hold cease upon their death. Until the passing of the act, the House was a largely hereditary institution but the arrival of life peers changed that: within a short time the award of hereditary membership had virtually ceased, and the activities of the House were much invigorated. Following the exclusion of all but 92 of the hereditary members in 1999, the House has in effect become an appointed senate-like body, unlimited by number and with no retirement age. In June 2014 there were 652 life peers. As we have seen, only the bishops retire. All temporal peers stay until they die. The average age of the House is currently just over 70 years!

The granting of life peerages allowed members to be appointed from a wide range of backgrounds and facilitated greater diversity by gender and ethnic background. The professional background of new appointments to the House since 1958, based on the ten years preceding their appointment, is as follows:

	1958–97	1997–2010	2010–14
MPs	38.3	28.0	24.7
Other politics/unions	4.5	9.4	16.7
Industry/trade	14.1	14.7	14.2
Military	1.4	1.4	1.9
Public service	6.1	12.4	8.6
Law	9.6	7.3	4.3
Academic/medical	10.4	7.8	4.9
Voluntary	2.3	5.0	5.6
Local government	4.2	3.6	6.8
Other	9.1	10.4	12.4

Closer scrutiny shows a continuing predominance of national and local politicians and their advisers among new members: in the period to 1997 they numbered 47 per cent and in the period from the 2010 general election to June 2014, 48.2 per cent. And there has been a falling off in appointments from the professions, which represented 20 per cent of new appointments in the period to 1997, and only 9.2 per cent since 2010. Professional diversity in the House clearly has its boundaries. Gender diversity has certainly improved in recent years. In 2005, 18 per cent of members were women: by 2014 this had risen to 23 per cent, just ahead of the 22 per cent in the Commons. Figures are not maintained on ethnic diversity but a much more ethnically diverse chamber than ever before is visible on all benches.

So how are members of the House of Lords appointed? The power to create new peerages belongs to the Crown, but in effect is exercised by the Prime Minister. He is the gatekeeper who decides when a list of new members is announced and the number of names it contains. By convention other party leaders are also asked to make nominations from among their own party faithful. This gives party leaders very considerable patronage. Until relatively recently it was possible to separate these lists into different categories – dissolution and resignation lists, honours lists and 'working peers' lists. But the award of a peerage through the honours system is now rare and neither Tony Blair nor Gordon Brown had resignation lists. There was a dissolution list of former MPs of all parties following the 2010 election but it was announced at the same time as, and hence was largely indistinguishable from, David Cameron's first 'working peers' list. So except for the shadowy survival of a dissolution list every five years, it is fair to say that at present all lists of new members are 'working peers' lists, particularly given the parties' presumption that members will attend faithfully. Occasionally a single person may be nominated; for example, if he or she is required to serve as a minister in the Lords.

In addition to these party political nominations, a non-statutory House of Lords Appointments Commission makes recommendations for non-political members and vets for propriety all other nominations. Following the establishment of the Commission in May 2000, a public nomination system was launched and in April 2001, 15 'people's peers' were announced with a further 7 in May 2004. The rate of nomination has now settled at two a year. In addition the Prime Minister can award a non-political peerage; for example, when a Chief of the Defence Staff or Cabinet Secretary retires.

There is in this process no attempt to pace the introduction of new members over time and, among those who make the nominations, no concept of what constitutes an ideal size for the House. As a result there are times, particularly following a change of administration, when the Lords must absorb large numbers of new members as supporters of the outgoing regime are rewarded and supporters of the incoming regime are found places. Thus, in the months following the 2010 election, 111 party nominees became members.

Life peers under the Appellate Jurisdiction Act 1876

Before the establishment of the Supreme Court as a separate institution in 2009, the House of Lords acted as the final court of appeal for the whole of the United Kingdom in civil cases and for England, Wales and Northern Ireland in criminal cases. The judges who heard these appeals, mostly sitting as a committee called the Appellate Committee, were specially appointed to the House as Lords of Appeal in Ordinary, or Law Lords, under the 1876 Act. These were the first life peers and they were able to engage in the wider parliamentary functions of the House too, though latterly many of them did not. In 2009 the serving Law Lords who became Justices of the Supreme Court were disqualified from sitting under the terms of the Constitutional Reform Act 2005. But, on retirement, that disqualification ceases and they can resume their seats. And of course the retired Law Lords never left. They are a dying breed as the 1876 Act has now been repealed, but there are currently 12 members in this category.

Hereditary peers

Until the passing of the Life Peerages Act, all members of the House of Lords, except for the bishops and Lords of Appeal in Ordinary, were hereditary. The principle of a hereditary peerage is that, at some historical point, an individual is created a peer or lord (in one of the different ranks of dukes, marquesses, earls, viscounts or barons), and the legal document conferring that peerage (the 'letters patent') stipulates that his heirs (normally only the males) may inherit his title and with it the right to sit in the House of Lords. Some peerages descend through the female line, as well as the male, and after 1963 women holders of hereditary peerages were also able to take their seats in the Lords.

Current membership of the House of Lords includes 92 hereditary peers who have seats as a result of the House of Lords Act 1999. This Act reformed the House's membership by excluding hereditary peers from sitting, but following an agreement between the government and the then Leader of the Opposition in the Lords, Lord Cranborne, the bill was amended so that 75 hereditary members were excepted from the general provisions of the Act by election from among their own party or group, a further 15 by election by the whole House to serve as Deputy Speakers and committee chairs, and 2 (the Earl Marshal and Lord Great Chamberlain both of whom are currently on leave of absence) *ex officio*.

These arrangements were expected to be transitional pending further reform of membership (see Chapter 12), but their effect meanwhile is to make the hereditary principle a continuing feature of British political life. From the passing of the House of Lords Act until the end of the 2001–02 session, vacancies arising out of the death of one of the ninety elected members were filled by the runners-up in the relevant category with the most votes. Two crossbench vacancies were filled in this way. Thereafter a system of by-elections came into force. Anyone in receipt of a writ before the passage of the Act, or anyone who has subsequently established a right to be included, may ask to be on the register of eligible candidates maintained by the Clerk of the Parliaments. The electors are the whole House in the case of the 15 Deputy Speakers or chairs but only the hereditary peers in a party or group in respect of the 75 elected by party or group. The Labour Party currently has four excepted hereditary members, and thus three electors! The first such election was held in March 2003, using a preferential voting system, and elections have since become commonplace, if increasingly bizarre.

Before the 1999 Act, the House of Lords was on paper at least a predominantly hereditary body, although in terms of regular attendance the hereditary element was just under 50 per cent. Now, the 92 hereditary members represent just 11.6 per cent of membership.

Attendance

We have already noted that members of the House are not representative. They are also part-time and do not always attend. Thus, in the 2012–13 session, of those eligible to attend, just over 50 per cent of members attended 75 per cent or more of the sittings; and just over 70 per cent attended 50 per cent or more of the sittings. Only six never came at all. Indeed, the average daily attendance is higher than it has ever been, and has risen steadily since 1999. The numbers for the sessions between 1999 and 2014 are shown below:

Session	Attendance	Rate of attendance
1999–2000	352	51%
2004–05	388	56%
2010–12	475	59%
2013–14	497	64%

Rates of attendance vary widely by political group. In the long 2010–12 session, the mean daily attendance per member was 68 per cent for Labour, 61 per cent for Conservatives, 76 per cent for Liberal Democrats and 45 per cent for crossbenchers. Thus two key facts emerge: first, attendance is on the increase both in absolute and relative terms, and second, there are still wide differences in individual behaviour, indicating that members interpret their obligations to attend Parliament in response to The Queen's Writ of Summons – and, indeed, the promises they may have made to their political sponsors or the Appointments Commission before their appointment – in a variety of different ways.

Politics

Although members of the House are not representative and are unelected, they are nearly all political animals. Most members of the House take a party whip, and of course most of the life peers owe their membership of the House to political patronage. The non-aligned crossbench members have political opinions on issues,

Table 2.2 Composition of the House of Lords, 1 May 2014*

	Life	Hereditary	Bishops	Total
Conservative	171	49	–	220
Labour	214	4	–	218
Liberal Democrat	94	4	–	98
Cross-bench	151	30	–	181
Bishops	–	–	26	26
Other	34	1	–	35
Total	664	88	26	778

*Excludes members on leave of absence, disqualified or suspended.

although none of them supports a political party. Party political allegiance on the eve of the 2014–15 session is set out in Table 2.2.

It is immediately apparent from Table 2.2 that the numbers of Labour and Conservative members are broadly balanced, though the Conservatives are far more dependent on excepted hereditary members than are Labour. Only with the support of the Liberal Democrat members or the Crossbench and non-affiliated members can either major party win votes. Party loyalty is much stronger in the House of Lords than might be imagined for an unelected chamber. Party cohesiveness, as measured in voting habits, is very high and there are few who rebel against the party whip. Thus, in whipped votes in the 2010–12 session the Labour Party achieved 99 per cent cohesion, the Conservatives 97 per cent and the Liberal Democrats 94 per cent. But what the whips cannot always enforce is attendance.

There is some evidence that the identification of members with party, or at least their readiness to turn out to vote, has increased greatly in the last few years. Between the 2008–09 and 2013–14 sessions, average daily attendance rose by just over 24 per cent from 400 to 484 but the average number of members voting in divisions rose by 103 per cent, from 194 to 394.

It is sometimes maintained that the relative size of the political parties in the Lords broadly reflects their relative share of votes cast at the last general election and that this accords the House as it is presently composed a form of legitimacy. To the extent that this may be true it is largely coincidental and as a proposition might well not survive a substantial swing from one party to another or a voting collapse. The Coalition Agreement of 2010 proposed that Lords appointments would be made so that the House is 'reflective of the share of the vote secured by the parties at the last general election'. Even were this precept to be observed the rate of change might be too slow to achieve the desired effect. The low rate of churn in membership is explored further in Chapter 12.

Leaving the Lords

Until now, it has not been possible for a member of the House of Lords – other than a bishop – ever, formally, to leave it. Life meant life and resignation was not possible. In 1957, in the days of the hereditary House, a scheme was instituted whereby a member who could not attend might apply for Leave of Absence for the remainder of a Parliament. At the beginning of the 2014–15 session, 44 members had taken leave. Such leave may be rescinded on three months' notice. In 2011, the House also introduced a voluntary retirement scheme which was essentially a variation of the Leave of Absence arrangements and by May 2014 four members had 'retired'. Real change in this area was effected when the House of Lords Reform Act 2014 was passed at the end of the 2013–14 session. The Act allowed members to retire permanently and cease to receive a Writ of Summons. Any member who did not attend at all in a session would be deemed to have retired at the end of it. This bill, promoted as a private member's bill in the Commons by Dan Byles MP, drew on elements of a Lords private member's bill first introduced by Lord Steel of Aikwood (see also page 381). For the first time it will be possible for members of the House to resign their seats permanently. Given the low take up of the voluntary scheme, it will be interesting to see whether the effect of this minor piece of legislation on membership figures will be any more than cosmetic. The same act also provided for the permanent disqualification from membership of a member convicted of a serious offence carrying a term of imprisonment of over one year, thus bringing the Lords into line with the Commons.

The Queen

It is easy to think of Parliament as consisting simply of the two Houses; but the sovereign is also part of the institution. Indeed, the words that precede every Act of Parliament remind us that, to become law, a bill must be approved by the Queen, as well as by both Houses:

> *Be it enacted by the Queen's most Excellent Majesty, by and with the advice and consent of the Lords Spiritual and Temporal, and Commons, in this present Parliament assembled, and by the authority of the same, as follows:*

The Queen's name appears again and again in the proceedings of Parliament. Bills go for Royal Assent; if a bill affects the Royal Prerogative or the Queen's personal interests, then the Queen's consent must be signified before it is passed; the spending of taxpayers' money in connection with a bill must have the Queen's recommendation; the government's legislative programme is set out at the beginning of a session in the Queen's Speech; many papers presented formally to the two Houses are presented 'by Command of Her Majesty'; Orders in Council – a category of delegated legislation – are made in her name; the government is 'Her Majesty's Government'; and ministers are 'Ministers of the Crown'.

This terminology may seem more appropriate to the mediaeval relationship between the monarch and his fledgling parliament, and in the early twenty-first century the language is entirely symbolic. The Queen does, indeed, give her consent to bills –

by signing a list of bills passed rather than each one – but she has no practical power of refusal. The last sovereign to refuse Royal Assent (to a bill for settling the militia in Scotland) was Queen Anne in 1707–08, and in subsequent centuries sovereigns have progressively distanced themselves from the business of politics.

Above politics: political neutrality

The conventional phrase is that the Queen is 'above politics' or, as Walter Bagehot said of royalty and Queen Victoria, 'Its mystery is its life. We must not let in daylight upon magic. We must not bring the Queen into the combat of politics, or she will cease to be reverenced by all combatants; she will become one combatant among many'. Nearly 150 years after Bagehot's *The English Constitution*, the Queen's political neutrality is still of constitutional importance. On the one hand, most people would regard it as unacceptable for the monarch to be identified with a particular political party (even a political party that they themselves supported); on the other hand, the Queen may have to perform a crucial constitutional task: deciding who should form a government after a general election.

Choosing a Prime Minister

Normally this is straightforward. The day after polling day the leader of the party with the most seats in the House of Commons – and so able to command the House and get the business of government through – is summoned to Buckingham Palace and asked as Prime Minister to form a government, which in practice means appointing the members of the Cabinet and other ministers and taking responsibility for the administration of the country.

Similarly, when a sitting Prime Minister resigns – as Harold Wilson did in 1976, or Margaret Thatcher did in 1990, having lost the confidence of her party – the sovereign's task is an easy one. The government party will choose a new leader under the procedure required by its party rules, and – assuming that that party still has a majority in the House – the Queen will invite the winner to form a government.

A hung parliament

However, in a hung parliament after a general election, where no one party has a majority, the Queen's task may be more difficult. When the final tally of seats is clear, there will probably be intense negotiation between the parties to see how much common ground there might be for the formation of a coalition (where ministers would be drawn from two or more parties) or for one party to govern with the formal support of another. When the Conservative Party lost its majority in the general election of February 1974, Edward Heath negotiated with the Liberal Party in an attempt to continue in government with Liberal support. When it was clear that he would be unsuccessful, the Queen asked Harold Wilson to form a minority government, which struggled on until a general election in October that year, at which Wilson won a narrow overall majority of three seats. In May 2010 the

Conservative Party under David Cameron was the largest party, but 20 seats short of an overall majority (306 seats to Labour's 258). However, the Coalition Agreement between the Conservatives and the Liberal Democrats (with 57 seats), negotiated between 7 and 12 May, meant that the Coalition had an overall majority and the Queen's task was an easy one.

More difficult for the sovereign would be a situation where a general election produced a three-way split in seats in the Commons but very little common ground between any of the three parties. If it was quickly clear that the party leader first asked to form a government could not sustain it – for example, by losing the vote on the proposed legislative programme in the Queen's Speech – she would probably invite another party leader to attempt to form a government.

It would be a matter of judgement as to how long this process could be allowed to go on. On the one hand, the argument goes, the people have spoken (as former President Clinton famously said of the 2000 US presidential election, 'but we're not sure yet what they've said') and it is for politicians to agree a constructive way forward. To force another poll so soon after the first (whether or not the Fixed-term Parliaments Act were still in force) would inflict another general election on a weary electorate, with no guarantee that it would produce any different result. On the other hand, the business of government needs to be carried on and a second general election might be preferable to months of inter-party squabbling and horse trading.

In these circumstances, the sovereign's political neutrality is crucial. While others may be concerned about party advantage, she must consider only the national interest. The process is not risk-free: when in Australia in 1975 the Governor-General dismissed the Prime Minister on the grounds that the two Houses of Parliament could not reach agreement on the budget and the business of government could not be carried on, that undoubtedly fuelled the flames of republicanism. By contrast, in Belgium, where coalition governments are the norm, there was little criticism of the King in 1985 when he refused the Prime Minister a dissolution because the coalition government had broken down.

Another method?

It is sometimes suggested that the Queen's powers to dissolve Parliament and invite a party leader to form a government should be delegated to the Speaker of the House of Commons (as has been the case in unicameral Sweden since 1974, where the King's functions are purely ceremonial). But even if it were acceptable to give the presiding officer of one House powers over the other – for a dissolution affects the Lords as well – and there were sufficient confidence in the Speaker, which is not a foregone conclusion, the same problems would remain to be solved.

The sovereign as statesman

To quote Bagehot again: 'the sovereign has, under a constitutional monarchy such as ours, three rights – the right to be consulted, the right to encourage, the right to warn'. He was speaking of Queen Victoria, who perhaps exercised more influence than does her great-great-grand-daughter, but those principles still hold good today. It is worth remembering that the present Queen has more experience of the nation's affairs than anyone in politics. She sees a wide range of state papers and is briefed frankly by the government on the issues of the day. British ambassadors ('Her Majesty's Ambassadors') and high commissioners call upon her when they leave to take up their posts and when they return, and she sees their most important despatches.

She has known twelve Prime Ministers, from Churchill to Cameron, and at weekly audiences has discussed with them the crises and dilemmas that they have faced. Almost all have had an excellent relationship with her, and some have described the weekly audiences in terms almost of therapy: being able to talk about major problems in total confidence with someone of immense political experience who is neither a political opponent nor a rival. The role of the present Queen demonstrates that Bagehot's rights of the sovereign are still invaluable.

3

Running Parliament

The House of Commons

The Speaker

The Speaker of the House of Commons is the most visible player on the parliamentary stage. His 'Order, order' opens every parliamentary day in the Chamber; he is usually in the Chair for the stormiest parliamentary events, and he is the representative of the House on occasions of state ceremony, sorrow and rejoicing.

Not only does the Speaker have the task of chairing the House; he is also an influential figure in most aspects of the way that the House and its administration are run. As the presiding officer of the Commons he may seem the exact counterpart of the Lord Speaker as the presiding officer of the Lords; but, as we shall see, their functions are very different.

The office of Speaker

The first member known as Speaker was Sir Thomas Hungerford in 1376, although it seems clear that individual members presided over the early mediaeval House before then, perhaps as early as Peter de Montfort in Henry III's 'Mad Parliament' at Oxford in 1258. The title of Speaker (Mr Speaker or Madam Speaker, as he or she is always referred to in the House) comes from the ancient position of official spokesman of the Commons to the monarch. In the days when sovereign and Commons were frequently at odds, this aspect of the job was rather more arduous than today, and more hazardous: between 1471 and 1535, six Speakers were executed.

Some of the ancient functions of the Speaker survive in more symbolic form. Once elected by the Commons, he makes claim to the Crown of the House's:

> *ancient and undoubted Rights and Privileges, particularly to freedom of speech in debate, freedom from arrest, freedom of access to Her Majesty whenever*

occasion may require, and that the most favourable construction should be placed on all its proceedings.

Although this may perhaps appear a little at odds with the modern relationship between the monarch and a House elected by universal suffrage.

The Speaker still occasionally acts as the House's spokesman and representative. After the terrorist atrocities on 11 September 2001 he expressed the House's condolences to the US Congress; and on the occasion of the Diamond Jubilee in 2012 he presented an Address of the House to the Queen in Westminster Hall. When parliaments around the world responded to the London bombings of 7 July 2005 it was to the Speaker that they sent their messages of sympathy.

The independence of the Speaker

In many foreign parliaments the presiding officer is a party politician. In the US House of Representatives, for example, the Speaker is a leading party politician and frequently takes part in controversial debate. In Germany, the president of the Bundestag is normally a senior member of the government party who continues to play an active part in his party's affairs, and the same is true of the president of the French Assemblée nationale.

However, in the House of Commons there is a long tradition of impartiality, which began with Arthur Onslow (Speaker for 33 years from 1728) and which is so strong that there is a powerful expectation that all Speakers should be seen as genuinely independent of party. The media keep every utterance of the Speaker under close scrutiny, for any perceived party or personal bias – and if there were to be any such bias, it would mean that the Speaker could not do his job effectively, exercise the considerable powers that the House has given him, or maintain the confidence of the House.

In practice, this means that the Speaker resigns from his party – perhaps after having been a party member for many years – and has nothing more to do with its internal affairs. When he stands at a general election, it is not under a party banner but as 'the Speaker seeking re-election'; and he is usually unopposed by the major parties. He draws the salary of a cabinet minister and can look forward on retirement to a generous pension and a peerage. The dress worn by the Speaker in the Chamber has grown somewhat less formal according to the preference of recent incumbents. Speaker Boothroyd abandoned the full-bottomed wig and, since Speakers Martin and Bercow followed suit, that particular tradition has probably ended for good. Speaker Bercow has gone further and now simply wears a gown over a lounge suit when in the Chamber. When the Speaker goes to and from the Chamber he is preceded by a trainbearer. Warned by cries of 'Speaker!' from the doorkeepers, even the most senior MPs are expected to stop what they are doing and bow as he goes by.

In the Palace of Westminster the Speaker has a personal staff to support him and splendid state apartments, which are his official residence, with a comfortable and less formal flat above. He no longer eats with other MPs in the dining rooms or takes part in the political gossip of the Tea Room. Members now come to him. Every Speaker must keep a finger on the pulse of the House and the concerns of its members, and much of his time is taken up with meetings not only with, for example, the Leader of the House or the Chief Whips, but also with a wide variety of MPs with concerns, problems – or bright ideas.

The Speaker is also the embodiment of the House as far as the outside world is concerned. He receives ambassadors, Speakers and ministers from other parliaments, delegations of all sorts, and he presides over a number of parliamentary associations and other bodies.

The Speaker still carries out constituency work and duties in the same way as any other MP. It is sometimes suggested that the Speaker should sit for a notional constituency, perhaps called St Stephen's – but this idea has never found much favour and has been rejected by the House's Procedure Committee. Speakers rightly want to understand and share at first hand the constituency pressures and problems faced by other MPs; and their own constituents are fortunate in having the Speaker for their Member of Parliament as ministers understandably give special attention to constituency cases raised by the Speaker.

The election of the Speaker

Since 1945, some Speakers have been former ministers (Morrison, Lloyd and Thomas had all been cabinet ministers, while Hylton-Foster had been Solicitor-General and Weatherill had been government Deputy Chief Whip); the careers of others had been mainly on the backbenches (King and Martin; Boothroyd had been a government assistant whip for two years; Speaker Bercow had briefly been an opposition frontbencher). However, since 1965 five out of the seven Speakers have been former Deputy Speakers (King, Thomas, Weatherill, Boothroyd and Martin); not only did they come to the Speakership with experience in the Chair, but also the House had been able to make some assessment of them in that role.

Perhaps surprisingly in view of the rigid political independence of the office, all post-war Speakers except Betty Boothroyd and John Bercow have come from the government side of the House, whichever party has been in power. Given that one of the roles of the Speaker is to protect the House's interests when they conflict with those of the executive, this may have required a rapid reorientation; but it is often said that, particularly at the outset, Speakers tend to be harder on their former party than on the other side of the House.

Since 1992 there have been elections for the Speakership each time it has come vacant. In 1992 the former cabinet minister, Peter Brooke, was defeated by 372 votes to 238, and Betty Boothroyd was elected. She was re-elected unopposed at the start of the 1997 parliament.

On her retirement in 2000 there was an unprecedented election for the Speakership, with no fewer than twelve candidates standing. Propositions are normally put to the House in the form of a motion to which amendments may be moved, and this had always been the procedure for the election of the Speaker, where the motion 'That X do take the Chair of this House as Speaker' could be amended by leaving out 'X' and inserting 'Y'. Thus in 2000 the motion named Michael Martin, and the other candidates were put to the House one by one in a series of amendments. Speeches proposing and seconding the candidates, and by the candidates themselves, together with the votes on each amendment and the final decision, took nine hours. As of course there was no Speaker, the member with the longest continuous service (the then Father of the House), Sir Edward Heath, presided.

In one sense, a day's sitting to fill a post of such importance to every single MP and to the House as a whole was not excessive; but there was understandable pressure to see whether matters could be handled differently. Following a report from the Procedure Committee, in 2001 the House agreed new arrangements. These favoured a Speaker who returns to the House after a general election; only if a motion that he or she should take the Chair is defeated does the new procedure for a contested election come into play.

In a contested election, nominations (supported by twelve to fifteen MPs, at least three of whom cannot be from the candidate's own party) are submitted to the Clerk of the House on the morning of the election. When the House meets later that day, the candidates address the House in turn, in an order chosen by lot, and MPs then vote by secret ballot. If one candidate gets more than half the votes, his or her name is put to the House straight away; but if not, the lowest-scoring candidate and any candidate with less than 5 per cent of the votes are eliminated, a second ballot is held, and so on until one candidate gets more than half the votes. The system is designed to be as fair as possible and not to give an advantage to the candidate who is proposed first (as did the previous system). It is unlike any voting system used in any of the House's other decisions and was first used in June 2009, following the resignation of Speaker Martin in the wake of the expenses scandal.

The 2009 election for Speaker was unprecedented for a number of reasons. It not only followed the new process outlined above, but the *behaviour* of the candidates was novel: the traditional air of reluctance adopted by putative Speakers was cast aside as the contenders set out their stalls in a series of hustings, including one that was televised. Debate about the role was informed not just by the candidates' distinctive approaches, but by the circulation by the then Clerk of Legislation of a paper (the so-called '75 point Plan') setting out possible reforms and innovations that a new Speaker might want to champion.

On the day of the election, after the 10 candidates had each addressed the House, the first round of voting failed to achieve an outright winner; the candidate with the fewest votes and three other candidates with fewer than 5 per cent of the votes were eliminated. The second round also failed to produce a winning candidate with more than half the votes; again, the candidate with the least support was eliminated and the three other lowest polling candidates each withdrew from the contest. Therefore, only two candidates went into the final round; John Bercow gained 322 votes compared with 271 for Sir George Young, the 50 per cent threshold was crossed and the House had a new Speaker. A subsequent review of the arrangements by the Procedure Committee concluded that they had generally worked well, although some minor changes were made. An argument has been made that, in the case of an incumbent Speaker seeking re-election at the start of a parliament, the vote on whether that Speaker should be allowed to continue in post should be carried out by secret ballot – as with the votes in any full-blown contest. That change has not been adopted, but support for it is growing.

The roles of the Speaker

Maintaining order

Perhaps the most obvious function of the Speaker and his deputies is to maintain order when the House is sitting. All speeches made in the Chamber are addressed to the Chair, and the Speaker 'calls to order' any MP who offends against the rules of the House. Some of these are conventions, and others are laid down in standing orders or in past resolutions of the House. The definitive guide to them is *Erskine May's Treatise on the Law, Privileges, Proceedings and Usage of Parliament*, usually known as *Erskine May*. Sir Thomas Erskine May, Clerk of the House from 1871 to 1886, edited the first 9 editions, and 15 more have been edited by his successors.

The House's rules range from the relatively trivial, such as requiring members to refer to each other by constituency rather than name, to the more serious, such as the *sub judice* rule (see page 265), which is designed to prevent criminal trials or civil actions in the courts being prejudiced by comment in the House. Other rules require speeches to be relevant to the matter before the House (and supplementary questions to be relevant to the subject of the question on the Order Paper), forbid the use of insulting words or 'unparliamentary expressions' (see page 265), specify when an MP may speak a second time in a debate, regulate the proper conduct of votes, and so on. The Speaker has both to make sure that these rules are observed and to give his rulings when MPs raise points of order about the application or interpretation of these rules.

In a democratic assembly passions can run high and tempers flare. It is then that the Speaker and his deputies need to be most sensitive in gauging the mood of the House. Will a humorous intervention from the Chair defuse the situation, or is there serious trouble that must be dealt with firmly from the outset? At need, they have powers to discipline individual MPs, either by ordering them to resume their seats, to leave the Chamber for the day or, for more serious offences (usually involving a disregard for the authority of the Chair), naming them. After a member has been named, a motion is moved by the senior minister present, to which the House invariably agrees, and which has the effect of suspending the MP, so barring him or her from the building for 5 sitting days on the first occasion, 20 sitting days on the second and indefinitely on the third (and stopping payment of the member's salary for those periods). If there is general disorder in the Chamber, the Speaker can suspend the sitting.

These are powers used with great reluctance by the Speaker. He does not want to create martyrs or give an individual MP's political protest added force by expulsion from the Chamber; but he has also to protect the reputation of the House and the business before it. Precipitate disciplinary action can rebound upon the Chair, as with the Victorian Speaker who was foolish enough to have the police called to deal with disorder in the Chamber. Thereafter, whenever the House was rowdy, his authority was routinely undermined by shouts of 'send for the police'.

Holding the ring

The Speaker and his deputies have absolute discretion over which members they call to speak. There may be some fixed points in a major debate: perhaps a cabinet minister will open the debate, responded to by his or her opposition shadow and the winding-up speeches at the end might be made by another member of the shadow cabinet and by another cabinet minister.

In between, the character of the debate is shaped by which MPs the Chair calls to speak. Balancing their claims is no easy task. Let us suppose that there is a full day's debate on policy towards asylum seekers: in practice, five or six hours' debating time. The opening and closing frontbench speeches might leave no more than three or four hours for everyone else who wishes to take part. Let us also suppose that pressure on existing reception centres for asylum seekers has led the government to propose a number of additional sites. Unrest in two or three centres has been followed by violence and extensive damage. There will be MPs with asylum centres in their constituencies; those who represent people who are up in arms that a new centre might be located near them; those who represent Channel ports; those who are close to the unions representing asylum centre staff; perhaps the chair and members of the Home Affairs Select Committee, who have just produced a critical report on asylum policy. And, as well as juggling these urgent claims to speak, the Speaker and his deputies have to ensure that the party balance is maintained.

During Question Time (see Chapter 9), the Speaker's ability to shape events is even more marked. He can cut short over-long supplementary questions (and ministerial answers), but he can also decide how long to go on calling MPs to ask supplementaries on a particular question. If the subject is one on which the government is vulnerable, eight supplementary questions – perhaps including some hostile ones from the minister's own side – instead of two or three may give a minister a torrid time at the despatch box. Speaker Bercow's practice of hurrying through the questions to reach as many as possible has had the perverse effect of giving ministers an easier time, as well as making Question Time harder to follow for the public by cutting off questions and answers before they are completed. However, if political and media pressure has forced a ministerial statement or urgent question (see pages 49 and 290) on some high-profile problem, the government's exposure will be much greater if questions run for one hour instead of half an hour, and the present practice is to allow every MP who wants to ask a question to do so, even though the later questioning may add little to what has already been elicited.

The Speaker's powers in the Chamber

In sharp contrast to the House of Lords, the Commons has given its presiding officer extensive powers. The House of Lords may largely regulate itself, but in the much more contentious and politically polarised Commons the Chair has a considerable armoury.

First, as we have seen, there is *the power to call MPs to speak in a debate or to ask a question*, described by Speaker Thomas as his most potent weapon. Although Speakers strive to be fair to every MP, the member who is disruptive or abusive, or disregards the authority of the Chair, may find it difficult to catch the Speaker's eye at Prime Minister's Questions for some little while thereafter. Allied with this is the power to decide *how long questioning on a particular topic may continue*.

In most debates, the Speaker also has the *power to limit the length of backbench speeches*, down to a minimum of three minutes. He can also intervene to *prevent deliberate time-wasting* by MPs either speaking repetitiously or calling for unnecessary votes. The decision on whether to accept the closure – in other words, to *allow the House to decide whether a debate should end and a vote be taken on the subject under discussion* – is entirely in the hands of the Chair.

The Speaker also has discretion on *whether amendments to bills or to motions before the House should be debated and voted upon*. This can be of great significance. For example, on 26 February 2003 the Commons debated a government motion calling upon Iraq to recognise this as its final opportunity to comply with its 'disarmament obligations'; the Speaker selected a Labour backbench amendment to the effect that the case for military action against Iraq was 'as yet unproven'. The amendment was defeated by 393 votes to 199, but the 199 included 122 Labour MPs voting against the government's policy – a rebellion of huge political significance.

Less than a month later, the government put before the House of Commons a motion authorising the use of all means necessary to ensure the disarmament of Iraq's weapons of mass destruction – in effect authorising war. Again, the Speaker selected a Labour backbench amendment asserting that 'the case for war against Iraq has not yet been established, especially given the absence of specific United Nations authorisation'. This time the amendment was defeated by 396 votes to 217; the 217 included 139 Labour MPs (29 of whom had not rebelled on the previous occasion), again a seismic political event.

The number of amendments selected for voting upon by the Speaker can be a matter of controversy. In May 2013, at the end of the debate on the Queen's Speech, the Speaker allowed separate divisions to be held on three amendments (in addition to one held on the penultimate day). The government viewed this as a break with precedent, as previously only two amendments had been called on the final day and they argued that the House would be in a confused position if the Speaker felt able to select an unlimited number of amendments to put to the vote. They also reasonably argued that the phrasing of the relevant Standing Order ('*a* further amendment') could be interpreted only as singular. Eventually, the situation was clarified by a change in the Standing Orders of the House which set out that up to four amendments in total could be selected (with an assumption that one of these would be voted upon during the penultimate day of the debate).

The Speaker can also set part of the political agenda, and allow the House to call the government to account, through urgent questions (or UQs), formerly called private notice questions because they are applied for to the Speaker privately rather than being printed on the Order Paper. If the Speaker thinks a matter is sufficiently urgent or important, and there is unlikely to be another way of raising it in the House in the next day or so, he allows a question to be put to a minister (often by the Opposition spokesman on the subject) at the end of Question Time. Although ministerial statements are made voluntarily by the government, urgent questions are granted when, in the Speaker's view, the House needs to be informed but no ministerial statement is forthcoming. Acting on one of the options included in the '75-point Plan' referred to on page 45, circulated to all candidates for the Speakership, Speaker Bercow has allowed many more UQs than did his predecessors, as shown below:

Session	*Number of urgent questions*
2013–14	35
2012–13	38
2010–12 (a notably long session)	73
2009–10	26
2008–09	11
2007–08	4
2006–07	9

Urgent questions are described in more detail in Chapter 9 (page 290).

The Speaker also has the power to decide whether *a complaint of privilege* – in other words, an allegation that an MP, or a servant of the House, or perhaps a select committee, has been obstructed or threatened – should be put to the House. Such an allegation must be made privately to the Speaker – a procedure designed to prevent frivolous complaints. If the Speaker believes that there may be grounds for action, he allows the matter to take precedence over other business and a motion to be moved referring the complaint to the Committee on Privileges for investigation. Such complaints are rare. Privilege is described in more detail in Chapter 5 (page 161).

The casting vote

Once put to the vote in the House, a matter must be decided; it cannot be left as a draw. If the numbers of 'ayes' and 'noes' are equal, then the occupant of the Chair must decide the question by casting a vote; and it is only on these occasions that the Speaker or his deputies do vote. However, the Chair is protected from controversy by clearly established historical principles. These are, broadly, that a decision should be taken by a majority of the House, not just on the basis of a casting vote; and that there should be opportunity for further discussion. Thus the Chair will vote 'aye' on a casting vote on the second reading of a bill, because the bill can continue its progress and be amended if the House wishes. But the Chair will vote 'no' if the vote on the third reading is tied, because that is the moment at which the Commons approves the bill, and the law should not be changed except by a majority of the House. If the vote is on a motion for the adjournment, the Chair votes 'no' in order to allow the House to proceed with other business.

In the Thatcher and the Blair years, big government majorities made the need for casting votes much less (although on issues of conscience, or unwhipped votes on private members' bills the possibility was always there; and it is worth remembering that the 80 per cent elected/20 per cent appointed House of Lords option was defeated only by 284 votes to 281 on 4 February 2003). However, when the government has a small majority the more likely is the need for a casting vote; it was used seven times between 1974 and 1979. It was almost needed when the Callaghan government fell as a result of losing a vote of confidence on the night of 28 March 1979; 311 MPs voted against the government, and 310 for.

Had the casting vote been needed then, it would have been 'no' on the principle that the decision had to be taken by a majority and not on a casting vote. But so clear is the principle that, even in the greatest political controversy, there is no question of political bias. The most recent casting vote is a good example. On 22 July 1993, the House was voting on the Leader of the Opposition's amendment to a motion on the Social Protocol of the Maastricht Treaty. The votes were 317 ayes and 317 noes. Speaker Boothroyd voted 'no' on the basis that the decision should be taken only by a majority. The government lost the vote on the motion itself and put a motion of confidence before the House the next day, which it won comfortably, without the need for a casting vote. There have been other close calls: in November 2005, with Conservative and Liberal Democrat Support, a Labour backbench amendment to the Terrorism Bill, limiting the definition of 'glorifying terrorism', was defeated by only one vote, and in January 2006 a Lords amendment to the Racial and Religious Hatred Bill was defeated by one vote.

Recalling the House

There have been 27 occasions since the Second World War when, because of some grave event, the House was recalled during a recess. There have been 11 such instances in the last two decades, as shown below:

Date of recall	Subject matter
31 May 1995	Bosnia
2–3 September 1998	Omagh bombing: Criminal Justice (Terrorism and Conspiracy Bill)
14 September, 4 and 8 October 2001	International terrorism and attacks in the USA

3 April 2002	Death of Her Majesty Queen Elizabeth the Queen Mother
24 September 2002	Iraq and Weapons of Mass Destruction
20 July 2011	Public confidence in the media and police
11 August 2011	Public disorder (additional statement on global economy)
10 April 2013	Death of Baroness Thatcher
29 August 2013	Syria

At such times the media normally report that it is the Prime Minister who has recalled Parliament. In fact, the standing orders provide that ministers may represent to the Speaker that the public interest requires an earlier meeting of the House; and, if the Speaker agrees, he appoints a time for the House to sit. This may be a distinction that is not much of a difference because, following precedent, the Speaker always agrees to the government's request. However, despite a Procedure Committee recommendation that the decision should be one for the Speaker alone, a proposal in Gordon Brown's Green Paper, *The Governance of Britain* that 'where a majority of members of Parliament request a recall, the Speaker should consider the request, including in cases where the government itself has not sought a recall', and an incomplete (because it ran into the 2010 election) inquiry by the Procedure Committee, no such change has been made.

Statutory and other functions

The Speaker is *ex officio* chairman of each of the Boundary Commissions mentioned in Chapter 2, although the work falls to the other members, led by a High Court judge (or Scottish equivalent). He also chairs the Speaker's Committee on the Electoral Commission and the Speaker's Committee for the Independent Parliamentary Standards Authority.

The most important and time-consuming of the Speaker's statutory responsibilities is as chairman of the House of Commons Commission, which is the financial and employing authority for the House administration, and whose work we describe on page 57.

The voice of the House

The Speaker's role as official spokesman of the Commons to the monarch may survive only in ceremonial form, but the core of his job is still protecting and expressing the interests of the House. He must protect the interests of the House through securing orderly proceedings, the courtesies of debate, and consistent and fair rulings on points of order and matters of contention. Expressing the interests of the House is more complex and potentially more politically exposed, as it centres upon the House's relationship with the government of the day. The Speaker can grant urgent questions, select unwelcome amendments, allow questions to run on, and ensure that a wide spectrum of opinion is called in debate if this helps Parliament better to air issues and hold the government to account.

One key area on which successive Speakers have expressed strong views is that the House is the first to hear of important developments in government policy. This is a sensitive area; governments of both political parties have wanted to set the media agenda outside the House, to brief selected journalists, perhaps to prepare public opinion for unwelcome news. But if Parliament is to be the focus of national attention, then, whether the news is momentous or not, the principle that the nation's representatives in Parliament are told first is an important one; and the Speaker must be its main advocate. The increased use of urgent questions, noted on page 49 – where ministers can be compelled to come to the House – has meant that the government must now routinely expect that the Commons will require an explanation about urgent and important matters with which it is engaged, even when it had not planned to make a statement.

Conferences and Commissions

Between 1916 and 1978 there were five Conferences on Electoral Law, held at the request of the Prime Minister and chaired by the Speaker. The first of these, in 1916–17, chaired by Speaker Lowther, paved the way for the franchise to be extended to women. In September 2007, Gordon Brown revived the practice, and called on the Speaker to chair a Conference looking at voter registration and turnout, weekend voting, the representation of women and ethnic minority people in the House of Commons, and the possibility of extending the franchise to 16-year-olds. The Conference was established as a committee of the House and reported in January 2010.

In November 2013, the Speaker announced he was setting up a Commission on Digital Democracy, the aim of which is to 'consider the effect of the digital revolution' on representative democracy. The Commission has examined the opportunities presented by digital developments to enhance scrutiny of government, passing legislation, representing citizens and promoting dialogue among them, and encouraging engagement with the political process.

Precedent and change

Precedent provides the framework within which any Speaker operates. It is a powerful ally in making rulings robust against challenge and – as with casting votes – emphasising the impartiality of the Chair. But no Speaker can simply rest on precedent. Parliament is constantly changing – not only internally in terms of its membership and political complexion, but also in terms of the influences and pressures upon it. There are always new problems and situations with which a Speaker must grapple, and set new precedents in the process. These may be as far-reaching as the procedures adopted by Speaker Brand in the 1870s and 1880s to deal with the Irish Home Rule

MPs who were obstructing the House's business; before his unilateral action to limit MPs' rights to speak by the introduction of the closure, members could speak for as long as they liked on any question before the House. More often, changes come about almost imperceptibly as a result of a series of Speaker's rulings.

The Speaker should work closely with the Clerk of the House and the Clerk's senior colleagues; he can draw on their professional knowledge and long experience, and has the political and professional advice of often highly experienced deputies. But the decisions are for him alone. Members may criticise the Speaker only by putting down a substantive motion for debate; if such a motion is not withdrawn, the government quickly finds time for a debate in order to resolve the matter. It was the tabling of such a motion in 2009 that triggered the resignation of Speaker Martin (before the motion was debated). Only three such motions have actually been debated since the Second World War.

The Deputy Speakers

The Speaker is assisted by three deputies – the Chairman of Ways and Means and two Deputy Chairmen. Before 2010, they were appointed by the House for the duration of the parliament, normally all at the same time on the first business day of a new parliament, and in a far less elaborate way than the Speaker; after informal soundings were taken, a motion to appoint them appeared in the name of the Prime Minister or the Leader of the House. This rather informal procedure was replaced in 2010 by elections of the Deputy Speakers. After consideration by the Procedure Committee, and agreement by the House, the first elections for the jobs were held in June 2010. The elections are held under the Single Transferable Vote (STV) system, with provisos that the Chairman of Ways and Means (the senior Deputy) and the Second Deputy Chairman must be a candidate from a party other than the party from which the Speaker was drawn; the First Deputy Chairman of Ways and Means must be drawn from the party from which the Speaker came; and that, across the four posts of Speaker and three Deputies, at least one woman and one man shall be elected. Under the STV system, candidates do not need a majority to be elected, only a known 'quota' or share of the votes, determined by the size of the electorate and the number of positions to be filled. Nine candidates stood in the 2010 election, and Lindsay Hoyle (Chairman of Ways and Means), Nigel Evans (First Deputy Chairman) and (now Dame) Dawn Primarolo (Second Deputy Chairman) were elected. The successful candidates were elected for the parliament, although Nigel Evans resigned in 2013 and was replaced, following an election, by Eleanor Laing.

The Chairman of Ways and Means is so called because, since the late seventeenth century, he presided over the Committee of Ways and Means (dealing with taxation), as well as the Committee of Supply (dealing with government expenditure), at that time the only two permanent committees of the House. It was not until 1853 that the Chairman began formally to deputise for the Speaker.

Today, the Chairman of Ways and Means exercises most of the powers of the Speaker in the Chamber (and has the power to select amendments in the Committee of the whole House, when the Speaker never presides). The Chairman also has three other distinct roles. He oversees the consideration of private bills (as distinct from private members' bills) (see page 220); he supervises arrangements for sittings in Westminster Hall (see page 259); and through his chairmanship of the Panel of Chairs (see page 189), he has general responsibility for the work of legislative committees. From 1902, a Deputy Chairman of Ways and Means was appointed, and a Second Deputy Chairman from 1971. They exercise the same powers in the Chamber as the Chairman of Ways and Means. No decision of any of the three may be appealed to the Speaker.

The three Deputy Speakers come from both sides of the House and, together with the Speaker, cancel out the loss of numbers from government and opposition sides of the House. Thus, Speaker Bercow came from the government (Conservative) side; Lindsay Hoyle, the Chairman of Ways and Means, from the opposition (Labour) side; Eleanor Laing, the First Deputy Chairman, from the government (Conservative) side; and Dame Dawn Primarolo, the Second Deputy Chairman, from the opposition side. The deputies are rigidly impartial in the Chair and other House duties, and they do not vote (except to resolve a tied vote). However, unlike the Speaker they remain members of their parties, and they fight general elections on a party basis.

The Speaker and the deputies have a rota of duty in the Chair; normally, the Speaker takes the first two hours, disposing of Question Time, one or more ministerial statements thereafter, and any points of order before the main business of the day begins. The deputies do stints of two hours or so, although the Speaker may return to preside over the end of the main business and any votes that take place.

In 2002, the Procedure Committee attempted a job description for the deputies:

> *an ability swiftly to command the respect of the whole House . . . a demonstrable knowledge of procedure and its application, as well as wider experience of the House and the way it works, together with an ability to chair the most challenging debates with demonstrable fairness and authority . . . a good team player. An appetite for hard work, unremitting punctuality and a sense of humour and proportion are also highly desirable.*

The Leader of the House

The Leader of the House of Commons – from July 2014, William Hague – is a key figure in both government and Parliament. He is a cabinet minister, as well as an MP; but although the Leader has collective Cabinet responsibility for defending the government's policies in the House, he also has the wider task of upholding the rights and interests of the House. With the Chief Whip, the Leader is responsible for the arrangement of government business in the Commons, and for planning and supervising the government's legislative programme as a whole by chairing the

Parliamentary Business and Legislation Committee of the Cabinet (known as PBL). He is also a member of the Cabinet's Home Affairs Committee.

The Leader reports weekly to Cabinet on forthcoming parliamentary business. He announces that business – firm for the following week, provisional for the week after – to the House every Thursday, an event that emphasises the control that the government of the day has over the time of the House of Commons. He also answers oral questions once a month on his wider responsibilities as Leader.

The Leader usually moves (and defends) motions to determine how Commons business is to be dealt with, or to introduce procedural change, and often winds up at the end of major debates on behalf of the government. He also plays a role in House administration as an ex officio member of the House of Commons Commission and as the minister responsible for the Members Estimate (see page 58).

The Clerk of the House

The Clerk of the House of Commons is the House's senior official and combines a variety of roles. He is the House's principal constitutional adviser, and adviser on all aspects of its business, procedure, practice and privilege; the editor of *Erskine May*; and a frequent witness before select committees and joint committees. He is the Speaker's and Deputy Speakers' principal adviser on a wide range of issues, but he answers not to the Speaker but to the House as a whole, and advises government and opposition, as well as any individual member of the House. He is Head of the House of Commons Service; chairs the Management Board; and is the principal adviser to the House of Commons Commission (see page 57). He is Accounting Officer for the House of Commons Administration Estimate and the Members Estimate and so is personally responsible for the propriety and economy of expenditure. He is the House's Corporate Officer and so formally holds property (including the Commons part of the Parliamentary Estate) and enters into contracts on the House's behalf, and is legally responsible for the actions of the House Administration. He is the Data Controller and so legally liable for the proper handling of information under the Data Protection Act 1998. In addition, he is the professional head of the cadre of Clerks in the House, most closely concerned with the work of the House and its committees.

It may seem strange that the Clerk combines the somewhat academic precision of procedural matters with overall responsibility for the management of the House's services. In fact, there is a strong argument for him to do so: he is the authority on all aspects of the House's core business – not just the drier matters of procedure – and no one is in a better position to understand from long experience how the main functions of the House need to be supported and how they can be made more effective.

In December 2014, the Select Committee on House of Commons Governance recommended that the Clerk should remain the House's principal official, but that some of the Clerk's executive functions should be delegated to a director general – in effect, a chief operating officer.

The first known Clerk of the House – formally styled 'Under-Clerk of the Parliaments, to wait upon the Commons' – was appointed in 1363; there has been an unbroken line since. The title 'Clerk' probably derives from the fact that in early mediaeval times literacy was by no means universal and was most widely found among priests, or clerks in holy orders. The Clerk of the House is appointed by the Queen by Letters Patent, which underpins his independence and ability to give advice no matter how unpopular that advice might be. For the first time, a competition open to staff from the UK's parliaments and assemblies was run for the role of Clerk and Chief Executive in 2011; and an open competition was run in 2014, but abandoned amid some controversy.

The House of Commons Service

The permanent staff of the House (some 1,750 people) are not civil servants but employees of the House of Commons Commission. This distinction may not be of great importance for those staff who are responsible for the upkeep of the buildings or for catering services, but for many it is of constitutional importance. The Clerk of a departmental select committee who manages a committee's inquiry into something that has gone wrong within government and then has to draft a report strongly critical of ministers and civil servants would face an intolerable conflict of loyalties if he or she owed allegiance to the Civil Service. To take another example, analysis prepared by the subject experts in the Library's research services is expected to be rigorous regardless of the possibility that their findings may not be palatable to the government of the day.

The House of Commons Service must also be politically impartial. Again, this is more important in some areas of work than in others. Staff in the Department of Chamber and Committee Services may find themselves in quick succession advising both government and opposition on procedural tactics for highly contentious business in the House, or within the space of a few minutes advising both the member in charge of a private member's bill and those MPs who want to scupper its chances of proceeding any further. If they are to retain the confidence of MPs, it is essential for their credibility that Clerks giving that advice are seen to be absolutely impartial as to both parties and issues.

The House administration

The administration of the House of Commons is fairly complex. This is not surprising; on the one hand, it has to deliver a wide range of disparate services, from regilding Pugin decoration in a Grade I listed building to supporting select committee work that covers every aspect of public life, to producing overnight a record of all the proceedings in the House and in Westminster Hall. On the other hand, professional management and planning must take into account the changing, and not always consistent, wishes of MPs, as well as the unpredictable pressures on Parliament itself.

A 1999 review of the way the House services were run summed up the problem.

The effective operation of the House is of enormous constitutional and public importance. The elector (and taxpayer) expects Governments to be held to account; constituents to be represented and their grievances pursued; and historic Parliamentary functions to be extended and adapted to changes in the wider world.

These things do not come cheap, and no-one should expect them to. Seeking to hold to account a complex, sophisticated and powerful Executive; dealing with an unremitting burden of legislation; and meeting ever-increasing expectations on the part of constituents; all this requires substantial, high-quality support. . . .

There is no shortage of complicating factors. Each Member of Parliament is an expert on what he or she wants from the system, and what the system should provide. With their staffs, Members are in effect 659 [now 650] small businesses operating independently within one institutional framework. Managers in both the public and private sectors have to meet the needs of demanding customers; but they do not have customers every one of whom can take a complaint to the Floor of the House of Commons – perhaps televised nation-wide.

At the same time the House and its Members are funded by the taxpayer. This spending is inevitably high-profile, exposed to media interest which is not always friendly and which may not pause to assess the wider value of Parliamentary expenditure. The House must be able to demonstrate proper stewardship of public money, and to show that expenditure is efficient, effective and economical.

That is the task facing the House administration.

The House of Commons Commission and the Members Estimate Committee

The Commission is the supervisory body of the administration, responsible for the House's finances and the employer of almost all its staff. Set up under the House of Commons (Administration) Act 1978, it is chaired by the Speaker; its other members are the Leader of the House, a member nominated by the Leader of the Opposition (in practice, always the Shadow Leader of the House), and three senior backbenchers, one from each of the main parties. The Commission operates in a wholly non-party way; in any event, it has never had a majority of government members. Established in 1978, it now falls short of modern governance expectations; for example, it so far has no independent external members, which would be best practice today.

The Commission meets monthly. Its meetings are private, usually with senior staff who are responsible for the subject under discussion; but it posts its minutes on the Internet and also publishes an annual report that is a mine of information about the activities of the House administration, its plans and performance. One member of the Commission acts as its spokesman and answers written parliamentary questions on its behalf, as well as oral questions in the Chamber once a month. The Members

Estimate Committee has the same membership as the Commission, and its role is to oversee the Members Estimate (see below).

The Commission is advised by two select committees of MPs: the Finance and Services Committee considers major items of expenditure, and financial and business plans; the Administration Committee advises on services more generally.

Strategic planning

The House of Commons itself may not have a mission statement, but the House administration is subject to normal public sector disciplines. Each year the Commission approves a corporate business plan for the administration. The 2014/15 to 2016/17 plan sets out four strategic goals:

- to make the House of Commons more effective;
- to make the House Service more efficient;
- to make sure that members, staff and the public are well-informed; and
- to work at every level to earn respect for the House of Commons.

The plan also outlines specific work to be completed, including delivering a new Education Centre, establishing a new Digital Office, and being fully prepared for the 2015 general election and the next parliament.

The Management Board

Responsibility for running the House services, and for employing staff, is delegated by the Commission to the Management Board. This consists of the six heads of the House departments and two external non-executive members, and is chaired by the Clerk of the House and Chief Executive. The Board is supported by the Office of the Chief Executive, which acts as a corporate office, providing internal audit, project and programme management assurance; risk management; business and strategic planning; and internal communications functions, as well as the Board's secretariat.

Estimates and the Audit Committees

The activities of the House of Commons are funded under two budgets or Estimates, which provide the legal authority for the House to finance its activities. The House of Commons Administration Estimate covers the staff of the House and its running costs, and the Members Estimate covers certain expenditure relating to MPs. Much of the expenditure previously authorised under the Members Estimate, including members' pay and allowances, was transferred to the Independent Parliamentary Standards Authority from the start of the 2010 Parliament.

The Administration Estimate Audit Committee (AEAC) is a sub-committee of the House of Commons Commission, and the Members Estimate Audit Committee (MEAC) is a sub-committee of the Members Estimate Committee. Both Committees support the Clerk as Accounting Officer in discharging his responsibilities under the relevant estimate. In particular, the Committees advise on: the effectiveness of the system of governance, risk management and internal control; the integrity of the Resource Accounts; the work of the internal audit service and the external auditor (the NAO); and other matters referred to them by the Accounting Office or the Commission/MEC. The Committees have identical membership, comprising three MPs and three external members, one of whom chairs the Committees.

The House departments

For reasons of good governance and economy, the House administration must operate as a corporate whole. There are also issues such as financial planning, the use of accommodation, ICT, health and safety, data protection, human resources and so on that can be dealt with effectively only across the board. However, both their historical origins and the specialised nature of the services they provide mean that the individual House departments have distinct characters and roles. The Departments of the House are: Chamber and Committee Services; Facilities; Finance; Human Resources and Change; and Information Services. In addition, a joint Department, PICT (Parliamentary ICT) (to be replaced by the Parliamentary Digital Service – see page 61) provides services to both Houses.

Department of Chamber and Committee Services (DCCS)

The DCCS was formed in January 2008, following a review of the House's management and services (the 'Tebbit review', after Sir Kevin Tebbit, the former Permanent Secretary of the Ministry of Defence, who led the work). The Department comprises the following Directorates: Chamber Business; Committee; Official Report; and Serjeant at Arms. It has 471 full-time equivalent staff. Senior members of the Department, along with the Clerk of the House, are perhaps the most visible of all the House staff; in television coverage of the Chamber, they are seen sitting at the Table of the House in front of the Speaker, dressed as a QC would be in court: court coat, wing collar (but with a white tie rather than barrister's bands), wig and gown. Their task there is to advise the Chair, ministers, whips and any other MP on the business the House is transacting; to record the decisions the House has taken (but not what has been said, which is taken down by the *Hansard* reporters in the gallery above them) and to help to conduct votes. The Clerks at the Table have other roles as well, usually as head of one of the offices of the Department.

The *Chamber Business Directorate* comprises: the Public and Private Bill Offices, which administer all business relating to legislation before the House, provide the staff for Public Bill Committees and other legislative committees, and advise members and others on legislation; the Journal Office, which advises on parliamentary privilege and procedure generally and compiles the daily permanent legal record of proceedings;

the Table Office, which prepares the Order Paper and processes parliamentary questions; the Vote Office, which is responsible for the provision of official papers to MPs; and the Ways and Means Office, which supports the Chairman of Ways and Means and his Deputies.

The *Committee Directorate* provides the secretariat of each investigative select committee and, with 202 full-time equivalent staff, is the largest Directorate in the Department.

The *Serjeant at Arms's Directorate* has operational responsibility for access and security in the House, as well as a range of ceremonial functions. The first recorded Serjeant at Arms was given office by King Henry V in 1415, the year of the Battle of Agincourt. In previous centuries, he was responsible for carrying out orders of the House, including making arrests; the splendid silver gilt Mace that the present Serjeant carries in the Speaker's Procession every day, and which then lies upon the Table while the House is sitting, was in times past a necessary symbol of the House's authority outside the precincts.

The *Official Report Directorate*, more commonly known as *Hansard*, records what is said in the Chamber, in Westminster Hall and in general committees. *Hansard* is substantially a verbatim report; repetitions and obvious mistakes are corrected, but the Editor strongly resists any attempt by an MP, no matter how senior, to make any change of substance.

The DCCS also includes the *Overseas Office*, which is responsible for the House's relations with other parliaments and international assemblies. The *Office of Speaker's Counsel*, which provides legal advice to the Speaker and Departments of the House, and the *Office of the Parliamentary Commissioner for Standards* are also within the DCCS for budgetary purposes.

Department of Facilities

With 540 full-time equivalent staff, the Department of Facilities is the largest House Department. The Department has three directorates: *Catering and Retail Services* provides all catering facilities for the House, operating 16 outlets and serving 1.5 million meals annually and more than 8,000 customers on a typical sitting day; the *Parliamentary Estates Directorate* has the formidable task of managing Parliament's complex and ageing estate; and the *Accommodation and Logistics Service* manages accommodation across the Estate.

Department of Finance

The Finance Department, with around 50 full-time equivalent members of staff, leads on financial strategy, financial management, and continuous improvement, and provides pension, payroll and payment and income collection services to the House Service and members. The Department supports the Accounting Officer, members on the Finance and Services Committee and the Audit Committees and Pension Trustees.

Department of Human Resources and Change

The Department of Human Resources and Change provides HR services to House Departments and staff, as well as to members. It is also responsible for supporting change management programmes in the House, as well as leading on diversity and inclusion, information security and health and well-being. It has approximately 100 members of staff, of whom about 80 are full-time.

Department of Information Services

Although the grand rooms running along the river front of the palace may seem reminiscent of the sort of Victorian library we mentioned in Chapter 1, the Department of Information Services, with some 340 full-time equivalent staff, is a very different institution. As well as offering the library and reference facilities one might expect, it also provides MPs with high-quality, impartial research and information services, as well as leading the House Service's efforts to engage with the public and provide information for them.

The researchers are highly qualified, and their work is respected both inside and outside the House. When a member says in the Chamber 'the Library have told me', what they have said is unlikely to be challenged. Library staff undertake research in response to specific requests from MPs, as well as producing research papers on bills and other current issues. This research back-up is highly valued by MPs, and especially by opposition spokespeople in shadowing ministers, when the latter can call upon the extensive resources of government departments.

The Department also works to ensure that the House of Commons is outward-looking and engages with the public, in particular by providing: support for schools and an educational visits programme through Parliament's Education Service; Public Information and Outreach services supporting awareness of, and engagement with, the activities of Parliament and answering inquiries on them; tours for visitors to Parliament arranged through members or offered commercially; Web and Intranet Services (for members of both Houses and their staff, parliamentary staff and the public), although this part of the department will move into the new Digital Service; media support for the House; and other opportunities for the public to engage, such as Parliament Week, TEDx Houses of Parliament and similar events.

Services shared between the Lords and the Commons

In 2005, the first – and, to date, only – joint department of the two Houses, the *Parliamentary Information and Communications Technology Service* (PICT) was established, charged with providing ICT support to peers, MPs, their staff and staff of both Houses. Following an externally commissioned, independent review, in 2014 the Clerks of both Houses announced that a new Digital Service was to be established, the intention of which is to bring together the management of all online and ICT services into a single organisation, with an aim of putting digital delivery at the forefront of the work done to support both Houses, prioritising the needs of users.

Despite the fact that the House administrations of the Commons and Lords are constitutionally separate, they share other services (although, unlike PICT, not via a formally constituted joint department), when it makes sense to do so; for example, on estates and works, communications, procurement, records, ceremonial matters, security and visitor access. Costs are apportioned between the Houses, under a variety of funding formulae. At the last count there were some 30 areas where costs were shared. Even in areas where each House has distinct needs, there is nevertheless informal consultation and cooperation.

MPs' pay, allowances and IPSA

MPs' pay and allowances

As we saw in Chapter 2, the expenses scandal of 2009 was a hammer blow to the public reputation and self-confidence of MPs and the House. Members of Parliament were first paid in 1911, when the rate was £400 a year. Ever since, their pay levels have been controversial, not least because, until the recent reforms, MPs were one of the few groups of people who could in effect set their own salaries. In order to provide an objective assessment, pay and allowances had, since 1970, been referred to an outside organisation, latterly the Senior Salaries Review Body (SSRB). The SSRB based its recommendations on general principles: that pay should not be so low as to deter or so high as to make it the main attraction; that, although some MPs take on work outside Parliament, pay should be at a level reflecting the full-time job that it is for most MPs; that there should be no compensation for job insecurity or reflection of length of service; and that there should be a clear distinction between pay and expenses.

However, the political fall-out of the expenses scandal meant that earlier attempts at objectivity were perceived as insufficient and the system in place for determining MPs' pay and allowances politically unsustainable. The Independent Parliamentary Standards Authority (IPSA) was established by the Parliamentary Standards Act 2009 with the intention of shifting the parliamentary allowances system in the House of Commons from a system of self-regulation to one of regulation by an independent body. While IPSA was originally given responsibility to pay members' salaries, and to determine the level of and to pay members' allowances, it was in 2011 given the additional responsibility of determining pay, as well as allowances. In 2013, it conducted a review of MPs' remuneration and found that 'Past increases in MPs' pay, judged to be justified and appropriate by review bodies, have been set aside or diluted because of concerns about the political consequences of their implementation. Quite simply, there is never a good time to determine MPs' pay'. It recommended a package that, without increasing the cost to the taxpayer, it said would involve five elements: 'a one-off pay rise, thereafter linking MPs' pay to what everyone else is paid; overhauling MPs' generous pensions; scrapping resettlement payments worth tens of thousands of pounds; further tightening expenses; and calling on MPs to produce an annual report to help constituents understand their work'.

IPSA intends that its recommendations on business costs and expenses will come into effect the day after the next general election. Its recommendations on basic pay, while not requiring agreement by Parliament, will only be implemented after a review that IPSA is statutorily required to make in 2015. If implemented, the proposals on pay will lead to a one-off salary increase of 9.26 per cent, to £74,000 p.a. Thereafter, MPs' salaries will be linked to average earnings. The other key impacts of its proposals would be: to place MP's pensions on a par with others in the public service and to increase MPs' own pension contributions; to replace the 'resettlement allowance' (previously paid when an MP stood down at an election, or lost his or her seat) with a more modest loss-of-office payment, made only to those who contest and lose their seats; and to tighten the rules about business costs and expenses, including scrapping a provision for claims for evening meals.

Even after the anger aroused by the expenses scandal, it is generally accepted that MPs need to be able to claim certain expenses – in order to be able to hire staff, to travel between Westminster and their constituencies and, where necessary, to rent accommodation to allow them to be able to live and work both in Westminster and their constituencies, for example. In 2013/14, the maximum amounts claimable available for such costs were:

Accommodation expenses

London area (rent)	£20,100
Associated expenditure (available to members who own their own home, to cover costs such as utility bills and council tax)	£8,850

Caring responsibility	£2,425
London area living payment	£3,760
London area living payment (addition)	£1,330

Staffing expenditure

London area MPs	£144,000
non-London area MPs	£137,200

Office costs expenditure

London area MPs	£25,350
non-London area MPs	£22,750

Start-up expenses	£6,000

Winding-up expenditure

London area MPs	£56,450
non-London area MPs	£53,350

Regardless of the amounts available to help MPs function, there is now greater transparency about what claims are made by them. Before responsibility moved to IPSA, the House had, for many years, published the total amounts claimed by each MP against the main allowances. IPSA continues to publish such information each September, but it also publishes individual claims submitted by each MP (other than those relating to security and disability assistance). Constituents are thus able to see exactly what their MP has claimed (and compare those claims with those of other MPs).

The reputational hangover of the expenses scandal persists, and evidence suggests that many people still do not trust their MPs. However, whether MPs are paid too much or too little, and whether their allowances regime is overly generous or penny-pinching, it has never been easier to see exactly what payments have been made to them; and they no longer take decisions about the levels of those payments. IPSA has had many criticisms made of it by MPs, and its Chairman has been ready to stand up to them; however, in a letter to the *Daily Express* in May 2014, he argued that:

> *Gone are the days of MPs and the House of Commons setting the rules, gone are the days of MPs receiving allowances without proving they incurred costs, gone are the days of MPs claiming for mortgage interest payments . . . and gone are the days of the public being in the dark about MPs' costs and expenses.*

MPs' staff

MPs are the employers of their staff, although staff are paid centrally by IPSA and are hired on standard contracts. In recent years, there has been a substantial increase in MPs' paid staff, from 1,850 in 2001 to 2,580 in 2005, to around 3,000 in 2013 (in addition to unpaid staff).

There is no one pattern of the way an MP uses staff, and there are many permutations. Some MPs, particularly those with a heavy constituency caseload, base all their staff in the constituency. This makes practical sense: staff in constituency offices can network more easily with local agencies and more conveniently make arrangements for surgeries, visits and so on, and staff costs are lower outside London. Others, especially London members, whose constituencies are not far away, have all their staff at Westminster (where they also have the advantage of free accommodation and other services). In the country as a whole, staff are split about one-third at Westminster and two-thirds in constituencies. There is concern that the structure of IPSA's staffing allowances provides a perverse incentive for MPs to base staff at Westminster rather than in their constituencies. Not only does this put additional pressure on the House administration and the Parliamentary Estate, it would be perverse if MPs' staff unnecessarily based at Westminster cost the taxpayer more per head than those in constituencies.

The types of people that MPs employ, and what they expect from them, vary from member to member, reflecting the fact that there is no standard way of doing the job of an MP. Some need caseworkers; some need a PA to organise a diary and act as their right hand; others need researchers to support work on their specialist subjects; yet others need a 'deputy MP' in the constituency, someone they can trust to handle their local profile and press relations, combined with a sure touch on constituency cases.

Opposition frontbenchers have a particular need for specialist support because they are taking on ministers who can draw on the non-party-political, but nevertheless substantial, resources of government departments. Sometimes, MPs pool their staff; for example, in opposition the Conservative Party established its own parliamentary research unit of a dozen or so graduates who researched topics in depth on request from subscribing MPs. Opposition frontbenchers are also heavy users of the independent researchers in the House of Commons Library.

A number of MPs have worked at Westminster before winning a seat of their own, and a post as a researcher is a recognised apprenticeship in a political career. But it is also not unusual to find staff who do not identify fully with their MP's political views and see themselves as servants of the constituency as much as of a party politician.

Some, especially the traditional secretary or PA, spend much of their working lives in the job. For others, such as the 'interns' in the US model, working for an MP may be more for the experience than the pay, as a prelude to a career in a different field. A few universities now have a sandwich year as a formal part of a politics degree.

Just as the use made of staff varies, so too does its effectiveness. Having personal staff is a new experience for many newly elected MPs. Some take to it readily and use staff to add real value to their work. However, too many MPs allow researchers to operate with a good deal of independence, which leads to criticisms that these are surrogate members pursuing their own agendas and encouraging MPs to commission Library research or table parliamentary questions that are more for the benefit of researcher than member.

Finance for opposition parties

'Short money': parties in the House of Commons

Since 1975, there has been financial support for opposition parties in the Commons (often called Short money, after Edward Short, Leader of the House at the time) to go some way towards redressing the imbalance between the support available to opposition parties and that available to the government through the Civil Service. In order to qualify, a party must have at least two MPs – or one MP, provided that the party also polled 150,000 votes nationwide. In either case, the MPs must have been elected for their party at the previous general election, which disqualifies new party groupings formed in the current parliament from claiming financial support.

There are three categories of support: the basic funding established in 1975; travel and associated expenses, introduced in 1993; and support for the Leader of the

Opposition's Office, which began in 1999. All are up-rated annually in line with the retail price index.

The current amounts for basic funding are £16,250.37 per MP and £32.46 for every 200 votes cast for the party in the last general election. The 2013/14 allocations were: Labour, £5,589,415; SNP, £177,224; DUP, £157,302; Plaid Cymru, £75,563; SDLP, £66,734; and Green, £62,473. For travel expenses, the opposition parties shared a total of £178,516 in the same proportions as their basic funding. Support for the Leader of the Opposition's Office was £757,097.

The basic funding may be used only for parliamentary business, which includes research to support shadow ministers and their work, and developing and communicating alternative policies. The money may not be used for political campaigning, fund raising or membership drives. Each party has to produce an auditor's certificate every year to verify that the money has been spent only on parliamentary business. In February 2006, the government's proposal to give the Sinn Féin MPs financial support along the same lines as Short money, although they had not taken their seats, was approved despite fierce opposition in some quarters.

Opposition salaries

Six opposition members in the two Houses receive a salary by virtue of the posts they hold. In the Commons, the Leader of the Opposition gets £63,098 a year, the Opposition Chief Whip gets £33,002 and her deputy and one other Whip get £19,239 – in each case, in addition to their salaries of £67,060. In the Lords, the Leader of the Opposition receives £69,138 and the Opposition Chief Whip £63,933 a year.

Why subsidise the opposition?

It may seem reasonable for a taxpayer to say: 'I'm prepared to fund hospitals, or the education system; but why should I pay for party politicians?' Fair enough; but there is a powerful counter-argument. Ministers are not allowed to use their civil servants for overtly party political purposes, although they can still use the huge resources of their departments to research, develop and present new policies. But no government has a monopoly of truth and right. It must surely be to the advantage of the country as a whole when opposition parties have the resources to test and challenge those policies in a reasoned, well-researched way, and to put forward credible alternative proposals.

This was recognised in the Political Parties, Elections and Referendums Act 2000, which made provision for 'policy development grants'. The sum of £2 million a year is now available for work on policies for inclusion in a party's manifesto. Under the supervision of the Electoral Commission, the money is divided between parties with at least two MPs at Westminster (who have taken their seats, so Sinn Féin are not eligible). The money is allocated in a similar way to Short money: £1 million is split in proportion to numbers of MPs; and £1 million in proportion to votes cast at the last election.

State funding for political parties?

More generally, the extent to which the non-parliamentary activities of political parties should be publicly funded remains contentious. The combined membership of the Labour and Conservative parties in 2011 was about 320,000, or about 1.7 per cent of those who actually voted for those parties in the 2010 election (and down from a total of about 800,000 at the time of the 1997 election). So the ability of major parties to fund themselves from their membership is declining. This inevitably makes them readier to look to major donations by wealthy individuals; but these, in turn, give rise to suspicions of peddling influence and politicians in hock to vested interests.

Although there are no caps on the amounts that may be donated to parties, they are required to report to the Electoral Commission all donations and/or loans from any single source which total £7,500 or more in any one year, and their accounts must be lodged with the Electoral Commission. In 2013, Labour was the best-funded party with an income of £33.3 million (including 'Short money'), the Conservatives were in second place with £25.4 million and the Liberal Democrats third with £7.3 million. UKIP's income doubled from its 2012 figure, to £2.5 million, and the other smaller parties were: SNP, £2 million, Sinn Féin, £1.2 million, the Green Party on £882,000 and the BNP on £605,000. At the same time, the paid-up membership of most parties was relatively low: Labour, 189,531, and the Liberal Democrats 43,451. (The Conservative Party does not declare membership figures but its membership income was £747,000.)

A review of party funding, chaired by Sir Hayden Phillips, was launched in 2006 and reported the following year. However, the parties were unable to agree on reforms, and so talks were suspended. Following the 2010 election, the coalition government said that it wanted to return to the issue and the Deputy Prime Minister was given responsibility for this. The Committee on Standards in Public Life reported on the financing of parties and the government accepted, in principle, the case for caps on donations and for funding of parties by trades unions to be reviewed. However, the cross-party talks that followed were not successful and, in July 2013, the government said that the full package of reforms would not be able to go ahead in the current parliament. However, the Transparency of Lobbying, Non-Party Campaigning and Trade Union Administration Act 2014 tightened the controls in place for non-party campaigning (for example, charities and unions) in the run-up to elections, and placed certain caps on what could be spent.

There is considerable opposition in some quarters to the state funding of *all* the activities of political parties (in contrast to the parliamentary functions of challenge referred to on page 66). And there are also the arguments that state funding tends to make recipient parties complacent and – because the obvious way of setting levels is to base them on the previous election results – that it over-rewards those who do well. The government seems to have accepted these arguments, whereas it has been reported that the Labour party intends to include proposals for a cap on donations, possibly opening the way for further state funding of political parties, in its manifesto for the 2015 election. It therefore seems likely that the outcome of the 2015 election may determine the extent to which the state will fund political parties.

The House of Lords

The Lord Speaker

Since July 2006, the House of Lords has elected its own presiding officer in the form of the Lord Speaker. The speakership had, until then, been held *ex officio* by the Lord Chancellor but the role ended with the passage of the Constitutional Reform Act 2005 and the effective dismemberment of that ancient office. The Lord Speaker is elected by the whole House using the alternative vote system and has assumed the parliamentary duties formerly performed by the Lord Chancellor, along with other functions befitting a full-time, salaried office. The current Lord Speaker, Baroness D'Souza, was a crossbench member and was elected in 2011.

First and foremost, the Lord Speaker presides in the Chamber of the House for up to three hours a day, seated upon the Woolsack or at the Table of the House when the House is in Committee. But the powers of the Lord Speaker in the Chamber are still relatively limited. The Lord Speaker does not arbitrate on rules of order. The preservation of order in the House is the responsibility of all the Lords who are present, and any Lord may call the attention of the House to any breaches of order or laxity in observing its customs. If the House is in need of advice on matters of procedure and order, it is to the Leader of the House (also a government minister) that they look. And the Leader – or, in her or his absence, the government Chief Whip – will often intervene to interpret and give voice to what he or she considers to be the wish of the House when procedural difficulties occur.

The Lord Speaker and Deputy Speakers do not call lords to speak. As we shall see on page 270, the order of speaking in debates is prearranged and set out in lists prepared by the Government Whips' Office. Each item of the day's business set out on the Order Paper is called on by the Clerk at the Table. The Lord Speaker or her deputies will call members to speak to their amendments when the House is considering legislation, but no one calls the subsequent speakers in a debate on an amendment. The Lord Speaker cannot curtail debate, and when debate is concluded, the function of this role is limited to putting the question – announcing what it is on which the Lords are about to vote – and then declaring the result of the vote. The Lord Speaker is expected not to vote in the House, even if a vote is tied. In such cases, the standing orders of the House decide the result and the amendment falls. The Lord Speaker has assumed responsibility from the Leader of the House in deciding whether to grant leave for an Urgent (Private Notice) Question to be asked at Question Time, and also in exercising discretion in the application of the *sub judice* rule.

A new and significant function is to chair the House Committee, which is the House's chief administrative body (see page 71). This gives the Lord Speaker a major role in most aspects of the internal administration of the House. Together with the Speaker of the Commons (and the Clerks of the two Houses as Corporate Officers), the Lord Speaker has responsibilities for the security of the precincts and meets regularly with the Speaker to discuss matters of joint concern. The Lord Speaker is empowered to recall the House of Lords whenever it stands adjourned if public interest requires it; for example, for the debate on the issue of possible intervention in Syria on 29 August 2013.

The representative role of the Lord Speaker has blossomed since the post became elected, both in promoting the work of the House to audiences at home, representing the House at meetings of conferences of Speakers overseas, and fulfilling bilateral visits to overseas parliaments. In June 2013, the Lord Speaker hosted the annual meeting of the Association of European Senates in the Queen's Robing Room. The Lord Speaker also represents the House on ceremonial occasions – hosting and, together with the Commons Speaker, making a speech of welcome to visiting heads of state and others; presenting Humble Addresses to The Queen, as on the occasion of her Diamond Jubilee in 2012; as a member of Royal Commissions for Prorogation; and at the State Opening of Parliament.

The Chairman of Committees, Deputy Speakers and Deputy Chairmen

Even after the election of a Lord Speaker in 2006, the need for a panel of deputies (albeit reduced in number to twelve) continued – to preside when the Lord Speaker cannot.

The principal Deputy Speaker is the Chairman of Committees, a member of the House who is appointed by the House at the beginning of every session to take the chair in all Committees of the whole House. The Chairman of Committees is a very influential figure in the Lords and is paid the salary of a minister of state in consequence. He organises the panel of Deputy Speakers and Deputy Chairmen and assigns them their duties week by week. He has considerable powers in the field of private legislation (see page 222) by selecting opposed private bill committees and himself presiding over unopposed bill committees. During the nineteenth century – the heyday of private legislation – this gave the holder of the post immense power and influence over many of the greatest public works projects of the day. This aspect of his work takes up far less of the Chairman of Committees' time today.

Indeed, most of his work is now concerned with the administration of the House. While the Lord Speaker chairs the House Committee, it is the Chairman of Committees who acts as the House Committee's spokesman in the House. He chairs the Select Committee on Administration and Works; the Liaison Committee, which meets from time to time to review and allocate resources to the policy select committees of the House; the Privileges and Conduct Committee; and the Procedure Committee. The current Chairman of Committees, Lord Sewel, as did his predecessor, also chairs the Refreshment Committee which oversees the House's catering services.

The Leader of the House of Lords

The Leader of the House of Lords is a government minister and attends meetings of the Cabinet. The allegiance of this role is to the government and its policies, but the Leader of the House of Lords also has a wider task of upholding the rights and interests of the House as a whole. It is the Leader of the House, for example, who assists the House in keeping its own order during proceedings – particularly during Question Time – and who makes representations on behalf of the House on such matters as members' allowances.

The Leader of the House of Lords works closely with the Leader of the House of Commons in planning and supervising the government's legislative programme; is a member of the Parliamentary Business and Legislation Committee of the Cabinet, together with the Government Chief Whip and their Liberal Democrat deputies; and reports to the Cabinet itself on business in the Lords. The role is responsible for delivering the government's business in the House, although most of the planning of this is undertaken by the Government Chief Whip and, in particular, by the Chief Whip's principal private secretary, a Clerk on secondment to the Cabinet Office, who also assists the Leader of the House in her parliamentary work.

Much of the Leader's influence is exerted behind the scenes; for example, through meetings of the business managers (as the Leaders and Government Chief Whips of the two Houses are known). Within the Lords, the Leader of the House of Lords secures agreement on matters relating to the business of the House and other matters by discussions with other party leaders. Similar negotiations are held by the Chief Whip with other party whips. As in the Commons, these contacts are known as the usual channels. They are entirely informal and by their very nature devoid of any ground rules, save perhaps one – that a deal struck through 'the usual channels' will normally stick. The Leader of the House, together with other party leaders, sits on all key decision-making bodies within the House – such as the House Committee, the Liaison Committee and the Procedure Committee.

The Clerk of the Parliaments and the staff of the House

The most senior official of the House of Lords is the Clerk of the Parliaments. In the same way as the Clerk of the House of Commons, he combines a variety of roles. He is the principal adviser to the House on all aspects of parliamentary practice and procedure, and the daily business of the House proceeds on the basis of briefs prepared by the clerks in the procedural offices. But he also has wide administrative responsibilities as Chief Executive of the House Service and Chair of the Management Board (see page 71) – a pre-eminence derived from his position as Accounting Officer for money spent under the two Lords Requests for Resources (formerly Votes), and as the employer of all House of Lords staff under the Clerk of the Parliaments Act

1824 and the Parliamentary Corporate Bodies Act 1992. The 1992 Act makes the Clerk of the Parliaments Corporate Officer of the House of Lords, and in this capacity he gives the House legal personality and enters into contracts on its behalf. The Clerk of the Parliaments is appointed by the Crown under Letters Patent, usually from among the longer-serving Clerks of the House, following advertisement and interview by the party leaders and Convenor. His immediate deputies, the Clerk Assistant and the Reading Clerk, are appointed by the Lord Speaker following a similar process.

Different offices of the House's administration deal with finance, committees, legislation, human resources, facilities (including works and accommodation), the Journal of the House, overseas business, the official report or *Hansard*, catering services, and information services including the Library and Parliamentary Archive. The Department of the Gentleman Usher of the Black Rod deals with ceremonial events and some in-House security matters including access, under the supervision of the Parliamentary Security Director. The total number of staff employed in these offices is about 480. This figure excludes staff in services shared with the Commons – for example, in the Parliamentary Works Services Directorate; the Parliamentary Estates Directorate; the Parliamentary Information and Communications Technology Service; the Visitor, Education and Outreach Services; and the security staff contracted to both Houses from the Metropolitan Police.

House of Lords administration

The chief decision-making body in the administration of the Lords is the House Committee, a select committee of twelve members, including the Leader of the House and other party leaders and the Convenor of the Crossbench Peers. The Clerk of the Parliaments attends and other senior officers attend as required. The committee's role was last reviewed in 2007–08 and is to set the policy framework for the administration of the House and to provide non-executive guidance to the Management Board; to approve the House's strategic, business and financial plans; to agree the annual Estimates and Supplementary Estimates; to supervise the arrangements relating to Members' expenses; and to approve the House of Lords Annual Report. Its work is assisted by a management board of senior officers of the House chaired by the Clerk of the Parliaments. Both the House Committee and the management board meet monthly when the House is sitting, and their decisions are published on the Internet.

Four further domestic select committees – on administration and works, refreshments, information, and works of art – have responsibility for determining policy in those areas within the strategic framework and financial limits approved by the House Committee. Thus, any decision requiring major unauthorised expenditure requires the agreement of the House Committee. To the extent that the House of Lords has an equivalent to the House of Commons Commission, it is the House Committee.

The administration is also assisted by an Audit Committee, whose membership – unusually – is determined by the House Committee. It consists of members of the House, none of whom holds any other office in the House, and two external members, one of whom also currently attends meetings of the Management Board. The Audit Committee oversees the House's internal financial controls, management responses to internal audit reports and risk management.

Expenses

Members of the House of Lords are unpaid, in the sense that, with the exception of certain office holders, they do not receive a salary. But they do receive free travel to and from Westminster, and financial support in respect of each day of attendance at the House or on other prescribed business. This may be claimed at one of two rates – £150 or £300, though a few members make no claims at all. This payment is tax free because members of the House of Lords, unlike MPs, are deemed to hold a 'dignity' rather than a paid 'office'. The current scheme was adopted in May 2010 and replaced a more elaborate scheme of day and overnight subsistence, and other allowances. The flat rate was introduced after it had emerged in 2009 that the allowances – the overnight allowance, in particular – were in some cases being improperly claimed. The rate of current financial support is due for review in 2015.

Finance for political parties in the Lords: 'Cranborne money'

For many years, the chief opposition parties in the Lords received funding from money made available from public funds to opposition parties in the Commons (see page 65). Since October 1996, the Official Opposition and the second-largest party have been provided with a separate allocation, funded by the House. Since 1999, the Convenor of the Crossbench Peers has received similar funding to provide secretarial support. These sums are determined by resolution of the House and are up-rated annually in line with inflation. With effect from 1 April 2014, the amounts available were £572,717 to the Labour Party as Official Opposition and £73,564 to the Convenor. Upon joining the Coalition government, the Liberal Democrats ceased to be eligible to receive opposition party funding.

House of Lords funding

The House of Lords is funded directly from the Treasury on the same lines as a government department, but for constitutional reasons – and unlike a department – the House is not cash-limited. That does not mean that it can spend what it wants. Great self-restraint is, in fact, exercised on the demands made upon the public purse, and a savings programme that was put in place in 2010 has had a considerable downward effect on spending. The House has two Estimates, one for resource costs of the administration (including members' financial support) and one for capital spending, chiefly works, which is more liable to fluctuation according to the projects in hand. Overall financial control rests with the House Committee; the Clerk of the Parliaments, who is head of the Lords administration, is the Accounting Officer and is responsible for all its expenditure, including its propriety and effectiveness. The House of Lords accounts are examined and certified each year by the National Audit Office (NAO).

How much does Parliament cost?

Parliament operates on the same resource accounting basis as central government, so the costs of Parliament include not only what is paid in cash – such as salaries, rates and electricity, but also notional costs for the use of buildings and other assets.

On this basis, in 2013/14 the House of Commons administration cost some £200 million, including £24.4 million of capital expenditure. In the same year, IPSA cost approximately £153 million, including the salaries of all MPs and their staff. In 2013/14, the House of Lords administration cost £73 million, and works £32 million – a total of £105 million (resource and capital costs). The total cost of Parliament was considerably less than one tenth of 1 per cent of total government spending.

4

Influences on Parliament

The House of Commons

The job is what you make it

Almost everyone in employment in the United Kingdom has a job description. And those who are self-employed – perhaps running a shop or other small business – have pretty clear indications of what constitutes success or failure. Members of Parliament have neither, unless it is to be re-elected at the next election. As we shall see, there is no shortage of people who will tell the newly elected MP what he or she should be doing; but there is no formal statement of what the job involves.

There are many good descriptions of 'what MPs do', but they are strictly *descriptions*, drawn from observing the many, and not *definitions*. And the truth is that no definition exists. As a newly elected MP, it is entirely up to you to decide how you do the job. No doubt you want to do all those tasks listed by the Modernisation Committee, but time is limited. The question is which of those tasks is the most important, and to which should you pay most attention? Will you devote yourself entirely to your constituents and their problems? (Unless you are both selective and realistic, you will rapidly discover that you could easily spend twenty-four hours in every day on this.) Will you become a standard bearer for some product of your constituency – apples, computer software, shellfish, sports cars? Will you pursue an abiding political interest that you had before you came into the House: perhaps debt in the developing world, or renewable energy? Possibly, you are attracted by select committee work, the business of calling the government to account, and making yourself an expert on a particular area of policy. Perhaps you might set yourself to contribute to better understanding between the United Kingdom and the Arab world, or to ensuring that the UK makes the most of commercial opportunities on the Pacific Rim. If you are in the party of government, might your ambitions be focused on ministerial office and getting a foot on the first rung of the ladder as a parliamentary private secretary (PPS; see page 76)?

In practice, most MPs will do some or all of these various aspects of the job. But few will do exactly what they expected when first they came into the House. And the main reason for that is the complex web of influences on the House and its members.

The government's control of the House of Commons

We saw in Chapter 2 how, in order to be invited to form a government, a prospective Prime Minister must have control of the House of Commons – that is, for his or her party (and, if necessary, its coalition partners) to have a sufficient parliamentary majority to be certain of getting approval for the legislative programme (announced in the Queen's Speech) and for government taxation and spending (through the Finance Bill and the Estimates). But having a numerical majority in order to be able to win votes and secure government business is only one kind of control; control of the House's time and agenda – what is debated, for how long, and on what terms – also matters. And while the government retains very significant control of what the House debates and when, this control was weakened in the 2010 Parliament by steps taken to give backbenchers greater influence over the House's time and agenda.

Control of time

Every Thursday, the Leader of the House announces what the business will be – that is, what items will be taken on each day – for the next fortnight. In many parliaments, particularly those on the continental model, there is a business committee or *bureau*, involving not only the business managers and other party representatives, but also the president of the assembly and his deputies, who decide what business to propose. And even then, that draft agenda is subject to approval by the assembly as a whole. At the start of the 2010 Parliament, it seemed that the House might soon adopt a similar approach: the Coalition Agreement included a commitment to implement in full the proposals of the Reform of the House of Commons Committee – or 'The Wright Committee' as it was better known, after its Chair, Dr Tony Wright, the former MP for Cannock Chase – including plans for a House Business Committee, which would have carried out *bureau*-style functions. In July 2014, however, the Leader of the House said that there was as yet no basis of agreement on the proposal.

The absence of a House Business Committee in the Commons means that it remains primarily for the government of the day to propose and to dispose. Ever since the Balfour reforms at the turn of the nineteenth/twentieth centuries, all House of Commons time that is not ring-fenced is at the disposal of the government of the day. This meant, before the 2010 Parliament, that in 150 or 160 sitting days in a parliamentary session, only 20 'opposition days', 13 days for private members' bills, some time for private bills, 3 'Estimates days' for debates on select committee reports, the daily half-hour adjournment debate, urgent questions and the daily Question Time were not in the gift of the government. Even then, it was for the government to decide *when* the opposition days, private members' bill days and Estimates days were to be taken.

It is still the case that non-ring-fenced time is at the government's disposal, but the big difference in the 2010 parliament was the appointment of the Backbench Business Committee (BBCom) (see also page 258) and its allocation of 35 days (27 in the Chamber, and the remainder in Westminster Hall) of backbench business. This has loosened the (still formidable) grip of the government on the timetable and agenda of the Commons. The statistics bear this out: the amount of time spent on business initiated by the government has fallen from nearly three-fifths in the 2003–04 and 2004–05 sessions to around one-third in 2012–13 and 2013–14, while time on business initiated by backbenchers has risen in the same period from around one-tenth to nearly one-quarter.

The 'elective dictatorship'?

A former Conservative Lord Chancellor, Lord Hailsham, described the Westminster system of parliamentary government as an 'elective dictatorship': that is, one in which a government, once elected, is free to do very much what it wants. To an extent, Lord Hailsham was and is right. The Westminster system is not government by Parliament but government through Parliament and (perhaps especially obvious when the government has a large parliamentary majority) one of the roles of Parliament is to legitimise what the government does. The difference between debating policies and enshrining them in legislation is important: while the recent changes to backbench business have increased the ability of backbenchers to initiate debates in the House, it remains the case that the vast majority of legislation passed by Parliament is government legislation, and even private members' bills stand little chance of enactment unless they have government support.

Government patronage and collective responsibility

The government's position is further entrenched by the Prime Minister's ability to choose ministers and for ministers to choose parliamentary private secretaries (PPSs), who are not ministers but who act as unpaid aides to secretaries of state or ministers of state. Collectively, these people make up the payroll vote: those individuals expected to vote with the government – a total of some 140 MPs in the Commons.

Not only is the power of ministerial appointment a key prime ministerial weapon, but it is also allied to the constitutional doctrine of collective responsibility, under which all the members of a government support any public statement of the government's policies. Ministers may (and often do) disagree privately and seek to change or modify their colleagues' minds and policies, but if they disagree publicly they are expected to resign (as did the Leader of the House, Robin Cook, in March 2003 over the government's proposed military action against Iraq) or face the sack from the PM of the day.

This concept has been strained but not broken under the Coalition government. It has held firm for the generality of government business: whatever spats ministers from each of the governing parties may have had with their counterparts in private (where that definition occasionally extends to off-the-record briefings to journalists), Conservative and Liberal Democrat ministers have generally been required publicly – and in the House – to toe the collective government line, with some exceptions.

The first category of exceptions comprises those divergent views sanctioned in advance in the Coalition's *Programme for Government*. This stated that the governing parties might adopt opposing positions on: the referendum to be held on the alternative vote system (but not the bill setting up the referendum); university funding; the renewal of Trident; and tax allowances for married couples. Such explicit 'agreements to differ' are not a constitutional novelty. In 1975, the Labour government agreed that its ministers could (outside Parliament) campaign against the collective line in the referendum on membership of the (then) European Economic Community; two years later, the government decided that ministers could vote against laws establishing direct elections to the European Parliament. There is a coalition precedent, too: on 23 January 1932, *The Times* published the then coalition government's agreement to differ on the issue of tariff reform. Ten days later, in the House, the Conservative Chancellor, Neville Chamberlain, introduced the government's policy, subsequently to be opposed by the Liberal Home Secretary, Sir Herbert Samuel.

However, the 2010 *Programme* failed to predict all those areas where it might be necessary for the Coalition partners to differ, and further disagreements emerged. In 2012, collective responsibility was suspended for the Electoral Registration and Amendment Bill and, specifically, on an amendment designed to delay a review of parliamentary constituency boundaries. The review – included in the Coalition Agreement – was scuppered after the Deputy Prime Minister instructed Liberal Democrats to vote against it. This was in response to the failure of House of Lords reform – a favourite policy of the Liberal Democrats, included in the Coalition Agreement – because of the refusal of sufficient numbers of Conservatives to support such reform.

Another high-profile disagreement between the two parties took place over the report by Lord Leveson on *The Culture, Practices and Ethics of the Press*. Following publication of the report in 2012, the Prime Minister and the Deputy Prime Minister made separate, successive, statements in the House of Commons in response to it, each answering questions from backbenchers. In that case, however, there was no collective government position on how to respond to the report and so, formally at least, the concept of collective responsibility was preserved. A more egregious departure from the convention concerned the 2013 Queen's Speech. On that occasion, Conservative MPs tabled an amendment regretting that an EU referendum Bill was not included in the Speech. The Queen's Speech, in setting out the government's legislative intentions for the forthcoming session (see page 124), can be seen as the epitome of collective responsibility. Therefore, when the Prime Minister indicated that ministers would be able to abstain on the vote and PPSs allowed to vote for the rebel amendment, this appeared to represent a flouting of the convention of collective responsibility as generally understood. However high-profile these disagreements, they represent a tiny fraction of the government business conducted since the start of the Coalition. In that sense, perhaps it is more remarkable that the concept of collective responsibility has survived coalition government as well as it has, rather than that it has occasionally broken down.

Theory and practice

It might appear that little stands in the way of the government doing precisely what it wants (or, perhaps more precisely, what the Prime Minister with the backing of the Cabinet wants). But the picture is more subtle than that. There is, indeed, an expectation that a government having won a mandate at a general election, with a majority in the House of Commons, will be able to get its business through. However, in practice this depends on a number of factors. A government must retain the support of its backbenchers; and, as we shall see, it is not enough to issue orders; persuasion is often needed. Public and media opinion also needs to be benign – or, at least, not so critical as to give government backbenchers cold feet.

In addition, all governments are aware of the fact that, perhaps not too long distant, they may be on the opposition benches. In the heady days after a big election victory, or with the insulation of a large parliamentary majority, this recollection may be sometimes less vivid, but it underpins any government's need to maintain a working relationship with the opposition, and especially with the largest opposition party ('the Official Opposition'). New MPs who have known only the government benches may want to press on regardless, but their enthusiasm tends to be tempered by longer-serving MPs who can remember all too many occasions when in opposition they won the arguments but lost the votes.

This working relationship with the opposition means, in House terms, general agreement on the arrangement and timing of business, and accord on less contentious matters such as the dates of parliamentary recesses, normally through 'the usual channels' (see page 82). An effective working relationship may also colour the relationships between the parties on much more significant matters, such as a measure of agreement on how to approach a firefighters' strike, or the possible imposition of sanctions against a foreign country.

The opposition, too, has a considerable interest in maintaining this working relationship. The traditional statement that the opposition's power is one of delay is now out of date, given the routine programming of government bills (see page 178). However, cooperation with the government in the arrangement of business will give the opposition the chance to express (and sometimes secure) priorities for debate, and to trade time and tactics, perhaps along the lines of 'no division on second reading of bill X and only half a day on its report stage', but in return 'an extra day on the report stage of bill Y'. The opposition gets the extra day on bill Y, which it sees as more important; the government saves some time on bill X and also knows that it can slacken the voting requirements for its MPs on the second reading of that bill.

Accountability and responsibility

A distinction is sometimes made between ministerial accountability (being answerable to Parliament for the government's actions) and ministerial responsibility ('taking personal responsibility for what has been done in the minister's name – even without the minister's knowledge – and, if necessary resigning') but, in practice, the second is really an extension of the first.

Arthur Balfour (Prime Minister 1902–05) described democracy as 'government by explanation'. Even if it is likely that the government will eventually get its way, Parliament is the forum in which it must explain itself and be held to account. Explanation may take various forms: responding to criticisms of proposed legislation at the second reading of a bill, or on detailed amendments put forward at report stage; explaining and defending a broader policy, perhaps on education reform or NHS funding, as part of a full day's debate initiated by the opposition or backbenchers; or giving a detailed account of its actions to a select committee inquiry. The requirement on governments to explain and justify can, in itself, be a brake on executive power; but it is up to members of Parliament in both Houses to make this process effective.

Ministerial accountability is a concept that it is easier to recognise than to define. There is extensive case law covering a number of years, beginning with the Crichel Down affair in 1954, when the Minister of Agriculture, Sir Thomas Dugdale, resigned apparently because he was taking responsibility for errors made by his civil servants (but more likely because he was left high and dry by a change in government policy); the Westland affair in 1986; and the special adviser Jo Moore 'burying bad news' in 2001, which led eventually to the resignation of Stephen Byers as Secretary of State for Transport, Local Government and the Regions. On Westland, Leon Brittan resigned as Secretary of State for Trade and Industry, taking responsibility for errors by officials but refusing to explain exactly what had happened. The Defence Select Committee, which investigated the saga, remarked drily: 'A Minister does not discharge his accountability to Parliament merely by acknowledging a general responsibility and, if the circumstances warrant it, by resigning. Accountability involves accounting *in detail* for actions as a Minister'.

The principle of accountability to Parliament is now underpinned by resolutions of both Houses in March 1997 (following the Scott inquiry into the supply of arms to Iraq) on how ministers should behave towards Parliament:

> *Ministers of the Crown are expected to behave according to the highest standards of constitutional and personal conduct in the performance of their duties. In particular, they must observe the following principles of Ministerial conduct:*
>
> i   *Ministers must uphold the principles of collective responsibility;*
> ii *Ministers have a duty to Parliament to account, and be held to account, for the policies, decisions and actions of their Departments and Next Steps Agencies;*
> iii *It is of paramount importance that Ministers give accurate and truthful information to Parliament, correcting any inadvertent error at the earliest*

opportunity. Ministers who knowingly mislead Parliament will be expected to offer their resignation to the Prime Minister;

iv   *Ministers should be as open as possible with Parliament and the public, refusing to provide information only when disclosure would not be in the public interest, which should be decided in accordance with relevant statute and the Government's Code of Practice on Access to Government Information;*

v   *Similarly, Ministers should require civil servants who give evidence before Parliamentary Committees on their behalf and under their directions to be as helpful as possible in providing accurate, truthful and full information in accordance with the duties and responsibilities of civil servants as set out in the Civil Service Code.*

In Chapters 9 and 10, we will look more closely at the ways in which the government is called to account.

The party

However close an MP's relationship with the constituency, the party to which he or she belongs is the key element in an MP's parliamentary life. This is not surprising; as we saw in Chapter 2, in general the only realistic prospect an aspiring politician has of being elected to the House of Commons is to join a political party and then have the backing of that party to fight an election. But for most MPs their relationship with their party has an element of compromise about it. No party is ever in the happy position that every one of its MPs would sign up to every last detail of every one of its policies. Some would prefer to see greater emphasis in this or that direction; others are uneasy about the party committing itself on something else. However, just as the collective responsibility of ministers has its strength in public unity, so MPs are content to exchange occasional disagreements or private doubts for the shelter and support of the party that best represents their political outlook.

Given the enormous importance of political parties in Westminster politics, it is perhaps surprising that they are not more explicitly recognised in the rules of the two Houses. In the Commons, the standing orders notice parties only so far as 'committee memberships reflect the composition of the House', that smaller opposition parties have a share of opposition day debates, that a small number of posts are reserved to (or have to be divided between) parties, and that one MP speaking for the second largest opposition party is exempted from any limit that may be imposed on speaking time for backbenchers in a particular debate. In a formal sense, party structures and disciplines exist in parallel with the regulation of the House and its proceedings although, in practice, they interlock at every level.

By contrast, in some parliaments – for example, the Canadian House of Commons – the role of parties is explicitly recognised in the allocation of oral questions and speaking time, which means that the Speaker plays a smaller role in allocation than at Westminster.

The whips

The whips are key players in party organisation and discipline, and in the arrangement and timing of business, on both sides of the House. The title derives from 'whippers-in' or 'whips' in the hunting field. Whips act as a two-way channel of communication between the party leadership and the backbenches; on the one hand feeding back MPs' views and warning of areas of possible difficulty or dissent and, on the other, making clear to backbenchers what the leadership wants from them.

An effective whip needs to be a strong character and a shrewd operator, but also has to balance personal authority with an understanding of the pressures on the MPs for whom she or he is responsible. Much is written, and more speculated, about the black arts of the whips – their techniques for bringing recalcitrant MPs into line – and of their intelligence gathering. There is no doubt that whips can, on occasion, be fearsomely effective, whether by use of stick or carrot, in persuading potential rebels to live with their doubts rather than express them; and there is no doubt, either, that a good whips office knows more about the views and foibles of its backbenchers than it would ever wish to see made public.

One player who should know – the Liberal Democrat Chief Whip, Don Foster – has claimed that these days the job of the whips involves more carrots than sticks. He said that:

> *In the past, the so-called black arts, the revealing of personal secrets, denying office space, denying membership of the committee, denying chairmanship of the committee, all these levers that were part of the [whips'] bag of black arts: they don't exist any more. Parliament has got sufficient office space for MPs, Parliament itself decides its membership of committees . . . so the power of the whips has been stripped away by quite rightly handing those powers back to Parliament itself . . . So what you've got to do is to persuade people of the importance of collegiality.*
>
> *But you've also got to make sure that you bring legislation before Parliament that's not going to cause great friction. The job of the whip, the whole whips' operation, has changed dramatically in recent years.*

Whips also need to be good personnel managers. New (and some more experienced) MPs may find life at Westminster difficult and frustrating; and spending much of the working week perhaps hundreds of miles from home and family, combined perhaps with constituency casework that is especially tragic or emotionally draining, can impose real strains. In such circumstances, a good whip is a source of advice and support.

Whips are ever-present in proceedings in the House and general committees (see Chapter 5). In the House, there is always a government and an official opposition whip sitting on the frontbenches keeping an eye on proceedings, jotting down notes on speeches (and speakers) in the debate and alert for any procedural or political difficulty that may arise. Whips have a talent-spotting role, and their good opinion (and especially that of the Chief Whip) may lead to ministerial office or a shadow post.

The Government Chief Whip is known formally as the Parliamentary Secretary to the Treasury (and sometimes as the Patronage Secretary – a reminder of the carrot rather than the stick of parliamentary discipline). It is his responsibility to get the government's business through the Commons with the greatest efficiency and the least dissent from government backbenchers. He normally attends Cabinet meetings and advises the Prime Minister and his senior colleagues on opinion within the parliamentary party, and how proposed policies are likely to play with backbenchers. On the government side, the next three senior whips carry formal titles of posts in the Royal Household: the Treasurer of HM Household, followed by the Comptroller and the Vice-Chamberlain. Traditionally, the Treasurer has also been the Deputy Chief Whip; in the Coalition government, this post has been held by a Conservative, and the Comptroller, also entitled 'Deputy Chief Whip', has been a Liberal Democrat (who is also the Liberal Democrat Chief Whip). There are six other whips (known as Lords Commissioners of the Treasury) and usually seven assistant whips (two of whom are Liberal Democrats).

The Labour Official Opposition has a Chief Whip and a deputy (who receive additional salaries even though they are in opposition) and twelve or thirteen other whips (one of whom receives an additional salary). The smaller parties each have someone who acts as a Chief Whip, although with relatively few MPs their role is more as their parties' voice in the arrangement of business than as organisers and disciplinarians. In the major parties, the whips have regional and subject responsibilities; for example, one may be responsible for both the north-east and defence.

The usual channels

This is deliberately vague shorthand for the informal discussions that take place between the business managers on both sides of the House. It embraces the Leader of the House and shadow Leader, and the government and opposition Chief Whips (and of other parties as circumstances require), but it also includes day-to-day and minute-to-minute conversations and arrangements between whips on both sides. A key player is the private secretary to the Government Chief Whip who, although a civil servant, plays a highly political role as a go-between.

The usual channels deal with a wide range of business, from issues such as the amount of time to be spent on a government bill in committee and which party should get which select committee chair, to extempore arrangements in which a whip will go round the Chamber asking his side's last two or three speakers to limit their speeches so that the 'winding-up' speeches from the frontbenches can start at the time agreed. Off-the-cuff arrangements are sometimes referred to as being done 'behind the Chair' – which is, indeed, where they happen when whips from both sides have whispered conversations behind the Speaker's Chair.

Discussions through the usual channels are private – were they to be made public, it is unlikely that they would take the same form or be so effective (this is the tension at the heart of proposals for a House Business Committee). But this secrecy, and the feeling on the part of some that deals cooked up behind the scenes may be more for the convenience of the participants than that of backbenchers on one side or another, has led to criticism: Tony Benn, for example, described the usual channels as 'the most polluted waterway in Europe'.

There is no doubt that, on occasion, the whips on both sides are closer to each other than to some elements of their own parties. It was widely thought, for example, that an alliance of the whips on both the government and opposition sides was responsible in October 2002 for defeating a proposal by Robin Cook as Leader of the House that would have greatly reduced the power of the whips over which MPs should serve on which select committees. (However, as we shall see in Chapter 10, wide-ranging and influential reforms were eventually made in this area.)

The Whip

A vital document for every MP is *The Whip*. This is circulated weekly by the whips of each party to their own members and lists the business for the following two weeks, together with the party's expectations as to when its MPs will vote. The importance of the business is reflected by the number of times it is underlined – hence the phrase 'a three-line whip' for something seen as an unbreakable commitment. An example is shown overleaf.

By arrangement with the whips, an MP may miss even an important vote if he or she is paired – that is, if an MP from the other side makes a formal arrangement not to vote, so that the effect is neutral. This is of less importance when the government of the day has a very large majority, but it may be of considerable importance when the numbers are close; for example, it allows the Foreign Secretary to be at the UN, or other ministers to take part in crucial negotiations in Brussels, rather than being called back to vote. When the government party can rely on a large majority, it will normally excuse some of its MPs from voting, on a rota basis, so that they can spend time in their constituencies.

Occasionally, it happens that the usual channels break down, and the opposition withdraws pairing arrangements. This can be a considerable inconvenience to the government, which must keep many more of its MPs in the precincts or nearby in case of a snap vote.

Party discipline

The whips are responsible for delivering the votes to give effect to their parties' policies and intentions. On matters that are likely to be contentious within the party, the leadership normally takes care to trail proposals in advance to assess whether there is likely to be dissent. It follows that, for the whips, a backbencher's cardinal sin is to abstain, or worse, vote against his or her party without giving any warning. An MP who expresses doubts about being able to support the party will normally be asked to discuss those doubts with his or her own whip, and probably also with the Chief Whip. For crucial votes, the Prime Minister (or other party leader) may want to try to change minds by meeting waverers, as in the vote on the EU referendum in October 2011 and the vote on possible military intervention in Syria in August 2013.

THE BUSINESS FOR THE WEEK COMMENCING 23RD JUNE WILL INCLUDE:

MONDAY 23RD JUNE
Last day for tabling: Business, Innovation and Skills
The House meets at **2:30pm** for **Work and Pensions Questions**
Conclusion of the Remaining Stages of the Deregulation Bill (Whip in Charge: Gavin Barwell)
THERE WILL BE A RUNNING 3-LINE WHIP FROM 3.30PM

TUESDAY 24TH JUNE
Last day for tabling: Communities & Local Government and Scotland
The House meets at **11:30am** for **Treasury Questions**
Remaining Stages of the Wales Bill (Whip in Charge: Stephen Crabb)
THERE WILL BE A RUNNING 3-LINE WHIP FROM 12.30PM

WEDNESDAY 25TH JUNE
Last day for tabling: Justice
The House meets at **11:30am** for **Cabinet Office Questions**
At 12 noon: Prime Minister's Questions
Opposition Day (2nd Allotted Day). There will be Debates on Opposition Motions, including on the Subject of the Private Rented Sector (Whip in Charge: Claire Perry)
THERE WILL BE A 3-LINE WHIP AT 3PM FOR 4PM AND 6PM FOR 7PM

THURSDAY 26TH JUNE
Last day for tabling: Prime Minister
The House meets at **9:30am** for **Business, Innovation and Skills Questions**
At 10:30: Business Questions
General Debate on the Programme of Commemoration for the First World War (Whip in Charge: Harriett Baldwin)
THERE WILL BE A 1-LINE WHIP

FRIDAY 27TH JUNE
The House will not be sitting.

A political party's 'Whip', which tells its MPs when they should be present for votes in the Commons

Source: Government Chief Whip's Office, 2014

A former Cabinet minister once advised his new MP colleagues 'to tread that narrow path between rebellion and sycophancy'. Although, as we shall see below, the 2010 Parliament is on course to be the most rebellious in recent history, party discipline is normally not a problem for most MPs. They accept that membership of a party, with all the advantages that its structures and organisation bring, involves some degree of compromise; and they are usually content to vote as the party wishes, especially in subject areas of which they have no close knowledge. They are also well aware that a divided party is a parliamentary, and certainly an electoral, liability. It is ironic that, on the one hand, there is public pressure for MPs to be more independent but, at the same time, a feeling that a party that cannot keep its own members on side has somehow failed.

Dissent and rebellion

An MP will think very carefully before voting against the party, or even abstaining, in an important vote. Unless it is unassailably on a matter of personal conscience, the action will be seen as disloyal and will often have an effect on the prospects for preferment; whips have long memories.

The reasons for rebellion are varied: the issue may be one of general principle, as on limiting the right to jury trial, or on the prospect of military action in Iraq or Syria. It may be on an issue that is seen by some of its members as contrary to a party's traditions and best interests; for example, for the Conservatives on the Maastricht Treaty in the 1992 parliament and on continued membership of the EU in the 2010 parliament, and for the Labour Party on university tuition fees in the 2001 parliament.

The size of a government's majority is obviously an important factor. In 1992, the Conservatives under John Major were returned with an overall majority of 21. By the end of the parliament, by-election defeats and defections to other parties had reduced this to a minority of three. Rebellions among Conservative MPs resulted in a total of nine defeats for the government during that parliament. By contrast, in 1997 Tony Blair had an extraordinarily high majority of 179 over all other parties. Actual defeat on the floor of the House was therefore much less likely; but rebellions were still of no less concern to the leadership. Coalition government since 2010 has made dissent even more of an issue for party leaders and whips.

Dissent since 1997

In the 1997 parliament, the level of dissent on the government backbenches was less than in previous parliaments, perhaps because of a feeling of being on trial after 18 years in opposition, perhaps because of memories of damaging divisions in the party during the last Labour government in 1974–79. Nevertheless, there were 104 occasions on which Labour members voted against the government on the floor of the House – the fourth largest number of rebellions in parliaments since 1945. In the 2001 parliament, Labour backbenchers rebelled in 20.8 per cent of votes, the highest *rate* of rebellion since 1945.

The biggest rebellions during the Labour administrations between 1997 and 2010 – and, in fact, the biggest for more than a quarter of a century – took place over the government's policy on military action against Iraq. On 26 February 2003, 122 Labour MPs voted against the government on an amendment asserting that the case for military action was 'as yet unproven'; and on 18 March, 139 Labour MPs voted for an amendment to the effect that the case for war had not been established.

Dissent in the 2001 parliament

Indeed, in the first two sessions of the 2001 parliament the government experienced the greatest level of backbench dissent since 1945, with more than two-thirds of

Labour backbenchers voting against the government on one or more occasion. This dissent continued throughout the parliament: in January 2004, 72 Labour MPs voted against the second reading of the Higher Education Bill on the issue of tuition fees, and the bill scraped through by only five votes. In November 2004, abstentions and votes against knocked 95 votes off the government's majority on second reading of the Gambling Bill, which would have authorised a number of 'super-casinos'; and, in March 2005, 62 Labour MPs voted against the government's proposals for house arrest of terrorist suspects on the authority of a minister and not of a judge.

Dissent in the 2005 parliament

In June 2005, the government's majority of 66 was reduced to 31 on second reading of the Identity Cards Bill, which suggested that the smaller majority in the 2005 parliament would need careful management. And so it proved. In the first nine months of the parliament, the government lost four major votes, on issues relating to the treatment of terrorist subjects and the definition of incitement to racial hatred. The habit of rebellion continued throughout the parliament. A further two defeats followed in 2009, on the rights of Gurkha veterans seeking to settle in the UK (unusually, this loss occurred on an Opposition Day motion – see Chapters 5 and 7); and on what was essentially a question of parliamentary privilege (see Chapter 5), on the permissibility of using as evidence in court material relating to parliamentary proceedings. No post-war government with a majority on the scale of the 2005 Labour government (60) had suffered so many defeats.

There were many more rebellions, of course, that did not result in defeats for the government. In all, Labour MPs rebelled in 365 divisions between 2005 and 2010, easily the highest number of rebellions in a parliament since 1945 (the second highest being between 1974 and 1979, when government MPs rebelled in 309 votes). This meant that Labour MPs voted against their government in 28 per cent of divisions; again, a post-war high, with the previous record being 21 per cent in the 2001 parliament.

Dissent in the 2010 Parliament

The scale of rebellions has increased yet further in the 2010 parliament. At the end of the 2013–14 session, four-fifths of the way through the parliament, there had been a revolt by government members in 37 per cent of divisions. Therefore, barring a dramatic drop in the number of dissenting votes in the final session, the 2010–15 parliament will have been the most rebellious since the Second World War. Given the scale of dissent, it is perhaps surprising that this has not translated into more government defeats. In fact, by the end of the 2013–14 session, the government could really only be said to have lost a vote as a result of backbench dissent on two occasions. The first, in October 2012, saw 53 Conservative rebels vote for an amendment tabled by a Conservative MP, Mark Reckless, calling for a reduction in the EU budget. The amendment was supported by the Labour opposition and the government lost by 307 to 294 votes. The second defeat sustained as a result of backbench dissent was of greater consequence, causing the government to shelve plans for likely military intervention.

The government recalled parliament on 29 August 2013 to debate the situation in Syria. Responding to the evident disquiet among their own backbenchers, the government committed not to engage in military action without a further vote. Despite that stance, 30 Conservative and 9 Liberal Democrat MPs voted against the government motion, which was defeated by 285 to 272. The story was very different in the vote on limited military intervention in Iraq during the recall of Parliament on 26 September 2014, when a cross-party alliance ensured that the government's proposed course of action was approved by 524 votes to 43.

What the small number of defeats does not expose is the sometimes quite dramatic steps taken by the government in order to avoid such defeats. We noted (page 77) that the *Coalition's Programme for Government* indicated that there would be an agreement to differ between the two governing parties on matters such as university funding, the renewal of Trident and tax allowances for married couples: all issues on which, in previous post-1945, non-Coalition governments, it would be very difficult to imagine circumstances in which government MPs would not be expected to vote as directed by their whips. We also saw how, on a rebel amendment to the Queen's Speech, in the knowledge that the alternative was a humiliatingly large rebellion, the Prime Minister sanctioned abstentions by ministers and votes for the amendment by PPSs.

But the most dramatic volte-face by the government as a result of near-inevitable rebellion was the abandonment of the House of Lords Reform Bill. Although the government achieved a large majority at second reading, it did so because of Labour support, and despite the 91 Conservative MPs who voted against the Bill. Knowing that a similar number of rebels would also vote against a programme motion for the Bill – crucial, if the Commons was not going to get bogged down in the minutiae of the Bill, to the near exclusion of all other legislation – and that Labour would not support such a motion, the government abandoned the motion and the Bill. So, while the government was not defeated in a vote, its policy was jettisoned because of the likelihood of such a defeat. The prospect of rebellion can be just as disruptive for government as the reality.

The dynamics of dissent

Voting against one's party, however good the reasons, is not a decision lightly taken. The aims vary. Quite apart from their views on matters of principle or what is in the interests of their constituency, MPs may want to make a point about being consulted by the party leadership. They may want to establish their credentials, both within the party as a whole and with their constituents, on a major issue.

Especially if the government's majority is small, a threatened revolt may secure substantial changes in policy. But small majorities work both ways; when the boat is low in the water, people are less inclined to rock it, and, however strongly they feel, government MPs will be reluctant to risk the 'nuclear option' of defeating their party on a major issue and perhaps triggering a vote of confidence (as happened when, in July 1992, the Conservative government was defeated by 324 votes to 316 over the Social Protocol to the Maastricht Treaty – even though it won the confidence motion the next day by the luxurious margin of 110 votes).

Dissent and rebellion can become a habit for some MPs. In each of the three full sessions of the 2010 parliament to date, the same three Conservative MPs – Philip Hollobone, David Nuttall and Philip Davies – have topped the charts of most rebellious MPs (albeit in a slightly different order in each session). And, of the 96 Conservative MPs who rebelled during the 2013–14 session, all but 10 had rebelled in at least one of the earlier sessions of the parliament; and of those 10, 7 had been ministers or whips for part of the time, and therefore precluded from rebelling as part of the payroll vote. Repeated rebellion sometimes indicates a growing disenchantment with the mainstream views of the party – for a few, this may be the first step towards defection to another party (see *crossing the floor* on page 89). It is also the case that rebellion becomes easier; an MP may think that, having damaged his prospects by voting against the government several times, full membership of the 'awkward squad' will not make things much worse. The presence of a major figure, perhaps a former Cabinet minister who is on the backbenches because he or she resigned over a major policy difference, may also be a potential focus of dissent. The number of sacked ministers and of MPs who are unpromoted and resentful (the 'ex-would-be-ministers') is also contributory. In 2005 and 2006, the wish of a number of Labour MPs to see Tony Blair step down was an additional factor.

Because of their wish to present a united front to the electorate and the media, political parties tend to undervalue dissent – or, at least, dissent in public. In most organisations and businesses, challenge is seen as a healthy process, leading to better decision-making.

Punishment

Voting against the party is not normally a good career move; most parties are unwilling to reward rebels with promotion. There are more formal sanctions. The Parliamentary Labour Party (PLP) has a code of conduct that requires its MPs to behave in a way that is consistent with the policies of the party, to have a good voting record and not to bring the party into disrepute. However, it does contain a 'conscience clause', which recognises a right of dissent on 'matters of deeply held personal conviction'. The Chief Whip may reprimand an MP in writing (which may also be reported to the member's constituency party). The PLP as a whole may 'withdraw the whip' from one of its MPs – in effect expelling them from the party.

The Conservative Party has similar rules, also with 'conscience' provisions. But, in the 1992 parliament, eight Eurosceptic Conservative MPs had the whip withdrawn from them for six months because of their repeated voting against the party on European issues, and crucially on the Maastricht Social Protocol, which became an issue of confidence for the government.

Whether to make an example of rebels is a matter of judgement. There is a balance between doing so *pour encourager les autres* and the risk of creating martyrs. And, if dissent is on a large enough scale, the whips may have little practical power; the solution then is for the party to re-examine its policy.

In the 2005 and 2010 parliaments, the whip has tended to be removed as a result of personal misconduct rather than because of rebellions arising from policy differences. For example, in 2009 three Labour MPs had the whip removed as a result of allegations about expenses, and in the following year three former Cabinet ministers lost the whip because of claims about lobbying.

Crossing the floor

In an extreme case, an MP who falls out with his or her party may leave altogether and join another party. This is relatively rare; there were eight in the period 1992–2005. Since then, one Conservative MP became an Independent UKIP MP briefly, and in August 2014 Douglas Carswell, and in September Mark Reckless, defected from the Conservatives to UKIP, but no MP has crossed the floor between any of the major parties. An MP changing parties does not normally trigger a by-election, as he continues to represent constituents whether or not they voted for him; but there is usually some local pressure for the defector to resign so that a new candidate can be chosen. This is one circumstance that might be covered by any 'recall' legislation (see page 369). Douglas Carswell and Mark Reckless did actually resign their seats in order to fight by-elections in Clacton and in Rochester and Strood, both of which they won decisively.

Large-scale defections may rewrite part of the political map, as in 1981 when 27 Labour MPs and 1 Conservative joined the newly formed Social Democratic Party founded by the 'Gang of Four' – former Labour ministers Roy Jenkins, David Owen, Shirley Williams and William Rodgers. The importance of established party backing was demonstrated by the fact that only 4 of the 28 survived the 1983 election (and 1 of those lost in 1987).

Party organisation in Parliament

The whips do not spring political surprises on MPs, for MPs are themselves part of the decision-making processes in their party, and their influence is felt in the committees and groups in each party. This organisation is obviously more complex in larger parties, but each party has a formal structure, supported by its own secretariat.

The Labour Party

The Parliamentary Labour Party (PLP)

All Labour MPs, backbench and frontbench, and Labour peers, are members of the Parliamentary Labour Party. The PLP meets at 6.00 p.m. every Monday for between 45 and 90 minutes. The main agenda item is normally forthcoming business in the House, and the Chief Whip tells MPs what the whipping will be. A Cabinet minister will normally be a guest speaker, reporting on plans and current issues (with a chance to shine in front of the party's rank and file). An important agenda item may be a topical subject raised under 'any other business'. Individual MPs may move motions to make a point or to test opinion; notice of these must be given to the Chief Whip at least a week before the meeting. Attendance at the weekly PLP meetings is usually between 100 and 150. The chair of the PLP (since 2012, Dave Watts) is elected by a ballot of all Labour MPs (not just backbenchers) and is a key party figure.

The Parliamentary Committee

When the Labour Party is in government, the Parliamentary Committee of the PLP – in effect, its executive committee – consists of the Prime Minister and Deputy Prime Minister, four ministers including the Leader of the House and the Chief Whip in the Commons, the chairman of the PLP and four backbench MPs elected by other backbenchers, and one peer elected by backbench Labour peers.

Subject committees

Each of these monitors the work of a government department from a party point of view; there is also a Women's Group, which only women members may join. Labour MPs may belong to a maximum of three subject committees (not counting the Women's Group) but may attend any other committee in a non-voting capacity. The committees meet approximately fortnightly, often with the participation of ministers; attendance varies greatly according to the interest of the agenda, down to half a dozen or so. When the party is in government, the chairman and officers of a subject committee keep in close touch with the ministers of the relevant department. Committees are consulted about forthcoming policy initiatives and legislation, and ministers report to the relevant committee on the work and plans of their departments.

Regional groups

Every Labour MP belongs to the appropriate regional group: for example, Greater London, the North-East or Wales. These usually meet fortnightly and focus on issues of particular local concern or interest. They can play an important part in setting the broader agenda within the party, and they are also a target for local government, agencies and institutions that want to shape opinion among the MPs for their area.

The Conservative Party

The 1922 Committee

The Conservatives' equivalent of the PLP is the 1922 Committee, which was founded in 1923 by MPs who came into the House for the first time at the 1922 general election. Despite its former formal title of 'the Conservative Private Members' Committee', it has always been known as 'the 1922 Committee' or 'the '22'. Every Conservative MP may attend meetings of the '22', although only backbenchers may vote. Conservative members of the European Parliament (MEPs) and peers may attend but do not vote. The 1922 Committee meets on Wednesdays at 5.30 p.m.; the business taken is similar to that in the PLP. The chairman of the 1922 Committee (since 2010, Graham Brady) plays an important role in the party as the representative of the interests of backbenchers, with direct access to the leader of the party, and he also sits as the representative of the parliamentary party on the Conservative Board, the governing body of the party.

The Executive Committee of the 1922 Committee

This consists of the chairman of the 1922 Committee, 2 vice-chairmen, a treasurer, 2 secretaries and 12 other backbenchers, elected each year. The Executive Committee has always had a significant influence on party policy and direction.

Policy committees

The 1922 has five elected backbench policy committees, with each committee covering the work of a number of government departments.

The Liberal Democrats

Liberal Democrat MPs meet on Wednesdays at 5.30 p.m. for an hour or more. The first item is usually a report by the leader of the party, followed by a discussion of forthcoming business in the House, and items submitted by individual MPs. Occasional longer meetings take place, including 'awaydays' outside Parliament during recesses. Partly attributable to the size of the party (57 MPs in the 2010 parliament), there is no formal committee structure.

Other parties

The six Scottish National Party and three Plaid Cymru MPs meet jointly on Wednesday evenings, with the chair alternating between the leaders of the parties. An important purpose of these weekly meetings is to arrange for the coverage of debates and to develop coherent tactics. This is a problem for small parties – business is arranged principally between the two major parties, and the Nationalists might find that they have to decide between support for the government and support for the opposition when they may not wholly support either. The option of abstention is not recorded officially and so is not distinguishable from absence.

The Democratic Unionists, with eight MPs, hold weekly meetings, usually on Wednesdays at 2.00 p.m. The five Sinn Féin MPs elected in 2010 have not taken their seats (neither did their predecessors elected in 2001 and 2005), and take no part in the business of the House.

Political groups

We said earlier that membership of a party involved a degree of compromise, that some MPs would prefer to see greater stress placed on some areas of policy or might be uneasy about other areas. For many years, in all political parties, these differences of emphasis have led to the formation of political groups within parties that more closely represent particular currents of opinion. The Conservative Party's dining clubs come and go, but the more enduring are the centre-left Nick's Diner and the No Turning Back group, which is to the right of the party. The Cornerstone Group is sometimes described as 'the religious right' and interviewed each of the candidates for the party leadership in 2005.

Party leadership

No assessment of influences on MPs within their own parties (and the influence that they, in turn, can exercise) would be complete without a mention of the way in which party leaders are elected. Dissatisfaction with a party leader, or the perception that there is a leader-in-waiting, can produce blocs of opinion within a party – as witness the press's enthusiastic labelling of Labour ministers in the 2005 parliament as 'Blairite' or 'Brownite'.

It can also give rise to an extreme form of dissent, as when in 1990 Margaret Thatcher was deposed as party leader (and so as Prime Minister) following a leadership challenge by Michael Heseltine, who had resigned from the Cabinet over the Westland affair almost five years before. Thatcher won the ballot by 204 votes to 152, but the scale of support for Heseltine led her to withdraw from the contest. In the early part of the 2005 parliament, dissent by some Labour MPs seemed to be aimed at Tony Blair's premiership almost more than the issues on which they voted against him.

In the Conservative Party, a challenge to the leadership may be triggered only if 15 per cent or more of Conservative MPs (in the present parliament, at least 46) ask the chairman of the 1922 Committee for a vote of confidence in the leader. If the leader then receives a majority of the votes cast, there can be no further challenge for a year. If the leader loses, votes of all Conservative MPs then reduce the number of candidates for the leadership to two, and the contest is decided by a ballot of all party members in the country at large (despite an unsuccessful attempt by Michael Howard in 2005 to make the views of party members advisory, and that of Conservative MPs decisive). In 2003, Iain Duncan Smith lost the party leadership following a vote of confidence among Conservative MPs (90 votes to 75); Michael Howard was the only candidate to succeed him, and became leader with neither a further vote by MPs, nor a ballot of party members. But in 2005, after ballots of Conservative MPs had eliminated Kenneth Clarke and Liam Fox, it was on a vote of party members, by 134,446 to 64,398, that David Cameron beat David Davis for the leadership.

In the Labour Party, in March 2014 rule changes were agreed so that in future leadership contests candidates must be nominated by 15 per cent of Labour MPs (39 in the current parliament) and all members (including affiliated and registered supporters) then vote on a one-member-one-vote basis. This replaced the previous system, under which the leader and deputy leader were elected by three elements of the party: Labour MPs and MEPs, party members, and affiliated organisations (mainly trade unions), each element disposing of one-third of the vote. A candidate with more than half of the votes was elected (after elimination ballots if necessary).

A nomination had to have been supported by 12.5 per cent of the PLP if there was a vacancy, and by 20 per cent (82 MPs) if there was a challenge. It was this system that was used in the dramatic election of 2010, which was contested by five candidates. Using the alternative vote system (where the candidate placed last in each round is eliminated and his or her supporters' next preferences are counted), after four rounds, Ed Miliband won the leadership, beating his brother David by a very narrow margin: 50.65 per cent to 49.35 per cent. David Miliband had been leading in each earlier round, and gained more votes from Labour MPs and MEPs and individual party members in the final round, but the votes of affiliated members (predominantly the unions) meant that his brother emerged victorious.

The Liberal Democrat leader is elected by a ballot of the party in the country as a whole under the alternative vote system. Candidates must be Liberal Democrat MPs, and they must have the support of 10 per cent of MPs in the parliamentary party, and of 200 party members in at least twenty local parties. In 2007, Nick Clegg won the leadership election by a narrow margin ahead of Chris Huhne, by 20,988 votes to 20,477. An election can be triggered by a vote of no confidence in the incumbent leader by MPs or by 75 local parties writing to the President of the Party to request a contest.

The party: conclusion

Political parties consist of much more than members of Parliament, but MPs are at the forefront of political activity, and they have an important role in the determination and presentation of their parties' policies. The multifaceted organisation of parties in Parliament is a constant influence on the individual MP, in terms of voting expectations, exposure to the views of other MPs and changing currents of opinion, and, in the major parties, interaction with ministers when the party is in government and with shadow ministers when it is not.

In turn, MPs have the opportunity to take part in the development of party policies through formal committee and group structures, and also through informal personal contacts and relationships – the newest MP may spark off an important new idea with the leadership in a three-minute conversation in the Tea Room or the division lobby.

Personal influences

People are shaped by their experiences, and MPs are no exception. They bring with them into the House what they have acquired in previous careers, whether as teachers, lawyers, social workers, as craftspeople (in the case of former Speaker Martin, as a sheet-metal worker) or in other fields, such as the Labour MP who was an Oscar-winning actress, the Liberal Democrat with a doctorate in logic or the Conservative who was a firefighter. MPs are also influenced by more personal experiences. In the present parliament, members' contributions have reflected, for example, the NHS treatment provided for a spouse who died in hospital, caring for a parent with dementia, and personal experiences of mental health issues. Many of these experiences will condition how an MP reacts to some of the myriad issues of parliamentary life.

The constituency: the MP's relationship

The constituency is a vital part of the life of every MP. As we noted in Chapter 2, it is a power base, and its voters must be wooed to maximise the chances of being elected. An MP's identification with the interests and concerns of a constituency is also sharpened by the fact that UK constituencies are small enough to be fairly homogeneous in terms of character, population and economic activity.

An MP represents all the people in a constituency, whether or not they voted for him or her – or, indeed, whether they were old enough to vote; an average constituency in England may have 76,000 electors but a total population of 90,000 if you count those under 18. This non-party representation of a constituency is emphasised by the fact that in most cases the majority of people entitled to vote will not have voted for the person elected as an MP. This is especially true of recent elections, at which turnout has been historically low (the 65.1 per cent turnout at the 2010 general election, while a modest increase on the 2005 level, was the third-lowest figure since universal male suffrage was introduced in 1918) and in safe seats (where turnout tends to be lower). For example, in 2010 in Manchester Central – a safe Labour seat – the winning candidate got 52.7 per cent of all votes cast. However, turnout was only 44.3 per cent (the lowest in the country), so less than one-quarter of eligible constituents voted for the new MP.

The closeness of an MP's relationship with the constituency, and the extent of its influence on the MP's actions in Parliament, has steadily increased. The classic statement of the relationship of member and constituency is that contained in Edmund Burke's speech to the electors of Bristol in 1774:

> *It ought to be the happiness and glory of a representative to live in the strictest union, the closest correspondence, and the most unreserved communication with his constituents. Their wishes ought to have great weight with him; their opinion, high respect; their business, unremitted attention. It is his duty to sacrifice his repose, his pleasures, his satisfactions to theirs – and above all, ever, and in all cases to prefer their interest to his own. But his unbiased opinion, his mature judgement, his enlightened conscience, he ought not to sacrifice to you, to any man, or to any set of men living . . .. Your representative owes you, not his industry only, but his judgement; and he betrays, instead of serving you, if he sacrifices it to your opinion.*

The first part of this antithesis – the close relationship with and unremitting attention to the constituency – may be seen as years before its time, even though Burke was speaking to electors a century and a half before universal suffrage. For the whole of the nineteenth century, and in many cases into the twentieth, constituencies were simply platforms on which MPs stood to take part in public life and that they visited rarely. Such absenteeism would not wash today, and we will shortly describe some of the constituency pressures on the modern MP.

The second part – the assertion that an MP is the representative of a constituency who votes according to his judgement and conscience, and not a delegate who votes according to constituents' instructions – has undergone a transformation. An MP may still exercise judgement and conscience, and in doing so may represent a minority of opinion in the constituency – for example, for rights for prisoners, or for additional powers for the European Union – but, as we saw earlier in this chapter, the main constraint on the way an MP *votes* is now the party to which he or she belongs.

Listening to constituents

Almost every MP has a constituency office to deal more effectively with constituency matters and to have a presence close to local issues; and many MPs base some or all their support staff in constituencies rather than at Westminster.

In recent years, the core of an MP's work on behalf of constituents has been the 'surgery', when the MP's availability to discuss problems is advertised on their websites, in the local press and elsewhere. In a small constituency, this may be at a central constituency office; in a larger one, it may be in a succession of town and village halls during the day, or even in a caravan that the MP tows around. Surgery work is on the increase; many MPs have moved to twice-weekly surgeries, and the changed sitting patterns of the Commons since 2002 have included many more non-sitting 'constituency Fridays'.

Constituents also raise issues and problems with their MP by letter. While MPs still receive many letters each day, evidence suggests the numbers are declining: in 2006, almost 4.8 million items of correspondence were delivered to the Palace of Westminster; by 2013, that number had dropped to just under 2.5 million. However, that falling off in the number of letters sent appears to have been more than counterbalanced by the huge numbers of emails received by MPs. This brings its own challenges: the speed of communication leads many constituents to expect an equal speed of reply on what may be a hideously complicated problem. One conscientious inner London MP estimated in 2013 that she received between 300 and 400 emails each day. MPs are also communicating via social media; a survey of new members elected in 2010 found that around 65 per cent of them used Facebook, just over 50 per cent of them used Twitter and 38 per cent of them had a blog.

Constituents' problems

People will raise literally any subject with their MP. They do so for a variety of reasons: they think the MP will be able to get action; they have exhausted all other possibilities; they do not know who to approach and so start with the MP; or they go to the MP as a personification of an establishment that they see as being the problem itself. This last category inevitably includes the desperate and the disturbed, and at surgeries security is often an issue; in 2000, an MP's researcher was killed and the MP himself badly injured, and other MPs have been attacked and occasionally seriously injured.

When a constituent seeks help, the MP must first establish exactly what the problem is. This is often much more difficult than it might seem. The constituent may be coming to the MP only after months or years of struggle with some organisation or agency, and his or her opening gambit may be to present a box file overflowing with documents of all sorts, some more legible than others. Unravelling the tangled skein to find out exactly what has happened, whose fault it was and what can be done about it can be enormously time-consuming. On the other hand, the problem – perhaps 'neighbours from Hell' – may be very straightforward, but what can be done without legal action, which the constituent cannot afford, may be much more difficult.

People often assume that an MP can do something about anything but, strictly speaking, an MP's role is limited to matters for which ministers are answerable to Parliament – in general, the responsibilities of government departments or executive agencies. This nevertheless covers a huge range of things that give rise to constituents' problems: immigration and asylum, pensions and social security, income tax, the Child Maintenance Service, the National Health Service, and animal health and farming subsidies being just a few.

The MP does not have a direct role in matters that are the responsibility of a local authority – the running of local schools, rubbish collection and recycling, council housing, council tax, and so on, as 'constituency cases' here are the responsibility of local councillors. But although an MP will be careful not to step on the toes of councillors (whether of the same party or not), he or she may on the basis of local difficulties pursue a broader issue of principle for which central government *is* responsible: for example, in the extent of central government funding for local authorities and what is taken into account in setting the level of that funding. In addition to respecting the remit of local councillors, one impact of devolution is that a wide range of issues are now the responsibility of members of the relevant devolved body, rather than Westminster MPs. A constituent may bring to the MP a 'private sector' problem: perhaps the mis-selling of pensions, rogue builders, or rocketing insurance premiums in an area prone to flooding. A letter from an MP may or may not have any influence directly with the company concerned, but in cases such as these the MP's best bet is to engage the responsibilities of ministers for regulating these sectors of industry in the public interest, or perhaps to seek the assistance of an industry's own watchdog body, which has an interest in the reputation of the industry as a whole. If the problem is a failing company and job losses, the MP may be looking for government support for European Union grants, or money for retraining redundant workers.

Even if the MP really has no direct role, and the possibility of doing something constructive is very limited, there is always the risk that an honest answer to this effect may be misrepresented by the constituent, the press or a political opponent as 'Ms X doesn't care' or 'Mr Z isn't prepared to put himself out'. There is thus a good deal of pressure on the MP to make some sort of positive or helpful response, even if it is only to suggest some other person or agency to approach.

MPs are extremely careful to check that the person raising a problem is, indeed, their constituent and not that of a neighbouring member (you can find out who your MP is from the parliamentary website: www.parliament.uk/mps-lords-and-offices/mps/). Occasionally, an MP faced with a case in which he or she might be thought to have a personal interest may ask another MP to take it on. This also happens from time to time when an MP has taken a strong public stand on an issue, in order to avoid a constituent with a contrary view feeling that there might be a conflict of interest. However, if an MP dies or resigns, it is usual for constituents' problems to be dealt with by one or more neighbouring MPs.

A new MP is always warned by colleagues not to take up planning cases; planning has its own machinery at both local and national levels, and the applicants and the objectors are usually all constituents; to favour one is to disadvantage another. Similarly, although the 'neighbours from Hell' may be a public nuisance for a whole local area, MPs are generally reluctant to take up neighbour or family disputes; all concerned are likely to be constituents.

What can the MP do?

An MP does not have executive power but is an analyst and advocate. In taking up a constituent's case, he or she must identify what the problem is and who is responsible (or direct a constituent elsewhere if someone else is more likely to be able to take effective action). Then, it is a matter of exposure and persuasion. A letter on House of Commons writing paper or an email from a parliamentary address may be enough to break a bureaucratic log jam or to persuade a company that it has treated someone unfairly.

On most things for which central government is responsible, the most usual first step is the letter to the minister. This may ask for a case to be reviewed, for the minister's observations on the problem or simply for a clear statement of the department's policy on the point at issue. We return to MPs' letters to ministers in Chapter 9.

If the minister's response does not solve the matter, and the constituent has a good case that the MP is determined to take forward, the possibilities are limited only by energy and ingenuity. The MP may seek a meeting with the minister. If the problem is a wider one within the constituency – perhaps involving mass redundancies, or a manufacturing or farming sector in crisis, this may take the form of leading a deputation to a formal meeting in the department, with the minister and civil servants present. The MP may make an informal approach – the classic way is to corner a minister in the division lobby during a vote in the House. Perhaps there are other members who have had similar problems in their constituencies, who can make common cause. Maybe the issue can be given a higher profile through parliamentary questions or an early day motion (EDM) (see page 262); or the MP may apply for a debate via the Backbench Business Committee (see page 258) or for one of the daily half-hour adjournment debates in the House or Westminster Hall, when there will be an opportunity to set out the case in detail and the responsible minister will have to reply. A case of maladministration may be referred to the Ombudsman (see page 309). At any of these stages, the support of the local – or, possibly, the national – media may be enlisted.

However good the constituent's case, success is not guaranteed. But, as with so many issues in parliamentary and political life, a good argument, persuasively and energetically deployed, the support of sympathisers and, above all, persistence and determination offer the best chance of success.

Constituents' views

Constituents also write to MPs on the issues of the day. These naturally vary with the political agenda, but a survey conducted in 2013 found that 34 per cent of MPs cited gay marriage as one of the main concerns raised with them by voters, ahead of welfare reform (23 per cent), NHS reforms (19 per cent), pensions (13 per cent), fuel prices (13 per cent), unemployment and jobs (8 per cent) and the Budget (8 per cent). In most cases, an MP's response will reflect party policy or personal views. However, the strength of popular opinion shown by the size of the postbag – provided that it consists of individually written letters and not duplicated campaign mailings – may influence both individual MPs and their parties.

Constituency profile

A new Labour MP for a Welsh valley constituency had previously been an energetic local councillor. Within weeks of being elected to Westminster, he was stopped in the street by a constituent he had known for a long time. 'We don't see much of you now', she said. He replied that he had been elected as an MP. 'Yes', she said. 'I voted for you. But we still don't see much of you'. He explained that he was very busy in the House for most of the week. 'So you're not going to be here as much as you were?' 'No', he said. 'I'm sorry, but I'm not'. 'Oh', she said. 'If I'd known that, I'd never have voted for you'.

This anecdote (not apocryphal) illustrates a tension in the life of the constituency MP. The centre of parliamentary life is Westminster, and to satisfy the requirements of the parliamentary party and the whips, to promote constituency interests and to take part in select committee work, as well as to pursue personal political priorities, that is where the MP needs to spend a good deal of time. But there is a strong gravitational pull from the constituency as well. The local MP is expected to be on the spot: to open bazaars and fairs; to speak to working men's clubs and the WI; to put in an appearance at school prize-givings or road safety days; to comment knowledgeably on livestock at an agricultural show or present quality awards at the diesel engine works; to read the lesson at the civic service; to attend the Remembrance Day parade; or to draw the fund-raising raffle.

Those activities are public duty rather than party duty; but an MP must also spend time cultivating local party links and support. This may involve party social events, from wine and cheese to beer and crisps, and a round of dinners and lunches (the so-called 'rubber chicken circuit'), as well as reporting back on the MP's work at Westminster.

For many MPs, constituency activity fills up the rest of the week not occupied by work at Westminster. Some constituencies are within easy distance of Westminster and the distinction is less sharp, but, for most members, the Westminster week finishes on Thursdays; they travel to their constituencies that afternoon, and Friday, the weekend and Monday mornings are given over largely, or even entirely, to activity in the constituency; they then travel back to Westminster on Monday in time for votes in the evening.

Fighting the corner

In 2001, the Senior Salaries Review Body reported on the work of MPs in representing the constituency as a whole:

> *Our interviewees [a sample of MPs] were nearly unanimous that expectations in this area had grown substantially from business, public institutions such as schools, and indeed the public generally. The Press have become much more insistent on the local MP contributing to local debate (for example through regular columns) and everyone expects them to 'fight the local corner' with Ministers and other influential players at national or European level.*

Dealing effectively with constituents' problems is only half of being a 'good constituency MP'. The local member is also expected to be an advocate and ambassador for the constituency as a whole. This may involve seeing that his or her patch is not left out when EU grants or subsidies are bid for, or ensuring that ministers do not forget how the crisis in farming is hitting the constituency, or perhaps (for some Scottish MPs with distilleries) making the case against a Budget tax rise on spirits. As well as direct approaches to ministers and the media, subject debates and, particularly, Question Time are good opportunities for this; but there is a convention that members should not use select committee work to make the constituency case.

In the last analysis, constituents expect important constituency matters to be paramount for the MP, even if that means rebellion against the party line. For example, more than 30 Conservative MPs voted against the HS2 high speed rail link bill, and a significant number have promised to continue opposing the bill, in large part because of its impact on their constituencies.

The constituency comes to Westminster

The closer a constituency is to London, the more likely an MP is to see his or her electors at Westminster. This may be an individual visit to put a problem to the MP; it may be an organised party to see around the Palace of Westminster and perhaps listen to a debate; it may be a school visit; or it may be tea on the Terrace for senior members of the party in the constituency and their spouses. MPs value these connections; they give constituents a chance of seeing the other side of an MP's life and understanding more about Parliament – and they may be a special day out that demonstrates the MP's regard for his or her constituents.

The changing role of MPs – from parliamentarians to caseworkers

Constituency work, and particularly casework on constituents' problems, has taken more and more of MPs' time over the last twenty to thirty years. But in recent years it has become the determining influence upon the great majority of MPs. Although the 'golden age' of Parliament yearned after by some commentators probably never existed, it is certainly true that fewer MPs than ever before are now classic 'parliamentarians', speaking with authority on the great issues of the day or developing the expertise to challenge the government on some complex or technical subject. For most of their time, the majority are caseworkers, more interested in effective intervention in local issues, or establishing a reputation as a constituency champion. There is no right and wrong about this, of course; but the change has meant that the parliamentary opportunities afforded by the House of Commons are used less effectively than they might be.

All-party parliamentary groups

'All-party parliamentary groups' (APPGs) bring together MPs and peers to discuss issues of common interest. They must contain at least four members from different parties, and, as the rules are administered by the Commons, the Chair must be an MP. Many such groups also involve outsiders. A reform in 2014 abolished associate parliamentary groups, in which people who were not members of one or other House could, in principle, vote, but there is no bar to groups containing non-parliamentarians in a non-voting capacity. Most notably, the Parliamentary and Scientific Committee brings together MPs, peers, scientific organisations, science-based companies and universities.

APPGs can be divided into subject groups, and country groups. The subject groups are most numerous – in May 2014, there were over 500 such groups, covering subjects from Accident Prevention to Zoroastrianism.

States such as Kazakhstan and Yemen, as well as many more familiar countries, have their own country group. Most groups receive briefings from the embassies of the countries in which they are interested, and their members are sometimes invited to visit or to receive overseas delegations to the UK. Country group members do not normally see themselves as defenders of the governments of the countries concerned but as people who know something of the politics, culture, economics and history, and so are able to make some contribution to the UK's relationship with that country. Most country groups cooperate with the Inter-Parliamentary Union or the Commonwealth Parliamentary Association.

APPGs meet as often as enthusiasm sustains them; they elect their own officers and (because they are often seen as potential lobbying targets and, in some cases, receive outside funding) they are officially – and publicly – registered. The principal groups are Westminster fixtures; others are established or disappear as the mood takes. Some have formal secretariats and planned programmes; others may simply have a social event from time to time, perhaps with a guest speaker.

The extent and variety of activity is well-shown by the meetings advertised in the *All-Party Whip* (this is not about party voting requirements but is a sort of Westminster noticeboard) for the last full week before the 2014 summer recess. On Wednesday 16 July, there were meetings of country groups for Azerbaijan, Italy, Sweden (with the newly appointed deputy British Ambassador), Australia, New Zealand (with the New Zealand High Commissioner), Jamaica, Canada, the South Pacific, Burma (a report back on a visit to Shan and Kachin states), the Holy See, Tanzania (a panel discussion on business and human rights), South Africa and Cuba. The APPG on Accident Prevention had a discussion on lighter evenings; the APPG on Arts and Heritage were on a visit to Sir John Soane's Museum; the APPG on Anti-Semitism held a seminar on 'integration and extremism'; the APPG on Occupational Health and Safety held its annual seminar on asbestos; the APPG on Cycling discussed cycling and HGVs; the APPG on Agriculture and Food for Development debated 'ICT and knowledge sharing in agriculture'; the APPG on Modern Languages heard about 'opportunities for the UK through the EU's Erasmus Programme'; the APPG on Opera heard about a recent production of *Benvenuto Cellini*; and there were meetings of the APPGs on Christians in Parliament, Small Shops, Child Health, Education, Shipbuilding, Motorcycling, Voter Registration, Boxing, Hepatology, Bridge, Environmental Health, and a dozen others.

All-party parliamentary groups give MPs and peers the opportunity to discuss a wide range of issues, often with major players. They give members the chance to develop policy, to focus opinion and, in turn, to influence ministers. APPGs driven by committed and knowledgeable Members can help bring about change: the APPG for Smoking and Health, for example, has been very influential

Lobby groups and lobbyists use such groups to assess and influence parliamentary and political opinion. While some APPGs are shoestring operations, run from a member's office, others have secretariats supported by external organisations, such as charities, industry associations, or learned societies. Opinion is divided over the relationship between APPGs and lobbying; lobbying is seen as part of the parliamentary process, but external funding imports a degree of risk. Even so, it should be noted that the rules prohibiting paid lobbying by members extend to APPG activity, and the fact that in 2014 an MP was forced to resign for attempting to set up an APPG in return for payment demonstrated that this rule could and would be enforced.

The new APPG regime agreed by the House, which will come into operation fully in the 2015 Parliament, is built on five principles:

- APPGs should be driven and controlled by Parliamentarians.
- Members playing an active part in an APPG's activities should recognise their responsibility for its governance and understand they may be held to account over any failings.
- There should be transparency about APPGs' activities and expenditure, as well as about the support they receive from external sources.
- Information should be provided in a way that makes it easier for the public to understand how APPGs work and how they are regulated.
- Regulation should be appropriate to an APPG's size and activities.

Although MPs and peers are free to work with external organisations outside the APPG regime, such groups may not describe themselves as parliamentary or use the Portcullis insignia; also, any significant benefit they receive must be registered by the Chair of such a group as if it were given to him or her alone.

Lobby groups and lobbyists

The word 'lobby' used in the sense of a House of Commons ante-room first appears in 1640. It later crossed the Atlantic to be applied to the geography of the US Congress. But 'to lobby' (meaning to seek to exert influence on parliamentarians) and 'lobbyist' (one who does so) are American coinages first appearing in 1850 and 1863, respectively. By the end of the nineteenth century, both had crossed the Atlantic the other way and became commonly used in the Westminster Parliament.

The term 'lobby group' is usually used of political pressure groups that might, for example, be campaigning for more resources to provide clean water in the Third World, or for healthier children's diets, or homeopathy – or for the ordering of new fighter aircraft, or lower taxes on electric cars. 'Lobbyist' is usually used of the professional advocate whose skills in presentation, making contacts and persuasion are for hire.

Modern lobbying is mainly directed at governments, whose executive power and power of initiative make them obvious targets, and covers the whole field of government activity. Political pressure groups, charities or commercial interests may try to have particular provisions included in (or, just as often, excluded from) forthcoming legislation, or seek favourable tax treatment in a forthcoming Budget. The government is a huge contractor and purchaser (for example, of defence equipment), and selling to government is a major area of lobby activity.

Single-issue politics – embracing campaigns such as those on, for example, animal rights and anti-globalisation, often with an international dimension – have become more prominent in recent years. They tend not to use traditional lobbying methods but use the Internet both to bring their supporters together and to target politicians who are seen as opponents, often running campaigns against those with slim majorities. Some organisations that have used more traditional techniques in the past are either switching to this approach or are running both methods in tandem. Lobby groups and lobbyists are interested in MPs for two main reasons. First, if they espouse a cause they can give it a high profile through writing to ministers, parliamentary questions, early day motions or tabling of helpful amendments to legislation. Second, they can influence opinion, both outside the House through the media and, more important, with their colleagues, both backbench and frontbench. This influence will usually be greater if their party is in government.

Effective lobbying means effective targeting, either through knowledge of an MP's interests and experience, or by exploiting the vital constituency link. Too many would-be lobbyists have an entirely unrealistic idea of how interested most MPs will be in what they have to say. In the view of the Conservative MP for North Wiltshire, who had been a director of one of the larger lobbying consultants:

> *Bombarding decision-makers with excess and useless information will often be counter-productive. Those people who believe that they are achieving something useful by sending their annual accounts out to MPs with a stereotyped covering letter with 'Dear James Gray' at the top (only worse is 'Dear James Gray, Esq., MP', which happens all too often) are mistaken . . . waste paper baskets round Westminster will be the only beneficiaries.*
>
> *By contrast, a simple letter along the following lines will hit the mark every time: Dear Mr Gray* [preferably handwritten], *the widget-makers of North Wiltshire are very concerned about the effects of a forthcoming government Statutory Instrument about widget specifications, which may put 25 jobs in your constituency at risk. I know that Mr Blodgett, the managing director of Widgets to the Gentry, Bumpers Farm, Chippenham, would very much welcome the opportunity of meeting you to explain the matter and to introduce you to his workforce if you could spare an hour or so, perhaps one Friday, in the near future.* [Handwritten:] *Yours sincerely, Fred Plunket, National Association of Widget-Makers.*

This description of an MP's reactions is reinforced by Lord Tyler, the former Liberal Democrat MP, who had run a public affairs consultancy:

> *Anything that looked like a real message from a real constituent – preferably a local postmark – got priority attention . . . Targeting from a constituency viewpoint, and timing to coincide with the parliamentary agenda, has always seemed to me to be much more likely to achieve impact than the most elaborate hospitality or printed material.*

Although lobby groups and lobbyists influence MPs, they are also extremely useful to MPs – and to others – as well. James Gray again:

> *Those of us in Parliament, and no doubt in government, find truly professional lobbying very useful indeed. A shadow minister handling an obscure statutory instrument debate; a back-bencher searching for an original line in a select committee or during oral questions; a journalist looking for a new perspective*

on legislation; a civil servant seeking to summarise an industry or public response to a ministerial initiative – all of these and others will value a truly professional, concise and targeted exposition of a particular argument.

Good lobbying (objective, factual, well-argued) provides some of the research resource that many MPs feel they lack, despite the support of their own staff and the work of the researchers in the House of Commons Library. And if it obeys the golden rule of being on an MP's particular political interest, or relating to the constituency, it is likely to be used.

Lobbyists, or parliamentary or public affairs consultancies, are used by many organisations and interests. Some simply want to have parliamentary and government activity monitored in order to have early warning of what is coming forward. Others feel they need help in making their case. A typical assignment might be to attempt to head off a policy proposal that the client believes might damage his business. The lobbyist will need to understand the proposal and its context and master the arguments against it.

Contacts between ministers, MPs, civil servants, journalists and others must then be used, or new ones developed, to get the message over. The EU dimension is increasingly important, both at the stage when a proposal is only a gleam in the eye of the European Commission and as it advances through the European Parliament. Above all, the earlier the problem is tackled, before political capital is invested and it quickly becomes much harder to get a proposal modified or dropped, the better.

One fundamental difference between lobbying in the USA and in the UK is that lobbyists in Washington are advocates for their clients; US politicians seem to prefer dealing with a 'hired gun' than directly with the client. In the UK, however, parliamentarians prefer to hear the message direct, and lobbyists prepare their clients for meetings rather than being the principal actors.

In the late 1980s and 1990s, some types of lobbying acquired a doubtful reputation, becoming associated with the parliamentary sleaze we shall describe shortly and appearing to be based more on lavish entertainment than strength of argument. In the 1990s, there were attempts to brighten the industry's rather tarnished image by promoting high ethical standards through voluntary codes of conduct and registers. In 2014, registration of lobbyists was put on a statutory footing by the Transparency of Lobbying, Non-Party Campaigning and Trade Union Administration Act 2014 which prohibits lobbying by unregistered consultant lobbyists (those who are paid to lobby for third parties).

There are also organisations that make it easier for members of the public to email MPs on a variety of topics, such as 38 degrees and Change.org. This can give MPs an indication of the strength of opinion on a particular topic, but is rarely as effective as a more personal approach, except where a member is already concerned about a particular subject. Members are well aware of the amount of effort and engagement needed to click a mouse rather than write a letter. As a result, they may respond to mass campaign tools in kind through standardised responses, often on websites, sometimes prepared centrally by party organisations or groups of MPs.

Parliamentary standards

Self-regulation and privilege

The House of Commons has long regarded its independence as paramount. Over the centuries, the House has evolved into a body that can, if it wishes, control the executive rather than one that was summoned by the Crown only when necessary, and was largely controlled by the Crown. The right of members to speak freely, and of the House to control its own precincts, was a key part of this evolution, and was fiercely fought for. It is enshrined in 'parliamentary privilege', which we examine in greater detail on pages 161 to 166.

Parliamentary privilege is not immunity. MPs are subject to the law of the land in the same way as anyone else. If they engage in criminal conduct, they can be (and have been) prosecuted. Civil suits can be brought against MPs. This is in itself a mark of British confidence in its judicial system. In many other countries, members of Parliament have complete immunity from criminal proceedings while they are MPs, unless the Parliament concerned chooses to waive it. In such countries, parliamentary immunity is often defended on the grounds that politically motivated prosecutions could be used to remove an awkward MP.

The principle of 'exclusive cognisance' means that only the House can regulate what is said or done in proceedings in the House. That does not mean there are no external sanctions: a political party may decline to select a sitting MP as its candidate in the next election or the electorate may choose to reject him or her. But the disciplinary powers for what is said and done in the House rest with the House itself, and it is for the House to decide the rules that should govern MPs' behaviour.

Although there is a constitutional principle behind it, the lack of parliamentary immunity means that the House's self-regulation is broadly similar to the self-regulation exercised by many professions. Nonetheless, parliamentary self-regulation has become a matter of some controversy.

The Committee on Standards in Public Life

The evolution of the disciplinary system in each House of Parliament – and, indeed, in many walks of public life – has been greatly influenced by the Committee on Standards in Public Life (CSPL). This was established in October 1994 by the then Prime Minister, John Major, in response to scandals about 'sleaze' – in particular, cash for questions.

The committee has ten members; it has no parliamentary character (although three peers are members); it is appointed by the Prime Minister and it reports to him. It covers the whole of the public sector, but has produced several reports on parliamentary standards, prompted first by the difficulties of the 1990s, and subsequently by the expenses scandal.

Following the first report of the CSPL in 1995, the House of Commons set up a Select Committee on Standards in Public Life to consider the Committee's findings and to recommend how they should be reflected in the rules of the House. The main changes made in 1995 were:

- the appointment of a Parliamentary Commissioner for Standards (PCS);
- the setting up of a new Committee on Standards and Privileges to replace the separate Committees on Privileges and on Members' Interests; and
- the drawing up of a Code of Conduct for MPs.

Subsequent changes have included:

- making provision for an investigatory panel to assist the Parliamentary Commissioner for Standards in making findings of fact in serious cases (this has not been used);
- introducing a non-renewable fixed term for the PCS as a guarantee of independence; and, most recently
- the involvement of lay members in House of Commons disciplinary processes.

Regulating influence: a history

It is clearly of the first importance for public confidence in Parliament that MPs act in the national and constituency interest rather than with the expectation of private gain. In 1695, the House of Commons passed a Resolution 'Against offering bribes to Members', stating that the offer of money or 'other Advantage' in respect of a matter that was to be transacted in Parliament was 'a high Crime and Misdemeanour and tends to the Subversion of the Constitution.' Although the seventeenth- and eighteenth-century approach seems to have been rather more relaxed about the acceptance of favours, when Sir John Trevor as Speaker received the then colossal bribe of £1,050 from the Common Council of London for helping to get a bill passed, the House expelled him in short order.

The Victorian House of Commons recognised the importance of MPs' advocacy in the House being divorced from private gain and, in 1858, resolved that: 'It is contrary to the usage and derogatory to the dignity of this House that any of its Members should bring forward, promote or advocate in this House any proceeding or measure in which he may have acted or been concerned for or in consideration of any pecuniary fee or reward'. This was aimed especially at MPs who were practising barristers, but it was reinforced in 1947 by a further resolution forbidding contractual arrangements under which, for any benefit, a member promoted any point of view on behalf of an outside interest. In 1974, the House agreed that MPs should be required to declare any financial interest that they might have in matters being debated or otherwise before the House or its committees, and that they should register their financial interests. A Select Committee on Members' Interests was established to supervise this process.

In the late 1980s and early 1990s, there was a steady growth in professional lobbying firms on the US model, many with multi-million or multi-billion pound businesses as clients. They saw parliamentary influence as a valuable commodity and, by 1995, more than one-quarter of MPs had paid consultancies with lobbyists (26) or with other bodies outside the House (142).

Whether or not this was against the public interest, public unease was greatly increased by some high-profile incidents: the 1994 'cash for questions' affair, in which *Sunday Times* journalists approached 20 MPs offering £1,000 for simply tabling parliamentary questions (which was accepted by two of them); and the allegations by the businessman and owner of Harrods, Mohamed al-Fayed, that he had rewarded MPs for lobbying on his behalf.

At the same time, there was a growing public suspicion – both reflected in and, to an extent, fuelled by a high media profile – of the uses that certain individuals made of their position or wealth. Donations to political parties to buy influence, newly retired or resigned ministers and senior civil servants obtaining lucrative directorships, important public appointments being made on the basis of personal connections rather than merit – however widespread (or not) this might have been, the important thing was that it was widely believed.

It was this unease that led to the establishment of the CSPL, and a great part of the Code of Conduct for MPs is aimed at preventing improper use of influence.

The expenses scandal

The Code of Conduct had prohibited misuse of resources from its inception, and the Committee on Standards and Privileges had dealt with a number of cases related to misuse of public money that caused public concern, including the case of a member who was found to have employed his son and paid bonuses when that son had, in fact, done no work. But the issue really ignited as a result of the publication of unredacted expenses claims by *The Daily Telegraph* starting in May 2009. There were three aspects to this. First, some MPs and peers had been acting in ways that were subsequently judged to be criminal; second, many MPs had claimed for money to which they were not entitled, either inadvertently or to obtain maximum benefit from the system; and third, the expenses system itself was seen as much too generous. The seeds of disaster had probably been sown in the early 1980s, when Margaret Thatcher's government backed down on a justified pay rise for MPs but contrived to imply that the difference could be made up on expenses.

As a result of the expenses scandal, a new statutory body, the Independent Parliamentary Standards Authority (IPSA) was established to set and administer MPs' pay and expenses. It is theoretically possible that if an MP claimed expenses in a way that was not criminal, but was felt to be improper, the IPSA Compliance Officer could refer the matter to the Parliamentary Commissioner to consider whether there had been a breach of the Code of Conduct. In fact, this has never arisen – although there have been several legacy cases – so the House has not yet had to consider complaints of misuse of expenses under the new system.

A further result of the expenses scandal was that the Committee on Standards and Privileges put it on record that criminal proceedings against members should take precedence over the House's own disciplinary proceedings. This principle has been reiterated by the successor Committee on Standards.

The rules

The House has agreed two distinct but overlapping and interdependent mechanisms for the disclosure of personal financial interests; these aim to 'provide information about any financial interest that might reasonably be thought by others to influence their parliamentary conduct or actions'. The first is registration of interests: information about certain financial interests has to be registered within four weeks of acquiring the interest. The Register is published in hard copy annually and regularly updated online. Currently, there are 12 categories of interest, although the Committee on Standards and Privileges recommended that they be reduced to 10. Members are required to register information about directorships; remunerated employment, including details of any client for whom they work directly; donations they may have solicited to their constituency party or association; gifts, benefits and hospitality above a certain threshold; land and property other than that used as a residence; and significant shareholdings. Journalists and members' staff also have to register financial interests that might be advantaged by their position.

The Register is intended as a register of interests, not a declaration of wealth. The thresholds for registration and the registration categories may be changed from time to time by the House. Indeed, during the expenses scandal, there were frequent changes to rules and thresholds – first, in an attempt first to tighten up rules that were deemed inadequate and, subsequently, to correct overreactions. The detailed rules are on the Parliament website.

An MP must disclose a financial interest when speaking in a debate, in a way sufficiently informative to allow a listener to understand the nature of the interest. Interests must also be declared when tabling parliamentary questions, when tabling early day motions or amendments to bills (or adding names to them), and when introducing private members' bills. When an interest is declared, the symbol [R] appears on the Order Paper beside the name of the member concerned.

An MP must also declare if he or she has a reasonable expectation of future financial advantage – for example, an MP whose family business made industrial cleaning equipment would be expected to declare an interest when speaking on a bill that would set up an inspectorate to monitor standards of cleanliness in schools and hospitals.

In select committees, all members declare their registrable interests before standing for election as chair, on the grounds that this aspect of an MP's independence is a factor in his or her suitability for the chair. Thereafter, members of a select committee must declare any relevant interest, or even withdraw from an inquiry completely, if there is a conflict of interest.

Lobbying for reward and paid advocacy

This rule, based on the 1858 and 1947 resolutions (see page 106) and borrowing some of their language, takes the declaration of interests several steps further. It outlaws paid advocacy – that is, doing anything in the House (speaking, voting, tabling amendments or urging other MPs to do so, or approaching ministers or civil servants) directly for payment. In practice, this means that an MP who is a director of a company, or a paid adviser for an organisation, may not try to get any preferential treatment for that company or organisation (for example, in tax relief, subsidies or some special treatment or opportunity) in any use of his or her functions as an MP.

Voting

The classic rule was stated from the Chair almost two centuries ago, when Speaker Abbott ruled that 'no Member who has a pecuniary interest in a question shall be allowed to vote upon it'. In modern times, this is interpreted as a direct financial interest, and in the context that an MP's interests have been declared. To take two examples: in 1983, the Speaker ruled that MPs who were solicitors might vote on a bill that removed their exclusive rights on conveyancing, as the bill was a matter of public policy; however, in 1981 MPs who were also members of Lloyd's were advised not to vote on a bill to regulate the Lloyd's insurance market.

The Ministerial Code

MPs (and peers) who are ministers are subject to the Code of Conduct of the relevant House. They are also covered by the Ministerial Code laid down by successive Prime Ministers with the aim of ensuring that there is no actual or apparent conflict between their private interests and their public duties as ministers. The Ministerial Code became more contentious with a series of high-profile cases (notably David Blunkett's second resignation from the Cabinet in November 2005 following allegations of a conflict of interest, and the financial dealings of Tessa Jowell's husband). It was increasingly argued that policing the Code should be a matter not for the Prime Minister, but for an independent figure. In March 2006, the Prime Minister appointed Sir John Bourn, the Comptroller and Auditor General, as an independent adviser on the Code; he was succeeded by Sir Philip Mawer and then has since been succeeded by Sir Alex Allan. It remains for the Prime Minister to decide whether an investigation is warranted and to judge whether a minister has breached the Code.

The Committee on Standards and the Parliamentary Commissioner for Standards

Two institutions are key to setting and enforcing standards; the Parliamentary Commissioner for Standards, and the Committee on Standards (formerly Standards and Privileges), which oversees the work of the Parliamentary Commissioner. The current Commissioner is Kathryn Hudson, who had been Deputy Parliamentary and Health Service Ombudsman. She is supported by a small secretariat, which includes the Registrar of Members' Financial Interests.

The role of Parliamentary Commissioner for Standards was intended to introduce an element of independence to the system. She is appointed for a fixed term, non-renewable contract to ensure she cannot be threatened with loss of office, or influenced by the prospect of a further term. Although the Parliamentary Commissioner is overseen by the Committee on Standards, the Committee neither manages her work, nor what she chooses to say in her memoranda or annual report. The Commissioner's power to propose changes in the rules is not limited in any way, and past Commissioners have, for example, consulted publicly on potential revisions to the Code and Guide.

Much of the work of the Parliamentary Commissioner, and the work of her office, is in maintaining the register, offering advice to members individually and collectively, and keeping the system under review. While it is for the Committee to decide what to recommend to the House, and for the House to make the final decision, the Standing Order requires the Commissioner to monitor the operation of the Code and registers, and to make recommendations to the Committee. The Committee's role in this work is to approve or modify the arrangements proposed by the Commissioner or the Registrar, and to support the Commissioner and her office in their work. So, for example, the Chair of the Committee has written to members advising them about how particular rules should be interpreted, or alerting her to the need to check their Register entries.

The Commissioner's independence provides a check on the self-regulatory system, while the Committee's oversight of her work means that the Commissioner cannot make unilateral recommendations or findings that could be unreasonable. This applies both to the generality of the Commissioner's work, and her findings on individual cases.

The Committee on Standards

The Committee on Standards now contains ten MPs and three lay members. The lay members are people who have never been MPs, and were selected on the basis of fair and open competition. Their tenure is limited to the Parliament in which they were first appointed plus a possible further term of up to two years. This regular turnover should have the effect of avoiding 'organisational capture'. As for the MPs, although the party balance on the Committee reflects the party balance in the House, no one party has a majority, and Committee members are expected to set aside their party loyalties. The Committee is generally chaired by a member of an opposition party.

The lay members do not have a vote because if they were full members – not being MPs but, in effect, co-opted – the committee would not be a proper select committee and its proceedings (and its members) would not be protected by parliamentary privilege. Nonetheless, they play a full part in the discussions of the Committee and, as the Committee normally proceeds by consensus, they have at least as much influence over proceedings as any MP. Arguably, they have more influence, in that they have the formal power to add an opinion to a report, setting out their views. If they wish to do this, the Committee report cannot be published until the opinion is ready, and there are no restrictions on what the opinion may cover. The power to append an opinion gives lay members the opportunity to set out their views in a free-standing and very public way. In contrast, an MP who disagrees with some or all of a draft report will simply have his or her dissent recorded in the formal minutes as defeated amendments to the draft.

Dealing with complaints

Although the Commissioner and the Committee each have an important role in preventing problems, their highest-profile activity is ensuring the rules are enforced. The Commissioner can 'self-start' inquiries if there is evidence of wrongdoing, or if the IPSA Compliance Officer asks the Commissioner to do so, but the vast majority of inquiries arise from complaints made by members of the public or, very frequently, other MPs.

When a complaint is made that an MP has broken the rules, the Commissioner decides whether the matter is within her remit or there is enough evidence to justify an investigation. Most cases fall at this stage. Many of the complaints made to the Commissioner are about the handling of constituency cases, which are outside the scope of the Code. Others are about the expression of political opinions, or even actions within parliamentary proceedings, which are not for the Commissioner. Others complain about matters that are not breaches of rules, or are not accompanied by any evidence. It is entirely for the Commissioner to decide whether or not a matter is within her remit or whether the evidence is sufficient to justify starting an investigation. The procedure for investigations (agreed with the Committee) is set out on the Commissioner's webpages. Although some evidence is required to start an inquiry, the Commissioner will usually gather more, particularly in serious cases.

An investigation may result in a finding that no breach of the rules has occurred, or that there has been a minor breach that the MP concerned can put right easily ('rectification'). For example, someone who has inadvertently sent political material in a prepaid envelope may be asked to refund the cost of stationery, or a member who has failed to declare an interest may do so in a point of order on the floor of the House. In such cases, the papers relating to the inquiry are simply published on the Internet.

In more serious cases, the Commissioner submits a memorandum to the Committee on Standards, accompanied by all the evidence gathered in the course of her inquiry. The Committee may make further inquiries and report to the House with its conclusions and recommendations, which may include repayment of money, written or oral apologies, or suspension from the House (with loss of pay). It is for the House itself to decide whether or not an MP should be suspended or even expelled.

In principle, the Commissioner and the Committee will not deal with criminal matters. But some serious cases still come before the Committee. In 2012, it had to deal with a case in which an MP had submitted invoices signed with a '*nom de plume*'. The Committee recommended suspension for a year, which resulted in the resignation of the MP concerned, possibly after party pressure. This case had earlier been referred to the police for investigation by the Commissioner (with the Committee's consent), but no charges had been brought. When the Committee's report was published, the case was reopened, and the person concerned was subsequently jailed. Similarly, in 2014, the Committee recommended a suspension of six months for an MP who, as a result of a journalistic sting, accepted a 'consultancy' and tried to found an APPG to further the interests of his fictitious clients. Once again, the member concerned resigned.

Checks and balances

The political class has always struggled to be trusted, and the expenses scandal was a major setback. Whether the current level of distrust is merited is another matter. People in the United Kingdom seem ready to believe the worst: the most recent EU anti-corruption report noted:

> *In the case of the UK, only 5 persons out of 1115 were expected to pay a bribe (less than 1%), showing the best result in all Europe; nevertheless, the perception data show that 64% of UK respondents think corruption is widespread in the country (the EU average is 74%).*

A body without an effective system for policing standards may look cleaner than one where those who break the rules are investigated and punished, and that may have a number of cases.

There are real dilemmas in self-regulation. It can, of course, be seen as the political class 'marking its own homework'. But there is already a robust legal framework setting out who can and cannot be an MP, and no blanket immunity for MPs. The Code of Conduct rightly sets higher expectations for MPs than their observance of the law. Handing the right to police compliance (and perhaps even to set such expectations) to an external body would mean non-elected people would decide who should sit in Parliament, whatever the decision of the electorate.

A system of 'recall' in which the electorate could force a by-election if a sufficient number wished, even where there was a sitting member, is often advocated – and, indeed, is an element in the Coalition Programme – might deal with these problems. There is a division between those who believe that recall should limited, and those who want 'total recall'. The first consider that recall should be available only when an MP has committed 'serious wrongdoing' as found by the House itself, since otherwise the system might be open to manipulation by political opponents, or those with deep pockets. The second believe that it should be possible to challenge a sitting MP's right to continue if a significant portion of the electorate lose faith in him or her, for whatever reason (including defecting to another party). Still others believe that any system of recall would be open to manipulation, and reduce MPs' freedom to speak and act in the way that they consider best.

There are those who believe that all MPs should be full-time; others believe equally strongly that current outside experience makes an MP more knowledgeable and effective. People are distrustful of lobbying and external interests. Many deplore the rise of what they see as the 'professional politician' with no experience outside Westminster (although a conscientious constituency MP sees much more of 'life' than do many of the critics). And we should not underplay the influence of the selectorate and the electorate. Local parties are free to choose candidates without outside interests, and will almost certainly do so if it is likely to increase their vote; and the voters are free to disagree.

No system will satisfy everyone, but if outside interests are to be allowed, then public disclosure of those interests, allied to rigorous investigation of complaints and effective sanctions when the rules are broken, seems a reasonable way to proceed. Whether it commands public confidence, in a society that is distrustful by default, is a separate issue.

The House of Lords

Lords and Commons

Members of the House of Lords are subject to much the same influences as MPs, except that they do not have constituencies. Perhaps the chief influence – constraint even – on the House of Lords is its unequal position in Parliament vis-à-vis the House of Commons. The limitations on Lords' powers to reject or amend bills are fully described in Chapter 6, but it is important to grasp at this stage that the Lords, by not being elected and therefore being unrepresentative, are put at considerable disadvantage in terms of power compared with the Commons. If the Lords always attempted to insist on its will against that of the elected House, especially if the Commons were giving effect to policies endorsed by the electorate as part of the election manifesto of the governing party, there would be a constitutional showdown between the two Houses that would almost certainly result in further diminution of the Lords' powers. Because of this, the Lords tacitly recognises the right of the government to govern and of the House of Commons to see its will prevail most of the time. They willingly sacrifice their power in the same sort of compromise as that involved in the supremacy of the government in the House of Commons.

Many thought that the introduction of an elected element into the House under proposals for reform of the House as set out in the government's House of Lords Reform Bill in 2012 (see page 379) would have necessitated a readjustment of these assumptions – assumptions that have held good since the House of Commons became a truly representative chamber following the extension of the franchise in the nineteenth and early twentieth centuries. That said, the House of Lords is also subject to government, party, personal and external pressures in just the same way as the House of Commons, although these influences are perhaps less obtrusive in the Lords.

Government

The position of the government in the Lords is not as well entrenched as in the Commons. Following a general election, the party with the majority of seats in the House of Commons forms the government, and it is this party that occupies the government benches in the Lords, too. The government frontbench in the Lords following the Government re-shuffle in July 2014 consists of six ministers of state, two of whom – the Leader of the House and the Lords Minister of State in the Foreign and Commonwealth Office – attend the Cabinet; 11 parliamentary under-secretaries of state; and 10 whips. (Until July 2014, the Leader of the House of Lords was traditionally a full member of Cabinet and both the Conservative and Labour parties have committed to returning to that position after the 2015 general election.) Standing at 27, the total number is very high by historic standards and reflects the need to include seven Liberal Democrats as ministers or whips. Reflecting the pressure on ministerial office brought about by the need to include the coalition partners and the fact that there is a statutory limit on the number of ministerial salaries, ten of these officeholders are currently unpaid – with six unpaid Conservatives and four Liberal Democrats. Even so, the government presence is, relatively speaking, much smaller in the Lords than in the Commons, and promise of ministerial office is accordingly much less influential. The government's influence over its own back-benchers and over other members of the House is, in the absence of a large 'payroll' membership, that much weaker.

However, there is an understanding that the government can expect to get its business through. As we shall see on page 211, under the Salisbury convention the Lords will not reject at second reading legislation relating to commitments contained in an election manifesto and, indeed, it is rare for the Lords to reject at second reading any government bill. But a more general understanding on business is indispensable for the proper functioning of the House, as there are no procedural devices for curtailing debate on legislation; neither do the Lords' standing orders give government business precedence over other business. In the House of Commons, we have seen that a high proportion of sitting time is reserved for government business. In the Lords, anything up to 60 per cent of sitting time can be occupied with government business, but none of it is formally reserved for government use. In the last resort, a government might try to suspend standing orders in order to give its own business precedence, but fortunately this is rarely necessary. Provided that the government business managers respect the conventions of the House, consult the opposition through the usual channels and do their best to accommodate the demands of the private member, the other parties and private members alike are content to leave the arrangement of business to the Government Chief Whip. Governments are able to get their business through because they make sure that they are seen to deal fairly with the other parties and interests in the House.

The political parties

Although the members of the House are not elected, many of them – but by no means all – belong to political parties. A breakdown appears on page 37. Because lords are not elected, it is important to remember that the political composition does not change after a general election.

Officially, the House scarcely recognises the existence of the political parties. They are nowhere referred to in standing orders, and they are barely mentioned in the *Companion to Standing Orders*, the House's own procedural handbook. But the reality is very different. Each party has its leader and its whips and a small secretariat. We have already seen how opposition parties (currently only the Official Opposition) and the Convenor of the Crossbench Peers receive public funding (the so-called Cranborne money) to assist them in their activities. The government party has the advantage of an office manned by civil servants to organise its affairs. Committees of the House tend to reflect the composition of the House, as in the House of Commons, and the government party negotiates through the whips' offices of the other parties (the usual channels) and, where appropriate, with the Convenor nominated by the crossbenches, in the arrangement of business.

As in the Commons, the party whips send their members statements of forthcoming business in the House, with items underlined to indicate their importance to the party leadership. But discipline is not as strong as in the House of Commons. For many members of the House, their political careers are not their principal interest, and the allure of office carries less weight. There is no pairing system. There are weekly party meetings – every Wednesday afternoon – at which future business is discussed and there is, even in the Lords, a general predisposition to toe the party line. Members of the House do not have to submit themselves to the rigours of selection by the constituency parties or to re-election by constituents. The voting record of members of the House of Lords is not subjected to the same level of scrutiny as is that of MPs. We have seen that party cohesiveness is high when the House votes: but no one has yet measured the effect of strategic absenteeism. The crossbenchers – who profess no party line – are all, theoretically, floating voters though in recent years they have shown remarkable cohesiveness on some votes, particularly when the mover of the proposition is a crossbencher. (An amendment moved by a crossbencher to the Immigration Bill in the 2013–14 session attracted 78 crossbench votes in support and none against!)

The leader of the government party in the Lords is the Leader of the House, who, together with the Government Chief Whip, advises ministerial colleagues on any problems that might be encountered in getting their business through the House. Similarly, the Leader and Chief Whip of the Official Opposition will have regard to the views of the wider parliamentary party and shadow Cabinet in determining their approach to more controversial business.

Personal interests

The composition of the House guarantees great diversity of interest. The table on page 33 shows the background from which new members have been drawn over the years. First and foremost, there are the politicians – either those elected hereditary peers who have taken up political careers based in the Lords, or those created peers who have formerly been MPs or prominent in local government. Then there are those, mainly but not exclusively life peers, who are drawn from other walks of life – business, the professions and so on. Very often they are retired or approaching retirement, but they bring valuable experience and sometimes genuine expertise which places them at an advantage where detailed scrutiny of policy is required – say, in debates on academic funding or the operation of the benefits system, or in scrutiny in committee of the lessons to be learned from the recent banking crisis, for example. The diversity of the members of the House ensures that personal interest and influences are very strong in the Lords.

Members' interests, the Code of Conduct, and the Lords Commissioner for Standards

It was a long-standing custom of the House that members spoke always on their personal honour; and where they decided to participate in debates on matters in which they had an interest, whether pecuniary or not, they were to declare it so that other members and the public might form a balanced view of their argument. These rules were clarified and a scheme of voluntary registration of interests put in place in 1995. Following a review of these arrangements by the Committee on Standards in Public Life, a compulsory registration scheme and a code of conduct came into force in 2001. In the wake of high-profile breaches of that code, a new and more prescriptive Code of Conduct and accompanying guidance came into force at the start of the 2010 Parliament, and a Commissioner for Standards was appointed. Let us now discuss the chief characteristics of the rules on conduct.

Members of the House must as a general principle comply with the Code, act on their personal honour, never accept or agree to accept any financial inducement or reward for exercising parliamentary influence (acting as a 'paid advocate'), or providing parliamentary advice or services (acting as consultants or lobbyists). Any conflict between personal and public interest should always be resolved in favour of the latter. The seven principles of conduct as defined by the Committee on Standards in Public life should be observed. Every member must sign an undertaking to abide by the Code as part of the ceremony of taking the oath of allegiance at the start of every Parliament, or on their first arrival in the House.

The Code requires every member of the House to register any 'relevant' interests, and keep that registration up to date. A relevant interest is one that might be thought by a reasonable member of the public to influence the way in which the member might discharge his or her parliamentary duties. Interests may be financial, such as a shareholding or paid employment, or non-financial, as with membership of an organisation. In certain cases, they will extend also to a spouse or partner. In addition to registration, members must declare their interests in debate when relevant to the matter under discussion, and when tabling written notices, for instance questions or motions, in House of Lords Business.

The Code also requires members to abide by the rules relating to financial support received from the House and the rules on the use of the House's facilities and services.

Since 2010, any investigation of a possible breach of the Code is carried out by the House of Lords Commissioner for Standards. His findings and conclusions are reported to the sub-committee on Lords' Conduct for review and, where appropriate, recommendation of a sanction. The reports of the Commissioner and the sub-committee then go to the parent Committee for Privileges, to which the member concerned may appeal. The Committee's determination is then reported to the House for final decision. Sanctions for a breach may vary from an apology, or repayment of moneys, to suspension from the service of the House. The power to suspend a member was reasserted by the House in May 2009 at the height of the expenses scandal, which in the Lords chiefly took the form of false claims for overnight allowances. The power of suspension does not extend beyond the end of a Parliament – though it could be renewed; neither can the House expel a member permanently because the House cannot require the Writ of Summons issued to each member at the beginning of a Parliament to be withheld. The possibility that this might be changed by legislation is further discussed at page 383.

Between May 2009 and May 2014, 11 members made formal apologies for breaching the Code, 6 members repaid moneys falsely claimed, and 10 members were suspended for periods ranging from 4 to 18 months. Two members were imprisoned following criminal prosecution and were also found to have breached the Code.

Territorial

Members of the House of Lords have no constituencies: they are not representatives. As Lord Birkenhead (F.E. Smith) once remarked of a member of the House who had incurred his ire, 'The noble Lord represents no one but himself and I don't think much of his constituency'. It follows therefore that they do not have 'surgeries', or make representations to government or other authorities in respect of individuals' problems or grievances. Neither are they answerable to local party organisations or selection committees.

However, sometimes members of the House will be approached by interests in the locality in which they live or whose title they bear by reason of some long – and sometimes extinct – association, asking them to take up a particular stance on a public matter. Members are undoubtedly responsive to such approaches.

Lobby groups

As we examine in detail later on, all legislation has to be considered in the Lords, as well as in the Commons, and some legislation begins its passage through Parliament in the House of Lords. Members of the House therefore find themselves courted in much the same way as members of the House of Commons by lobby groups either directly, from their government and parliamentary relations officers, or through parliamentary consultants. The dramatic increase in lobbying since the end of the 1970s has been a conspicuous feature of the revival in House of Lords influence in recent years – part cause and part effect. Some lobbyists are skilful and selective in their targets. Others resort to an indiscriminate 'mail-drop'. These organisations will prepare evidence for committees, draft amendments to be moved to bills and provide briefing notes, offer to take peers on visits, or arrange lectures at which their policies are expounded. Over 30 organisations lobbied members on the Communications Bill in 2003. Of these, one organisation was a consortium of 12 well-known charities, and another represented over 1,000 businesses active in IT, telecommunications and electronics. More recently, in the 2012–13 session, the wide-ranging Enterprise and Regulatory Reform Bill attracted the attention of many different lobbyists. A provision to remove the general duty of the Equality and Human Rights Commission pro-vided for in the Equality Act 2006 was opposed by the PCS Union, Unite, the Law Society, the British Institute of Human Rights and others; changes to civil liability for breaches of health and safety duties were opposed by the TUC, Unite and the Scottish TUC; while the provisions on copyright law attracted briefings from the British Library, Universities UK, the Wellcome Trust, the Libraries and Archives Copyright Alliance and UK Music.

As a result of these contacts, some peers form potentially close associations with, for example, local authority organisations, industry groups, charities, bankers, major exporters or libertarian groups. These contacts not only influence members of the House, but also help to provide briefing and a wide range of assistance to what is essentially still a part-time Chamber of the legislature. They help to fill a void left by the highly effective but relatively limited research resources of the House of Lords Library.

There are drawbacks to this reliance on third-party organisations. Some members' associations with lobby groups are so close that they can appear to be their mouthpiece; the arguments advanced are inevitably to the advantage of the group, however worthy, often with insufficient regard for the wider consequences; and the lengthy briefing can lead to some debates being unnecessarily long.

Peers, in the same way as MPs, also belong to the all-party and registered special interest and country groups (see page 100).

5

The parliamentary day and the organisation of business

The parliamentary calendar

Before we look at the various items of business that make up a typical day in Parliament, and how members of both Houses are likely to spend their time, it is worth looking more broadly at the parliamentary calendar and the cycle of business in each House.

A parliament

In Chapter 2, we encountered the main division of parliamentary time: *a parliament*. This is the period between one general election and the next. Under the Septennial Act of 1715, the maximum life of a parliament was set at seven years. This was reduced to five years by the Parliament Act of 1911, although during the First and Second World Wars, to avoid a wartime general election, the life of the 1911 parliament was extended to eight years; that of the 1935 parliament was extended to ten years. Although the maximum life of a parliament – that is, the period between the day of first meeting and dissolution – was five years, few parliaments ran their course, because the Prime Minister of the day would seek a dissolution at a time that he or she saw as giving the best electoral advantage. The average length of parliaments between 1945 and 2010 was around three years ten months, and four years or so being the modern norm.

The Fixed-term Parliaments Act 2011

That changed with the passage of the Fixed-term Parliaments Act 2011 (FTPA). The FTPA, which was a key element of the 2010 Coalition Agreement between the Conservatives and the Liberal Democrats, set the date of the next UK general election as Thursday 7 May 2015; and thereafter, the first Thursday in May in the fifth calendar year following the previous general election. The dissolution of Parliament was set for a specified period (originally 17 working days, later extended to 25) before the date of the general election, and Parliament could not otherwise be dissolved. Thus, the Prime Minister's power to set the date of the general election was abolished, and the duration of a Parliament fixed at five years (subject to the provisions for an earlier, or later, election).

The main purpose of the Act was widely seen as being to ensure the continuance for a full five-year term of the coalition government between the Conservatives and Liberal Democrats, preventing the Conservative Prime Minister from 'pulling the plug' early and forcing a new election at a time of his choosing (although some commentators and constitutional reformers had been advocating such a change for some time, and the proposal was included in the Liberal Democrat manifesto for the 2010 election). The Act necessarily makes provision for early elections, but sets high hurdles to be crossed before that can occur. Section 2 provides for early general elections when either of the following conditions is met:

- if a motion for an early general election is agreed either by at least two-thirds of the whole House (including vacant seats), or without division; or
- if a motion of no confidence is passed and no alternative government is confirmed by the Commons within 14 days by means of a confidence motion.

For the avoidance of doubt (because defeat on other types of motion, such as key parts of the Budget or the Address in response to the Queen's Speech setting out the government's legislative programme, might be taken as a demonstration of no confidence), the Act provides explicitly that a no confidence motion must be in the form 'That this House has no confidence in Her Majesty's Government'.

These provisions leave open the theoretical possibility of a Prime Minister who commands a majority in the House of Commons engineering a no confidence vote that will enable a general election to take place at a time of his choosing: but the political consequences of attempting such a move make it unlikely that anyone would ever do so.

A more significant disadvantage of the Fixed-term Parliaments Act is that it does not cater for the situation where a government is, indeed, defeated on the Queen's Speech or on a major matter of public policy. Unless the House of Commons then agrees a motion for an early general election, or the government loses a motion of no confidence (and there is no motion of confidence within 14 days), presumably the government limps on until one of those motions is passed, but in the meantime it has lost credibility and much of the authority to govern.

Where an early election has taken place, the date of the next election reverts to the first Thursday in May, either in the fourth calendar year following the early election, if that election takes place before the first Thursday in May of that year, or the fifth calendar year, if the early election takes place after the first Thursday in May of that year. So, if an early election were to take place in February 2017, the next election would be fixed for Thursday 6 May 2021; if the early election took place in October 2017, the next election would be fixed for Thursday 5 May 2022. Thus, the usual May date is restored and provision is made so that a Parliament cannot last more than five years.

The Act also makes provision for the date of a general election to be delayed by up to two months beyond that set by the Act, by an order made by the Prime Minister following its approval in draft by both Houses of Parliament. The draft order laid before Parliament must be accompanied by a statement setting out the Prime Minister's reasons for proposing the change in the polling day. The drafters of this provision presumably had in mind the events of 2001, when the general election expected in, and the local elections set for, May 2001 were delayed for a month as a result of a widespread outbreak of foot-and-mouth disease that necessitated movement restrictions across much of the country.

Why five years?

Given that the average length of a Parliament in the post-war period was less than four years, why set the length at five years – previously the maximum length of a Parliament defined in the Parliament Act 1911 – rather than, say, four, which is closer to the actual average period between general elections in recent times? The government argued that a Parliament limited to four years would mean that a government's useful life would be closer to three, which was 'not adequate to deliver effective governance of the UK'. A Parliament limited to five years, it said, will allow a full four years for action, and the consequences to become clearer, allowing both better accountability, and a stronger incentive to sustainable long-term decision-making. Readers will make their own judgement about the extent to which this has been the case, or whether the FTPA has instead resulted in the final year being one of tetchy electioneering and not a lot more. Repeal of the Act – and a return to the use of the prerogative power to dissolve Parliament and set an election date of the Prime Minister's choosing – may prove attractive in the event of the return of a majority government in May 2015, though it is perhaps less likely in the case of the formation of another coalition.

Parliaments are numbered; the 2010 parliament is the fifty-fifth parliament of the United Kingdom since the Union with Ireland in 1801.

The beginning of a parliament

Some events always happen at the start of a parliament. Both Houses assemble on the day specified in the Sovereign's proclamation following the dissolution of the previous parliament. In the House of Commons there is a real advantage in a longer gap between polling day and the day of first meeting, as it allows longer for the induction and initial briefing of what may be a substantial number of new MPs (in 2010 there were 227, or 35 per cent of the House).

On the day of first meeting, the Commons go to the House of Lords, where they are directed to elect a Speaker (see page 44). Having gone back to their own House and done so, the Commons return to the Lords the next day, where the Queen's approbation of the Speaker-Elect is signified. (These ancient usages reflect a mediaeval relationship with the Sovereign; but should it ever happen that the Commons were unwilling to go to the Lords on either occasion, it would be difficult to imagine that their choice of a Speaker could be challenged as being somehow illegal or ineffective.)

The Commons then return to their own Chamber, and the new Speaker takes the oath of allegiance, or makes the affirmation required by law, standing on the upper step of the Speaker's Chair. Other MPs then take the oath or make the affirmation, starting with the Prime Minister and the Cabinet, and the shadow Cabinet, then Privy Counsellors (usually former Cabinet and other senior ministers), then other backbenchers. The order of taking the oath is of significance only when the longest-serving MPs were elected in the same year; if their seniority is equal, the Father of the House (there has not yet been a Mother of the House) is the member who takes the oath first.

MPs queue up before the Table; the oath is administered by the Principal Clerk of the Table Office; under the supervision of the Clerk Assistant each MP then signs the test roll, a bound parchment book, and is then formally introduced to the Speaker by the Clerk of the House. The swearing in of members goes on for three or four hours that day and then continues on the next three or four days.

The wording of the oath and affirmation and the way they are taken was established in the Oaths Act 1978. An MP takes the oath by holding the sacred text in his or her uplifted hand and saying the words:

> *I (name of Member) swear by Almighty God that I will be faithful and bear true allegiance to Her Majesty Queen Elizabeth, her heirs and successors, according to law. So help me God.*

The Act also permits the oath to be taken in the Scottish manner, with uplifted hand but not holding the sacred text. Members who want to do so may also take the oath as prescribed in the Promissory Oaths Act 1868, by kissing the book and using the words:

> *I (name of Member) do swear that I will be faithful and bear true allegiance to Her Majesty Queen Elizabeth, her heirs and successors, according to law. So help me God.*

Alternatively, members may make a solemn affirmation instead of taking an oath, using the words:

> *I (name of Member) do solemnly, sincerely, and truly declare and affirm, that I will be faithful and bear true allegiance to Her Majesty Queen Elizabeth, her heirs and successors, according to law.*

The sacred texts available for those who wish to use them are the New Testament (in English, Welsh or Gaelic), the Old Testament (in English and Hebrew, or in Hebrew), the Koran and the Granth. The last two texts are kept in slip-cases so that they are not handled directly by those not of the faith. The oath or affirmation must be taken in English, but it may be said additionally in Welsh, Scots Gaelic or Cornish. An MP must take the oath or affirm before sitting, speaking or voting in the House (except for the election of a Speaker); and if by chance he or she does not, the penalty is severe: the seat is vacated and there must be a by-election. The additional penalty of a £500 fine seems trivial by comparison.

Most MPs take the oath or affirm in these first days of a new parliament, but those remaining may do so in the days following the first Queen's Speech of the new parliament (and, occasionally, much later if prevented by illness). When the 'swearing days' are completed, the House adjourns to the day of the State Opening, which takes place at the start of a new parliament and also at the start of each of the subsequent sessions of that parliament.

Similarly, the Lords sit for two swearing-in days for oaths and affirmations, and for signing the undertaking to abide by the Code of Conduct and then adjourn until the State Opening. For the purpose of taking the oath, they may choose from a variety of religious texts – from the New Testament to the Hindu Gita and Parsee Avesta.

A session

This is the period that begins with the State Opening of Parliament and the Queen's Speech outlining the government's plans for legislation during the remainder of the session. It ends with prorogation (see page 128), or with a dissolution (see page 22) if it is the last session of a parliament.

Before the passage of the Fixed-term Parliaments Act 2011, a session would normally last from a State Opening in the first or second week in November until prorogation a year or so later. Following a general election in the spring or summer (as has been the case since 1979), the first session of a parliament was usually a long session lasting until the November of the following year. Conversely, the final session of the Parliament was usually a short one, lasting from November until the election the following summer. This pattern had some advantages, providing a long first legislative period for a new government and a foreshortened final period as members' and ministers' thoughts inevitably turned towards the forthcoming election.

Although it was not a necessary consequence of the FTPA, following its passage the government decided that a five-year Parliament should contain five sessions of more or less equal length. State Opening was moved from November to the spring, in line with the May general election, to last until the following spring. A session is denoted by both years (thus, the '2013–14 session'). The government announced, however, that the session that began in 2010 would be extended rather than shortened and it lasted for nearly two years: its 295 sitting days make 2010–12 the longest ever session of the UK Parliament.

The State Opening

A session begins with colourful ceremony, centuries old (Queen Elizabeth I opened Parliament in much the same way), as the Queen drives in procession to Westminster with an escort of Household Cavalry, normally arriving at 11.30 a.m. The processional route is lined with troops and thronged with tourists; bands play; the police even wear white gloves. The Queen arrives under the Victoria Tower at the south end of the Palace of Westminster and proceeds to the Robing Room, where she puts on the Imperial State Crown and then moves in procession to the House of Lords, which is a bright theatre of peers' scarlet and ermine, judges' robes and wigs, and ambassadors and high commissioners in evening dress and decorations.

Black Rod ('the Gentleman Usher of the Black Rod') is directed to summon the Commons. In a symbolic reminder of the right of the Commons to exclude any royal messenger, the doors leading to the Chamber are closed in his face; he knocks, is admitted and delivers the summons. Led by the Speaker and Black Rod, and followed by the Clerk of the House, Prime Minister and Leader of the Opposition, and members of the Cabinet and shadow Cabinet, MPs walk the 100 metres or so to the House of Lords, where they crowd behind the Bar of the House (the formal boundary of the Chamber) to hear the Queen's Speech.

The Queen's Speech

The Queen's Speech is the parliamentary core of this state ceremony. The speech is drafted by the government and will have been approved by the Cabinet. It normally refers to any recent or forthcoming royal events or state visits, and it contains some very broad policy intentions; the 2013 speech began: 'My Government's legislative programme will continue to focus on building a stronger economy so that the United Kingdom can compete and succeed in the world. It will also work to promote a fairer society that rewards people who work hard.' A sentence in the speech tells the Commons (because they, rather than the Lords, have financial authority) that estimates for financing the public services will be laid before them.

The meat of the speech is the legislative agenda for the coming session: the 2013 speech foreshadowed 15 bills and two draft bills. Bills are usually described in very broad terms; in 2013, for example, Parliament was told that 'Legislation will be brought forward to introduce new powers to tackle anti-social behaviour, cut crime and further reform the police'. Bills do not have to be in the Queen's Speech to be introduced, but the speech outlines the main legislative activity for the year ahead.

When the Commons return to their Chamber, the sitting is suspended until 2.30 p.m. At this point, the Speaker will make a statement reminding the House of the duties and responsibilities of members. The details of this statement will vary, but it will usually include a reminder of members' responsibilities under the Code of Conduct, a reference to the ancient privileges by which the House is free to conduct its debate without fear of outside interference, together with a warning about the necessity of exercising those privileges responsibly, an enjoinder to ensure that all members are heard courteously in debate, regardless of the views that they may be expressing, and a reminder of the need to protect the security of the House and those who work there. The House then gives a formal first reading to the Outlawries Bill 'for the more effectual preventing clandestine outlawries', whose purpose belongs to the distant past but which is a symbol of the right of the House to proceed with its own business before considering what the Sovereign has just told Parliament.

The Lords sit at 3.30 p.m., when certain sessional orders, including that to prevent 'stoppages in the streets', are passed; some office-holders such as the Chairman of Committees are appointed; and a *pro forma* bill (in the Lords it is the Select Vestries Bill) is read the first time.

Debate on the Queen's Speech

This is the first debate of the session, normally lasting four or five days. The debate is formally on a motion to present 'an Humble Address' to the Queen thanking her for the 'most Gracious Speech' addressed to both Houses, but it is in practice a review of the government's policies and intentions. The debate is opened by a mover and a seconder from the government backbenches (the only occasion on which a motion in the House of Commons is seconded). It is something of an honour to be selected (by the whips) to make these first two speeches. The MPs concerned (usually one new and one long-serving) are expected not to be contentious but to be reminiscent and witty, and to extol the virtues of their constituencies.

Then the business gets more seriously under way. The Leader of the Opposition speaks next, with the disadvantage that he gets no advance text of the Queen's Speech and has only a couple of hours to decide on much of what he will say. Then, the Prime Minister makes what is, in effect, the keynote speech, outlining the government's plans and programme, and going into much more detail than in the Queen's Speech itself. The leader of the Liberal Democrats, as the second largest Opposition party, follows (unless the Liberal Democrats are in government, as has been the case in the 2010 Parliament), and then the debate is open to MPs generally. The first day is a general debate, when any aspect may be raised; the subsequent debates are themed as agreed through the usual channels, perhaps on home affairs, foreign affairs and defence, health, and the economy, and are opened and closed by the relevant ministers or shadow ministers. On the last two days, amendments in the name of the Leader of the Opposition are moved and voted upon, usually regretting the fact that the Gracious Speech contains no plans to legislate to do this or that. When the government has a comfortable majority, the outcome is not in doubt; but were there to be a minority government or a shaky coalition, these votes, and that on the substantive motion at the very end of proceedings, would be the first test of whether the Prime Minister of the day could command a majority in the House. On the last day, further amendments may be voted upon. When the Liberal Democrats were in opposition, an amendment standing in their name would generally be called, providing an opportunity to have a formal vote on the key policy priorities of that party. In the

2010 Parliament, with the Liberal Democrats in government in coalition with the Conservatives, practice has varied, with amendments in the name of either the Scottish or Welsh nationalist parties being called each year, and in 2013, additionally, an amendment standing in the name of a number of mostly Conservative backbenchers regretting the absence from the Queen's Speech of a bill to provide for a referendum on the UK's membership of the European Union. In 2014, the standing orders were amended so that no more than three amendments could be called on the last day, and in 2014 only one (the Official Opposition amendment) was called on the last day.

In the Lords, the motion for 'an Humble Address' in reply to the Queen's Speech is moved and seconded from the government backbenches, but the debate proper is then adjourned and takes place over the subsequent four days. As with the Commons debate, each day has a theme but, unlike the Commons, no vote is taken at the end.

The pattern of the session

The reference points in any parliamentary session are a combination of the sacred and the secular: the State Opening, Whitsun, the summer adjournment, the September sitting, a brief adjournment in November, Christmas, February half-term, Easter and prorogation.

Early business in a session usually includes a government motion to fix the 13 Fridays on which private members' bills will be taken (7 for second readings and 6 for 'remaining stages'; see page 201). The House does not usually sit on Fridays other than those on which private members' bills are debated, though occasionally the government will arrange for one of the days of debate on the Queen's Speech or the Budget (see page 258) to take place on a Friday.

In the first few days of a new session, the first two or three of the major government bills foreshadowed in the Queen's Speech will be introduced (at that stage they will be given a purely formal first reading, with second reading debates on the principle of each bill following ten or so days later). *Second readings of government bills starting in the Commons* (others will be beginning their parliamentary journey at the other end of the building in the House of Lords) are a feature of business in the Chamber up to the summer break and, again, after the House returns in September and October, usually into November. Also before the summer adjournment, the Commons will normally approve the *Departmental Estimates* on the first *Estimates day* (see page 245).

After their second reading in the Chamber, the *government bills will go into public bill committees* (see page 188) and, in the period up until Christmas, public bill committee activity builds up. At its peak, six or seven public bill committees may be sitting for much of Tuesdays and Thursdays, occupying 100 to 150 MPs altogether, with big bills taking several weeks in committee, and each being the main focus of activity for the ministers responsible for each bill and for the shadow ministers opposing them. As the bills complete their committee stages, they return to the House for *report stages* and, in the period up to Easter and beyond, this starts to take up time on the floor of the House. Government legislation will usually be contentious between the parties and so will require the presence of MPs to vote even if they are not directly involved in the business.

Most *second readings of private members' bills* will normally be taken from July through to October, but many will fall by the wayside. By November, the successful (up to then!) private members' bills will be coming through their public bill committee stages and queuing up for the *six remaining stages days* in the latter part of the session. An MP's presence on a private members' bill Friday is less likely to be required by the whips (with the exception of the payroll vote of ministers and PPSs), so unless the MP has agreed to support a colleague's bill (or wants to obstruct or kill a bill) these may be days when the MP can work in the constituency, as on other Fridays.

From late October onwards, *bills that started in the Lords begin coming down to the Commons* and going through all the same stages as those bills that originated in the Commons. By January, the government may be starting to introduce for second readings those bills that will be subject to the carry-over procedure – with those that were introduced in the previous session and carried over going into public bill committee or taking their report stages in the early part of the session.

Before Easter, the House approves the remaining *Supplementary Estimates* for the current financial year, and any *Excess Votes* for the previous financial year (see page 245). A key event before Easter is the Budget, usually in March or early April, followed by four days' debate on the Chancellor of the Exchequer's proposals. At a fairly late stage in the session (although increasingly this is spread throughout the year, there is sometimes a queue late in the session), the two Houses consider the amendments each has made to bills that started in the other House: *Commons amendments* and *Lords amendments*, sometimes abbreviated to *CCLA* (Commons Consideration of Lords Amendments) and LCCA (Lords Consideration of Commons Amendments). If amendments made by one House are not accepted by the other (most often this arises because the government wishes to reverse a defeat it has suffered in the Lords) a passage of 'ping-pong' between the two Houses may ensue, with alternative amendments being offered in an effort to get agreement before the bill is killed by the end of the session.

The end of the session after Easter is usually a final tidying up of the to and fro of bills between the two Houses, often with other business being inserted as a makeweight while waiting for one House or the other to complete proceedings on this or that bill.

We have described the pattern of the session largely in terms of legislation and financial business, but a great deal else is going on. Time must be found for the 20 *opposition days*, each of which is a full day's debate on a subject on which the opposition feels the government may be vulnerable, or for which it wants a parliamentary shop window; the second and third *Estimates days*, on which select committee reports linked to particular Estimates are debated; time may need to be found for private bills; and the 27 days of *backbench business*, debate on subjects chosen by a committee of backbenchers on the basis of representations made to them by members of the House. And on every day except Friday there is the framework of Question Time, ministerial statements, and the half-hour adjournment debate at the end of each day's proceedings, as well as debates in Westminster Hall on Tuesdays, Wednesdays, Thursdays and occasionally Mondays (see page 259).

Business in the Lords follows a slightly different cycle. Although the business managers make every effort to introduce a certain number of bills in that House to occupy it in the early part of the session, most bills start in the Commons and arrive in the Lords in the late summer or early autumn at the earliest. This makes for longer sitting hours and more sitting days in the latter part of the session. Also, the Lords often sit later in July than the Commons and return earlier after their summer break. September sittings have been tried but have not taken root in the House of Lords. Unlike the Commons, the Lords have no fixed points in the calendar for consideration of financial matters, except for their formal consideration of the Finance Bill in July.

Prorogation

This is the formal end of a session. It is a 'prerogative act' of the Crown, another survival of the early relationship between sovereign and Parliament (and used on occasion by monarchs to curb an inconvenient House of Commons). In modern times, such royal powers are exercised by the government of the day, so it is the government that decides the length of the parliamentary session. There is no formal requirement for an annual May to April session, but the constitutional convention of an annual session is a strong one. The first session of a Parliament was always longer – spanning the period from the election, usually in May and the October/November of the following year. The first session of the 2010 Parliament was even longer as it was decided to extend the session even further till the following May – that is to say, to two years – to bring the parliamentary session into line with the expectations of the five-year electoral cycle imposed by the Fixed-term Parliaments Act 2011. So, there will have been four sessions in this Parliament, rather than five. There is no expectation of a similarly long first session in the next Parliament, but it would be open to the next government to return to the pattern of November–November sessions, other than in general election years, if it wished.

The timing of prorogation is often settled in the last few days of the session; the government business managers want to be sure that they have left enough time to get the last bills through – those that have not been made subject to the carry-over procedure – which may involve a degree of brinkmanship in achieving agreement between the two Houses.

At prorogation, the House of Commons goes up to the House of Lords just as at the State Opening, although in rather fewer numbers; but on this occasion the Queen will not be there. The Queen's Speech – a retrospective of the session – and the proclamation proroguing Parliament and setting the date for the State Opening will be read out by one of the five peers who form the Royal Commission to do this on the Queen's behalf. The date to which Parliament has been prorogued may be changed in either direction by a royal proclamation. During the period of prorogation neither House, nor any committee, may meet.

Clearing the decks

A prorogation brings to an end almost all parliamentary business (which is why the business managers are so keen to secure the passage of government bills before the end of the session). The exceptions are those bills that are 'carried over' from one session to the next. This has long been possible for private bills (see page 220) and hybrid bills (see page 222) and, in 1998, the Commons agreed to a procedure whereby public bills may also be carried over. The explicit consent of the House is required for a bill to be carried over, and it requires careful planning by the business managers – it cannot simply be applied at the last minute to a bill that has failed to complete its parliamentary stages at the end of a session. A bill may be carried over only if it is still in the House in which it originated and, in the case of Commons bills, the procedure applies only to government bills; a bill may only be carried over from one session to the next, and not over again into a further session; and a time limit is set of one year from its introduction within which the Bill must complete its passage (subject to the possibility of extension, which can only be granted by the further approval of the House, and not beyond the end of the session into which the bill has been carried over). In most sessions, only about three or four bills are carried over, including the Finance Bill (as the Budget now takes place only about two months before the end of the session). In some ways it is surprising that the procedure has not been used more often for government bills. Although in some ways it is convenient for the business managers, it can also allow longer scrutiny of legislation – the pressure of time is both a bone of contention between government and opposition, and a source of criticism of the quality of legislation. It could also smooth the legislative programme by allowing major bills to be introduced later in the session.

This 'sudden death' at the end of the session is practised by relatively few parliaments and may have disadvantages in the case of legislation; but it also acts as a clear-out of the parliamentary agenda and imposes some discipline on the legislative process. Early day motions (of which there may be more than 2,000 by the end of the session) lapse, and private members' bills die – both those that are clearly going to make no progress however much time might be available and those that their backers feel might have had a chance 'if only'.

Adjournments

The standing orders prescribe when the House of Commons sits, both in terms of time and days of the week, so when the House finishes its sitting ('adjourns') on any day, it will automatically meet on the next sitting day. Longer times of adjournment, commonly called 'recesses' – although strictly speaking this word applies only to the time during prorogation – are discussed through the usual channels and decided by the House on the basis of a motion moved by the Leader of the House.

The normal pattern of recesses and sitting periods (sometimes called 'terms') is:

May	State Opening
	Whitsun adjournment: one or two weeks
June	–
July	House rises in the second half of July (summer adjournment)
August	–
September	A two-week sitting, after which the House adjourns for the party conferences
October	–
November	A brief three-day break around the middle of the month
December	Christmas adjournment: about two weeks
January	–
February	A 'constituency week' coinciding with school half-term
March	Easter adjournment: one or two weeks
April/May	Prorogation

It should be clear from the earlier account of constituency pressures that recesses are not MPs' holidays. Constituents do not stop writing because the House of Commons is not sitting, and many MPs will do more surgery work, and certainly more constituency engagements, than during a sitting week. But every year when the House rises in July, the media remorselessly report that 'MPs are off on x weeks' summer holiday'.

Sittings of the Lords follow the same pattern but with some small variations; for example, in 2013, the Commons rose for the summer recess on 18 July and the Lords on 30 July. Both Houses returned on 8 October. Later in the session, the Commons rose for Easter on 10 April 2014 and returned on 28 April, while the Lords rose on 9 April and returned on 6 May, and rose in July a week later than the Commons (but with no September sitting to follow).

The annual calendar

Although the pattern of sitting times has always been broadly predictable to within a week or two, exact dates used not to be announced until a short time before each recess. In October 2002, a parliamentary calendar for the next 12 months (something that has long been routine in many parliaments) was introduced, and a motion setting the dates of 'periodic adjournments' is now routinely agreed in December to cover the whole of the following year. This has proved extremely useful, allowing those who deal with Parliament, as well as those in it, to make long-term plans. There is a tension between announcing sitting times a long way ahead and the wish of business managers to retain flexibility; and any change (as, for example, when an extra Friday sitting was arranged to prevent the Budget debate straddling, or intruding into, the Easter recess in 2013) may lead to criticism.

The annual calendar is a prediction of *likely* sitting and recess dates. Some suggestions for reform have gone further, with proposals for a fixed parliamentary year (so that, for example, the summer adjournment would always begin on the third Thursday in July), and the other non-sitting periods would be fixed in the same way. This, it is argued, would mean that the government would have to make concessions to get its business through without running out of time and could not use the threat of sitting into late July or even August. However, if such a fixed calendar were to be introduced (and it is hard to see any government's business managers being enthusiastic about such a change), the result might be a greater proportion of parliamentary time given over to legislation, and stricter programming of bills to ensure that time did *not* run out.

As long as the pressure of government legislation remains at the levels of the last few years, the same might be the result of the more radical suggestion that the Commons should meet in alternate weeks, with the rest of the time being allotted to constituency or committee work. Given the size of the House, a net reduction in parliamentary time would limit the debate and question opportunities for back-bench MPs.

Recall of parliament

In Chapter 3, we noted the Speaker's role in recalling the House if, as Standing Order No. 13 says, 'it is represented . . . by Her Majesty's Ministers that the public interest requires' that the House should meet during an adjournment. The Speaker always grants such a request; and since 1990 there have been 13 days on which the House has been recalled to debate events, including the invasion of Kuwait (1990), the UK's withdrawal from the European exchange rate system (1992), the Omagh bombing and subsequent emergency legislation (1998), the terrorist attacks in New York and Washington (2001), to mark the death of Queen Elizabeth the Queen Mother (2002), public confidence in the media and police in the wake of the phone hacking affair (2011) and possible military action against Syria (2013). It was also by an emergency recall that, on 3 April 1982, the House met on a Saturday to debate the invasion of the Falklands. The only Sunday sitting in the last century was on 3 September 1939, on the outbreak of the Second World War.

The sitting week in the Commons

From April 1946, the House sat at 2.30 p.m. each day, with the moment of inter-ruption (see page 141) normally ending the main business at 10.00 p.m., and on

Fridays at 11.00 a.m., with the moment of interruption at 4.00 p.m. In each case, after the disposal of the business before the House (including business that was exempted and so could proceed after the moment of interruption) there would be the daily adjournment debate (see page 258) for a further half-hour. In 1980, Friday sittings were moved to 9.30 a.m., with the moment of interruption at 2.30 p.m.

In 1994, following the recommendations of a select committee chaired by the former Conservative Chief Whip Michael Jopling, attempts were made to rein back the amount of business and the impact it had on the hours the House sat, particularly late at night. One of the changes was the introduction of Wednesday morning sittings starting at 9.30 a.m. As with the brief experiment under the 'Crossman reforms' in the 1960s (named after the then Leader of the House, Richard Crossman), these were used primarily for non-contentious business and debates initiated by back-benchers. From 1999, Thursday sittings began at 11.30 a.m.; and at the end of 1999, with the additional backbench opportunities afforded by the establishment of Westminster Hall as a second debating forum, the House went back to sitting on Wednesdays at 2.30 p.m.

A new timetable – and second thoughts

As a result of changes recommended by the Modernisation Committee chaired by Robin Cook as Leader of the House, 2003 saw a radical rearrangement of sitting hours. The original hours were kept for Monday (or for a Tuesday or Wednesday if this followed a recess), but with an 11.30 a.m. start Tuesday to Thursday, and an earlier finish on Thursday. The few remaining Friday sittings stayed at 9.30 a.m. The Modernisation Committee pointed out that, over history, the House's hours had changed in response to changes in social custom and business practice. Later hours were convenient when MPs were unpaid and could do much of a day's work in the City or the courts and still be at Westminster for the main business of the House. The committee felt that this was no longer appropriate when most members were full-time MPs.

It also observed that major events such as statements and PM's Questions came relatively late in the day; and the House responded to an agenda of public debate – in effect, media coverage of events – which had already been set by then. Major votes usually came at 10.00 p.m., often too late for adequate coverage in the next day's papers.

In making its proposals, the Modernisation Committee warned that there was no consensus on sitting hours, and so it proved. Earlier sittings on Wednesdays were approved by 288 votes to 265, and those on Tuesdays by a narrower margin: 274 to 267. Opinion among MPs was sharply divided: on the one hand, some believed that more conventional working hours make Parliament seem less alien, and that a more family-friendly approach would encourage more people with family responsi-bilities to become MPs. Others disliked earlier starting times for committees and the House sitting during a morning that could be used for constituency and other parliamentary work.

Those with constituencies (and families) in or near London tended to prefer the new hours; those hundreds of miles from Westminster were less enthusiastic.

The new sitting hours remained contentious and, in January 2005, the traditionalists reclaimed the old sitting hours for Tuesdays, by a majority of 292 to 225. The start of the Thursday sitting was advanced to 10.30 a.m. to allow more substantial business to be taken on that day. Those sitting hours prevailed throughout the 2005 Parliament, but the advocates of reform did not give up, and early in the 2010 Parliament the Procedure Committee, picking up the baton from the now defunct Modernisation Committee, considered the matter again.

Very much the same issues arose as when the Modernisation Committee had considered the matter, and the Procedure Committee largely avoided coming to firm conclusions, stating rather that 'in looking at the sitting hours of the House there are no mainstream options which are necessarily "right or wrong", "out-dated or modern", or "effective or less so". The whole issue is largely a matter of individual preference', and that 'there are differing views which will need to be resolved by the House'. The eventual result was a narrow vote (256 to 241) in favour of the House meeting earlier again on Tuesdays, and slightly more convincing vote in favour of a further advance, by an hour, of sittings on Thursdays. The existing sitting hours on Mondays and Wednesdays were endorsed without anyone pressing the matter to a vote.

The current sitting pattern is shown in Table 5.1.

A perverse result of the move to change sitting times is that on only two days of the week is the Commons timetable the same. Most parliaments have a consistent timetable to which members, parliamentary staff, the public and the media easily adapt. The House of Commons no longer does.

The sitting day in the Commons

This is often complicated and, although the business is taken in a prescribed order and subject to the House's rules, is never entirely predictable. Here, we describe both the unchanging parts of the day and events that may happen only occasionally. Some of the more important proceedings are described in greater detail later in this book. The Order of Business for a typical day appears on page 136.

Before the sitting, the *Speaker's Conference* will have taken place. Here, the Speaker goes over the business for the day with the Deputy Speakers and the Clerk of the House and his senior colleagues, assessing possible problems or procedural complexities – deciding, for example, what will be a reasonable scope of debate on a particular item, or what response he will give to a likely point of order. The Speaker will also take a view on applications for urgent questions or urgent debates that may have been submitted. The Serjeant at Arms is also present and may know of a planned demonstration or mass lobby, which may affect access to the palace or may delay MPs getting to the House to vote.

The start of a sitting

Every sitting begins with the *Speaker's Procession* from Speaker's House. The Speaker, preceded by a doorkeeper and the Mace carried by the Serjeant at Arms, and followed by his trainbearer, secretary and chaplain, walks to the Chamber by way of the Central Lobby. Here, the police inspector shouts 'Hats off, Strangers!', even though these days it is very unlikely that any man present (except for the police officers) will be wearing a hat. This is now a rare use of the term 'strangers' meaning visitors. The Speaker, his chaplain and the Serjeant at Arms then enter the Chamber. The Serjeant places the Mace on the Table to show that the House is sitting, and the Speaker and chaplain kneel at the Table for *Prayers*. These Anglican *Prayers for the Parliament* take about four minutes and are in private. (A member who wants to reserve a seat in the House for the whole of a sitting may leave a prayer card on a place to show that he or she will be there for Prayers.)

As the Speaker rises, the doorkeepers shout 'Prayers are over'; the galleries are opened to guests and visitors; the Clerks' chairs are set at the Table; and, as the Speaker rises to begin proceedings with 'Order, order', television coverage starts.

Up to the end of Question Time

Although infrequent, any *report of the Queen's answer to an Address* (for example, the 'Humble Address', which was formally before the House during the Queen's Speech debate) will come at the start of business. The sovereign's response is normally read out by one of the government whips who holds a post in the Royal Household (see page 82), and is generally very brief, as 'I have received with great satisfaction the dutiful and loyal expression of your thanks for the speech with which I opened the present session of Parliament'.

There may be a *formal communication by the Speaker*. The death of a member is notified to the House in this way: this used to be done in brief, formal terms, but more recently the Speaker has paid a brief tribute. There is normally no opportunity for a eulogy, although the House adjourns on the death of the Prime Minister or a former Prime Minister, or the Leader of the Opposition, after tributes from the party leaders and others (and on the death of Baroness Thatcher in April 2013, the House was recalled for a day of tributes). The Speaker may also announce that he has sent or received messages of condolence or congratulation (for example, to the Royal Family, or to foreign parliaments or heads of state). Early in a Parliament, there will be arrangements for the election of select committee chairs or Deputy Speakers to make known, and later the Speaker will announce vacancies for those positions as they arise. He may, very rarely, announce the outcome of an 'election court' set up to resolve a dispute about the conduct of an election, which can declare a particular candidate to have been elected or can order a rerun of the election. He may even report the imprisonment of an MP (of which the courts must inform the House).

A *motion for a new writ* may be moved. This triggers a by-election in a seat made vacant by the death, resignation or disqualification of the sitting MP. It is normally moved by the Chief Whip of the party to which that member belonged but has

Table 5.1 Programme for a normal sitting week in the House of Commons

	Monday	Tuesday	Wednesday	Thursday	Friday
House sits	2.30 p.m.	11.30 a.m.	11.30 a.m.	9.30 a.m.	9.30 a.m.
Prayers (every day, for about four minutes) private business after Prayers (not on Fridays) Question Time (not on Fridays)					
Urgent questions, statements by ministers	3.30 p.m.	12.30 p.m.	12.30 p.m.	10.30 a.m.	11.00 a.m.
(On Fridays, the main business will begin after Prayers and will be interrupted if there is a statement or urgent question at 11.00 a.m.)					
Main business (perhaps legislation, an opposition day or a debate on a topic in government time)					
Main business interrupted	10.00 p.m.	7.00 p.m.	7.00 p.m.	5.00 p.m.	2.30 p.m.
	After the end of any votes (or of proceedings on 'exempted business'): daily adjournment debate (up to half an hour)				
Sittings in Westminster Hall:					
Begin	4.30 p.m.*	9.30 a.m.	9.30 a.m.	2.30 p.m.	
Suspended		11.30 a.m.	11.30 a.m.		
Resume		2.30 p.m.	2.30 p.m.		
End	7.30 p.m.	5.00 p.m.	5.00 p.m.	5.30 p.m.	
Select committees (typically)	4.00 p.m.	9.15 a.m. 2.00 p.m.	9.15 a.m. 2.00 p.m.	9.30 a.m.	
Legislative committees (typically)	4.30 p.m.	8.55 a.m. 2.00 p.m.	8.55 a.m. 2.00 p.m.	11.30 a.m. 2.00 p.m.	
(Sittings in Westminster Hall, and in committees, are suspended for divisions in the House)					

*for debate on e-petitions, if allocated by the Backbench Business Committee

HOUSE OF COMMONS

Monday 27 October 2014 Order Paper No.49: Part 1

SUMMARY AGENDA: CHAMBER

2.30pm	Prayers
Afterwards	Oral Questions: Education
3.30pm	Urgent Questions, Ministerial Statements (if any)
No debate	Presentation of Bills
Until 10.00pm	Recall of MPs Bill: Committee (Day 1)
No debate	House of Commons Members' Fund (Motion)
Until 10.30pm or for half an hour	Adjournment Debate: Closure of JTI Gallaher factory

URGENT QUESTIONS AND STATEMENTS

3.30pm

■ **Urgent Questions (if any)**

■ **Ministerial Statements (if any)**

PRESENTATION OF BILLS

Presentation of Bills: no debate (Standing Order No. 57)

■ **International Trade Agreements (Scrutiny)**

Geraint Davies
Bill to require scrutiny of and enable amendments to international trade agreements, including investor state dispute settlements, by the European and UK Parliaments; and for connected purposes.

BUSINESS OF THE DAY

1. RECALL OF MPs BILL: COMMITTEE (DAY 1)

Until 10.00pm (Standing Order No. 9(3) and Order of 21 October)

> Notes:
> Proceedings on Clauses 1 to 5, new Clauses and new Schedules relating to how an MP becomes subject to a recall process will, if not previously concluded, be brought to a conclusion at the moment of interruption (Order of 21 October).
> For amendments see separate paper (also available on the documents webpage for the Bill).

2. HOUSE OF COMMONS MEMBERS' FUND

No debate (Standing Order No. 118(6) and Order of 14 October)

Mr William Hague
Tom Brake
Mr Peter Lilley
That pursuant to section 4(4) of the House of Commons Members' Fund Act 1948 and section 1(4) of the House of Commons Members' Fund Act 1957, in the year commencing 1 October 2014 there be appropriated for the purposes of section 4 of the House of Commons Members' Fund Act 1948:

(1) The whole of the sums deducted or set aside in that year under section 1(3) of the House of Commons Members' Fund Act 1939 from the salaries of Members of the House of Commons; and

(2) The whole of the Treasury contribution paid to the Fund.

> Notes:
> An Explanatory Memorandum is available from the Vote Office.
> If this item is opposed after 10.00pm, the division will be deferred.

ADJOURNMENT DEBATE

Until 10.30pm or for half an hour (whichever is later) (Standing Order No. 9(7))

■ Closure of JTI Gallaher factory: Ian Paisley

Parts of a typical Commons Order Paper (a page containing oral questions is on page 282)

Source: Copyright House of Commons, 2014

occasionally been moved by a backbencher wishing to make a point about a delay in holding a by-election, or to frustrate later business. By convention, new writs are moved within three months of the vacancy occurring, but there is no formal limit. If a motion for a new writ is opposed at this time, it is taken later in the sitting, after statements but before the main business.

After these uncommon proceedings comes private business – that is, private bills and related motions (including motions relating to the Committee of Selection (see page 312). At this time in the sitting day, only private business to which a blocking motion has not been tabled, or that is not opposed by even one single MP shouting 'object', can pass. Much private business is uncontroversial, and it is not unusual for private bills to go through all their stages on different days at this time.

A *motion for an unopposed return* may be moved. It may be that an official inquiry has criticised individuals who might sue if the report were published in the conventional way (for example, Lord Hutton's inquiry into the death of Dr David Kelly in 2004, the Bloody Sunday inquiry in 2010 and the report of the Hillsborough Independent Panel in 2012). This device gives the report the protection of parliamentary privilege.

Even if all the items of business listed above were to take place, they would probably delay the House for only four or five minutes. *Question Time* then follows and continues for an hour (although it may be extended by anything between twenty minutes and an hour if an *urgent question* has been granted, or if a minister has decided to answer a *question at the end of Question Time*). This is described in greater detail in Chapter 9.

After Question Time and up to 'the commencement of public business'

After the first hour of oral questions, any new member of the House elected at a by-election is formally introduced to the House and takes the oath or makes affirmation (see page 122) – normally on the Tuesday following the by-election. He or she waits below the Bar of the House (in other words, within the Chamber but just outside what is formally the floor of the House; the Bar itself does exist, but as it consists of two heavy metal rods that slide back into the woodwork of the benches on each side it is seldom seen). When the moment arrives, the new MP, flanked by two members who act as sponsors (perhaps old friends or constituency neighbours), comes forward, clutching paper from one of the Clerks in the Public Office certifying that the Clerk of the Crown has received the 'return' that is proof of election. He or she bows at the Bar, again halfway up the Floor of the House, and again at the Table, and then takes the oath (or affirms), signs the test roll and is announced to the Speaker and the House by the Clerk of the House. There will have been considerable political interest in the by-election campaign and its outcome – particularly if the seat has been captured by a different party – and the introduction of the new MP is in some ways the culmination of the campaign, hailed with cheers from MPs of the victorious party and fairly good-natured heckling from other parts of the House.

The main events at this time are *statements by ministers*. These may announce a new policy initiative, inform the House about some international crisis, or perhaps give the government's reaction to the outcome of a court case or an official inquiry. A statement may report on an international meeting, perhaps of the UN or European Council, or the outcome of significant EU negotiations. Statements are also used to inform the House about serious accidents or terrorist crimes and to set out the government's response. In cases of great urgency, a statement may be made at another time; on 29 April 2009, the Secretary of State for Health updated the House on what the government was doing to strengthen its contingency plans following the confirmation of three cases of swine flu in the UK, after the main business and before the half-hour adjournment debate.

Significant statements are made by the responsible cabinet minister (or by the Prime Minister); less important statements are made by more junior ministers directly responsible for the subject. Ministers notify the Speaker in advance of their intention to make a statement, but (although they conventionally begin a statement with the words 'with permission, Mr Speaker') they need neither his permission, nor that of the House, to do so. Notice that a statement is to be made appears on the television annunciators around the House between one and two hours beforehand, and a minister will as a courtesy give his or her opposition 'shadow' an advance copy of the text an hour or so before it is delivered. However, unless the subject is one that has been simmering on the political agenda, much of the initiative rests with the government (especially so if the statement announces a surprise policy development), and the opposition will have to be quick on its feet to react effectively.

As we saw in Chapter 3, it is up to the Chair to decide how long questioning goes on. This will depend on the significance of the statement, but the Speaker will also have in mind the need to protect any important business that follows, at the same time as exposing the minister fully to questioning.

On Thursdays, the Leader of the House's *weekly statement of forthcoming business* is formally a reply to a question from the shadow Leader (and so follows immediately after Question Time) rather than a conventional ministerial statement. However, if on a Thursday there is a statement by a more senior minister, or a statement that needs to be made a soon as possible, the Leader's announcement may follow it and be technically a statement in its own right.

After statements, MPs have the opportunity of *requesting an urgent debate*, sometimes known as 'an S.O. No. 24 application', on what the standing order calls 'a specific and important matter that should have urgent consideration'. The MP must seek the Speaker's permission beforehand and has three minutes in which to make the case for an urgent debate. The Speaker then gives his decision (and is forbidden by the standing order from giving any reasons). If he allows the application and the House agrees, a debate of up to three hours will take place the next day (or the same day if there is sufficient urgency).

Urgent debates are infrequent, though perhaps becoming less so; there have been four such debates since 2010, but there were only 17 in the previous 30 years. Applications may be used as a means of raising a constituency crisis, as well as events on a bigger scale: in January 2011, an MP sought a debate on a factory closure and consequent job losses in her constituency; in March 2013, an MP tried for a debate on the proposed appointment of a special administrator for his local hospital; and, in April 2014, an MP applied for a debate on the closure of two collieries in his constituency.

There is then a slot for (rare) *ceremonial speeches* – perhaps on the death of a former Speaker or some other distinguished figure, *motions to give the Speaker leave of absence* for some specific reason, and *personal statements*. These may be of apology, perhaps for failing to register an interest or for using 'unparliamentary language', or a minister may apologise for giving the House wrong information; or they may be of explanation after resignation. This second category can be dramatic. Sir Geoffrey Howe's statement after resigning as Deputy Prime Minister in 1990, delivered in an electric atmosphere in the House, was a defining moment just before the end of Margaret Thatcher's Prime Ministership. Equally memorable were Norman Lamont's statement in June 1993 after he had been sacked as Chancellor of the Exchequer; Robin Cook's in March 2003 after he resigned from the Cabinet on the eve of war against Iraq (his personal statement was unusually made at 9.45 p.m., but that was just after the equally unusual timing of a statement by the Foreign Secretary that talks in the UN had broken down); and Clare Short's attack on the Prime Minister's style of government following her resignation in May 2003.

Personal statements may be made only with the permission of the Speaker, and because the practice of the House is to hear statements in (near) silence, and not to allow interventions, the Speaker sees the text beforehand (except in the case of ministers who have resigned).

Matters relating to privilege (see page 164) may be taken at this time. Alleged breaches of privilege have to be raised privately with the Speaker, so matters of privilege are raised on the floor of the House only if he is prepared to give them precedence over other business. An opposed motion for the issue of a new writ in a by-election would also be taken at this stage of the day.

Usually at about this time, MPs will raise *points of order* with the Speaker (although points of order on the business actually before the House may be raised at any time). The test of a 'genuine' point of order is whether the Chair can actually rule upon it because it relates to the rules and practice of the House – for example, whether a phrase is acceptable parliamentary language, or perhaps in some complex business, the order in which the House will take decisions, or whether something was amiss in one of the House's working papers. The Speaker will either give his decision on the spot (particularly if the MP has given him notice of the point to be raised) or undertake to give a decision later. These rulings are part of the case law that is an important element in the practice and procedure of the House.

Even if a point of order is genuine, Speakers will normally not rule on something that is hypothetical, or on something that has happened in committee; that is the responsibility of the occupant of the chair concerned. Neither will the Chair give detailed procedural counsel, normally suggesting that the MP seeks the advice of the Clerks.

Genuine points of order sometimes relate to the administrative responsibilities of the Speaker, such as access to the precincts or the use of facilities. But the majority of points raised at this stage in the parliamentary day are, to a greater or lesser degree, bogus in that they make political or debating points. One of the most frequent from the opposition benches is an inquiry as to whether the Speaker has received a request from a minister to make a statement on some contentious subject (usually implying undue reticence on the part of the government). Assertions by ministers, or the content of their replies to parliamentary questions, are often raised. There is a Catch-22 in that the Chair has to allow the MP to go some way towards making the point, as it is only then that it becomes clear that this is not a real point of order. However, because of the limited opportunities that MPs have to raise current issues other than in relevant Question Times or debates (many parliaments have a period each day in which the members may speak briefly on any subject of current concern), these points of order can act as something of a safety valve. (A point of order specifically on the business before the House at that moment may be raised with the Chair at any time during a sitting.)

'At the commencement of public business'

It may seem strange that this title occurs only at this stage of the sitting day; but for almost all the preceding business most of the very few decisions that arise have to be taken by unanimity, and for much of the time there is no *question* before the House – that is, a matter put forward for decision by the House. Confusingly, there is no 'question' in this technical sense before the House during Question Time.

Three main types of business are taken at this time. The first is the *presentation and first reading of public bills* – a formality, which is explained in Chapter 6. Then may come government motions to regulate the business of the House for that day – perhaps to allow several items to be debated jointly, or to allot time to a particular item of business, or to allow an urgent bill to be taken through all its stages at one sitting. Such motions can be debated and may be voted upon. To avoid the (perhaps unpredictable) loss of time for the main business, these are usually taken on a previous day.

The best-known category of business 'at the commencement' is the *ten-minute rule bill* (strictly a motion, because the member seeks permission to bring in the bill rather than a decision by the House on the bill itself). Every Tuesday and Wednesday, a backbencher has the chance to propose new legislation in a speech lasting not more than ten minutes; if there is opposition, one MP may put the contrary case, again for no more than ten minutes, and if necessary there is a vote. These are very popular opportunities for backbench MPs, not least because a backbencher's opportunities to initiate business on the floor of the House are very limited, but also because they take place in 'prime time', which may be immediately before a major debate. Ten-minute rule bills are discussed further in Chapter 6.

The main business

It is unusual for the events described so far (apart from urgent questions and ministerial statements) to go on longer than 15 or 20 minutes after the end of Question Time. The House then embarks on the main business of the day, which consists of *orders of the day* (typically, a stage of a bill) and *notices of motions* (typically, a debate either on a substantive motion, as on an opposition day, or a neutral motion that the House has considered a particular matter).

It often happens that the usual channels have agreed that the main business should be in two halves, or that the Liaison Committee has recommended two estimates for debate on an estimates day. In that case, the halfway point is at about 7.00 p.m. on a Monday, 4.00 p.m. on a Tuesday or Wednesday, or 2.00 p.m. on a Thursday ('half days' do not happen on Fridays).

The moment of interruption

At 10.00 p.m. on Mondays, 7.00 p.m. on Tuesdays and Wednesdays, 5.00 p.m. on Thursdays and 2.30 p.m. on Fridays comes the 'moment of interruption'. This is normally the end of the main business and is the time when most major votes are taken. Unless there has been a previous decision of the House to the contrary, business still under way when that moment comes will stand adjourned to a future day (or, for adjournment motions or neutral motions, lapse). Thus, an MP can 'talk something out' by continuing to speak as the Speaker says 'Order, order' to signify that the business is being interrupted. To prevent this, the closure (see page 201) must be moved, which will be granted by the Chair after a full day's debate and is normally agreed without a vote, the House passing straight on to a vote on the main business itself.

Talking out is a traditional weapon used against private members' bills; 100 MPs must vote for the closure for it to be effective, and the sponsor of a private member's bill may find it difficult to round up enough supporters at the end of business on a Friday. In addition, if the bill is second or third on the order paper on a private members' Friday, the Chair may think that there has been insufficient debate to allow the closure to be put to the House. Strictly speaking, 'talking out' happens only when there is opposition to further proceedings. Theoretically, if the Chair detected no objection from any member, debate on 'non-exempted' business could survive the moment of interruption, and the House could then take a decision at the end of that debate; but such cases are extremely rare.

Non-exempted business, which is not expected to be debated, is sometimes described as 'nod or nothing after seven o'clock' (or ten o'clock); in other words, either it is agreed 'on the nod' without any objection, or there is objection and the matter cannot be put to the House.

Exempted business

Not all business has to end at the moment of interruption. A motion moved (only by a minister, and only if notice has been given on the order paper) may allow an item to be proceeded with 'until any hour' or for a specific time.

Some other business is automatically exempted: finance bills (unlimited time); statutory instruments and European Union documents (an hour-and-a-half – although any that have already been considered in committee cannot be debated again); and some thirty other types of business, although not debatable, may nevertheless be decided.

After decisions and votes taken immediately after the moment of interruption have been disposed of, *public petitions* may be presented. Petitions are described in more detail in Chapter 9. There is then the *half-hour adjournment debate*, which is covered in Chapter 8.

The last words spoken in the Chamber are the same as the first: 'Order, order'. The occupant of the Chair (by this time, usually one of the Deputy Speakers) leaves the Chair, and the Serjeant at Arms takes the Mace from the Table and joins the Deputy Speaker behind the Chair. The Deputy Speaker says '11.30 [or whatever the next day's sitting time is] tomorrow' or '2.30 on Monday', which is repeated by the Serjeant. The doorkeepers shout 'Who goes home?' – usually abbreviated to a long drawn-out 'ho-oo-me', a relic of days when MPs homeward bound in the same direction would band together as a defence against footpads and highwaymen – the division bells ring for the last time, and the parliamentary day is over.

Late sittings

Late sittings were a regular feature of the House of Commons in the 1970s and 1980s. The average time the House rose in the decade to 1990–91 was well after midnight (so – taking Fridays into account – an average sitting of some nine hours), with some sittings lasting much longer. More than one-fifth of sitting time was after the moment of interruption. Sometimes, proceedings were greatly prolonged by backbenchers or by opposition parties to emphasise criticism of the government or its proposals. This occasionally went as far as sitting beyond the House's scheduled time of meeting the next day, thus 'breaking the sitting' and losing the government's planned business for the following day.

By contrast, since 2005 the average sitting day has varied between about seven-and-a-half and eight hours, and the sitting time after the moment of interruption has been less than 10 per cent of the total. There have been various reasons for this change – although all have their critics. They include the *routine programming of bills* (see page 180), whereby time limits are imposed on bills at an early stage in their passage through the House; *the move of a substantial amount of debating time to Westminster Hall* (and, indeed, a net increase in debating time thereby; sitting time in Westminster Hall amounts to the equivalent of nearly two-and-a-half hours for each day on which the House sits); and the taking of *more business in public bill or delegated legislation committee rather than on the floor of the House*.

Time in the House

The Modernisation Committee pointed out that the House of Commons (and, by extension, the House of Lords, which has similar sitting patterns):

> *spends far less time in recess than most other democratic parliaments. The House of Commons meets for more days than any of the parliaments of the larger*

Commonwealth countries and indeed for twice as many days as all of them except Canada. The typical pattern among European parliaments is for the legislature to sit around 100 days in the year, compared with 150 days for the UK Parliament.

Comparisons with continental legislatures, where the work of the plenary is fuelled to a much greater degree by committees, are not exact; but there is no doubt that the Westminster Parliament is one of the longest-sitting parliaments in the world. There are a number of reasons for this: principally the unremitting legislative programme of successive governments; but also the number of members and so the pressure for parliamentary time to raise a wide range of issues; even, perhaps, a degree of habit.

Scheduling of time and the Backbench Business Committee

House of Commons Standing Order No. 14 states that 'Save as provided in this order, Government business shall have precedence at every sitting.' The business to be taken in the House each day is decided by the government business managers, after consultation through the 'usual channels', and announced by the Leader of the House at the weekly Business Question which takes place on a Thursday morning. This announcement of the business is provisional, and generally covers two weeks ahead: the business to be taken the following week is usually pretty firm and likely to be displaced only by a serious unforeseen occurrence but the business for the second week may be more likely to change, which would be announced at the next business questions on the following Thursday.

The extent and appropriateness of this government control over the parliamentary agenda was considered by the 'Wright Committee' on Reform of the House of Commons (chaired by Dr Tony Wright MP), which reported in 2009. The Committee examined the then current system for scheduling business in the House in detail, and set out for each category scheduled by ministers how far they were really to be regarded as ministerial, as opposed to House or backbench, business. In place of the arrangements by which the government was in control of the vast majority of the House's time and business, the committee recommended an alternative system. Backbench business would be organised by a Backbench Business Committee, responsible for all business that is not strictly ministerial. That Committee would then join with the representatives of the government and opposition in a House Business Committee that would be obliged to come up with a draft agenda for the week ahead, working through consensus, with the Chairman of Ways and Means in the chair. The agenda would then be put to the House for its agreement, replacing the weekly business questions.

In 2010, following the general election of that year, a Backbench Business Committee was duly established, and tasked with determining the business to be taken in the Chamber and in Westminster Hall on 35 days each year (of which at

Table 5.2 Breakdown of sitting time in the House of
Commons, sessions 2012–13 and 2013–14

Business	Percentage of time
Daily prayers	1.1
Questions	10.9
Ministerial statements	7.0
Urgent questions	1.9
Business statements	2.4
Ten-minute rule motions	0.9
Points of order	0.8
Government bills	25.9
Private members' bills	5.1
Private bills	0.5
Estimates	1.2
Affirmative instruments	0.7
Negative instruments	Nil
Government motions	5.5
Opposition motions	10.6
Backbench business (including select committee statements)	12.5
Petitions	0.2
End of day adjournment motions	6.1
Miscellaneous	6.6

least 27 are to be in the Chamber). The Coalition Agreement between the Conservative and Liberal Democrat parties also spoke of establishing a House Business Committee 'by the third year of the Parliament', but that aspiration was not achieved and in accordance with Standing Order No. 14 the government remains in control of most of the business in the House that is not either determined by the Backbench Business Committee or taken on private members' bill Fridays. The Leader of the House still announces the business for the next two weeks, including which days are to be allocated to backbench business, at the weekly Business Question. The Backbench Business Committee meets weekly to hear representations from members about the debates that they would like to take place on backbench business days, which it judges against a published list of criteria. Its decisions on what is to be debated, including select committee statements (see page 366), are reported to the House formally and published in the relevant section of the 'Vote bundle' (see page 151).

Use of time

Taking the 2012–13 and 2013–14 sessions together to give a more representative picture, the sitting time of the House of Commons broke down as shown in Table 5.2.

The amount of time spent on business initiated by the government has fallen from nearly three-fifths in the 2003–04 and 2004–05 sessions to around one-third in

2012–13 and 2013–14, while time on business initiated by backbenchers has risen in the same period from around one-tenth to nearly one-quarter, showing the impact of the creation of the category of 'backbench business' and the creation of the Backbench Business Committee to determine what is debated then. In addition, there were some 789 hours of backbench- and select committee-initiated debate in Westminster Hall, representing around 33 per cent of total House sitting time.

Just under one-third of time on the floor of the House is spent on legislation – not counting the hundreds of hours that are spent on legislation in public bill and delegated legislation committees.

An MP's day

There are as many ways of doing an MP's job as there are MPs. The influences upon them, which we surveyed in Chapter 4, and the variety of priorities that they have, mean that there is no standard working week or day, although there are some common ingredients. An MP will normally come to Westminster from midday onwards on a Monday, depending on how far away the constituency is, and go back to the constituency on a Thursday or Friday, subject to the business in the House.

Some of the parliamentary agenda is set by the media, and devouring a variety of newspapers, together with breakfast news or the *Today* programme (or sometimes appearing on it), is a usual start to the day. An amount of time in the office at the House, talking over the in-tray with researcher and assistant, may be followed by attendance at a public bill, delegated legislation or select committee, and then to the House for Question Time (especially on a Wednesday, when Prime Minister's Questions are at noon). Or the morning may be given over to constituency work, perhaps also seeing a delegation representing an important local industry and then taking them to meet a minister in Whitehall.

Lunch – these days for many MPs more likely to be a sandwich and a yogurt than anything more elaborate – may be in the office, hearing the case a pressure group wants to put, or chatting with other members in the Tea Room. In July 2005, a new Muslim MP remarked ruefully: 'Nothing is done without eating or drinking with colleagues, so I've drunk more water and Diet Coke than I thought possible'. The afternoon might include writing the MP's weekly column for the local newspaper, signing letters, an interview with local or national media, telephone calls following up constituency cases, or back to general committee or select committee business – perhaps interrupted by votes in the House. If the MP retains business or professional interests outside the House, he or she may find time for these. Later in the day, there may be a meeting of a party committee and an all-party group on a subject in which the MP is heavily involved.

Perhaps the MP wants to speak in the Chamber; in that case, most of the afternoon may be taken up waiting on the green benches, leaping up to catch the eye of the Chair at the conclusion of each speech, and then being in the Chamber again for the wind-up speeches by the frontbenches at the end. Or possibly he or she has been able to secure the half-hour adjournment debate; in that case, much of the time that day will have been spent looking over notes for the speech, and perhaps discussing the issues with the constituent whose case has been raised, or a group interested in the subject to be debated; and, as the parliamentary day nears its end, narrowly watching the progress of business so as to be in the Chamber in time. Thereafter, a telephone call home to a distant family to exchange news about the day.

Ministers

If the MP is one of the 90 or so ministers in the Commons, the day will be very different. Whitehall, not Westminster, is their focus; their departments' concerns rule their day, and their officials feel that they own a minister's time. As well as work at the desk, there will be a range of meetings – with civil servants, ministerial colleagues (for the more senior, in Cabinet and in Cabinet committees), official visitors and delegations (perhaps led by one of their backbench colleagues). There will be opening ceremonies, keynote speeches at conferences, ministerial visits, EU negotiations in Brussels, press conferences. Their relationship with the House will change; now they are concerned only with one subject area, and their time in the House will centre on when their department is due to answer Questions (see page 279), when they open or reply to a debate, take 'their' bill through its stages or appear as a witness before a select committee. Their weekends are dominated by red despatch boxes with papers they need to read or approve by Monday morning – in effect, the homework set by their department. And they still have to keep up with their constituency work. Most ministers' workloads are very heavy; just how heavy often comes as a surprise to newly appointed ministers.

To a lesser extent, the same is true of opposition shadow ministers, who have fewer resources to support them. Although they do not have the burden of departmental work, much of their day is spent in keeping up with developments in their subject brief, or perhaps leading for the opposition on a bill in committee or a debate on the floor of the House.

Attendance in the Chamber

Most visitors to the galleries, or viewers of coverage of the House of Commons, comment on the relatively small attendance of members in the Chamber Even though the Chamber is packed weekly for Prime Minister's Questions and at other times for major debates or statements, the routine level of attendance for some debates can be embarrassingly low, and is often a source of criticism from those who see on television an important subject being debated by only 1 or 2 per cent of the House's membership.

The level of attendance is influenced by various factors: there is continuous television coverage over the annunciator system, and there have been improvements in members' office accommodation, both of which have limited the tendency to 'drop in' to the Chamber rather than planning to be there for a particular item of business.

When debate is predictable and the outcome certain – especially if it is by a large majority, this too will have an effect.

However, it will be clear from the description of an MP's day that members are also drawn away from the Chamber simply because there is so much else to do. For most of the day, there is a great deal of formal parliamentary activity going on elsewhere – in Westminster Hall, and in legislative or select committees – in addition to the huge variety of party and group activity, as well as constituency work. Much is sometimes made of 'activity statistics': how many times an MP has voted, or how many times he or she has spoken in debate. These give a rather two-dimensional picture and can be misleading. Whips will score highly on divisions, because they are on the premises most of the time the House is sitting and votes are their business. But they will not feature in debates, because by convention they do not speak. Members with distant constituencies may not score as highly as London members; other MPs may decide that they can do more through select committee work than by interventions in the Chamber. And the shift towards constituency casework may be an additional reason why attendance in the Commons Chamber is often much lower than in the Chamber of the House of Lords.

Sittings and use of time in the House of Lords

The House of Lords usually sits from Monday to Thursday, and on Fridays once a month. In the 1999–2000 session – a very busy one – it sat for 177 days, an average of 7 hours 29 minutes each day (the Commons sat for 170 days, averaging 8 hours 29 minutes per day). In 2013–14, by contrast, it sat for 149 days, averaging 6 hours 47 minutes each day. On Mondays and Tuesdays the Lords meets at 2.30 p.m., on Wednesdays at 3.00 p.m. and on Thursdays at 11 a.m. On Fridays, sittings begin at 10 a.m. and continue without interruption until the business before the House has been completed. There are target rising times too – 10.00 p.m. on Mondays to Wednesdays, 7.00 p.m. on Thursdays and 3.00 p.m. on Fridays. The convention of rising at 10.00 p.m. was introduced in 2002 and is now fairly well-established, though on occasion due to pressure of business and the need to reach targets it is simply not observed. Thus, in 2013–14, 31 per cent of sittings exceeded the 10.00 p.m. cut-off. As in the Commons, Saturday and Sunday sittings have taken place only at times of national crisis. The length of Lords sittings has grown gradually. In the 1974–75 session, the average sitting lasted under six hours, while in 2010–12 the average sitting lasted over seven hours.

Sittings of the House and its committees are rarely if ever impeded by not having enough members present to transact the business as the quorum is only three! Exceptionally, for the joint committees on Human Rights and on Statutory Instruments, and for sub-committees of the European Union Committee, the quorum is set by the House at two. A higher threshold of 30 is set for divisions on bills and secondary legislation. If fewer than 30 vote – a rare but occasionally a tactically engineered event to delay business – the debate on the question is adjourned and the House proceeds to its next business. So, when the House is considering government bills the government whips always ensure that there are at least 30 government supporters in the House. But, as we have seen, attendance is normally far in excess of the procedural minimum.

As in the Commons, the day begins with *Prayers*. In the Lords, a psalm and prayers are read by a bishop, and many members kneel on the benches. Immediately after Prayers, new members go through their ceremony of introduction and take the oath or affirm, as does any member who has not yet taken the oath or affirmed so far in the parliament. The business starts with a short *question time* when four oral questions are taken. Private notice questions when they are allowed by the Lord Speaker come immediately after oral questions. *Business statements* – indicating the limitations on speaking time to be observed in time-limited debates, or the hour of adjournment for dinner during a particularly long piece of legislative business, for example – follow. *Ministerial statements* come next in theory, but only if the minister making the statement is a lord. Most statements are made in the Commons and repeated in the Lords. Occasionally statements to be made in the Commons are deemed by the usual channels not to be sufficiently important to the Lords to be repeated. When they are important, they will usually have been delivered in the Commons after questions in that House and are repeated in the Lords as soon thereafter as is convenient. In the Lords, brief comments and questions for clarification from the opposition front-benches and from backbenchers of all parties are allowed for a total period not exceeding forty minutes following the end of the statement. Members clearly value this opportunity to comment and probe the government further on statements.

The substantive business then begins. Discussion of *private legislation* comes first, followed by *Business of the House motions*, usually moved by the Leader of the House and signifying a change in the order of business. Then, when necessary, comes *Chairman of Committees' business*. This usually relates to the discussion of any reports by committees for which the Chairman of Committees has responsibility – such as reports of the House Committee on some matter of internal management, or the Procedure Committee. Discussion of *public bills, delegated legislation and reports from select committees* come next, followed by other motions. At the end of business, any *questions for short debate* (*QSDs*) that have been tabled for oral answer by the government may be taken. Proceedings on QSDs are time-limited to one-and-a-half hours when taken at the end of business. They are somewhat akin to adjournment debates in the Commons. Indeed, so popular have they become that, if time permits, they are now sometimes taken during the adjournment for dinner of proceedings on a major bill, or in Grand Committee, when they are time-limited to one hour

The order of business is slightly different on Thursdays when, by standing order, motions have precedence over bills and other business. The practical effect of this is to make Thursday, for most of the session, a day of debates. Any other business has to come last.

It would be very unusual to find all the different kinds of business set down for any one day. A typical day might begin with Prayers, followed by oral questions and business statements; proceedings on a private bill might come next but would usually be very brief (discussion of a controversial nature will, at the Chairman of Committees' discretion, usually be deferred until later in the day); there may then come a business motion; then would follow the legislative stages of one or more bills. If the principal business consists of a lengthy stage of a major bill requiring constant attendance, then at 7.30 p.m. that stage may be adjourned for an hour, in which time short items of business – say, an uncontentious piece of delegated legislation, or a private member's bill, or a question for short debate might be taken. The adjourned proceedings on the major bill will then be resumed and the House might adjourn at any time between about 9 p.m. and 10 p.m. If it is likely that business will finish earlier in the evening, a question for short debate may have been set down as last business.

A day's business in the Lords is illustrated by the Order Paper reproduced overleaf.

On the day shown, after questions, a Business of the House motion was moved to advance an item of business to a time earlier than that for which it had been set down for the following day; this was followed by an item of Chairman of Committees business, making an appointment to a committee, in this case the Refreshment Committee which the Lord Chairman also happens to chair; then came a government motion of 'instruction', moved by a minister, to provide that amendments to the Pensions Bill be considered in a particular order for report stage; and next we find two motions to approve items of delegated legislation already debated in Grand Committee but requiring formal approval by the House. These five items would have been taken very quickly. Finally, we come to the substantive business of the day: the third day in committee of the whole House on the Water Bill and – to be sandwiched into the one hour break for dinner – a Question for Short Debate. Meanwhile in the Moses Room, another government bill, the Defence Reform Bill, continued its committee stage in Grand Committee. The House on that day rose at 9.20 p.m., well within the target rising time of 10.00 p.m.

The sitting time of the House of Lords in the 1995–96, 2003–04, and 2010–12 sessions broke down approximately as shown in Table 5.3.

The relative apportionment of time in the Chamber remains fairly constant, save for a slight increase in the amount of time taken up by government bills and statements relative to other kinds of business.

We conclude this chapter with four topics that are ever-present in a parliamentarian's day: parliamentary papers, voting, the media and the broadcasting of Parliament; and two that form a preface to the more detailed examination of some of the functions of Parliament that follows: privilege and procedure.

Parliamentary papers

The parliamentary process generates a great deal of paper. Much of it is private and relates only to a particular group – for example, the working papers of a select committee – but there is also a central core of printed and electronic material that provides MPs with their bread-and-butter information and that is also available to people outside Parliament.

HOUSE OF LORDS BUSINESS

No. 113

Tuesday 11 February 2014 at 2.30pm

*Oral Questions, 30 minutes

*Lord Bach to ask Her Majesty's Government what assessment they have made of the extent to which section 10 of the Legal Aid, Sentencing and Punishment of Offenders Act 2012, dealing with "exceptional cases", is working as intended.

*Lord Spicer to ask Her Majesty's Government what are their latest projections for the economic growth of (1) the British, and (2) the Scottish, economy in 2014.

*Baroness Morgan of Ely to ask Her Majesty's Government what representations they have made to the food and drink industry about reducing levels of sugar in processed products in the United Kingdom.

*Lord Alton of Liverpool to ask Her Majesty's Government what is their assessment of the humanitarian situation in Darfur and other parts of the Republic of Sudan following the decision of the government of Sudan to suspend the work of the International Committee of the Red Cross.

Business of the House Lord Hill of Oareford to move that the question for short debate in the name of Lord Mawson, set down for Wednesday 12 February, be advanced to after that in the name of Baroness Jones of Moulescoomb.

Refreshment The Chairman of Committees to move that Lord Fink be appointed a member of the Select Committee in place of Lord Howard of Rising, resigned.

Pensions Bill Lord Freud to move that the amendments for the Report stage be marshalled and considered in the following order:

Clauses 1 to 5	Schedules 8 and 9	Clauses 26 to 31
Schedules 1 and 2	Clause 14	Schedule 16
Clauses 6 and 7	Schedule 10	Clauses 32 and 33
Schedules 3 and 4	Clause 15	Schedule 17
Clauses 8 and 9	Schedule 11	Clauses 34 to 43
Schedule 5	Clauses 16 to 23	Schedule 18
Clauses 10 and 11	Schedule 12	Clauses 44 and 45
Schedule 6	Clause 24	Schedule 19
Clause 12	Schedules 13 and 14	Clauses 46 to 49
Schedule 7	Clause 25	Schedule 20
Clause 13	Schedule 15	Clauses 50 to 56.

continued

House of Lords Business (the Lords Order Paper)

Source: Copyright House of Lords, 2014

Consumer Credit Act 1974 (Green Deal) (Amendment) Order 2014 Baroness Verma to move that the draft Order laid before the House on 9 January be approved. *18th Report from the Joint Committee on Statutory Instruments, considered in Grand Committee on 4 February*

Localism Act 2011 (Consequential Amendments) Order 2014 Baroness Stowell of Beeston to move that the draft Order laid before the House on 7 January be approved. *17th Report from the Joint Committee on Statutory Instruments, considered in Grand Committee on 4 February*

Water Bill Committee (day 3) [Lord De Mauley] *20th Report from the Delegated Powers Committee*

Lord Morris of Aberavon to ask Her Majesty's Government what are the reasons for the delay in the completion of the Chilcot Inquiry. (*Dinner break business, 1 hour*)

Grand Committee in the Moses Room at 3.30pm

Defence Reform Bill Committee (day 3) [Lord Astor of Hever] *17th and 21st Reports from the Delegated Powers Committee*

Table 5.3 Comparison of sitting time breakdowns in the House of Lords

	Percentage of time spent		
	1995–96	**2003–04**	**2010–12**
Prayers	1.2	1.3	1.5
Introductions	0.5	0.5	0.5
Oral questions	6.7	7.4	6.6
Private bills	0.1	0.4	0.2
Statements	3.1	3.6	4.9
Public bills (government)	47.8	52.7	53.7
Public bills (private members)	4.3	1.9	2.3
Statutory instruments	5.7	5.6	3.0
Debates	25.1	20.1	21.1
Questions for Short Debate	3.0	4.8	4.6

The Vote bundle

Every MP receives a daily bundle of papers known as 'the Vote'. This will be no more than a few pages in the first few days of the session, but for many sitting days it may be as much as 200 pages. The front page is the *Summary Agenda*, which lists the titles of business to be taken in the House and Westminster Hall. Then follows the *Business Today* or Order Paper, a detailed agenda that gives all the items for which notice is required; so, for example, the texts of oral questions and of any motions to be debated (or to be put for decision without debate), in the order in which they will be taken. The agenda for the Chamber is followed by that for Westminster Hall. The Order Paper 'freezes' at the moment when the House adjourns on the previous sitting day; nothing can be slipped in thereafter (although, of course, some things are permitted to be done without notice). Statements may appear on the Order Paper but do not have to, and urgent questions are not included; both are in any case notified by way of the television annunciators before the start of the sitting. The Order Paper tries to be informative without being misleading (for example, by implying that a practice normally followed will necessarily be followed). After all, it is often the opposition's aim not to achieve the agenda; and the government does not have to proceed with every item of business simply because it is on the Order Paper.

There is then a list of *written ministerial statements* to be made that day (for less important announcements, an alternative to making an oral statement to the House), followed by notice of *committee sittings that day*, giving the time and place of each, and the witnesses for public sittings of select committees. This section of the Vote ends with a list of committee reports to be published that day, and a section for other announcements such as the arrangements for future end of day adjournment debates and debates in Westminster Hall.

The next section is *future business*, which comes in two parts. Section A is the calendar of business that has been provisionally announced by the Leader of the House or chosen by the Backbench Business Committee for dates in the next two weeks. It also includes private members' bills that have been set down for future Fridays, and notices of motions for leave to bring in 'ten minute rule' bills on future Tuesdays and Wednesdays. Section B, *remaining orders and notices*, contains items of business that have not yet been scheduled for a specific date.

Other items in the Vote bundle are *lists of amendments* put down to bills to be debated that day, both on the floor of the House and in public bill committee; and the *Votes and Proceedings*. This is the formal legal record of what the House *did* the previous day rather than what was said: decisions on motions, amendments made to bills, papers laid before the House, the record of reports from select committees, and so on. All of the papers listed here are available on the parliamentary website (www.parliament.uk) and increasingly MPs access working papers delivered to their mobile devices.

Also in the Vote bundle are the parliamentary questions and amendments to bills that were tabled the previous day, and new early day motions (or those up to a fortnight old to which new signatures were added the previous day). These are all printed on blue paper to show that they are new notices rather than papers for the current working day. All parliamentary questions already tabled for that day or for a future day are contained in the separate *Question Book*, which is now no longer printed but is available online.

Hansard

T.C. Hansard was the nineteenth-century printer and publisher whose daily record of the Commons was published privately. From 1909, staff of the House took on the recording of debates, but the name 'Hansard' stuck and was officially adopted in 1943. Properly called *The Official Report*, *Hansard* is the record of what is said in the House. It is substantially verbatim; *Official Report* staff tidy up obvious mistakes and repetitions, but they do not allow any change of substance.

Hansard contains not only everything that is said in debates in the House and Westminster Hall the previous day, but also lists of MPs voting in divisions and a large section devoted to the answers given by ministers to written questions, as well as written statements by ministers. There are two columns on each page of *Hansard* (a column accounts for about three minutes of debate), and references are always to column or 'col.' rather than to page. Unlike many parliaments, Westminster does not allow speeches prepared but not delivered to be put into the record. The full text of every day's *Hansard* is published at 7.30 a.m. the following morning and put on the parliamentary website at 8.00 a.m. At the end of 2005, a 'rolling' *Hansard* of the Chamber was introduced, with chunks of text being posted on the Internet about three hours after the words were spoken in the Chamber. *Hansard* staff also record all the debates in general committees; these appear a little more slowly than the Chamber *Hansard*. Evidence given by witnesses before select committees is recorded by *Hansard* or by contractors working for them. Select committee evidence is also posted on the parliamentary website, on the pages of the relevant committee.

Other parliamentary papers

A wide range of papers are presented to Parliament, which MPs may obtain in hard copy from the House's Vote Office, and members of the public may buy from the Stationery Office. Most papers generated by Parliament itself are also available at www.parliament.uk; those produced by government departments are usually on www.gov.uk.

Bills are published when they are first introduced and again at subsequent stages if they are amended. More than 300 *Command Papers* (so called because they are formally presented by the government 'by command of Her Majesty') are presented each year. These may be treaties and other agreements with foreign governments, reports of non-parliamentary committees of investigation or Royal Commissions, *White Papers* (statements of government policy) or *Green Papers* (documents for consultation on possible policy options). *Act Papers* are laid before Parliament because an Act of Parliament requires it; the majority are Statutory Instruments (see page 223) – about 1,500 a year – but this category also includes reports and accounts of a wide range of public bodies, government statistics, and reports by the Comptroller and Auditor General (see page 248).

House of Lords working papers

The most important of these is *House of Lords Business* which is, broadly speaking, the Lords equivalent of the Commons Order of Business, Votes and Proceedings and other notices rolled into one. It is compiled each day and sent out to peers overnight. It begins with the orders of the day for the following day, which are also printed separately as the *Order Paper* each day (see page 150). Next comes future business – the motions and orders of the day for the coming month in so far as business will have been set down, followed by motions of various kinds awaiting debate but with no day allocated, questions for written answer newly tabled since the last print of House of Lords Business, lists of bills and statutory instruments of various kinds currently awaiting consideration, and a list of forthcoming committee meetings. The last item in the document is the Minutes of Proceedings, a formal record of the business conducted in the Chamber and Grand Committee that day along with a list of papers laid before the House.

The Government Whips' Office also publishes its own *Today's Lists*. This combines elements of business from the Order Paper with lists of names of speakers in debates and lists of groupings of amendments, as necessary.

The House of Lords has its own *Hansard* and each session, based on the daily *Minutes of Proceedings*, the House publishes a *Sessional Journal*. Two other unofficial documents are also useful working papers. The Government Whips' Office publishes each week its *Forthcoming Business* which contains more information than *House of Lords Business* about what might be taken in coming weeks. Deadlines for tabling amendments and enrolling for debates are also included. The Committee office publishes online daily a *Committee Bulletin* of all current committee inquiries, their remit, and forthcoming programme. The *Bulletin* has a very wide circulation. All these documents except the Committee Bulletin are published in paper and electronic form.

Nearly all the papers presented to the Commons are also laid before the House of Lords (but not financial statutory instruments (see page 226)).

Voting

Votes are called 'divisions' because MPs 'divide' physically, going through different lobbies depending on which way they are voting. Although during a sitting day many things are decided without a division, disagreement between government and opposition (or dissent by a smaller group of MPs on either side of the House) will produce a vote. Forcing votes as a means of taking time and disrupting or delaying the business is a tactic used in every parliament.

Voting in both Houses of Parliament is on the basis of approval or disapproval; there is no provision for formally recording abstentions and no means of ranking competing choices in a single decision (which might have led to a rather different outcome on the future composition of the House of Lords); the only exception is in the procedures for the election of a new Speaker, of deputy speakers and of select committee chairs (see pages 44, 53 and 317).

When a proposition has been put before the House for debate (for example, when a member has moved that a bill 'be now read a second time', or that an amendment be made), when the mover sits down, the Speaker *proposes the Question* – in other words, says formally to the House 'The Question is, that the Bill be now read a second time' or whatever, making clear exactly what it is that the House then has to decide or debate. This may seem a pointless duplication, but it is important as a formality – and vital if the House is proceeding rapidly through a flock of amendments. At the end of a debate the Speaker *puts the Question*, saying 'The Question is, that the Bill be now read a second time. As many as are of that opinion say "Aye". Of the contrary, "No"'. If the matter is uncontroversial, the only response he hears is a muffled 'Aye' from the government whips, and the matter is decided without a vote.

But if there is disagreement and the opposition as a whole, or a group of backbenchers, wants to press the matter to a vote, the two sides will shout out 'Aye' or 'No' in response to the Chair. The Speaker, in what is known as *collecting the voices*, says, judging what he thinks is the louder cry, 'I think the Ayes/Noes have it'. If his decision is challenged by the other side still shouting 'Aye' or 'No', then he says 'Division. Clear the Lobby' (in the singular, this refers not to the division lobbies but to the Members' Lobby beyond the Chamber, which the doorkeepers now clear of all but members and House staff to allow MPs easier access to vote). The division bells ring throughout the parliamentary precincts (and in nearby flats, pubs and restaurants whose owners pay to be connected to the system). A division is under way, and the division clerks hurry to the division lobbies to be in place before the tellers are appointed.

After two minutes, the Speaker *puts the Question again* to check that there is still disagreement between the two sides. He then *names the tellers*. These are usually two whips on each side, although any MP may act as a teller. 'The Ayes to the right, the Noes to the left [referring to the two division lobbies]. Tellers for the Ayes, Mark Hunter and Jenny Willott. Tellers for the Noes, Heidi Alexander and Tom Blenkinsop' [or whoever it may be]. If no teller (or only one) has come forward on one side, the Speaker declares the result in favour of the other side.

The tellers, one from each side so that they agree on the numbers, then go to the exit door of each division lobby and count MPs as they emerge (whips will be at the other end of the lobby to encourage their own MPs to vote the right way). Inside the lobby their names will have been taken by the division clerks, and the lists that result will be published in *Hansard* the following day. After eight minutes from first calling the division, the Speaker says 'Lock the doors'; the doorkeepers lock the doors leading into the lobbies and no more MPs can get in to vote. When every member has passed the division clerks and then the tellers, the results are reported to one of the Clerks at the Table, who writes them on a 'division slip', which is handed to one of the tellers on the winning side. The tellers then form up at the Table, by the Mace and facing the Speaker, with the Clerk at the despatch box to one side, and the teller with the division slip reads out the numbers of Ayes and Noes to the House – a soundbite often used on the television news when a major vote has taken place. The Clerk takes the slip to the Speaker, who repeats the numbers and declares the result: 'The Ayes to the Right, 307. The Noes to the left, 271. So the Ayes have it, the Ayes have it. Unlock'. The doorkeepers unlock the doors to the division lobbies, and the House moves on to the next part of the business of the day. From start to finish, the division has taken anything from 12 to 15 minutes.

This may seem unnecessarily complicated, but there is a good deal of common sense about it. Collecting the voices allows an expression of disagreement but does not commit the House to a division unless the disagreement is persevered with. Putting the question again after two minutes allows for second thoughts; and if no disagreement is expressed, then (or if it is not enough to provide two tellers for one side or the other) the matter is decided. This avoids unnecessary votes (and in complicated proceedings allows for the occasional mistake; for example, when a group of MPs actually wanted a vote on the next amendment rather than this one). Requiring tellers on each side to agree on the number of votes they have counted also means that the numbers are unlikely to be challenged.

If the result of a division shows that fewer than 40 MPs were present (that is, fewer than 35 actually voting, plus the two tellers from each side and the occupant of the Chair), then the division is not valid and the House proceeds to the next business. In fact, many MPs may be present but not voting; staging an inquorate vote in this way is, for example, a very good way of killing a private member's bill.

Electronic voting?

But for many people the idea of taking a quarter of an hour of valuable parliamentary time on a vote is inexplicable. Why not vote electronically? There is a good case for it, but also some powerful arguments against. From a practical point of view, the fact that MPs do not have individual seats in the Chamber means that there would have to be voting stations outside the Chamber. Then, because MPs would have to come to the Chamber to vote, perhaps from offices some distance away, and queue up at the voting stations, not much time might be saved after all. Remote electronic voting is canvassed by some – after all, if you can pay your London congestion charge by text on your mobile phone, why could you not vote? However, for many proponents of electronic voting, this goes too far. The public perception of MPs not even having to come to the Chamber to vote on some vital issue, at a time when Parliament is struggling to 'reconnect' with the public, might not be favourable. The same might go for a more modest solution, such as voting stations in more distant parts of the precincts.

There is also the question of security; how do you ensure that in every case a vote is registered only by an MP entitled to do so? Swipe cards may not be enough and may need validation by biometric systems such as palm prints or iris recognition. After all, what is at stake is not whether you can get £100 out of a cash machine. A vote 'to take note' of a particular EU document may not be of huge significance, but the House of Commons also votes on the biggest national issues – whether a government survives a vote of confidence, or, in August 2013, whether the UK should engage in military action. Any system of electronic voting has to deliver the same confidence in the result as the present system; and it is interesting to note that, in the later days of the Major government, with close results on important votes and even the government's survival in the balance, the accuracy of those votes was never challenged.

However, for many MPs, a powerful argument for the present system is that it collects large numbers of members together for a few minutes, often at a predictable time. This brings backbench and frontbench MPs together (and many backbenchers may not actually see very much of those in government) and is a valuable opportunity to buttonhole ministers, or to gather support for some initiative or signatures for an early day motion. For most MPs, this adds a great deal of value to the otherwise often mundane business of voting.

Deferred divisions

In June 2000, the Modernisation Committee recommended a new procedure to 'reduce the number of occasions on which [the House's] judgements have to be delivered in the small hours of the morning' and to allow debate without requiring other members to be on hand for a vote that might, in the event, not take place. Following an experimental period, this procedure was made permanent in 2004.

The procedure does not apply to bills or to motions that authorise expenditure or charging in relation to bills; neither does it apply to consideration of Estimates and to some types of motion to regulate the business of the House. But where it does apply, if after the moment of interruption (see page 140) an attempt is made to force a vote, that vote is held between 11.30 a.m. and 2.00 p.m. on the next sitting Wednesday. In one of the division lobbies, members mark 'Aye' or 'No' on a form that lists all the votes to be taken, the numbers are totalled by the Clerks, and the Speaker announces the result to the House later during that sitting.

The procedure is a departure from the general practice of the House of taking a decision immediately following a debate (although this could already happen on Estimates and on some amendments to bills (see page 195)), and it has some strong critics. To an extent, it reduces the power of the opposition (or dissenters anywhere in the House) to force votes on the spot to demonstrate disagreement and to have that disagreement reflected in inconvenience for the government. Others see it as preserving the opportunity to vote, but at a more sensible time (although the fact that the change in sitting hours means that on three days of the week votes that are now able to be deferred would have taken place in the early evening has somewhat weakened this argument).

Some would wish to go further, and have all votes delayed to a single 'decision time'. Although some parliaments have this system, it also has strong critics, on the grounds that it would be seen by the public simply as a means of making MPs' lives easier, and would reinforce the image of MPs as 'lobby fodder'. In some types of proceedings, it might actually distort the process of decision-making. For example, on the Terrorism Bill in November 2005 there was an amendment to reduce the government's proposed 90-day detention without charge to 28 days, and another to 'sunset' any such period (that is, to make it law only for a limited time). If the decisions had been postponed to a later time, the debate on 'sunsetting' would have taken place with no idea of what period of detention without charge was being discussed.

Voting in the Lords

Voting is broadly similar in the Lords, in that the count is manual and the members file through lobbies where their names are recorded. The most obvious difference is that Lords members shout 'Content' or 'Not Content' rather than 'Aye' or 'No'. When a division is called, three minutes elapse for the appointment of two tellers for each side. If tellers are not appointed, the division is called off. The question is then put for the second time and the Contents go to the lobby 'to the right by the throne' and the Not Contents 'to the left by the bar'. A further five minutes elapse before the doors are locked. When voting in the lobbies is complete, the tellers report their figures to the Clerk at the Table who adds in the numbers he has recorded as having voted in the Chamber. The winning teller takes the result to the Lord Speaker or Deputy to be announced. The numbers taking part in divisions is now very high (see page 37) and not only do they often take longer than the eight-minute minimum, but it is frequently impossible to lock the doors. Doorkeepers simply prevent latecomers from joining the line. But the frequency of divisions has mercifully decreased: there were 250 divisions in 1985–86, 165 in 1992–93, 110 in 1995–96, 176 in 2003–04, 89 in 2008–09 and 89 in 2013–14.

As in the Commons, there has as yet been no appetite among members of the House to vote electronically in the lobbies, though it is technically feasible. On the other hand, the present system is reliable and mistakes are rarely made. The sandglasses used by the Clerk at the Table to time the vote and the ivory sticks used by the tellers to count their flock through may seem archaic, but the recording of names by the Division Clerks is now done electronically for *Hansard* and for rapid publication on the Internet, along with a breakdown of figures by party. There are no deferred votes in the Lords.

The media

The gallery and the lobby

The relationship between politicians and journalists has always been, and will always be, an equivocal one. Politics is about publicity; opinions will gather force and support if they are positively presented to a mass audience. But good political reporting has to be critical; it must show up weaknesses, as well as strengths, which politicians find less attractive. And political disasters make the best copy of all. There is a partnership – or perhaps a fatal attraction; journalists need the stories that politicians provide, and politicians need the oxygen of publicity to further their own aims.

For many years, the House of Commons treated reporting of its proceedings with the gravest suspicion. In 1694, the writer of a newsletter that carried an account of debates was summoned to the Bar of the House and there – on his knees – was rebuked by the Speaker. In 1738, the House resolved that:

It is a high indignity to, and a notorious breach of privilege of, this House for any news writer, in letters or other papers . . . or for any printer or publisher . . . to give . . . any account of debates or other proceedings of this House . . . and that this House will proceed with the utmost severity against such offenders.

However, by the end of the eighteenth century, although the resolution still stood, reporters were starting to appear in the gallery of the House (where they had to compete for space with members of the public). The 'press gallery' was established in 1803, when Speaker Abbott directed that seats should be reserved for the press. In the eighteenth and nineteenth centuries, literary luminaries appear as parliamentary reporters: Johnson, Hazlitt, Coleridge, Cobbett and Dickens, as well as (before note taking was permitted) 'Memory' Woodfall, a prodigy who could remember hours of debate verbatim and would later return to his office to dictate from memory.

Today, there are more than 300 print, radio and television journalists in the gallery and the lobby. Many of these represent national papers or channels, but others report for a regional audience; given their constituency focus, MPs are particularly keen to establish good relations with these. All journalists must be accredited by the Serjeant at Arms before they get a pass – and they, too, must make a declaration of their interests. Members of the gallery used to report proceedings in the House and in committees, and members of the lobby were more concerned with interpreting parliamentary and political events to the outside world; but in practice the distinction has disappeared. Most national newspapers also have sketch writers, who contribute satirical – and more or less witty – pieces about one or two events the previous day. When they are at Westminster, journalists inhabit cramped and somewhat Dickensian quarters behind the actual Press Gallery in the House.

The lobby have access to a number of places around the palace frequented by MPs but denied to the general public; principally, the Members' Lobby and some of the bars. They will also receive advance copies of documents, such as government White Papers or select committee reports 'under embargo', which allows them a vital 24 to 72 hours to write their stories on what may be a complex subject in time for publication. More importantly, lobby correspondents have access to MPs and ministers in both Houses on lobby terms; the journalists are given information on the basis that it may be disclosed but not attributed. Politicians will use this channel in a number of ways: a secretary of state whose policy has proved damagingly unpopular may be able to hint at a U-turn; public opinion may be prepared for some new initiative; or disenchantment with the party leadership may be aired, and a warning shot fired, without actually putting a head over the parapet.

There are more formal ways in which the lobby is briefed, and ministers and others may be questioned. On sitting days, the Prime Minister's official spokesman or his deputy holds twice-daily briefings usually at 11.00 a.m. and 3.45 p.m. On Wednesdays after Prime Minister's Questions, there is a rather informal briefing by the PM's special advisers in a huddle outside the Press Gallery, followed by a similar briefing by the Leader of the Opposition's advisers. More generally, press conferences are held by ministers and others as occasion demands.

The lobby system has its critics; it is alleged to be too cosy and open to manipulation by those – especially governments – eager to spin the best story. Partly in response, after the 2001 general election the No. 10 briefings became attributable (although not by name, but as the Prime Minister's official spokesman (PMOS)), and summaries of these briefings are put on the No. 10 website. The Prime Minister also holds regular televised press conferences.

Politicians and journalists each have something the other wants – information on one side, and a national or local platform on the other – but journalists can also exercise a great deal of influence on politics. MPs and, more important, senior ministers take notice of Nick Robinson's acute dissection of an issue, or of the results of a mugging in an interview by John Humphrys. But whether the relationship is by turns supportive or critical, suspicious or friendly, the media are an integral part of British politics and, so, of the Westminster Parliament.

Broadcasting Parliament

Although it was as long ago as 1923 that the BBC sought unsuccessfully to broadcast the King's Speech at the State Opening of Parliament, it was not until 3 April 1978 that regular sound broadcasting of both Houses and their committees began. The Lords has been televised since 23 January 1985 and the Commons since 21 November 1989. Both Houses began with an experiment, which was then made permanent. The initial reluctance to be televised – the Commons rejected it in 1966, 1971, 1975 and 1985 – is slightly reminiscent of the House's view of journalists in previous centuries. Even when the Commons approved televising, the majority was not over-whelming: 320 in favour and 266 against; but now it is very hard to imagine Parliament not being televised.

Committees of the two Houses have drawn up rules of coverage concentrating on what is actually being said rather than distractions elsewhere in the Chamber: 'a full, balanced and accurate account of proceedings, with the aim of informing viewers about the work of the House'. This means that the use of cutaway shots is limited, which can be frustrating to broadcasters who want more atmospheric coverage; but the pictures ('the clean feed' – in other words, with no captions or other material added) are also used by broadcasters who want brief inserts for a news bulletin and so need pictures of MPs speaking rather than reacting. The rules for the use of material prohibit it being used for comedy or satire, or for advertising.

Proceedings in both the Commons and the Lords are covered gavel to gavel by remote-control cameras in each Chamber operated from a control room across the road at 7 Millbank – eight cameras in the Commons and five in the Lords. All sittings in Westminster Hall are televised, but broadcast quality coverage of committees is arranged (and charged) on the basis of bids received from broadcasters and is limited to five at any one time. All Chamber and committee meetings are streamed online, primarily in vision but occasionally in audio only. These arrangements, and the rules of coverage and use, are supervised by the Director of Parliamentary Broadcasting, who is an officer of both Houses.

The opening of Portcullis House, with six camera-equipped rooms (four of which are primarily for select committees) and two permanent control rooms, brought in digital broadcasting for the first time. All parliamentary broadcasting is now digital and is available in widescreen format. BBC Parliament, the digital channel, carries the House of Commons Chamber live, time-shifted coverage of the House of Lords and unedited coverage of about ten committees each week. BBC 2, BBC News 24 and Sky News take Prime Minister's Questions live, together with some ministerial statements and committee evidence. The main domestic channels, regional companies and some international organisations use recorded extracts. In 1989, when televising of the Commons began, there were four parliamentary broadcast licence holders. Today, there are in excess of 190 broadcast licence holders and 90 Internet licence holders.

All material is archived by the Parliamentary Recording Unit, which keeps the material for about two years before it is deposited at the National Film Archive. This is developing into a fascinating historical record; many will regret that televising or filming was not permitted many years before, and that the archive does not show us debates at the time of Munich, during the Second World War or during the Suez crisis; and that we have only the written word and contemporary recollections to tell us how Chamberlain, Churchill, Bevan, Macmillan, Wilson and many others performed in the House of Commons.

In January 2002, the two Houses launched experimental webcasting, transmitting audio and audio-visual coverage of proceedings over the Internet (www.parliament live.tv). This was made permanent in May 2003 and automated cameras were introduced into the majority of committee rooms by 2008.

The microphones used in the Chambers are highly selective and directional to reduce extraneous noise, especially in the often noisier Commons. Perversely, this makes the coverage slightly less realistic. A minister may be under a great deal of pressure, being barracked as he or she winds up a debate; but if the minister keeps going, talking directly at the microphone, it sounds as though the ride is fairly smooth – and the one-line interjections that spice proceedings are often heard by the House (which reacts) but are inaudible to the bemused listener or viewer.

It is understandable that broadcasters should make the most use of moments of confrontation on the floor of the House, but a good contrast is provided by coverage of select committee hearings, which can be compelling television. Overall, televised proceedings are an excellent way of making Parliament and its proceedings much better known and more accessible to the country at large.

Privilege

The privilege of Parliament allows the Houses, and their members, to perform their duties without outside threat or interference: rights absolutely necessary for 'the due execution of [Parliament's] powers' as the eighteenth-century Clerk of the House of Commons John Hatsell described them. 'Privilege' is an unfortunate term, as it implies a special advantage rather than a special protection. The word derives from the Latin phrase *privata lex*, meaning private or special law, and 'immunity in the public interest' would be a better description.

The privileges of Parliament, and especially of the House of Commons in its struggle for power with the sovereign, have been established over many years in a series of cases that are charted in *Erskine May*. In later years, assertion of privilege became less important, and in the nineteenth and twentieth centuries these cases became more a matter of defining the limits of privilege – actions to which it did or did not apply.

From 1997 to 1999, the whole question of privilege was examined by a joint committee of both Houses, chaired by a law lord. The committee made a number of detailed recommendations, including setting out the extent of privilege clearly in an Act of Parliament; its overall approach was that privilege was needed for the proper functioning of Parliament in the public interest, but that it should be limited to what was essential in practice. The difficulty of defining precisely the nature and extent of privilege – and fears that doing so would, perversely, risk increasing the extent to which proceedings in Parliament were open to judicial questioning – meant that the committee's recommendations remained largely unimplemented. Concerns about the possible extent of privilege grew in the wake of the expenses saga when four members accused of fraudulently claiming expenses attempted to argue that the expenses system was covered by parliamentary privilege and that their cases could therefore not be heard in the criminal courts. Responding to that case, the 2010 Coalition Agreement contained a pledge to 'prevent the possible misuse of parliamentary privilege by MPs accused of serious wrongdoing', raising again the possibility of legislation to define the extent of privilege.

In the event, the Supreme Court rejected the (always very dubious) notion that the House's system of expenses and allowances might constitute a 'proceeding in Parliament' and the government's eventual Green Paper on Parliamentary Privilege published in April 2012 concluded that there was no need for legislation. As the Green Paper noted, 'Courts remain respectful of parliamentary privilege and exclusive cognisance; but statute law and the courts' jurisdiction will only be excluded if the activities in question are core to Parliament's functions as a legislative and deliberative body.' It is worth noting that Westminster MPs are less protected than those of many other parliaments, where a parliamentary immunity from arrest or civil suit exists.

The Green Paper was considered by a further joint committee of both Houses which reported in July 2013. The Joint Committee largely endorsed the conclusions of the government's Green Paper so far as the need for legislation was concerned, arguing that 'it would be impracticable and undesirable to attempt to draw up an exhaustive list of those matters subject to exclusive cognisance' and that 'legislation should only be used when absolutely necessary, to resolve uncertainty or in the unlikely event of Parliament's exclusive cognisance being materially diminished by the courts'.

Freedom of speech

There are two key elements in modern parliamentary privilege: the first is *freedom of speech*. The classic statement of this is in Article 9 of the Bill of Rights 1688–89: 'That the freedom of speech, and debates or proceedings in Parliament, should not be impeached or questioned in any court or place out of Parliament'. This means that no MP or peer can be sued or prosecuted for anything he or she says as part of the proceedings of that House or any of its committees. This ensures that a member of Parliament can speak up on behalf of constituents, or can express any opinion on a public issue, without fear of legal action. Rich and powerful individuals or companies cannot use the threat of writs to silence criticism. Anyone giving evidence to a committee of the House also has the absolute protection of privilege; no civil or criminal action can be brought against them on the basis of what they have said.

The protection of privilege is balanced by a need for it to be used responsibly, as has been emphasised by successive Speakers (and the Chair, both in the House and in committees, does have some control over MPs' opportunities to speak). Nevertheless, it does happen that individuals are unfairly criticised, or even unjustly accused of a crime, but freedom of speech has to include the freedom to make mistakes, and there would be no freedom of speech if everything had to be proved true before it was spoken. However, this freedom of speech is limited to *proceedings*. This includes anything said in debates on the floor, or in general or select committees; it also includes anything put in writing that forms part of a proceeding, such as the text of any question (or a minister's written answer), amendment or early day motion, and, by virtue of the Parliamentary Papers Act 1840, any document published by order of the House (select committee reports, *Hansard* and potentially sensitive reports by outside bodies that are the subject of a motion 'for an unopposed return' (see page 137)).

The privilege of freedom of speech does not include press conferences, letters to constituents or to ministers, or words said at ordinary public meetings (even if they are held within the parliamentary precincts). Strictly speaking, it does not even include distributing a speech from *Hansard*, as the protection applies to the whole of the document rather than excerpts; but, unless the excerpts were selected and edited in a distorting and malicious way, it would be very unlikely that any action would succeed.

Exclusive cognisance

The second key element in modern parliamentary privilege is *the freedom of each House to regulate its own affairs* – to use the language of the Bill of Rights, not to have its proceedings questioned. This freedom is sometimes known as 'exclusive cognisance' and, in practice, it means that the validity of what one House or the other has done – whether in making amendments to a bill, deciding not to proceed with some matter, or in regulating the conduct of its own members – cannot be adjudicated upon by any other body.

Exclusive cognisance: the 'Damian Green affair'

The freedom of each House to regulate its affairs extends to control of its precincts. A formal protocol requires that if the police, in the course of investigating a suspected crime, wish to come onto the Parliamentary Estate and access offices or papers, they may do so only on production of a properly executed warrant, and the

Speaker will take legal advice before granting access. This was a principle that was not observed in the 'Damian Green affair', when in 2008 the Metropolitan Police had arrested Damian Green, an MP and shadow immigration minister, in connection with a series of leaks from the Home Office. No charges were brought against him, but the actions of the police in searching his office, and the actions of the House authorities in not insisting on a warrant, were the subject of criticism, and a select committee inquiry.

Following these events, a similar protocol was put in place by the House of Lords relating to police access to papers and offices of members of that House. This ensures that the Clerk of the Parliaments and Black Rod are notified beforehand and the authority of the Lord Speaker sought; and, as in the Commons, procedures are followed to ensure the confidentiality of any material that may be covered by parliamentary privilege.

Parliament and the courts

The scope of exclusive cognisance has contracted in recent years, as Parliament has made certain legislation – for example, on employment protection, anti-discrimination, health and safety, and latterly the Freedom of Information Act 2000 – applicable to itself. It is also the case that the courts may find legislation incompatible either with the Human Rights Act 1998 or with EU law; but both these possibilities arise as a result of decisions by Parliament itself, and in both cases what is at issue is the final content of the legislation rather than the way in which Parliament has passed it. In addition, following the *Pepper* v. *Hart* case in 1993 (where the Inland Revenue interpreted a piece of tax law in a way at odds with what a Treasury minister had said about it when the bill was before Parliament), the courts may try to resolve ambiguities in law by looking at ministerial statements and speeches, and the explanatory notes on a bill, setting out the intention of a piece of legislation.

With the exception of these closely defined categories, the courts are careful to follow the principle set out by the jurist Blackstone in 1830, that 'the whole of the law and custom of Parliament has its origin in this one maxim, that whatever matter arises concerning either House of Parliament, ought to be examined, discussed and adjudged in that House and not elsewhere'. The rules of both Houses seek to return the compliment, through the rules on matters *sub judice* (see page 265) and on criticism of judges.

If the extent of parliamentary privilege were to be set out in an Act of Parliament, as recommended by the 1999 Joint Committee on Parliamentary Privilege, the courts would have a bigger interpretative role (as they do in Australia, for example, and will shortly do in New Zealand, following the passing of a Parliamentary Privilege Act there), which might not make the relationship easier.

Privilege

Until 1978, complaints that parliamentary privilege had been infringed could be made by any MP in the Chamber, and this became a regular slot (in much the same way as the 'bogus point of order') for raising political matters that had nothing to do with privilege. Now, MPs have to write privately to the Speaker; in the exceptional cases where he agrees that there has been a serious breach, he makes a statement to the House and allows the MP the opportunity to move a motion relating to the matter, normally the following day, and usually referring the matter to the Committee of Privileges for detailed examination. The most recent reference was in October 2013, of the addressing by Sussex Police of a Police Information Notice to a member following a dispute between him and a constituent.

Contempts

The privileges of free speech and exclusive cognisance protect the proceedings of Parliament in the public interest. Attempts to interfere with proceedings in Parliament, or to obstruct or threaten MPs in the performance of their parliamentary duties, are known as 'contempts'. Examples of contempts might include disrupting a sitting, giving false evidence to a select committee, or threatening an MP on account of something he or she had said, or intended to say, in the House, or for voting in a particular way – or for threatening or taking action against a witness because of what he or she had said to a select committee. A contempt may also be committed by an MP: examples in the last 30 years are the leaking of a draft select committee report to a government department and agreeing to ask parliamentary questions in return for payment. In 2004, for example, the Lord Chancellor and others were found to have committed a contempt by dismissing Judy Weleminsky from the board of the Children and Family Court Advisory and Support Service (CAFCASS) on account of evidence she had given to a select committee.

There is no automatic definition of whether something is a contempt or not. Only if the Committee of Privileges finds that a contempt has been committed, and its view is endorsed by the House, is the matter decided.

Punishment

From early times, both Houses have had the power to imprison, fine or reprimand anyone (including an MP), and to suspend or expel MPs from the House. The last time the Commons imprisoned someone was in 1880, and it is difficult to see the House attempting to do so in modern times. The last time the House fined someone was in 1666; but the power has never been formally discontinued. The 2013 Joint Committee recommended that the two Houses re-assert their historic penal jurisdiction – albeit adding that, at the same time, they would need to set up procedures for exercising that jurisdiction which would meet modern expectations of fairness and due process.

The sixteenth to eighteenth centuries are dotted with expulsions of members from the House, from the rather grand crime of 'being in open rebellion' through forgery, fraud and perjury to the social discrimination of 'having behaved in a manner unbecoming an officer and a gentleman'. Expulsion became less frequent in the nineteenth and twentieth centuries; the last occasion was in 1954, for a criminal conviction.

Suspension, on the other hand, is used more frequently; when an MP is named by the Speaker in the House (usually for disorderly conduct challenging the authority of the Chair), the House suspends the member for 5 sitting days on the first occasion, 20 sitting days on the second occasion and indefinitely (until the end of the session or until rescinded by the House, whichever happens first) on the third.

Suspensions are also used as punishments for other offences: 20 days for damaging the Mace (1988); 10 and 20 days for 'cash for questions' (1995); 3, 5 and 10 days for leaking a draft select committee report (1999); 2 weeks for conflict of interest, followed by indefinite suspension if an apology was not made (2005); 18 days for misuse of parliamentary resources and failure to cooperate with an inquiry (2006); and 7 days for misclaiming allowances and supplying misleading information in support of those claims (2011). An MP who is suspended is not paid during the period of the suspension.

In recent times, the expectation of a long suspension has tended to prompt a member to jump before he is pushed: although the Committee on Standards stopped short of recommending the expulsion of either Denis MacShane, for misclaiming expenses, or Patrick Mercer, for paid advocacy, both members took the Chiltern Hundreds before the House had the opportunity to consider a motion to apply the lengthy suspension recommended by the committee.

As the Joint Committee on Parliamentary Privilege confirmed in 1999, the House of Lords – as with the Commons – has power to imprison its members, and the House of Lords can also fine them. In fact, the House has attempted neither in recent times. While the House cannot expel its members, significantly the Lords in 2009 asserted the right to suspend its members for serious infringement of its rules, on the basis of advice tendered to the Committee for Privileges by the former Lord Chancellor, Lord Mackay of Clashfern (see page 117).

Procedure

Procedure regulates the proceedings of the Commons and its committees. It has four sources. *Practice*, sometimes called 'ancient usage', refers to matters so clearly established over centuries that there is no need to set them down formally; for example, the process of moving a motion, proposing the question on it to the House, debating that question, and then deciding it by 'putting the question'.

Standing orders are general rules for the conduct of business and are amended or added to as the House alters its procedures. They govern matters as diverse as the election of the Speaker, the appointment and powers of most select committees, and the length of debate on different types of business. It is probably not a coincidence that standing orders became significant in the early nineteenth century when the government began to exert more control over the time of the House. Today, 202 standing orders occupy 192 pages of the blue booklet which these days is republished annually – sometimes more often – to keep up with changes.

Rulings from the Chair are an important part of the case law of procedure. These usually arise because the view of the Speaker is sought on a point of interpretation, or some new matter not otherwise covered. The rules on admissibility of parliamentary questions, motions and amendments to bills have grown up in this way. Rulings have a close relationship with precedent – that which has been done before, and judged to have been in order by the Speaker of the day. Rulings and precedents are distilled in successive editions of *Erskine May*.

Finally, some parliamentary proceedings are regulated by *Acts of Parliament*, covering such things as the way Royal Assent to bills is signified to Parliament, how secondary legislation (see page 223) is dealt with, and making an affirmation or taking an oath.

As with the Commons, the House of Lords derives its procedure from practice, from standing orders, and to some limited extent from Acts of Parliament. But as the House has no Speaker with powers of order, there are no Speaker's rulings in the Lords. Instead, procedure is developed and refined by the House itself by agreeing recommendations from its Procedure Committee. Sometimes, these may result in amendments to standing orders, but more usually they are set out in the House's own procedural handbook, the *Companion to Standing Orders*.

Why procedure? And why is it complicated?

Every deliberative body, from a parish council to the General Assembly of the United Nations, needs rules to a greater or lesser extent. Rules regulate how business is initiated; they provide a framework for consideration; and they define how a valid decision is reached.

Many organisations can manage with simple rules, and perhaps no great damage is done if even those rules are not followed very closely. The procedure of Parliament is not simple, for three main reasons.

- *Contention*. If a group of people are in complete agreement about something, rules are barely necessary. The Supreme Soviet in the old USSR had little need of procedure. The Westminster Parliament is a forum where often profound disagreements on politics and principles are argued out and decided. Procedure thus has to provide a means of focusing points for decision, allowing challenge to take place, and balancing the will of the majority against the arguments of the minority.

  In addition, procedure has to protect the rights not only of the opposition parties, but also of groups of MPs, or individual members, wherever they may sit in the House. In a House the size of the Commons, this is especially important; one MP out of 650 may be in a very small minority, but he or she may have constituents whose interests might be threatened by a decision of the majority.

  Where the balance should be struck between the will of the majority (in effect, the government of the day) and the arguments of those who disagree is controversial. There has always been an understanding that a government that has a majority will eventually get its way; but governments are always impatient.

- *Control*. The standing orders are about setting limits – defining what powers select committees may have, how long various types of business may be debated, when certain things happen, and so on. The more tightly those limits are drawn, and the more circumstances that have to be controlled, the more complex the rules. For example, the standing orders on the programming of bills run to twelve pages.
- *Complexity of business.* Parliament has to deal with a huge range of material: every issue for which the government is responsible, and legislation on any subject, often extremely detailed. It approves taxation and grants the government the money required to run the country. At the same time, it must try to fulfil its role of calling government to account. Small wonder that procedures to regulate this business are often complicated.

Consistent, certain and clear

We have seen why there have to be rules, and why they are complicated. But rules are not an end in themselves. As the United Kingdom has no written constitution, and as the way Parliament operates cannot be reviewed by any other body, its rules must be robust. Good procedural rules have three qualities:

- They must be *consistent*; things of the same type must be dealt with in the same way; when something is not, that must be on the basis of a formal decision to handle it in a different way.
- They must be *certain*, with notice given of matters for substantive decision and rules enforced firmly but fairly. Punctuality is an important part of this; if the moment of interruption is 7.00 p.m., the Commons Speaker will say 'Order, order' precisely on the stroke of seven o'clock, not a moment earlier or later.
- Rules may be complex, but they must be *clear*. Vagueness will mean that the rules themselves, not what they regulate, will become a source of disagreement; and it will also tend to cast doubt on the validity of what has been done.

In his book *Last Man Standing: Memoirs of a Political Survivor*, Jack Straw, the former Foreign, Home and Justice Secretary, and former Leader of the House of Commons, said: 'Procedure may be boring to some, but it's about the distribution and exercise of power. It really matters.' We concur.

6

Making the law

Is Parliament 'sovereign'?

Before looking at how Parliament operates as a legislature, this may be a good place to consider the nature of Parliament's powers. In the past, writers on the constitution would have described these as constituting the 'sovereignty of Parliament', but a better modern term might be 'legislative supremacy', because Parliament, strictly speaking, is not sovereign:

First, Parliament is clearly not sovereign in the sense that it embodies any concept of national sovereignty, although it may contribute to the sentiment.

Second, it is not sovereign in the sense that it vies with the Queen to be head of state.

Third, it is not the centre of the day-to-day decision-making of government. It is the government that conducts the business of the state, often acting within the powers and resources that have been granted by Parliament, and claiming its authority to govern by virtue of its majority in the House of Commons. Although Parliament may try to influence the government's actions by a variety of means, it does not and cannot micro-manage the affairs of state. Parliament does not govern.

Fourth, Parliament is not the sole source of the government's powers, many of which are derived from the prerogative powers of the Crown with little or no recourse to Parliament at all. Prerogative powers and the concept of prerogative range widely. The government exercises patronage through honours and appointments; the Civil Service answers to the Executive, not to Parliament (although Accounting Officers answer to the Public Accounts Committee (see page 249)). Prime Ministers can restructure or abolish government departments with little say by Parliament, and can appoint and dismiss even the most senior ministers. Parliament does not *have* to be consulted before the armed forces are used – although, as a matter of practical politics, the votes on involvement in Iraq in 2003 and, especially, on Syria in 2013 have made it unlikely that a government could now go to war without the authority of Parliament. The balance has shifted a little in some areas – for example, a formal opportunity to express a view on international treaties (see page 174), and the increasing numbers of select committee hearings before appointments are made to important public offices – but Parliament is a long way from mastering the prerogative powers of the Crown that are exercised by ministers.

Parliament's legislative supremacy

So, when people use the phrase 'the sovereignty of Parliament', what they really mean is the *legislative supremacy* of Parliament - that is to say its unique ability, in the words of the nineteenth-century constitutional writer A.V. Dicey, to 'make or unmake any law whatever'.

The principle was set out elegantly in 1844, when Thomas Erskine May published the first edition of his *Treatise on the Law, Privileges, Proceedings and Usage of Parliament* – a work that was to become the authoritative text on the procedures of Parliament (see page 55). He began his second chapter with this paragraph:

> *The legislative authority of Parliament extends over the United Kingdom, and all its colonies and foreign possessions; and there are no other limits to its power of making laws for the whole empire than those which are incident to all sovereign authority – the willingness of the people to obey, or their power to resist. Unlike the legislatures of many other countries, it is bound by no fundamental charter or constitution; but has itself the sole constitutional right of establishing and altering the laws and government of the empire.*

Parliament no longer legislates for an overseas empire, but Erskine May's words are in all other respects still applicable.

Characteristics of legislative supremacy

Legislative supremacy is essentially a legal concept, and it manifests itself in a number of different ways. For example, the courts of law are under a duty to apply legislation, even if that legislation might appear to be morally or politically wrong. This is a powerful reason why legislation needs to be technically correct to minimise the possibility of unexpected consequences. Moreover, unlike countries with written constitutions – the United States, for example – it would not be possible to challenge an Act of the United Kingdom Parliament in the courts on the grounds that it was 'unconstitutional'. The 2005 challenge to the Hunting Act (which was appealed all the way to the House of Lords) was based on the alleged effects of the Parliament Acts (see pages 209), not on a conflict with the constitution. And, in any event, even the constitution can be subject to statute. New constitutional principles can be established, such as reform of the membership or powers of the House of Lords, or devolved government in Scotland, Wales and Northern Ireland. Moreover, existing constitutional principles can be changed, as in making male and female heirs equal in succession to the throne.

One of the consequences of Parliament's legislative supremacy is that one parliament cannot bind its successor parliaments, which have an equal claim to that legislative supremacy. In some cases, things that Parliament does by legislation are in practical terms so difficult to reverse that successor parliaments are, in effect, bound by those Acts – such as the Acts that gave self-government or confederation to the former dominions, or independence to the former colonies, or votes to women, or even devolution to Scotland and Wales. (Devolution in Northern Ireland, however, has been revoked, restored, revoked and then restored again by Parliament.)

But in other areas the principle of legislative supremacy remains strong – even in the field of human rights. It was for many years held that a bill of rights – in modern language, a bill to incorporate the European Convention on Human Rights into UK law – could never be entrenched into law so as to protect such fundamental rights from the possibility of subsequent infringement by a future parliament. Indeed, when the government brought forward its Human Rights Bill in 1997–98, it made no attempt to do so.

Limitations on legislative supremacy

Parliament's legislative supremacy is a powerful concept, but it has its limitations. Erskine May put his finger on the chief limitation – 'the willingness of the people to obey, or their power to resist'. Most of the time, in these days of universal suffrage, this manifests itself through the ballot box rather than in mass civil disobedience, but the repeal of the much disliked community charge or poll tax legislation in 1992 was undoubtedly hastened by the mass demonstrations of 1990.

Other limitations derive from the radical changes in society since Erskine May first wrote. On the one hand, the law has covered more and more areas that formerly went unregulated or were considered private matters not deserving the intervention of the state – such as education, working conditions, social security, health, and so on. But on the other hand, modern technology, and in recent years especially information technology, has placed some activities almost beyond the reach of UK law-making – electronic international transfer of funds, for example, or intellectual property rights in material placed on the Internet.

Apart from the ultimate limitations of public consent and of practical constraint, the legislative supremacy of Parliament has been limited in practical ways in recent years, by:

- the passing of the Human Rights Act;
- accession to the European Union (at that time the European Economic Community); and
- devolution to Scotland and Wales, and, with some qualifications, to Northern Ireland.

We now look at Parliament's legislative function – the means of exercising this legislative supremacy.

Who makes the law?

If asked 'Who makes the law in the UK?' most people would instinctively reply 'Parliament'. It seems to be an obvious feature of our democracy that the law under which it operates has been decided by elected representatives in Parliament. And if we were asked 'Where can one find the law?' we might consult 'Statutes' or 'Acts of Parliament', each of which begins with the formula:

> *Be it enacted by the Queen's Most Excellent Majesty, by and with the consent of the Lords Spiritual and Temporal, and Commons, in this present Parliament assembled, and by the authority of the same, as follows:*

However, if we look at the law in operation, the picture is less simple. The way the law works in practice may differ from the intentions of Parliament when the law was passed, or the application of the law may vary in different parts of the country.

For example, the driver of an antique lorry used in a steam fair is stopped by the police as he drives the wrong way down a one-way street. The police find that he has no tachograph in his cab, and they take the view that this is required by law to record his hours of work and the miles he has travelled. The driver is charged with driving the wrong way down the street and with not having the tachograph and is convicted by the magistrates on both counts. He accepts the first but goes all the way to the Court of Appeal on the second, on the grounds that his lorry is an exhibit and is not used for commercial haulage purposes, so it is not required to have a tachograph. The appeal court judges agree and quash the conviction.

What has Parliament to do with this process? The enforcement of the law was the duty of the police. The interpretation of the law was a matter for the courts. The street was not designated as one-way by Parliament but by the local council. The law about tachographs was set out in regulations made by the Secretary of State for Transport, not by Parliament. And all the Secretary of State for Transport had done was to give effect in the UK to European Union legislation brought forward by the European Commission and agreed by the Council and the European Parliament.

However, all those involved were operating within a framework that derives from statute law as made by the Westminster Parliament. The local council was able to make the street one-way because an Act of Parliament gave it the power to do so; the European Union was able to legislate because an Act of Parliament – in this case, the European Communities Act 1972 – provides that such European legislation shall apply to the UK; and the Secretary of State for Transport was able to make regulations because the same Act of Parliament allows the translation of general EU legislation into detailed domestic law. The Westminster Parliament undoubtedly retains the power to repeal the European Communities Act 1972 and end the power of the EU to make any law applying to the UK, although this would mean moving into uncharted constitutional waters. This chapter looks in detail at these Acts of Parliament and how they are made. It also examines delegated legislation; that is, legislation made directly by the government and other bodies that have been authorised by Parliament to do so.

Types of legislation

First, some definitions. The *Acts of Parliament* we have been talking about are a level of legislation known as *primary legislation*. A piece of draft primary legislation is a *bill*. When a bill is passed, it becomes an *Act* and part of *statute law*. An Act is referred to by its title and the year it was passed; for example, the Immigration Act 2014.

There are two types of bill and Act: *public* and *private*. The vast majority, and by far the more important, are public. They affect the public general law, which applies to everyone in the UK – although some Acts may apply specifically to England, Wales, Scotland or Northern Ireland (or to London), and the Scottish Parliament and Welsh Assembly have power to make primary legislation for Scotland and Wales on a range of subjects defined by the Westminster Parliament in the Scotland Act 1998 and the Government of Wales Act 2006, as does the Northern Ireland Assembly on 'transferred matters' (those not reserved to Westminster under the Northern Ireland Act 1998).

Private Acts confer private and particular rights, or are local and personal in their effect. A private Act might allow a local authority to close a cemetery, or to confer powers to manage and control access to areas of common land. A private Act may also allow an exception to the general law; for example, to allow an individual local authority to do something within its own area that needs specific legal authority. In recent years, the rare cases of personal legislation (once used for divorces) have been to allow people to marry who otherwise would be prevented from doing so (for example, stepfather and stepdaughter).

Sometimes, a public bill contains provisions that do not apply generally but affect particular individuals or bodies differently from others who would otherwise be in the same situation. If these were the only provisions in the bill, it would be a private bill; but combining them with changes to the general law turns the bill into a *hybrid bill*. These are usually bills promoted by the government relating to large-scale infrastructure projects, such as Crossrail and the proposed HS2 London to Birmingham high-speed rail line. Different procedures apply to public bills, private bills and hybrid bills.

Private members' bills are sometimes confused with private bills, but they are public bills to change the general law; their title comes from the fact that they are brought forward by a private member (that is, a backbencher) rather than by the government.

Bills of all types may start their parliamentary passage in either House, although those whose purpose is mainly or entirely financial will generally start in the Commons. At the beginning of a parliamentary session, the government business managers will try to maximise their use of parliamentary time available by deciding which bills will start in the Lords and which in the Commons. A bill that begins in the Lords has [*Lords*] in its title when in the Commons and [HL] when in the Lords.

Delegated legislation is made by a minister (or occasionally a public body) under powers conferred by an Act of Parliament. Individual pieces of legislation may be called *orders*, *rules*, *regulations*, *schemes* or *codes*, depending on what the original Act (called the 'parent Act') says; but they are generally known as *delegated legislation*, *secondary legislation* or *Statutory Instruments* (SIs). A special type of order, an *Order in Council*, requires the approval of the Queen in the Privy Council.

Delegated legislation is normally used for detailed arrangements that flesh out broader provisions in the parent Act, or to specify matters – such as, for example, the arrangements for licensing some activity – the details of which may need to be changed and for which an amending bill would be a poor use of time. But the balance between what is contained in primary legislation, which can be examined in detail during the passage of a bill, and what is left for ministers to determine in much less scrutinised secondary legislation, is an important issue. We deal with delegated legislation in greater detail on pages 223 to 233, which also cover *regulatory reform orders, remedial orders* and *Church of England measures.*

Government bills

Origins

After a general election, the legislative programme is dominated by *bills reflecting commitments that the winning party has made in its manifesto* or, as happened in 2010, which are the subject of a coalition agreement between parties in the event of a hung parliament. Reversing the policy of the previous government on a key issue may also be a priority. During a government's term of office, its legislative programme will *reflect new and developing policies* as a result of changing circumstances, subjects moving up the general political agenda, or sometimes the personal priorities of a senior member of the Cabinet in his or her area of policy – although he or she will also need Cabinet support.

Financial bills are required both to raise revenue and to authorise how it is spent. The Finance Bill, introduced following the Budget, authorises taxation, as well as embodying the Chancellor of the Exchequer's proposals for tax changes; and Supply and Appropriation Bills authorise government spending.

Bills may be needed to *give effect to international commitments in domestic law,* such as the European Union (Amendment) Act 2008 to implement the Lisbon Treaty. In general, treaties are not required to be approved by legislation, but the Constitutional Reform and Governance Act 2010 put on a statutory footing the previous convention under which a treaty was laid before Parliament but the government did not proceed with ratification until 21 sitting days had elapsed. Under the new formal arrangements, the government lays a treaty before both Houses with an explanatory memorandum, and the Houses have 21 sitting days in which one or the other may resolve that the treaty should not be ratified. If necessary, there is then a subsequent stage in which a minister lays a statement of why the treaty should be ratified and can be prevented from doing so only by a further resolution against ratification within a further 21 sitting days.

Government bills may also *respond to events*. Fear about the potential for fraud in postal voting gave rise to the Electoral Administration Bill in 2005, and London's success in the competition to host the 2012 Olympic Games was followed by the Olympic Games and Paralympic Games Bill in 2005 to set up the Olympic Delivery Authority. In addition, most government departments will want what might be called *housekeeping bills*. These may or may not be substantial, are often not controversial in party political terms and are about keeping the business of government and public affairs up to date.

Also in the housekeeping category are consolidation bills, which set out the law on a particular subject in a clearer and more up-to-date form without changing its substance.

From proposal to bill

Political and day-to-day departmental pressures – to say nothing of the proposals from special interest groups for changes in the law – ensure that no government department is ever short of ideas for legislation. When those ideas have been formulated, a process of consultation begins, the length and detail of which depends on what sort of legislation is being considered and how quickly it is needed. Inside government, the Treasury will be consulted, as well as other departments with an interest, together with the devolved administrations in Scotland, Wales and Northern Ireland. Outside government, the views of pressure groups, public bodies, industries or trade unions affected will be sought.

The process of consulting outside government is covered by a Cabinet Office Code of Practice. Consultation documents are widely circulated and available on the Internet. Nevertheless, the process is sometimes open to criticism. Political pressures may mean that there is, in fact, little time for *effective* consultation. The process may sometimes focus too much on 'the usual suspects' – those organisations with a national profile – rather than opinion more widely. Consultation often has to be on the broad intentions of a proposal, but 'the devil is in the detail', and some important elements of a proposal may be decided only when the business of drafting begins. Finally – and crucially – there is no point in consulting if the opinions expressed are ignored and the government of the day steams ahead regardless.

These criticisms are met to a certain extent if legislation follows a Green Paper, where the government has sought views on various legislative options, or a White Paper, where is has made its intentions clear. Increasingly, though, the use of draft bills (see page 181), where a complete legislative proposal can be considered in detail before it begins its formal parliamentary stages, is seen as a way of allowing the widest consultation, as well as resulting in better legislation.

In due course, the sponsoring government department will have proposals to put before a policy committee of the Cabinet. This will often be done by correspondence, and only if disagreements arise or if major issues are at stake will the subject need to be discussed at a meeting of the committee itself. In 2014, there were 14 ministerial committees of the Cabinet, covering broad areas such as Public Expenditure and National Security, but also specific areas of current concern, such as Banking Reform, and Flooding.

But even if the relevant ministerial committee endorses a proposal, this does not mean immediate legislation. A minor change may have to wait until a more extensive bill in that subject area comes along. A major policy development, or a series of related proposals, may need a whole bill and so a place of its own in the government's legislative programme.

Parliamentary time is scarce, so further decisions need to be taken centrally about priorities and about balancing the programme of bills for each session of a parliament. This is the task of the Parliamentary Business and Legislation Cabinet Committee (PBL), which includes the Leaders and Government Chief Whips in both Houses. That committee recommends to the Cabinet what proposals will actually find a place in the next Queen's Speech. As the new session approaches, PBL will decide which bills will start in the Commons and which in the Lords, and which should be published in draft; and it makes an assessment of how much parliamentary time will be needed for each and any difficulties on the way – perhaps dissenting government backbenchers in the Commons, or a critical reaction in the Lords.

Meanwhile, those proposals that have been approved for the next session's programme have been moving from concept to detail. The sponsoring department prepares drafting instructions for parliamentary counsel. These instructions will set out what the bill needs to do but not the detail of how it will do it. This is the job of parliamentary counsel, an elite group of lawyers specialising in legislative drafting. Despite the name, they are servants of the government rather than of Parliament, and they draft all government primary legislation (secondary legislation is normally drafted by lawyers in the government department concerned).

In converting a department's instructions into a bill, parliamentary counsel have a number of tasks. They must achieve clarity and precision, not only so that the bill's provisions will be tightly defined, but also so that, once it is passed, the possibility of legal challenge is minimised. They must ensure that the bill fits with legislation already in existence – both the statute book of primary legislation and any relevant EU or delegated legislation. This may mean that the bill must amend or repeal provisions of UK legislation that may be scattered through a number of Acts of Parliament. Ministers will want them to draft the bill tightly to minimise the possibility of unwelcome amendments in either House being in order – a tough assignment when dealing with major bills with a broad scope. Finally, they must ensure that the provisions of the bill work – in terms of logic rather than political policy. To take a simple example, if you make something illegal you need to ensure that there is an appropriate penalty for doing it, and you also need to define what will constitute evidence that the offence has been committed. Small wonder that it is said to take seven years to acquire the skills needed to draft a medium-sized bill.

This process of turning instructions into drafting often throws up new questions of policy, and for most bills there will be a continuing dialogue between the sponsoring department and parliamentary counsel while the bill is being drafted. Even then the bill may go through several further drafts before it is finally approved by its sponsoring department and minister, agreed by PBL, and is ready to begin its parliamentary journey.

Just before it does so, the text must be submitted to the authorities of the House in which it is to start. In the Commons, the Clerk of Legislation ensures that the bill complies with the rules of the House; that its short title is appropriate and not misleading or sloganising; that everything in it is covered by the long title – the passage at the start of a bill that says that it is 'A Bill to . . .' and then lists its purposes; that any provisions that would require expenditure or would levy charges or taxes are identified (and are printed in italics); whether the Royal Prerogative is affected (in which case the Queen's or Prince of Wales's Consent will be required); whether any uncertainties exist as to what sort of amendments might be in order; and whether it conflicts with or duplicates a bill or part of a bill that has already been introduced. In the Lords, the Public Bill Office offers advice on the same range of issues, except on financial matters. Once these consultations are complete, the bill is ready for introduction.

Is a government bill really draft legislation?

Parliamentary and politics textbooks say that a bill is a draft Act of Parliament, but governments do not see it in that way. For each bill, there has been a lengthy process of development and debate between departments and ministers, the government has consulted those it feels have an interest, the contents of the bill have been minutely considered by officials and by parliamentary counsel, and the bill has been through a series of drafts.

So, by the time the bill reaches Parliament it is not so much draft legislation for discussion and amendment as word-for-word what the government of the day wants to see on the statute book. Moreover, ministers identify personally with major bills; 'their' bills are part of their political achievements as ministers, and significant amendment of a government bill – such as the major rewrite of the Health and Social Care Bill in 2011 – is seen as a loss of face.

The pressure of legislation

This might matter less if there were more time to consider legislation and the lead times were longer. However, governments of both parties are always in a hurry: to demonstrate their dynamism; to seek to deliver on commitments; and to put their stamp on key areas of policy. This means, in turn, that the machinery for preparing legislation is frequently overloaded. The result is that the consultation process is rushed or curtailed, too many large and complex bills are attempted in a session, policy is sometimes not settled well in advance of drafting (and sometimes it changes after introduction of a bill) and instructions from departments to parliamentary counsel are sometimes late.

This often leads to 'drafting on the hoof', when significant amendments to a bill are made not because of effective criticism inside or outside Parliament but in order to reflect the government's changing views. Some government amendments are brought forward to meet such criticism (and one of the strengths of a bicameral system is that it allows an undertaking to amend to be given in one House and the time to bring forward the amendment in the other House).

Although it is difficult, if not impossible, to be sure of the genesis of every amendment that a government puts down to one of its own bills, a large proportion is the result of second thoughts rather than a response to a measured critical process. To give examples of the general and the particular: in the 2010–12 session, 2,537 amendments were made to government bills in the Lords, and only 45 were forced upon the government by a vote. For the session 2012–13, the figures were 1,132 (of which 835 were to bills coming from the Commons) and 21. In the 2010–12 session, the government tabled at the Commons report stage of the Health and Social Care Bill some 1,100 amendments. To be fair, about 700 of these amendments simply changed the name of a type of body created by the bill ('commissioning consortia' became 'clinical commissioning groups'); but many of the others related to major matters of policy. This was presented as a measured response to a 'listening exercise' that had seen the Bill re-committed to a public bill committee, but the sheer number of amendments involved made the report stage unwieldy for everyone involved. It is worth noting also that drafting on the hoof has an additional perverse effect in that it occupies the time of parliamentary counsel, who could be working with a longer lead time on the next session's bills.

There has been pressure both from within and outside government to reduce the need for government amendments (especially late amendments), but the results have been patchy. One example of poor practice was the return of the Transparency of Lobbying, Non-Party Campaigning and Trade Union Administration Bill, considered in the Commons on 22 January 2014 having been considered by the Lords the previous day, with 116 amendments occupying 17 pages of text.

Programming and guillotines

In the Lords, the intervals between the different stages of the passage of a Bill are prescribed by a recommendation of the Procedure Committee in 1977: two weekends between introduction of a bill and second reading, 14 days between second reading and committee, 14 days between committee and report for large and complex bills, and 3 sitting days between report and third reading. Intervals in the Commons are governed by practice and a degree of negotiation between the two sides but are usually much shorter than in the Lords. The 1985 Commons Procedure Committee recommendation for two weekends between introduction and second reading, and ten days between both second reading and committee, and committee and report, was never adopted.

Bills may need little – or sometimes no – debating time if they are narrow and technical, or if they command support on all sides (although all-party agreement may not make for good legislation, as was shown by the oft-quoted cases of the Dangerous Dogs Act 1991 and especially the Child Support Act 1991). However, for most bills there is pressure, both from the opposition and from government backbenchers, for more debating time than the government is prepared to concede. The purposes and motives of such debate are varied: to set out a contrary political position; to seek explanation and clarification from the government; to explore and criticise the details of the legislation and its likely effects, and to make alternative proposals; and, in the case of the more contentious bills, to make opposition clear, and to inconvenience the government, by delaying the bill.

There are various ways in which debate may be limited. We have already looked at the closure (see page 141), where, after what in the view of the Chair is a reasonable period of discussion, the use of the government's majority can bring debate to an end and have the particular question before the House at the time put; but this is of little practical use to the government where legislation is concerned. A more draconian power was introduced into the Commons in the nineteenth century following the disruption of proceedings over several sessions by Irish MPs campaigning for Home Rule. It was generally recognised that the rights of the majority needed to be preserved and, despite considerable reservations at the time, the *guillotine* or *allocation of time order* was introduced. In essence, this allows the House to agree, at any stage in proceedings on a bill, strict time limits for the remainder of its progress. A timetable is set out in a motion that is put to the House. If it is agreed, then delaying tactics are of no use; committee and report stages come to an end after a fixed period whether all amendments selected by the Chair have been discussed or not, and sometimes with many clauses of a bill not having been debated at all.

At one time, guillotines were considered wholly exceptional and could arouse outrage both inside and outside the House. The procedure was used just over 70 times in the 90 years 1881–1970. However, from the late 1970s its use increased under governments of both parties, and it was routine for three or four, or more, bills to be guillotined in each session. The highest numbers were in 1988–89 (10 guillotines out of 37 government bills passed), 1998–99 (11 out of 27) and 1999–2000 (13 out of 39).

In 1985, the Procedure Committee argued that the weapon of delay probably does nothing to change a government's mind, and that the guillotine response usually meant patchy scrutiny. It recommended that for controversial bills (those likely to need more than 25 hours in what were then known as 'standing committees') there should be a timetable agreed by a Legislative Business Committee on which all parties were represented, which would allocate time in committee and on report to reflect the importance of different parts of the bill. This proposal had a good deal of support on the backbenches but not on the frontbenches, and in February 1986 it was defeated in the House by 231 to 166. The Jopling Committee (see page 132) returned to this in 1992 and endorsed the earlier approach. In the event, this was introduced in an informal way, with some timetabling agreed through the usual channels and guillotines avoided whenever possible (and, indeed, from 1994 to 1997 there were only six guillotines).

In 1997, the newly established Modernisation Committee returned to the issue. It recommended a halfway house between informal agreement and guillotine, to be known as *programming*. When a bill was selected for programming, there should be discussions that would take account of representations from all sides of the House, including backbenchers. In the light of those discussions, the government would move an amendable motion immediately after second reading specifying the type of committee to which the bill should be sent and the day by which it should be reported. The committee would then decide how to use that time.

A *programme order* differs from a guillotine in that it is imposed on proceedings on a bill immediately after second reading rather than later, when the speed of progress (or extent of delay) is known, and, if taken immediately after second reading, is not debatable (guillotines are debatable for three hours). And, as noted above, unlike a guillotine it specifies the type of committee to which the bill should be sent. The programme order may be amended later; for example, if the opposition persuades the government to provide more time.

When under a programme order the time allotted for part of a bill expires, only certain specified questions may be put to the public bill committee or the House: in particular, on the amendment already under discussion, on any amendment selected by the Chair for a separate vote (in practice, amendments already debated on which the opposition parties particularly want to register their position); thereafter, government amendments and new clauses may be taken en bloc.

When a programme order applies to proceedings in public bill committee, the number of sittings and allocation of time is proposed by a sub-committee comprising the chair of the committee and seven of its members. The sub-committee's resolution may be debated by the committee for half an hour (and may be amended). A public bill committee can also make proposals to the House for changes in the date for reporting a bill, or in the programming of the report stage and third reading.

Following its introduction early in the 1997 parliament, programming has operated on a fairly consensual basis, even when applied to controversial bills such as the devolution measures. Though it has on occasion been bitterly disputed, it has become an established, even (as the Procedure Committee put it in 2013) a 'broadly accepted' part of the Commons legislative world.

Where it does continue to be criticised is when the knives of a programme order fall and large parts of a bill, and many proposed amendments, are undebated (just as with a guillotine). The fact that this has caused particular problems at report stage has been commented on in reports by various House committees, most recently the Procedure Committee in 2013. In the 2013–14 session, when 26 bills were subject to programming, 20 groups of amendments went undebated in this way.

It is worth noting that although programming offers the prospect of more effective use of time, it can do nothing to increase the total time available; neither in itself can it reduce the pressure of the government's legislative programme. One way of improving scrutiny – and perhaps of saving time in the long run – might be the use of draft bills.

Draft bills and 'pre-legislative scrutiny'

It was the case for many years before the introduction of public bill committees – and remains the case today – that a bill may be sent to a select committee for detailed examination after second reading. The select committee format has several advantages. The committee is not just a debating forum but can take oral and written evidence, involving many more people in a formal process of consultation and making the legislative process more accessible to those outside Parliament. A select committee has to return to the House the text of a bill just as a public bill committee (see page 188) does, but unlike a public bill committee it can also report its views and the reasons for its decisions. Even on highly contentious issues, select committees have a long history of operating in a consensual rather than an adversarial way, which is likely to make for more effective scrutiny of legislation.

Scrutiny of bills *in draft* by select committees (or joint committees of both Houses) goes several steps further. A draft bill has not begun its formal parliamentary progress, and it really is draft legislation in a way that a bill, once introduced, is not. Ministers have invested less political capital in it, and changes will not necessarily be seen as defeats. The Liaison Committee, consisting of the chairs of all select committees, described the scrutiny of bills in draft as 'a development of great significance. It offers the prospect of properly examined, better thought out and so higher quality legislation'.

The numbers of draft bills each session is on what seems to be an upward trend: rising from three, four and nine in the sessions 2005–06, 2006–07 and 2007–08, respectively, to 11 in the admittedly long 2010–12 session, an impressive 14 in the session 2012–13, then falling back a little to six in 2013–14. So, the numbers are going up, but they need to be seen against a background of typically more than 20 government bills in most sessions.

However, draft bills are not a panacea – at least, not for governments. They add to the time before a proposal passes into law (and circumstances may change during that time); they tie up more resources in the preparation and drafting of bills, as substantial changes may be needed in the bills eventually introduced; and, as there is the opportunity for criticism well-supported by argument and evidence, they may make it harder for the government of the day to get its way. However, unless a way is found of slackening the *overall* pressure on a government's legislative programme, the contribution that draft bills can make may be limited.

For pre-legislative scrutiny to work, it must be allowed enough time. We now follow the passage of a government bill (formally introduced into the Commons and not a draft bill) through Parliament. A chart showing the stages of legislation in the two Houses is overleaf.

Anatomy of a bill

Part of the Local Audit and Acountability Bill [*Lords*] of the 2013–14 session is reproduced on pages 183 to 185 and shows some of the main features of any bill.

House of Commons		Timing
First Reading	• Formal reading out of title by the Clerk at the Table. • Ordered to be printed.	
Second Reading	• Main opportunity to debate the principle of the Bill. A 'reasoned amendment' may be tabled. A division at this stage represents a direct challenge to the principle of the Bill. • After Second Reading, Government Bills are usually timetabled by Programme Motions which, amongst other things, set an end-date for the committee stage.	Usually two weekends after First Reading.
Committee Stage	• Chance to consider and vote on the detail, line by line. • Amendments selected and grouped by the Clerk under the authority of the Chair. All Bills go to one of three Committee types: (i) Committee of the whole House — for "constitutional" and some other bills, and parts of the Finance Bill; (ii) Public Bill Committee — most usual procedure; 16–50 Members, in proportion to overall party strengths. One or two days of oral evidence in select committee mode is followed by more formal debate on amendments as the committee goes through the bill 'line-by-line'. (iii) Select Committee - infrequently used.	Usually starts shortly after Second Reading and can take anything from one meeting to two per week for some months.
Report Stage	• A further chance to consider amendments, new clauses and for MPs, not on the Committee, to propose changes.	Usually shortly after Committee Stage.
Third Reading	• Final chance to debate the Bill, as amended at previous stages. • A vote gives chance to show dissatisfaction with amended Bill. • The Bill now goes to the Lords.	Usually immediately after Report Stage on the same day.
House of Lords		
First Reading	▪ Formal. ▪ The Bill is reprinted in the form finally agreed by the Commons.	No significant delay in the transfer of a Bill between the two Houses.
Second Reading	• Debate on general principles of the Bill. • Government Bills included in the election manifesto are, by convention, not opposed at their Second Reading, but 'reasoned amendments' may be tabled as a means of indicating dissent and can be voted on.	Two weekends must elapse after First Reading.
Committee Stage	• Bills usually go to a Committee of the Whole House or Grand Committee away from the Chamber and rarely to other types of committee. • Detailed line by line examination. • Unlike the Commons: (i) no selection of amendments – all can be considered, and (ii) no timetabling; and debate of amendments is unrestricted.	Usually starts at least 14 days after Second Reading, often taking place over several days.
Report Stage	• Further chance to amend the Bill. • May take place over several days.	Usually starts at least 14 days after the end of Committee Stage.
Third Reading and Passing	• Unlike in the Commons, amendments can be made provided the issue has not been voted on at an earlier stage. • Passing: the final opportunity for peers to comment and vote on Bill.	Usually at least three sitting days after the end of Report Stage.

The stages in the passing of a public bill

Source: Copyright House of Commons, 2014

Every bill has a *short title*, which is the title by which it is known during its passage and which will normally be the same as the title of the Act that will result. Also on the cover page of the bill will be a statement by the relevant minister as to whether the provisions of the bill are compatible with the European Convention on Human Rights. After the cover page will be a list of contents, if the bill is long enough to need one. At the start of the bill is the *long title*, which sets out the contents of the bill; all the provisions of the bill must fall within the long title. This is followed by the words of enactment: 'Be it enacted by the Queen's Most Excellent Majesty'.

Clauses are the basic units of a bill; they are divided into *subsections, paragraphs and sub-paragraphs.* This particular bill contained 47 clauses, but a long bill may contain 100 to 500 clauses or more and be divided up into several *parts* (which, in turn, may be divided into *chapters*). When a bill becomes an Act, the clauses become known as *sections.* To reduce complexity, the *schedules* to a bill fill in some of the fine detail (for example, one of the schedules will usually list amendments and repeals affecting existing legislation). A schedule is always dependent on the clause that introduces it and has no effect unless the clause is agreed to. Any provisions that would cost public money (other than routine administration by the government department concerned), or that would impose taxes or levy a charge, are printed in italics in bills introduced in the Commons, although sometimes a single 'sink' clause will cover all the expenditure implied by the bill.

Local Audit and Accountability Bill [HL]

EXPLANATORY NOTES

Explanatory notes to the Bill, prepared by the Department for Communities and Local Government, are published separately as HL Bill 4 – EN.

EUROPEAN CONVENTION ON HUMAN RIGHTS

Baroness Hanham has made the following statement under section 19(1)(a) of the Human Rights Act 1998:

In my view the provisions of the Local Audit and Accountability Bill [HL] are compatible with the Convention rights.

Typical front page of a Bill

Source: Copyright House of Commons, 2014

A

BILL

TO

Make provision for and in connection with the abolition of the Audit Commission for Local Authorities and the National Health Service in England; to make provision about the accounts of local and certain other public authorities and the auditing of those accounts; to make provision about the appointment, functions and regulation of local auditors; to make provision about data matching; to make provision about examinations by the Comptroller and Auditor General relating to English local and other public authorities; to make provision about the publication of information by smaller authorities; to make provision for directions to comply with codes of practice on local authority publicity; to make provision about council tax referendums; and for connected purposes.

B E IT ENACTED by the Queen's most Excellent Majesty, by and with the advice and consent of the Lords Spiritual and Temporal, and Commons, in this present Parliament assembled, and by the authority of the same, as follows:—

PART 1

ABOLITION OF EXISTING AUDIT REGIME

1   Abolition of existing audit regime

(1)   The Audit Commission ceases to exist.

(2)   The Audit Commission Act 1998 is repealed.   5

(3)   Schedule 1 (abolition of Audit Commission: supplementary provision) has effect.

(4)   In that Schedule—
   (a)   Part 1 makes some arrangements in connection with the abolition of the Audit Commission, and   10
   (b)   Part 2 contains consequential repeals and revocations of Acts and instruments that amend the Audit Commission Act 1998.

Typical first substantive page of a Bill

Source: House of Lords, 2014

Local Audit and Accountability Bill [HL]

A

BILL

To make provision for and in connection with the abolition of the Audit Commission for Local Authorities and the National Health Service in England; to make provision about the accounts of local and certain other public authorities and the auditing of those accounts; to make provision about the appointment, functions and regulation of local auditors; to make provision about data matching; to make provision about examinations by the Comptroller and Auditor General relating to English local and other public authorities; to make provision about the publication of information by smaller authorities; to make provision for directions to comply with codes of practice on local authority publicity; to make provision about council tax referendums; and for connected purposes.

Baroness Hanham

Ordered to be Printed, 9th May 2013

PUBLISHED BY AUTHORITY OF THE HOUSE OF LORDS
LONDON — THE STATIONERY OFFICE LIMITED
Printed in the United Kingdom by
The Stationery Office Limited

HL Bill 4   55/3

Typical back page of a Bill: The Local Audit and Accountability Bill [*Lords*] passed by Parliament in January 2014

Source: House of Lords, 2014

The last page of the bill is the *backsheet*, which repeats the long and short titles, gives the bill number and the session it was introduced, and lists the MP introducing the bill (the 'member in charge') and his or her 'supporters'. For a government bill, the member in charge will be the secretary of state heading the relevant department, and the supporters will be senior ministers with an interest in the subject matter.

Explanatory Notes are a separate document that accompanies a bill. They set out the bill's intention and background, explain the clauses in non-legal language and give an assessment of the bill's resource implications and its impact on businesses (for example, if a bill were to introduce a new system of regulation or licensing). They must be in neutral terms, objectively explaining the bill and not making a case for it.

Commons stages

Introduction and first reading

The most usual method of introducing a bill is by the member in charge giving notice of the bill's long and short titles, and of the intention to introduce it on a particular day. This notice appears on the Order Paper for that day, the MP is called by the Speaker at the commencement of public business (see page 140) and brings the so-called 'dummy bill' (merely a sheet of paper with the short and long titles and the names of up to 12 supporters) to the Clerk of the House at the Table. (In the case of a government bill, a dummy bill is not brought to the Table: it is already there.)

The Clerk reads out the short title and the Speaker says 'Second reading what day?' For all government bills the response is 'tomorrow' (or the next sitting day if there is a break for a weekend or recess) as the government can bring any of its bills forward on any sitting day. For a private member's bill, however, naming a day can be a matter for careful tactics (see page 201).

The bill is now said to have been read the first time; it is recorded in the Votes and Proceedings as having been ordered to be printed and to be read a second time on whichever day has been named. A bill introduced in this way is known as a *presentation bill*; bills may also come before the House by being *brought from the Lords*, by being *brought in upon a resolution* (the Finance Bill is founded upon the resolutions agreed by the House to give effect to the Chancellor's Budget proposals) or when an MP gets *leave to bring in a ten-minute rule bill*.

Second reading

This is the first time the bill itself is debated, and it is a discussion of the principle of the bill rather than the details of individual clauses. In the Commons, it is considered good practice for second reading to be delayed until at least two weekends have passed since the bill's introduction (although, if the bill has not been seen before in draft, even this does not give much time to assess it). The government does not always comply with the 'two weekends' convention; neither, less importantly, do backbenchers with private members' bills. In the Lords, the requirements are more formal.

A second reading debate on a major government bill will normally take a day (in practice, about six hours; on a Wednesday, for example, from about 1.00 p.m. to 7.00 p.m.). Less important bills will get less time, and wholly uncontroversial measures (including some private members' bills) can receive their second reading 'on the nod' – that is, without any debate at all. It is also possible – but very unusual – for uncontroversial bills to be referred either to a *second reading committee* 'upstairs' or, in the case of a bill relating to Wales, second reading may be taken in the Welsh Grand Committee. The Scottish and Northern Ireland Grand Committees may in theory consider bills in relation to their principle, but following devolution this is now much less likely. Second reading committees are also used for bills prepared by the Law Commissions; but these are usually technical reworkings of the law and will normally have started in the Lords and have been considered by a select committee there.

Some major bills have, in the past, had lengthy second reading debates on the floor of the House. In 1972, the bill to enable the United Kingdom to join the then EEC was debated over three days on second reading, and the 1976 bill on Scottish and Welsh devolution (which eventually failed) was debated for 32 hours over four sitting days.

A second reading debate on a government bill takes place on a motion moved by a minister 'That the bill be now read a second time'. At the end of this debate, on bills that are opposed, a vote is taken. This can be a straight vote against second reading, or a vote on what is known as a 'reasoned amendment' (if it has been selected by the Speaker). This spells out the reasons why the bill's opponents do not wish it to have a second reading. If the reasoned amendment is carried, or the House votes against second reading, the bill can go no further – neither can exactly the same bill be reintroduced in the same session. It is extremely rare for a government bill to be defeated on second reading; the last example was in 1986, when the Shops Bill, which had been intended to relax the law on Sunday trading, was passed by the Lords but defeated in the Commons by a majority of 14. However, as we saw in Chapter 4, voting against the second reading of a controversial bill may be a powerful way for government backbenchers to register dissent.

These days, the second reading of a bill will normally be followed immediately by a *programme motion*, which is decided without debate (although sometimes with a vote), followed if necessary by a motion to authorise government expenditure in relation to the bill (a *money resolution*), or the raising of a tax or charge (a *ways and means resolution*). These also give the committee on the bill authority to consider provisions that would require expenditure or impose a tax.

'Fast-track' bills

Certain types of bill are dealt with on a 'fast-track' procedure. *Consolidation bills* are prepared by the Law Commissions as a sort of housekeeping of the statute book. These bills draw together the law on a particular subject, which may be in a series of Acts of Parliament, and present it in a more logical and user-friendly way. *Statute law repeal bills* remove parts of the law that have become redundant. Bills of both sorts are checked by a joint committee of both Houses to ensure that no change of substance has been made in the process of restating the law, and that no 'live' legislation is to be repealed. If no amendments are put down, such bills are passed without debate. *Supply and Appropriation Bills*, which authorise government spending, have no committee or report stage; the questions on second and third reading are put successively without debate.

Committee

As soon as a bill has had its second reading, it is sent to a committee for a detailed examination of the text. The choices are *public bill committee*, *Committee of the whole House* or *select committee*. The Finance Bill is routinely divided between Committee of the whole House for its most important provisions and a public bill committee for the rest, and other bills are occasionally treated in the same way. As public bill committees are the default setting – if no other decision is taken, a bill goes automatically to a public bill committee – we start with this method of consideration.

Public bill committees

In November 2006, the House of Commons approved changes recommended by the Modernisation Committee. 'Standing' committees (a misleading name because they were not permanent) were renamed 'public bill committees'. New members, and a new chair or chairs, are appointed to a public bill committee specifically for each bill; and, when the committee has reported the bill back to the House, it is dissolved. At the same time, the Modernisation Committee also proposed that public bill committees should be empowered to receive oral and written evidence, in addition to line-by-line consideration, thereby taking on many of the features of what were called 'special standing committees' (which had been used very rarely since their invention in 1981, and were abolished as part of the reforms). For the 26 bills considered in public bill committee in the 2013–14 session, there were 195 consideration sittings, 34 oral evidence sessions and 383 written submissions. Government bills starting in the Lords do not have an oral evidence-taking stage, although this is purely government practice rather than a procedural restriction.

Membership

A public bill committee must have between 16 and 50 members but, in practice, the membership is usually between 16 and 30. Its members are chosen by the Committee of Selection, which includes whips of the three main parties. Membership of a public bill committee reflects the party proportions in the House as closely as possible. Where there was a free vote on second reading (as on the Hunting Bill in the 2002–03 session), the membership reflects the numbers of supporters and opponents in the House on the second reading vote. The Committee of Selection appoints members directly to a public bill committee; the names do not have to be approved by the House, unlike the membership of select committees.

At least one government minister will always be a member of a public bill committee (including public bill committees on private members' bills), together with a government whip, and frontbenchers from the other parties. The backbenchers are a combination of those who are interested in the subject (and who spoke in the second reading debate) and those who are drafted in by the whips but are ready loyally to support their party's line on the subject. Obviously, the strength of the second group becomes more important when very contentious legislation is being considered, but the Committee of Selection has generally appointed a spread of MPs, so that dissent within a party is represented as well.

The Law Officers (Attorney General, Advocate General and Solicitor-General) may, if they are members of the Commons, attend a public bill committee and speak (but not vote), although this is in practice very rare. Any minister may do the same in the committee on the Finance Bill but, in practice, this is handled by Treasury ministers. Other MPs not appointed to a committee on a bill may not take part in its proceedings (although they may table amendments – see page 190).

The Chair

Each public bill committee is chaired by a member of the Panel of Chairs. The Panel is a group of thirty to thirty-five senior MPs chosen by the Speaker to chair public bill and other general committees. It also includes the Deputy Speakers (and is itself chaired by the Chairman of Ways and Means), thus connecting the business of chairmanship in the House with that of public bill and general committees. The Panel meets from time to time as a committee to consider wider issues affecting general and public bill committees (for example, whether MPs should be allowed to use laptops, or drink coffee and tea, in committee), and also matters relating to Westminster Hall. Since November 2005, public bill committee chairs have been paid a salary depending on their experience on the Panel: from £2,970 per annum for under one year's service to £14,876 per annum for those with more than five years' service.

If a public bill committee is taking a big bill, there will normally be two or more chairs sharing the duties. The chair has most of the powers to control proceedings that the Speaker has in the House, including power to select amendments (see page 191), but not including the disciplinary powers listed on page 46. As in the House, he or she does not vote unless there is a tie, and then strictly according to precedent (see page 49). And an MP who has chaired the public bill committee does not take part, or vote, in the bill's subsequent stages on the floor of the House.

Meetings

For any initial oral evidence sessions, public bill committees meet in a select committee room, with the typical horseshoe arrangement. When they proceed to the line-by-line consideration stage, they move to rooms laid out in very much the same way as the Chamber, with the two sides facing each other across the floor. The chair sits on the dais at one end, with the clerk on his or her left (see the plan on page 192).

Meetings of public bill committees are open to the public and, as in the House, debates are webcast and recorded verbatim by *The Official Report* (*Hansard*) and published on the parliamentary website. Public bill committees may meet on any day on which the House sits, but committees on government bills normally meet on Tuesdays from 8.55 a.m. to 11.25 a.m., resuming at 2.30 p.m., and on Thursdays from 11.30 a.m. to 1.00 p.m., breaking for lunch and resuming at 2.00 p.m. Depending on how keen the government is to make progress with the bill, and how contentious it is, the committee may then go into the evening.

The normal first business of a public bill committee is to consider the resolution of the *programming sub-committee* (the chair of the committee and seven members), which makes proposals about the witnesses who will be giving oral evidence and, sometimes, the time to be allotted to the various parts of the bill and the order in which parts of the bill are to be taken.

Amendments, selection and grouping

Once any oral evidence sessions have been concluded, the committee deals with the clauses of the bill one by one. Any MP may put down an amendment to a bill in public bill committee (or an entire new clause or schedule), but only a member of the committee may actually move it. MPs may supply brief factual explanatory notes for publication with their amendments (and this may also be done at report stage).

Amendments can serve a variety of purposes. If the bill is highly contentious in party political terms, many amendments will be pegs for debate to give publicity to government and opposition viewpoints – although this is more the case in Committee of the whole House (see page 196) as public bill committees get little media coverage. So-called 'probing amendments' are used to get the minister to clarify provisions of the bill and outline the thinking behind them. However, for the reasons we have seen, it is extremely unlikely that the opposition will table an amendment, convince the government of its merits and have it agreed to.

The chair of a public bill committee, like the Speaker in the House or the Chairman of Ways and Means in Committee of the whole House, has the power of *selection and grouping* (which does not exist in the House of Lords). This is crucial in allowing an orderly and logical debate on amendments, and it also prevents the proceedings of the committee being clogged up by hosts of amendments being tabled for their own sake.

Amendments are tabled on the days before the committee first meets (usually, at this stage by the opposition parties and possibly government backbenchers but, as we have seen, the government may even at this stage want to modify its own bill, and amendments may go down in the name of the minister in charge of the bill).

The day after they are tabled, amendments will appear on blue paper in the Vote bundle (see page 151); but, on the day the committee first meets, it will have before it a *marshalled list*, printed on white paper, of all the amendments that have been put down up to and including the previous day. This list of amendments is the committee's order paper.

The marshalled list sets amendments down by reference to where they apply to the bill. As each amendment is tabled, it is given its own unique reference number, so the numbering will jump about: for example, if the very first amendment tabled was to the last schedule, it will still be 1; and if, after 500 amendments have been tabled, an amendment is put down to the first line of the bill, it will be 501.

The process of selection and grouping, in which the chair is advised by the clerk of the committee, begins with weeding out amendments that are *out of order*. Disorderly amendments include those that are irrelevant or outside the scope of the bill (or of the clause to which they are tabled); inconsistent with a decision that the committee has already taken (or that the House has taken in approving second reading – so-called 'wrecking' amendments); ineffective or incomplete; tabled to the wrong place in the bill, or to a part of the bill that the committee has already considered; 'vague, trifling or tendered in a spirit of mockery'; or that would impose charges outside the scope of any money or ways and means resolutions agreed to by the House. These rules are sometimes quite complex in their application, but they are a common-sense way of clearing out amendments that are irrelevant or ineffective (although an MP whose pet amendment is ruled out of order may not always see it in that way).

Then begins the process of *selecting* from among the remaining amendments those that will be debated. Selection in public bill committee is fairly generous (at report stage, it is less so), and unless an amendment is fairly trivial, or one of a multiplicity on the same point, it is likely to be selected. Amendments proposed by the member in charge of a bill, whether a minister or a private member, are normally selected automatically provided they are in order. An amendment that has been tabled the previous day or the day before that, rather than the minimum three days in advance, will usually not be selected, although the chair has power even to select a 'manu-script' amendment put forward within the previous few minutes if the circumstances warrant it.

At the same time, the chair and clerk will be looking for themes that will help to *group* amendments. There are three main ways of doing this: the first is to group amendments that offer *alternative proposals on the same point*. An example might be where the bill proposes that a search can be authorised by any police officer. The opposition think that this is not stringent enough and so have put down an amendment that would require the authorising officer to be of the rank of inspector. Backbenchers on the committee (on both sides) would prefer to go further, and amendments are down variously specifying a superintendent, a magistrate and a High Court judge. If the 'inspector' amendment were selected on its own, the debate would take place only on the issue of whether the minimum authority should be constable or inspector. Separate debates would have to take place on the other proposals – and

1 CHAIR
2 CLERK
3 *HANSARD* SUB-EDITOR
4 CIVIL SERVANTS
5 MINISTER(S)
6 OPPOSITION FRONT-BENCH SPOKESPERSON
7 THIRD PARTY SPOKESPERSON
8 GOVERNMENT BACK-BENCHES
9 OPPOSITION BACK-BENCHES
10 PRESS
11 PUBLIC

Layout of a Public Bill Committee room

Source: Copyright House of Commons, 2014

if the 'inspector' amendment were to be agreed to, then that would rule out debate on any alternative as being inconsistent with the decision the committee had reached. So all the amendments about the level of authorisation are grouped.

The second method is to group *interdependent amendments*. An example here might be where the opposition has an amendment early in the bill to appoint a statutory investigator of complaints. It has a raft of other amendments throughout the bill that specify how different types of case will come to this investigator. If the principle of appointing an investigator is defeated early on, all the later amendments will fall, so it is sensible to debate them together.

The third method is to group *amendments on a theme*. For example, there might be a number of amendments designed to require the secretary of state to make a regulatory impact assessment before using any of a number of powers that the bill would confer. Grouping these together allows a debate on the principle of requiring such an assessment. If the amendments were not so grouped, the result would be a series of very similar debates as the committee got to each of the clauses that would give the secretary of state each of those powers.

The result of this is a *selection list*, a new edition of which appears for each sitting day. The chair gives no reasons for his or her decisions on selection, and there is no appeal to the Speaker. Two examples of selection lists appear on pages 194 and 195: one for the first day of a public bill committee's consideration of a bill; and one for part of the report stage of a bill in the House. Both of these proceedings were programmed.

How the committee goes through the bill

Once the recommendations of the programming sub-committee have been considered and any oral evidence sessions have been held, the committee begins with the first clause of the bill. Let us suppose that the first amendment in the first group – *the lead amendment* in that group – is to Clause 1. That amendment is moved, and the debate on the question 'That the amendment be made' then includes debate on any other amendment (or new clause) that is grouped with it. At the end of the debate the question is decided, on a vote if necessary: after a short interval, the doors of the committee room are locked, the clerk rises and reads out the names of members of the committee. MPs say 'Aye' or 'No' or 'No vote'; the clerk totals the votes and hands the list to the chair. He or she declares the result, says 'unlock' and moves on to the next question to be decided.

If a second group has its lead amendment to Clause 1, that group will be dealt with in the same way. But if not, the chair proposes the question 'That Clause 1 stand part of the bill'. This gives the opportunity of a 'stand part debate' on the clause as a whole. If debate on a number of amendments to a clause has covered the ground, the chair can decide to put the question on clause stand part without further debate.

An important feature of this way of going through a bill – and one that often causes confusion – is that the *amendments are decided not in the order in which they are grouped for debate but in the order in which they apply to the bill*. This can mean

---

TUESDAY 19 NOVEMBER 2013
LOCAL AUDIT AND ACCOUNTABILITY BILL [*LORDS*]

Chairs' provisional selection of amendments

Schedule 8
141 + Gov 48 + Gov 51

Clause 29

Clause 30

Clause 31
142

Clause 32

Schedule 9
Gov 53 + Gov 104 + Gov 54 + 143

Clause 33

Schedule 10
Gov 55 + Gov 56 + Gov 57 + Gov 105 + Gov 58 + Gov 59 + Gov 60 + Gov 61

Clause 34

Clause 35

Schedule 11
144 + 145

Clause 36

Clause 37

Clause 38
146 + 147 + 148

Clause 39
149

Clause 40
Gov 130 + Gov 134 + Gov NC 4 + Gov 135
150

Clause 41

Clause 42

Schedule 12
Gov 66 + Gov 67 + Gov 68 + Gov 131 + Gov 106 + Gov 132 + Gov 107 + Gov 133 + Gov 108 + Gov 109 + Gov 110 + Gov 111 + Gov 69 + Gov 112 + Gov 113 + Gov 70

Clause 43
151

Clause 44

Schedule 13

Clause 45

Clause 46

Clause 47
71

New Clauses
NC2
NC3
Gov NC 5 + Gov 136

New Schedules

Remaining proceedings on the Bill

Proceedings to be concluded by 5pm on Thursday 21 November

Mr Mike Weir

Sir Edward Leigh

A typical selection list for a Commons public bill committee considering a bill under a programme order

Source: The House of Commons 2014

LOCAL AUDIT AND ACCOUNTABILITY BILL
Consideration of Bill: Tuesday 17 December 2013
The Speaker's provisional selection of amendments

Audit and accountability of local authorities
NC1 + NC2 + NC4 + NC5 + NC6 + Gov 1 + 13 + Gov 2 + Gov 3 + 12 + Gov 4 + Gov 5

Code of practice on local authority publicity
14 + 15 + 16

Council tax referendums
17 + Gov 6 + Gov 7 + Gov 8 + 18 + Gov 9 + Gov 10 + Gov 11

6.00 pm

17 December 2013   By order of the Speaker

A typical selection list for the report stage of a bill in the House of Commons under a programme order
Source: The House of Commons 2014

that an amendment to a clause near the end of the bill may be debated with the first group at the first sitting; but it will be put to the vote only when the committee gets to that clause, which may be after many hours of consideration. If amendments have already been debated (unless they are in the name of the member in charge of the bill), they are often passed over in silence when they are reached. But if the opposition or a backbencher wants a vote – a separate division – and the chair agrees, a vote on a specific amendment may take place, but without further debate. Government amendments that are reached in this way are called formally whether or not a vote is expected; the minister says 'I beg to move' and the question on the amendment is put to the committee.

If no lead amendment is down to any clause, the committee must nevertheless agree whether or not the clause should stand part of the bill. When the committee has got to the end of the bill, any new clauses and new schedules (and any amendments to them) are decided upon (and debated, if they have not been grouped with earlier amendments).

When the committee has completed its consideration of a bill, the formal report of the bill appears in the Votes and Proceedings for that day, and the bill – if it has been amended – is reprinted for the *report stage* (see page 198). The process of going through the bill may have taken only a few minutes at a single sitting, or it may have taken 100 hours of often fierce debate over 20 or 30 sittings in the space of several weeks.

Scrutiny by debate and amendment: how useful is it?

Richard Crossman, Labour Leader of the House in the 1960s, wrote 'The whole procedure of standing committees is insane . . . under the present system there is no genuine committee work, just formal speech-making, mostly from written briefs'. Consideration in what are now public bill committees occupies a great deal of time: in the sessions 2010–12 to 2013–14, public bill committees held a total of 690 sittings, and it is reasonable to ask how good a use of the time of the MPs involved this was, and how effectively the legislation was scrutinised.

Unlike select committees, public bill committees have no research or staff resources of their own (the main concern of the clerk of a public bill committee is the conduct of the proceedings, not the merits of the bill – though, alongside departmental select committee staff and the Scrutiny Unit, they prepare a brief for oral evidence sessions). Other than this, MPs have to rely on input from outside pressure groups (which are naturally often advocacy for a particular point of view). However, the minister taking a bill through public bill committee has the support of the 'bill team' of civil servants, and behind them the substantial resources of his or her own department.

It is rare for the government to accept opposition (or individual backbench) amendments in public bill committee, although a 2013 study by the Constitution Unit concluded that many ideas raised at this stage go on to be debated at later stages in both Commons and Lords, and often result in government concessionary amendments. But however attractive measured, non-partisan scrutiny may be, one should not lose sight of the role of the Commons as a place where political ideologies clash and where deep divisions between parties (often reflecting different views in the country at large) are played out in an adversarial way.

Committees of the whole House

At one time, almost all bills were considered in Committee of the whole House. As its name suggests, it consists of all MPs (although only a relatively small proportion of those will be present during its proceedings) and takes place in the Chamber during part of a normal sitting of the House. The only evident differences are that it is presided over by the Chairman of Ways and Means and his deputies and not by the Speaker, that the Chairman sits not in the upper Chair but at the Table in the place of the Clerk of the House (who is absent when the House is in Committee), alongside the Clerk at the Table, and that the Mace is placed on brackets below the Table rather than on it. Votes are taken in the same way as in the House.

The manner of going through a bill is similar to that in public bill committee; and, as in committee, an MP may speak more than once in any debate. Selection and grouping of amendments is the responsibility of the Chairman of Ways and Means.

In recent years, Committees of the whole House have been confined to three types of bill. For convenience, *uncontroversial bills* (for which there would be no point in setting up a separate sitting of a public bill committee) are considered in this way to save time. Also taken in Committee of the whole House are *bills of great urgency* that need to become law quickly, such as, in April 2006, the Northern Ireland Bill to pave the way for the restoration of the Northern Ireland Assembly.

The third category is of major *bills of first-class constitutional importance*. Since 1945, governments have been committed to having such bills dealt with in this way, but there is no formal definition, and whether a bill does or does not fall into this category can be a matter of political argument. Legislation to incorporate EU treaties into domestic law, to devolve powers to Scotland and Wales, or to reform the House of Lords clearly qualifies. In the 2013–14 session, the Transparency of Lobbying Non-Party Campaigning and Trade Union Administration Bill, the Wales Bill, parts of the Finance (No. 2) Bill and two other bills were taken in Committee of the whole House at a total of nine sittings.

It may thus be a matter of argument (or negotiation) as to what measures are treated in this way. The opposition will want time on the floor of the House and the higher profile of Committee of the whole House, but the government business managers will generally be reluctant, not only to take floor time on a bill they feel could be dealt with in public bill committee, but also to have the burden of votes taking place in a forum of 650 MPs when they would otherwise take place in a committee of 20 members upstairs. And, historically, Committees of the whole House have presented problems for government business managers: the Parliament (No. 2) Bill to reform the House of Lords was considered for 12 days before it was dropped; and devolution to Scotland and Wales took up 34 days in Committee of the whole House in the 1976–77 and 1977–78 sessions. Nowadays, the prospect of being able to programme proceedings and so make them much more predictable and controllable may make government business managers slightly less reluctant to take committee stages on the floor of the House.

Select committees

We considered earlier the advantages of scrutinising *draft* legislation in a select committee. A bill that is on its *formal* passage through the House may be committed to a select committee after second reading, although this is rare. The main example is the bill every five years to renew disciplinary law for the armed forces (most recently in 2010–12).

More frequently, it happens that a select committee seizes the moment and conducts a swift inquiry into a bill (without the bill having been formally committed to it) and reports in time to influence later proceedings upon it, as when in 2014 the Political and Constitutional Affairs Committee reported on the Transparency of Lobbying, Non-Party Campaigning and Trade Union Administration Bill twice during its passage through the Commons, the second report being produced in time for Commons consideration of the Lords Amendments to the Bill. However, if the bill has not been formally referred to a select committee by the House, the committee cannot make amendments to it.

Report stage

Except for bills that are considered in Committee of the whole House *and* are not amended there, all bills come back to the floor of the Commons for their *report stage*, properly called *consideration*. The bill returns in the form in which it left committee, and report stage is a further opportunity for amendments to be made. The important difference is that all MPs have an opportunity to speak to amendments on report.

Few bills will have more than two days on report – between 2010 and 2014 only the Finance (No. 3) Bill and the Legal Aid, Sentencing and Punishment of Offenders Bill were given three days, and only three bills were given that amount of time in all the sessions between 2001–02 and 2009–10. Report stages of government bills in the session 2013–14 occupied about 11 per cent of the total time on the floor of the House.

New clauses and amendments for debate on report are selected by the Speaker on the same principles as in public bill committee. However, selection is a little tougher than in committee; the Speaker is unlikely to select amendments on a topic that has been fully aired in committee, unless the government indicated in committee that it was prepared to think again. Even so, major matters of public policy that were debated in committee may reappear, on the grounds that the House as a whole, rather than a small group of MPs, should have the opportunity of expressing a view.

Procedure on report is somewhat different from Committee of the whole House. The Speaker (or one of the deputies) is in the Chair, and the Mace is on the Table. New clauses and schedules are normally taken first (although, as in committee, the minister may propose a particular order in which proceedings should be taken). The House is now revising the bill as a whole rather than going through it clause by clause, so there is no 'clause stand part'.

Third reading

When all the selected amendments have been disposed of (or when the time allotted to report stage under the programme order has expired), the House moves on to the third reading (usually at the same sitting). If there are no amendments on report, that stage is omitted and the third reading is taken immediately.

Third reading is the final review of the contents of the bill (debate is limited now to what is actually in the bill rather than, as at second reading, what might have been included). Except on highly controversial bills, where the opposition has the opportunity to fire some last shots, third reading debates tend to be quietly valedictory affairs in which those most closely involved (frontbenchers and other MPs who were on the public bill committee) look back rather sentimentally on the bill's progress through the House. Since the introduction of programming, however, the opposition frontbench has often taken the opportunity to express hopes that the House of Lords will deal in more detail with this or that provision that they feel has had inadequate scrutiny in the Commons.

The procedure is akin to second reading: a minister will move 'That the bill be now read the third time', and a debate takes place on that question. As at second reading, it is possible to move a reasoned amendment (if selected by the Speaker), but this is very rare. As programme orders normally allow no more than one hour for third reading debates, these occupy relatively little time on the floor of the House – just under 1 per cent of the total in the 2001 parliament.

Once the third reading has been agreed to, the bill has been passed by the Commons. One of the Clerks at the Table, in wig and gown, then 'walks' the bill to the Lords. The doorkeepers shout 'Message to the Lords', the doors are thrown open, and the Clerk proceeds in stately fashion through the Members' Lobby, the Central Lobby and eventually to the Bar of the House of Lords. There, the bill – tied up in Commons green ribbon (known as 'ferret', from *fioretti*, a sixteenth-century Italian name for a kind of silk) – is handed over to one of the Lords Clerks.

This may seem a somewhat archaic way of taking a bill from one House to the other, but bill text is compiled and amended using highly sophisticated software and, at the same time, an electronic version of the bill text has gone from the Public Bill Office in the Commons to its counterpart in the Lords. It can happen, though, that near the end of a session, with the 'ping-pong' of amendments between the Houses, the exact moment of a bill's formal arrival is of some importance. Handing it over in the Chamber makes this publicly evident in a way that its electronic appearance in a distant office does not.

Private members' bills

Before we move to the other end of the building to see how the House of Lords considers legislation, let us look at a category of legislation that often attracts publicity even though many more bills in this category fail than ever find their way onto the statute book: private members' bills.

These are not private bills but public bills that aim to change the general law of the land. They are introduced in one of four ways: the first private members' bills in each session appear following the *private members' bill ballot*; then there are *presentation bills* (described on page 186), sometimes called 'back of the Chair bills'; when leave is given under the ten-minute rule; and private peers' bills that have been passed by the House of Lords may be *brought from the Lords* and *taken up* by a private member in the Commons.

Ballot bills

Ballot bills are introduced in the same way as presentation bills, but an MP gets the right to introduce such a bill through success in the ballot, a sort of legislative prize draw. On the Tuesday and Wednesday in the second week of each session, MPs sign a book kept in the No Lobby, being allotted a number in the process. On the Thursday at 9.00am in Committee Room 10, normally televised live, the Clerk Assistant draws 20 numbers from a despatch box. The Chairman of Ways and Means matches the numbers to the MPs who have signed in and calls out the names (recently, to increase the suspense, these have been announced in reverse order, so the 20th number drawn wins the ballot). The 20 MPs get priority in introducing their own bills – but absolutely no guarantee that any of those bills will become law.

Some MPs are enormously keen to win the ballot; others strenuously hope not to be successful, as they have a good idea of how much sponsoring a private member's bill may interfere with their daily work. However, the reluctant are 'encouraged' by their whips to sign in, as the whips would prefer to see their own people successful rather than the other side. In most sessions, 400 MPs will enter the ballot. Those whose names are drawn – especially those in the first seven places – are immediately mobbed in person, and by telephone and e-mail by pressure groups who hope to persuade an MP to take on their special cause (and who may just happen to have a bill ready for the MP to adopt).

The ballot bills are presented on the fifth Wednesday of the session; and each of the 20 MPs has up to the rising of the House the previous day to decide what sort of bill to introduce. For some, this will be a simple matter; this may at last be the opportunity to introduce legislation for which they have spent much of their parliamentary careers campaigning. For others, there are choices to be made. Should they accept that any bill is unlikely to become law and so produce a sort of manifesto on a subject they think important, hoping that as a bonus they might get a chance to debate it? Or should they temper their ambitions and go for a narrow bill that is likely to be uncontroversial but could make a modest but worthwhile change to the law?

One of the factors that will help an MP to come to a decision is the extent of outside support likely to be available. A pressure group may be a large and influential body, with resources including lawyers who can help with drafting the bill and people who can write speeches and briefings on hostile amendments. In these circumstances, an MP will feel a little less like David pitted against Goliath.

In a sense, the ultimate pressure group is the government itself. We saw earlier that it can be difficult for a government department to get its bills included in the legislative programme for any session. Persuading a friendly MP (not always from the government party) to take on one of its smaller hoped-for bills can be another route to the statute book. If an MP decides to take on one of these so-called *hand-out bills*, he or she will act in a similar way to a minister, supported by departmental civil servants; and the bill itself will have been drafted by parliamentary counsel. However, the bill itself will proceed in the same manner as any other private member's bill and will get no special treatment (unless it is one of the very small number of private members' bills to which the government of the day is prepared to give some of its own time; years may pass without this happening).

By the evening before the fifth Wednesday of the session, the MPs successful in the ballot must have given in the short and long titles of their bills (the latter will limit the scope of the bill when drafted), and they will have collected the names of their supporters for the back of the bill. At the commencement of public business (see page 140) the next day, the 20 MPs form a queue at the back of the Speaker's

Chair, and as their names are called they come forward and hand their bills to the Clerk, who reads the title. The Speaker says 'Second reading what day?' and the MP names a day.

Tactics and procedure

It is at this point that the tactics essential for success in private members' legislation begin. There are normally seven days for private members' second readings. Obviously, it is best to be the first bill on any day, because that means a full day's debate and the prospect (if 100 MPs can be found to vote for the closure) of getting a second reading and going into committee; and the earlier one can do that, the better. So, if the 20 MPs name the days strictly according to those criteria, the bills will come on like this (the dates of the Fridays below are illustrative):

9 January	16 January	23 January	6 February	20 February	12 March	19 March
1	2	3	4	5	6	7
8	9	10	11	12	13	14
15	16	17	18	19	20	

However, it may be that the sponsor of bill 5 is not too concerned about his or her bill and cannot be in the House on 20 February anyway. So, he or she names 9 January, which leaves a first-place slot open on 20 February. A quick-witted MP with a much lower-placed bill may then be able to get the first slot on 20 February, and a full day's debate. And unless the sponsor of bill 8 has those quick wits, and when it comes to his turn he names 9 January as he had planned, he will find that he is now the third bill on that day and not the second as he had hoped. And once a day is named, there is nothing to be done; a bill can be deferred but not advanced. The picture may be further complicated by MPs guessing that a particular bill will be fairly uncontroversial and may get through quickly, and so putting their bill on for that day rather than the earlier day they could have taken (but when they would have been behind a fiercely contested bill and would have had no chance of getting debating time).

The next step for all the MPs successful in the ballot is to get their bills drafted. They may have the help of an outside body, of parliamentary counsel for a hand-out bill, or a kindly Public Bill Office (although this is not a formal part of the office's role). The drafting does not have to be perfect at this stage. If a bill gets into committee and looks to have a chance of getting further, the government will normally put down amendments so that if the bill is eventually successful it will be in properly drafted and workable form.

For those in the top slots on the second reading days, it will not be enough simply to have a majority of those in the House on the Friday in question. Even a few opponents can 'talk the bill out' by continuing to debate it up to the moment when the Deputy Speaker says 'Order, order' at 2.30 p.m. It will be important to muster at least 100 supporters, so that when the sponsor of the bill claims the closure just before 2.30 p.m. by saying 'I beg to move that the Question be now put', the closure is agreed with at least 100 MPs voting in the majority. With most MPs wanting Fridays for constituency work, this may take some silver-tongued persuasion – private members do not have the armoury of the whips at their disposal.

The rule that financial initiative rests with the Crown means that only a minister may bring in a bill whose main purpose is to create a charge. However, if a private member's bill that gets a second reading would incidentally involve an increase in public spending, the government will normally put down a money resolution to authorise such expenditure and to allow the bill to be considered in committee.

As with government bills, the next stage after second reading is public bill committee, where opponents may seek to delay the bill by putting down a great many amendments, or – more subtly – may hurry the bill through to report because they can put amendments down at that stage, not to kill this bill but to deny time to the bill that is behind it on report. Under Standing Order No. 84(5) not more than one committee on a private member's bill can sit at any one time unless sanctioned by the government.

The next hurdle will be the six 'remaining stages' days. On these Fridays – with Darwinian ruthlessness – the bills are ranked with the most advanced stage first: so, Lords amendments, third readings, report stages, Committee of the whole House (which is an option, although a high-risk one, for the private member) and second readings, in that order. Much the same tactics (and the need for closures) will apply, but at this stage it is much easier for opponents to take up time with amendments rather than on the single question of second reading, and so easier to kill the bill (which may be allowed only one day, because new report stages take precedence over those that have already started). The MP who is successful at this stage and secures third reading will rely on a colleague in the Lords to sponsor the bill there, and he will hope that that House does not amend the bill, as this will produce another chance of 'sudden death' when the Commons considers those Lords amendments.

When a stage of a private member's bill is on the Order Paper on any of the first twelve private members' days but is not completed (because it is talked out or objected to after 2.30 p.m.), the member in charge may name one of the later private members' days for continuing with the bill. As the session proceeds, unsuccessful bills are put off from Friday to Friday, until on the thirteenth and last day (widely known as 'the massacre of the innocents') there may be 50 or 60 to be 'called over' at 2.30 p.m. Even if an MP is lucky enough to get third reading at this stage, eventual success will depend on the Lords agreeing to the bill without amendment in the relatively short time that then remains in the session.

Presentation, ten-minute rule and Lords private members' bills

Much of what we have said about the procedure and tactics of ballot bills also applies to ordinary presentation bills, to ten-minute rule bills and to bills brought from the Lords. However, all of these have more of a hill to climb, as none may be proceeded with until the ballot bills have been presented (and those will have taken up two or three slots on each of the days devoted to second readings).

Both presentation bills and ten-minute rule bills are thus used more often to make a point than seriously to seek to change the law. Ten-minute rule bills have the additional advantage that an MP has the opportunity to gauge opinion in the House. Beginning in the seventh week of the session, on every Tuesday and Wednesday before the main business of the day, one MP is called to make a speech of not more than ten minutes setting out the case for a bill and seeking the leave of the House to introduce it. Other MPs are alerted to the subject matter by a brief description on the Order Paper. If there is objection to the proposal, one opponent may speak against, again for a maximum of ten minutes; and, if necessary, there is a vote. If the proposer is successful, the bill is introduced in a little ceremony that involves the MP walking from the bar of the House to the Table, bowing three times en route. (In a strange historical survival, the second of those bows, halfway up the Chamber, is just at the point where the great chandelier hung in the Chamber destroyed by fire in 1834, where MPs presenting a bill would stop and bow two centuries and more ago.)

Ten-minute rule bills are very popular with MPs. They could, of course, introduce exactly the same bill by the ordinary presentation method, without seeking the leave of the House. However, ten-minute rule bills come on at prime time immediately after questions and statements, and they are often a high-profile way of floating an idea and getting media attention – and perhaps laying the foundations of a later successful attempt. The right to introduce them is on a first come, first served basis. In the past, an MP would spend the night in a room next to the Public Bill Office in order to be the first to give notice 15 sitting days before the slot came up; but informal arrangements between the parties have, on the whole, ended this 'January sales' tactic.

Success and failure

Even with government backing, the success of a private member's bill is not assured. Against government opposition, failure is virtually certain; and even half a dozen determined backbench opponents can make it exceedingly difficult to get a private member's bill on the statute book.

In recent years, up to ten private members' bills a session have become law; but these figures are skewed by 'hand-out bills' (see page 200) where an MP is, in effect, taking through legislation on behalf of a government department. The numbers of bills passed in the last three complete sessions are shown in Table 6.1.

Table 6.1 Bills dealt with by Parliament, 2010–14

Session	2010–12 long session		2012–13		2013–14	
Passed	6	(43)	10	(28)	5	(23)
Not passed	224	(4*)	93	(6*)	144	(6*)

Figures for government bills are in brackets.

*Including bills not passed in that session because they were carried over to the next.

It is difficult to categorise successful backbench legislation. Many bills are minor pieces of tidying up of the statute book to remove generally recognised anomalies, and a number of these will have been suggested to sympathetic private members by government departments. Other Acts have dealt with small social reforms, particularly in areas affecting the rights of the disabled; marriage, children and the family; gaming and alcohol; care and control of animals; and the environment.

Overall, though, the scope has been very wide. Examples include the British Nationality (Falkland Islands) Act 1983, which gave British nationality to the inhabitants of the islands; the Race Relations (Remedies) Act 1994, giving industrial tribunals new powers in cases of racial discrimination; the Law Reform (Year and a Day Rule) Act 1996, which abolished the old rule of law that a person could not be found guilty of murder if the victim died more than a year and a day after being attacked; the Christmas Day (Trading) Act 2004, which prevented supermarkets and other large stores from opening on Christmas Day; and the Anti-Slavery Day Act 2010, which introduced a national day to raise awareness of the dangers and consequences of slavery, human trafficking and exploitation. Although the scope of these private members' bills may have been relatively small compared with major government bills, they have had important consequences in particular areas.

Some private members' bills have had a much wider application; they have brought about the abolition of the death penalty, the legalisation of abortion and homosexuality, and the end of theatre censorship.

Success can be measured in other terms. Sometimes, the government will take over the intention of a private member's bill and it will appear in a subsequent session as a government bill. In 1994, the then government's embarrassment following its blocking of a private member's bill on disability discrimination led to a government bill being introduced, which became the Disability Discrimination Act 1995. The Wild Mammals (Hunting with Dogs) Bill failed in the 1997–98 session but appeared in the 2000–01 session as the Hunting Bill, was passed by the Commons but overtaken by the dissolution of Parliament in 2001; a similar bill was introduced by the government in 2002–03 but was not passed by the Lords; and in 2005 the Hunting Act, still not passed by the Lords, became law using the provisions of the Parliament Acts.

It is possible for the government to give a private member's bill government time in the same session that it began as a private member's bill. This was done in the 1950s and 1960s on such subjects as the abolition of the death penalty and the legalisation of abortion, but it is now very unusual – no doubt because of the 'me too' principle; the government would find it hard to pick and choose among worthy bills. In 1976, the Sexual Offences Bill, which provided for anonymity in rape cases, was given government time; so, too, was the Census (Amendment) Bill [*Lords*] in 2002. A slightly different case occurred in 2002, when the Tobacco Advertising and Promotion Bill [*Lords*], a private peer's bill, was taken over as a government bill when it arrived in the Commons. (An identical bill had originally been introduced in the 2000–01 session as a government measure but had been lost at the general election for want of time.)

Success may have nothing to do with eventual legislation. As a backbencher, Tony Benn used substantial presentation bills to put forward his ideas on a Commonwealth of Europe to replace the European Union, on giving Parliament control over Crown prerogative, and on the reform of Parliament. None of these had a chance of succeeding, but setting out these detailed political proposals was an end in itself (and an MP whose bill is printed can receive up to 150 free copies of it).

The MP who seeks leave to bring in a ten-minute rule bill rarely expects that his or her bill will get on to the statute book (none have since the 2005–06 session, although ten did so in the period 1992 to 2005); and many bills for which leave is given are never actually printed. The ten-minute rule slot is a way of attracting attention to a subject, gauging opinion and putting it on the future political agenda. In the twelve-month 2013–14 session, 39 bills were brought in under the ten-minute rule. None became law (although one got as far as report stage); but the others gave an opportunity to air subjects for possible legislation such as nuisance phone calls, hate crime and access to mental health services.

Should it be easier?

Private members' bills are fragile vessels. The sponsor of a bill from scratch (rather than a government hand-out) will have to compromise on what is desirable to achieve what is realistic; he or she has to be an astute tactician, must try to ensure that the government is at the least neutral on the proposal, will have to persuade doubters and potential saboteurs, and needs a bit of luck. And even then success is by no means guaranteed.

This process can be frustrating – perhaps never more so than when a bill gets a second reading by a large majority but is then defeated by guerrilla warfare in public bill committee, on report or in the House of Lords. The EU (Referendum) Bill is an example; it received a second reading by 304 votes to nil, and was eventually passed by the House of Commons: but it did not become law because it was not passed by the House of Lords.

It may be said that the principle is one thing but the details another, and that scrutinising details is what the committee and report stages are for. And even if the degree of scrutiny – as opposed to obstruction – that a bill gets in those circumstances is open to question, many would argue that protecting the rights of the minority to disagree is especially important in the case of private members' legislation – in contrast to the assumption that a government with a majority will get its bills eventually.

Most proposals for making it easier for private members' bills to pass into law centre on providing more time, although, to make real difference, a substantial amount of time would have to be provided (and in a House that already sits for longer than many other parliamentary chambers).

The Procedure Committee reported twice on these issues during the 2013–14 session, with a wide-ranging initial set of proposals that it revised later in the session when they did not receive a positive response from the government. Its second, more modest, set of proposals have not yet been agreed to by the House. The committee considered, but rejected, moving private members' business to an earlier day of the week; for example, a Tuesday, Wednesday or Thursday evening. Another suggestion floated was to make some private members' bills subject to a form of programming that would allow them to be voted upon at all their stages and would prevent their simply being 'talked out'.

Opinion is divided, even among MPs themselves. Some believe that taking initiatives to change the law should be a key part of an MP's role, and one in which MPs generally could act more independently of government; others are reluctant to see the amount of legislation already made every year increased, and they take Churchill's view that 'not every happy thought which occurs to a Member of Parliament should necessarily find its way on to the statute book'.

Lords stages

Bills can begin the parliamentary process in either House, and they have to be agreed by both Houses before they can be presented for Royal Assent, unless the Parliament Acts (see page 209) are used. A bill introduced in the Commons, and passed by that House after it has completed the various stages just described, is sent to the Lords. A bill introduced in the Lords will, after going through its stages in that House, be sent to the Commons for similar treatment. Consideration by the two Houses is – unlike the practice in the United States – never simultaneous, although on very rare occasions, to save time, identical bills are introduced in both Houses. One is later dropped, but the other can then proceed more quickly because its main points have been discussed already by both Houses.

The Lords spend a great deal of their sitting time discussing bills. All stages are normally taken on the floor of the House, despite the development of the grand committee procedure with a view to considering more bills in committee off the floor. Indeed, a greater proportion of time is spent on bills in the Chamber in the Lords than in the Commons – between 50 and 60 per cent of the total sitting hours as opposed to one-third.

Bills in the Lords go through the same stages as in the Commons – a formal first reading, a substantial debate on second reading, detailed amendments at committee stage and report, and further debate (and, in the Lords only, consideration of amendments) at third reading. But outward appearances hide substantial differences in procedure, many of which reflect the more flexible and less constrained procedures that have survived in the Lords long after their demise in the late nineteenth-century House of Commons.

Characteristics of Lords legislative procedure

Lords legislative procedures have some particular characteristics that are quite distinct from those of the House of Commons. First, consideration at committee stage is very different. A bill can, in theory, be committed to five different kinds of committee for consideration but only two are usual – *Committee of the Whole House* where most bills are still considered and *Grand Committee*, which is increasingly used. The Grand Committee was first set up in 1995 following the recommendation of the 1994 Group on Sittings of the House, and in a normal session between six and eight bills will be sent off the floor in this way. The Grand Committee is unselected – any member may attend – and it sits in a specially adapted room near the Chamber, the Moses Room. The procedure is exactly the same as in the Chamber but, because the committee membership is unselected, amendments may be made only by agreement and no divisions may take place. (Therein lies the secret of the Grand Committee's success and it has supplanted an unsuccessful earlier *public bill committee* procedure which was a selected committee with power to amend and vote. The procedure was seldom used and need not be considered further.)

From early and tentative beginnings in the late 1990s, the Grand Committee has evolved into a parallel chamber for many kinds of business in addition to committee stages on bills: motions to consider affirmative or negative statutory instruments, motions to take note of select committee reports, Questions for Short Debate, debates on National Policy Statements, and general motions for debate. In addition, Second Reading debates on Law Commission Bills also now take place in the Moses Room, in an unselected Second Reading Committee different in name only from a Grand Committee. In the 2013–14 session, the Grand Committee sat on 92 days – well over half the total sittings of the House – for over 310 hours, equal to about 45 extra sitting days in the Chamber. It has become indispensable.

A fourth way for dealing with a committee stage is to commit a bill to a *special public bill committee*. Although in theory any bill could be so committed, in practice the procedure is used exclusively for bills that have been prepared by the Law Commission, implementing normally uncontroversial proposals for law reform emanating from Commission reviews. The committee is selected and may take oral and written evidence on a bill within the first 28 days of its appointment. After a short break, the committee then considers clauses and amendments in the usual way. In the first three sessions of the current parliament, four bills had this treatment; and all of them had received their second reading off the floor in Second Reading Committee.

Finally, it has always been possible for a bill to be committed to a *select committee* at any stage between second and third reading, usually after second reading, for consideration of its merits. The committee undertakes detailed investigation of the subject matter and reports on the main provisions, recommending whether the bill should proceed or not and, if so, in what form. If a bill is to proceed, it is recommitted to a Committee of the whole House. The procedure is not used for government bills because of the delay that would be caused and, arguably, because such a bill should not be in need of forensic scrutiny of the policy it enshrines. But it is more often used as a way of considering controversial issues raised in private members' bills, such as the Assisted Dying for the Terminally Ill Bill in 2004. Exceptionally, after the government lost a crucial vote in the House, the Constitutional Reform Bill (a government bill) was committed to a select committee in March 2004.

The committee, which included the Lord Chancellor as a member, sat until the end of June, hearing evidence, reporting on the policy of the bill and making amendments. Despite vigorous efforts in the 1990s to move legislative work off the floor, the norm is for the committee stage of bills containing any controversial material to be taken in Committee of the whole House.

A second difference between the Lords and Commons legislative procedures is that there is no selection by a chairman of amendments to be discussed. Provided they are relevant to the bill, all the amendments that have been tabled may be considered, even if they have already been discussed at an earlier stage. While this can in some cases lead to a constructive dialogue with ministers – the same points are often made at second reading, committee and report, it also leads to a great deal of repetition of argument. Since the mid-1980s, amendments have been grouped at the initiative of the Government Whips' Office. Groupings are informal and not binding, so every amendment still has to be called and if necessary moved, even if it is unlikely to be further discussed.

Third, there is no guillotine or programme procedure so, in theory, proceedings could be very protracted indeed. Fortunately, filibustering is rare. Most members – and especially the party whips – realise that the excellent opportunities that arise in the Lords to consider all clauses and to take all amendments could not long survive persistent abuse by any one member or any one party. Early in 2011, this long-standing freedom came perilously close to being ended. The Parliamentary Voting Systems and Constituencies Bill (see page 215) took 17 days in committee because of the delaying tactics used by certain opposition members. Parliamentary counsel drafted a timetable motion for the government to use as a last resort. Eventually, it proved unnecessary and the House shied away from the abyss.

Another substantial difference is that, in the Lords, it is possible to move amendments at third reading. The principal purposes of amendments at this stage are to clarify remaining uncertainties, to improve drafting and to enable the government to fulfil undertakings given at earlier stages of the bill. It is not permissible to raise an issue that has been fully debated and decided upon at a previous stage. And amendments raising new issues, or amendments similar to ones tabled and withdrawn at an earlier stage, should not be tabled. A general debate may also take place on the motion 'that the bill do now pass', after any amendments have been considered, although this practice is now discouraged.

Since 1992, all government and some private members' bills are considered by a Lords Select Committee on Delegated Powers and Regulatory Reform, which reports to the House whether the provisions of any bill inappropriately delegate legislative powers to ministers using statutory instruments; or whether they subject the use of any delegated powers to insufficient parliamentary scrutiny. All bills are considered – usually on the basis of memoranda supplied by the government – after Lords first reading, and the committee reports quickly so that its findings can, if necessary, be acted upon by the House at committee stage. There is no equivalent committee in the House of Commons. All bills, whether introduced in the Lords or Commons, are also scrutinised by the Joint Committee on Human Rights in respect of any human rights issue, and by the Lords Constitution Committee for any constitutional issue. Reports are published by these committees on the issues raised, but the bills themselves are not committed to them and they cannot amend them.

It is worth noting that the government has no formal priority over other peers in introducing or debating legislation. In practice, government business is recognised to take priority, but at the same time – possibly as a quid pro quo – generous provision is made for private members' bills in the Lords. Because there is no limitation on the number of days on which they can be considered, the government has little control on the number of these bills that will actually be considered on the floor of the House. Indeed, the House now tends to sit on Fridays once a month to consider private members' bills. From the start of the 2014–15 session, a ballot is held on the day of the State Opening of Parliament to determine the order in which bills handed in on that day will receive a first reading. Although the dates of second reading debates are likely broadly to follow that order, it offers no other priority and, of course, it is no guarantee of eventual success. Ultimately, Lords private members' bills do not cause any trouble for the government, because a private member's bill to which the government is opposed and that survives in the Lords can always, if necessary, be blocked in the Commons.

Limitations on Lords powers: ancient practice and the Parliament Acts

Before we consider the impact of the House of Lords on bills, we should note that the Lords do not have free rein in amending certain types of Commons bill. By ancient practice set out in Commons resolutions dating from the late seventeenth century, the Lords may not amend bills of 'aids and supplies' – a type of bill that includes the annual Finance Bill, which implements the tax proposals made by the Chancellor of the Exchequer in his Budget, and Supply and Appropriation Bills, which sanction government expenditure. Based on this constitutional principle that only the Commons may authorise taxation and spending, any Lords amendment to a bill that has financial implications and that is rejected by the Commons – whether on policy or on financial grounds – will be returned to the Lords with a 'privilege reason': that it offends Commons financial privilege (see page 234). Lords practice is not to insist on such an amendment and, where an amendment in lieu is proposed, it should not be couched in a way that would invite the same response. In fact, the Commons waive their privilege in many cases, particularly in respect of government amendments made in the Lords. Commons financial privilege in respect of Lords amendments is not well-understood and when it has been invoked recently in respect of certain high-profile amendments – for example, to the Welfare Reform Bill in 2012 – some Lords members have felt frustrated by the application of these ancient, and fundamental, constitutional principles. They have felt that financial privilege has somehow been invoked at the whim of the government, which is not the case. The judgement on whether a Lords amendment has a financial implication is made by the Clerk of Legislation in the Commons, who does so on entirely objective grounds.

If the Lords insist on their amendments to any other public bill in a manner that renders the bill wholly unacceptable to the majority in the Commons and to the point that the bill is lost by the close of the session, or if they reject altogether a bill passed by the Commons, the procedures of the Parliament Acts 1911 and 1949 may be invoked. These Acts were passed to ensure that important reforming legislation introduced by the Liberal and Labour governments of the time was not frustrated by the then overwhelming Conservative majority in the Lords.

The severest restrictions in the Parliament Acts apply to 'money bills'. These are bills that deal only with certain specified central government finance matters. The most important of them are pure taxation bills or the Supply and Appropriation Bills that formally vote money to the government. These are described in more detail in Chapter 7. (The annual Finance Bill, which implements the budget proposals, is often not certified as a money bill because it contains wider provisions than those defined in the Parliament Acts. This is somewhat paradoxical, since the 1911 Parliament Act was passed as a reaction to the Lords' rejection of the 1909 Finance Bill.) Under the Parliament Acts, money bills passed by the Commons are allowed one month to pass through the Lords. If the Lords do not pass them within a month, they can be sent for Royal Assent without Lords approval. The provisions relating to money bills have never had to be invoked for the purpose of giving Royal Assent. When, through inadvertence or the interruption caused by a parliamentary recess, a money bill has not been passed within the prescribed time frame, it has subsequently been speedily passed under normal procedures.

All other public bills passed by the Commons may be delayed for a minimum effective period of 13 months by the Lords. The rule is strictly as follows: any bill that passes the Commons in two successive sessions (whether or not a general election intervenes) can be presented for Royal Assent without the agreement of the Lords, provided that there has been a minimum period of one year between the Commons giving it a second reading for the first time and a third reading for the second time, and provided that the Lords have received the bill at least one month before the end of each of the two sessions. The effect of this is to limit the Lords' power of delay to about 13 months, though it can be longer.

The rigours of these provisions of the Parliament Acts have on only four occasions been taken to their final stage since the 1949 Act (which reduced by one year the delaying time of the 1911 Act) was itself passed without the agreement of the Lords. In 1991, the War Crimes Act received Royal Assent under these provisions after the bill had been passed by the Commons and rejected by the Lords at second reading in two successive sessions. This bill sought, retrospectively, to create a new criminal offence so as to enable charges to be brought against alleged perpetrators of atrocities, chiefly against Jews, in continental Europe during the Second World War. Many lords felt that such prosecutions would be difficult to secure and that too many legal principles were offended by the proposed legislation. As the bill was not a manifesto commitment by the government, the Lords felt entitled to reject it. In 1998, the European Parliamentary Elections Bill was lost following disagreement over the electoral system proposed. The Lords rejected the reintroduced bill at second reading in the following session, thus enabling Royal Assent to take place in time for the elections to proceed notwithstanding the initial delay. In 2000, Royal Assent was also given under the Parliament Acts to the Sexual Offences (Amendment) Bill, which lowered the age of consent for homosexual activity and buggery to 16. In 2004, the Hunting Bill, which outlawed hunting deer, foxes and hares with hounds, received Royal Assent in the same way.

The Parliament Acts procedures are the fundamental limitation on the legislative power of the Lords. They enable any administration with a majority in the Commons to exert its will and ultimately to pass its legislation without Lords agreement. Indeed, when the government introduced its proposals to reform the House of Lords in 2012, it based its view of the legislative subordination of the Lords to the Commons in large measure on the continued application of these Acts. But Parliament Act procedures are like a nuclear deterrent and, of course, they involve delay. For practical reasons, government business managers often find it easier to accept Lords amendments than to attempt to overturn them every time, let alone threaten the use of the Parliament Acts. While they may well serve to underscore Commons primacy in legislative matters, as a tool of business management they are clunky.

The Salisbury convention

Members of the House of Lords accept that the elected government of the day must be allowed to get its business through. The nearest that this idea has come to formal expression is in the Salisbury convention – an understanding reached between the Conservative opposition in the House of Lords (led by the fifth Marquess of Salisbury) and the Labour government immediately after the Second World War in 1945. The convention is that the Lords should not reject at second reading any government legislation that has been passed by the House of Commons and that carries out a manifesto commitment – that is to say, a commitment made to the electorate in the government party's election manifesto.

The convention had its origin in the doctrine of the mandate developed by the third Marquess of Salisbury in the nineteenth century. He argued that the will of the people and the views of the House of Commons did not necessarily coincide and that the Lords had a duty to reject – and hence refer back to the electorate at a general election – contentious bills, particularly those with constitutional implications. As did the doctrine of the mandate before it, the Salisbury convention is perhaps more a code of behaviour for the Conservative Party when in opposition in the Lords than a convention of the House. The Liberal Democrats – whose precursors, the Liberal Party, were not privy to the 1945 agreement – have not considered themselves to be bound by it. Indeed, it is a moot point whether, following the passage of the House of Lords Act 1999, the expulsion of the hereditary members and the ending of the overwhelming numerical advantage of the Conservative Party, the Salisbury convention as originally devised can have any continuing validity.

In 2006, a Joint Committee on Conventions of the UK Parliament suggested that the Salisbury convention took the following form: that a manifesto bill is accorded a second reading; it is not subject to 'wrecking amendments' that would change the manifesto intention; and that the bill is passed and sent to the Commons. Interestingly, the Joint Committee also observed that the evidence it had heard pointed to the emergence in recent years of the practice that the Lords usually gave a second reading to any government bill whether related to a manifesto commitment or not.

In 2010, following the inconclusive result of that year's general election, the Conservative and Liberal Democrat parties' Coalition Agreement supplanted the party manifestos laid before the electorate so, at present, the Salisbury convention as originally conceived is a very dead duck indeed. Of greater significance by far is the broad acceptance that government bills will usually be given a second reading and dealt with in reasonable time. But whatever one's view of the Salisbury convention, or a broader understanding on government bills, the right of the Lords to amend bills has never been compromised, and this leaves the House with considerable room for manoeuvre, as we shall see.

Lords impact on legislation

House of Lords practice and procedure gives a persistent member far more oppor-tunities and time for getting a point of view across than the equivalent MP has in the House of Commons. We have already observed that, while party voting is very cohesive, the powers of the whips to compel attendance are relatively weak. Since the expulsion of the hereditary members in 1999, the House is more than ever a House of no overall control. In these conditions, members of the House are able, by persuasion or imposition of their will in the division lobbies, to have considerable impact on bills.

But the first thing to remember is that most of the changes that are made to bills in the Lords are by agreement, for the fact remains that most of the Lords work is of a revising character – whether in respect of its own bills or of bills received from the Commons. Detailed examination by a second chamber of legislature is perhaps a unique feature of the UK parliamentary system, allowing time for reflections and time to 'get things right'. Whichever party is in power, this aspect of the Lords' legislative work continues unchanged, and the biggest source of amendments of this kind is the government itself. During the passage of a bill, the government is continually seeking to improve the clarity of drafting of a bill, introducing detailed or even new provisions that were not ready at the time of introduction and – to some degree, at least – making changes in response to pressure within either House of Parliament. We saw earlier how, in the long post-election session 2010–12, 10,127 amendments were tabled to government bills and 2,537 were made, of which only 45 had been forced on the government following defeat in the voting lobbies; and, in 2013–14, a session of normal duration, 4,790 amendments were tabled and 1,686 made, of which only 14 had been forced on the government on a vote. Practically all of these amendments which were agreed to consensually, though often after debate, were government amendments moved by a minister.

These instances will have included occasions when the government has been persuaded to bring forward amendments in response to argument in the House at an earlier stage, or in the Commons. A good example is an amendment on pay day lending moved at the third reading of the Financial Services (Banking Reform) Bill in December 2013. After heavy pressure at earlier stages and strong support from the Archbishop of Canterbury, the amendment required the Financial Conduct Authority to make rules protecting borrowers from excessive charges. This change, resisted in the Commons, represented a significant change of heart. Another good example of responding to pressure relates to the Public Bodies Bill in the 2010–12 session. The purpose of the bill was to make it easier for the government to merge or abolish public bodies and it allowed the minister by order to move any body on a long list in schedule 7 to the list for abolition or merger – to death row, so to speak. After huge pressure on the floor – and from the Constitution and Delegated Powers and Regulatory Reform Committees – the government agreed to delete the schedule. It also signed up to a Labour amendment proposing a sunset clause, so that provisions on abolition or merger will lapse after five years. There are many other examples.

Recent research provides some very useful quantitative evidence in support of what otherwise would be a series of anecdotes. Meg Russell of the Constitution Unit at University College London has analysed the Lords amendments to 12 varied bills, 7 from the 2005–10 Parliament and 5 from the 2010–12 session of the present parliament. She found that 88 per cent of the 498 amendments made in the Lords to those bills were government amendments and, of these, 130 had policy significance. Of these, 84 (or 65 per cent) were traceable to other members' amendments or recommendations of Lords bill scrutiny committees. So, as part of the 'revising' process it is clear that the government does take on board the representations made to it in the House – particularly in those areas where it is prepared to shift, or where it thinks that change will be forced upon it if there were to be no shift at all. On the other hand, it should be remembered that 2,384 amendments were tabled from all parts of the House to these bills, most of which were successfully resisted.

More dramatic by far than changes secured by persuasion are those forced on a reluctant minister in the division lobbies, though their net effect on a government's legislative programme is not necessarily greater than amendments voluntarily made or conceded. Table 6.2 shows the number of times the government has been defeated on a vote in the Lords in each parliament from 1979 to 2014. It covers some 35 years of legislative history and tells us some interesting things. Until the passage of the House of Lords Act in 1998, the House was – at least, on paper – a predominantly Conservative body. All the more remarkable, then, that between 1979 and 1997 the Lords were often highly critical of aspects of government policy. Targeted by lobbyists, the Lords became recognised as the Chamber in which Mrs Thatcher's bills were vulnerable. Notwithstanding the departure of most of the hereditary members in 1999 and a very great increase in Labour members relative to Conservative members over the period, the years between 1997 and 2010 saw more government defeats than

Table 6.2 Government defeats in the House of Lords

Parliament	Number of defeats
1979–83	45
1983–87	62
1987–92	72
1992–97	56
1997–2001	128
2001–05	245
2005–10	144
2010–14	80

ever before – a reflection of the increased assertiveness of the House following the passage of the House of Lords Act. Finally, the 2010–15 Parliament has seen rather fewer occasions when the government has lost votes, despite the fact that the two main parties remain numerically broadly in balance – evidence that when it comes to voting, the coalition in the Lords has held firm most of the time.

Many of the amendments made to a bill on a defeat in the lobbies may be reversed in the lobbies during the exchanges between the Houses known as 'ping-pong' (see page 217). But some are not overturned, or will be met with a compromise. Here are some recent examples where the Lords have had a substantial effect on policy.

- *Prevention of terrorism*. The House has been especially vigilant in ensuring that the government's response to terrorism has been proportionate. In the 2001–05 Parliament, the Lords successfully modified aspects of anti-terrorism legislation that they considered excessive, particularly the Anti-Terrorism, Crime and Security Bill – a 126-clause bill containing measures in response to the terrorist attacks in New York and Washington on 11 September 2001. Although proceedings were accelerated, the Lords spent 53 hours seeking to amend this bill. As a result, changes were made in key areas, in some cases after the Lords had insisted on their amendments. Thus, among other things: an appeal mechanism against deportation was provided for; the additional police powers conferred by the bill were confined to anti-terrorism and national security matters; the offence of inciting religious hatred was struck out; and a 'sunset clause' was inserted to time-limit many of the bill's provisions. Similarly, the Lords were to insist on a number of amendments to the Prevention of Terrorism Bill in March 2005, chiefly aimed at making the proposed control orders subject to judicial rather than political decision, under rules of court, consistent with the ECHR and subject to clearer statutory definition. The passage of the bill was eventually secured by agreement to Commons amendments in lieu of Lords amendments and an undertaking on the part of the government (not on the face of the bill) to review the bill's provisions with a view to renewal one year later. These final exchanges obliged the House to hold its longest sitting in modern times – beginning at 11 a.m. on

Thursday 10 March 2005 and ending at 7.31 p.m. on Friday 11 March. This included four long adjournments for Commons consideration and the necessary negotiations. An attempt to increase the period of pre-charge detention of terrorist suspects (from 28 days to 42 days) in the Counter-Terrorism Bill in the 2007–08 session was rejected by the Lords and the government failed to persuade the Commons to reverse the Lords amendment.

- *Trial by jury.* The Lords have been doughty opponents of attempts to encroach upon the right to trial by jury, going back to their opposition to key provisions in the Criminal Justice (Mode of Trial) Bill in 1999–2000. These sought to abolish trial by jury in so-called 'either way' cases, which can be heard either by a magistrate or a jury. The provisions were removed by the Lords and the bill abandoned. Reintroduced as a 'No 2' bill late that session, it was – unusually – rejected by the Lords at second reading when it arrived from the Commons. Further attempts to limit access to trial by jury in certain cases were effectively seen off by amendments to the Criminal Justice Bill 2002–03 and a final attempt to end jury trial in complex fraud cases was resisted when, in 2007, the Fraud (Trials without a Jury) Bill was rejected at second reading.

- *Incitement to religious hatred.* In the 2005–06 session, the Racial and Religious Hatred Bill, which sought to create a new offence of inciting religious hatred, was amended radically in the Lords so as to separate the two offences, to provide that only intentional behaviour would be caught by its provisions and, as part of a 'freedom of speech' provision, confine the offence only to 'threatening speech and behaviour' rather than the looser 'abusive and insulting behaviour' in the original bill. In the Commons the government, while accepting the separation of the offences and the amendment on intention, sought to introduce the new concept of 'reckless behaviour' and to reinstate the 'insulting and abusive' provision. The government lost two critical votes, failed to modify the Lords amendments, and so the bill received Royal Assent in the form in which it left the Lords.

- *Identity cards.* The Lords were dogged in their opposition to the provision in the Identity Cards Bill 2005–06, which would have compelled all applicants for a new passport from 2008 to accept an identity card too. The Commons was eventually obliged to accept an amendment in lieu offered by the Lords which, while allowing applicants' details to be entered in a new national identity register, would not have required them to accept a card until 2010 – after the next general election – thus making the acceptance of a card an election issue. Another Lords amendment removed the provision whereby the secretary of state might, by statutory instrument, make what was intended to be a voluntary scheme a compulsory one. (The legislation was repealed by the coalition government.)

- *Constituency boundaries.* In the early months of the 2010 Parliament, the government introduced the Parliamentary Voting System and Constituencies Bill. It provided for a referendum to be held on whether or not to change the voting system for a general election to the alternative vote (AV) system; and, following a review by the Boundary Commission, to reduce the number of Commons constituencies by 50, and provide for greater equality in the size of electorates. The Lords failed to make much impact on the bill and it received Royal Assent in 2011. The referendum decisively rejected the AV system. It was expected that the orders making the boundary changes would be made in time for the 2015 election. In 2013, the Lords amended the Electoral Registration and Administration Bill so as to postpone the implementation of the boundary changes until after 2015. Because this amendment – in the opinion of the Clerks, not even relevant to (in Commons terms 'within the scope of') the bill – had been made with official Liberal Democrat support, it proved irreversible in the Commons. On this occasion, the Lords motives were more than usually political; the Labour Party had vigorously opposed the original bill fearing the loss of many urban seats and the Liberal Democrats sought vengeance against their coalition partners for what they considered to be the premature abandoning of the House of Lords Reform Bill in September 2012. Irrespective of the circumstances in which the Lords made their amendment, its effect on the outcome of the 2015 election may be significant.

- *Employment rights.* A provision in the Growth and Infrastructure Bill in the 2012–13 session proposed an employee shareholder scheme whereby employees might receive company shares in return for giving up certain employment rights – such as the right to redundancy pay or protection against unfair dismissal. The Lords removed this provision. Although overturned in the Commons, concessions agreed to in lieu required employees to set out the advantages and disadvantages of the scheme to their employees and to pay for legal advice for any employees before entering into such a contract.

These case histories make good reading, and there are more of them. Why, one may ask, does the government not reverse all Lords amendments in the Commons? There are a number of reasons why not: very occasionally, it cannot muster the votes in the Commons; sometimes, particularly if the amendments have been made with support from its own backbenches, it will seek to compromise or live with the change; sometimes it will have a change of heart and accept the amendment, particularly if public opinion has been engaged; and often, at the end of a busy session when time is of the essence and bills are passing from one House to the other, it will deliberately avoid unnecessary confrontation with the Lords.

And what is the overall success rate? Again, Meg Russell has provided a useful analysis of government defeats on bills in the period 1999–2012 and the degree to which the amendments were accepted, overturned in the Commons, or subjected to compromise in the form of 'amendments in lieu'. Of the 406 individual defeats analysed, 33 per cent were accepted, or largely accepted, and a further 11 per cent were met halfway by amendments in lieu. This represents a win or draw rate of 44 per cent. In some sessions, the success rate was higher. In 2008–09, for example, the win or draw rate was as high as 67 per cent.

Disagreement between the Houses: the balance of power

Ping-pong . . . or poker?

The previous section dealt with disagreements between the two Houses on a bill, and we now explore this more fully, together with the constraints on the Lords powers to amend bills. A bill that passes without amendment through the second House then needs only the Royal Assent – or formal approval by the Queen – before it becomes law. It does not go back to the House where its progress began. However, if the second House makes amendments to a bill, those amendments (but no other part of the bill) must be considered by the first House. If they are agreed, the bill is ready to become law. If they are not, the second House looks at the matter again and can either insist upon its amendments or attempt compromise proposals. Theoretically, alternative compromises can be shuttled between the two Houses indefinitely until the session ends. Each time, messages are exchanged between the two Houses. These can become fiendishly complicated.

The final stages of the Prevention of Terrorism Bill in 2005, which we looked at earlier in this chapter (page 214) are a good example. The Commons sat from 11.30 a.m. on Thursday 25 March until nearly eight o'clock in the evening of Friday 26 March, and during that time the Bill (which had the previous week gone from the Lords to the Commons and back again without agreement on the most contentious provisions) went back and forth between the Houses seven times, with proposals and counter-proposals being considered each time (with new working papers being printed on each occasion – even at three in the morning). The Lords finally gave in, and their message to the Commons read:

> *The Lords do not insist on their Amendment to the Prevention of Terrorism Bill to which this House has disagreed and do agree with this House in its Amendments in lieu thereof; they do not insist on an Amendment in lieu of certain other Lords Amendments to which this House has disagreed, and do agree to the Amendments proposed by this House in lieu thereof; and they agree to the Amendments proposed by this House to words so restored to the Bill.*

Shortly after the arrival of this message, Royal Assent to the Prevention of Terrorism Act 2005 was announced to both Houses. Although dressed in archaic language, the exchanges were a classic political struggle between two Chambers of a bicameral Parliament, in one of which the government had a majority, and where the second had the power to destroy the government's bill, but was mindful of the possible political consequences of doing so. The process was perhaps more poker than ping-pong.

If a compromise were not reached, the bill would be lost, as happened to the House of Commons (Distribution of Seats) (No. 2) Bill in 1969 (which was not reintroduced); to the Trade Union and Labour Relations Bill and Aircraft and Shipbuilding Industries Bill in 1976 (reintroduced in 1977 and enacted in the conventional manner following compromise); and to the Hunting Bill in 2002–03 (enacted under the Parliament Acts at the end of the 2003–04 session). The point of *final disagreement* is normally thought to have been reached when each House has taken up its position and insisted upon it without an alternative proposition being offered (*double insistence*).

In the past, final disagreement has usually been defined with respect to individual amendments even where they may have been grouped for purposes of debate. In the Commons, since 1997 the practice had arisen of grouping amendments together for the purpose of both debate and decision. This Commons practice of 'packaging' created difficulties in the Lords in May 2004 in respect of the Planning and Compulsory Purchase Bill. The Lords authorities took the view that double insistence had been reached on an amendment and that the bill was lost, whereas the Commons intention was that the bill could be further considered because that amendment had been decided as part of a 'package' with another amendment to which an amendment in lieu had been offered. Exceptionally, the bill was further considered by the Lords.

It was, however, subsequently agreed by the House that it would consider packages of amendments during ping-pong only if they were confined to single or closely related issues, not disparate issues joined together simply for convenience. In the case of the former, the House would be willing to consider such amendments in packages, in which case the double insistence rule would apply to the whole package. This development has the benefit that consideration of Commons amendments may often become procedurally easier as the amendments can be printed together, whether consecutive or not. On the other hand, on complex issues it may be that the moment of double insistence will be longer deferred unless opposition parties remain vigilant.

Royal Assent and implementation

A bill passed by both Houses needs the Royal Assent – from the Sovereign as the third element of Parliament, in addition to the Lords and the Commons – before it can become law. The Queen's agreement is automatic (Queen Anne in 1707–08 was the last monarch to refuse to accept a bill passed by both Houses). Although, in theory, the Royal Assent can be given by the Sovereign in person, this was last done in 1854, and in 1967 it was decided to stop the procedure by which Black Rod would interrupt the proceedings of the Commons, summoning them to the Lords Chamber to hear the Lords Commissioners announcing Royal Assent. This now occurs only at prorogation. At other times, the Speaker in the Commons and the Lord Speaker in the Lords announce the Royal Assent at a convenient break in each House's proceedings.

Although Royal Assent to a bill turns it into an Act and makes it law, the law does not necessarily come into force immediately. The Act will normally contain *a commencement provision*. Typically, this allows the secretary of state concerned to make an order at some future date to bring part or all of the Act into force, although a date may be specified; for example, three or six months after Royal Assent. Sometimes, the appropriate date never comes: the Easter Act 1928, which would have fixed the date of Easter, was never brought into force; neither was the Employment of Children Act 1973. In June 2010, a Lords Written Answer revealed that elements of over 100 Acts of Parliament passed by the Labour government between 1997 and 2010 had not been commenced – ranging from a few sections to whole parts.

The question of whether it was legal for a minister simply not to bring into force something that had been decided by Parliament was considered by the Court of Appeal in 1994. That court decided that, as Parliament had not set a time for commencement, the minister had not acted illegally; but the then Master of the Rolls, in a dissenting judgement, suggested that the power given to the minister was to decide *when* rather than *whether* an Act should come into force. However, it is not clear when delay becomes long enough to regard the Act passed by Parliament as ineffective.

If there is no commencement provision (whether a date, or a power given to a minister), the Act comes into force from midnight at the beginning of the day on which Royal Assent was given.

What is the law?

Acts of Parliament are available in bound copies of the statutes for any particular year, and the government website www.legislation.gov.uk contains Acts of Parliaments as passed and also Acts as currently in force, back to 1267. The website shows the extent to which an Act has been brought into force, or amended or repealed by subsequent legislation (although it is not always entirely up-to-date: details are given against each individual Act). UK legislation is not codified; in other words, there is no single Act – covering, say, immigration law – which is republished every time there is an amending bill. To some extent, the work of the Law Commissions addresses this problem by compiling *consolidation bills* that bring together the existing law in a more logical and convenient form. For want of resources, the programme of consolidation has produced very little in recent sessions of Parliament. So the reader who wishes to know what a particular Act says needs to be careful to consult a fully revised and updated version; as well as www.legislation.gov.uk there are printed publications such as Halsbury's *Laws of England* and online subscription services from law publishers such as Halsbury or Butterworth.

Post-legislative scrutiny

It has always been possible for a select committee to examine the workings of an Act of Parliament relevant to its subject area, but there have been recent moves to make such *post-legislative scrutiny* more systematic. Following various exchanges between Parliament and government, in 2008 the government undertook that in most cases it would produce a memorandum assessing each Act between three and five years after Royal Assent; 58 of these had been published by January 2013. It is then up to the relevant select committee to decide whether to take up the memorandum and make it the subject of an inquiry. In late 2012, the Liaison Committee was able to point to only three specific examples of such inquiries, though there had been wider inquiries that had included evaluations of previous legislation. The House of Lords began setting up select committees to carry out post legislative scrutiny in 2012 when adoption legislation was considered and, in the 2013–14 session, further committees were set up to consider the Mental Capacity Act 2005 and the Inquiries Act 2005. Overall, this is an initiative that promised more than it has delivered. This may well be because, if a particular legislative provision is clearly not working and this really matters to the government of the day, it will be dealt with by subsequent legislation; and, if it is a matter of party contention, it may be repealed upon a change of government. A *systematic* assessment of how an Act of Parliament is working is no doubt worthy, but may be better carried out in an academic rather than a parliamentary context. If there is a specific problem with a piece of legislation, a select committee is well-placed to investigate it.

Private legislation

The reader of the House of Commons Order of Business will often see at the beginning of the day's agenda on Mondays to Thursdays references to private business. Occasionally, the words 'Private business set down under Standing Order No. 20' can be seen. The private business is not private in the sense of being confidential or related to the internal affairs of the House; it is business related to private legislation.

As we saw earlier in this chapter (page 199), private bills are nothing to do with private members' bills. Private members' bills seek to change the general law, but private bills affect individuals, groups of individuals or corporate bodies in a way different from other individuals, groups or bodies. Their effect is private and particular as opposed to public and general. For example, the Dartmoor Commons Act 1985 was promoted by Dartmoor farmers to give powers to stop the overgrazing of the moors, the Southampton International Boat Show Act 1997 allowed a park in Southampton to open for one extra day a year, and the City of London (Ward Elections) Act 2002 made changes to the franchise for local elections in the City. The Hereford Markets Act 2003 allowed a livestock market that, by royal charter, had to be held within the city limits to be moved outside and so release a prime site for other uses. Around ten recent private bills were recently promoted by local authorities to regulate street trading and pedlars in their areas.

The first step in private legislation is for the person or group seeking the legislation to petition for the bill. Private bills are not presented by MPs or peers but by the promoters of the legislation, who are represented by special lawyers known as parliamentary agents. Throughout the bill's passage – but especially before it is even introduced – the promoters will be working to ensure that the bill attracts as little opposition as possible. Promoters need to comply with an elaborate set of standing orders, which try to ensure that interested parties (who may know nothing of the promoters' intentions) are given notice of the bill. When this has been done, the bill is allocated to one House or the other for first consideration, and, after second reading, is sent to a special committee. Private bill procedure is particularly complex and is set out in detail in *Erskine May*, but the main elements are described here.

Anyone who is aggrieved by the bill's provisions has the right to petition against it, but only someone directly affected by the bill (who has what is known as *locus standi*) has the right to be heard. If the bill is not opposed by petitions, or if all the petitions are withdrawn because the promoters have been able to meet the petitioners' wishes, the bill is considered by a committee on unopposed bills, through which it usually passes swiftly after an explanation of its purposes by the promoters. Opposed private bills are considered much more elaborately over many days by a committee of four MPs (or five peers), who must have no personal interest in the matter.

The committee acts in a semi-judicial capacity, examining witnesses and hearing barristers who appear for and against the bill. In effect, it displays the character of Parliament both as a court, inquiring into and adjudicating on the interests of private individuals, and as a legislature, safeguarding the public interest. The committee has to decide whether the promoters have demonstrated that the bill is necessary, whether those affected by it have been treated fairly, and whether there is any objection to it on public policy grounds. The committee has the power to make amendments, or even to recommend that the bill should not proceed (as happened with the first Crossrail Bill in 1994, which failed).

After their committee stage, private bills are considered on report (in the Commons, but not the Lords), read a third time and passed to the other House for similar stages to be taken. It is quite usual for a private bill not to complete all its stages in one session; an order is made that allows it to be taken up in the following session at the stage it had reached. Private bills are not covered by the Parliament Acts, so there is no restriction on the power of the Lords to delay them.

Most private bills do not encounter sustained opposition from MPs or peers, but the opportunities for delay are considerable. Each stage of a bill's progress is advertised on the Order of Business 'at the time of unopposed private business' and can be stopped from proceeding further by an MP shouting 'Object!' and then by the tabling of a 'blocking motion'. If this objection is sustained on each appearance of the bill on the Order of Business, the bill cannot proceed without time being found for a debate. This is in the hands of the Chairman of Ways and Means, who has a general responsibility for the way that private bills are handled (but not for the success or failure of any bill). He can set a bill down for a three-hour period, which according to the standing orders is the last three hours before the moment of interruption (for example, from 7.00 p.m. to 10.00 p.m. on a Monday), but is usually changed nowadays to a three-hour period at the end of government business.

The government business managers are naturally anxious not to have much scarce parliamentary time taken up with opposed private business, so an MP who objects to an aspect of a private bill has a strong bargaining counter with the promoters. Unless they go some way towards meeting the MP's wishes, he or she can delay the bill by insisting on a debate at each stage, and this may eventually mean that the bill is lost.

In the Lords, private bills that have been reported from a select committee are not usually opposed further on the floor. The Chairman of Committees oversees private legislation proceedings in the Lords in the same way as the Chairman of Ways and Means in the Commons.

The amount of private legislation has fallen dramatically in recent years, especially following the Transport and Works Act 1992. This removed from the parliamentary process private bills dealing with matters such as railway, tramway and harbour building, and other types of development. These were often the most controversial private bills, and there were usually more than 20 bills each session. Nowadays, parliamentary involvement in such projects will occur only when a project is seen by the government as being nationally significant, when a single debate on its desirability will take place on the floor of the House. An example is the debate on the proposal to build a new railway from Leicester to the Channel Tunnel via Rugby, which was rejected by the Commons in 1996.

The timetable for presenting private bills has not yet been amended to match the move of the start of sessions from November to June; petitions for new bills are still presented in November, and in the last five years (2009 to 2013) the numbers were 2, 3, 0, 2 and 1, respectively.

There will no doubt be private bills in the future that do not deal with transport and works but that will still prove controversial – as, for example, did the City of London (Ward Elections) Bill, which encountered opposition on the grounds that it provided for a weighted franchise, and which took nearly four years to get through Parliament, and the bills relating to street trading, which were opposed by both members and street traders, which also took several years to be passed. Any private bill may be of great importance both for its promoters and for those who will be affected. But, compared with their nineteenth-century heyday, private bills have become something of a parliamentary backwater.

Hybrid bills

These bills – which are fairly unusual – combine characteristics of a public bill and a private bill. Bills that are introduced by the government but that would otherwise be private bills are also treated as hybrid. Examples of hybrid bills include the Channel Tunnel Bill in 1987, the Cardiff Bay Barrage Bill (which was enacted in 1993 after starting out as a private bill and then being taken over by the government), the Channel Tunnel Rail Link Bill in 1994, which became law in 1996, the Crossrail Bill introduced in 2005 and enacted in 2008, and the current High Speed Rail (London - West Midlands) Bill. One of the classic examples of a hybrid bill was the Aircraft and Shipbuilding Industries Bill of 1976, which was intended to nationalise these two industries. It was discovered that this bill did not apply to one shipbuilding company that otherwise fulfilled the bill's criteria for nationalisation. Because this company was thus being treated differently from all other companies in the same class, the bill was ruled by the Speaker to be hybrid. Although this ruling was set aside by the Commons, the bill was committed to a select committee in the Lords.

Hybrid bills are treated as public bills, and the promoters do not need to prove the need for the bill. Bills are examined to see whether they comply with the standing orders that relate to private bills, and there is an additional stage – they are referred to a select committee in each House, which can hear petitions from those affected. This may be a major exercise; the committee on the Channel Tunnel Bill received several thousand petitions. The Crossrail Bill attracted 358 petitions and the High Speed Rail (London - West Midlands) Bill has so far attracted 1,925 petitions.

Delegated legislation

Definitions

Delegated legislation is law made by ministers or certain public bodies under powers given to them by Act of Parliament, but it is just as much part of the law of the land as are those Acts. The volume of delegated legislation is huge, and this presents particular challenges for parliamentary scrutiny.

Individual pieces of delegated legislation, often called *secondary legislation* to distinguish them from primary legislation contained in Acts of Parliament, or *subordinate legislation*, are found under many different names. They can be *orders*, *regulations*, *Orders in Council*, *schemes*, *rules*, *codes of practice* and *statutes* (of certain colleges rather than in the sense of Acts). Even the Highway Code is a form of secondary legislation.

Delegated legislation may be made by any person or body empowered to do so by an Act of Parliament ('the parent Act'); and although some institutions and professional bodies have this power in particular cases, the bulk of such legislation is made by ministers.

Before the Second World War, there was very much less delegated legislation, and parent Acts prescribed a variety of different parliamentary procedures, often designed for the particular case. Most of these were unified by the Statutory Instruments Act 1946, which describes what a statutory instrument is and prescribes the principal procedures for parliamentary approval. Not all pieces of delegated legislation are *Statutory Instruments*, but this general term (abbreviated to SI, with individual instruments numbered in an annual series; for example, 'SI 2006/875') will serve. About half of the 3,000 or so statutory instruments made each year have only a local effect and may be for only a temporary purpose. Our concern is with the general instruments that form part of the law of the land.

Purpose

The original idea of an SI was to supplement what was set down in an Act of Parliament, for two particular purposes. The first was to prescribe things that were too detailed for inclusion in an Act of Parliament. The second was – again, for fairly minor matters – to provide the flexibility to change the law to meet changing circumstances without the sledgehammer (and the delay) of new primary legislation.

As long as this remained the guiding principle, one would expect there to be little difficulty. However, over the years the boundaries of delegated legislation have been tested. The increase over the last 30 years has been of the order of 50 per cent, although it appears that the upward trend may have levelled out. However, the *volume* of delegated legislation is huge: the last set of annual volumes of SIs (for 2009) took up 11,888 A4 pages.

The second area of strain has been in the *use* of SIs. Ministers naturally find it more convenient to be able to legislate in a way that is subject to more limited parliamentary scrutiny than primary legislation, and there is thus a temptation to leave to delegated legislation matters that arguably should be set out in a bill and so in an Act. The most extreme examples of this have been in so-called 'skeleton' or 'framework' bills, where the use of delegated powers is so extensive that the real operation of the bill would be entirely by the regulations made under it. The Education (Student Loans) Bill in 1990, the Child Support Bill in 1991 and the Jobseekers Bill in 1995 all attracted criticism on these grounds, as have 'Henry VIII powers', which allow ministers to amend primary legislation by the use of secondary legislation (see also page 230).

The speed of the legislative process encourages an overuse of delegated powers. A minister may want to put a new provision into a bill during its passage, but the limited time available to settle the details may lead to the provision being drafted in very general terms, with even quite significant matters being left to delegated legislation. There is also the question of where the threshold should be set between the more important *affirmative instruments*, which Parliament must approve explicitly, and *negative instruments*, which have effect unless Parliament says otherwise.

Since 1992, the House of Lords has sought to address the balance between delegation and control through the work of the Delegated Powers and Regulatory Reform Committee (formerly the Delegated Powers and Deregulation Committee). For each bill introduced into the Lords (and for substantial government amendments), this committee examines the powers to make delegated legislation that are proposed to be given to ministers. It reports on both whether those powers are justified and whether the level of parliamentary control is appropriate (in other words, which powers should be exercised through negative instruments, which through affirmative instruments, and which should be matters for an Act of Parliament rather than delegated legislation). The vast majority of the committee's recommendations have been accepted, and it plays an important role in striking a balance between executive freedom and parliamentary control.

Table 6.3 Number of SIs made in selected years 1950–2013

1950	2,144
1955	2,007
1960	2,495
1965	2,201
1970	2,044
1975	2,251
1980	2,051
1985	2,080
1990	2,667
1995	3,345
2000	3,433
2005	3,602
2010	3,117
2013	3,314

Two other features of the system should also be mentioned. The first is that the vast majority of SIs are not amendable. This is inevitable in that both Houses must take the same view on an SI, and amendable instruments would be like another class of bills going back and forth for both Houses to agree on any amendments. But it also means an element of 'take it or leave it', especially when an SI is substantial or complex.

The second is that the way the threshold is set between affirmative and negative instruments can become out of date with changes in society. For example, in an Act passed in 1950 it might have been thought essential to require a minister to come back to Parliament for permission to exercise a power that by 2014 would be thought to be routine. But the requirement remains in the 1950 Act, and only further primary legislation will remove it. The phenomenon may also work the other way – something routine in 1950 may have taken on a different significance 60 years later.

Parliamentary control

There are five levels of parliamentary control:

1   Delegated legislation that may be made and come into effect *without any reference to Parliament*. This category includes a large number of SIs with only local effect, and many of these will be printed only if the responsible minister wishes them to be. Among non-local SIs in this category are commencement orders for bringing into force all or part of an Act of Parliament.

2   Delegated legislation that may be made and come into effect, and that *must be laid before Parliament, but on which there are no parliamentary proceedings*. These are really for information.

3   *Negative instruments*: these are *laid before Parliament* and may *come into effect* immediately or on some future date *unless either House resolves that the instrument be annulled*.

4   *Affirmative instruments*: these do not normally (except in cases of urgency) come into effect until they have been *approved by resolution of each House*. (Urgent affirmative instruments come into force before approval but lapse unless approved within a certain time.)

5   *Super-affirmative instruments*, such as *legislative reform orders* (see page 230).

These require the minister concerned to have regard to the results of consultations, House of Commons and House of Lords resolutions, and committee recommendations made within 60 days of laying the draft instrument, in order to decide whether to proceed with the draft order, whether as laid or in an amended form.

The third and fourth categories are the most significant; in the last two complete sessions, they averaged 214 affirmatives and 724 negatives a year.

Instruments considered by the Joint or Select Committees on Statutory Instruments

Type	Session 2012–13	Session 2013–14
Unlaid (general)	164	177
No procedure, laid	32	22
Negative	685	763
Affirmative	186	242
Total	1,067	1,204

Procedure

When an instrument has been laid before Parliament, it is examined by the Joint Committee on Statutory Instruments (with members from both Houses), which is supported by specialist lawyers and reports on various technical aspects: whether in making the instrument the minister has exceeded the powers given by Parliament (this is also something that can be challenged in the courts); whether the drafting is defective or unclear; whether the instrument has retrospective effect, and so on. The Committee also examines instruments not laid before Parliament, but only if they are general, not local. The committee reports its conclusions but, even if it finds fault, the progress of the instrument is not automatically halted. Some instruments, on finance and taxation, are laid before the Commons only and are examined by the Select Committee on Statutory Instruments, which consists of the Commons members of the Joint Committee.

Negative instruments

In the case of a negative SI, nothing will happen unless an opposition party, or a group of backbenchers, tables what is known as a *prayer*. This has nothing to do with religious devotion but is so called because of the form of the motion; because the instrument has been made by one of Her Majesty's ministers, it is the Sovereign who has to be asked to undo what has been done. To take a real example from the 2013–14 session (the SI that raised fees for judicial review in immigration and asylum cases), the motion would read:

> *That an humble Address be presented to Her Majesty, praying that the Upper Tribunal (Immigration and Asylum Chamber) (Judicial Review) (England and Wales) Fees (Amendment) Order 2014 (S.I., 2014, No. 878), dated 27 March 2014, a copy of which was laid before this House on 1 April, be annulled.*

Any annulment of an instrument must take place during a period of 40 days (excluding time when both Houses are adjourned for more than 4 days) from the laying of the SI; this time is unsurprisingly known as *praying time.*

In the Commons, debate on a prayer on the floor of the House is unusual; most are taken upstairs in a *delegated legislation committee*, which is very similar to a public bill committee on a bill but which debates the prayer on a motion 'That the committee has considered' the instrument, for a period of one-and-a-half hours (two-and-a-half hours in the case of Northern Ireland instruments). Only a minister can move a motion in the House to refer a prayer to a delegated legislation committee, so even debates of this sort are in the gift of the government and are normally only granted to the principal opposition parties, and almost never to backbenchers. Moreover, the committee cannot reject the instrument, so any vote that is not on the floor of the House is purely symbolic; and on the floor of the House no prayer has been carried since 1979.

In an average session, five to ten prayers are taken in delegated legislation committee; but only one or two on the floor of the House.

Affirmative procedure

Because any instrument in this category must be explicitly approved, a decision of each House is required. In the Commons, affirmative instruments are automatically referred to a delegated legislation committee. These operate in exactly the same way for affirmative instruments as for prayers against negative instruments, and they offer an opportunity for debate rather than substantive decision. When an affirmative has been debated in committee it returns to the floor of the House for decision, and a vote if necessary, but without further debate.

It is also possible for an affirmative to be 'de-referred': that is, so that it is both debated and decided on the floor of the House. The automatic referral to standing committee has existed since 1995; it was introduced as part of an effort to reduce sitting time on the floor of the House, but there was an understanding that the government would accede to a reasonable request to take particular affirmatives on the floor of the House.

Although, to begin with, substantial numbers of affirmatives were taken on the floor (73 in 1994–95, 47 in 1995–96 and 42 in 1996–97), there was a sharp decline thereafter, and now fewer than a dozen affirmatives are considered on the floor of the House in an average session. Recent subjects taken in the Chamber have included: local government finance and the financing of police authorities, up-rating of social security benefits and urgent orders to proscribe organisations under the Terrorism Act 2000.

Every sitting week, the Journal Office in the House of Commons produces a *Statutory Instrument List* showing the state of play on all affirmative and negative instruments and, in the latter case, the number of 'praying days' remaining on each. It is available on the parliamentary website.

Lords proceedings on Statutory Instruments

Most SIs that are laid before the Commons are also laid before the Lords – except for some financial ones – and the same rules apply, The House of Lords spends quite an amount of its time debating secondary legislation though much of this discussion is off the floor in Grand Committee. In 2012–13, discussion of SIs took just over 35 hours (or 3.9 per cent) of total Chamber time, but a further 67 hours in Grand Committee. Indeed, 28 per cent of Grand Committee time was spent debating no fewer than 205 SIs. The more controversial debates, any debates potentially leading to a vote, and formal motions to approve affirmative instruments debated in Grand Committee are reserved for taking in the Chamber.

Although delegated legislation is not subject to the Parliament Acts, the House of Lords rarely opposes negative or affirmative instruments. As we have seen, they are not amendable, so if the House pressed its opposition to a vote, the result could be the wholesale rejection of the instrument. As the Lords usually consider instruments after they have been taken in the House of Commons, this has constrained opposition parties from pressing their disagreement. Between 1955 and the end of the 2013–14 session, 119 SIs were divided on, but such was the unease of the two major parties while in opposition about using the House's powers to the full that 61 of those divisions were on motions that would not, if carried, have proved fatal to the instrument in question.

Only five times has the government of the day ever been defeated on a vote directly on an order. The Conservative Opposition divided the House against the Southern Rhodesia (United Nations Sanctions) Order 1968 and defeated the government, so provoking a constitutional furore. A virtually identical version of the order was approved a few weeks later. Two other instances occurred in February 2002 on a prayer to annul the Greater London Authority Election Rules 2000 and on a motion to approve the Greater London Authority (Election Expenses) Order 2000. In 2007, the House declined to approve the Gambling (Geographical Distribution of Casino Premises Licences) Order 2007, following an adverse report from the Merits of Statutory Instruments Committee as it was then called questioning the decision-making process. And, in December 2012, the House declined to approve the Legal Aid, Sentencing and Punishment of Offenders Act 2012 (Amendment of Schedule 1) Order 2012 on the grounds that it did not provide support for welfare claimants at first-tier tribunals. The Royal Commission on Reform of the House of Lords recommended in 2000 that the Statutory Instruments Act 1946 be amended to enable the Commons to override a Lords rejection of an affirmative or negative instrument. By diminishing the theoretical powers over delegated legislation slightly, it was argued, the House might make more use of the powers that remained to it. But this recommendation was not taken up. Meanwhile the House's powers in this area lie largely dormant but by no means extinct.

Improving parliamentary control

Parliament's control of secondary legislation has been criticised on a number of grounds. The remit of the Joint Committee is limited to technical issues of *vires* and drafting; opportunities for debate, particularly in the Commons, are limited; and SIs may not be amended in either House.

Lords Select Committee on Delegated Powers

The House of Lords, while cautious in the use it makes of its powers to reject affirmative or negative instruments in the Chamber of the House, has in recent years taken considerable steps in other directions so as to ensure that delegated powers are appropriately used. We have already noted the major contribution made by the Lords Select Committee on Delegated Powers and Regulatory Reform. Since 1992, this committee (originally the Delegated Powers Scrutiny Committee) has scrutinised all government and some private members' bills so as to establish whether any legislative power is inappropriately delegated to ministers, or whether any delegation is subject to sufficient parliamentary scrutiny. This 'up-stream' policing of the use of delegated powers has been very successful (see page 338). The Committee also scrutinises and makes recommendations on draft orders laid under the Legislative and Regulatory Reform Act 2006 (see page 230). By the end of the 2013–14 session, 12 such orders had been considered and, in July 2013, it recommended for the first time that one such order – on the regulation of providers of social work services – should not proceed.

In 2004, the House established the Secondary Legislation Scrutiny Committee (formerly the Merits of Statutory Instruments Committee) to sift those of political significance from the rest. The establishment of such a committee had originally been recommended by the Royal Commission on Reform of the House of Lords in 2000 and endorsed by the Group on the Working of the House in 2002 and the Liaison Committee in 2003. The committee finally began its work in April 2004. The committee's remit is to consider every instrument laid before each House subject to parliamentary proceedings (the so-called 'super-affirmative' procedure where draft proposals are first laid for a 60-day period of consideration and possible amendments), and every draft statutory instrument. The committee does not consider human rights remedial orders, regulatory reform orders or Church measures. The committee draws to the attention of the House any instrument that is important politically, legally or in policy terms; is inappropriate in view of developments since the passage of the parent Act; imperfectly achieves its objectives; is insufficiently explained by the government in explanatory material; or inappropriately implements EU legislation. (This latter provision arose out of fears that such regulations were overly elaborate and 'gold plated' the original EU requirements.) The committee has also been empowered to conduct inquiries into general matters relating to the scrutiny of merits of instruments and, since 2011, to scrutinise draft orders laid under the Public Bodies Act 2011 (see page 213) where it has power to recommend changes to any draft.

The workload is very considerable and the committee is supported by two full-time advisers in addition to the usual Clerk and clerical support. During the 2013–14 session, the committee considered 998 instruments. It reported on 29 affirmative instruments and 30 negative instruments, chiefly on grounds of public policy interest. Between 2011 and May 2014, 8 Public Bodies Orders had been considered. The Commons Procedure Committee has twice recommended a sifting committee on merits of instruments such as that now in place in the Lords (in 1996 and 2000), saying that 'the existing system of scrutinising delegated legislation is urgently in need of reform'. The committee also recommended that praying time for negative instruments should be increased from 40 days to 60; that no decision on an SI should be taken by the House until the Joint Committee on Statutory Instruments had completed its consideration; and that the most substantial and complex SIs should be given a super-affirmative treatment, being subject to pre-legislative scrutiny in the same way as a draft bill. The government has not so far taken action on these recommendations. We return to this in Chapter 12.

Legislative reform orders

There are some Acts of Parliament that allow a minister to amend primary legislation by secondary legislation – to amend an Act by an SI. Such a provision in a bill is known as a 'Henry VIII clause' – reflecting that monarch's somewhat broad-brush approach to his powers. It is generally undesirable for a minister to be able to change what normally only Parliament may decide; however, in 1994 the Deregulation and Contracting Out Act gave ministers just those powers, but subject to a stringent system of parliamentary control.

As part of the then Conservative government's wish to lighten the weight of regulation, the 1994 Act allowed ministers to amend or repeal primary legislation that imposed a burden affecting any person carrying on a trade, business or profession. It introduced an entirely new parliamentary procedure whereby a minister had to consult on a proposal, which would then be laid before Parliament and examined by Deregulation Committees of both Houses, which could suggest amendments before the deregulation order was laid as a formal draft for approval. Nearly 90 deregulation orders were made under the 1994 Act, ranging from greyhound racing to the registration of marriages to the selling of salmon roe; but it is in the nature of deregulation that after the early quick hits it becomes harder to find areas to deregulate.

The scope of the procedure was then widened by the Labour government's Regulatory Reform Act 2001 to cover 'burdens affecting persons in the carrying on of any activity'; and some other limitations in the 1994 Act were relaxed. A power to make 'subordinate provisions' (a sort of further delegated legislation, but also to be considered by the committees) was introduced. The committees were renamed: that in the Commons became the Regulatory Reform Committee, and the Lords committee became the Delegated Powers and Regulatory Reform Committee.

Regulatory Reform Orders have now, in turn, been superseded by Legislative Reform Orders under the Legislative and Regulatory Reform Act 2006, which was initially intended to widen considerably the purposes for which such orders could amend previous acts, but which was made more limited following protests during the passage of the bill.

Before a minister may make a legislative reform order, he or she must *consult widely with those who would be affected*. This is part of the procedure on which the committees have been particularly insistent. After the consultation, the minister may lay before Parliament *a draft order, together with an explanatory statement, and a recommendation as to the procedure that should apply (super-affirmative, affirmative or negative)*. There is then a period of time for consideration by the committees (either 40 days or 60 days, depending on the procedure, and, as with praying time, not including recesses). Either committee can 'upgrade' the procedure (strengthen it from negative to affirmative or super-affirmative, or from affirmative to super-affirmative) and then tests the proposal against various criteria, including whether this is the right method of changing the law; the adequacy of the consultation; whether the right balance of burdens and benefits has been struck, and whether the proposal would continue any necessary protection for those affected; whether it would limit any reasonable rights or freedoms; and whether the minister is acting within the powers given by the Act.

In assessing the proposal, the committees often take written or oral evidence, both from the government and from those who might be affected, and they then report separately on whether the proposal should go forward, with or without amendments. If a committee wishes to propose amendments, it will also upgrade the procedure to super-affirmative, to enable the minister to lay a revised draft order, taking into account the views of the committees and of anyone else who has commented during the 60-day period, and setting out what changes have been made, and why. The committees look at the draft order within 15 sitting days and report to each House upon it.

In the Commons, there is then a graduated procedure. If the committee has unanimously recommended that the draft order be made, it is put to the House without debate; if the committee had a vote on the matter, there is an hour-and-a-half's debate in the House; but if the committee recommends that the draft order not be approved, there must be a debate of up to three hours on a motion to disagree with the committee. If that motion is successful, the question on approval of the draft order is put without further debate.

Once the draft order has been approved by both Houses (or for the negative procedure, so long as the draft order has not been the subject of a negative resolution in either House), the minister may *make it* and so bring it into law. A list of legislative reform business, and the stages each draft order has reached, is published weekly. The number of draft orders per year has varied and is currently about four.

This procedure, under all three Acts, has been innovative and effective. It has all the advantages of pre-legislative scrutiny: detailed, evidence-based scrutiny and analysis; wide consultation and public access to the legislative process; and the testing and amendment of proposed legislation to produce a better quality of outcome. Moreover, it is systematic; it is not up to the government of the day to decide, as with bills, whether they should be examined in draft before being formally introduced. If the legislative reform route is taken, then the procedure outlined above applies automatically.

It has been rigorous; indeed, so much so that several government departments decided early on that they would not take this route but wait for an opportunity for the easier ride of primary legislation. It has been effective and has allowed backbenchers to have a real influence on the content of legislation; governments of both parties have almost always accepted the committees' recommendations. And it has been consensual; the committees have worked in a remarkably non-partisan way. The procedure is seen by many as offering lessons that could be applied more widely.

Remedial orders

The Human Rights Act 1998, which came into effect in October 2000, allows ministers to make a new form of delegated legislation known as 'remedial orders'. These come about when a UK court finds that some provision of an Act of Parliament is incompatible with the Human Rights Act. A remedial order may amend primary legislation; the procedure for considering it is similar to that for a regulatory reform order, except that it is the task of the Joint Committee on Human Rights, rather than the two committees described in the preceding sub-section, to consider and report on proposals and draft orders. Once it has been considered by the Joint Committee on Human Rights, and the statutory periods have passed, a draft order is treated in the same way as any other affirmative instrument.

If swift action is required, a minister may make an order, laying it before both Houses. It has immediate statutory effect, but it must be confirmed by both Houses approving it within 120 days of its being laid (as for praying time, excluding times when both Houses are in recess). During the first 60 of those days, representations may be made to the minister; and if as a result the minister decides to make a new order, it must be approved by both Houses within the remaining 60 days.

Details of remedial orders are included in the Statutory Instrument Lists (mentioned on page 228). There have so far been only six remedial orders, the most recent of which was the Sexual Offences Act 2003 (Remedial) Order 2012.

Church of England measures

As the established church of the state, the Church of England has to have its legislation approved by Parliament, including the Royal Assent of the Sovereign. These *measures* are a form of delegated legislation, although they eventually form part of the statute book. They are first agreed by the Church's parliament, the General Synod, which has procedures for debate and amendment very similar to the Commons and Lords. A draft of the measure is then sent to the Ecclesiastical Committee, which consists of 15 members of the House of Lords nominated by the Lord Speaker and fifteen MPs nominated by the Speaker. This is not a conventional joint committee appointed by the two Houses but a statutory body set up under the Church of England Assembly (Powers) Act 1919.

The purpose of the Committee is 'to determine whether or not the measure is expedient'; it cannot make amendments. To assist the Committee in coming to a view, comments and explanations are submitted by the General Synod, and members of its Legislative Committee assist the Ecclesiastical Committee in its deliberations. On difficult issues, a conference with the full membership of the Legislative Committee may be held, but this is rare. The committee presents a short report on each measure, together with its decision on whether the measure in question is 'expedient'. The measure is at the same time laid before each House of Parliament for approval.

The role of Parliament in the governance of the Church is sometimes a cause of controversy. After all, the General Synod as the Church's own representative body has already approved a measure by the time it reaches Parliament. It is arguable that, in its consideration of a measure, Parliament should not seek to second guess the Synod. Very occasionally, the Ecclesiastical Committee has, on some point of principle, suggested that a measure be laid in a slightly different form. Once the Ecclesiastical Committee has found a measure expedient, the proceedings in the two Houses are uncontroversial, although in 1989 a measure dealing with the ordination of divorced men was actually rejected by the Commons.

7

Parliament
and the taxpayer

Total government expenditure in 2014–15 was expected to be £732 billion, or about £11,350 for every man, woman and child in the United Kingdom. Taxation and public spending touch everyone's daily lives, from the amount of income tax we pay to the levels of state pensions and benefits we receive, and from standards in our local hospitals and schools to the quality of the environment and the number of police on the beat. It is not surprising, then, that management of the economy and of the nation's finances are always at the heart of political controversy. Are levels of public spending helping or hindering economic growth? What services should be protected from the full effects of reductions in public spending? Is the taxpayer getting good value for money? How will decisions on spending affect levels of taxation and public borrowing?

These questions are central to much of the work of Parliament but, as we shall see in this chapter, while Parliament provides the main forum for debate on the big issues, it exercises little detailed control.

The constitutional principles

The modern role of Parliament (and especially the House of Commons) in financial matters reflects the ancient relationship with the Crown. The Sovereign needed the authority and agreement of the Commons for levying new taxes; but from early times the House sought the redress of grievances before approving the Crown's taxation proposals, and this was the cornerstone of Parliament's growing status.

It is now a basic constitutional principle that it is for the Crown (in fact, the government of the day) and not for Parliament to propose expenditure and taxation. This *financial initiative of the Crown* means, in practice, that only ministers may make proposals for spending and taxes. If Parliament agrees to those proposals, then they are given authority through legislation.

The House of Commons has a special role in financial matters, asserted in a resolution of 1671, which stated 'That in all aids given to the King by the Commons, the rate or tax ought not to be altered by the Lords', and reinforced seven years later by a resolution that said in splendidly comprehensive language:

> *All aids and supplies, and aids to his Majesty in Parliament, are the sole gift of the Commons; and all bills for the granting of any such aids and supplies ought to begin with the Commons; and that it is the undoubted and sole right of the Commons to direct, limit and appoint in such bills the ends, purposes, considerations, limitations, and qualifications of such grants, which ought not to be changed or altered by the House of Lords.*

The Lords did not endorse these views, and remained willing to reject tax measures outright.

Thus, in 1860 the Lords rejected the Paper Duty Repeal Bill and, more seriously, in 1909, the Finance Bill, which would have given effect to Lloyd George's controversial Budget. In the latter case, the result was the passing of the Parliament Act 1911 and the permanent restriction of the powers of the House of Lords to thwart the legislative will of the Commons.

One consequence of the *financial privilege* of the House of Commons is that *bills of aids and supplies*, principally Finance Bills, which authorise the government's taxation proposals, and Supply Bills, which authorise government spending, originate in the Commons and are not amended by the Lords. Finance Bills are debated on second reading in the Lords, but other proceedings are formal only.

The Parliament Act 1911 defines a *money bill* as a bill whose *only* purpose is to authorise expenditure or taxation, a definition that does not always apply to Finance Bills, but may cover other Bills. If the Commons passes a Bill certified by the Speaker as a money bill and it is sent to the Lords at least one month before the end of the session and has not been agreed by the Lords within a month, it may be sent directly for Royal Assent. Although it remains, in theory, possible for the Lords to amend money bills – and such amendments have in the past been made – the Commons are not obliged to consider them, and it is now inconceivable that any amendment would be attempted. The stages of money bills in the Lords are abbreviated and no money bill has ever had to be presented for Royal Assent under the terms of the 1911 Act.

A bill whose provisions involve an increase in public expenditure or taxation may begin in the House of Lords, but it may proceed in the Commons only if a minister takes charge of it. In such a case, the constitutional niceties are preserved by a *privilege amendment*: a subsection at the end of the bill that says 'Nothing in this Act shall impose any charge on the people or on public funds' or vary any such charge. This is a fiction, of course; and the provision is removed when the bill is in committee in the Commons.

Another practical effect of Commons financial privilege is that any Lords amendments to a Commons bill that involve a charge upon the public revenue not sanctioned by the Commons money resolution in respect of that bill are deemed disagreed to upon the Speaker's declaration, 'by reason of privilege'. A privilege reason for disagreeing to such amendments is now not questioned by the Lords. This is

Table 7.1 Parliament and financial cycles

Month	Budget cycle	Estimates cycle	Reporting cycle
Start of parliamentary session			
May	Finance Bill in Committee of the whole House and standing committee		
June	Finance Bill report stage and third reading		
July	Formal consideration by Lords (Finance Act)	First estimates day (debates on select committee reports) Supply and Appropriation (Main Estimates) Bill passed	Annual report and accounts (with audited accounts for year 1 and plans for years 3 and 4) published Select committees review and report.
July/October		Spending Review (usually plans for years 3, 4 and 5) published in certain years	
November/ December		Autumn Statement published Treasury Committee reports	
December/ January		Presentation of – Supplementary Estimates (for year 2); – Votes on Account (for year 3); – Excess Votes (for year1); – Ministry of Defence Votes A (for years 2 and 3) (for approval by 18 March)	Departmental Mid-Year reports published with updates on progress against objectives Select committees review
March	Budget statement and debate	Second and third Estimates days (debates on select committee reports) Supply and Appropriation (Anticipation and Adjustments Bill) passed (must be by 31 March)	
April		Main Estimates (for year 2) presented (for approval by 5 August)	
End of parliamentary session			

what is termed 'unwaivable privilege', as such amendments do not simply infringe the Commons financial primacy so that when they are disagreed to the 'financial privilege' reason is given (see page 209), but they have no financial cover and so are disagreed to without formal consideration by the Commons.

The financial pre-eminence of the Commons in matters of legislation does not mean that the Lords are inhibited in discussing or investigating financial subjects. Both in debate and through the work of select committees such matters are frequently pursued. The Economic Affairs Committee has often reported on certain policy aspects of the Finance Bill and, in 2013–14, an *ad hoc* select committee examined the consequences of the use of personal service companies for tax collection. The legislative primacy of the Commons in financial matters rests to some degree on the self-restraint of the Lords. Whether a reformed House of Lords would be equally restrained, and how the Commons might react, have been vigorously debated in the context of Lords reform proposals.

The annual cycles

Financial procedure is hideously complex; this is partly because of the complexity of the subject matter but is also because the process takes place in three largely separate cycles. The *Budget cycle* deals with broad financial issues, the management of the economy and the authorisation of taxation. The *estimates cycle* covers the authorisation of public spending; and the *reporting cycle* provides information on what money has been spent and how effectively it has been used. We will examine these individually (and hope to make them slightly less confusing); but Table 7.1 shows how events in all three relate. The fact that the parliamentary year, which now usually begins in May, does not exactly coincide with the financial year starting in April is a further complication.

Table 7.1 shows the main events in each of the Budget, estimates and reporting cycles. Dates are indicative rather than exact (except for the approval deadlines). The financial year beginning in April is designated year 2; during the session the House will also consider business relating to year 1 (the financial year that ended shortly before the start of the new session) and examine plans for the year 3 (which starts shortly before the end of the session) and beyond.

Some important economic decisions are scrutinised by Parliament but are not under parliamentary control: interest rates are set by the Bank of England rather than by the government; and the level of the public sector borrowing requirement does not require parliamentary authorisation.

The Budget cycle

The word 'budget' comes from the archaic French *bougette*, a little bag, which in English had its literal meaning from the fifteenth century; later, 'to open one's budget' meant 'to speak one's mind'. In 1733, Sir Robert Walpole – then Chancellor of the

Exchequer, as well as Prime Minister – was depicted in a satirical pamphlet as a quack doctor opening a bag of pills. The term rapidly became applied to the Chancellor's review of the national finances, given annually from Walpole's time onwards.

The Chancellor of the Exchequer normally delivers the Budget in March. There will also usually be a Budget not long after a general election if there has been a change of government. In recent years, the Budget statement has been on a Wednesday, although for most of the post-war period it was usually a Tuesday. Budget day is always something of a media event, with the Chancellor being photographed outside his residence at No. 11 Downing Street before leaving for the Commons, holding up the despatch box containing his Budget speech.

The Budget speech comes immediately after Question Time; in order not to upstage the Chancellor, the ten-minute rule bill slot (which is normally on Tuesdays and Wednesdays) for Budget day is deferred to the following Monday. Before the Chancellor's statement begins, the Speaker's place in the Chair is taken by the Chairman of Ways and Means, a tradition reflecting the fact that until 1967, when it was abolished, taxation proposals were made in the Committee of Ways and Means.

The Chancellor begins with the review of the nation's finances and the economic situation. Some of the form would be familiar to the Chancellor's predecessors over three centuries, but following the creation of the independent Office for Budget Responsibility (OBR) in 2010 – placed on a statutory footing in the Budget Responsibility and National Audit Act 2011 – the economic and public finance forecasts are those of that Office rather than of the Treasury. In the latter part of the speech – in which interventions are not usually taken – the Chancellor moves on to taxation proposals. Modern Budget statements last an hour or so: a far cry from Gladstone's four-and-three-quarter-hour marathon in 1853. When the Chancellor's statement is complete, the motions to give effect to its tax proposals – usually around 70 of them, although there were 89 in 2014 – are made available to the House. Strict secrecy should be maintained on the Budget proposals until the Chancellor announces them – not least because of their market sensitivity – so, exceptionally, no notice is given of these motions. However, Budget secrecy generally no longer has its former magic and, in the days leading up to the Budget statement, it is now not unusual to find remarkably authoritative media comment on possible proposals.

The Chancellor then usually moves a motion to give immediate legal effect to certain Budget proposals (four in 2014) to forestall the speculation that might take place if it were known that the duty on cigarettes or whisky, for example, would be raised, but not for days or weeks. Under the Provisional Collection of Taxes Act 1968, when this motion is agreed to, the proposals it covers have the force of law, but the House must agree to the motions on the individual proposals within ten sitting days. This procedure may apply to any proposal continuing a tax or altering its rate, but not to new taxes.

The Chancellor then moves what is known as the 'amendment of the law' motion. This is a general statement that 'it is expedient to amend the law with respect to the

National Debt and to make further provision in respect of finance', and it is the vehicle for the very broad Budget debate that follows. The Chancellor is followed not by the shadow Chancellor but by the Leader of the Opposition, who must make some shrewd guesses in advance to enable swift reaction to what the Chancellor has said, in addition to setting out the Opposition's economic policies.

The Budget debate normally lasts for four or five days, and at its conclusion all 70 or so motions are put to the House, providing the opposition parties with an opportunity to vote against – usually three or four – individual proposals with which they particularly disagree. The Finance Bill is then formally introduced on the basis of what have now become the *founding resolutions*.

The Finance Bill

The Finance Bill is a substantial document, often running to 250 or more clauses with many schedules. Its provisions combine changes to levels and types of taxation with much detailed administration of the tax system, which makes for greater complexity. It also provides for the renewal for the financial year just starting of taxes already in force.

The Finance Bill's second reading debate will be a single day, providing a further opportunity for a general debate on the government's fiscal policy. Proceedings on a bill based on founding resolutions such as the Finance Bill need not end at the moment of interruption, which formerly led to many late sittings, but a programme motion agreed at the time of second reading usually now supersedes these open-ended arrangements. At the same time, the House usually now agrees a motion to carry over the bill into the next session (see also page 129). The bill is then divided; clauses dealing with the major, or most controversial, proposals are taken in Committee of the whole House. The rest of the bill is committed to a public bill committee. The report stage and third reading usually occupy a further two days on the floor of the House.

Public bill committees on the Finance Bill have a character rather different from those on other bills. They are larger, often with 30 to 40 members rather than 20 or so; because of the regularity of Finance Bills, and of debates on economic affairs, the participants will know each other well and be old sparring partners; and the level of expertise is high. Both the opposition parties and government backbenchers will be extensively briefed by groups that will be affected by the Chancellor's proposals and assisted by them in drafting amendments to the often highly complex provisions of the bill. In addition to the usual rules about the admissibility of amendments (see page 191), MPs' ability to propose changes is restricted by the scope of the resolutions to which the House has agreed and, where the resolutions simply said 'that provision may be made about the level of' such and such a tax or charge, the levels actually proposed in the bill. For example, if the House agreed to a resolution that said that the rate of corporation tax should be 20 per cent, amendments seeking to raise that rate would not be in order, although it would be possible to move to reduce it.

Governments are usually even less willing to accept substantial amendments to the Finance Bill than they are in the case of other legislation, although disquiet among backbenchers can cause changes, whether following defeat on a vote, as with the scrapping of the second tranche of VAT on domestic fuel in December 1994, or by the government altering its proposals to head off possible defeat, as in the halving of the increase in petrol duty that was proposed in the 1981 Budget. However, to a great extent the Budget is a package and, for MPs of governing parties in particular, voting to defeat one proposal implies voting to increase revenue elsewhere – or to reduce public expenditure. However, less dramatic changes are occasionally made as a result of the committee stage of the Finance Bill. One example in 1998 was the proposal to tax agricultural earnings applied to the upkeep of historic houses. The Historic Houses Association briefed MPs on the committee, they took up the case, and the taxation was phased in rather than being introduced immediately, with considerable benefits for the national heritage.

The Finance Bill then goes to the Lords. A general economic debate is held on second reading of the Finance Bill, and remaining stages are then taken formally, without debate.

Budget information

On Budget day, the Treasury publishes the *Budget Report*, often known as the Red Book. The document, running to around 120 pages in 2014, provides an overview of the state of the economy and the public finances, sets out the detail of the Budget measures and their financial implications, and places those measures in the wider context of government policy. It is accompanied by a distributional analysis of the impact of the Budget on households and more detailed policy costings, as well as around fifty documents from HM Revenue and Customs on specific proposals.

At the same time, the OBR publishes its *Economic and Fiscal Outlook*, which sets out the forecasts for the economy and the public finances, and the OBR's assessment of the prospects for the government meeting its targets for the future health of the public finances periodically set in the Charter for Fiscal Responsibility. The OBR also provides a commentary on whether it considers the Treasury's costings to be reasonable.

Although the range and scale of the Budget documentation has fallen back from its peak during the Chancellorship of Gordon Brown, this single parliamentary event is the occasion for announcing a vast array of measures of great complexity. The audience for the proposals is, of course, much wider than Parliament, and the proposals and analysis are closely examined in the financial, commercial and industrial sectors. Nevertheless, the Budget proposals and information set the House of Commons a substantial task of scrutiny, which the legislative stages of the Finance Bill struggle to perform.

However, the Treasury Committee reports rapidly upon the Budget in order to inform consideration of the Finance Bill. It takes oral evidence not only from the Chancellor himself and senior Treasury officials, but also from the OBR, as well as from outside financial and economic experts. It often exposes otherwise neglected aspects of the Budget; for example, in 2014 highlighting the proposal to grant HM Revenue and Customs the power to recover money directly from taxpayers' bank accounts.

The Autumn Statement

In late November or early December, the Chancellor makes a second major economic statement to the House of Commons – the Autumn Statement. This statement provides an opportunity for the Chancellor to update the House on the government's plans for the economy and to set out the economic and fiscal forecasts of the OBR in its second *Economic and Fiscal Outlook* which is published at the same time. As with the Budget, the Autumn Statement contains policy measures and is accompanied by substantial documentation. The statement itself is not followed by formal financial proceedings comparable to those after the Budget, although the Chancellor can expect to answer questions after his statement for far longer than is usually the case with a Ministerial statement – for over two-and-a-half hours in 2013. The Autumn Statement is considered by the Treasury Committee in an inquiry almost comparable in scale and intensity to that on the Budget, albeit with a lesser focus on fiscal measures.

From the early 1980s until the early 1990s, the Autumn Statement also reported on the outcome of an annual spending round. From 1993 to 1996 public spending plans and taxation proposals were briefly combined in a 'unified Budget' in November. This was followed, from 1997 to 2010, by a return to the traditional spring Budget, but with a Pre-Budget Report in the Autumn including consultation on proposed Budget measures. From 2010, George Osborne reverted to the pre-1993 pattern, although the separation of this statement from the announcement of spending plans, introduced by Gordon Brown, was retained.

In 2010, the government established a tax consultation framework, setting out ideas on prospective tax changes. Although the Autumn Statement is not theoretically as consultative as the Pre-Budget Report, tax proposals in the Budget and Autumn Statement often involve consultation exercises rather than immediate legislative provisions. This can enable the government to modify the measures in the light of public responses, or withdraw them altogether.

The estimates cycle

The process of voting 'supply' has its origins in a time when monarchs needed to spend money that the Crown did not have, usually on wars. Parliament then had to be asked to supply the funds. Initially, Parliament authorised taxation alone and decisions on expenditure were for the Crown, but in the eighteenth century a settled practice emerged whereby separate parliamentary authorisation was required for how money was spent, as well as how as how it was raised. Thus, even when tax receipts are held in the government's bank account – the Consolidated Fund – distinct statutory authority is needed to spend them. The main method of authorising that spending in the Commons is through 'Supply' proceedings, as distinct from 'Ways and Means' proceedings that relate to taxation. Most public expenditure is authorised annually on the basis of government requests in the form of the estimates.

There are large areas of public expenditure that are not subject to annual parliamentary control based on the Supply estimates, either because there is standing statutory authority for such expenditure – for example, for net contributions to the European Union budget, or because the spending is funded by means other than taxation – such as national insurance contributions or council tax.

Resource accounting

Since 2001–02, as a result of the Government Resources and Accounts Act 2000, the estimates have been presented to Parliament on a 'resource' accounting basis (although they still also include a request for total cash (the *Net Cash Requirement*) to give effect to the spending). 'Resource' accounting – also known as 'accruals accounting' – records the economic costs of the provision of services and the consumption of assets (including depreciation and future liabilities such as those for compensation for early retirement). It is designed to give a more accurate picture of how resources are being used and makes government accounts much more like company accounts. It also allows a better assessment of how resources have been applied to the achievement of policy objectives. Cash accounting, the method used until 2001, merely tracked the movement of cash, creating an incentive to bring forward or delay cash payments at year end to stay within voted limits, and thus distorting longer-term spending patterns.

Public spending plans

Since 1998, successive governments have replaced the annual spending round with multi-year spending plans announced every two or three years. Initially, a spending review every other July (in 1998, 2000, 2002 and 2004) announced plans for three subsequent years, including revised plans for the year covered previously. In October 2007, the Labour government set three-year spending plans in a single exercise. In October 2010, the Coalition government announced spending plans for a four-year period up to 2014–15, supplemented in June 2013 by a single year spending round for 2015–16. In each case, an overall government expenditure ceiling has been set, and departments negotiate with Treasury Ministers to agree departmental totals and what will be achieved with such spending. The results are announced in a statement and accompanying publication, but there is no role for Parliament in the negotiation process.

For each department, spending reviews have set a *Departmental Expenditure Limit* (*DEL*) (split between resource and capital totals) within which that department must operate, even though some elements will be demand-led. Spending reviews also set out forecasts for *Annually Managed Expenditure* (*AME*). AME covers expenditure that is less predictable or controllable than DELs; for example, social security and Common Agricultural Policy payments. In 2010, within a context of considerable budgetary restraint, the spending review also sought to bear down on the growing costs of AME (particularly welfare benefits), and this is being extended from 2015–16 with a requirement for the House of Commons to approve spending on welfare above a preset 'welfare cap' based on past forecasts of spending from the OBR. Together, the DEL and AME total constitute *Total Managed Expenditure* (*TME*).

These multi-year spending reviews provide an important opportunity for debate on expenditure by the House of Commons, and for consideration of departmental priorities by select committees.

Votes on Account

Because the main process for statutory authorisation of departmental expenditure is not completed until nearly four months into the financial year in question, advanced authorisation is given on the basis of Votes on Account presented in January or February. These normally cover about 45 per cent of the amounts already authorised for each government department for the previous financial year. Votes on Account must be agreed by the House within a roll-up motion by 18 March each year (see page 245).

Ministry of Defence Votes A

The Bill of Rights 1688–89 prevented the Crown from maintaining a standing army in time of peace without the approval of Parliament. This control is exercised in part through Supply proceedings, and the Ministry of Defence 'Votes A' laid before the House by the Secretary of State for Defence alongside the Votes on Account and the Supplementary Estimates invite the annual authorisation by the House of Commons of the maximum numbers of personnel in the regular and reserve armed services for the coming year, and any modification of those limits for the current year.

Main estimates

The main estimates, one for each government department (and for other bodies such as the Office of Rail Regulation and the NHS Pension Scheme), are published within five weeks of the Budget, usually in late April. They form the principal request from the government to the House of Commons for the resources required to run the state in the following financial year. They vary from small departments such as the Cabinet Office, which in 2014–15 had a combined resource and capital voted budget of £557 million, to major areas of government expenditure: in 2014–15, the Department of Health had an equivalent budget of £103 *billion*.

Part I of each estimate provides the key information on which the House of Commons is being asked to vote: the net resource and capital totals within DEL, the equivalent totals for AME, any net non-budget requirement (principally the block grants for the devolved governments) and the *net cash requirement*. Even though government accounting is on a resource basis, the amounts sought are expressed in cash terms, as well as in resource terms, to control the cash flowing out of the Consolidated Fund. The Estimates now include totals for non-voted expenditure (that not requiring annual authorisation) so that estimates can be aligned with the budgets set in spending reviews and monitored by the Treasury.

Each estimate also contains a formal description of the services to be financed from each relevant budgetary boundary within the estimate (known as the *ambit*). The ambit also specifies the income that may be retained by the department. The ambit is an important part of the process of authorisation because it describes the purpose for which the money is sought, and expenditure must fall within that description. Finally, Part I of the estimate notes any amounts already allocated in the *Vote on Account*.

Part II of the estimate shows the resource requirement from Part I, broken down into more detail of what is going to be provided with the money. This breakdown forms the basis for in-year control of expenditure by the Treasury. If there is an underspend in one area and a requirement in another, funds may be moved between these subheads without further parliamentary authority (a process known as *virement*), although departments need prior Treasury approval to move income between subheads. The rationale for this is that Parliament approves the headline figures but not the detailed breakdown. The flexibility that virement gives also means that there is less need to build in a contingency into each subhead, which would encourage an over-provision in the estimate as a whole. Part II also contains a detailed reconciliation between a department's net resource requirement and the net cash requirement.

Part III provides detailed reconciliation between all expenditure and income within the accounting boundary. It also gives further information on departmental income (which was formerly subject to separate parliamentary control), including income that will be surrendered to the Consolidated Fund rather than used to finance its own expenditure. Finally, Part III states who will account for the estimate; for each estimate there must be an *Accounting Officer*, usually the Permanent Secretary of the government department concerned or the chief executive of an executive agency. Accounting Officers have a personal responsibility for the regularity and propriety of expenditure – including ensuring that money is spent only on purposes authorised by Parliament – as well as for the quality of internal financial controls in the department concerned.

The notes to each estimate describe any *contingent liabilities*: commitments that, if they were to be called upon, would require further expenditure. Although ministers may give guarantees or indemnities, Parliament is not bound in advance to honour any liabilities arising unless by law the liability is charged on the Consolidated Fund. Liabilities outside the normal course of business and above £300,000 or of a non-standard kind must be reported to Parliament.

When the estimates are published, departments send an explanatory memorandum on their estimates (the Estimates Memorandum) to the relevant select committee.

This explains differences between current and previous estimates, the reasons for major changes and the impact of the changes sought, facilitating more rigorous scrutiny of the estimates.

Supplementary estimates

Supplementary estimates are presented in February and seek authority for any additional funds that government departments have found to be necessary since the main estimates were prepared and can also now reduce the amounts sought. They are also accompanied by an Estimates Memorandum. *Revised estimates* may be presented in the early summer to replace the main estimate for a department prior to parliamentary approval, usually to reduce the amount sought or vary the way in which it is spent.

If emergencies arise, the government can have recourse to the contingencies fund. This is limited by law to 2 per cent of the previous year's total authorised supply expenditure, and any money drawn out of the fund must be repaid. Alternatively, the House may be asked to agree an out-of-turn estimate at any time. The motion to approve any such estimate would be separately debateable.

Excess Votes

Both main and supplementary estimates are timed to be approved within the financial year to which they relate, in order to set statutory limits that provide the benchmark for audit. Where a department's spending in a financial year is found by that process to have exceeded what Parliament authorised (or has been incurred for a purpose that was not authorised), Excess Votes are presented (usually in February) in the following or a subsequent financial year. These are examined by the National Audit Office (NAO), which advises the Public Accounts Committee; no excess vote may be put to the House for approval without debate unless that committee has no objection.

Roll-up motions and estimates days

In the later Victorian period, Supply motions provided the occasion for exhaustive (although not always relevant) debate, so that the Parliament sat well into August before the main estimates could be approved. In 1896, the Leader of the Commons, Arthur Balfour, obtained its agreement to a deadline of 5 August for votes on all outstanding estimates to 'give even the hardest worked of us some chance of enjoying, at all events, the end of an English summer'. All outstanding main estimates are now approved without debate on a single 'roll-up' motion prior to 5 August, with matching provision for roll-up motions on supplementary estimates, Defence Votes A and Excess Votes before 18 March. The only estimates that are now debated are those selected for debate on three estimates days each session, the first usually on the day of the summer roll-up, and the second and third shortly before and on the day of the spring roll-up (see Table 7.1 on page 236). Given the huge sums involved, and the myriad purposes for which they are used, three days may not seem much, and the process is, indeed, highly selective. The Liaison Committee, consisting of all the chairs of select committees, proposes one or two estimates for debate on each of these days. However, rather than inviting the House's detailed examination of a particular part of the estimate concerned, there is normally a reversal of the process. The estimate is used as a peg for a debate upon a select committee report that is usually much more about policy than about the money the government is seeking from the House of Commons. In order to allow debate on the maximum number of select committee reports, estimates days are almost always divided into two parts, each with a different subject.

Because of the financial initiative reserved to the Crown – in effect, to ministers – any amendment proposed to an estimates motion may only reduce the total of a request for resources, not increase it, although amendments to such motions are now rare, the last one that was moved being in June 2002. All questions on estimates day motions are deferred until immediately before the relevant roll-up, even if the debate is on a preceding day.

Supply Bills

Statutory authorisation to the Supply motions agreed at the time of the summer roll-up is given by the *Supply and Appropriation (Main Estimates) Bill* which is introduced when that motion and any motions arising from the first estimates day are agreed. The Bill gives parliamentary authority for total resources and capital requested to be used, and cash to be issued from the Consolidated Fund, but also limits the way in which the resources and capital can be used by *appropriating* the specified amounts to particular budgets in order to finance specified services, set out in the ambits that are reproduced in the Bill. The Bill also sets limits on defence numbers in accordance with Votes A. The questions on second and third reading are put without debate on a day subsequent to the roll-up; and there is no committee stage. Consideration in the Lords is purely formal.

The spring roll-up and any associated motions debated on the second and third estimates days are given effect in the Supply and Appropriation (Anticipation and Adjustments) Bill. This Bill authorises the amounts requested in the supplementary estimates, the Excess Votes and the Votes on Account, appropriates the first two of these and modifies limits on personnel numbers in the *Votes A*. This Bill, too, is passed without debate and is dealt with only formally by the Lords.

The reporting cycle

We have seen so far how the government seeks authorisation for the taxes it wishes to levy and the different stages by which its proposed spending is approved. What about the other side of the process: how does the government account for how it has spent the money?

Departmental annual reports and accounts

The main means by which departments account to Parliament for their spending and performance is their *annual report and accounts* which are usually published in June or July. The first element of these – the annual report – has been produced since 1991 and has developed substantially since then through initiatives by departments themselves and recommendations by select committees. The Treasury exercises general supervision and lays down guidance. The report element varies in format and presentation, but contains core elements. Each sets out the names and responsibilities of the department's ministers and senior officials and the department's structure and purpose, and surveys the principal activities of the previous year.

Departmental reports also give figures for planned spending over the remainder of the planning period, together with the estimated spending for the current year and the actual spending for the five previous years. Other elements include changes to previously published plans, value-for-money initiatives, and departmental running costs and staffing.

The Coalition government introduced a requirement for departments to produce *Departmental Business Plans* to identify their objectives (or 'structural reform priorities'), their plans for implementation and the data that can be used to measure progress. This framework superseded the public service agreements that served as the framework for objective-setting under the previous government. The report and accounts must include assessments of progress in relation to the business plans, using a series of measurable data on activity and performance.

The second element of the document comprises the accounts for the financial year ending in March that year. Accounts are prepared according to government standards adapted from International Financial Reporting Standards and, in many respects, are similar to annual accounts of private sector businesses. In addition to the standard primary financial statements, the consolidated statement of overall expenditure (equivalent to an income statement or profit and loss account), the statement of financial position (or balance sheet) and a statement of cash flows, there is a *Statement of Parliamentary Supply* comparing voted and non-voted budgets in the final estimate with final audited outturn. These are followed by a number of notes giving further information on categories of expenditure, on income and on assets and liabilities. The format of accounts is reviewed annually, and there are plans for more radical changes to make the accounts more useful to parliamentary and other users, while retaining the components necessary for parliamentary and public accountability.

The accounts of government departments (and many other public bodies, with some controversial exceptions, such as the BBC) are audited by the NAO, headed by the Comptroller and Auditor General (C&AG) (see page 248). Each set of accounts is preceded by the C&AG's certificate and report which sets out how the NAO has audited the accounts, and whether they represent a true and fair statement of the position. The C&AG may qualify his opinion on the accounts, if there are concerns that the financial statements do not fully comply with accounting standards; for example, spending may be misstated due to large fraud and error rates. In rare cases, the C&AG may even 'disclaim' the accounts or aspects of the accounts if there is insufficient audit evidence to support a 'true and fair' opinion.

Mid-year reports

The information in the first element of the annual report and accounts has, since 2013–14, been complemented by *Mid-Year Reports*, which are published by departments in December or January. These supersede the Autumn Performance Reports that were published until 2009. The mid-year reports are shorter than the annual reports, and only cover the period from April to September, and are not subject to audit, but provide a more focused commentary on performance.

Select committee scrutiny of expenditure and performance

As part of the core tasks for departmental select committees agreed in 2002 and revised in 2012 (see page 329), select committees are expected 'to examine the expenditure plans, outturn and performance of the department and its arm's length bodies, and the relationships between spending and delivery of outcomes'. Some committees conduct inquiries focused on expenditure, so that the Defence Committee has regularly examined the supplementary estimates for the financing of military operations in Iraq and Afghanistan, for example. In 2014, the Justice Committee drew the House's attention to a supplementary estimate from the Serious Fraud Office seeking an in-year increase in budget of over 50 per cent.

In its 2012 report on select committee effectiveness, the Liaison Committee encouraged select committees to broaden their scrutiny of departmental performance, focusing more on future plans and expected outcomes, including alternatives that could be considered. That committee also pressed for financial implications to be considered as a matter of routine when policies are examined. Select committees are aided in their examination by the Committee Office's *Scrutiny Unit*, which, in addition to providing analysis for individual committees, also supports the Liaison Committee in discussions with government on improvements to financial transparency and reporting.

The Comptroller and Auditor General and the National Audit Office

Although accounts may be examined by departmental select committees, across government and other public bodies as a whole, audit and control is the task of the Comptroller and Auditor General backed by the Public Accounts Committee (PAC).

The C&AG heads a staff of about 820 (about two-thirds of whom are either professionally qualified or training for professional qualifications) in the NAO, whose main building is about a mile from the Houses of Parliament. The C&AG has a direct responsibility to Parliament and works closely with the PAC. This relationship is recognised by the C&AG's personal status as an Officer of the House of Commons.

The C&AG's work has four main elements. In his function as Comptroller, the Bank of England releases money to the government from the Consolidated Fund only on the authority of one of the C&AG's officials, who certifies that the release does not exceed the amount voted by the House. The C&AG also carries out an audit of the propriety and regularity of accounts – a total of some 430 accounts examined every year, including government departments, executive agencies and associated public bodies. The National Audit Act 1983, which established the NAO (previously the Exchequer and Audit Department), also gave the C&AG the task of examining the economy, efficiency and effectiveness of public spending. This leads to the publication each year of about 60 value-for-money studies. Examples from 2014 are the privatisation of Royal Mail, whistleblowing policies and adult social care. Finally, the NAO supports select committees and individual MPs in their scrutiny of public spending and service delivery.

The C&AG is independent in matters of audit judgement, although (under the Budget Responsibility and National Audit Act 2011) the operation of the NAO is now overseen by a Board. The budget for the NAO is considered by a statutory body, the Public Accounts Commission, composed of MPs.

The Public Accounts Committee

The PAC was first established at Gladstone's instigation in 1861. The committee has up to 16 members and is always chaired by an opposition MP. The standing orders give it the narrow task of 'the examination of the accounts showing the appropriation of the sums granted by Parliament to meet the public expenditure, and of such other accounts laid before Parliament as the Committee may think fit'; but for some years the committee has ranged more widely, principally drawing on the value-for-money reports of the C&AG. This routinely takes it into areas of policy (which it is always said not to investigate) and produces sometimes unhelpful overlap with the work of departmental committees.

The PAC's consideration of the C&AG's reports enhances their status, and the committee's work is made more credible by the very substantial back-up of the C&AG and his staff. Although the most frequent witnesses at the twice-weekly meetings of the PAC are Accounting Officers, the Committee has expanded its range of witnesses in recent years, including contractors and (in the case of high-profile sessions on tax arrangements) individual companies. The PAC publishes some fifty reports a year, achieving a high public profile and keeping many senior mandarins on their toes. In recent years, though, it has given in too readily to the temptations of confrontational questioning and media headlines, and has undoubtedly lost some effectiveness as a result.

Conclusion

Because the role of the House of Commons in the authorisation of taxation and expenditure is of such long standing and involves so many procedural peculiarities, the House is open to criticism for the imbalance between the ink expended in describing that role and the level of parliamentary engagement in practice. Such criticism has a point, although in forming a judgement it is important to take into account the opportunities for scrutiny, as well as the formal processes of authorisation.

On taxation, the House of Commons does its job quite well, at least in comparison with its examination of expenditure. There are still multiple opportunities for debate on tax measures on the floor of the House, and the Public Bill Committee on the Finance Bill takes its job seriously. However, the Finance Bill has largely escaped the reforms that have benefited legislative proceedings as a whole. There is little or no pre-legislative scrutiny and no evidence sessions are held at the start of the public bill committee stage. The Treasury and HMRC continue to use the annual opportunity of the Finance Bill to make manifold changes to the ferociously complex law on tax, sometimes after public consultation, but proposals for systematic pre-legislative scrutiny of the tax administration elements, or for their inclusion in a separate bill, have met with Treasury resistance.

So far as expenditure is concerned, opportunities for debate and consideration closely linked to the formal decisions on authorisation are almost non-existent. The separation between debate and decision is of long standing, and a cause of complaint by select committees for nearly 100 years. In 1981, a Procedure Committee referred to 'the myth of effective control'. The subsequent introduction of three estimates days provided some formal link between debate and decision, but the connection is still tenuous, with the priority for select committees and participating MPs invariably being with policies rather than expenditure, and what discussion on expenditure that does takes place seldom arises from the estimates.

In 2008, the Liaison Committee identified three preconditions for progress in recreating financial scrutiny – less complex financial reporting within government, reforms to expenditure proceedings in the Chamber and higher levels of engagement by committees themselves. Reforms introduced by the Treasury with parliamentary support as part of the Alignment Project have made it easier to read across between the budgetary limits set in spending reviews, the more detailed plans in departmental reports and the estimates for each year. Select committees have more information about changes as a result of estimates memoranda. In 2009, the Liaison Committee encouraged select committees to focus more on future spending plans. It envisaged that estimates day debates might consider motions on a department's future spending plans, including proposals for increased expenditure, and that the Procedure Committee might look again at the idea of referring some estimates for debate in a general committee.

Some have advocated institutional changes to galvanise financial scrutiny. In 2006, the Hansard Society proposed that some departmental select committees might pilot a Finance and Audit Sub-Committee. In 2012, Edward Leigh and John Pugh, two MPs who had served, respectively, as Chair and member of the PAC, proposed the creation of a Budget Committee to examine spending plans and propose debates for estimates days, as well as the appointment of a Parliamentary Budget Officer to give a higher profile to the support given to financial scrutiny.

The reform moment that gripped the Commons in the wake of the expenses scandal has not itself led to changes to financial scrutiny and control, but has opened up opportunities. The Liaison Committee proposal for debates on future spending plans, and for motions about spending priorities in the future, could be given effect in backbench time. The Treasury is unlikely to support institutional reforms, but it has led the way in improving the consistency of the information reported to the House. The power lies within the hands of select committees, if the will is there.

8

Debates

The *Oxford English Dictionary* defines the principal meaning of 'debate' as 'to dispute about, argue, discuss, especially to discuss a question of public interest in a legislative or other assembly'. Most proceedings in Parliament, whether on legislation or any other matter, take the form of debates. The main exceptions are questions and the examination of witnesses by select committees. In this chapter, we look at how debates take place on the floor of each House and elsewhere, how motions are moved and amended, and at some of the conventions of parliamentary debate.

Substantive motions

A substantive motion is one that expresses an opinion about something. The subject matter may range from 'That this House welcomes the Natural Capital Committee's first annual State of Natural Capital report; and urges the government to adopt the report's recommendations and to take concerted action to embed the value of natural capital in the national accounts and policy-making processes as early as possible', for which there may be a dozen MPs in the Chamber, to 'That this House has no confidence in Her Majesty's Government', which will be a full-dress occasion, with intense media interest and the Chamber packed, perhaps to see the Prime Minister of the day fighting for his or her political life and the survival of the government.

A motion is *moved*, or proposed, by an MP who sponsors it. No seconder is required in the House of Commons; the seconding of the motion for the reply to the Queen's Speech is a tradition rather than a requirement.

If the motion requires notice, then the names of that member and any others who are putting the motion forward will appear on the Order of Business (although any minister, including a whip, may move a government motion, and any member of the relevant committee may move a motion in the name of the Chair on behalf of a committee). The MP moving the motion argues for its approval by the House. When he or she sits down, the Speaker will *propose the Question*, stating to the House what must be decided. Rather than read out a long text, he will normally say 'The Question is, as on the Order Paper'. A debate then takes place, with the Chair normally calling MPs alternately from one side of the House and then the other.

If an *amendment* is down to the motion and is *selected* by the Speaker (see page 48), then at some point in the debate the Chair will ask one of the MPs whose names are to the amendment on the Order of Business to move it (although any MP could do so). It is possible for the Speaker to select a *manuscript amendment* – that is, one that was not tabled before the rising of the House at the previous sitting and so does not appear on the Order of Business, but this is unusual.

Once the amendment has been moved, the Speaker proposes the Question upon it, saying 'The original Question was [as on the Order Paper]. Since when an amendment has been moved [as on the Order Paper]. The Question is, that the amendment be made'. Strictly speaking, the debate then takes place on the amendment rather than on the motion that was first moved, but in most cases the scope of debate covers both.

When the time for the debate has elapsed, because the Question must be put at any particular time, or because the closure (see page 141) has been moved and agreed to – or simply because there are no more MPs wishing to speak – the Speaker *puts the Question* on the amendment first ('The Question is, that the amendment be made') and the House decides that question, if necessary, by dividing (see page 154). Once the House has made its decision on the amendment, the original motion – whether or not amended – is decided, again by dividing if necessary. If an amendment was moved, the original motion is also known as the *main Question*.

If the motion is agreed to, it becomes a *resolution* or an *order* of the House. The distinction is that a resolution expresses an opinion (for example, 'that this House has no confidence in Her Majesty's Government'); an order is something on which the House can exercise power directly ('that a select committee be appointed to examine . . .').

The Syria debate

As an example of the House dealing with a substantive motion – in this case, a very high-profile one – let us take the debate on Syria, for which the House was recalled on 29 August 2013. The government tabled a motion deploring the use of chemical weapons in Syria, describing the diplomatic activity at the United Nations, and noting that before any British involvement in military action a further vote of the House would take place. As there was no opportunity to table amendments to the motion the previous day, the Speaker agreed to select a manuscript amendment from the Leader of the Opposition. He also announced a five-minute limit for backbench speeches (which was later reduced to three minutes). The Prime Minister opened the debate by moving the motion: he spoke for 41 minutes and accepted 22 interventions. The Leader of the Opposition spoke next, moving his amendment, which left out all the words in the motion after 'That this House' and added other words that were similar to those in the Prime Minister's motion, although seeking to limit the type of action that might be the subject of a further vote. He spoke for

26 minutes and took 13 interventions. The Speaker then announced that 99 MPs had asked to speak: in the end, 60 of them were successful. At about 9.30 p.m., the Speaker called an opposition spokesman and then the Deputy Prime Minister to wind up. At 10.00 p.m., the House divided on the amendment, which was defeated by 332 votes to 220. The Speaker then put the 'main Question', on the original motion in its unamended form, which was defeated (the Ayes were 272 and the Noes 285). Thirty Conservative and nine Liberal Democrat members voted against the government. Following the declaration of the result, the Leader of the Opposition, on a point of order, sought a government assurance that they would not use the Royal Prerogative to commit troops without another vote, and the Prime Minister, on another point of order, gave that undertaking. There was an unrelated point of order about Colombia and the House then adjourned.

This was for many reasons an unusual debate, but it contained all the key elements of debate on a substantive motion. By contrast, when the government sought approval for limited military intervention against Islamic State (IS) fighters in Iraq, Commons approval was given with 524 votes in favour and 43 against. While the Lords were not asked to vote, sentiment in that House was very similar. As we saw in Chapter 6, debate on legislation is structured in much the same way: a member moves 'that the such and such Bill be now read a second time'; it is possible to move a 'reasoned amendment'; and at the end of the debate the amendment and the main Question are disposed of. Similarly, when an amendment to the text of a bill (or a new clause or schedule) is proposed in Committee of the whole House or public bill committee, or in the House on report, the amendment is moved, and the question is proposed and debated. Amendments to amendments or to new clauses or schedules are treated in the same way as amendments to motions.

The moving of an amendment, whether in the House or in committee, is subject to the Chair having selected it. As we saw in Chapter 3, this is a power through which the Chair exercises great influence on the shape of proceedings. However, the power of selection does not exist in select committees (when, for example, they consider draft reports).

Neutral motions

A different type of motion is tabled when what is wanted is a debate, rather than a decision. These debates used to take place on the motion 'that this House do now adjourn', and this is still done in Westminster Hall and for the half-hour debate at the end of each day in the Chamber. The subject for debate is shown on the Order Paper but does not form part of the text of the motion. Since 2007, however, a motion on the floor of the House of Commons that is purely a vehicle for debate has been in the form 'that this House has considered the matter of X', and a standing order provides that if the motion is expressed in neutral terms, no amendments may be tabled to it. (This is intended to replicate the rule that an adjournment motion cannot be amended, but it can be a matter of dissension if the government tables a neutral motion when the opposition would prefer an amendable one.) If debate finishes before the moment of interruption (see page 141), a division could still be forced, but this is unusual. Normally, the motion is passed without opposition, or debate is allowed to continue till the moment of interruption, when the motion simply lapses.

Before being replaced by 'has considered' motions, some debates on adjournment motions were great parliamentary occasions. One such in 1940 ('the Norway debate') led directly to the replacement of Neville Chamberlain by Winston Churchill as Prime Minister. In recent years up to 2007, the debates at emergency sittings of the House (for example, on the invasion of the Falkland Islands and on the 11 September 2001 terrorist attacks in the USA) were on motions for the adjournment.

Disposing of a motion

Once a motion has been moved and the question proposed, it may be disposed of by being decided one way or the other, as outlined above. It may also stand adjourned or lapse because the moment of interruption arrives and there is no provision for it to be debated beyond that hour. It will then have been 'talked out' (see page 141). A motion may also be *withdrawn* or *superseded*.

Withdrawal

Once a motion of any sort has been moved, and before it has been put to the House or a committee for decision, it is possible to seek to withdraw it. But because the motion has been moved, it is in the possession of the House or committee and may be withdrawn only 'by leave' – that is, by unanimous consent. The MP who moved it says 'I beg leave to withdraw the motion [or amendment]'; and the Chair says to all and sundry 'Is it your pleasure that the motion [amendment] be withdrawn? . . . Motion [amendment], by leave, withdrawn'. But even one objection is enough to prevent this happening, and in that case the motion or amendment must eventually be put to a decision.

Superseding

It is possible to supersede debate on a question before the House or committee by what is known as a *dilatory motion*. This may be a motion for the adjournment of the debate, or of the committee, or of the House. In consideration of legislation, it may also be a motion that further consideration of the bill be adjourned, or 'that the Chair do report progress'. The moving of such a motion is subject to the permission of the Chair, who must be satisfied that it is not an abuse. If it proceeds, however, debate upon it supersedes the original debate, which is not resumed until the dilatory motion has been decided (or, indeed, which will not be resumed at that sitting if the dilatory motion is successful).

A rare and old-fashioned motion similar to a dilatory motion is *the previous Question*: a motion 'that the Question be not now put'. If it is agreed to, the House immediately moves on to the next business; but if it is not agreed to, whatever matter was interrupted must be decided immediately (as when a closure is agreed to).

Debate may also be interrupted by a motion 'that the House sit in private'. This might be in earnest if extraordinary circumstances arose during some national emergency; the House sat in secret several times during the First and Second World Wars. Modern use of the motion (formerly in the words 'that Strangers do now withdraw') has been to attempt to disrupt business or express strong objection to some proceeding. The Chair must put the motion immediately to the House for decision; but it may not be moved more than once during a sitting. It is rarely successful; the most recent occasion was in December 2001, during proceedings on the Anti-Terrorism, Crime and Security Bill (as an expression of objection rather than to allow some confidential matter to be discussed). The government was unprepared for such a motion to be moved, the motion was agreed to, and the House sat in private for nearly an hour. As the *Hansard* reporters withdraw when the House sits in private, there is no record of what was said during that time.

Quorum

A motion to sit in private may also be used to test whether a quorum is present, which in the House or Committee of the whole House can be demonstrated only when a vote takes place. If the result of the vote shows that fewer than 40 MPs are present (35 voting, 2 tellers on each side and the occupant of the Chair), then the business that was under discussion beforehand stands over until the next sitting of the House. If the business is not government business, this may well be fatal, and this tactic is used from time to time to attempt to kill private members' bills.

In general committees and select committees, no such procedure exists; the specified quorum must be present throughout or the chair must suspend the committee. In select committees, the quorum is three or one-quarter of the membership, whichever is the greater; in general committees, it is one-third of the membership (subject to a maximum quorum of 17). In both cases, fractions are rounded up. Somewhat illogically in general committees, the chair is not counted in calculating what the quorum is but does count towards whether a quorum is present. In Westminster Hall (see page 259), the quorum is three.

If the number of members present on the government side of a committee alone does not provide a quorum, the opposition sometimes uses the tactic of removing its own MPs from the room and thus stopping the business. The rule of the business standing over does not apply 'upstairs', however, and as soon as a quorum is again present (provided it is within twenty minutes), debate proceeds.

We now look at several different types of motion.

Motions on opposition days

Each session, 20 days are set aside for debates initiated by the opposition parties. Seventeen of these are allocated to the Official Opposition and three to the second-largest opposition party, which usually shares them with other, smaller, opposition parties. Opposition day debates account for about 11 per cent of the total time of the House.

These days are ring-fenced opposition time; but, although their scheduling is normally agreed through the usual channels (see page 82), exactly when opposition days are taken is formally in the gift of the government. Each is the main business of a parliamentary day, so usually about six hours' debate – although ministerial statements can cut into this (often producing objections from the opposition). Days are often informally divided into two parts of roughly equal length so that two subjects can be debated.

These days are a key opportunity for the opposition parties, and especially for the Official Opposition, to try to expose the government over an issue on which it may be vulnerable, or to provide a shop window for one of its own policies. Among the subjects selected by the Labour Party in 2014 were housing, fixed-odds betting terminals, banking, the national minimum wage, Syrian refugees, and the quality of teaching.

The motion moved in the House is usually a strongly worded criticism of government policies; the government usually tables an amendment that seeks to remove all the words of the motion after 'That this House' and substitute a warm endorsement of what the government is doing. The frontbench speakers will be the relevant shadow secretary of state and shadow minister, and their counterparts in government. The debate is often combative. Some can be testing for ministers, as well as a proving ground for opposition frontbenchers; and opposition days can give newer MPs an opportunity to shine and perhaps catch the selectors' eye as possible ministerial material.

At the end of an opposition day debate, the Question is put in an old-fashioned form that survives only in this case. Normally, the government amendment would be decided first and would no doubt be approved. The next Question would be the main Question, as amended; so both votes would take place on the government's words, not those of the opposition. The device that is used to avoid this is that the first Question put is 'That the original words stand part of the Question' – in other words, a vote on keeping the opposition motion as it is. When this proposition has been defeated, the second Question put is 'That the proposed words be there added' – a vote to approve the government's amendment. When this is agreed to, the Chair declares the main Question, as amended, to be agreed to, without a further vote (which would be pointless, as it would be a second vote on the government's text).

This may seem a rather complex minuet, but it is important to opposition parties to be able to put their own proposition to the House rather than to be forced simply to vote upon the government's counter-proposition.

Sometimes (and more frequently in the 2010 Parliament) the government does not table an amendment to an opposition motion and simply votes against it.

Government substantive motions

Most of the occasions on which the government needs to seek the approval of the House of Commons are on legislation or spending. Exceptionally, as in the debate on Syria, it may wish to have the backing of an explicit resolution of the House of Commons. On most substantive motions in a session, the government is in the position of defending or explaining in the face of opposition challenge. However, there are some occasions when the government puts a substantive motion before the House for debate. These are often when procedural changes are being proposed; when the Committee on Standards reports on the conduct of an MP; domestic business such as approving arrangements for the summer opening for visitors; or money and ways and means motions that are taken other than immediately after second reading. The four or five days of debates on the Queen's Speech and on the Budget – although each is very much a special case – may also be counted as government substantive motions.

Backbench business

Until 1995, four half-days and ten Fridays were set aside for motions moved by backbenchers chosen by ballot. As part of the Jopling reforms (see page 132), these were abolished and replaced by extra opportunities for backbenchers to raise subjects on the adjournment on Wednesday mornings (later moved, with increased time, to Westminster Hall). Private members' motion days gave individual MPs an opportunity to put a proposition to the House – which could be as controversial as they wished.

Between 1995 and 2010, there was no way for an ordinary MP to put a proposition to the House and have it voted on (except in a limited way for legislative proposals under the ten-minute rule (see page 203). However, the Backbench Business Committee, established in 2010 as a result of the Wright Committee recommendations (see page 75), is allotted at least 27 days in each session (and a further 8 days in Westminster Hall), and decides the business to be tabled on these days on the basis of proposals made by MPs. This business normally consists either of substantive motions or of neutral ones. Select committee statements (see page 366) are also backbench business.

Daily adjournment motions

Every day, after other business has been disposed of, backbenchers have an opportunity to raise a subject in the half-hour adjournment debate. The government whip on duty formally moves 'That this House do now adjourn', and the backbencher then has fifteen minutes or so to speak, followed by a minister replying for the remainder of the time. Brief speeches from other MPs are allowed with the permission of the initiator of the debate and the minister, and either may give way to interventions within their own speech.

MPs apply to the Table Office for an adjournment slot (by the end of a Wednesday for the following week), and their applications are put into a ballot operated by the Speaker's Office. The Speaker himself chooses the subject for the Thursday slot, often picking an MP who has an urgent constituency matter to raise or who has been consistently unlucky in the ballot.

Any subject can be raised, provided that it falls within the responsibilities of the government so that a minister can reply to the debate. MPs are, in theory, not allowed to use the half-hour adjournment primarily to call for legislation but, in practice, this rule is not especially restrictive. As an illustration of the topics raised, five successive sitting days in February 2014 produced debates on national parks, European Union funding, safety of young drivers, the Post Office Museum and the Post Office Railway, and community radio licences.

The half-hour adjournment is a sought-after opportunity for backbenchers, providing about 150 to 160 mini-debates each year and occupying about 6 per cent of the total time of the House. Unlike the Westminster Hall debates (see below), the timing of the half-hour adjournment is not always predictable because it depends on the main business that precedes it; but many MPs see such debates in the Chamber as having a higher status. If the main business finishes early, the debate may none-theless continue until thirty minutes after the moment of interruption, and therefore could last considerably more than half an hour.

The half-hour adjournment often shows the extraordinary flexibility of the House of Commons. Some great matter may have been decided at the end of the day's main business, eagerly reported by the media; but as MPs stream out of the Chamber after a dramatic vote, the House – albeit much depleted – may turn to a very specific local problem: perhaps the difficulties faced by a single constituent.

Recess debates

Before each recess, there is a debate arranged by the Backbench Business Committee on 'matters to be considered before the forthcoming adjournment'. This gives an opportunity for backbenchers to raise topics similar to the half-hour adjournment debates, although in this case they are replied to not individually by the departmental ministers responsible for the subjects but in an omnibus reply given by the Leader or Deputy Leader of the House (although sometimes some of the subjects have been grouped by department and the departmental ministers have replied to those). This is parliamentary time valued by backbenchers, as evidenced by the number of takers, which often means that a time limit on speeches is imposed.

Emergency debates

In Chapter 5 (page 138), we described how an MP can make a case for an emergency debate; if granted by the Speaker, a debate of up to three hours takes place on a motion that the House has considered the subject the MP wishes to raise. However, such debates are rare; there have been only six in the last ten years. Debates during a recall of the House (see pages 50 and 131) also have the character of emergency debates, although these happen on the initiative of the government.

Westminster Hall

Much of the business in Westminster Hall takes place on the adjournment, so this may be a good place to describe this important debating forum.

Following the House's approval of a recommendation from the Modernisation Committee, from the beginning of the session 1999–2000 a 'parallel chamber' was established, known as 'Westminster Hall' but, in fact, in the Grand Committee Room, a large committee room off the northern end of Westminster Hall. The idea had its origin in the 'Main Committee', a parallel but subordinate chamber used by the Australian House of Representatives in Canberra.

The Westminster parallel chamber was intended to allow debates, open to all MPs, on less contentious business for which it would be difficult to find time on the floor of the House. Such business was to be referred by agreement through the usual channels, and decisions in Westminster Hall would be taken only by unanimity. The more consensual approach of Westminster Hall was emphasised by a seating layout closer to the hemicycle found in many other parliaments, with two rows of seats on each side as in the Chamber but with two more rows in a semicircle at the end, facing the Chair.

The Modernisation Committee was keen to avoid two possible disadvantages of a parallel chamber; that the additional time available should not simply provide an outlet for more government business – and especially not more legislation, and that the Chamber of the House itself should remain clearly pre-eminent.

Westminster Hall sittings take place on Tuesdays and Wednesdays from 9.30 a.m. to 11.30 a.m., when they are suspended to allow MPs to attend the main Chamber, resuming at 2.30 p.m. until 5.00 p.m. On Thursdays, the sitting time is 1.30 p.m. to 4.30 p.m. There is also a Westminster Hall sitting on a Monday from 4.30 p.m. to 7.30 p.m. when the Backbench Business Committee has set down a debate on an e-petition. Sittings in Westminster Hall are suspended for any votes in the House but have 'injury time' to compensate.

On Tuesdays and Wednesdays, Westminster Hall is given over to backbench adjournment debates, two of one-and-a-half hours each – which are intended for broader subjects on which a number of MPs will want to speak, and three of half an hour each. The Backbench Business Committee chooses the subject for one of the longer debates on a Tuesday, and two ballots are held on the Wednesday of the previous week for the six half-hour debates and the remaining three longer ones; MPs may enter for both categories but cannot be successful in both. To minimise the disruption to ministers' work, each government department is on call to respond to debates every other week rather than (as in the House) whenever a relevant debate comes up. The business for Thursdays may include debates on select committee reports chosen by the Liaison Committee, which has given the work of those committees a higher profile, or other matters chosen by the Backbench Business Committee, and (not for some time) *cross-cutting oral questions* (see page 289). Forthcoming business in Westminster Hall is set out in Part B of *future business* (see page 152).

In a typical week in April 2014, broader hour-and-a-half subjects included the funding of schools, taxis and private hire vehicles, bowling greens and admissions to Catholic schools.

Table 8.1 Sitting time in Westminster Hall compared with sitting time in the House, in hours and minutes

Business	Session 2012–13	Session 2013–14
Backbench debates (ballotted)	270:55	284:18
Backbench debates (BBCom)		23:24
BBCom debates	34:55	39:05
Liaison Committee debates	36:23	49:52
Petitions	7:09	5:43
Select Committee statements		0:23
Miscellaneous	0:07	0:01
Total	349:29	402:46
House total	1135:30	1273:24

Note: Suspensions are left out of Westminster Hall sitting hours.

In Westminster Hall, the chair is taken by a member of the Panel of Chairs under arrangements supervised by the Chairman of Ways and Means (who has overall responsibility for proceedings in the same way as the Speaker in the House). The proceedings are recorded in *Hansard* and published in hard copy and on the parliamentary website in the same way as proceedings in the Chamber. Westminster Hall sittings are also televised in their entirety.

Decisions in Westminster Hall may be taken only by unanimity; if a decision is challenged, it is referred to the House. In addition, if six MPs object to further proceedings, a debate stands adjourned. This has not yet happened, as no substantive business has been taken in Westminster Hall; all debates have been on the adjournment (except for those on e-petitions, which are specifically exempted from objection).

In the sessions 2012–13 and 2013–14, Westminster Hall has thus provided an additional 31 and 32 per cent of the total time available in the House, largely to the benefit of backbench debates on the adjournment. In an average year, it is likely that there will be 320 such debates, about 130 of the longer hour-and-a-half slots and 190 of the half-hour debates.

Debates in the Grand Committees and the Standing Committee on Regional Affairs

The Scottish, Welsh and Northern Ireland Grand Committees (not to be confused with the select committees on each of those parts of the UK) consist of all the MPs sitting for constituencies in each country. Additional MPs from elsewhere are added to the Welsh and Northern Ireland committees. In the years immediately before devolution, the roles of all three committees were widened, allowing them to hear statements from ministers (including ministers in the Lords), to hold sessions of oral questions, to consider bills and delegated legislation, and to hold adjournment debates. Post-devolution, the committees have met less frequently, and the Scottish Grand Committee has not met at all since 2003. All three committees may, with the approval of the House, meet away from Westminster in their respective parts of the UK.

In the sessions 2012–13 and 2013–14, the Welsh Grand Committee sat six times (to discuss such matters as the Queen's Speech, the Budget, and the Silk Commission on Devolution), and the Northern Ireland Grand Committee has sat once (in Belfast, to discuss 'Peace and progress'). The Regional Affairs Committee consists of thirteen MPs sitting for constituencies in England, although any MP with a seat in England may attend and speak. The committee considers matters referred to it by the House and, with the leave of the House, may sit away from Westminster. A sitting of the committee may begin with a ministerial statement, followed by questions, for one hour; then a debate for three hours. The Committee has not met since 2004. From January 2009 to April 2010, this Committee was replaced by a set of experimental Regional Grand Committees, which could meet either at Westminster or in the relevant region.

Early day motions

Every sitting day, about ten motions are tabled 'for an early day' – that is, for debate on an unspecified day. Almost all these 'early day motions' (EDMs) are tabled by backbenchers (although 'prayers' – see page 226 – first make their appearance as EDMs), so the chances of their being debated are negligible. Very occasionally, as in the case of the 1989 EDM on war crimes, a really significant EDM will be given debating time by the government or may figure in an opposition day debate. In addition, a motion critical of the Speaker will first appear as an EDM but, by convention, the government will quickly find time to debate it.

An EDM is simply an expression of a view that could be debated by the House (they all begin 'That this House'). They may be tabled by any MP, must not be longer than 250 words and must conform to other rules of order (for example, no unparliamentary language, and no reference to matters *sub judice*). An EDM appears in the Vote bundle, printed on blue pages, the day after it is tabled, and is reprinted for the rest of that week and the following week if any other MPs add their names to it or if an amendment is tabled. Thereafter, an up-to-date list of signatories is available only electronically. All EDMs fall at the end of the session.

EDMs are used for a wide variety of purposes: an MP may want to put on record the success of his local football team (perhaps attracting only the signatures of his constituency neighbours – and perhaps a hostile amendment from supporters of a rival team), or criticise somebody's opinion or action – almost like writing a letter to a national newspaper. EDMs are also used by MPs to defuse pressure from constituents and others by being seen to be doing something about an issue, or to put material on the parliamentary record under the protection of parliamentary privilege. EDMs are also used to test and gather support on major issues (recently, on reducing the tax on bingo, the future of the BBC Three television channel, the live export of horses and the use of animals in scientific research), and they are a useful source of political intelligence for the whips.

A random selection of EDMs tabled in April 2014 condemned human rights violations in Colombia, called for consultation on proposals to close ticket offices at London Underground stations, commemorated the author Sue Townsend following her death, called for the reversal of an EU ban on the importation of Alphonso mangoes, and celebrated Scout Community Week.

Over 1,000 EDMs are tabled each session and may attract a total of 600 or 700 signatures from MPs on a single sitting day. The number of EDMs, and the fact that many are on relatively trivial matters, have led to criticism of them as 'parliamentary graffiti'. On the other hand, it can be argued that they act as a safety valve, and that MPs (and people outside the House) value them as a means of expressing and testing views – although their increasing numbers are devaluing the currency. Apart from the 'prayers' referred to, none is ever likely to be debated, although it is sometimes suggested that time should be found for those with substantial numbers of signatures. This may be a superficially attractive suggestion, but a good debate needs opposition, and the prospect of a debate on a matter on which all agree does not appeal.

The rules and conventions of debate

An MP is called to speak by the Speaker (or by the chair in a committee). MPs who want to take part in debates in the House or Westminster Hall, but not when a bill is in Committee of the whole House or at report stage, write to the Speaker beforehand. This is not to say that those who do not write cannot be called, but those who do write have preference.

When there is great pressure to speak in a particular debate, the Speaker may impose a time limit on speeches, as in the Syria debate described earlier (see page 253). This does not apply to the two frontbenches (neither does it apply to one MP per debate speaking on behalf of the second largest opposition party: but this provision was not operated during the 2010 Parliament). The time limit is usually somewhere between 4 and 12 minutes, and may be varied upwards or downwards during the course of a debate. In order to preserve the custom of 'giving way' (see page 264), MPs get 'injury time' for the first two interventions they take from other members; the clock stops while the other member is intervening, and then the MP speaking gets an extra minute so that he or she can reply to the intervention. This injury time can be profitable if the reply to the intervention is very short! On occasions, the chair will suggest an informal time limit for speeches. Unlike the practice in the House of Lords and in many other parliaments, no list is made available of those who are to speak (although has been some pressure for the introduction of such a list). When the previous MP sits down, all those in the Chamber wanting to speak will bob up, hoping to 'catch the Speaker's eye'. The Speaker then says 'Mr Smith' and Mr Smith begins his speech. It is said that the practice of calling out a member's name originated with the corrupt Speaker Trevor at the end of the seventeenth century (see page 106). Up to then, the Speaker merely looked meaningfully at the member he wished to call; but Speaker Trevor had a truly grotesque squint, which is supposed to have led to widespread misunderstanding as to which member he had intended to call. This may be apocryphal, but Trevor's portrait confirms the squint, at least.

MPs must address the House through the Chair, referring to other members in the third person, and by their constituency or the office they hold rather than by name. So, an MP cannot say to another 'What do you mean by that?' but must say 'What does the honourable member for Loamshire East mean by that?'; and an MP cannot talk about 'Ed Miliband' or 'You in charge of the Labour Party' but must instead refer to 'the right honourable member for Doncaster North' or 'the Leader of the Opposition'. All MPs are referred to as 'honourable members' or 'the honourable lady' or 'the honourable gentleman'; those who are privy coun-sellors (usually present or former senior ministers) are styled 'right honourable'. This may sound rather antique, but it avoids the direct confrontation of two MPs addressing each other as 'you' and often helps to lower the temperature.

The practice of referring to QCs as 'honourable and learned' and officers retired from the armed forces (or still in the reserves) as 'honourable and gallant' is no longer a convention of debate, but the terms are still used by traditionalists.

When they enter or leave the Chamber, MPs are expected to bow to the Chair as a gesture of respect to the House itself (it is not a bow to the Speaker, but almost certainly a survival of the days when there was an altar in St Stephen's Chapel, where the Commons sat from 1547). They should not cross the line of sight between the Speaker and the member who has the floor; and – very important – should sit down as soon as the Speaker or a deputy rises. Dress conventions – jackets and ties for men – are generally upheld. Eating, drinking (except water) and smoking are forbidden: the House of Commons has been a no-smoking area since the resolution of 1696 'That no Member do presume to take tobacco in the gallery of the House or at a committee table'. MPs may not use mobile phones to make or receive calls, but MPs may now use hand-held electronic devices (but not laptop computers) in the Chamber so long as they do not cause a disturbance and do not 'impair decorum', and in committees laptops may be used as well.

MPs must speak from the place where they are called, which must be within the formal limits of the Chamber (so, not from the crossbenches below the Bar of the House or from the parts of the galleries reserved for members). MPs may refer to notes, but they should not read questions or speeches at length – although notes, and even whole written speeches, are used to a greater degree than was the case a few years ago, with an adverse effect on the quality of debate. An MP should be present for the opening and winding-up speeches of the debate in which he or she takes part, and after speaking should stay in the Chamber for at least the next two speeches. The Speaker will not call an MP to ask a question following a ministerial statement (or an urgent question) unless he or she has been there for the whole of the opening statement.

The House of Commons has a long tradition of MPs seeking to intervene in each other's speeches, to ask a question or to make a point. This – different from the practice in many other parliaments – makes debate much more lively than would otherwise be the case and is easier in the relatively intimate style of the Chamber than it would be in a large hemicycle (see page 12). Interventions must be brief; and they may be made only if the MP who has the floor 'gives way', although the expectation is that the MP speaking will, indeed, give way. The Chair will stop an MP whose speech is irrelevant or tediously repetitive, although with a certain amount of ingenuity most things can be made relevant and unrepetitive.

In most debates, MPs may speak only once but this does not apply, for example, in a committee on a bill. The *sub judice* rule prevents any MP referring to a current or impending court case (more precisely, when someone has been charged in a criminal case or, in a civil action, when a case has been set down for trial). This is to avoid debate in the House – under the protection of privilege – possibly influencing the outcome of a case; but it also reflects the relationship between Parliament and the courts (see page 164). However, the rule may be relaxed at the Speaker's discretion, and it does not prevent the House considering legislation.

'Good temper and moderation'

The language of debate must be restrained. An MP may not accuse another of lying, or of deliberately misleading the House; the Chair will intervene immediately to require the withdrawal of the charge. In July 2013, Nigel Dodds was ordered to leave the Chamber for refusing to withdraw his allegation that a minister's reply had been 'deliberately deceptive'.

However, in June 2012 the Labour MP Chris Bryant was allowed to accuse the then Health Secretary Jeremy Hunt of having lied to the House. Although the style of the accusation was a little immoderate, it was not disorderly because the House was debating a motion that centred on the Health Secretary's veracity before the House; it would have been a nonsense if members could not have addressed the issue directly.

Erskine May no longer lists the words ruled to be 'unparliamentary', although the lists in earlier editions are entertaining. 'Villains' got a red card in 1875, as did 'Pecksniffian cant' in 1928. Rather surprisingly, so did 'rude remarks' in 1887. Animal words of all sorts ('jackasses', 'swine', 'rats' and even 'stool pigeons') have always been required to be withdrawn. The important thing (and the reason why *Erskine May* no longer lists examples) is the context in which language is used. However, *Erskine May's* dictum 'that good temper and moderation are the characteristics of parliamentary language' remains the gold standard.

MPs are expected to inform their colleagues when they intend to refer to them in the Chamber; when they table parliamentary questions that specifically affect the constituency of another MP; and when they intend to visit another constituency (except in a purely private capacity).

All these conventions and constraints may sound a little like school rules, and some occasionally come in for criticism from new MPs and others. But where political views clash and passions can run high, a little formality can make the House more dignified and tolerant. It is a pity that many people judge the House of Commons from what they see on television of the gladiatorial Prime Minister's Questions; the House is actually a much more courteous place than many might think, while still allowing challenge and lively disagreement. At a time when Parliament is seeking to reconnect with the people, this is no bad thing.

The purpose of debate

As has been shown, the House of Commons itself, Westminster Hall and a variety of committees provide a great many different occasions and circumstances where debate takes place. What is the purpose of the millions of words spoken as a result?

Much of debate is, in one way or another, about deploying political argument: seeking to make the case for a particular philosophy or interpretation and applying it to the issue of the moment. Although many in the country at large see a clash of ideologies as rather sterile and negative, it is part of political reality.

But debate is also about challenge, testing and explanation. Parliament is a place where the government should be forced to justify its policies and actions. That process is part of checking an executive that will always tend to be over-mighty. It is also a process that crosses political divides, and it involves both the shadow minister who aspires to be in government and the government backbencher who is uneasy about a course that the government is taking. In these circumstances, debate provides the opportunity to point out the weakness in a case, to offer alternative solutions and to ask 'why?'

Debate is also about exposure. One purpose of this is to force – or provide an opportunity for – the government to set out its view and its policy. This may be on some major issue – the achievement of peace in the Middle East, or the renegotiation of the terms of the United Kingdom's membership of the European Union. It may be on something with a lower profile but of great importance to those affected; for example, a school closure, an accident black spot or a local industry. This will produce a statement of government policy, or a response to criticism, but it will also act as a mind concentrator, not only for the minister but also for the civil servants in his or her department, who should be asking 'Is this a reasonable line to take? How vulnerable are we on this? Should we do more?'

The uses of debate

Exposure through debate is a way of attacking and defending – but, above all, testing – policies and ideas. It is also a way of putting subjects on the political (and media) agenda. It may be some abuse – perhaps a holiday timeshare scam, or perhaps an ethical or moral issue – such as stem cell research, battery hens or cluster bombs. It may also be a way of swinging the spotlight on to some injustice – sometimes affecting only one person or one family, perhaps children kidnapped by an estranged father, a disability pension denied or the perverse application of some planning law.

Debate is also about representation: industries, regions, constituencies, pressure groups and individuals have a parliamentary voice through MPs taking up causes, setting out the case and gathering support.

Does debate change minds? On the spot, rarely. On most matters that come to the House of Commons, the parties will already have their view; individual MPs will have their opinions. On a non-partisan issue, a compelling speech may be influential; on a highly charged issue, the trend of debate may change minds (a significant number of MPs said that they finally made up their minds which way to vote on military intervention in Syria only during the debate in August 2013). In the case of most debates, effective advocacy will, indeed, change minds, but more slowly. It may modify the government's view, influence public opinion and put new subjects on the agenda. How effectively it does this is very much down to MPs themselves.

Debates in the House of Lords

Just over one-quarter of House of Lords Chamber time is taken up with debates of various kinds on issues of public policy, and nearly 60 per cent of sitting time in the Grand Committee. In 2013–14, the House spent just over 453 hours in debate – that is to say, 34 per cent of the total time available to it in the Chamber and Grand Committee. Debates take place, as in the Commons, on a motion moved by the initiator. The form of the motion used will vary according to the purpose of the debate. Most debates in the Lords will take place on a neutral motion 'to take note': when it is desired that the House express a view on the subject matter under debate, a motion 'for resolution' is moved – usually resulting in a vote at the end. The Lords also has a unique procedure that allows for short debate on a question (a QSD).

Opposition and backbench debates

Debates on motions moved by opposition parties and backbenchers take place on Thursdays, when motions have precedence over bills and other business. Most of these Thursdays are given over to the political parties to initiate debates, usually on the neutral 'take note' motion. The days for these debates are allocated to the various parties by agreement between party whips, with the majority going to opposition parties and crossbench peers. Although they are not time-limited in any procedural sense, the Leader of the House usually moves a Business of the House motion limiting the time. This can create the opportunity for two debates to be held. The limit on a single debate is usually five hours: the limits where two debates are held can vary but must not exceed a total of six hours.

In the earlier part of the session, up until the end of December, one Thursday a month is set aside for two balloted debates limited to two-and-a-half hours each and initiated by backbenchers or crossbenchers. The subjects are chosen by a ballot conducted some weeks beforehand by the Clerk of the Parliaments in the presence of the Chief Whips and the Convenor of the Crossbenches. Members may not hedge their bets by tabling both a motion for the ballot and a QSD on the same topic at the same time. And after the ballot is drawn, all motions fall and have to be retabled, in an attempt to keep the House's debates current.

In the 2012–13 session, Thursday opposition and backbench motions included such themes as foreign affairs (the Middle East, Afghanistan, Syria, Sudan); energy policy, including nuclear power; education; the NHS and social care; child care and the economy.

Government motions

Sometimes the government will itself wish to initiate a debate on a matter of public concern or potential concern to the House. Thus, debates on reform of the House in recent sessions have usually been held on government motions to take note. Debates on pressing issues of foreign policy fall into the same category. On 18 March 2003, the Lords, as did the Commons, debated the situation in Iraq, but on a take note motion, in the full knowledge that war was probably imminent. Unlike the Commons, however, no vote followed the end of the debate. On 29 August 2013, a similar debate on a take note motion took place on the use of chemical weapons in Syria, following a recall of Parliament. In fact, it was a debate on how the UK should respond to these developments and very few speakers favoured any form of military intervention. Although the government's decision not to interfere followed an un-favourable vote in the Commons (because the representative House of Commons acts as the forum of the nation in such matters), the doubts raised in the Lords debate by participants – including the Archbishop of Canterbury, former senior officers in the armed services and diplomats, ex-Cabinet Ministers and others – will have carried weight, too. The tenor of the Lords debate on limited military intervention against Islamic State (IS) fighters in Iraq, which was held following the recall of Parliament on 26 September 2014, was more supportive of government policy.

But there have been occasions in recent sessions where the government has sought to test the opinion of the two Houses of Parliament on issues of policy, placing a series of options before each House. Thus, in March 2002 the government itself tabled motions for resolution on a series of options relating to hunting with dogs; in February 2003, although the debate had already taken place, a series of votes were held on seven motions to approve one or other of the options relating to the reform of the composition of the House that had been proposed by the Joint Committee on Reform of the House; and, on 12 July 2005, the House resolved, after a short debate, that it should elect its own presiding officer (an issue that had been debated at greater length in early 2004). In March 2007, the House again voted on the seven options for reform of House of Lords membership, with various proportions of elected to appointed members. The Lords rejected all except one – that of an all appointed chamber. (The Commons had already voted the week before in favour of an 80 per cent or 100 per cent elected body.)

Debates on reports of select committees

Select committees on public policy (see page 335) – such as the Economic Affairs Committee, Science and Technology Committee or European Union Committee – make their reports to the House in the expectation that, at some stage, they will be debated. In recent sessions, 3 per cent of sitting time in the Chamber and up to 16 per cent of time in Grand Committee was spent debating these reports, almost invariably on a motion to take note. Sometimes, motions to take note of reports on similar subjects are debated together. The debates on the Economic Affairs Committee's reports on the Finance Bill are usually debated as part of the second reading of the bill.

Chairmen and members of select committees were, in the past, often critical that insufficient time was offered by the Government Whips' Office for debates on select committee reports or that time, when offered, tended to be at short notice or subject to last-minute change. But the availability of Grand Committee time has helped to ease the pressure. There are those who point out that such debates rarely attract interest from the wider House and, save for a few members with knowledge of the subject matter, most of the participants tend to be members of the committee that made the report. In some ways, this does not matter. The dialogue with the government over a committee's recommendations takes place not only on the floor of the House, but also in the direct exchanges between the committees and ministers.

Questions for Short Debate

Some debates arise on Questions for Short Debate (QSDs) and take the form of short debates time-limited to an hour-and-a-half at the end of the day's business. A minister answers the question at the end of the debate, and there is no right of reply. These debatable questions can also be held during dinner adjournments in the course of legislative business, when they are limited to one hour. They may also be taken in Grand Committee when either time limit may be applied. Since 2013, up to the end of January in any session, the opportunity also exists for a topical QSD to be taken on Thursdays between the two main motions for debate. They are chosen by ballot on the previous Monday and the criterion by which topicality is measured is that of media coverage in two mainstream outlets over the preceding three days. Select committee reports can also be debated in this way provided the topicality criterion is met. QSDs are hugely popular and have proliferated in recent years. In 2013–14, they took up no less than 8 per cent of Chamber time and 25 per cent of Grand Committee time. There was a time when QSDs were fitted into the margins of other business, but now they are a much more central feature of Lords proceedings.

Conventions of debate

Certain conventions apply to all debate in the House, whether on legislative business or on the general motions that are the subject of this chapter. We saw in Chapter 2 that the Chair does not call members to speak in the Lords. Peers usually give advance notice to the Government Whips' Office of their intention to speak in debates, and lists of speakers are prepared by the Government Whips' Office in consultation with the usual channels and published before the debate begins. Any lord not on the list may speak, but only after those already on the list and before the winding-up speeches, and then only briefly. So, there is no problem in the Lords of 'catching the Speaker's eye'. And, of course, the House keeps its own order.

As in the Commons, there are conventions and standing orders – some dating from as early as 1621 – governing the way in which other members are addressed. Thus, remarks are addressed to the House as a whole. Other participants are addressed in the third person, never as 'you'. And the style of address is always 'The Noble Lord, Lord . . .' or 'The Right Reverend Prelate, the Bishop of . . .'. A suggestion in 2011 by Lord Goodlad's Working Group that these forms of address might be simplified was rejected by the House.

Generally speaking, a lord may speak only once in debate, except when the House is in committee on a bill, and must not read (although many do). Unless speaking from the frontbench, where lords speak from a despatch box, members speak in their places. Speeches must be relevant and, indeed, in 1965 the House even resolved that they should be shorter. Today, a rather generous fifteen-minute rule applies in debates that are not time-limited, with a twenty-minute limit for members opening or winding up. Most debates are now time limited and the whips are vigilant to ensure that the limits are observed. Members must avoid 'asperity of speech' and reading. And relevant interests must be declared (see page 117).

In addition to these rules of debate, various rules of conduct apply – such as speaking 'uncovered' (without a hat!) or the custom of making obeisance to the Cloth of Estate behind the throne on entering the Chamber. Such customs help to lend the House a veneer of good, even courtly, manners that are sometimes sorely tested in the debates themselves.

Value of debate: the chamber of experience

It is no easier to set a value on Lords debates than it is for the Commons. We take it for granted that debate is free and open. It is, of course, protected by parliamentary privilege. That in itself is something to be cherished. But what purpose is served? Minds are certainly not swayed, especially where arguments follow party lines. Given that most speeches are prepared beforehand and then scrupulously read out, that is hardly surprising.

The value of debates is that they offer different opportunities and attractions to different participants. For a backbencher initiating a debate, they offer the chance to air a policy matter of personal interest with the guarantee of a government response that is likely to represent the latest government thinking on the issue. For opposition parties, they offer the chance to set out their wares: to expose some aspect of government policy of which they do not approve, perhaps to say how things might be done better or differently, and to try to put the government on the spot. And for government itself, they offer the opportunity to set out some new policy development or change in world events, and to test opinion across the parties.

Are the debates of good quality? Many are. In most debates a few speakers can be deemed to have experience that is relevant to the subject matter, and a few may have current and genuine expertise – a rare commodity in a parliamentary body. This high level of knowledgeability stems in part from the fact that the House of Lords has never been a chamber of salaried members. Many, whether life peers or hereditary, have or have had full-time careers elsewhere. And life peerages have been bestowed on a wide range of men and women distinguished in their field – some irrespective of party, others because they have espoused a party cause. Thus, among the speakers in the debate on China and multilateral nuclear disarmament in November 2012, there were a former Foreign Secretary who negotiated the terms of the handover of Hong Kong, a former Secretary of State for Defence, a former defence minister, a former Deputy Prime Minister, a former Governor of Hong Kong, and a former UK Permanent Representative to the United Nations. Among those speaking in a debate on the impact of the UK's visa policy on university admissions in January 2013, there were a former Secretary of State for Education and Science, a former director of a research council, a recently retired chief executive of Universities UK, two former university or college principals, three honorary university chancellors, three university council members, and two professors. Some commentators now view the House of Lords as a chamber of experts. This is perhaps to exaggerate the expert element in the House. Most of the peerages bestowed in the last 50 years or so have gone to politicians, active at either the national or local level. And many of the 'experts' have retired, or are about to retire, when they become members of the House. Their expertise might be thought a little dated. It is more apposite to regard the House of Lords as currently composed as a chamber where experience abounds. It is a knowledgeable place in a way that distinguishes it from most other parliamentary assemblies in the world.

9

Calling to account: questions

In this chapter, we will look at one of the best-known inquisitorial functions of Parliament: parliamentary questions, often known as PQs. This will also be a convenient place to look at public petitions and MPs' letters, which are other ways in which the actions of government can be influenced or exposed.

Questions in the Commons

By comparison with the processes of debate, legislation and examination by select committees, questions evolved relatively late in parliamentary history. Although the first recorded question to a minister was in the House of Lords in 1721, questions in the Commons did not develop until the nineteenth century, when all questions were asked orally; questions for written answer (now a major part of parliamentary activity) were not introduced until 1902.

What are questions?

Erskine May states the purpose of a question as 'to obtain information or to press for action'. The people who have the information – and the ability to act upon it – are government ministers, and it is they who have to answer questions. Some questions are asked (or, in parliamentary language, 'tabled' or 'put down') of MPs who are not ministers but who speak on behalf of bodies such as the House of Commons Commission (see page 57) or the Church Commissioners. However, well over 99 per cent of all PQs are asked of ministers by backbenchers, and this process is part of the way in which government can be held to account.

Questions are one of the best-known, but often misunderstood, features of the House of Commons, and it is on that House that we will concentrate. Questions are also asked in the House of Lords, but in much smaller numbers and less restricted by rules than in the Commons.

There are two types of question: oral, and written (which are split into the unrationed ordinary written, and written questions for answer on a named day, of which each Member can ask five in a day). Questions for written answer now far outnumber oral questions, and the two types of question have steadily grown apart. Questions for written answer are still designed to seek information or press for action; oral questions are increasingly rhetorical in purpose. The introduction of 'topical' oral questions (see page 279) has increased this divergence: one can foresee a point at which all oral questions are 'open' or spontaneous.

The rules for questions

First and foremost, questions must be about something for which a minister is responsible. In many cases this is clear-cut: the Secretary of State for Defence is responsible for ordering a new aircraft carrier, and the Secretary of State for International Development is responsible for how the UK's aid budget is spent. But, although the government has an overall responsibility for local government finance, it is not responsible for the detail of how local authorities spend their money. Neither, for example, is it responsible for what the courts do, for the operational details of policing, or the actions of EU institutions (although it is responsible for its own policy towards them).

Ministers are responsible to Parliament for their own policies and actions, not for those of the opposition parties; so, a government backbencher could not table a question that asked 'What would be the effect on the economy of the deficit reduction plans announced by the Labour Party', even if the minister were eager to answer. But if the MP were to ask the Chancellor of the Exchequer an oral question such as 'What recent progress he has made on deficit reduction', then that is a matter for which he is responsible, and the reply may well take a side-swipe at the policy of the Labour Party.

There a variety of other rules. Matters that are *sub judice* (see page 265) cannot be raised. Questions must not offer information 'If she is aware that . . .' or be argumentative 'Does he agree that it is unacceptable that . . .' They must have some reasonable basis in fact, rather than being purely speculative – they cannot, for example, ask whether a press report is correct. Government is treated as a single entity, so it is not in order to ask one minister to intervene with or influence another (although the same result may be achieved by asking the Prime Minister a question about improving coordination between two government departments).

A question that has been already been answered in the current session may not be asked again unless there is reason to think that the situation may have changed (although in practice, with the exception of historic statistics, this is interpreted as allowing a question to be repeated after three months). This is a common-sense rule that prevents cluttering up of both the Vote bundle and *Hansard* with identical exchanges. The tabling of numerous, but very similar questions is not allowed for the same reason. A related rule prevents an MP asking for information that is readily available – for example, in official publications. Now that huge amounts of information and statistical data are published by the government on the Internet, this rule is increasingly applied. The amount of information now published in this way, combined with the impact of the Freedom of Information Act has greatly altered the role and status of parliamentary questions.

Since devolution to Scotland, Wales and Northern Ireland, ministers at Westminster may not be asked about things for which responsibility has passed to the devolved administrations. They may, however, be asked about matters on which they have the power to require information from the administrations, or about concordats or liaison arrangements. Adherence to this rule has relaxed somewhat now that some of the early sensitivities about devolution have diminished.

The rules about questions have developed over the years; for the most part, they either reflect other rules of the House (such as the *sub judice* rule) or try to ensure that questions keep to their principal purposes of obtaining information or pressing for action. The rules are applied more rigorously to questions for written answer than to oral questions. MPs can find the rules frustrating; but it is remarkable how often a slightly different question – or the same question in a different form – avoids running foul of the rules, and may even get closer to what the MP really wants the answer to.

Tabling a question

Whatever type of question, whether written or oral, MPs must table questions in writing, either personally with the Clerks in the Table Office (a small room behind the Speaker's Chair), by post or via a secure electronic tabling (e-tabling) system. By the end of the 2013–14 session, 534 members were signed up for e-tabling. Written questions e-tabled are subject to a limit of 20 per day; there is no limit on written questions handed in personally at the Table Office or posted.

An MP's question is examined by one of the Clerks, who checks that it does not fall foul of any of the rules for questions and who will, where possible, suggest to the MP how to avoid breaching the rules, or perhaps how to put the question in a more effective form. As well as conforming to the rules that operate for all questions, an oral question should seek no more than three pieces of information and, except in the case of topical questions and questions to the Prime Minister (see page 288) must be precise enough to give an indication of the intended supplementary – 'open' questions are not allowed.

The answers

There is a rather hackneyed story of a minister and a senior civil servant being driven to some remote government establishment. The fog closed down, the car went slower and slower, and finally the driver, dimly seeing a passer-by, rolled down the window and said 'Where are we?' Back came the answer 'You're in a car, in the fog'. 'Do you realise, Minister', said the civil servant, 'that's a perfect answer to a parliamentary question. It's short, it's absolutely true, and it tells you nothing you didn't know already.'

In Chapter 4, we quoted the 1997 resolution of the House of Commons on ministerial accountability, which states the duty of ministers to account for policies, decisions and actions. So far as questions are concerned, the key passages are those that require ministers 'to give accurate and truthful information to Parliament' and to be 'as open as possible with Parliament, refusing to provide information only when disclosure would not be in the public interest'. The language of the resolution is reflected in the Ministerial Code, most recently published in May 2010.

The coming into force of the Freedom of Information Act in January 2005 has given all citizens a right to information, subject to a number of exemptions, and a public interest test. The Public Administration Select Committee's (PASC) report of 2003–04 on *Ministerial Accountability and Parliamentary Questions* was concerned that the rights of members to information through answers to parliamentary questions should not be disadvantaged compared with the rights of ordinary citizens through Freedom of Information (FoI). The government response to the PASC report reiterated the government position that, if PQs are properly handled, FoI requests should not reveal information that has been refused in answer to PQs:

> *A Code of Practice providing guidance to all public authorities (as required by section 45 of the Act) will include advice on procedures for dealing with complaints about the handling of requests for information. This will make clear that there should be no inconsistencies between the provision of information in answer to Parliamentary Questions and information given to citizens under the Act.*

Answers to parliamentary questions provide a huge amount of information on the whole range of government responsibilities, but attention inevitably focuses on occasions when answers are not given. Before the coming into force of the Freedom of Information Act, ministers' judgement of 'not in the public interest' was normally based on the *Code of Practice on Access to Government Information*, first introduced in 1994, which listed 15 categories of exemptions to the provision of information, on grounds including harming international relations, or the frankness of discussion inside government, or the ability of the government to manage the economy, or the proper and efficient conduct of the business of a government department.

Although it was expected that the government would continue to provide reasons, analogous to the exemptions contained in the Act, this has not happened. The government informed the PASC that it did not believe it would be possible to interpret the public interest by analogous reference to Freedom of Information Act exemptions, and that reference to the Freedom of Information Act exemptions in answers would give members 'the impression that the request for information in the Parliamentary Question has been subject to a full public interest test when, in fact, it is not possible to do this within the time constraints for answering Parliamentary Questions.'

However, the Freedom of Information Act has marked a step change in the status of PQs. Before that Act, MPs had a privileged status in terms of access to government information; and journalists, researchers and others (quite legitimately) had to seek the help of an MP to prise information out of the government. Now, everyone has the right to ask questions of the government and it is legally obliged to answer them. This has devalued the PQ to an extent, and the impact of this change of status is just one more of those challenges that the House of Commons has come to terms with in the way it organises its practices and procedures in the information age.

There are some subjects on which few would expect information to be given in answer to a PQ, such as the operations of the security and intelligence services, or where an investigation into major VAT fraud might be under way.

But on many other issues, interpretations and expectations can differ. From a government perspective, it is easy to understand a reluctance to answer particular types of questions – not least because answering one question may produce a flood of questions on a sensitive topic. Nevertheless, MPs find a minister's refusal to answer extremely frustrating when it prevents them pursuing a subject that they see as of political or constituency importance. If a minister refuses to provide information on a particular subject for a stated reason, it usually also prevents the same question being asked for the remainder of the session, which adds to the frustration.

In the 2010 Parliament, the Procedure Committee has monitored unsatisfactory and late answers to parliamentary questions, reporting sessionally and receiving from the Leader of the House a memorandum providing statistics in a standard format on departments' performance in answering written PQs within a reasonable time.

The Committee received 50 complaints from MPs about unsatisfactory answers from ministers in the long 2010–12 session, and 12 complaints in 2012–13. In a number of cases where the Committee chose to pursue the complaint, it was successful in obtaining on behalf of the members concerned the information they sought. The Committee's role in monitoring the timeliness of answers to questions has also had results. Concerns about the record of the worst-performing department of 2010–12, the Department for Education (DfE), which answered only 18 per cent of ordinary written questions, and just 17 per cent of questions for named-day answer, within acceptable timescales, and the absence of a marked improvement in 2012–13, led to two oral evidence sessions, the second of which in January 2013 was with the Secretary of State. The Procedure Committee recorded in its latest monitoring report (for the 2012–13 session) that the Secretary of State had written to the Committee in November 2013 giving the latest position for the 2013–14 session, showing that 96 per cent of ordinary written questions and 88 per cent of named-day questions were answered within acceptable timescales. That now puts the DfE among the best-performing departments.

Although the form and content of Questions is subject to the rules of the House, the content of answers remains a matter for ministers, and in those answers ministers are sometimes not above a sideswipe at the performance or practices of the previous administration rather than the current one. And, of course, while the majority of Questions are seeking information and their answers giving it, questions – and especially oral questions – are an important dimension of the party clash between opposition and government.

For example, in the 2010–12 session, a number of members tabled Questions on Government Procurement Card spending by the Office of the Deputy Prime Minister. The Questions included one seeking information on spending in Doyles Seafood Quay and Sydney Aquarium (related to an official visit to Australia), which received the answer 'Ministers in this Administration are of the view that such transactions – which are all associated with the visit of Lord Prescott when Deputy Prime Minister – did not represent value for money for the taxpayer.' Lord Prescott complained to the Cabinet Office and the media that the Questions and their answers were part of a 'dirty tricks' campaign to prevent him from becoming a police and crime commissioner, and that the answers being given were designed to convey the impression that he had inappropriately been enjoying hospitality at taxpayer expense when that had not been the case.

In the 2013–14 session, a question from Hilary Benn about budgets for catering and hospitality in the Department for Communities and Local Government received a detailed answer on the various budget heads and then concluded with the observation that 'his spending in his last year in office is equivalent today to buying 720,479 packets of Jammie Dodgers from Waitrose (albeit, with a free cup of coffee thrown in).' In the same session, the eagle-eyed would have spotted a number of One Direction song titles hiding in an answer to a question on the contribution to the UK economy of One Direction.

Successive Speakers have refused to comment on the ways in which ministers answer – or avoid answering, and many backbenchers feel that it is unfair that ministers can decide, without any independent check, to refuse to answer particular questions that everyone accepts come within their responsibilities. The reality is that, if questions really are a means of holding the government to account, one cannot expect them always to be a friendly volunteering of information.

Cost

Ministers may refuse to provide an answer to a PQ if the cost of doing so would exceed a certain amount, known as the *advisory cost limit*. In February 2012, this was raised to £850. A minister's 'disproportionate cost' answer can be a source of annoyance to MPs: not only may they think that the expenditure limit of £850 does not represent a large amount of civil service time, they may also suspect that estimating the cost of answering is a fairly rough-and-ready business, and that if ministers wanted to answer the question, they would do so (and, indeed, a minister may decide that a question is to be answered irrespective of cost). However, the government's internal guidance emphasises that even if to give a full answer would cost more than the limit, any readily available information should be given.

In February 2012, the Treasury estimated the average cost of answering a written question at £164, and of answering an oral question at £450. These figures are averages, not the price-tag of each question; it does not cost very much to reply 'No' to a question asking for a particular document to be published, for example.

The higher cost of answering oral questions is because of the additional research and briefing needed for possible supplementaries (see p. 287), so the extra cost is more that of defending the minister's position than of actually answering the question.

The cost of answering has, in the past, been used against the more assiduous questioners. In the 2001–02 session, the Conservative MP for Buckingham, John Bercow, tabled only 4 oral questions, but 4,206 written questions (the next place went to Andrew Turner, the Conservative MP for the Isle of Wight, who tabled 15 oral and 1,337 written questions). It was perhaps not surprising that Mr Bercow's questioning was described by his opponents as 'costing the taxpayer half a million pounds' rather than 'calling ministers to account'.

In the 2013–14 session, 43,919 written questions were tabled; 536 MPs tabled at least one question, but half of all written questions were tabled by the top 68 questioners. The most questions, 1,575, were tabled by Chris Ruane MP, who tabled nearly double the number of written questions tabled by the second- and third-placed MPs combined.

Oral questions

Civil Service guidance for answering oral PQs says of Question Time:

> *Supplementary questions vary from the factual to the highly political in content, so that the notes for supplementaries have to anticipate every ramification of the original Question. While some questions are genuinely seeking action or information, others are designed to highlight the merits of an alternative policy or the perceived shortcomings of the Minister's Department. The task facing civil servants is to 'get behind the Question' and provide a range of brief subject headings and corresponding short speaking notes (often drafted in the first person) which the Minister can easily pick up and use to answer the supplementaries in the House. He or she may also reflect upon which other Members the Speaker may call for supplementaries and the type of point they may raise.*

Many questions for oral answer receive a written reply, either because time runs out before they are reached, or because the MP concerned cannot in the event be in the House that day, and asks for a written rather than an oral reply.

But even though oral questions account for a relatively small part of the total, Question Time, when they are answered, is one of the liveliest parts of the parliamentary day, and Prime Minister's Questions (PMQs) each Wednesday is normally the highest-profile event of the week.

Question Time

Question Time takes place every day except a Friday, and begins immediately after Prayers are over and any private business (see page 137) has been disposed of. This means that, on Mondays, it runs from about 2.35 p.m. to 3.35 p.m.; on Tuesdays and Wednesdays from about 11.35 a.m. to 12.35 p.m.; and on Thursdays from 9.35 a.m. to 10.35 a.m.

The ministers from each government department answer questions every five weeks according to a rota that the government itself decides. Most departments answer substantive Questions (of which they have received notice and which are printed in the Order Paper) for 75 per cent of their slot, and topical Questions (of which no notice is given) for the remaining 25 per cent. Members may enter and be successful in both the substantive and topical Question ballots. All government departments answer topical Questions with the exception of the Attorney-General; the Northern Ireland, Wales and Scotland Office; and the non-government answering bodies (such as the House of Commons Commission and the Church Commissioners).

Topical Questions were introduced from the 2007–08 session, with the first session on 12 November 2007. This took place in response to the perception that the parliamentary question process was unable to react to events on the day of the PQ or just before it. The change resulted from a recommendation by the Modernisation Committee, whose intention was to create the opportunity for 'topical and spontaneous questions' on issues of the day selected by members. The arrangements for topical questions are broadly similar to those for PM's 'engagements' questions. The pro forma topical Question is 'if she or he will make a statement on her/his Department's responsibilities'. The minister answers this question once at the start of the topical questions slot and then members who have been successful in the ballot, and others, are called by the Speaker to ask questions. The rota for a typical fortnight is shown below.

2014 Issue No. 3 (12 May)

DATES AND DEADLINES FOR ORAL QUESTIONS
Monday 12 May 2014—Thursday 11 December 2014

(T) indicates that a topical Question may also be tabled to the answering Department

	Monday 12 May	Tuesday 13 May	Wednesday 14 May	Thursday 15 May
Question Time	Defence (at 2.30pm; T at 3.15pm)	Deputy Prime Minister (at 11.30am; T at 11.50am) Attorney General (at 12.10pm)	Wales (at 11.30am) Prime Minister (at 12 noon)	The House will not be sitting
Deadline at 12.30pm (Date of Question Time)	Environment, Food and Rural Affairs (T) Church Commissioners and Public Accounts Commission and Speaker's Committee on the Electoral Commission (Thur 15 May)	Education (T) (Mon 19 May) Northern Ireland (Wed 21 May)	Health (T) (Tue 20 May)	

	Monday 2 June	Tuesday 3 June	Wednesday 4 June	Thursday 5 June
Question Time	The House will not be sitting	The House will not be sitting	No Question time this day	No Question time this day
Deadline at 12.30pm (Date of Question Time)	No deadline this day	No deadline this day	Health (T) (Tue 10 June) Northern Ireland (Wed 11 June)	Prime Minister (Wed 11 June)

Extract from the rota for Government departments' oral questions and related deadlines for tabling

Source: Copyright House of Commons, 2014

The day on which a department is top for questions can be a testing time for ministers answering at the Despatch Box, but can also be a shop window for the department concerned, in which ministers have the opportunity of emphasising their successes and putting on the record their interpretation of events. The balance between the two depends on how quick ministers are on their feet, how well they prepare, and how sharp opposition MPs (or, indeed, backbenchers on their own side) are with their supplementaries.

Tabling oral questions

An MP can table a PQ for oral answer any time after the previous Question Time for a particular department up to 12.30 p.m. three sitting days before that department's next Question Time. So if the department is top for questions on a Tuesday, questions have to be tabled by 12.30 p.m. the previous Wednesday (for questions to the Secretaries of State for Northern Ireland, Scotland and Wales, the notice period is five days because of the extra complication of there being devolved administrations in those parts of the UK). An MP may table only one oral question to a department on any one day, and no more than two in total on that day (which, for example, allows an MP to have a question to the Prime Minister, as well as the secretary of state answering the same day).

Questions are tabled to the responsible secretary of state rather than to an individual minister within a department, although there are slots for government departments and offices that do not have a secretary of state, such as those for the Leader of the House and the ministers for Women and Equalities.

Just after 12.30 p.m. on the last tabling day, there is a random computer shuffle of the questions that have been tabled to the department or departments concerned. The successful questions are printed next morning in the blue pages of the Vote bundle (see page 151) and in Future Day Orals on the parliamentary website in the order in which they will be called on the day. Not all questions tabled are printed; if a single department is to answer for the whole of Question Time (in practice, 55 minutes), then 25 questions to that department will be printed. If the slot is for 45 minutes, 20 will be printed, and so on down to a 15-minute slot, for which 10 questions will be printed. The remainder are treated as 'lost', are not printed and do not receive answers.

If a question is put down to one government department, but is more properly the responsibility of another, it will be transferred, and answered by a minister from the second department. This does not matter for written questions, but an MP who has an oral that is transferred after the shuffle has taken place will lose the opportunity to ask the question orally. When this happens, it sometimes results in a row; but it is a matter within the discretion of the government, and the Speaker will not intervene, although Speakers have criticised the transfer of a question where there is some shared responsibility.

Both government and opposition parties are keen to get their MPs to table questions, because it shortens the odds of being successful in the shuffle, and so beginning a question exchange with a friendly (or, for the opposition, a critical) supplementary. Both opposition and government frontbench teams, through their PPSs, will also identify themes they want to raise in a forthcoming Question Time, and encourage their backbenchers to table (sometimes identical) questions on these subjects, a practice known as 'syndication' or 'hand-outs'.

Question Time: on the day

The Speaker announces 'Questions to the Secretary of State for the Home Department' (or whichever department is top), 'Mr Peter Bone' (or whoever). Mr Bone simply says 'Number One, Mr Speaker' (there is no point in reading out the question because it is printed on the Order of Business), and the minister gets up to reply. Mr Bone is then called to ask a supplementary question, to which the minister replies. Two or three (or more) backbenchers (called alternately from each side of the Chamber) ask supplementaries. If the subject is an important one, the Opposition shadow minister may ask the final supplementary, and the Speaker calls the name of the next MP with a question down for answer. As we saw in Chapter 3 (page 47), the number of supplementaries called is entirely a matter for the Speaker; on a subject on which the government is vulnerable, calling more MPs to put supplementaries may put the minister under greater pressure; conversely, if fewer supplementaries are called, more questions on the Order of Business will be reached. The current Speaker is very keen to call as many members who have a question on the paper as possible, but this haste (although popular with members who have a question down) makes Question Time an easier ride for the government of the day.

Question Time is, above all, a political exchange; it is not about seeking information, which is what written questions are for. Oral questions are about exposing and criticising, or helping and supporting. All the ministers in a department – in a large department, the secretary of state, two ministers of state, and two junior ministers (parliamentary under-secretaries) – will be present for their slot at Question Time. Which questions they answer will depend on their particular responsibilities within the department, but the secretary of state will usually take the biggest 'political' subjects.

The list of questions on the Order of Business may not be followed exactly. A minister may 'group' similar questions for answer if they are reasonably close together on the list, and the MPs who tabled those questions are called first to ask supplementaries. If an MP is unable to be present, he or she may withdraw a question, or convert it from an oral to a written question (known as 'unstarring' because oral questions were historically denoted by a star against them on the Order of Business).

The art of the supplementary

If Question Time is seen as a duel, the tabling of the question and the minister's often low-key reply are rather like two fencers squaring up to each other before the swords clash. The real conflict of Question Time is in the supplementaries. Thus, an

BUSINESS TODAY: CHAMBER

2.30pm Prayers

Followed by

QUESTIONS

■ **Oral Questions to the Secretary of State for Work and Pensions**

1 **Rosie Cooper** (West Lancashire)
What steps he is taking to improve the administration of the work capability assessment. (904358)

2 **Ann McKechin** (Glasgow North)
What steps he is taking to improve the claims and decision-making process for personal independence payments. (904359)

3 **Mel Stride** (Central Devon)
What assessment he has made of recent trends in employment figures. (904360)

4 **Mr David Amess** (Southend West)
What assessment he has made of recent trends in employment figures. (904361)

5 **Mrs Sharon Hodgson** (Washington and Sunderland West)
How many wage incentives for recruiting unemployed young people have been paid under the Youth Contract to date. (904362)

- -

20 **Clive Efford** (Eltham)
What steps he is taking to improve the administration of the work capability assessment. (904379)

21 **Graham Jones** (Hyndburn)
What estimate he has made of the number of people below the threshold for auto-enrolment in a workplace pension.   (904381)

22 **Pat Glass** (North West Durham)
What steps he is taking to improve the administration of the work capability assessment. (904382)

At 3.15pm

■ **Topical Questions to the Secretary of State for Work and Pensions**

T1 **Rehman Chishti** (Gillingham and Rainham)
If he will make a statement on his departmental responsibilities.   (904383)

T2 **Nic Dakin** (Scunthorpe) (904384)

T3 **Mr Andrew Love** (Edmonton) (904385)

Oral questions on the Commons Order Paper for 23 June 2014 (questions 6–19 and topicals T4–T10 omitted)

Source: Copyright House of Commons, 2014

opposition MP may table a question that simply asks the Home Secretary how many police officers there are in England. The Home Secretary gives the figure, and the MP then asks 'But is the right honourable Member aware that in the police authority that covers my constituency, police numbers have fallen by 9 per cent over the last three years, and violent crime has increased by 13 per cent? Doesn't that demonstrate that the government is soft on crime? Will the Home Secretary tell my constituents why she is not committed to improving their safety?' This not only makes the political point on behalf of the MP's party, but will play well in the MP's local press.

A government backbencher may table exactly the same question, but the supplementary will be very different: 'Will the Home Secretary accept the thanks of my constituents for the government's commitment to beating crime, for reducing bureaucracy allowing extra officers to be on the beat, and for the reduction of [some category of crime that has gone down rather than up]'.

Short and sharp

By comparison with the *tabling* of oral and written questions, there are very few rules for oral supplementaries. If they are evidently wide of the original question, or if they refer to matters *sub judice* (see page 265), or if they clearly have nothing to do with the minister's responsibilities, the Speaker will call the MP to order. There is, however, a Catch-22 about this; it is not easy to tell that a supplementary is out of order until the MP is a fair way through asking it. However, one type of disorderly supplementary from the government side is usually spotted very quickly: inviting the minister to comment on the policies of the opposition. Ministers are responsible for the government's policies, not those of their opponents. Even in the more knockabout atmosphere of Prime Minister's Questions, the Speaker has stopped the Prime Minister overtly responding to supplementaries that seek criticism of Labour policies.

Long supplementaries are tempting as a way of getting one's point on the record, but they also make things much easier for ministers. Not only is there plenty of time to turn to the relevant part of the briefing file for ammunition in reply, but long supplementaries are less focused and less likely to hit the target. Ministers are much less comfortable with the classic sharp supplementaries like 'Why?' or 'How much?' or 'How many?'

In this respect, Question Time is a perfect example of the law of unintended consequences. There used to be a long-standing rule against any member (other than a frontbencher) reading out a supplementary question; and even a brief glance down to a discreet note was met by cries of 'Reading!'. The sensible purpose of the rule was to keep Question Time moving and to encourage shorter supplementaries. Similarly, the rule against quoting in a supplementary question discouraged long-windedness. The feeling in some quarters that this was too restrictive upon back-benchers led to a change in the rule, and the immediate result was to encourage the use of written notes to make lengthy assertions, often backed with quotation, to which ministers were expected to respond. Question Time slowed down, and has never recaptured its former immediacy and speed.

THE
PARLIAMENTARY DEBATES

OFFICIAL REPORT

IN THE FOURTH SESSION OF THE FIFTY-FIFTH PARLIAMENT OF THE
UNITED KINGDOM OF GREAT BRITAIN AND NORTHERN IRELAND
[WHICH OPENED 18 MAY 2010]

SIXTY-THIRD YEAR OF THE REIGN OF
HER MAJESTY QUEEN ELIZABETH II

SIXTH SERIES   **VOLUME 583**

SECOND VOLUME OF SESSION 2014–2015

House of Commons

Monday 23 June 2014

The House met at half-past Two o'clock

PRAYERS

[Mr Speaker *in the Chair*]

Oral Answers to Questions

WORK AND PENSIONS

The Secretary of State was asked—

Work Capability Assessment

1. Rosie Cooper(West Lancashire) (Lab): What steps he is taking to improve the administration of the work capability assessment.   [904358]

The Minister of State, Department for Work and Pensions (Mike Penning): I am committed to continually improving the administration of the work capability assessment. I am pleased to say that since the announcement in the House during our last Question Time, the backlog has fallen from 766,000 to 712,000.

Rosie Cooper: On 10 June, the Minister admitted to the Select Committee that 712,000 work capability assessments were outstanding. That number includes 234 recipients of incapacity benefit who are to be assessed for employment and support allowance, and 84,000 incapacity benefit recipients who have not yet been migrated. My constituents would like to know who is at fault, Atos or the Minister.

Mike Penning: When the coalition Government came to office, the WCA backlog did not suddenly happen; the problem already existed. However, we take responsibility for what we are doing. [Interruption.] There is no point in Labour Members' shouting us down. They have short memories, but their backlog existed. If they do not wish to admit that, perhaps we can see the documents, which will enable us to know the facts. We have carried out 1 million incapacity benefit assessments, and 700,000 people are currently being helped into work or are looking for work.

Mr Julian Brazier(Canterbury) (Con): Does my right hon. Friend agree that it would have been cynical if we had simply turned our back on all the existing claimants and not considered them too? That, of course, has been the cause of much of the backlog.

Mike Penning: I entirely agree. If we had not assessed those 1 million incapacity benefit recipients, those people would have been left, as the Labour party left them for 13 years. At least they now have an opportunity to look for work, and those who are not capable of going to work, or seeking work, are receiving the assistance that they require.

22. [904382] **Pat Glass** (North West Durham) (Lab): Leaked memos reported by the BBC on Friday show that ESA is one of the largest fiscal risks that the Government currently face. What is the Minister going to do about that?

Mike Penning: No Government of any description talk about leaked documents, but I can say that the information in that document was not new. I had released most of it earlier, and I believe that the BBC worked up the story for its own benefit.

Charlie Elphicke (Dover) (Con): The Minister said that the WCA problems were long-standing. Is there a process whereby the last Government's figures could be made available to the House? Who entered into the Atos contract?

Extracts from Hansard's reporting of Question Time on 23 June 2014

Mike Penning: There is no doubt that the Atos contract was taken out by the last Labour Administration. I would love to know exactly what the backlog was, but, as an incoming Minister, I am not allowed to see the figures. Perhaps Her Majesty's Opposition would be happy to release them. If those documents were published, we would all know exactly what the backlog was before the present Administration came to power.

Dame Anne Begg (Aberdeen South) (Lab): The backlog does not involve only ESA. There are also huge backlogs of decisions relating to personal independence payments and universal credit. Only 7,000 universal credit claimants have been dealt with, although at this stage the number should be about 1 million. In comparison with figures such as those, the passport fiasco pales into insignificance. Does the Minister not think that his Department has bitten off far more than it can chew?

Mike Penning: No, I do not. As the Chair of the Select Committee knows, there is no universal credit backlog, so her statement about that is not particularly helpful. I think that we need to concentrate on ensuring that benefits go to the people who deserve them. That is what is most important.

Andrew Bridgen (North West Leicestershire) (Con): Can the Minister confirm that Atos Healthcare will not receive one penny of compensation from the taxpayer for the early termination of its contract?

Mike Penning: There is no doubt that the contract was taken out by the last Labour Administration. Her Majesty's Opposition called for me to sack Atos. If we had done so, we would have had to pay it a huge amount of compensation, but, instead, it will pay substantial damages to the Government when the contract is terminated.

20. [904379] **Clive Efford** (Eltham) (Lab): Judge Robert Martin has said that Her Majesty's Courts and Tribunals Service has seen a huge reduction in the number of work capability assessment appeals, not because of the quality of decisions, but because of the huge backlog and the quality of the service that is being provided.

Mike Penning: I am afraid that that is factually incorrect. I read Judge Martin's comments, and I do not think that that is quite what he said. There has been a reduction of more than 80% in the number of people who are appealing. That is because better decisions are being made, which is right and proper for everyone.

Stephen Timms (East Ham) (Lab): It is high time that Ministers took responsibility for their failings. It was their decision, after the election, to migrate all recipients of incapacity benefit to employment and support allowance. That was the decision that triggered the delays and backlogs about which we have heard. Now, the memos that were leaked last week have revealed that ESA

"is not delivering more positive outcomes for claimants"

than incapacity benefit did, and the Work programme has proved hopeless, with a 94% failure rate. How long will Ministers allow this shambles to continue?

Mike Penning: Clearly Her Majesty's Opposition have a short memory as to what happened when they were in government. This problem started under Labour, Atos was in place under Labour— *[Interruption.]* Opposition Front Benchers are saying "No, not us"; then they should release the documentation that proves what the backlog was before the last election.

Personal Independence Payments

2. **Ann McKechin** (Glasgow North) (Lab): What steps he is taking to improve the claims and decision-making process for personal independence payments. [904359]

12. **Fiona O'Donnell** (East Lothian) (Lab): What steps he is taking to improve the claims and decision-making process for personal independence payments. [904370]

16. **Nick Smith** (Blaenau Gwent) (Lab): What steps he is taking to improve the claims and decision-making process for personal independence payments. [904375]

The Minister of State, Department for Work and Pensions (Mike Penning): Yet again I am committed to improving our performance and that of our contract providers. I want to make sure the right decisions are made as soon as possible. With that in mind, I have looked, particularly working with Macmillan, at how we can reduce waiting times for terminally ill people waiting for PIP. That stood at 28 days when I first met the Work and Pensions Committee, and I said that was unacceptable. It is inside 10 days now, and I want it to become lower.

Ann McKechin: As the Minister of State is aware, by his own Department's statistics it will take 42 years to clear the current backlog. In the meantime people are running out of money, and they are becoming more stressed and more ill as a result of his Department's failure to get a grip on a payment which his Government introduced. When will the backlogs be reduced to a decent level, as people have a right to entitlements in this country?

Mike Penning: It is really important that we get the decisions right and that the right people get those payments. I said before the Select Committee that I promise to do that within my own Department's administration, and we are addressing that. There was a real performance issue as to how many people were coming through the schemes. I am addressing that now with the providers, and it will improve, and not in the length of time the hon. Lady mentions, which is scaremongering.

Fiona O'Donnell: An awareness campaign last week by the MND Association and MND Scotland informed us that about half of people diagnosed with motor neurone disease die before 14 months. They do not fit into the Minister's definition of "terminally ill", so how long does he think those people should wait for their claim to be assessed?

Mike Penning: Now I have addressed the issue of the terminally ill, we are particularly addressing progressive illnesses. We want to look at that very quickly.

Esther McVey: I thank my hon. Friend for asking that question because we have seen the biggest annual fall in long-term unemployment since 1998—108,000 fewer people on long-term benefits. That is a significant change. When we came into office we said that we would help those whom the Labour Government left behind and forgot about. We have set up the Work programme and other schemes, and the consequences are more of them in work.

T9. [904392] **Heidi Alexander** (Lewisham East) (Lab): Last week I met a constituent who received her husband's personal independence payment only after he had passed away. Will the Minister guarantee that no one else will suffer that deeply distressing situation in the future?

Mike Penning: Of course I cannot guarantee that, but we need to do everything we possibly can on this. Perhaps the hon. Lady will pass on our thoughts to her constituent for her loss. It is very import that we get the scheme to run faster, but the quality needs to be right. I am very sad when that sort of thing happens, but I cannot possibly guarantee to the House that it will not happen again. We just have to make sure that it does not happen very often.

Mr David Winnick (Walsall North) (Lab): I have been here since the beginning of Question Time and may I tell the Secretary of State that I have been sickened—there is no other way to describe my feelings—by his complacent indifference to the agonising hardship suffered by the most vulnerable in our society? He should be ashamed of the policies he is pursuing.

Mr Duncan Smith: The only sickening thing is the last Government plunging the economy into such a crisis that more people fell into unemployment and hardship as a direct result of the incompetence of the people whom the hon. Gentleman has progressively supported.

Daniel Kawczynski (Shrewsbury and Atcham) (Con): Under this Government, how many more women are now in employment?

Esther McVey: The rate is the highest it has ever been, at nearly 68%. The number and rate of women in employment is the highest we have ever seen.

Mr Andy Slaughter (Hammersmith) (Lab): After nine months, fewer than 200 people in Hammersmith and Fulham are on universal credit. This morning the shadow ministerial team visited Hammersmith's citizens advice bureau to hear directly from my constituents about the catastrophic failure of the Secretary of State's Department

in every area of operation. Is his failure to roll out universal credit just a cover-up of another DWP crisis in the making?

Mr Duncan Smith: Isn't that interesting? What a revealing statement. We have endlessly offered the Opposition Front Bench team the opportunity to visit jobcentres where universal credit is rolling out, but only one spokesman went— *[Interruption.]* No, the shadow Secretary of State never went and is refusing to go. Now she would rather visit citizens advice bureaux than the people who are actually delivering universal credit. Surely that is the most pathetic excuse I have ever heard.

Dr Eilidh Whiteford (Banff and Buchan) (SNP): I have a number of very sick constituents who have been pushed into severe financial hardship as a result of unacceptable delays in the PIP process. Some of them are now dependent on food banks. I listened carefully to the Minister earlier, but will he set out a timetable for clearing the backlog for all applicants, not just the terminally ill? What interim support will he offer to those having to wait more than 28 days?

Mike Penning: I repeat that it is taking too long. I accept that and am determined to get the time down. We are working with the providers to ensure that we get it down. I will look into individual cases if the hon. Lady wants to bring them to me, but we are doing everything we possibly can. I would rather see people being assessed than left without any assessment, as the previous Administration did, or with paper-based assessments.

Andrew Gwynne (Denton and Reddish) (Lab): Underlying the overly positive spin that Ministers have put on the employment figures is the fact that for the first time ever the majority of families living below the poverty line are in work. What are the Government going to do to make sure that work is always a route out of poverty?

Mr Duncan Smith: Nothing is more revealing than when the Opposition start claiming that we somehow have to spin the fact that there are more people in work now than when we came into office. We will soon break through the barrier and have the highest proportion of people in work. Unemployment is falling, youth unemployment is falling, and adult unemployment is falling. We do not need to spin facts, because facts in this case tell us that our welfare reforms are working.

Several hon. Members *rose*—

Mr Speaker: Order. I am sorry, but as usual demand exceeds supply and we must move on.

Preparing for Question Time

For the government, Question Time is an opportunity to tell the story the way ministers see it. It can also be a high-risk occasion, and government departments prepare very carefully. Ministers will have had briefing meetings with their civil servants, and each minister will take into the Chamber a ring-binder with the answer he or she is to give to each question, together with a 'survival pack' of information and briefing, according to a fairly standard template:

The reason for the question: why is the MP asking it? Is there a particular constituency focus? What has he or she raised with the department recently?

When a government MP puts down a question, he or she will often helpfully let the department know what is behind it, or what he or she plans as a supplementary question. Opposition MPs will also do this on occasion, especially if their intention is to flag up some issue of constituency concern rather than to attack the government. It is much better for them (and for their local media) to have a minister give a full answer on a matter of local concern rather than simply saying that he or she will write to the MP.

Elephant traps: 'any information that the minister should know about potential gaps in the policy or problems with the figures on the main issues likely to be raised';

Positive/defensive: '3 or 4 key best positive lines and 3 or 4 key defensive lines to take on the main issue . . . covering government achievements and positive activity in the area of policy, and defending against the most likely lines of criticism';

Key background facts and figures and, with a page for each issue, *other issues that may be raised* with bullpoint lines to take;

Key quotes: 'any useful third party endorsements or supportive comments from members of the opposition'.

The Official Opposition team shadowing the government department will also lay its plans for Question Time, highlighting areas where they believe the government is open to criticism, and seeking the help of backbenchers to reinforce the line being taken by the frontbench team.

Question times to major government departments now end with 10 or 15 minutes of 'topical' questions. For this period, just a list of names of MPs drawn in the shuffle is printed; there is no text of a question. The session starts with a very brief response from the secretary of state to the first topical question (often of a self-congratulatory nature) setting out some recent initiatives or successes of the department. After this, the rest of the topical question time is a series of spontaneous questions, technically supplementaries. They can be on any topic within the department's responsibility. The ministerial team must make a snap decision as to who is going to answer, and it is fascinating to watch the silent exchanges of body language by which they negotiate in a matter of seconds.

Although there was some trepidation about introducing topical questions in 2007, the House (and ministers) now value them. But topical questions rarely reveal any new information; they are much more of a political joust. In this way, they are a version of Prime Minister's Questions, to which we now turn.

Prime Minister's Questions (PMQs)

The Prime Minister answers for half an hour every Wednesday from 12 noon to 12.30 p.m. Only the top fifteen questions in the shuffle are printed, and the vast majority are in the form 'If he will list his official engagements for [Wednesday 9th July]'. Only the first such question is printed out in full on the Order of Business; if other MPs want to ask the same question their names alone are printed alongside the question numbers.

Why the 'engagements question'?

It may seem strange that so many MPs want to ask the Prime Minister what he happens to be doing on a particular Wednesday. The reason is historical, but the habit persists even though, in practice, it is not really necessary. Thirty and more years ago, the Prime Minister of the day would transfer a specific question to the relevant secretary of state if the latter had ministerial responsibility for the subject, and the MP concerned would lose the chance of an oral question to the Prime Minister. Prime Ministers are, in a sense, responsible for everything, but there are relatively few things for which they have *specific* responsibility and a departmental minister does not; examples include coordination between government departments, sacking and appointing ministers, setting up Cabinet committees, and the intelligence services as a whole.

So, the 'transfer-proof' question was devised by the Clerks in the Table Office: either to ask the Prime Minister his official engagements for the day, or a related open question – whether he would visit some particular place (usually the questioner's constituency) or country. When she became Prime Minister, Margaret Thatcher indicated that she would not transfer specific questions, as also did John Major and Tony Blair when they came to office, and this practice was continued by Gordon Brown and David Cameron. However, the open question persisted for two reasons. It allowed MPs to raise the issue of the moment even though the question had been tabled a fortnight before; and it was easy – no thought had to be given to researching and constructing some cunning question when it was odds-against that it would be successful in the shuffle. And even though the period of notice has shortened from ten sitting days to three with the express purpose of allowing more topical questions, the 'engagements question' is still the norm.

Prime Minister's Questions: on the day

As for departmental questions, the Speaker calls (say) 'Mr Crispin Blunt'; Mr Blunt stands up and says 'Number One, Mr Speaker'. The Prime Minister gives the stand-ard response: 'This morning I had meetings with ministerial colleagues and others.

In addition to my duties in this House, I shall have further such meetings later today.' The Prime Minister often takes this opportunity to offer condolences to the families of service personnel who have died on active service, victims of other tragedies, or, more cheerfully, to congratulate winning sports teams or other national heroes. Mr Blunt is then able to ask a supplementary on anything that is the responsibility of the government. After the Prime Minister has replied, the Speaker will call other MPs who were successful in the shuffle, interspersed with other backbenchers. Unlike departmental questions, MPs whose names are on the printed list simply ask their supplementary; they do not go through the process of calling out the number and having the Prime Minister repeat his original answer.

If the Leader of the Opposition rises, the Speaker will call him; he has a normal allocation of six questions in PMQs, which he can take either all in a run, or split into two groups of three (or any other pattern that he chooses).

Questions in PMQs are the usual mixture of the supportive and the critical, but the main event is the gladiatorial contest between the Prime Minister and the Leader of the Opposition. The House is full, noisy and partisan, which raises the stakes; and national newspapers carry 'post-match' comment the next day, sometimes rating the encounter in terms of goals scored or punches landed. The Prime Minister of the day has a built-in advantage; he is centre-stage for the whole play, while the Leader of the Opposition has only six appearances; and the Prime Minister can build on questions from his own backbenchers to project a positive presentation of government policy and achievements. The duel between the Leader of the Opposition and the Prime Minister usually occurs for just ten minutes or so; after it has concluded, things often quieten down and exchanges can be quiet and constructive.

Is PMQs too noisy?

Opinion is sharply divided between those who revel in the heady atmosphere of PMQs, the roars of support or opposition, and the gladiatorial exchanges; and those who see in PMQs the worst of a highly adversarial parliamentary system, with echoes of the junior common room. It would be unrealistic to expect that, having corralled 500 people of deeply held and opposing views in a small room, contentious assertions will be heard in reverent silence; they won't. But in the process it is important not to lose the value of PMQs. It is an opportunity to question for half an hour, every sitting Wednesday, the chief executive of the nation (even if the occasion is more about trying to put the Prime Minister under political pressure than exploring policies and intentions). It is reasonable for the Chamber to be boisterous, but when the volume (and, especially, collective barracking) prevents questions and answers being heard, then the House and the country are the losers. A welcome antidote is the regular appearance of the Prime Minister before the Liaison Committee (see page 308) in calm and courteous circumstances.

As well as Question Time in the House, oral questions may be asked at some sittings of the Scottish, Welsh and Northern Ireland Grand Committees (see page 261), although these are not frequent occurrences. The Standing Orders also provide for 'cross-cutting' oral Question Times in Westminster Hall, where questions are about a subject that involves a number of departments rather than about the responsibilities of a single department. After a number of such Question Times in the 2003–04 session – including on youth, domestic violence, drugs and older people – no further cross-cutting Question Times have been held, and the idea was not taken up by the coalition government in the 2010 Parliament.

Urgent questions

On any sitting day, an MP can seek privately the Speaker's leave to ask an urgent question. These were formerly known as 'private notice questions' (PNQs) because notice of them was given directly to the Speaker and not printed on the order paper as for other oral questions. The MP must make a request before 10.00 a.m. on a day when the House sits at 11.30 a.m., before 8.30 am on a day when the House sits at 9.30am and before noon on a Monday. The Speaker considers the application at the daily conference with the Deputy Speakers, attended by the Clerk of the House, the Clerk Assistant and the Principal Clerk of the Table Office. The Speaker, if he is satisfied that the matter is of public importance and is urgent, grants the application. Warning is displayed on the annunciators around the parliamentary estate, and the MP concerned is called to ask the question at the end of Question Time (or, on a Friday, at 11.00 a.m., interrupting the business then under way). Urgent questions on a Friday are rare.

The Speaker's power to grant an urgent question is a significant one. It brings a minister to the House at very short notice to answer on something on which the government may be in some disarray, and is still deciding how to respond to a problem that may have arisen only a few hours before. On major issues, the minister concerned has been exposed to questioning for up to an hour, though sometimes it can be for a shorter period.

The number of urgent questions granted under the current Speaker has increased sharply. This has become a way for the House to engage immediately with a high-profile issue of the moment that would not otherwise find its way on to the House's agenda. It puts the government under pressure to respond, report and explain; and the mere tabling of an urgent question, of which the government is immediately informed, is sometimes enough for ministers to volunteer a full statement.

In the 2013–14 session, the Speaker granted 36 urgent questions. Occasionally, two were granted on a single day. Subjects included the recommendation of the trust special administrator to close the A&E at Lewisham Hospital and reports that the Free Schools programme was £800m over budget. In April 2012, the granting of the Question 'if he will refer the conduct of the Secretary of State for Culture, Olympics, Media and Sport [Jeremy Hunt], in respect of his dealings with News Corporation, to the independent adviser on ministerial interests' brought the Prime Minister himself to the despatch box to answer.

The 'Business Question' every Thursday at 10.30 a.m., in which the shadow Leader of the House asks the Leader of the House to announce forthcoming business in the House, is technically an urgent question, although of a specialised type. The Leader of the House sets out the main items of business on the House's agenda, usually firm for the following week, more provisional for the week after, and then answers questions. Strictly speaking, these must relate to the forthcoming business, are often on more general political matters; and it does not take much ingenuity to ask for a debate on 'the government's failure to deliver on targets' or on 'the government's successes in carrying through public service reform'.

Since the creation of backbench business (see page 143), the Leader's answer is often to encourage the member to apply to the Backbench Business Committee for a debate. During business questions, the Leader will list forthcoming backbench business, but as he has no sway over the allocation of such business he is simply reporting the decisions made by the Backbench Business Committee.

Questions answered at the end of Question Time

A minister may choose to answer an oral question not as it is reached during Question Time, but at the end of oral questions (3.30 p.m. on Mondays, 12.30 p.m. on Tuesdays and Wednesdays and 11.30 a.m. on Thursdays). This is relatively unusual, but tends to happen when a question on the Order of Business is a convenient hook for an announcement a minister wants to make, but at greater length than would be permissible in answer to a conventional oral question. As this is, in effect, a mini-statement, the Speaker allows more supplementaries than during Question Time. A minister may answer an oral question in this way even though it would not have been reached during Question Time (and may even answer a written question in this way if it is down for answer on that day).

Written questions

In the 2013–14 session, 4,380 questions received an oral answer in the House. By contrast, 45,347 written questions were tabled during that session. Just over 11 per cent of these – some 5,267 – were to the Department of Health. Three other departments (Department for Work and Pensions, the Home Office and the Ministry of Justice) answered more than 3,000 each (between 7 per cent and 8 per cent of the total in each case). At the other end of the scale, the Scotland Office answered 275 and the Wales Office answered 289.

Written questions are of two types: *ordinary written questions*, which are put down, in theory, for answer two sitting days after they are received but which, by convention, the government is expected to answer within two weeks. There is no limit to the number of this type of question that an MP may table. *Named-day questions* are for answer on a stated day, with a minimum period of three working days, although an answer may be given only on a sitting day. The named-day system was originally intended for genuinely urgent questions (and used to be called 'priority written questions'), but it became greatly over-used, and increasing numbers of question got holding replies ('I will reply to the Hon. Member as soon as possible'). From January

2003, the House agreed to introduce a limit of five named-day questions per member per day.

Written questions have a wide variety of purposes. They are used by MPs to raise the profile of particular subjects, to tease out details of the government's policy on some issue with a view to deploying the material in political debate inside or outside the House, or to press ministers in an area where the government appears vulnerable. They are tabled to gather information in order to be able to respond to constituency concerns, or to give a constituent's case wider publicity. Shadow ministers use them to monitor what the government is doing in their policy areas. Outside organisations will ask MPs to put down questions in order to assist a campaign, or to obtain an authoritative statement on a situation or of the government's policy towards it.

Written questions have one great advantage over oral questions: they can be pursued much more relentlessly. Whereas in Question Time an MP gets one supple-mentary and the moment is past, with the ministers concerned not answering again until one month later, written questions can follow up in detail, almost as a barrister would in cross-examination, the precise conduct of government policy in a particular area.

Although, as we noted, there are rubbing points when MPs see no good reason for the government refusing to answer, replies to written questions put a staggering amount of official information into the public domain, even though some feel that their increasing use has devalued the currency. The total numbers of written answers published per financial year soared from 32,821 in 2000–01 to a peak of 73,601 in 2008–09. Although the figure reduced after that, it plateaued in the mid to high 40,000 range and, in 2013–14, 43,030 answers were published. Such questions used to occupy forty to fifty pages of *Hansard* on a typical day. Since September 2014, the House of Commons has stopped printing the answers to written parliamentary questions as part of a much wider move 'from print to web', making information electronically available to MPs and to the public. Members receive answers to their questions to up to three nominated email addresses. Answers are also fully searchable on the parliamentary website and available in a downloadable daily digest form. A sample screen from this 'Q & A system' is reproduced on page 294.

In the 2008–09 session, the Procedure Committee again reiterated that it did not believe that the tabling of written questions by MPs should be restricted, stating 'The use of WPQs is vital to the scrutiny of Government and, in line with previous recommendations of the Committee, we believe that no restriction should be placed on the number of ordinary written parliamentary questions Members may ask'.

Written statements

It used to be the case that, if the government wanted to put something formally on the record in the House that was not important enough for an oral statement (see page 138), a friendly backbencher would be found to put down an 'arranged question' drafted in the department concerned, for answer the very next day, in answer to which the government could make the statement it wanted. These arranged or 'planted questions' were a rather opaque way for the government to make an announcement and, from October 2002, a system of written ministerial statements was introduced. In June 2013, the House agreed to the Procedure Committee's recommendation that the provision to make written statements should be extended to answering bodies (such as the House of Commons Commission and the Church Commissioners) that already had slots to answer oral questions. Written statements to be made on any day are listed on the Order Paper at the end of the day's business, and statements on a future day appear in Section A of the *Future Business* part of the Vote bundle (see page 152), although advance notification is fairly rare. When made, the statements are printed towards the end of the next day's *Hansard* (and so are available online).

Are questions effective?

There is no doubt that, whereas 30 or 40 years ago, an MP would often first write to a government department for information, or seek a meeting to put some point to a minister, and would table a PQ only if he or she had to, in 2015 putting down a question is often the first, not the last step. As the Procedure Committee has acknowledged, the scale of the increase in written questions risks a reduction in the quality of government replies – although this is not to suggest that, if there were half the number of questions, the answers would be twice as helpful. And although many PQs engaged the efforts of the MP asking them very closely, the sheer number (and the poor level of authentication for 'e-tabling') has led to unease that significant numbers of PQs are actually drafted and tabled by MPs' staffers with minimal involvement of the member concerned.

However, as in so many areas of parliamentary life, the determination and hard work of an individual MP can produce remarkable results. For example, it was the written questions tabled by the backbench Labour MP Tam Dalyell in the 1980s that led to the admission from Margaret Thatcher's government that, during the Falklands War, the Argentinian heavy cruiser *General Belgrano* had been torpedoed when steaming away from British forces rather than towards them, as the government had previously implied. There are many less-celebrated examples of assiduous MPs doggedly plugging away at some area of a department's activities until they elicit enough information to reveal that the official account of events is inconsistent with the facts.

The processes of oral and written questions are key functions of the House of Commons. Both can be means of exposing the government to criticism, and of requiring explanation and justification. Oral questions, although inquisitorial in theory, are also part of the political debate. Written questions, on the other hand, are a way of calling governments to account in detail, and should be an important discipline on individual government departments and their ministers – the requirement to reply truthfully to a direct and precise question can mean that the spotlight swings onto something that the government would have much preferred to have kept to itself.

Parliamentary online Q&A system

Source: www.parliament.uk. Artwork by Nick Battley

Although, as we have seen, frontbenchers use questions extensively, they are also one of the main opportunities for backbench MPs on all sides of the House to pursue and expose issues, and to get the government of the day to put information on the public record. If the average costs of answering oral and written questions are correct, the system costs about £11.5 million per annum, or about £17,500 for each of the House's members. Set against expected total government expenditure in 2014/15 of some £732 *billion*, this does not seem excessive.

The great constitutional theorist Ivor Jennings described parliamentary questions as 'of the utmost constitutional importance'. The effect of the Internet, digital government and the coming into force of the Freedom of Information Act have all contributed to making PQs a less privileged and special way of eliciting information from the executive. But parliamentary questions still symbolise the ultimate accountability of ministers to Parliament, and in that respect are as important as they ever were.

Questions in the House of Lords

The House of Lords also has a variety of ways of scrutinising the actions of, and eliciting information from, the executive by means of questions. These questions are always addressed to Her Majesty's Government. (Questions on domestic House of Lords matters are usually addressed to the Leader of the House or Chairman of Committees.) It follows that the government must have responsibility for the subject matter of the question. Fewer questions are tabled in the Lords than in the Commons, and the rules governing their content are less strict. It is ultimately for the House itself to determine what is in order and what is not. But there are some conventions, nevertheless, and the guidance offered to members in the Companion to Standing Orders is now much more specific than it used to be. Questions casting reflections on the royal family or relating to the Church of England, or on devolved matters, or questions phrased offensively, are inadmissible. Questions that are *sub judice* (which are on matters awaiting decision by the criminal or civil courts) are also inadmissible – subject only to the discretion of the Lord Speaker, who may allow such a question if the case is of national importance and there is no danger of prejudice to the proceedings. It is held to be undesirable to table hypothetical questions, or to incorporate statements of fact or opinion in the text of a question. And, in the interests of 'comity', questions should not criticise decisions of the House of Commons.

Questions for oral answer (starred questions)

Every sitting day, except on Fridays, four questions for oral answer may be put to the government immediately after Prayers and before other business. They are marked on the Order Paper with a '*' and, provided that they are not 'topical questions', may be tabled up to one month in advance. In the sessions 2002–03 and 2003–04, the House experimented by taking a fifth question on Tuesdays and Wednesdays, but subsequently reverted to former practice.

As in the Commons, questions in the Lords were losing their currency from being tabled too far in advance and some members were, it was felt, hogging the Order Paper by tabling too many, too far ahead. In recent years, the Procedure Committee has recommended that no member should have more than one on the Order Paper at any one time; and that on Tuesdays and Thursdays one, and on Wednesdays two, of the questions should be 'topical questions' selected by ballot by the Clerk Assistant two working days before they are to be asked. No starred question may be tabled less than 24 hours before it is to be asked.

Unlike the Commons, questions are not limited to any particular government department on any particular day and there is, of course, no equivalent to Prime Minister's questions. Every member asking a question is allowed one supplementary before other members' supplementaries are put. Supplementary questions must be in terms confined to the subject of the original question but frequently go wider. They must not give rise to debate. Question time may not exceed thirty minutes. In the 2013–14 session, 543 oral questions were asked, which is now typical for a session of normal duration.

When, towards the end of Gordon Brown's premiership, two secretaries of state sat in the Lords (Business and Transport) in the period 2008–10, the House agreed in late 2009 to institute an additional question period for Lords secretaries of state. Three questions to a particular secretary of state would be taken additionally on Thursdays once a month, following a ballot on the previous Monday. The period allotted was 15 minutes. As there are currently no secretaries of state in the House, the procedure no longer applies, but it will be revived the next time there is one.

Questions for short debate

A question that may give rise to debate may be put down for any sitting day. Originally taken at the end of business by agreement with the Government Whips' Office, they may now be taken during dinner adjournments or in Grand Committee. They are discussed more fully on page 269.

Questions for written answer

Members of the House may also obtain written answers by tabling questions on the Order Paper under the heading 'Questions for written answer'. The minister concerned will then write to the Lord and the answer will also be published in *Hansard*. There is no limit to the number of questions a Lord may ask in this way, though members are discouraged from tabling large numbers of questions or multiple requests for information masquerading as a single question, and no more than 6 per day may be tabled by a single member, with a cap of 12 per week. During the long summer recess, written questions may also be tabled on the first Monday in September and the first Monday in October. Questions for written answer are answered within a fortnight. As in the Commons, the government itself often used the medium of a written answer to a question to make an announcement or publish information, but written statements are now published in *Hansard* instead – no fewer than 1,117 in the session 2013–14. In 1961–62, only 72 questions for written answer were tabled; in 1998–99, 4,322; and in 2013–14, 7,007. Written answers on matters delegated to executive agencies are filtered through an appropriate member of the government and printed in the Official Report in letter form.

Private notice questions

A Lord may seek to ask a question on a matter of urgency on any day, just as an MP may apply for an 'urgent question'. But it is the Lord Speaker who, in the first instance, decides whether the question is of sufficient urgency or importance to justify an immediate reply. Notice of such a question must be given by noon on the day it is proposed to ask it. Private notice questions are allowed relatively rarely – there were nine in 2013–14. They occur more frequently when a Cabinet minister with major departmental responsibilities sits in the Lords and during those periods when the House sits while the Commons remains in recess. But answers to many Commons urgent questions are repeated as statements in the House of Lords, if the opposition requests it. Questions and answers on any repeated Commons urgent questions are limited to ten minutes.

Statements

The making of a government statement also gives rise to a question and answer period. Except when the relevant secretary of state sits in the Lords, statements are made first in the Commons and repeated at a convenient time in the Lords. Following the conclusion of the statement, 20 minutes are allowed for questions from the opposition frontbench and a further 20 minutes for other members. In 2013–14, 65 statements were made – just under one every other sitting day.

Public petitions

The right to petition Parliament is an ancient one, summarised in a resolution of the House of Commons of 1699: 'That it is the inherent right of every commoner in England to prepare and present petitions to the House of Commons in case of grievance, and the House of Commons to receive the same'. The first recorded petitions date from the reign of Richard II (1377–99); in 1571, a committee with the splendid name of the Committee for Motions of Griefs and Petitions was appointed to examine petitions.

Petitions were originally read at the start of a sitting, and debates could arise upon them. Huge numbers were presented during the nineteenth century; for example, 17,000 per year between 1837 and 1841; and 34,000 in 1893. The twentieth century saw a sharp fall in the numbers of public petitions, but they remain a way of giving local or more widespread concerns a higher profile.

Petitions must be presented by an MP. They may have hundreds of thousands of signatures, or only one, but the procedure is the same in each case. The basic rules are that they should state from whom they come, should be in 'respectful language' and should ask for something that it is in the power of the House of Commons to grant. (It is important to make a distinction between these 'public petitions' and the petitions presented against a private or hybrid bill (see page 221).) The MP has the petition checked by the Clerk of Public Petitions to make sure it is in order, and can then, at any time during a sitting of the House, simply put in the green baize bag that hangs on the back of the Speaker's Chair. The MP can also present a petition formally in the House. Just before the daily half-hour adjournment debate, he or she is called by the Speaker, and briefly introduces the petition and reads the text. The MP then brings the petition to the Clerk at the Table and hands the petition to them. The Clerk announces the title of the petition and hands it back to the MP, who places it in the petition bag. All petitions are printed in *Hansard* and are sent to the government department responsible for the subject area, as well as the select committee that shadows that department. In October 2007, the House agreed that all 'substantive petitions should normally receive a response from the relevant government department' and select committees should 'formally place them on their agendas'. There is an expectation that observations should be made within two months of the petition being presented to the House. The observations are also printed in *Hansard*. Recent statistics are:

Session	Petitions	of which presented formally	Government observations
2004–05	43	51	44
2005–06	207	293	257
2006–07	112	161	142
2007–08	220	221	195
2008–09	97	123	111
2009–10	343	393*	135
2010–12 (long session)	176	187	159
2012–13	128	146	132
2013–14	163	175	137

Note: *Including 248 on the single subject of the Badman Report on home education.

Petitions cover a wide variety of subjects, both national and local. On the last sitting day before the 2014 summer recess, for example, petitions were presented on deaths and injuries in disturbances in Lahore, on dangerous dogs, on home-to-school transport for the Colne Community School in Essex, on the direct bus service from Hounslow West to West Middlesex Hospital, on human rights in Sri Lanka, on development proposals for 34 Hatton Avenue, Wellingborough, and on the proposed closure of Barclays Bank branches in the Suffolk Coastal constituency – a typical mix of international, national and local issues.

Petitions are not formally taken up, either by a committee of the House, or by an outside authority such as the ombudsman. Committees may occasionally write to the member who has presented the petition to share the work that they are doing on that subject area with them. In that sense, they are not a particularly effective way of making a case. But they can achieve a great deal of publicity; and on a local issue can have a snowball effect. On national issues, either the sheer numbers of signatories to a petition, or the fact that similar petitions from scores of constituencies are presented week after week, can be a powerful statement of concern which, for practical political reasons, the government must heed.

However, in December 2014, the Procedure Committee recommended the establishment of a Petitions Committee, which may presage a much higher profile and effectiveness for public petitions.

Petitions may also be addressed to the House of Lords by a member of the House. No speech or debate takes place beyond the formal words of presentation and they are not printed. Though largely defunct, petitions are very occasionally still presented there.

e-Petitions

The House of Commons had, for some years, grappled with whether to introduce an electronic system of petitioning. As early as 2006, in its first report of the 2006–07 session, the Procedure Committee had undertaken to examine 'the practical and procedural implications of introducing e-petitioning with a view to proposing a worked-up and practicable system to the House in due course'. On 6 April 2008, the Committee published a report on e-petitions that recommended that the House of Commons adopt a system of e-petitions, a recommendation that was agreed to by the government in July 2008. But the costs and complexities involved meant that no such system was introduced, despite a follow-up report from the Committee calling for government action in 2008–09.

The No. 10 Downing Street e-petitions system was launched on 14 November 2006 and rapidly attracted a large number of petitions and petitioners, and a high level of publicity. One petition, entitled 'Scrap the vehicle tracking and road pricing policy', attracted over 1.8 million signatures. The system allowed No. 10 to send a maximum of two emails to petitioners, enabling the government to respond directly to petitioners, but had no role for Parliament. A number of members, including the then Leader of the Opposition David Cameron, voiced concern that the No. 10 e-petitions system risked by-passing Parliament, or even taking on a role that is more properly one for Parliament.

In 2010, the new Coalition government, with David Cameron as Prime Minister, made a commitment as part of its *Programme for Government* 'that any petition that secures 100,000 signatures will be eligible for formal debate in Parliament'. The government gave effect to this commitment through the relaunching of the No. 10 Downing Street petition website in July 2011 as a government petitions website and the Leader of the House notifying the Backbench Business Committee of any petition that had been accepted and had passed a 100,000 signature threshold and that was therefore 'eligible' for debate.

The Backbench Business Committee treats e-petitions in the same way as other requests for debate; one or more MPs must apply for the debate, and e-petitions compete with subjects that have been raised in other ways. But e-petitions do have the advantage of some reserved time in Westminster Hall on Mondays between 4.30 p.m. and 7.30 p.m., when allocated by the Backbench Business Committee

By the end of the 2013–14 session, 28 e-petitions on the government website had reached the 100,000 signature threshold, making them eligible for consideration for debate. The topics of 22 had been the subject of debate in the House of Commons, most as a direct result of the e-petition. Seven of those debates had taken place in Westminster Hall on a Monday afternoon, in the additional time for e-petitions. Issues debated have included financial education in schools and the cost of fuel, and the e-petition calling for the release of documents relating to the Hillsborough tragedy, a release subsequently agreed to by the government.

There is still a feeling that the system of e-petitioning should be more squarely within the control of Parliament. A debate on petitions was held in the House of Commons on 8 May 2014. At the end of the debate, the House agreed the following motion:

> *That this House supports the establishment, at the start of the next Parliament, of a collaborative e-petitions system, which enables members of the public to petition the House of Commons and press for action from Government; and calls on the Procedure Committee to work with the Government and other interested parties on the development of detailed proposals.*

The Procedure Committee's detailed proposals were made in December 2014.

MPs' letters

MPs' letters to ministers can be seen as part of the questioning process, though they are not 'proceedings in Parliament' (see page 163). The level of correspondence between MPs and ministers is very high. The government's figures, from which Table 9.1 is drawn, include correspondence from peers, but the vast majority of letters are from MPs (who in this case also include ministers and the Speaker in their constituency roles).

It is not surprising that the departments that deal with the matters that touch people's lives most closely – health, law and order, education and immigration – have heavy post-bags.

Typically, an MP receives a complaint from a constituent, perhaps that he was discharged from hospital too soon, or that he has a fiancée who is not being allowed to settle in the UK from Pakistan, or that his son is being kept in poor conditions in a remand prison. It would be impossible for the MP to investigate these complaints personally. He or she could table parliamentary questions, or apply for an adjournment debate; but usually the MP begins by forwarding the constituent's letter to the minister

Table 9.1 Correspondence in calendar year 2013

Department for Business, Innovation and Skills	7,968
Cabinet Office	3,072
Department for Communities and Local Government	9,832
Department for Culture, Media and Sport	6,317
Ministry of Defence	4,853
Department for Education	16,898
Department of Energy and Climate Change	6,920
Department for Environment, Food and Rural Affairs	10,362
Foreign and Commonwealth Office	10,043
Department of Health	18,918
Home Office	8,761
UK Visas and Immigration	57,582
Her Majesty's Passport Office	1,123
Department for International Development	3,407
Ministry of Justice	4,985
Office of the Leader of the House of Commons	147
Department for Transport	8,041
Treasury	9,608
HM Revenue and Customs:	
Where Minister replied	1,915
Where CEO replied	6,331
Department for Work and Pensions	21,005

Note: Department for Education statistics include Education Funding Agency, National College of Teaching and Leadership, and Standards and Testing Agency.

responsible for the subject and asking for comments. Not all letters are of complaint. A small firm may want to know what government or EU grants it can apply for, or seek the MP's help in negotiating some tangle of bureaucracy.

The constituent could have written directly to the department, whether with a complaint or query, but the fact that the letter is coming from an MP means that the issue will be dealt with at a more senior level. The reply – usually from a minister personally, but also from officials with operational responsibility for the subject, or the chief executive of an executive agency – will be in a form that the MP can forward to the constituent as a response, but it may also give the MP useful background if similar cases arise.

Letters from members of the House of Lords to ministers are treated in the same way inside government departments as letters from MPs. No separate figures are published, but the numbers are much lower because peers have no constituency work.

Letters have several advantages over parliamentary questions. They can be sent at any time, whereas questions may be tabled only when the House is sitting or on non-sitting Fridays. They can raise confidential matters, or the personal details of a constituent's case, and can go into great detail about the point at issue. And, unlike questions, there are no rules restricting what an MP may say in a letter. The contents of letters between MPs and ministers are private unless one side or the other releases them; and although by convention the minister does not do this unless the MP does, ministers are always aware that the MP may 'go public' and their letters are, whenever possible, written in a form that can be forwarded directly to the constituent.

One disadvantage of letters is that they are more prone to delay than the answers to PQs. All the departments in Table 9.1 above have targets for replying to MPs' letters, of between 10 and 20 working days. In 2013, the Department for Transport responded to 97 per cent of letters within its 20-day target; the Department of Health and the Foreign and Commonwealth Office both replied to 95 per cent of letters within their target times of 18 and 20 working days, respectively; and the Department for Business, Innovation and Skills responded to 93 per cent of MPs' and Peers' letters within its 15-working day target. At the other end of the scale, the Department for Culture, Media and Sport trailed behind, responding to only 51 per cent of letters within its target of 20 working days. All other departments managed a response rate of over 70 per cent.

Most matters raised by constituents and taken by MPs with ministers are dealt with by correspondence. However, if the MP is unhappy with the government's response, he or she can seek a meeting with the minister, or put down parliamentary questions, or seek an adjournment debate, either in the Chamber or in Westminster Hall, to which a minister will have to reply. Proceedings in the House often start with a constituent's letter.

10

Calling to account: select committees

Select committees in the House of Commons

Introduction

People often associate select committees of the House of Commons with the system of departmental select committees set up in 1979; but, in fact, the House has used select committees for centuries to investigate, to advise, to consider complex matters – in fact, for any task that is more effectively carried out by a small group of MPs than by the House as a whole. Indeed, the very name 'select committee' indicates that a task or function has been given, or *committed*, to that body, composed of MPs *selected* to sit upon it.

We have already encountered general committees (see pages 188 and 227) – with the exception of European committees (see page 353), these do not have permanent memberships: each one ceases to exist when it has finished considering the particular item of business committed to it. Some select committees are also appointed for a single purpose – to examine a draft bill, perhaps – and are dissolved when they have completed their work, but most are permanent institutions. They are appointed under standing orders and so do not die at the end of a session or the end of a parliament.

When the House meets after a general election, the permanent select committees are technically in existence but have no members. It can take several weeks before select committees can begin their work. First, the House must decide which party chairs each departmental select committee and some of the other cross-cutting and internal committees. The chairs of these committees are now elected by the whole House, usually within about three weeks of the Queen's Speech. The parties must then nominate the other committee members. Both the Conservative and Labour parties hold internal elections for select committee places. Finally, the names are agreed by the House. Following the 2010 election, most select committees were appointed on 12 July, just under eight weeks after the beginning of the parliamentary session.

The development of select committees

Select committees have long been a feature of the work of the House of Commons. If you look at the Journals of the House for the end of the sixteenth century, you will find select committees involved in, and advising the House on, some of the most sensitive political issues of the day. In 1571, there was a Committee for the Uniformity of Religion – a matter of life and death in Elizabethan England. The following year there was a Committee on the Queen of Scotts [*sic*] – in this case, a matter of death. In 1571, there was also a Committee for the Examination of Fees and Rewards taken for Voices (that is, votes) in this House – an early example of the House looking at appropriate standards of conduct. Just after the turn of the seventeenth century, select committees dealt with the Confirmation of the Book of Common Prayer and with the Union with Scotland (both in 1604).

Some committees were virtually permanent: committees on Grievances, on Privileges and on the Subsidy (the grant of money to the Crown) were regularly appointed. There were also select committees with wider responsibilities, such as the splendidly named Grand Committee for Evils (1623).

But most committees were ephemeral; something came up that the House wanted looked at, and it set up a committee. These would often operate very informally: the members nominated to the committee would go straight out of the House into another room, would deliberate, perhaps examine witnesses, and then come back to the House (possibly even later in the same sitting), when one of their members would report orally what view they had come to.

Until well into the twentieth century, most select committees were set up *ad hoc* to examine a particular issue of public policy, or often some disaster or scandal (and their appointment was often used as a political weapon). A classic case was the Sebastopol Committee, set up in 1855, which – with some resonances for the aftermath of the Iraq war in 2003 – investigated the conduct of affairs but also sought political scapegoats in the process. The committee sat almost every day for more than two months, asked some 7,000 questions of witnesses and was bitterly critical of Lord Aberdeen, the former Prime Minister (who gave evidence to the committee). Unlike a modern select committee, the Sebastopol Committee had no staff (the role of committee clerks then was largely to ensure procedural rectitude), and the final report was written by one of its members, Lord Seymour (the draft report proposed by the fiery chairman, Mr Roebuck, was rejected by the committee).

The reputation of select committees as a means of inquiring into events was dealt a serious blow by the committee investigations into the Jameson Raid (a botched attempt to overthrow President Paul Kruger of the Transvaal Republic in 1895, often thought to have led to the Boer War) and the Marconi scandal of 1912, involving allegations of insider trading against senior politicians. Both were marked by extreme partisanship and were almost wholly ineffective. The contemporary lack of confidence in select committees as investigators led to the Tribunals of Inquiry (Evidence) Act 1921 providing a non-parliamentary means of investigation.

Unsystematic scrutiny

Committees such as the Sebastopol Committee played some part in calling governments to account (often after the event) but, with the possible exception of the Public Accounts Committee (see page 249), set up in 1861 to see whether public money had been properly expended, until the twentieth century there was little use by the House of Commons of select committees to monitor the detail of what the government of the day was actually doing.

A move in this direction was made with the appointment in 1912 of the Estimates Committee, which lasted until 1970, when it was succeeded (until 1979) by the Expenditure Committee. Both committees worked mainly through subject sub-committees, but their coverage of government activity, although occasionally influential, was very patchy. In the late 1960s and 1970s, various 'subject' select committees (for example, on agriculture, education and science, and overseas aid) were set up; but there was no real system of select committees; and the Agriculture Committee, for example, was wound up in February 1969 after a campaign of opposition by government departments.

The real change came with the election of the Conservative government in 1979. The new Leader of the House, Norman St John-Stevas, was quick to put before the House the recommendation of the Procedure Committee the previous year that there should be select committees to shadow each government department. The committee had also recommended that eight days per year on the floor of the House should be devoted to debating the committees' reports (and that their chairmen should be paid a small additional salary). These latter recommendations were not adopted by the government, but the key principle of a system of select committees related to government departments was approved in June 1979.

Had St John-Stevas not moved so quickly, the change would probably never have been made; by the autumn the Prime Minister, Margaret Thatcher (who had other things on her mind in the first few months of office), would have realised how inconvenient for the government these committees might be, and would have vetoed the proposal. But, for the first time, the House of Commons now had at its disposal a means of systematic scrutiny of the government of the day potentially much more rigorous than the traditional methods of debate and question.

Today, these departmental select committees account for the majority of select committee activity; but they number only about half of the House's select committees. We now look at what select committees there are and what they do; then at their appointment and powers; and we will then use the example of a departmental committee to see how they work.

The committees

Departmental committees

There are 19 of these (number of members on each committee in brackets):

- Business, Innovation and Skills (11)
- Communities and Local Government (11)
- Culture, Media and Sport (11)
- Defence (12)
- Education (11)
- Energy and Climate Change (11)
- Environment, Food and Rural Affairs (11)
- Foreign Affairs (11)
- Health (11)
- Home Affairs (11)
- International Development (11)
- Justice (12)
- Northern Ireland Affairs (14)
- Science and Technology (11)
- Scottish Affairs (11)
- Transport (11)
- Treasury (13)
- Welsh Affairs (12)
- Work and Pensions (11).

The departmental committees have a very broad remit: 'to examine the expenditure, administration and policy of [the relevant government department] and associated public bodies'. They are thus concerned not only with the doings of 'their' department, but also with any related executive agencies, and with regulators and inspectorates that operate in their field. All the committees have power to set up a sub-committee.

Because each committee shadows a government department, the system of committees has to change to match alterations in the structure of government. Thus, the Justice Committee followed on from the Constitutional Affairs Committee, which was itself a successor to the Committee on the Lord Chancellor's Department. Similarly, when particular responsibilities move from one government department to another, the task of monitoring them moves from one committee to another.

'Cross-cutting' committees

The departmental committees look 'vertically' at all the responsibilities of a single department and its ministers (although the Scottish, Welsh and Northern Ireland

Affairs Committees have a broader range of interests). The cross-cutting committees, on the other hand, look 'horizontally' across Whitehall at themes or actions in which all or most departments are involved:

- Environmental Audit
- European Scrutiny
- Liaison
- Political and Constitutional Reform
- Public Accounts
- Public Administration
- The Joint Committee on the National Security Strategy

Environmental Audit Committee

This was set up in November 1997. It has 16 members, and its task is 'to consider to what extent the policies and programmes of government departments and non-departmental public bodies contribute to environmental protection and sustainable development', and 'to audit their performance against such targets as may be set for them'. The committee inquires into a range of sustainability issues. Recent work has covered issues as diverse as air quality, the environmental impact of high speed rail, marine protected areas, and the sustainability of the UK's Overseas Territories. It has power to appoint a sub-committee.

European Scrutiny Committee

This committee (formerly known as the European Legislation Committee) was established shortly after the United Kingdom joined the EEC in 1973. It examines a range of European Union business: not only European Union policies, spending and draft legislation, but also institutional issues – it reported in detail on the processes that led to the Maastricht, Amsterdam, Nice and Lisbon Treaties. It has 16 members and has power to set up as many sub-committees as it wishes. The work of this committee is covered in Chapter 11.

Liaison Committee

This is an unusual committee whose work includes both detailed housekeeping (and so might be classed with the internal committees) and some of the most high-profile hearings (with the Prime Minister) of any select committee. The committee consists of the chairs of the permanent select committees. The membership thus varies with the number of committees, but at present it stands at 33. It has power to set up two sub-committees, one of which has a limited role in relation to organising the scrutiny of government proposals for National Policy Statements on planning matters.

The Liaison Committee has the general task of considering 'general matters relating to the work of select committees'. This may be a change in the format of committee reports, for example, or the resources available to committees, or the rules of engagement for pre-appointment hearings with senior public officials. The committee also decides how the budget for overseas travel by select committees is allocated, and it chooses reports for debate on the floor of the House on estimates days and in Westminster Hall (see pages 246 and 259).

In 2000, however, the committee changed its spots entirely and launched into a campaign to make select committees more effective. Its three reports, under the general theme of *Shifting the Balance* (between the executive and the legislature), put forward a reform programme that produced something of a confrontation with the government and with the then Leader of the House, Margaret Beckett. Her replacement by Robin Cook in 2001 led to the adoption of a number of the committee's proposals. The committee has followed up its work by publishing periodic reports on the select committee system, assessing its effectiveness and examining innovations and problems.

One Liaison Committee recommendation produced an important result, although not immediately. In December 2000, the chair of the committee wrote to the Prime Minister inviting him to give evidence to the committee on the government's annual report 'to spell out your policies in an atmosphere very different from that on the floor of the House'. The request was turned down on the grounds of precedent and what was described as 'the important principle that it is for individual Secretaries of State to answer to the House and its individual Select Committees for their areas of responsibility, and not the Prime Minister' – even though the Prime Minister answers on those areas of responsibility every week during Prime Minister's Questions.

However, just over a year later the Prime Minister did, indeed, offer to appear before the committee twice a year to discuss domestic and international affairs, and the first session took place on 16 July 2002. The Prime Minister's appearances have become important parliamentary occasions, televised live and carefully analysed by the media. The size of the committee makes the normal style of examination more difficult, but questioning is focused on themes decided by the committee beforehand, each led by one MP. The Prime Minister is given notice of the themes but not of the detailed questions; the calm questioning in depth at these sessions has been a valuable antidote to the knockabout of PMQs, and it is difficult to see a future Prime Minister being able to discontinue the practice.

Committee of Public Accounts

The work of this committee, usually known as 'the PAC', and of the Comptroller and Auditor General who supports it, is described in Chapter 7.

Public Administration Committee

This committee was set up in 1997, taking on the functions of two previous committees, the Public Service Committee and the Committee on the Parliamentary Commissioner for Administration. In its public service role, the committee has conducted inquiries into matters that affect the government as a whole: for example, during 2013–14 it published reports on the future of the census, the implications of open data, problems with statistics and reform of the civil service. The committee has 11 members and the power to appoint a sub-committee.

In its other role, the committee considers the reports of the Parliamentary and Health Service Ombudsman. The Ombudsman is an entirely independent official who reports to Parliament. Assisted by a staff of 435, investigating complaints about maladministration and the actions (or inactions) of government departments and other public bodies that seem to have caused injustice that has not been put right. The main aim of the Ombudsman is to obtain a remedy for those who have suffered injustice, and the secondary aim is to ensure good standards of public administration. If serious faults are found, the Ombudsman can recommend to the public body concerned what redress it should offer and the action it should take to avoid a repetition of the failure. The Ombudsman has no power to enforce recommendations, but they are almost always accepted. There are separate Ombudsman posts in Scotland, Wales and Northern Ireland that report to their respective devolved parliamentary bodies.

The relationship between the Ombudsman and the Public Administration Committee is not unlike that between the Comptroller and Auditor General and the Public Accounts Committee (see page 249). The Ombudsman has the additional clout of the committee's backing, and the committee is able to draw on the work of the Ombudsman's office with its substantial resources. The committee considers the Ombudsman's annual reports; but, rather than following up the details of individual investigations, it draws more general lessons for public administration as a whole.

Joint Committee on the National Security Strategy

This joint committee was established in 2010 to consider not only the National Security Strategy, but also the government structures for decision-making on national security, particularly the role of the National Security Council and the National Security Adviser. It has taken evidence on national security and the EU, the nature of the UK's alliance with the US; and energy security. In January 2104, it took evidence from the Prime Minister. It is chaired by a member of the Lords (Margaret Beckett, a former Foreign Secretary) and has 22 members, including the chairs of 7 Commons departmental committees with an interest in the subject matter (Business, Innovation and Skills, Defence, Energy and Climate Change, Foreign Affairs, Home Affairs, International Development, and Justice), and the chair of the Intelligence and Security Committee.

'Legislative' committees

Although most legislation is considered by general committees, several select committees are concerned with different types of legislation:

* Consolidation, &c., Bills
* Human Rights
* Regulatory Reform
* Statutory Instruments.

The European Scrutiny Committee might also be included in this list but, as it deals with a wide range of EU policy matters, as well as legislation, we have treated it as a cross-cutting committee.

Joint Committee on Consolidation, &c., Bills

This is a joint committee of both Houses on which both MPs and peers sit (we look at joint committees more closely on page 340). Established in 1894, the committee has 24 members, half from each House, and is chaired by a retired judge, who does much of the scrutiny work. Its task is to examine bills that 'consolidate' the law – that is, restate it in a more logical and convenient form without changing its substance, although errors and ambiguities may be corrected. Such bills are always introduced in the House of Lords rather than in the House of Commons. The committee considers the form rather than the merits of legislation. It meets only when a bill is referred to it: only four times since 2006.

Joint Committee on Human Rights

Following the enactment of the Human Rights Act 1998, the Joint Committee on Human Rights was appointed in 2001. It has a general remit to consider matters relating to human rights in the United Kingdom (but not individual cases). In 2013–14, its inquiries included violence against women and girls, the human rights aspects of UK extradition policy, and the implications for access to justice of the government's proposals to reform legal aid. It also has an important role in legislation. It examines every government bill as soon as possible after introduction to see whether the bill, if enacted, might risk violating a human right, and it reports its views to both Houses. The committee also examines proposals for, and drafts of, remedial orders, which come about when a court finds that an Act of Parliament is incompatible with the Human Rights Act, and amendment of the legislation is necessary (see page 232).

   This joint committee has 12 members, 6 from each House. It is an active committee that, in the first 3 sessions of the 2010 parliament, published 46 reports. Its staff includes an eminent human rights expert as legal adviser.

Regulatory Reform Committee

This is a Commons select committee (the Lords equivalent is the Delegated Powers and Regulatory Reform Committee), consisting of 14 MPs. The committee considers certain orders and draft orders under the Legislative and Regulatory Reform Act 2006, the Regulatory Reform Act 2001, the Localism Act 2011, and the Fire and Rescue Services Act 2004; this process is described in Chapter 6 (page 231). Its staff include legal advisers. The committee has the power to set up a sub-committee. It may also invite members of the House who are not members of the committee to attend oral hearings and ask questions, but they may not vote or count towards the quorum.

Joint Committee on Statutory Instruments

This joint committee is responsible for examining the technical aspects of delegated legislation rather than its merits – unlike the Secondary Legislation Scrutiny Committee in the House of Lords (see page 229). It has six members from each House with an opposition MP as chair; it normally meets weekly when Parliament is sitting, but it reports only when it wishes to draw the attention of both Houses to some defect in a statutory instrument. The analysis of well over 1,000 statutory instruments each year is carried out by a staff that includes three specialist lawyers. Delegated legislation on financial matters, which is laid only before the House of Commons, is examined by the *Select Committee on Statutory Instruments*, consisting of the Commons members of the joint committee. Delegated legislation is described in more detail in Chapter 7 (page 223).

Internal committees

These committees are concerned with the way the House and its members work, both procedurally and administratively:

- Backbench Business
- Procedure
- Selection
- Privileges
- Standards
- Finance and Services
- Administration

Backbench Business Committee

The Backbench Business Committee was first appointed in 2010, following a recommendation by the Wright Committee on reform of the House of Commons (see page 143). It determines the business to be debated in the House or Westminster Hall on days (or parts of days) allocated to it by the government. There are eight members of the Committee. All are backbenchers and are elected by the House at the start of each session. The Committee can invite members of the House who are not members of the Committee and who either are of a party not represented on the Committee, or are of no party, to attend its meetings and take part in its proceedings, although they may not move a motion or an amendment, or vote.

The Committee usually meets weekly when the House is sitting. It hears representations from members, or groups of members, advocating debates, before deciding which to choose – a process that has been compared with the *Dragon's Den* television programme, and has also been described as the *salon* of the Chair of the Committee.

Procedure Committee

Procedure Committees used to be appointed *ad hoc* to examine particular aspects of the House's business, or to address some problem. A Procedure Committee was appointed in each parliament from 1979, but the committee did not become permanent until 1997. The committee has not more than seventeen members, and it has the job of considering the practice and procedure of the House in the conduct of public business (so, not including private legislation – see page 220) and making recommendations.

The committee considers matters that are referred to it, usually informally by the Speaker or the government rather than formally by decision of the House. It also chooses its own subjects for investigation, although these are often picked because the committee is aware of a general feeling that some topic needs examination. Over the last few years, the committee has reported on such things as the arrangements for private members' bills, early day motions, the e-tabling of parliamentary questions, and debates on government e-petitions. The committee's recommendations must be approved by the House before they are implemented.

Committee of Selection

The main task of this committee, which meets weekly while the House is sitting, is to select MPs to serve on general committees on bills and statutory instruments and private bill committees. At the beginning of a parliament, it also puts forward names of MPs to serve on all the permanent select committees (except for Liaison, Standards, and Privileges), and it nominates any replacements needed thereafter (see page 317). It has nine members, most of whom are whips, but a non-whip is in the chair.

Committee of Privileges

The House has long appointed a committee to investigate and report on privilege matters and complaints of breaches of privilege (see page 164). In its current guise, the committee was first appointed in 2012: from 1996 to 2012, the House appointed a Committee on Standards and Privileges that dealt with complaints about members' conduct, in addition to privilege.

The committee has ten members and is chaired by a senior opposition back-bencher. It has the power to appoint sub-committees. Unusually, it has the power to order an MP to give evidence to it, or to produce documents; most committees have these powers only in respect of people who are not members of either House. Following the split of the former Committee on Standards and Privileges, the Committee of Privileges has, for the time being, the same membership as the Committee on Standards.

Committee on Standards

There has been a permanent committee to examine issues relating to members' conduct since the Committee on Members' Interests was first established in 1974. The current Committee on Standards was first appointed in 2012. It works closely with the Parliamentary Commissioner for Standards (see page 109), considers reports on complaints against MPs – taking evidence if necessary, and recommends to the House what action (such as suspending an MP for a specified period or withholding salary) should be taken. The committee also oversees the operation of the rules of conduct, and the compilation and publication of the registers of interests.

The committee is made up of ten members of the House of Commons (who are also the members of the Committee of Privileges) and two or three external (or 'lay') members, who can make a full contribution to the work of the committee except that they cannot move motions or amendments to reports or vote. However, any comments that the lay members wish to make about a report must be published with that report. The committee is chaired by a senior backbencher and has the power to appoint sub-committees. As with the Committee of Privileges, the Standards Committee has the power to order an MP to give evidence to it, or to produce documents. The operation of the standards regime is dealt with in greater detail on pages 105 to 113.

Finance and Services Committee and the Administration Committee

As we saw in Chapter 3 (page 58), the 11-member Finance and Services Committee (usually known as 'F&S') advises the House of Commons Commission on the financial and business plans of the House administration. The Committee is chaired by a member of the Commission and has 10 other members. The 16-member Administration Committee reflects the views of MPs generally in the planning and provision of services provided to and by the House. Its role is to advise the Speaker and the Commission.

Ad hoc committees

The House can set up new committees at any time, although the formal initiative to do so is invariably a motion moved by the government (in the nineteenth century and earlier, this was not the case; the Sebastopol Committee described earlier was appointed in the teeth of ministerial opposition, and the approval of the motion to set it up finished the government led by Lord Aberdeen).

In the more recent past, *ad hoc* committees have considered domestic matters such as MPs' pay (1980–82), the televising of the House (1988–90), the sitting hours of the House (1991–92, known as the 'Jopling Committee') and matters of public policy such as the royal family's pay and expenses (1971–72), a possible 'wealth tax' (1974–75), abortion (1974–75) and violence in the family (1975–76). The existence of a permanent Procedure Committee means that select committees are now less likely to be set up to consider individual in-House issues; and the existence of the departmental committees (two or more of which are able to conduct joint inquiries if they wish) means that select committees are also less likely to be appointed to consider specific issues of public policy. However, from time to time, special circumstances arise, usually, but not always, when a particular subject affects both Houses (see pages 162 and 340 for the joint committees on parliamentary privilege and Lords reform).

In July 2012, in the wake of the LIBOR interest-rate rigging scandal, both Houses established the Parliamentary Commission on Banking Standards, to examine professional standards and culture in the UK banking sector and to make recommendations for legislative and other action. Although called a 'Commission' it was, in fact, a joint committee, albeit a rather unusual one. It published five reports over the course of one year, including two relating to the Financial Services (Banking Reform) Bill, the last of which was published in nine volumes in June 2013. The Commission had a number of unusual features. It had the power to use counsel to examine witnesses, which it used on occasion. It established panels to look at specific issues, some of the panels comprising only one or two members of the Commission. The Chair was given the power to report to the House matters that had not been agreed by the Commission meeting formally, but on which all members of the Commission had been consulted. These innovations enabled the Commission to operate more flexibly than a select committee, but the call on the time of its members over a considerable period suggests that this may not be a model whose use is easily extended. However, there remains pressure (initiated by the Commons Public Administration Select Committee) for a similar Commission to be set up on the Civil Service.

Another significant example of a recent *ad hoc* committee was the 2009 Committee on Reform of the House of Commons (known as the 'Wright Committee') (see page 143).

These days, most *ad hoc* committees are appointed to consider bills or draft bills. In 2013 and 2014, the Modern Slavery Bill, Deregulation Bill, and Voting Eligibility (Prisoners) Bill were examined in draft by *ad hoc* committees. Other draft bills were considered by departmental select committees (see page 329).

Intelligence and Security Committee

The Intelligence and Security Committee was set up under the Intelligence Services Act 1994, and its role was developed in the Justice and Security Act 2013. It has a parliamentary character but is not a select or joint committee, being created by statute – and so parliamentary privilege does not attach to its proceedings (although it has some protections by statute). It oversees the work of the intelligence agencies and provides broader scrutiny of intelligence and security matters. The committee consists of nine parliamentarians, drawn from both Houses, all backbenchers, and is usually chaired by a former senior minister. When it was first set up, the committee was a government body, made up of parliamentarians appointed by the Prime Minister and reporting to him. Since 2013, Parliament chooses the members of the committee, on the basis of nomination by the Prime Minister after consultation with the Leader of the Opposition. The committee reports to Parliament although, on matters of national security, it may report first to the Prime Minister. In 2013, the committee heard oral evidence in public for the first time from the heads of the intelligence agencies.

How committees work

Although in this section we have a departmental committee particularly in mind, most of it applies to most select committees.

Orders of reference and powers

A committee's task is set out in its orders of reference, which also define its powers and specify how many members it shall have. In the case of permanent committees, these orders of reference will be in the House's standing orders; but the House can set up a committee for as long or short a time as it sees fit and can give it other tasks or instructions (such as reporting by a certain date).

Tasks are usually widely defined: for example, departmental select committees must 'examine expenditure, administration and policy', although other committees, such as those on statutory instruments or regulatory reform, are much more circumscribed. Most committees thus have a good deal of latitude; and it is also a basic principle that (subject to any instruction from the House) the interpretation of their orders of reference is a matter for them. Committees generally do not take kindly to being told by the government or by witnesses that they should not be looking at this or that subject; indeed, such comments are normally entirely counterproductive.

Committees are subordinate bodies of the House; they have only those powers that the House gives them and cannot exercise any power that the House itself does not have. The normal menu is 'to adjourn from place to place', which means that they do not have to sit only at Westminster ('within the United Kingdom' is added for those committees that may not travel abroad); to report 'from time to time', which means that they may continue reporting on their subject area rather than making one report at the end of their work; to appoint specialist advisers; (in most cases) to appoint one or more sub-committees; to exchange evidence with other committees (and with the Scottish Parliament, the National Assembly for Wales and the Northern Ireland Assembly); and to meet jointly with any other committee of either House. This last power provides a good deal of flexibility when a subject affects several committees: for example, the Defence, Foreign Affairs, International Development and Trade and Industry Committees have formed what is, in effect, a joint committee on arms exports. The Welsh Affairs Committee may invite members of any specified committee of the National Assembly for Wales to attend and participate in its proceedings (but not to vote).

The power of compulsion

A key phrase in a committee's powers is 'to send for persons, papers and records' (known as 'PPR'). This means that they have the formal power to compel witnesses 'within the jurisdiction' (that is, within the UK) to attend, answer questions and deliver up any papers that the committee may wish to see.

Most witnesses before select committees are willing, even enthusiastic; they want the opportunity to make their case on a very public stage. But some are not, for a variety of reasons from a generalised reluctance to answer a committee's questions to having something discreditable or damaging to hide. In such cases, the committee may make an order to attend (or produce documents), which is served personally on the witness. If he or she does not comply, the committee may report the matter to the House as a breach of privilege. But there are disadvantages to this: the matter is put into a wider political forum, which means that the committee loses control of events; the procedure is cumbersome; and – especially if the matter becomes a party political football – there is no guarantee that the committee will ultimately get what it wants.

A select committee's strongest weapon is publicity rather than the use of formal powers. A recalcitrant witness looks as though he or she has something to hide; the trick is for the committee to make *not* giving evidence more embarrassing or awkward than acceding to the committee's request. These factors will have influenced the decision by Rupert and James Murdoch to give oral evidence to the Culture, Media and Sport Committee on phone hacking in 2011, both having been formally summoned.

It has sometimes been suggested that the powers of select committees should be formalised in legislation, and that a refusal to attend, or the giving of false or misleading evidence should be punishable by law. This may be superficially attractive, but the practical implications are daunting. Any court, in considering an allegation of refusal to attend, would need to satisfy itself that the summons was fair. Was the witness given alternative dates? Sufficient notice? An indication of why the committee wanted him or her to attend? Was the witness allowed to bring advisers? Even, was the witness really relevant to the inquiry?

False or misleading evidence would pose even more problems. Was the committee oppressive in its questioning? Was the witness badgered? Was the committee's behaviour fair? Was the witness allowed to take advice? It is perfectly possible that a court would want to see the video-recording of the evidence session. Turning the process over to the courts would also slow the process down, and would certainly result in witnesses in contentious inquiries coming 'lawyered-up' to give evidence, refusing to answer certain questions on legal advice.

The Joint Committee on Parliamentary Privilege (see page 162) considered these issues and, in July 2013, sensibly came down against the involvement of the courts (as it also came down against the codification of privilege).

Ministers and civil servants have a special status that occasionally leads to conflict with select committees. Civil servants are agents of their secretary of state and carry out his or her instructions; they cannot be forced to divulge information against the secretary of state's wishes. A committee can ask a minister for information but (although the 'embarrassment factor' can come into play here as well) cannot demand it. The House could do so (technically by an address to the Crown, because the information is in the hands of Her Majesty's ministers), but the House does not delegate this power to select committees.

There have been celebrated tussles between investigating select committees and reluctant governments. In its investigation of the Westland Affair in 1986, the Defence Committee sought to interview the civil servants most closely involved with the selective leaking of an opinion of the Solicitor-General. The government refused to allow them to attend, but the Cabinet Secretary appeared twice before the committee, which – because of the political pressure building on the government – also secured internal government documents that had previously been refused. Although the government's internal guidance states that, when there is disagreement between a minister and a committee about the attendance of a civil servant, the minister should appear personally, this issue is still an occasional source of friction. This is particularly the case in relation to the intelligence agencies: several committees have tried and failed to call their heads or more junior intelligence personnel to give oral evidence.

Membership

Select committee members are almost invariably backbench MPs. Committees normally consist of between 9 and 18 MPs in as near as possible the party proportions in the House as a whole; thus, in the 2010 parliament, a committee of 11 usually had 5 Labour, 5 Conservative and 1 Liberal Democrat or other third-party member. Once MPs are appointed to a committee, they remain on it for the whole of a parliament, unless they resign or become ministers or frontbench spokesmen.

The quorum of a committee – the number of members who must be present for business to be transacted – is three or one-quarter of the number of members, whichever is the larger, with fractions counted as one.

Some committee chairs are elected by the House as a whole – we discuss this in more detail in the next section. The other members (or, where the committee chooses its own chair, all members) are selected by their parties using their own internal procedures. The names are then put to the House for approval in a motion proposed by the Committee of Selection. The memberships of the Liaison Committee, the Committee of Privileges, the Committee on Standards, any committees established under a temporary standing order, and the Committee of Selection itself, are proposed to the House by the Deputy Chief Whip.

Chairs

Until 2010, committees elected their own chairs. In most cases, among the MPs put on a committee at the start of a parliament was an obvious (or agreed) candidate for the chair. Following the recommendation of the Wright Committee on reform of the Commons, most select committee chairs (including the chairs of the departmental committees) are now directly elected by the House. Candidates must come from the party to which the House has allocated the position of chair, but all MPs may vote. Chairs elected in this way can be removed if their committee passes a motion of no confidence in the chair, either unanimously or with a majority of the members (including at least two members from the largest party represented on the committee and at least one member from another party) voting in favour. This mechanism has not yet been used.

If a Chair resigns (by writing to the Speaker), dies, or is subject to a no confidence vote, a by-election is held to replace them.

No MP may be elected chair of a committee that she or he has chaired for the two previous parliaments, or for eight years, whichever is the longer.

The chair is the key figure on any select committee, all the more so since direct elections. He or she takes a full part in the committee's work (unlike the chair of a general committee, who presides impartially over proceedings) and is usually the committee's spokesperson. The committee itself decides subjects for investigation and what witnesses to call, but the chair's views will be highly influential, and the chair has the power of initiative, particularly in relation to the content of draft reports for consideration by the committee.

Chairs operate in a variety of different ways: some are less interventionist 'chairmen of the board'; others are much more 'managing directors' driving the committee's work. Whichever style they adopt, the role of a good chair is crucial in keeping the committee together: giving all its members a chance, promoting consensus, foreseeing political problems, establishing good – but not cosy – relationships with ministers in the relevant department, and providing leadership when the going gets tough.

Since 2003, most select committee chairs have been paid a supplement to their salary of £14,728 per year, in recognition of their additional responsibilities.

There is no formal post of 'deputy chair'. If the chair is absent, then the senior opposition MP (or government MP, if the chair is from an opposition party) often takes the chair; but the committee can decide to put any of its members in the chair on a temporary basis.

Election of chairs of most select committees by the House as a whole has been widely welcomed, but on those select committees it has had a subtle effect on the relationship between chair and members. When it was the committee that elected the chair, they were the power-base and the chair was answerable to them. With election by the House, the relationship has changed, and on several committees the rank-and-file members have resented what they have seen as the high-handed style of a chair who does not feel answerable to the committee.

Staff

Select committees are supported by small teams of staff from the Department of Chamber and Committee Services; some thirty investigative committees are supported by about 210 staff in the Committee Office. A departmental select committee usually has six full-time posts. They are led by the *Clerk of the Committee*, a deputy principal clerk (equivalent to a Band 1 official in the Senior Civil Service – what used to be called Assistant Secretary/Grade 5) usually with 15 to 20 years of experience in the service of the House or, in some cases, an experienced senior clerk (Civil Service

Grade 7). In a nutshell, the Clerk's job is to help the committee to be as effective as possible in doing the job the House has given it. He or she is the committee's principal adviser, manages the staff team and the specialist advisers, works closely with the chair on all aspects of the committee's work, and will be responsible for some of the committee's inquiries. *The Second Clerk* deputises for the Clerk, manages inquiries and will usually clerk any sub-committee. One or two *committee specialists*, who are subject experts, or generalist *inquiry managers*, provide in-depth research and briefing and manage inquiries. The *senior committee assistant* oversees arrangements for hearings, committee visits, the website, and the publication of reports and evidence. He or she will have the support of a *committee assistant*, whose duties include preparing draft reports for publication. Even substantial committee reports are published extraordinarily quickly; sometimes, agreed one afternoon and published online and in print the next morning.

The committee also has the support of a *media officer*, shared with three or four other committees. He or she helps plan communication and public engagement work throughout the course of an inquiry, drafts press notices, promotes reports to the media, and organises the chair's media appearances on committee matters. There is also a *select committee outreach officer* in the Department of Information Services who assists select committees with outreach activity, such as meetings away from Westminster or public surveys in particular localities.

The permanent staff are augmented by *specialist advisers*, who work for the Clerk of the Committee. They are people, often of great eminence, who assist the committee part-time and are paid on a daily rate. This is a flexible and effective system; a committee can draw on a lifetime's experience in the precise area of what may be a very technical or complex inquiry. Some committees maintain panels of 12 or 15 advisers; others appoint 1 or 2 for specific inquiries. There are normally about 120 specialist advisers at any one time.

Committees also draw on the resources of the *Scrutiny Unit*, a group of 17 staff who specialise in the analysis of estimates, departmental annual reports (see page 247) and other financial information; and also in the scrutiny of draft legislation (which allows a committee to deal at short notice with a draft bill without having its programme of work blown off course). In addition, a *Web and Publications Unit*, comprising ten staff, has recently been established to help committee teams with digital publication.

A committee's work

Select committees always meet in private except when they are taking oral evidence; as we shall see later, this has advantages. When a committee meets for the first time at the start of a parliament, its members first make a formal declaration of their registered interests. They will then discuss their working practices and agree a programme of work. The chair will put proposals before the committee, based on work by the committee staff: work outstanding from the last parliament; current and expected events in the subject area (including possible draft bills); previous recommendations on which the committee needs to maintain pressure; policies still in the process of formation, where the committee could have an influence; or perhaps some serious problem where the committee needs to keep up with developments. Committee members will have their own suggestions and, after discussion, the committee will agree and announce its initial programme of work.

In addition, the House has set *core tasks* for departmental select committees. These are listed on pages 329–30 together with examples of activity on each.

Just as a departmental select committee has wide discretion about *what* it investigates, so it also has great flexibility about *how* it does so. Inquiries may range from an in-depth examination of a complex subject lasting several months to a short sharp inquiry carried out in a week, perhaps with five or six oral evidence hearings crammed into that time. Inquiries may aim to analyse and influence a developing policy, to review a whole subject area, to carry out a 'what went wrong' investigation, or to look at a topical issue of the moment.

Most formal inquiries lead to reports to the House, but a committee may hold hearings without then publishing a report; and most committees hold regular one-off hearings with public bodies, chief inspectors or regulators within their area, or with ministers or senior officials on current issues. However, let us take as an example a typical 'subject area' inquiry.

The start of an inquiry

The committee decides on a subject – let us say the government's policy towards domestic violence. The committee approves terms of reference for the inquiry, which are really to help potential witnesses who want to know what the main areas of interest will be – they do not bind the committee. Indeed, once an inquiry is under way, its focus often changes as the committee identifies particular aspects as more important. The committee publishes a press notice about the inquiry, and it may also publish an 'issues and questions' paper to stimulate debate and the submission of evidence.

As well as issuing a general invitation to submit evidence, the committee will make more specific requests for written evidence. For our example of an inquiry into domestic violence, several government departments – the Home Office, the Department of Health, the Government Equalities Office and the Ministry of Justice – are involved in different aspects of the subject. The committee may ask each department to prepare a paper on its own area of responsibility, or more likely (and to test coordination between the departments), will ask the government to provide a single paper addressing a series of written questions. At the same time, requests for evidence will go out to other key players: the NHS, the British Medical Association as representing GPs, the NSPCC, and national organisations representing social service providers, the police, and support groups for those who have suffered domestic violence. Committees usually publish written evidence online shortly after receipt.

The committee will, at the same time, draw up a list of likely witnesses. Oral evidence will often start with academics or expert commentators who can 'set the scene' and usually concludes with an appearance by the minister. Committees try to make the process as open as possible, not limiting it to 'the usual suspects'. For example, in an inquiry into the Probation Service, the Justice Committee's star witnesses were a group of convicted offenders who gave evidence about the use (or otherwise) of their probation officers; and the Transport Committee has taken evidence from people whose relatives had been accidentally killed at level crossings. On the basis of the written evidence that comes in – often, not formal papers from prominent organisations but letters from local bodies or individuals who have heard about the inquiry – committees will select other people to give evidence

Some time after the call for written evidence first went out, the first oral evidence hearing takes place.

Taking evidence

The members of the committee sit around a horseshoe-shaped table with the chair at the head and the clerk on his or her left. Reflecting the more consensual approach in select committees, the members often do not sit by party affiliation (unlike general committees). Witnesses sit at a table between the arms of the horseshoe. The transcribers who take a verbatim record of the evidence sit either in the middle or at the side of the room.

The MPs on the committee will have a detailed brief prepared by the committee staff. This will cover the background to the hearing, the key points from the witness's written evidence, including areas that could be explored further, anything that the committee especially needs to get on the record for its eventual report, and a list of suggested questions for the witness. Committees have sometimes used social media to get suggestions from the public of the key issues and questions: a prominent example was the Education Committee's #AskGove initiative in 2012 before taking evidence from the Education Secretary, which attracted over 5,000 responses.

The committee will often tell witnesses in advance the areas it wants to cover, but it does not normally give notice of particular questions unless some time for preparation would be needed to provide a full answer. Typically, the chair opens the questioning, and other MPs follow. An oral evidence session usually lasts between two and two-and-a-half hours, but several witnesses, singly or in groups, may appear during that time. The hearing will usually be webcast and may be televised as well. Seats are provided for the public (but it is not possible to reserve a seat) and the press.

The vast majority of evidence is given in public, but committees can take evidence in private, usually if matters of personal or commercial confidentiality, or national security, are involved. Select committees, mainly the Defence Committee and the Foreign Affairs Committee, have dealt with national security or 'classified' material up to the highest levels of sensitivity. In 2007, the Defence Committee held an inquiry in secret to scrutinise the Fulton Report into the capture of Royal Navy personnel

1 CHAIR
2 CLERK
3 MEMBERS
4 SHORTHAND WRITER

5 COMMITTEE STAFF
6 PRESS
7 WITNESSES
8 PUBLIC

Plan of a select committee room

Source: Copyright House of Commons, 2014

Commons Work and Pensions Committee gathering evidence on disability issues, February 2011

Source: Copyright House of Commons, 2014. Photography by Catherine Bebbington

by the Iranian Revolutionary Guard in March 2007 and establish whether it was comprehensive and whether its recommendations were sufficient.

Most hearings are fairly relaxed; the process is one of exploration and discussion of a subject about which the witnesses have special knowledge, on which the committee wants to draw. However, some hearings, usually if a committee is investigating something that has gone wrong, or where it believes that a government department or other witness is not being open, can be more adversarial. Committees can take evidence on oath if they wish, although this is unusual, and the witness or witnesses should, as a matter of natural justice, certainly be given notice of a committee's intention to do so.

Those giving evidence before a select committee are taking part in a proceeding in Parliament (see page 163), so they are fully protected by parliamentary privilege – that is, neither their oral nor their written evidence may give rise to a criminal prosecution or civil action, nor, for example, to disciplinary action by an employer.

The transcript of the hearing usually takes a few days to prepare but is sometimes expedited. It is published online straight away.

As the inquiry progresses, the committee will be following up oral evidence with requests for further papers, the staff will be researching other sources of information or possible evidence, and some thought will be given to possible visits. Committees may also commission research to support their work, such as opinion polling or analyses of a project's business case or likely economic impact.

Travel

Travel by select committees often gets a hard time in the media – but it contributes a great deal to a committee's effectiveness. In the inquiry example we have taken here, the committee will want to make visits within the UK – perhaps to see shelters for the victims of domestic violence in different parts of the country; to talk to social services, the police, GPs and support groups on their home ground; and possibly to take oral evidence as well. Visits make a select committee inquiry more accessible: not only do they bring the committee to a local community, but they also mean that people can talk informally to the MPs rather than giving evidence in the often daunting surroundings of Westminster.

Visits also mean that MPs see and hear for themselves; the often rather impersonal formal evidence is supplemented by the first-hand experience and opinions of the people actually involved, and a suggestion or criticism by a single individual often finds its way into the committee's final report.

Travel overseas plays a similar role. It may be that policy on domestic violence in Sweden, say, is better coordinated than in the UK; or that the Canadians have the most effective risk registers and techniques for early warning of violence. No amount of background reading and written evidence is a substitute for seeing for oneself, and finding out first-hand about the benefits and the problems.

The report

Towards the end of an inquiry, the staff member who has managed the inquiry will usually prepare a 'heads of report' paper – identifying the possible main themes of the report and recommendations, and questions on which the committee itself will need to form a view. Thereafter, the report will be drafted, usually with the assistance of specialist advisers and under the direction of the clerk. The draft report will be submitted to the chair and then, after his or her comments are incorporated, presented to the committee in the chair's name. In a contentious inquiry, other members may want an alternative draft report (and a clerk may be called upon to draft two entirely incompatible reports!). However, most select committee reports are unanimous and are the more effective for it.

Most committees go through draft reports very informally and then agree to the whole report as a single decision. However, if amendments are considered formally or there are any votes, these are set out in full in the formal minutes at the back of the published report. The same is true of any alternative draft report that may be put forward (although there is formally no such thing as a 'minority report', the same aim is achieved by publication in the formal minutes).

'Embargoed' copies of reports are often issued to the press a day or two before the publication date so that they can have their stories ready for the moment of publication, and copies will usually go to witnesses and others who have contributed to the inquiry. The committee may hold a press conference, and the chair and individual members of the committee will also give interviews to get their own perspective on the record. (In a sensitive inquiry, they may have to choose their words with care, as a press conference is not a proceeding in Parliament, and there is no protection of privilege.)

A type of report known as a 'special report' is used as a vehicle for publishing government replies to committees, or sometimes for informing the House of some difficulty encountered in the committee's work.

The government reply

Reports are made to the House, although the intended audience includes everyone concerned with the subject, the media and – crucially – the government. Every select committee report should receive a formal government reply within two months. This is a convention rather than a formal rule, but committees have found that asking the minister concerned to appear to explain a delay often means the rapid appearance of the reply.

No one expects a government to put on sackcloth and ashes in this formal reply. If the committee has been highly critical, the government is more likely to be defensive and to restate its case than to say 'It's a fair cop'. If the committee has put forward challenging recommendations, the government is likely to be cautious rather than to accept them right away. But the 'delayed drop' effect of select committee reports should never be underestimated. Ambitious recommendations may change the whole public debate on a subject; they may be taken up by public bodies and pressure groups; and months (or sometimes two or three years) later, they may contribute substantially to a major shift in government policy. Similarly, the effect of justified criticism may not be immediately apparent; but a department may be quietly changing its procedures to avoid making the same mistake again.

Whatever the contents of the government reply, committees are more influential if they follow up on their reports. Most departmental select committees have a 'continuous agenda' in which major policy issues recur, but returning to the detail of previous recommendations, and pursuing vague promises or non-committal responses through further inquiries, maintains the pressure and keeps the subject in the public eye.

Consensus

Select committees seem to be held in generally high regard – perhaps more than anything else that Parliament does. There may be several reasons for this: they provide access to the political process; they provide challenge and an alternative point of view based on evidence; but probably most of all they show how politicians of different parties can work together.

A typical inquiry

A timeline for a committee inquiry with four oral evidence hearings and a foreign visit, might look something like this:[*]

Week 1:	Committee agrees to hold an inquiry into a topic (let us say, the future of aspects of social care). Staff are asked to draw up draft terms of reference.
Week 2:	Terms of reference are agreed and published in a call for evidence.
Week 4:	The Chair brings forward a proposal for a visit to Sweden and Finland to investigate social care arrangements there (different models to the UK, generally well regarded). The Committee agrees to this proposal and the Chair bids for funding from the Liaison Committee (in the Commons).
Week 5:	Funding for the visit is confirmed, staff work with the embassies in both countries to draw up a programme.
Week 7:	Deadline for written evidence.
Week 8:	Committee agrees witnesses for its four oral evidence hearings and agrees to visit social care facilities in Birmingham. A communications plan for the inquiry, including the use of social media to request questions to put to the minister, is also agreed.
Week 9:	First oral evidence hearing.
Week 11:	Committee visit to Sweden and Finland (3 days).
Week 13:	Second oral evidence hearing.
Week 14:	Committee visit to Birmingham.
Week 16:	Third oral evidence hearing.
Week 17:	Final oral evidence hearing (with the minister).
Week 18:	Chair writes to minister with further questions arising from his or her evidence.
Week 19:	Committee agrees on the outline for its report ('heads of report').
Week 22:	Draft report, prepared by the staff, is considered and agreed by the Chair.
Week 24:	Committee considers and agrees the Chair's draft report (with amendments). Note, this may sometimes require more than one meeting. The report is finalised for publication. A press notice is agreed by the Chair.
Week 25:	Report is published. Chair makes a statement about the report on the floor of the House.

Two months later . . . Government sends its reply to the report to the Committee, which is considered at the Committee's next meeting and published. The Committee agrees to apply for a debate on the report in Westminster Hall, which takes place four weeks later.

[*] This would also be typical of one of the shorter inquiries by a Lords select committee; but both in the Commons and the Lords the complexity of the issues and the amount of oral evidence tend to determine the length of an inquiry.

There is no doubt that unanimous committees are more effective. They speak with a single voice, and it is much harder for governments to dismiss cross-party agreement. Some people see consensus as implying flabby compromise, but select committees show time and again that they can reach a tough agreed view on politically hot subjects. Given that select committees are made up of party politicians, how does this happen?

There are three main reasons. *First*, when they are not taking public oral evidence, *select committees meet in private*. Their discussions, working papers and draft reports are private. This means that it is much harder for party political pressure to be put on them – for example, by the whips – and it also means that the MPs can be remarkably frank with each other. For example, an individual backbencher can put forward ideas totally at odds with party (or government) policy; and the readiness to see the other side of the argument is a key factor in getting cross-party agreement.

Second, the members of a select committee usually get to know each other well (even if, as can happen in a House of 650 members, they have never spoken to each other before the committee's first meeting). They will work together over many months, both formally and informally; there will be a good basis for trust; and they will then often see themselves as members of the committee more than as party representatives.

Third, select committees proceed on the basis of evidence (as shown by the wealth of footnotes in most select committee reports!). They do this because basing their conclusions firmly on evidence is part of the due process of investigation, but also because recommendations firmly grounded in fact, and explicitly supported by expert opinion, are much harder to challenge. This approach also helps to maintain consensus; a weight of evidence can lead MPs on a committee to agree on a conclusion even if it does not match their previous personal opinions or their party's position.

Dealing with a select committee

As more and more people in all walks of life come into contact with the work of select committees, it may be helpful to say something about how to have an input into an inquiry (a fuller guide for witnesses is available on the parliamentary website, together with information about current inquiries and planned meetings).

First, *make sure that what you want to say is relevant to the committee's work*. Look at the call for evidence and see what ground the inquiry will cover. If you are submitting written evidence – and this goes for government departments and some major national bodies, as well as individuals – do not simply top and tail a paper prepared for some other purpose; make sure it is tailored to the requirements of the inquiry. If the inquiry is already under way, *look on the committee's home page at transcripts and written evidence that have already been published* to see what the government and other bodies are saying to the committee. You may also be able to follow an inquiry via webcasts or the BBC Parliament channel.

Keep written evidence concise and to the point; number the paragraphs and, for more than two pages or so, begin with a summary of what the paper says (and a table of contents if necessary). *Say if you want any part of the paper to be kept confidential.* Evidence should be submitted online in Word format. Once you submit written evidence, it becomes a committee document and, if you want to use it publicly before the committee publishes it, you should seek permission (which is almost always given).

You can ask to give oral evidence, but remember that the committee will have a full programme for the inquiry and will certainly not be able to accommodate all those who wish to do so. A witness who submits a constructive written paper that suggests solutions rather than simply rehearsing criticism may be more likely to be called to give oral evidence. If you are called, the committee staff will talk to you about the details and will usually be able to give you an indication of the committee's likely areas of interest. Let them know if you have a disability and need any adjustments made to assist you in giving evidence.

When you appear, do not expect to be able to make an opening statement; this is better done in writing in advance, as most committees want to get straight on with questioning. The MPs on the committee will all have name-plates in front of them, but it is best to address your answers to the chair. Remember that giving oral evidence (or submitting a written paper) is not the one and only chance to contribute. You can provide additional information in writing (for example, if you feel you did not answer a question fully), or comment on the evidence given by someone else. If you want to give any of your evidence in private, talk to the Clerk of the Committee well before your appearance.

Whether you are contributing to an inquiry or not, you can attend the public hearings (subject to there being space; it is not possible to book seats in advance) either in the Palace of Westminster itself or in Portcullis House, or if a select committee takes evidence elsewhere in the UK.

Select committee activity

Activity is at a high level. Formal meetings of select committees (not including informal meetings, seminars and visits) are running at about 1,300 a year, of which some 900 are public evidence hearings. Committees publish over 300 reports each year. On average, about 390 MPs are members of select committees of one sort or another. With the advent of Westminster Hall (see page 260), there is more debate on select committee reports in addition to the three estimates days in the Chamber (see page 246); and there has been a noticeable increase in the use of committee reports in major debates in the House. Chairs can now make oral statements in the House announcing the publication of a report, summarising its contents, and dealing with questions on the report from other members, which has further increased their profile.

Investigative select committees are also engaging in a wider range of activity. They hold seminars, often with outside experts, to focus and plan major inquiries; they undertake scrutiny of legislation; and they have a role in examining major public appointments. Committees have also widened political debate, taking evidence from opposition spokespeople on their alternative policies, European Commissioners, and ministers from devolved governments, as well as from UK government ministers. Committees have a constant presence on the news agenda, and it is now routine for high-profile television and radio programmes to turn to select committee chairs and members to comment on current issues, regardless of what inquiries their committees may be undertaking at the time.

Particularly in the context of the core tasks and with the help of the Scrutiny Unit, committees now conduct more financial scrutiny of government departments, particularly the annual estimates and annual reports. There is also more 'joined-up scrutiny'; for example, on European issues, between the European Scrutiny Committee and the departmental select committees. But in both these areas there is much more to do.

Committees themselves have become more accountable, most notably by using Twitter to communicate with their followers and seeking views on inquiry topics from people using online forums such as Mumsnet, as well as through annual reports on their work, which are published by the Liaison Committee.

These 'core tasks' for select committees, developed by the Liaison Committee and set out below, are a good starting point for a look at the sorts of things select committees were doing in 2013–14. In each case, the examples give only a flavour of the range of activity.

What are select committees doing?

Task 1: strategy. Examples of inquiries into strategic issues included the future of the European Union (Foreign Affairs); the retail sector (Business, Innovation and Skills); deterrence in the twenty-first century (Defence); and online safety (Culture, Media and Sport).

Task 2: policy. Specific areas of policy examined by committees included the Spending Review and Budget (Treasury); government policy on the drug Khat (Home Affairs); wild animals in circuses (Environment, Food and Rural Affairs); and 2012 GCSE results (Education).

Task 3: expenditure and performance. The Defence Committee published reports on the Ministry of Defence's annual report and accounts, its Main Estimate, and Supplementary Estimate. The Justice Committee reported on the Serious Fraud Office's Supplementary Estimate. The Health Committee published a report on public expenditure on health and social care.

Task 4: draft bills. Draft bills considered by committees in 2013–14 included the draft Consumer Rights Bill (Business, Innovation and Skills), and the draft Dangerous Dogs (Amendment) Bill (Environment, Food and Rural Affairs).

Task 5: bills and delegated legislation. The Joint Committee on Human Rights continued its routine scrutiny of government bills for human rights implications. In addition, the Culture, Media and Sport Committee published a report on the draft Public Bodies (Abolition of the Registrar of Public Lending Rights) Order 2013.

Task 6: post-legislative scrutiny. Committee work often involves assessing how legislation is working, as part of wider consideration of policy or strategy. The government now routinely publishes post-legislative memoranda on Acts of Parliament, five years after they passed into law. Examples of specific post-legislative scrutiny include work on the Greater London Authority Act 2007 (Communities and Local Government) and the Mental Health Act 2007 (Health). (See also page 219.)

Task 7: European scrutiny. In addition to the work of the European Scrutiny Committee on legislation and legislative proposals emanating from Brussels, the Justice and Home Affairs Committees both reported on whether or not the UK should opt in to EU police and criminal justice measures and the Transport Committee examined EU proposals on land transport security, railway legislation and sulphur emissions by ships. The Science and Technology Committee looked at the work of the European Space Agency.

Task 8: appointments. Scrutiny of public appointments is now routine for many committees. During 2013–14, the Treasury Committee scrutinised numerous appointments to the Bank of England's monetary and financial policy committees. It has recently held a pre-commencement hearing with the incoming Governor of the Bank of England. The Committee has a statutory veto over the appointment of the head of the Office of Budget Responsibility, a public body that is independent of government and publishes the economic forecasts used by the Treasury. Other examples of recent pre-appointment hearings included the chairs of OFGEM (Energy and Climate Change) and Monitor (Health).

Task 9: support for the House.. There were numerous examples of committee reports debated in the House or Westminster Hall, or launched in the House, with a short statement by the committee chair (this recently introduced procedure is a good way of exposing a report to the House and to the public without needing to have a debate). Committees have also formally contributed to scrutiny of proposals for National Policy Statements on strategic matters (Transport) and sentencing guidance (Justice).

Task 10: public engagement. Committees are becoming increasingly inventive in the ways in which they reach out to the public, in order to hear a wider cross-section of views than would otherwise be the case and to promote their work. For example, the Communities and Local Government Committee has used a 'speed dating' format to hear the views of serving and former councillors on standing for election. The Education Committee worked with the BBC on ways of making an inquiry into school sports accessible to children.

So far, so good. But what does all this activity achieve?

How effective are select committees?

Objective measurement of the effectiveness or influence of select committees is impossible. Governments have accepted a great many select committee recommendations, even when they have not originally been disposed to do so, but it is always difficult to judge how far this has been down to the committee in each case and how far the committee has been the decisive advocate for a growing body of opinion. Sometimes, the mere fact of an inquiry leads to a change in government policy before the committee reports and public exposure can have wider influence.

There is no point in trying to measure effectiveness by totting up how many recommendations are accepted by the government. This process makes no distinction between 'soft' recommendations, on which the door is already ajar, and 'hard' recommendations, which have no chance of being accepted now, but that change the whole nature of public debate, and that may end up as government policy – perhaps the policy of an incoming government after a general election – months or years later (the 'delayed drop' effect; see page 325).

The Constitution Unit at University College, London, discussed difficulties in measuring the effectiveness of committees in a report published in 2011. Its conclusion was that:

> *Select committees are taken increasingly seriously by government, and have become an established and respected part of the system. Twenty-five years ago [it was] suggested that 'the effect of these committees on ministerial and departmental policymaking has been indirect and marginal, contextual rather than substantive'. It would be hard to claim the same today. The committees to a significant degree condition the everyday behaviour of ministers and civil servants, and sometimes outsiders. They have achieved a high profile for their inquiries which enables them to threaten 'exposure', as well as the more mundane, day-to-day role of government accountability. And many of their recommendations . . . are taken up.*

However, having even tough recommendations accepted is not what effective scrutiny is about (although it may be one of the results). Scrutiny of government is the process of examining expenditure, administration and policy in detail, on the public record, requiring the government of the day to explain itself to parliamentarians as representatives of the citizen and the taxpayer, and to justify its actions. As a recent academic study noted, an important role for select committees is in providing 'an arena within which the credentials of a secretary of state are publicly tested. A competent performance before a committee by a minister may not boost [his or her] standing but a poor performance can certainly damage it'.

This process of accountability is never comfortable for those being scrutinised; and it should not be. But the fact that the government's actions can be put under the spotlight of public examination at any time makes for better decision-making; as Robin Cook when Leader of the House said, 'good scrutiny makes for good government'.

A sample of the work of just one departmental select committee over a period of 12 months or so gives a flavour of this process. The Transport Committee published a major report on aviation that argued in favour of the expansion of

Heathrow Airport to alleviate capacity pressures in south-east England. This report was based on research it had commissioned on the impact on Heathrow of opening a new hub airport east of London and was widely discussed in the media. A follow-up report on transport preparations for winter weather looked at the implementation of earlier recommendations. The Committee recommended against a government proposal for more claims for whiplash injuries, following a road traffic accident, to be dealt with using the small claims court procedure: the government later accepted the recommendation. An inquiry on safety at level crossings elicited a public apology from Network Rail's chief executive to families of accident victims whom his organisation had treated badly. A report on access to transport for disabled people was critical of aspects of the government's accessibility plan: the Committee initiated a debate on this issue in Westminster Hall. Several of the Committee's recommendations on parking enforcement were taken up by the government and published for consultation. The government's overall strategy for transport was criticised in reports on road and rail access to sea ports, the strategic road network, and a draft statement of the government's policy on the development of the strategic road and rail networks, published under the Planning Act. These criticisms were widely reported and discussed in the specialist transport press. The Committee maintained a long-running interest in maritime safety with continuing correspondence with ministers and the Maritime and Coastguard Agency on the reform of the Coastguard Service and legislation on maritime pilotage. Executives from Gatwick Airport and easyJet endured a difficult 90 minutes in front of the Committee explaining why passengers were so badly affected by flooding at the airport on Christmas Eve 2013. The Committee asked the airport and airlines to deal with all of the complaints it had received from members of the public about what had happened and checked that this was done. In addition, the Committee asked the public to suggest subjects for inquiries and held an outreach event at Coventry University on low carbon vehicles, as well as a seminar on women in transport during the annual Parliament Week.

In this chapter, we have described the role of Commons select committees largely in terms of scrutinising the government of the day. This accounts for much of their activity, but they also have a wider role. Their reports and recommendations may be aimed at particular public bodies, sectors of industry, or the professions. Select committees are often good at 'blue skies' thinking; they can examine some difficult topic of public policy and analyse possible courses of action – relaxation of the law on drugs is a good example – that political parties would find more difficult. Where there is controversy about the factual basis of public debate, perhaps on a topic such as climate change or genetic engineering, a select committee is an excellent vehicle for analysing conflicting claims and setting out common ground. As with written questions (see page 293) but to a far greater degree, select committee written and oral evidence puts a mass of information, from both the government and other sources, into the public domain.

Nevertheless, there is scope for select committees to be more effective. In the Liaison Committee's vision for the future:

Committees should be respected, listened to and feared by departments and ministers for the quality of their investigations, the rigour of their questioning, the depth of their analysis, and the value of their reports . . . The role of committees – and the powers which they can draw upon – will be understood by the public, and they will engage with a wide diversity of people in gathering evidence . . . Their work will be respected for its integrity and relevance to people's lives and will contribute to reviving faith in the value of parliamentary democracy.

This is a bold agenda that will require committees to be clearer about their objectives, more strategic in using the resources at their disposal, more agile and inclusive in their inquiry processes, and capable of publishing shorter, sharper reports while still seeking to achieve consensus between different political viewpoints.

Effort equals success: the role of committee members

Whatever a select committee does, its effectiveness depends, above all, on its chair and members. Their commitment and effort are crucial. As the Liaison Committee said in its 2000 report *Shifting the Balance*:

no pain, no gain: there is no easy route to success. A determined and hardworking committee, in which Members are prepared to devote substantial effort and put the interests of the citizen and taxpayer first, can be extraordinarily effective.

MPs on select committees need an up-to-date understanding of the subject area. They do not have to be great technical experts – and, indeed, there is some reason for them not to be; it could be said that one of the strengths of select committees is that they are made up of well-informed lay people who can ask common-sense questions of the experts and make sure they get proper answers. Occasional attempts to browbeat witnesses for some easy headlines do nothing for the select committee system and are usually counter-productive. As a wise select committee chair of another era used to say, 'more flies are caught with honey than with vinegar'.

On individual inquiries, members of a committee need to keep up with the written and oral evidence and to prepare for oral evidence sessions. The committee staff support the committee through briefing, and summarising and analysing evidence, but there is no substitute for individual MPs having command of the subject. Although, as we have seen in earlier chapters, there are many other calls on MPs' time, the most effective oral evidence sessions – especially with difficult and well-briefed witnesses – are those at which all the members of a committee are present throughout; are well-prepared; divide up the areas of questioning between them; ask questions rather than make statements; follow up each other's questions – and do not spend time tweeting during the evidence.

It is sometimes suggested that committees should have counsel to undertake part of the examination of witnesses: and counsel was used in this way in the work of the

Banking Standards Commission. However, it is relatively rare for this sort of forensic examination to be required: other types of inquiry are frequently more valuable and play to other select committee strengths, and when forensic examination is required, a good many MPs are perfectly capable of extremely effective questioning. There is also an important principle at stake. MPs are elected by the people to speak in Parliament, ask questions and take part in parliamentary proceedings: they should be wary of delegating these functions to the unelected.

Being an effective member of a select committee is time-consuming. A chair can easily spend the equivalent of two to three days a week on committee business, having to combine this with all the other pressures on an MP, and the time commitment for members of a busy committee may not be much less (which demonstrates that membership of more than one investigative committee, which happens too often, is not a practical proposition). The average attendances each session for the most well-respected committees routinely top 80 per cent.

A bargain price

The Liaison Committee described the achievements of the select committee system as having been 'at a bargain price'. This is still the case. Staff costs relating to select committees (other than those relating to the National Audit Office and the Ombudsman) run at around £14 million a year, and all other costs, including printing, transcription of evidence, specialist advisers, travel, and commissioned work, amount to a little over £3 million. 'Bargain' seems a fair description.

Select committees in the House of Lords

The committees

Since the early 1970s, the House of Lords has also developed an increasingly elaborate array of permanent select committees reappointed every session to scrutinise various aspects of public policy. (For legislative committees, see pages 229–31; for domestic committees, see page 71.) Some of these policy scrutiny committees enjoy a high reputation. Unlike the Commons, the Lords committee structure developed in a way that was thematic and cross-cutting rather than departmental, and there is now general acceptance that this, in theory at least, should enable Lords committee work to complement rather than compete with or duplicate that of the Commons (as is true of the two Houses more generally).

Sessional (or permanent) select committees

At the beginning of the 2014–15 session, the House of Lords had established the following permanent committees on public policy:

European Union: First established in 1973 and now possessing six sub-committees, this is the most elaborate of all Lords committees involving some 70 members at any one time. Its work is described more fully in Chapter 11.

Science and Technology: Set up in 1979, its remit is to consider science and technology across the board, including public policy that ought to be informed by science, technological challenges and opportunities, and public policy towards science itself. (14 members)

Economic Affairs: Set up in 2001, this committee evolved from an earlier *ad hoc* (temporary) committee to monitor the Monetary Policy Committee of the Bank of England. While it mainly conducts inquiries into topical areas of economic policy, since 2003 it has also established a sub-committee each year to inquire into policy aspects of the Finance Bill. (13 members)

Constitution: Also set up first in 2001, the committee conducts inquiries into constitutional issues and also examines all bills for any constitutional implications. (12 members)

Communications: This committee was established in 2007 following on from an *ad hoc* committee on the renewal of the BBC Charter. Set up initially for a series of terms of years, it was finally made permanent with effect from the 2013–14 session. It conducts inquiries into policy relating to the media, communications and creative industries. (13 members)

Ad hoc (temporary) committees

From the 1970s, the House occasionally set up temporary or *ad hoc* select committees which ceased to exist once they had reported. They often considered the merits of public bills, invariably private members' bills, that raised important policy issues, such as the Infant Life Preservation Bill in 1987–88 (on abortion), or the Assisted Dying for the Terminally Ill Bill in 2004–05 (on euthanasia). In both cases, the bills did not proceed further though, in theory, after hearing evidence it is open to a select committee on a bill to amend it and report it to the House, whereupon it is re-committed to a Committee of the whole House and continues its passage. The delay and possibility of amendment make the procedure unsuitable for the consideration of government bills, so the setting up of a committee on the government's Constitutional Reform Bill in 2004 – on a motion in the House moved by Lord Lloyd of Berwick, a crossbencher – was most unusual. Committees are also set up *ad hoc* to consider policy matters – embryonic stem cell research in 2001, religious offences in 2002–03, and HIV and AIDS in 2010–12 to name but a few.

    Ad hoc committees are popular among members and allow specific contemporary issues to be examined without setting up a permanent vehicle to do it. Now that they have become an established part of the Lords committee structure, every year there are many bids for such committees to be set up, invariably reflecting the interests of those members who put them forward. In order to give greater focus to this area of the House's work and to balance members' expectations with the capacity of staff, member resource, and infrastructure to cope with the demand, the Liaison Committee (see below) has recently advocated the appointment of *ad hoc* committees on both policy issues, and on post legislative scrutiny of bills. Thus, in the 2014–15 session three *ad hoc* committees were appointed to look at affordable child care, the Arctic, and ICT competitiveness and skills, and one to give post-legislative review to the Extradition Act 2003.

The process

How does the House decide when to establish a committee? Following a study of the House's committee work in 1991–92, a Liaison Committee chaired by the Chairman of Committees was set up to allocate resources between select committees and to make recommendations to the House on the appointment of committees. Discussions about committee work, which used to take place between the usual channels, now take place in the Liaison Committee, on which the party leaders, the Convenor of the Crossbench Peers and a small number of backbench members also sit. The role of the Liaison Committee is an unenviable one. A sessional select committee once established is difficult to abolish or modify and the pressure for new activity is high. Recently, the Committee has appeared to be more assertive – reducing the number of EU and Science and Technology sub-committees, and subjecting all *ad hoc* committee activity to an annual review and bidding process. But there have been occasions when the House has rejected the Liaison Committee's advice – in setting up a committee in 2001 on the crash of Chinook Helicopter ZD 576, for example. And sometimes the House has set up committees without reference to the Liaison Committee at all – on stem cell research in 2001 and on the Constitutional Reform Bill in 2004. Moreover, the requirement to set up joint committees to give pre-legislative scrutiny to draft bills or, indeed, to respond to any Commons initiative for a joint committee – such as the Parliamentary Commission on Banking in 2012 – cannot always be foreseen.

Sessional select committees are renewed at the beginning of every session, on a motion in the House setting out their orders of reference and powers. *Ad hoc* committees are set up by motion as required. The members are selected by the Committee of Selection on the advice of the Whips and Convenor and reflect party balance in the House. While there is no formal rule to this effect, a typical committee of 13 members might have 4 Conservative, 4 Labour, 2 Liberal Democrat and 3 Crossbench members. Chairmen are in theory appointed by the committees or sub-committees themselves but, in fact, are agreed upon through the usual channels. In the Lords, a rotation rule prevents a committee member from serving for more than four sessions on a committee in one stretch but, notwithstanding this sensible provision, there have been some serial re-appointments as soon as a year's grace has elapsed. To increase turnover of membership, with effect from the beginning of the 2015 Parliament the rotation period will be reduced to three sessions and members must be off a committee for at least two sessions before becoming eligible to re-join it.

Once established, select committees in the Lords operate in a way that is almost identical to Commons committees and they encounter many of the same logistical difficulties. Each committee or sub-committee is supported by its clerk, a secretary/ administrator, a committee researcher or specialist, and the assistance of an outside specialist adviser or advisers appointed for each particular inquiry in return for a daily fee. The permanent staff of the Committee Office is about 60 – even more modest than that in the Commons. The total spending of the Lords Committee Office in the financial year 2013–14 was just over £3.5 million in support of up to 17 active committees and sub-committees, and the current marginal cost of a unit of committee activity per year is about £225,000. In addition, under a different budget, about £450,000 was spent on the delegated legislation committees described on pages 229–31. These costs of select committees do not include any element for accommodation, IT, security or utilities. Neither do they have regard to the cost of members, whose expenses are paid by virtue of their attendance at the House. But the fact is that, as with Commons select committees, the monetary costs are modest (especially by comparison with Royal Commissions and non-parliamentary committees).

Lords committees have powers to send for persons (witnesses) and papers (evidence). Usually, witnesses attend and evidence is provided voluntarily but, were

House of Lords Constitution Committee taking evidence on the role of the Lord Chancellor, July 2014

Source: Copyright House of Lords, 2014. Photography by Annabel Moller it necessary, a committee could issue a formal summons and failure to respond would be reported to the House as a contempt. But enforcement of the summons would not be easy. As with Commons committees, the prospect of embarrassment and potential adverse publicity in failing to comply has proved to be a powerful persuader. Lords committees have power to meet concurrently with Commons committees, although this rarely occurs. The quorum of a Lords committee is usually three but for two joint committees – on Human Rights and Statutory Instruments – it is two for each House.

As in the Commons, there are no minority reports in the Lords. Dissent – were there to be any – would have to be recorded by moving amendments to the text and having these amendments printed in the minutes of proceedings. Lords committees usually succeed in achieving unanimity as members know that, unless their conclusions can be supported by all, they are unlikely to achieve the greatest impact. The chairman in the Lords has no casting vote.

The House usually finds time to debate the reports of its committees, although the timing may not always be to the liking of committee members (see page 269). Through these debates, the committee seeks to elicit a response from the government. In 2013–14, between 4 per cent and 5 per cent of the House's sitting time was spent debating select committee reports – that is to say, just over 46 hours, but a further 12 hours of debate were held in Grand Committee. In all, 32 reports were debated – a record high for a session of normal duration. A written response is also provided by the government within two months of publication, unless otherwise agreed with the committee in question.

Outcomes

It is difficult to say how far government policy adapts to the findings of Lords select committees, but where those committees produce reports that accord with government thinking, rather than being deeply critical, they seem to have effect.

In some areas of select committee activity, the influence is largely preventative. Thus, the very existence of the Delegated Powers and Regulatory Reform Committee means that the government is more likely to ensure that delegated powers are appropriately used in legislation and, if an adverse report is made, it usually complies with the committee's recommendations. Since the establishment of the Secondary Legislation Scrutiny Committee, precious few instruments have been reported on unfavourably on grounds of 'gold plating'. The bill scrutiny role of the Joint Committee on Human Rights has raised the profile of human rights in government, creating a culture of rights according to some commentators. The Constitution Committee's recommendations on fast track bills (expedited for urgent policy reasons) have been accepted by the government and are now addressed in the explanatory notes accompanying such bills.

In other areas, select committee reports – usually on ethical issues – will have helped to frame the debate. The select committee on the Infant Life Preservation Bill undoubtedly helped to focus the debate on the appropriate maximum period of gestation after which abortion would not be lawful, and its subsequent setting at 24 weeks. More recently, the Select Committee on the Assisted Dying for the Terminally Ill Bill in 2004–05 set the boundaries for a debate on this difficult issue that has continued ever since and on which Lord Falconer of Thoroton, former Lord Chancellor, introduced a private member's bill in the 2014–15 session.

Some Committees can point to instances where they have been influential in quite specific ways. For example, in 2012, the Constitution Committee reported on a problem that had occurred at the 2010 general election whereby those queuing outside a polling station when it closed at 10.00 p.m. had not been allowed to vote. The committee recommended a change in the law. The government failed to address this issue in their Electoral Registration and Administration Bill in 2012, so members of the committee tabled amendments. Faced with likely defeat, the government brought forward its own amendment to the bill and the law was changed. In 2014, the Communications Committee published a report on Broadcast General Election Debates with a number of recommendations aimed chiefly at the broadcasters. One of the recommendations – the creation of an online hub where the debates could be viewed on demand – was quickly picked up. Within two days of publication, the *Guardian*, *Telegraph* and YouTube announced that they were in discussion with the political parties with a view to hosting an online debate in the run up to the 2015 election, thus going some way to meeting the Committee's recommendation. In this case, the recommendations had been aimed not at the government but the media moguls themselves, and they responded.

The House of Lords Select Committee on Science and Technology has exerted demonstrable influence on government policy over recent years. The Committee's inquiry into nuclear research and development in the 2010–12 session, for example, spurred the government into taking a wide range of actions to address long-term planning for the UK's nuclear energy future. The key recommendation that resulted from its 2013 inquiry into scientific infrastructure – the pressing need for a long-term, strategic plan for science capital investment – was accepted by the government and is currently being implemented.

Committee members in the Lords, as in the Commons, often identify strongly with their committees and become very committed to the work. It follows that they are most anxious that their reports receive the widest possible publicity. Committee staff maintain elaborate and informative web pages containing the committees' programmes of work, publications, and written and oral evidence relating to current inquiries. Part of the House of Lords Information Office press and publicity team is dedicated to promoting committee work; meetings are publicised; many are webcast; the publication of every report is accompanied by a press notice; and, for the more significant reports, press conferences are held and the publication of most reports will have regard to newspaper deadlines and that highly sought after slot on Radio 4's *Today* programme. Coverage in online publications is also sought, and increasingly important. But timeliness is all. A report of the European Union Committee on future financing of the EU was widely reported because it appeared in print just before the unproductive Luxembourg Summit of 2005; a report of the Economic Affairs

Committee on the economics of climate change received extra coverage because it was published on the eve of the meeting of the G8 heads of government at Gleneagles, where climate change issues featured prominently on the agenda.

Committee work has featured conspicuously in the renaissance of the House of Lords in recent times. It suits the more reflective character of the House, and it is certain to remain a permanent – and one suspects ever expanding – feature of its activities.

Joint committees

We have seen elsewhere that the two Houses are able to appoint joint select committees. There was a time when the best-known and most established, such as the Joint Committee on Statutory Instruments and the Joint Committee on Consolidation, &c., Bills were legislative in character (see pages 311 and 310). But, nowadays, the Joint Committee on Human Rights (see page 310) and the joint committees established *ad hoc* to scrutinise the policy in draft bills (pre-legislative scrutiny committees, see page 181) are probably better-known because they consider policy matters. First set up in the 1998–99 session at the behest of the new Labour government, 26 pre-legislative scrutiny joint committees had been set up by the end of the 2013–14 session. Joint committees are also occasionally set up for certain kinds of opposed private business – opposed Special Procedure Orders and opposed Scottish Provisional Order Confirmation Bills (though, following devolution, the latter are now seldom necessary).

Joint committees are also set up *ad hoc* to consider particular issues of concern to both Houses, such as the privileges of the two Houses (see page 162) and reform of the House of Lords.

The first joint committee on Lords reform was set up in July 2002 to report on options for the composition and powers of the House once reform had been completed. After free votes in both Houses on the options, the committee would, it was envisaged, define in greater detail the proposed composition, role and powers of the second Chamber and recommend a transition strategy for transforming the Lords into its fully reformed state. The committee's first substantive report, published in December 2002, recommended no change in powers but set out seven options for composition ranging from fully nominated to fully elected. In February 2003, both Houses voted on these options. The Lords voted for continued nomination and rejected all other options. The Commons rejected all the options.

In a further report published in May 2003, the joint committee reported again, identifying areas of consensus and inviting the government to indicate what view it now took of Lords reform. In its response published in July 2003, the government indicated that, in the absence of consensus, its interest now would be in making the existing House work more effectively and the joint committee was not re-appointed the following session.

Following the 2005 general election and references yet again in the Labour Party manifesto to further Lords reform, a joint committee was set up in April 2006 to examine the conventions of the House (the Salisbury Convention and the practices on delegated legislation), the time taken on bills, and the practices governing the resolution of disputes over bills ('ping-pong').

In 2012, a further joint committee was set up to consider Lords reform, this time as a pre-legislative scrutiny committee on the Coalition government's draft House of Lords Reform Bill. The draft bill made provision for a largely elected and smaller House. This very large joint committee – with thirteen members from each House – was deeply divided on some of the key issues, including the principle of election. Nonetheless, albeit with qualification and on occasion on a majority, the joint committee reported favourably on most of the draft bill's key provisions. The work of all these committees, and in particular the 2012 bill and its eventual fate, are discussed more fully at page 379.

Until recently, it could have been said that joint select committees were seldom, if ever, set up to consider general issues of public policy – issues that would normally fall to a select committee of either of the two Houses to consider. But recently there have been two, on the Joint Committee on Privacy and Injunctions in 2011 and the Parliamentary Commission on Banking Standards in 2012–13. In 2010 and 2011, there was much media comment about so-called 'super-injunctions', which many celebrities were thought to have used to cover up alleged infidelities. Following the naming of one such celebrity under the protection of parliamentary privilege in the House of Commons, the government announced there would be a joint committee to examine the broad area of privacy, injunctions, their connection to parliamentary privilege and the future of media regulation. The Joint Committee on Privacy and Injunctions had 13 members from each House and took an extensive amount of evidence. Early in its life, the 'phone hacking' scandal gained great prominence, leading the committee to focus on the future of media regulation. This aspect of its inquiry had limited influence, though, as the Leveson Inquiry into press regulation was by then the centre of attention. The Parliamentary Commission on Banking Standards (we considered its work earlier at page 314) was also set up as a joint committee at the government's behest.

It is not yet clear how much appetite there is in either House for *ad hoc* scrutiny of policy by joint committee other than in the context of pre-legislative scrutiny. Nevertheless, the possibility remains that from now on, for reasons of its own, the government may well decide on occasion to use its influence to set up a joint committee on a pressing policy issue rather than establish some other kind of inquiry.

11

Parliament and Europe

Background

The relationship between the United Kingdom and its parliament and the European Union has been a key theme of British politics for more than 40 years. On 1 January 1973, the UK joined what were then three 'European Communities': the *European Economic Community* (EEC) or 'Common Market', together with the *European Coal and Steel Community* and the *European Atomic Energy Community* (Euratom). The 1992 Maastricht Treaty renamed the European Economic Community simply the 'European Community' and made it part of the new European Union. The system introduced by that Treaty and amended by the Amsterdam Treaty in 1999 was – with the notion of the European Community – abolished by the Lisbon Treaty, which came into force on 1 December 2009 and created a comprehensive legal identity for the European Union (EU).

Membership

There were six members of the EEC established by the 1957 Treaty of Rome: Belgium, France, Germany, Italy, Luxembourg and the Netherlands. In 1972, they were joined by Denmark, Ireland and the United Kingdom; in 1979 by Greece; and in 1985 by Spain and Portugal. In 1995, these countries were joined by Austria, Sweden and Finland. The biggest ever enlargement of the EU took place on 1 May 2004, with the addition of Cyprus, the Czech Republic, Estonia, Hungary, Latvia, Lithuania, Malta, Poland, Slovakia and Slovenia; Bulgaria and Romania joined in 2007 and Croatia in 2013. Currently, the Former Yugoslav Republic of Macedonia, Turkey, Iceland, Montenegro and Serbia are candidate countries; and Albania, Bosnia-Herzegovina and Kosovo (under UN Security Council Resolution 1244) are potential candidate countries.

Closer union

The preamble to the Treaty of Rome set ambitious objectives of 'ever closer union of the peoples of Europe and elimination of the barriers which divide Europe'. However, it also set the EEC apparently less politically sensitive tasks such as 'establishing a common market and progressively approximating the economic policies of Member States' . . . harmonious development of economic activities'.

For nearly 30 years, the EEC was concerned mainly with commercial and economic affairs; and during that time the Community managed with only modest amendments to the original treaty (such as those required when new member states joined). Subsequent changes were more profound, and have fuelled intense and continuing political controversy about the balance between national sovereignty and an 'ever closer union'.

In 1987, the *Single European Act* allowed legislation for the completion of the Community's internal market to be made by qualified majority voting (QMV) in the Council of Ministers. The use of QMV, which has since been applied to many other areas of EU legislation, means that the Council makes decisions by a weighted system of voting in which larger countries have more votes. It also means that no single member state can exercise a veto. The Single European Act also increased the legislative role of the European Parliament and provided for political cooperation on foreign policy.

In some ways, it is surprising that the then Conservative government led by Margaret Thatcher accepted the concept of QMV, which eliminated member states' powers of veto in most areas. The completion of the internal market, which was due in 1992, was no doubt seen as a higher priority; and the introduction of QMV allowed some 280 internal market measures to be passed that would otherwise have been blocked by one state or another.

The *Treaty on European Union* of 1992 (*the Maastricht Treaty*) established three 'pillars' of the EU: the European Communities, and two intergovernmental pillars, a common foreign and security policy (CFSP) and cooperation on justice and home affairs (JHA); and it instituted the machinery to bring about monetary union.

The *Treaty of Amsterdam* (1997) formalised for the first time the concept of 'flexibility' in providing for some countries to cooperate on aims that were not necessarily shared by all member states. It moved the free movement of persons from the JHA pillar to the Communities pillar, making it a subject for legislation rather than simply cooperation, and it also incorporated the provisions of the social agreement.

The *Treaty of Nice* (2001) established a European Security and Defence Policy and extended the application of QMV. It also made provision for the institutional change that would be necessary on enlargement of the Union, including the size of the European Commission and a new weighting of votes for QMV.

In December 2001, the European Council set up the *Convention on the Future of Europe* to examine how the EU could be made more democratic and efficient, and to propose a constitution for the Union. The convention, which included representatives from national governments and parliaments, both of current member states and the applicant countries, as well as representatives of the European Commission and the European Parliament, reported in the summer of 2003. Its draft constitutional treaty, including additional powers for the European Parliament and a longer-term President of the European Council, led to opposition calls for it to be subject to a referendum in the UK.

A period of some confusion followed. Although agreed by heads of state and government, and ratified by several member states, the draft Treaty was rejected in referendums in France and the Netherlands in May and June 2005. There was then a time of reflection and negotiation, after which, in 2007, work on a new Reform Treaty started in earnest during the Portuguese Presidency of the EU, and which accordingly came to be known as the Treaty of Lisbon. Again, the process of ratification by member states was not at all straightforward and involved a referendum that succeeded only at the second attempt (in Ireland), an appeal in Germany to its Constitutional Court and something of a smorgasbord of caveats, declarations and opt-outs for the Czech Republic, Denmark, Ireland and the United Kingdom.

The European debate

The European Communities Act 1972, which took the UK into the Common Market, was passed by the narrow majority of 17 (and the majority on second reading after 3 full days of debate was only 8). The UK's relations with the EU have been a matter of political controversy ever since. In 1975, the Labour government led by Harold Wilson held a national referendum on renegotiation of the terms of the UK's membership; and the subject was so divisive that collective Cabinet responsibility was suspended so that senior ministers could campaign for opposite sides of the issue.

Disagreements about Europe, both between and within parties, were never absent in the succeeding years; but it was institutional change within the European Union that brought them to centre stage. In the 1992–97 parliament, John Major's government was dogged by dissent and open rebellion on European issues, made more hazardous by the Conservatives' small majority.

Major came into office with an overall majority of 21, but after the loss of 8 by-elections and the defection of 4 MPs to other parties, the Conservatives lost their overall majority and were in a minority of 3 before the end of the parliament. This meant that rebels on European issues – and especially on the Maastricht Treaty – had a real prospect of bringing about a government defeat. In July 1992, the government did, indeed, lose a significant vote on the Maastricht Social Protocol, by 324 votes to 316, and had to put a motion of confidence – which it won comfortably – before the House the next day. Serious 'Eurosceptic' dissent nevertheless continued, leading to the withdrawal of the whip from eight persistent rebels from November 1994 to April 1995. And, in June 1995, Major resigned the leadership of the Conservative Party, standing immediately for re-election in an attempt to bring matters to a head. Although he won by 218 votes to 89, the size of the minority indicated the level of (largely Europe-fuelled) dissent.

The broadly pro-European stance of the incoming Labour government in 1997 (and also its huge overall majority of 179) meant that European issues were less prominent in the 1997 parliament; but in the 2001 parliament the Convention on the Future of Europe and the draft EU constitution were issues between the parties, as well as within the Conservative Party; and in the later stages of the 2005 parliament the intense debate resumed, with some of the same protagonists.

In the 2010 parliament, the debate about the UK's membership of the EU returned to the centre stage of British politics. The freedom of action of the Conservative party was, however, curtailed by its coalition with the Liberal Democrats and it was a private member's bill, the European Union (Referendum) Bill, introduced by the winner of the 2013–14 session ballot, James Wharton, that sought to make provision for a referendum on EU membership before the end of 2017. As is usually the way with contentious private members' legislation, the bill failed to become law because it ran out of time, in this case in the House of Lords, having got as far as passing the Commons. However, the strength of opposition in the Lords might have been fatal to the bill even if it had had a great deal more time.

As the 2014 elections to the European Parliament demonstrate, this is a debate that is increasing in intensity, not only in the United Kingdom but also elsewhere in the EU.

Law-making and sovereignty

It is easy to see why the EU has been a divisive issue. On the one hand, the argument runs, our interests are so similar to those of our neighbours that we should act with them, giving up some freedom of action so that we can be more effective and influential as a union of states. On the other hand, this closer union can also be seen as an unacceptable loss of sovereignty to an EU in which distinct UK interests will be submerged.

It is certainly the case that the United Kingdom Parliament has effectively lost its primacy in law-making in a practical sense. EU regulations automatically become law in this country without the involvement of Parliament. And EU directives set out what is to be the effect of the law in all the member states without specifying detailed terms; it is up to each country to decide on the wording. Under the European Communities Act 1972, implementation of EU directives in the UK takes place through delegated legislation (see page 223). Although the Lords Secondary Legislation Committee examines these statutory instruments for 'gold plating', there is no other scrutiny of the merits, even were the two Houses capable of amending delegated legislation, which they are not. Estimates of how much UK legislation 'comes from Europe' are notoriously difficult to make, but – according to the House of Commons Library – it is possible to justify any measure between 15 per cent and 55 per cent, depending on what is included in the calculation.

The Court of Justice of the European Union in Luxembourg has long asserted that EU law has precedence over the laws of member states. It is therefore possible for the Court to declare an Act passed by the Westminster Parliament to be incompatible with Union law and for a British court then to declare the law to be of no effect. This happened, for example, with the Merchant Shipping Act 1988 in the 1991 *Factortame* case, brought by a Spanish trawler company, and in which the United Kingdom was found to have breached EU law by requiring ships to have majority British ownership if they were to be registered in the UK. However, this is a complex and evolving area of law. In the UK, the Supreme Court, in its judgement in *HS2 Action Alliance Limited* v *Secretary of State for Transport and others*, raised the question (but did not answer it definitively) of whether the primacy of EU law as given expression in the European Communities Act 1972 extended to certain fundamental constitutional principles.

As recognised by section 18 of the European Union Act 2011 (which explicitly states that EU law is recognised in law in the UK 'only by virtue of' the European Communities Act 1972'), it would be theoretically possible for Parliament to repeal that Act and the other legislation that has incorporated successive treaty changes into UK law. To that extent it remains a sovereign parliament; but how far repeal would be a practical possibility, with the withdrawal from treaty commitments and the unscrambling of the UK's relationship with the EU that would be involved, is a matter of intense debate and speculation.

What, then, is the role for Westminster (and for the national parliaments in each of the other member states, as well as the Scottish Parliament, Northern Ireland Assembly and National Assembly for Wales), in this combination of political drama and day-to-day law-making at EU level? Before we consider this in more detail, it may be helpful to review the institutions of the EU and how EU laws are made.

The European Council

The European Council is the highest-level decision-making forum in the EU, its role having been formalised by the Treaty of Lisbon. It consists of the heads of state or government of member states, together with its own President (elected by a qualified majority of the Council) and the President of the Commission. It meets a minimum of twice every six months in Brussels but it can, and does, meet more frequently if needed. It defines the general political direction and priorities of the EU but does not legislate.

The Council of the European Union

The Council (formerly called the 'Council of Ministers' and not to be confused with the European Council) is one of the two principal legislative and decision-making bodies in the EU, together with the European Parliament. It consists of ministerial representatives from each of the member states' governments, who vary according to the business under discussion. Thus, for agricultural matters the Council will consist of agriculture ministers, finance ministers will deal with economic and financial matters, and so on. The great majority of Council meetings are held in private (although under the Treaty of Lisbon it now meets in public when it formally deliberates and votes on legislation); most decisions are taken by consensus, but if votes are necessary they are usually by QMV (see page 343). Most Council meetings take place in Brussels. The presidency of the Council is held by each member state in turn for a period of six months; this can be demanding for small states and can also lead to problems of continuity. The UK will next hold the presidency in the second half of 2017.

The Council is supported by the Committee of Permanent Representatives (member states' ambassadors to the EU), known as COREPER, which prepares Council business and negotiates agreement between member states so that the Council need take only a formal decision. COREPER is itself supported by more junior gatherings of officials known as the Mertens and Antici Groups which, in turn, receive reports from meetings of specialist officials on particular proposals. The office of the United Kingdom's permanent representative – essentially, the Brussels arm of government departments in Whitehall and elsewhere – is known as UKREP.

The European Commission

The Commission (based in Brussels) is the EU's executive – in some ways like a civil service, but with extensive powers of initiative, and of decision on a range of delegated matters. There are 28 Commissioners (one from each member state), each of whom is responsible for an area of policy, and the work of the Commission is carried out by 33 Directorates-General. The President of the Commission is highly influential, and his or her selection a matter for both the European Council (which proposes a candidate) and the European Parliament (which has the power to approve or reject the Council's nominee). The Lisbon Treaty states that the Council must take the European parliamentary election results 'into account' when making its proposal, a wording that was subject to varying definitions following the elections in 2014, especially in the context of David Cameron's opposition to the eventually successful candidate, the former Prime Minister of Luxembourg, Jean-Claude Juncker.

The European Parliament

Since 1979, members of the European Parliament (MEPs) have been directly elected for fixed terms of five years. The total membership is 751, of whom 73 represent UK constituencies (60 in England, 6 in Scotland, 4 in Wales and 3 in Northern Ireland). Following the 2014 elections, the largest party in the parliament was the European People's Party with 221 seats, closely followed by the Socialists and Democrats with 191. The Alliance of Liberals and Democrats for Europe includes the sole British Liberal Democrat MEP. The UK Independence Party, UKIP, has 24 MEPs and is affiliated to the Europe of Freedom and Democracy (EFD) group, which has 48 seats in the parliament. Labour's 20 MEPs sit with the Socialists and Democrats Group, and the Conservative party's 19 MEPs are part of the European Conservative and Reformist (ECR) group. Other United Kingdom MEPs are Green (3), SNP (2), Liberal Democrat (1) Plaid Cymru (1), Sinn Féin (1), Democratic Unionist (1), and Ulster Unionist (1).

Most business in European Parliament plenary sessions originates from the 20 permanent committees and their sub-committees, which carry out most of the legislative scrutiny. Somewhat surprisingly, the European Parliament continues to sit both in Strasbourg, for a week of plenary sittings each month, and in Brussels, for a number of two-day plenaries and the majority of committee meetings.

The European Parliament employs some 6,000 people. The budget for 2014 was £1.4 billion, including MEP's salaries. Exact comparisons are difficult but, in broad cash terms, the European Parliament costs well over twice as much as the Westminster Parliament.

Other institutions and associated bodies

The *European Court of Auditors* (in Luxembourg) audits EU revenue and expenditure, and makes both an annual report and special reports on particular expenditure programmes. *The Court of Justice of the EU* (also in Luxembourg) has a general duty of ensuring that in the operation of the treaties the law is observed. It decides on actions that challenge the legality of actions of the institutions of the EU, or that allege a breach of a treaty by a member state. It is assisted by the *General Court*, which used to be called the Court of First Instance. The 353 members of the consultative *European Economic and Social Committee* are drawn from trade union, employer, consumer and other interests; and the 353 members of the consultative *Committee of the Regions* represent the interests of regional and local government. The *European Central Bank* in Frankfurt has become the central bank for those countries that have joined the euro zone, while the *European Investment Bank* in Luxembourg is the EU's financing institution, providing long-term loans for capital investment.

European legislation: types

There are three forms of European legislation provided for under the Treaty on the Functioning of the European Union (TFEU) in its latest form following ratification of the Lisbon Treaty. *Regulations* have the force of law throughout the EU without member states having to take any action. *Directives* are binding on member states in terms of the result to be achieved by a specified date, but it is up to each country what form and method of implementation are to be used. *Decisions* adopted by an institution are binding on those to whom they are addressed; they are used for a range of matters, but especially to secure fair commercial competition through-out the EU. Regulations and directives must be published in the *Official Journal* of the EU.

European legislation: procedure

The legislative and decision-making processes of the EU are complex and this book is not the place to set them out in fine detail. However, following the reforms introduced by the Treaty of Lisbon, they are simpler than they used to be. In nearly all cases, the Commission has the exclusive right of initiative to propose draft legislative acts. There are then two categories of legislative procedure: the first is the ordinary legislative procedure (formerly known as co-decision) under which the Council and European Parliament both have to agree before the proposal can come into effect. As in Westminster, this is achieved through 'readings', but in the EU draft legislation is read *up to* three times, and most of the time a deal is concluded at the first reading stage through informal (and private) discussions between the Council presidency, European Parliament and Commission known as 'first reading deals' or 'trilogues'. Other provisions are subject to special legislative procedure, which means that the Council has either to 'consult' the European Parliament or seek its 'consent'. Under the ordinary legislative procedure the Council normally acts by qualified majority. Where the member states take decisions inter-governmentally, rather than legislatively, they do so through *common positions, joint actions, declarations, common strategies* or *conclusions.*

How to influence European legislation

We said earlier that a European regulation could become part of the law of the United Kingdom without the involvement of the British Parliament. Let us take a hypothetical example and then see whether British parliamentarians might have been able to affect what happened.

A virus that causes severe food poisoning has been found in cockles and small clams harvested in the western Mediterranean. Several people have died. During questions to the Fisheries Commissioner at a sitting of the European Parliament he is urged to take action, and undertakes to do so. The Commission then goes rather over the top and produces a whole new regulatory regime for shellfish, which among other things would require people catching shellfish of any kind to have their catch screened for the virus, and dealers to have similar checks carried out before selling shellfish to retailers.

The regulations go to the European Parliament and are considered in its fisheries committee. The Greens, who hold the balance of power on the committee, want the proposal strengthened to impose a ban on any catching or selling until procedures for the checks are in place EU-wide, and the Commission amends its proposed regulations. These are then discussed in the Council. The Irish fisheries minister argues that the regulations are too sweeping, and has the support of several others but not enough for a blocking minority; the British fisheries minister is doubtful but is unwilling to vote against for fear of unstitching an entirely separate agricultural negotiation on which the UK needs the support of countries that are in favour of the shellfish proposal.

The proposal comes into effect, and – because there is a three-month delay in manufacturing and supplying the equipment needed for the screening – effectively closes down the shellfish industry in northern Europe, as well as in the Mediterranean. The proposal applies not only to the cockles and clams that were the cause of the problem, but also to lobsters, crabs, prawns, scallops, mussels and oysters. Fishermen and fish merchants in Devon and Cornwall, and many other parts of the UK, face the loss of their livelihood and are outraged, as are their constituency MPs (and members of the Scottish Parliament, the National Assembly for Wales and the Northern Ireland Assembly). The only people who are delighted are the importers of shellfish from Thailand and the Philippines, outside the virus area; they are unaffected and can now sell their shellfish with very little competition.

How could the shellfish industry's case have been put more effectively? In this case, there have been three main actors: the Commission, the European Parliament and the Council. As soon as the Fisheries Commissioner gave his undertaking to the European Parliament, industry representatives could have lobbied the Commission; and constituency MPs, alerted by lobby groups, could have made the case to the Commissioner; but after having given the undertaking to the European Parliament, he might well have been unwilling to change his proposal.

MPs (and interest groups) could have contacted their European Parliament counterparts to emphasise the damage that could be done by the proposal. This might well have been effective with the MEPs (of whatever party) who had a constituency interest and were already concerned about the proposal – although with their much larger constituencies it might not have been quite such a priority as for some Westminster MPs. British MPs could also have approached British MEPs of their own party who did not have a direct constituency interest but who would appreciate the potential political damage. Once they had taken up the cause, the MEPs could have enlisted support from MEPs from other northern European countries that would be affected; and it might well have been that the proposal would have been toned down, or limited to the Mediterranean only, in the European Parliament's fisheries committee, rather than being toughened, as was actually the case.

But a critical point at which to try to secure changes was in the Council, through the stance taken by the British fisheries minister on behalf of the UK government. This is where the European scrutiny systems of both Houses would have come into play.

European scrutiny at Westminster

Two select committees – the European Scrutiny Committee in the Commons and the European Union Committee in the Lords – examine over 1,000 EU documents each year on behalf of Parliament. For each one, they assess its importance (and seek any additional information or evidence they need in order to form an opinion), report upon it and, if necessary, recommend it for debate at Westminster. The Commons committee works quickly, reporting on a large number of documents it judges to be of importance (some 500 each year) and recommending some for debate; the Lords committee reports on many fewer (25 or so each year) but in much greater depth, through inquiries by its sub-committees that are similar to the sort of inquiry carried out by departmental select committees in the Commons. Many other documents are scrutinised by the Lords committee by way of correspondence with the relevant minister. The two committees are doing their job in rather different ways, so they complement each other's work rather than duplicating it.

What is subject to scrutiny?

EU documents subject to the scrutiny process include draft regulations, directives and decisions; Commission Green and White Papers setting out future policy, including the Commission Work Programme; and a range of other papers including proposed actions on foreign affairs and defence and reports of the European Court of Auditors. Any document that is subject to scrutiny must be deposited in Parliament and provided to the committees within two working days of its arrival in the Foreign and Commonwealth Office in London.

The explanatory memorandum

Within ten working days of deposit, the Whitehall department primarily responsible for the subject matter must submit an *explanatory memorandum* (EM) on the document. The EM sets out which minister is responsible for the subject matter); the legal base of the Treaties under which the proposal is made, and what EU legislative and voting procedure applies; what the impact would be on UK law; whether the proposal meets the requirements of subsidiarity (in other words, whether action at EU level rather than at a national level is necessary); the government's view of the policy implications; a regulatory impact assessment if a proposal is likely to impose burdens on business; when required, a risk assessment and scientific justification; a note of what consultation has taken place; an estimate of the financial implications for the EU and the UK; and the likely timetable on which EU decisions will be taken on the proposal. EMs also include information on the interests of the devolved administrations.

EMs are an important element of accountability; one is submitted on every document and is signed by the responsible minister as formal evidence to Parliament. EMs are public documents, available on the Cabinet Office website, and so are useful sources of information for businesses and the public. Another advantage is that the process concentrates minds, both of the civil servants who draft the EM and the minister who signs it (especially when responsibility is shared between several departments and there is a risk of a subject not being gripped early enough). An EM can be a very comprehensive document; in our shellfish example, it would have set alarm bells ringing immediately, not least on the risk assessment, the scientific justification and possible burdens on business.

Once an EM has been submitted, the two Houses have different ways of dealing with documents.

The European Scrutiny Committee of the House of Commons

This is a select committee of 16 MPs. It has a staff of 13 (larger than that of any other Commons committee), which includes experts in EU law and former senior civil servants with experience of negotiating in Brussels. As well as its main work of scrutinising EU documents, it produces frequent reports on EU constitutional issues, including improving democracy and accountability within the European Union. It also conducts pre- and post-Council scrutiny, in which ministers involved in particular meetings of the Council explain, usually in writing, their approach to the agenda or the outcome of the meeting and the UK's role in it.

The committee is assisted by the National Parliament Office (NPO), which the House of Commons established in Brussels in 1998, and which now serves both Houses. This small office, staffed by two officials representing the House of Commons and one representing the House of Lords, acts as the committee's 'eyes and ears' in Brussels, gathering intelligence on likely proposals from the Commission, views in European Parliament committees, and so on. The NPO also publicises the reports of the EU committees in both Houses and assists other select committees investigating EU issues.

The European Scrutiny Committee meets every Wednesday when the House is sitting, and may consider 40 or more documents at each meeting. On each document, the committee has an analysis and recommendation from the committee staff. In an average year, the committee considers about 1,000 documents. It reports on about 500 of them and recommends around 50 debates a year.

The committee must first decide whether it has enough information to make a judgement. A comprehensive EM may be enough; but the committee may ask the government for further written evidence or, occasionally, call a minister to give oral evidence; this dialogue is a crucial part of the scrutiny process and of ministerial accountability. The committee decides whether the document is of political or legal importance. Our shellfish proposal would definitely be of political importance because of its likely impact on a UK industry. It might also be of legal importance if the proposal went beyond the EU's legal powers, for example. The committee may ask any departmental select committee (or the Public Administration, Public Accounts or Environmental Audit Committees) for a formal opinion on an EU proposal. There is increasing informal cooperation with other select committees, which often draw on the expertise of the Scrutiny Committee's staff.

If the committee decides that the document is, indeed, of political or legal importance, it will cover it in detail in its report on that week's crop of documents. The committee's weekly reports, which are published and put on the parliamentary website, are in effect a critical commentary on the EU agenda and a useful source of analysis and information for anyone monitoring developments in the EU.

Debates

A further decision for the committee is whether the document should be debated. It can choose to recommend a debate in one of the three *European committees*. These used to have permanent memberships but, since 2005, members are appointed afresh for the debate on each document. Any MP can attend and speak (although not vote). Committees categorised 'A' deal with matters affecting energy and climate change, the environment, food and rural affairs, transport, communities and local government; 'B' committees deal with finance, work and pensions, foreign affairs, home and legal affairs, and international development; and 'C' committees deal with business, innovation and skills, education, culture, media, sport and health.

A European committee is a combination of questions and debate; the meeting begins with a brief statement by a member of the European Scrutiny Committee, explaining why the document was referred for debate, following which a minister makes an opening statement. There is then up to an hour of questions to the minister (extendable to an hour-and-a-half), followed by debate on a motion. The committee lasts for a maximum of two-and-a-half hours. The motion is moved by the minister (amendments may be tabled and voted on), and usually formally takes note of the documents with some words supportive of the line the government is taking. European committees can be a testing time for a minister; in addition to the normal debate format, he or she normally has to answer questions alone and without notice. One former minister has described them as 'the scariest meetings you can go to'. Attendances at European committees are not high, however, and many finish short of their allotted time; it is surprising that MPs do not make more use of these opportunities to question ministers on what may be hot political issues. The Scrutiny Committee recommended in 2013 that permanent memberships should be re-established, but the government has repeatedly argued that there is insufficient interest among MPs to sustain this.

After the committee proceedings, the government puts down a motion in the House, which may be the same as the motion agreed to in the European committee (even if that was defeated) or may be an entirely new motion. That motion is taken without further debate, but it may be voted on.

On the most important documents, the European Scrutiny Committee can recommend that a debate should take place on the floor of the House; but it is up to the government to agree to such a recommendation, and it has not always done so. However, if the Scrutiny Committee has recommended a debate, it must take place, in a European committee if not in the Chamber. The precise timing is up to the government, but ministers will usually want the debate to take place soon so that they can get 'scrutiny clearance'.

The European Union Committee of the House of Lords

The House of Lords established its Select Committee on the European Communities in 1974. Renamed the European Union Committee in 1999, it scrutinises the government's policies and actions in respect of the EU. Alongside this scrutiny of the government the committee considers, and seeks to influence, the development of EU legislation. It receives the same documents and explanatory memoranda as the Commons committee, but has established a markedly different scrutiny system, in the form of its chairman's sift and the establishment of sub-committees. It draws the attention of the House to Commission proposals or other documents that raise issues of policy or principle with a recommendation as to whether or not a debate is desirable. The committee considers the merits of proposals for European legislation, and it uses Commission consultative documents or action programmes to undertake wide-ranging investigations of EU policy in a particular area. As with the Commons committee, it also undertakes inquiries into broader EU issues. In the 2012–13 session, for example, the committee reported on the future of EU enlargement.

The committee also monitors EU affairs in general. Thus, irrespective of the more specific policy work, regular meetings are held with Foreign and Commonwealth Office ministers, particularly following each European Council, and from the ambassadors of countries holding the EU presidency. The committee now makes a point of scrutinising the Commission's annual work programme and entering into correspondence on its views with the relevant Commissioners.

The committee has 19 members and 6 sub-committees that are divided into broad policy areas: economic and financial affairs; the internal market, infrastructure and transport; EU external affairs; agriculture, fisheries, environment and energy; justice, institutions and consumer protection; and home affairs, health and education. There is a total working membership (including co-opted members) of about 70 lords. The sub-committees consider whatever documents are 'sifted' to them by the chairman of the committee (many are deemed not to require scrutiny and so are not 'sifted'), as well as conducting free-standing inquiries. These sub-committees take evidence and make reports that draw on the knowledge and experience of their members: for example, in 2014 the Common Foreign and Security Policy Sub-Committee (Sub-Committee C) included a former Minister for Europe, former UK Permanent Representatives in Brussels, former Members of the European Parliament, senior diplomats, former MPs and a former Vice-President of the European Commission.

Every year, about one-third of the 1,000 EU documents deposited by the government are referred ('sifted') by the chairman for more detailed consideration by sub-committees, but only a fraction of these will become the subject of a full-scale inquiry. Some reports of the committee are made for information only, and some for debate. Inquiries may be based upon deposited documents received from the government and European institutions, while some are conducted on particular policy areas. An example of the latter was the Internal Market, Infrastructure and Employment Sub-Committee's report on youth unemployment in the EU, published in April 2014. Whether a report is debated or not, it is replied to in writing by the government within two months of publication. However, a substantial number of other documents are considered in detail by way of correspondence with the relevant minister. This is published, and much of it is available on the parliamentary website.

The reports are useful as a source of both information and informed opinion. Although their target is, theoretically, the House and, through the House, the government minister and government policies, the Lords reports, as those of the Commons committee, also have a wider market in the EU institutions, including the European Parliament itself and other national parliaments of the EU engaged in the scrutiny process.

Scrutiny clearance and the scrutiny reserve

The 1998 *scrutiny reserve resolution* of the House of Commons, and the 2010 Lords equivalent, constrain ministers from giving agreement in Council to an EU proposal that has not 'cleared scrutiny'. *Clearance* in the Commons means *either* that the European Scrutiny Committee has reported on it but has not recommended debate, *or* that the committee has recommended debate, the debate has taken place and the House has expressed a view on the proposal. In the House of Lords, *clearance* means *either* that the chairman of the European Union Committee has cleared the proposal at the weekly sift; *or* that the committee or one of its sub-committees has reviewed the document in more detail and decided to clear it from scrutiny, following correspondence, an inquiry or a debate in the House. A minister may give agreement to an uncleared proposal, but only with the Committees' agreement in both Houses, or if the minister believes there are 'special reasons' for agreeing – such as urgency, or if UK interests might otherwise be damaged – in which case the minister must provide an explanation, or be called in to explain in person.

For the scrutiny system to work effectively, there must be time for examination and debate in national parliaments. Over-rapid legislating is just as much of a problem at the European level as it is at the national level. This is particularly so when a proposal has been through the Westminster scrutiny process but is then changed substantially in later negotiations.

The Commons committee had a remarkable success in getting included in the Amsterdam Treaty a protocol on the role of national parliaments that requires a six-week period of notice before the Council decides on a piece of legislation (now eight weeks); but late changes to proposals often mean that this requirement is circumvented.

In 2013, the Committee concluded that things were not getting better and that developments since the Lisbon Treaty (for example, the increasing frequency of first reading deals) mean that national parliaments are still, too often, being shut out of crucial stages of the legislative process. It also proposed a new version of the scrutiny reserve resolution, not least because the current situation of operating on the basis of a text agreed before the Amsterdam, Nice and Lisbon Treaties came into force was absurd. The House of Lords European Union committee's inquiry into the role of national parliaments in the EU in the 2013–14 session similarly concluded that, by the time that national parliaments had an opportunity to consider EU legislation, those institutions that had prepared it would be resistant to change, taking the view that early sight of legislation is needed in order for there to be a greater role for national parliaments in the legislative process. Clearly, it would be in the Commission's interests to involve national parliaments earlier in the consultative process in order to head off later challenges to proposals.

To return to our shellfish example, things might have proceeded in this manner. The European Scrutiny Committee recommends a debate, which takes place in European Committee A. The minister is subject to some very hostile questioning from opposition MPs with fishing constituencies, and even some critical interventions from her own side. The government puts down a fairly bland motion about 'protecting public health and ensuring that all relevant factors are taken into account' but is unable to prevent the motion being amended to condemn 'an ill-thought-out proposal that will have a devastating effect on fishing communities throughout the United Kingdom'.

The same week, the Environment, Food and Rural Affairs Select Committee, which deals with fisheries, announces its intention of mounting a rapid inquiry into the possible effects of the proposal and invites the minister to be the first witness. There is now no way that the minister can support the proposal in the Council. The minister votes with her Irish and other northern European colleagues; there is a blocking minority, and it is clear that the proposal cannot get through in its present state. It later reappears in a modest form that applies only to certain species of shellfish in a limited part of the western Mediterranean.

How effective is the scrutiny process?

The institutions of the EU are not directly accountable to any national parliament, so parliaments can exercise influence mainly through their own governments and ministers. No matter how strongly the shellfish proposal was criticised, the most the House of Commons could have done would have been to agree to a motion instructing the government to vote against in the Council. The minister would have had a strong political imperative to obey that instruction, but could well have been out-voted in the Council.

The European scrutiny process is nevertheless valuable. It is comprehensive, and it catches a wide range of European proposals and other documents, on which ministers have to state their policy and provide evidence. It is open: EMs are public documents, and the committee's reports are published. It also means that proposals are normally investigated – and, if necessary, debated – before ministers vote on them in the Council, although last-minute drafting can still be a problem.

But the process depends crucially on the use that is made of it. It is a little like a burglar alarm. The scrutiny process can identify an EU proposal that might damage UK interests; and a burglar alarm can tell you that someone is attempting to get into your house through the kitchen window. But just as a little more action is required to apprehend the burglar, so the scrutiny system depends on MPs (and anyone else affected by an EU proposal or policy) making effective use of the information.

The Commons Scrutiny Committee produced a comprehensive report on the current system in late 2013. It concluded that, in general, its own sifting role was working reasonably well, but proposed changes to the system of European committees (in particular, the reintroduction of permanent memberships) and improved liaison with select committees, including the introduction of 'reporters' (named MPs with responsibility for EU issues in each committee). It also proposed much more radical change in a form of a national veto over EU legislation.

National parliaments and the Lisbon Treaty

The Treaty of Lisbon ostensibly gave national parliaments a greater role in Europe. It gave them, in particular, a specific role in monitoring whether EU proposals comply with the principle of subsidiarity (that is, whether action at EU rather than national level is necessary). Any national parliament or any chamber of a national parliament of a member state may send a reasoned opinion to the Council, Commission and European Parliament stating why it considers that a proposal does not comply with the principle. Bicameral parliaments have one vote per chamber; unicameral parliaments, two votes. Where reasoned opinions on the same proposal received within eight weeks amount to at least one-third of all the votes allocated to national parliaments – one-quarter for proposals in the area of freedom, security and justice – a yellow card is said to have been played, and the Commission has to review its proposal and give a reasoned decision.

So far, this threshold has been reached twice, once in 2012 for proposals relating to the rights of workers 'posted' to another member state by their employer, and in 2014 in respect of the establishment of a European Public Prosecutor's Office. There is also provision for an orange card, with a more stringent review requirement on the Commission, if reasoned opinions are issued in respect of more than half of the allocated votes – a threshold that has not been reached to date. If either the Commons or Lords committees decide that a proposal infringes the subsidiarity principle, they recommend a text and the respective House debates a motion on whether or not to issue a reasoned opinion (in the Commons, the debate may take place in a European committee, although the motion then must be approved – without debate – on the floor of the House). The House of Commons has issued 14 Reasoned Opinions since Lisbon; the House of Lords, 7. Finally, national parliaments can challenge EU legislation before the Court of Justice for non-compliance with the principle of subsidiarity.

In 2014, five years after the Treaty came into force, the low overall number of yellow cards, and the lack of any orange cards, is fuelling debate on whether the current system works. A factor may be that, although most parliaments of member states have some form of scrutiny process, relatively few have the means (or, perhaps, the will) to make it effective. There have been suggestions for a longer time limit (perhaps three months). Furthermore, the Commission seems to act with little regard to the views of national parliaments when they disagree with legislative proposals, and reacts slowly to correspondence; and some Commissioners have carved out personal fiefdoms, within which draft legislation reflects only the views of that Commissioner and of no one else.

This perceived lack of accountability from the Commission, and the democratic deficit present in the structure of the European institutions, has not only made the role of national parliaments even more crucial in European affairs, but is likely to have contributed to the rise in Euroscepticism in the recent era of financial crisis and imposed austerity.

What future role for national parliaments?

The European Parliament sees itself as the democratic institution representing citizens across the European Union. It is reasonable to ask, in that case, what is there for national parliaments to do? The answer is that the European Parliament is, in practice, remote from the citizens it seeks to represent and it lacks key powers expected of a parliament: it does not sustain a government in office (it must agree the appointment of the President of the Commission and can dismiss the entire Commission, but it has no power over the Council); it cannot impose taxes (although it must agree the EU budget); and, although with the agreement of the Council it may make amendments or block proposals for legislation, it cannot initiate legislation.

While there is no cause for complacency about the relatively low 65 per cent turnout in the 2010 British general election, total EU turnout in European Parliament elections is lower and has fallen from 63 per cent at the first direct elections in 1979 to 43 per cent in 2014 – despite voting being compulsory in several member states. In the UK – perhaps a country more publicly Eurosceptic than some – turnout has never reached 40 per cent. In 2014, it was 35 per cent – seventeenth out of 28 member states.

It is clear that, in many member states, voters see MPs, not MEPs, as their representatives; and that in European elections they tend to vote on national issues, just as they would in a general election, and not on broader European policies. Nevertheless, the European Parliament has the important roles of considering legislation in detail (with the power to block it) and supervising the unelected Commission.

Overall, national parliaments seem certain to remain the key democratic element in the EU for at least the foreseeable future, and the debate about their role and that of the European Parliament continues.

Closer cooperation between national parliaments

So, how can national parliaments be more involved at EU level, other than through the subsidiarity protocol? It has been suggested that the European Parliament could have a second chamber composed of national MPs representing each member state parliament; but the idea has gathered little support to date, and it is difficult to see how national MPs could spare the time to make such a chamber much more than a symbol.

The *Conference of European Affairs Committees* (usually known by the French acronym COSAC), which every six months brings together representatives of the European committees in all the national parliaments of the member states and of the Constitutional Affairs Committee of the European Parliament, acts as a forum for exchanging ideas and best practice on European scrutiny. Although COSAC has no formal powers, the protocol on the role of national parliaments in the European Union (part of the Lisbon Treaty) recognises that it has a role to play, with the right to transmit any contribution to the European Parliament, Council and the Commission, as well as the promotion of information and best practice between national parliaments and the European Parliament.

In 2014, the House of Lords European Union Committee suggested a range of ideas that could enhance the role of national parliaments in the EU. Its proposals would not require Treaty change; they would rely upon a habit of cooperation and collaboration between different member states' legislative chambers being developed, and similarly between the European institutions and national parliaments. The committee's recommendations included the idea that, if groups of like-minded national parliaments, acting together, made constructive suggestions for EU policy or legislative initiatives (a so-called 'green card'), those should be properly considered; that the Commission should take seriously its duty of review if a yellow card were issued under the reasoned opinion procedure; and that COSAC could increase its efficacy by improving the content of the biannual conferences and acting as a forum for the dissemination of best practice between national parliaments.

As well as the COSAC meetings, there are contacts between policy and legislative committees of parliaments of member states that deal with similar subject areas. Arrangements for holding meetings of representatives of these committees have, in the past, been somewhat *ad hoc*, falling either to the initiative of the European Parliament or to the national parliament of the country holding the presidency, but are now becoming more codified and, in some cases, written into Treaty provisions, such as that established by Article 13 of the Treaty on Stability, Co-ordination and Governance. Though not established by such a mechanism, the Interparliamentary Conference for the Common Foreign and Security Policy and the Common Security and Defence Policy has also become formalised.

Equally importantly, if national parliaments operate effective scrutiny systems, they can play an important part, not only in influencing their own governments, but also in publicising the possible effects of European proposals.

Increased cooperation and understanding – whether through joint meetings of subject committees, the work of COSAC, the annual meetings of national parliament Speakers, or contacts between individual MPs – are factors in maintaining and strengthening national parliaments as an essential democratic element in the European Union, and are a network in which governments and the EU institutions are becoming increasingly interested. It is worth noting in this context that the chairs of both scrutiny committees hold discussions with a range of ambassadors, members of parliament and foreign ministers of EU member states.

A closer relationship between MPs and MEPs?

How could MPs and MEPs be brought closer together, given that their roles are complementary? MEPs with dual mandates as MPs or peers used to provide something of a link between the institutions, but dual mandates have now been abolished. There is, however, informal contact through party organisations; and most MPs will have a working relationship with the MEP whose constituency covers their 'patch'. There are also regular meetings of the Scrutiny Committees of both Houses and UK MEPs. This kind of informal joint working will no doubt continue, complemented by the contacts between MPs and MEPs at the conferences mentioned above.

Other international relations

In this context, we should note the involvement of UK MPs and Lords (and staff of both Houses) in a number of international assemblies. The *Parliamentary Assembly of the Council of Europe*, based in Strasbourg, was established in 1949 as the parliamentary organ of the Council of Europe, in some ways a forerunner of the EU. The Council of Europe has had an important role in a range of social and cultural issues, but especially in human rights matters. It consists of 636 members drawn from the national parliaments of 47 countries (the British delegation has 36 members drawn from both Houses), and in recent years it has acted as a 'waiting room' for the new democracies of Eastern Europe that have become candidates for membership of the EU.

The *NATO Parliamentary Assembly* brings together 257 parliamentarians from the 28 NATO countries. It is based in Brussels but holds its sessions by turn in member countries. The *Parliamentary Assembly of the Organisation for Security and Co-operation in Europe (OSCE)*, based in Copenhagen, was set up in 1991. It consists of 326 delegates from the 56 OSCE participating states. The *British-Irish Inter-Parliamentary Body* brings together parliamentarians from Westminster and Dublin, and the devolved parliaments and assemblies.

The UK branches of the *Inter-Parliamentary Union (IPU)* and the *Commonwealth Parliamentary Association (CPA)* are based at Westminster. Although they are not part of the parliamentary administration, they are funded by annual grants from the two Houses. The IPU represents parliaments worldwide, the CPA those within the Commonwealth. Both aim to increase international cooperation and understanding, and they play a considerable diplomatic role; for example, the first formal contacts between the United Kingdom and Argentina after the Falklands War between parliamentarians of the two countries under the auspices of the IPU, and the IPU-organised visit to the UK by Mikhail Gorbachev just before he became leader of the USSR proved hugely significant.

The Overseas Offices of the two Houses also organise a large number of inward visits of officials and members of overseas parliaments, particularly Commonwealth parliaments, to Westminster. And there is increasing demand for staff and members to participate in parliamentary strengthening programmes in the parliaments of new and emerging democracies. These contacts are greatly valued and reflect the wider world beyond the frontiers of the European Union, whose parliaments were in many cases modelled on Westminster principles.

12

The future of Parliament

Modernisation, reform and effectiveness

Many people would say, usually without thinking, that Parliament needs 'modern-isation' or 'reform'. But these are words to be used with some care. To the person speaking, they really mean no more than 'change of which I approve'. After all, the 'Balfour reforms' of more than a century ago, which entrenched the government's control over the business and time of the House of Commons, were hardly a milestone in the democratic accountability of the executive. And in the present debate over the role of Parliament, 'modernisation' and 'reform' mean different things to different people.

It is much better to focus on the concept of 'effectiveness'. The traditional roles of Parliament include representing constituents, legislating, authorising taxation and spending, calling government to account, and acting as a forum for the testing of beliefs and opinions and a focus for national feeling. What do we expect Parliament to do for us, and how could it do those tasks more effectively?

Before we look in detail at some of the issues, it is worth establishing a sense of proportion. First, slagging off parliaments and parliamentarians is a national sport – all over the world, as well as in the UK. It is also a strange irony that, even though most democratic rights have been purchased with blood, they often seem to be little valued by those who live in democracies. 'Oh, I don't vote', you hear people say, 'I don't know anything about politics, and I'm really not interested'. Yet the stuff of politics, and the business of Parliament, affects every aspect of our everyday lives: peace and war, the education of our children, the safety of our streets, the quality of the air we breathe, our civil liberties. This lack of interest may be a symptom of the disconnection between people and Parliament, but it is also the case that, however Parliament changes, there will always be a significant number of people who 'don't want to know'.

However, the fall in turnout at general elections, from nearly 78 per cent in 1992 to 61.5 per cent in 2005 – even though there was a slight improvement to 65.1 per cent in 2010 – continues to be a matter of concern. As we saw in Chapter 2, the Hansard Society *Audit of Political Engagement* 2014 paints a discouraging picture, with only 49 per cent of respondents saying that they were certain to vote in the next general election, and 11 per cent saying that they were certain not to vote. These are things to be taken seriously, but there are no easy answers. The really frustrating thing is that, as we have seen in this book, Parliament is more independent-minded, vibrant and capable than it has been for decades; but this is not itself a guarantee of re-engagement with those it serves.

A reality check

Any proposal for changing the way Parliament – and particularly the House of Commons – works has to take into account the political and constitutional constraints. Here are ten practical factors:

- Some criticisms imply that Parliament should somehow simply stop the government doing things that are misguided or unpopular. As long as the UK has a constitutional system in which the government is *in* Parliament, *the execu-tive is always going to get its way eventually, provided that it has a majority in the House of Commons and can persuade its backbenchers to support it issue by issue.* A separation of powers – a system in which the executive and legislature are entirely separate, as in the United States – could greatly increase the independent powers of Parliament, but it would require seismic constitutional change, and – without buttressing Parliament's powers in a written constitution – could lead to Parliament being completely sidelined.
- Although many people are attracted by the more measured and slightly less partisan approach of the House of Lords, *parliamentary politics is party politics.* Like it or not, free elections involve a clash of party policies and ideologies, and in any elected House – at Westminster or elsewhere – party discipline will always be a powerful factor.
- *Parliament is by its nature reactive.* It responds to events, to public opinion and constituency pressures, and to the proposals and actions of governments. There are relatively few genuinely parliamentary initiatives: at Westminster, the main ones are private members' bills (when these are, indeed, at the initiative of the individual MP and not government hand-out bills), policy proposals made by select committees, and expressions of view as a result of debates initiated by backbenchers.
- *A wholly fresh start is impossible.* The more starry-eyed reformers of Parliament might wish to see a new Parliament on a greenfield site somewhere in the centre of England, breaking the ties with London and shrugging off the burdens of history and tradition. But the executive arm of government would have to move

as well, and it is difficult to see much enthusiasm for the establishment of a new administrative capital. However, as we shall see, the restoration and renewal of the Palace of Westminster may challenge the way the two Houses operate.

- *Parliament means different things to different people.* There are many who yearn for a measured, consensual approach to parliamentary politics. But there are also those who revel in the party battle, and see Parliament as an adversarial institution. As this book has shown, there is no reason why both cannot be accommodated; but one certainty is that there is no general agreement on *how* Parliament should change.

- *Parliament is not executive.* It approves principles (and, in the case of legislation, detailed instructions) about what is to be done; but it is the government of the day that is responsible for the business and administration of the state and is answerable to Parliament and the electorate.

- *Parliament is an organism rather than an organisation.* It is made up of individual members, often unpredictable, who react to a range of influences but who also have their own views. This means that the law of unintended consequences is a powerful factor in parliamentary reform; it is easy to set out detailed procedural prescriptions but difficult to predict what effect they will have, or how they will be used.

- *Politicians – not just MPs and Lords – but those involved in party and political organisations, and those in a position to bring pressure on them, must see the need for change and support it.* Theorists can propose wonderful schemes for parliamentary reform but, unless they get traction among those who will make things happen, those schemes will be dead in the water. A good example is the cultural change needed to make the House of Commons more representative. As long as those who select prospective parliamentary candidates select largely in their own image, we will go on as before.

- *A constraining factor on all change within Parliament is parliamentarians themselves.* It is pointless to propose new systems of select committees or legislative scrutiny if parliamentarians do not have the time and commitment to devote to making them work. This is especially true in the Commons, where the multiplicity of pressures on an MP may mean that new tasks must displace existing commitments if they are to be done at all.

- Perhaps most important, *Parliament – and especially the House of Commons – cannot easily change itself. It is the government of the day that has the majority of votes,* and which largely controls the business. Parliament's interests and those of the government are often at odds; change may come about because of wider political pressure, but it has usually depended on there being something in it for the government, as well as for Parliament. The ability of backbenchers to initiate debate and decision through the Backbench Business Committee has loosened that control, but has not yet altered the centre of gravity.

We now look at the issues as they affect each House.

The House of Commons

The credit side

We need to avoid the 'pre-emptive cringe' – a default setting of apology; the fact is that the Westminster Parliament does many things rather well, and some things better than many other parliaments. This is not an argument for complacency, but for valuing what we have. Westminster is well-regarded by people in the same business, as shown by the constant stream of visiting Speakers, members, committees and senior officials from overseas – from parliaments of all types, not only those in the Commonwealth that use the 'Westminster model'.

Over the last decade, there have been significant changes in the procedures of the House of Commons, and the pace has accelerated in the 2010 Parliament. However, at the same time, the ambitious programme of broader constitutional initiatives championed by Nick Clegg as Deputy Prime Minister in the 2010 Parliament has achieved very little, for a variety of reasons.

No survey of the last decade could ignore the savage blow dealt to the reputation of Parliament by the expenses scandal of 2009. However, as we have already emphasised, the 2010 general election made a profound difference to both composition and approach. The Commons had an intake of 227 new MPs; they knew what they were getting themselves into, and their refreshing determination to make a difference communicated itself to their returning colleagues, battered by their experiences in the previous Parliament.

With the additional factor of coalition government, it was perhaps not surprising that, as we saw in Chapter 4, the 2010 Parliament seems likely to be the most rebellious in modern times. And the change in culture could not be better demonstrated by the fact that, with the election of select committee chairs, two MPs from the 2010 intake now chair key departmental select committees: Rory Stewart on the Defence Committee and Dr Sarah Wollaston on the Health Committee. Only a few years ago, such a thing would have been unthinkable.

We now look at the changes that have recently taken place, the underlying strengths of the institution, and areas of possible future change.

Changes in the Commons

- Public bill committees were created in November 2006, enhancing legislative scrutiny by providing (for bills starting in the Commons) two days of select-committee-style evidence-taking before the more traditional debating stage of legislative committees; and the period of notice for amendments in committee was increased from two days to three;
- the experiment of the chair being able to impose speaking time limits in the Chamber was made permanent, November 2006;
- 'topical' (that is, open) oral questions, along the lines of those in PMQs, were introduced for departmental question times, November 2007;

- nominations to the statutory Intelligence and Security Committee were made comparable with those for select committees, July 2008;
- following the Baker Review, final decision-taking on MPs' pay was removed from the House and given to the Senior Salaries Review Board (but see IPSA below);
- provision was made for scrutiny of National (Planning) Policy Statements, May 2009;
- July 2009, the Parliamentary Standards Act 2009 created the Independent Parliamentary Standards Authority, entirely separate from the House of Commons, and gave it the task of devising a scheme for MPs' allowances and for determining claims (extended by the Constitutional Reform and Governance Act 2010, see page 62 and below);
- establishment of Speaker's Advisory Council on Public Engagement, November 2009;
- establishment of Joint Committee on the National Security Strategy, January 2010;
- Deputy Speakers were elected for the first time (rather than appointed), May 2010 (the procedure had been approved in March 2010);
- the Constitutional Reform and Governance Act 2010 provided for IPSA to be given responsibility for determining MPs' pay and pensions; responsibility for pay was transferred in May 2011 and for pensions in October 2011;
- election of select committee chairs and members, June 2010 (the procedure had been approved in March 2010);
- creation of the Backbench Business Committee and allocation of backbench time in the Chamber and in Westminster Hall, June 2010;
- Fixed-term Parliaments Act received Royal Assent, September 2011;
- changes to the procedures for financial scrutiny and passage of Finance Bills following the change from November–October sessions to May–April sessions, December 2011;
- creation of the Committee of Privileges and the Committee on Standards from the former Committee on Standards and Privileges; lay members added to the Committee on Standards, March 2012;
- changes to sitting hours: House sits at 11.30 a.m. on Tuesdays and 9.30. a.m. on Thursdays, July 2012;
- Monday sittings in Westminster Hall were introduced for debates on e-petitions;
- establishment of Speaker's Commission on Digital Democracy, November 2013;
- introduction of select committee statements (the introduction in the Chamber of a just-published select committee report by the chair of a committee, followed by questions to the chair), December 2013;
- notice period for amendments at report stage in the Chamber was increased from two days to three, on an experimental basis, June 2014.

Some changes did not survive: topical debates (introduced in 2007) were not a great success and were, in any event, overtaken by opportunities for backbench business in the 2010 Parliament. The publication by the government of a draft legislative programme in 2007 did not last long and seems unlikely to reappear. Regional committees, to scrutinise public services in the eight English administrative regions outside London, were set up in November 2008, as a number of ministers were given regional responsibilities; but they were not a success and did not make it into the next Parliament; but it is possible that something along these lines may be reintroduced as a response to the September 2014 referendum on Scottish independence.

Present strengths

The *close relationship with constituencies* means that Westminster MPs put considerable effort into an ancient function of the House of Commons: representing constituents, and getting their voices heard by ministers who are often seen as remote and inaccessible. Success in solving constituents' problems depends on the tenacity of the MP and the strength of the case, but the 'satisfaction factor' of constituency cases was rated highly by MPs in a recent survey, and this aspect of MPs' work generally gets a good rating from the public.

Select committees are a key part of the work of the Commons. The system is flexible and comprehensive; it encourages independence of view among committee members; it produces well-researched and well-written reports; as well as exposing a wide range of government activity to scrutiny, it publishes a great deal of official information that would not otherwise be in the public domain; and, perhaps most important, it provides public access to the political process. The election of chairs and members of most select committees in the 2010 Parliament has increased the authority and independence of the system, and innovations in scrutiny techniques and engagement with the public continue.

The complementary systems of European scrutiny in the Commons and the Lords are some of the best in any EU parliament (although their product is sadly underused).

Parliament attracts and retains high-quality staff, and its work is supported by committed and expert people who are highly regarded by their equivalents in parliaments worldwide. Other parliaments, when faced with a problem, often want to know 'How does Westminster tackle this?' It is to be hoped that the misconceived and botched process for the appointment of the new Clerk of the House of Commons in 2014 has not inflicted lasting damage on Westminster's professional reputation and its ability to attract and retain its staff.

Parliamentary questions, used on a larger scale than in any other parliament, have their critics but are an important means of requiring governments to put information on the public record and, in the hands of a determined MP, they can be remarkably effective. However, as we noted in Chapter 9, there is a risk that overuse may devalue them.

The House of Commons is *a natural focus of attention on historic occasions. It is the forum of the nation.* In 2013, it was a forum for tributes to Nelson Mandela and Margaret Thatcher, and more happily in the previous year for celebration of The Queen's 60 years on the throne. An important development took place in August

2013, when the House was recalled to debate developments in Syria, where civil war was raging and there was evidence that government forces had used chemical weapons against civilians. The government proposed a motion that envisaged the possibility of military action if certain conditions were not fulfilled. An Opposition amendment (not fundamentally different) was defeated by 332 votes to 220. The government's motion was then defeated by 285 votes to 272 and, at the dispatch box, the Prime Minister immediately undertook to be bound by the House's decision. This was an example of the House acting as a focus of national attention, but it was also a game-changer. The House had imposed its will on a determined executive, and had made it certain that formal military intervention would require parliamentary approval. The decision of the House of Commons had a wider resonance: shortly after the vote, in the United States President Obama announced that he would consult Congress before taking action; and in France President Hollande reacted in similar fashion, saying that he would seek parliamentary authority. The role that the House asserted for itself will be a continuing area of strength, as was seen in the government's need to seek parliamentary approval for limited military intervention in Iraq during the recall of Parliament on 26 September 2014.

We should not forget the more informal role that the House of Commons fulfils. It is *a place where opinions are exchanged and formed and laid open to the scrutiny of the media and the public*; where pressure groups and campaigners, as well as industries, the professions and a range of other players, put their case or seek a higher profile for their cause.

What next?

We now look at possibilities for the future. This is necessarily a highly selective list and many other proposals for change are considered in the relevant chapters.

Engagement and reconnection

Everyone agrees that Parliament needs to engage better with the people it serves, and to 'reconnect with the public', in the hope that this will raise levels of participation in the democratic process, and especially turnout in elections. However, there is no agreement on how to achieve this, beyond a general acknowledgement of the difficulty of making progress and the number of factors involved, which include:

The reputation of Parliament and its members

The foreword to the July 2013 determination of MPs' pay by the Independent Parliamentary Standards Authority (never a soft touch) said of MPs:

> *The importance of the job of an MP should be recognised, something which is all too often overlooked. These are the 650 people we have chosen to represent us. They sit at the pinnacle of our democracy. This is a fact that we ought to record and respect.*

Brave words; but despite the impressive turnaround and change of culture in the 2010 Parliament, there is a long way to go yet, and even one rotten apple out of 650 can be a severe setback for the institution.

Recall

In the 2014–15 session, the government introduced a bill for 'recall' of an MP who had committed serious wrong-doing, punished either by a period of imprisonment (less than a sentence of more than one year, which disqualifies a MP from membership of the House in any event) or by a suspension from the House of at least 21 days. Either of these circumstances could trigger a recall petition: if at least 10 per cent of voters registered in the MP's constituency signed, then the MP would lose the seat, and a by-election would be held (at which the MP would still be entitled to stand). These criteria are unlikely to satisfy the proponents of a less limited recall, in which the trigger would include, for example, changing parties once in the House.

Ease and attraction of voting

Many possible changes have been suggested: *mobile polling stations*, so that people can get to them more easily; *voting on a Sunday* (as in France), as this is the day on which most people can get to the polls; *holding several types of election on the same day*, as has been done for the European Parliament, local and Greater London Assembly elections; *making voting compulsory*, which is superficially attractive but which presents real practical problems and seems unlikely to make much of a difference; *reducing the voting age from 18 to 16*, as was done for the referendum on Scottish independence, and which seems likely to be part of the Labour Party's 2015 manifesto. *A change in the basis of political party funding* is sometimes canvassed, but agreement on this seems as far away as ever.

Making individual votes more influential has been the key aim of the campaign for proportional representation and, in 2010, it took 33,400 votes to elect a Labour MP; 35,000 votes to elect a Conservative MP; but 119,900 votes to elect a Liberal Democrat MP. As part of the Coalition Agreement, a referendum took place in May 2011 on replacing the first-past-the-post electoral system with the alternative vote system (where the voter ranks candidates in order of preference; the lowest scoring candidate on first preferences is eliminated and other preferences redistributed among other candidates). The proposal to change the voting system was heavily defeated, by 67.9 per cent to 32.1 per cent, and it seems likely that this issue is dead for some time to come.

Sometimes, efforts to improve the electoral system appear counter-productive. The introduction of Individual Electoral Registration was a logical response to concerns about electoral fraud. However, it seems likely that 6 million potential voters are not on UK electoral registers. This may – even after so long – owe something to the poll tax (the Thatcher government's local tax levied on individuals rather than on properties), but the fact remains that the equivalent of 85 constituencies are not even registered to vote.

Digital democracy

The increase in the use of the Internet, and the extraordinary growth in social media, has meant that these are seen as ways of revitalising democracy. Provided that security issues can be dealt with, the possibilities are unlimited. The Speaker's Commission on Digital Democracy, set up in 2013, has made recommendations about the use of new technology. But one constraining factor will still be the *digital divide*. In the first quarter of 2014, 44.6 million adults (87 per cent) had used the Internet, an increase of 1.1 million over the previous year; but 6.4 million (13 per cent) had never used it. As one might expect, the divide is sharpest among the growing population aged 75 and over, where only 37 per cent had used the Internet, but also among adults with a disability, where 30 per cent had never used the Internet. It is obviously important that the use of new technologies does not create new communities of the disenfranchised.

Referendums

If participation in conventional voting cannot be increased, what about direct involvement in decision-making through the use of referendums – an opportunity for all electors to vote on a specific proposition? Most democracies use referendums from time to time; in some systems (Switzerland and California, for example) the result has the force of law; but elsewhere, as has so far happened in the United Kingdom, the result is advisory only (although a government may pledge itself to abide by that result).

Referendums have been used from time to time in the UK: in 1973, in Northern Ireland on the province's constitutional future; and in 1975, throughout the UK on the issue of continued membership of the EEC. They were used twice, in 1979 and 1997, on proposals for devolution to Scotland and Wales, then on proposals for elected mayors, and in 2005 on the setting up of a regional assembly in the north-east of England. In 2011, there was a national referendum on a change to the electoral system and, in 2014, a referendum on Scottish independence. It seems possible that during the 2015 Parliament there will be a referendum on the United Kingdom's membership of the European Union.

There are several disadvantages of referendums as a way of supplementing conventional democratic decision-making in the UK. They can only be advisory; and they cannot be requisitioned by the people but are held at the government's initiative (and legislation is needed to authorise each referendum). The UK, without a written constitution, has no clear guidance about when referendums should be used; if, say, they should be used on constitutional issues, who decides what a constitutional issue is? For example, the government consistently refused the opposition's request for a referendum on the proposed new EU constitution, even though some other EU states held referendums as a matter of course.

If a referendum is held, what is a valid result? Should a minimum percentage of the electorate vote in favour, or should the requirement be an absolute majority, regardless of turnout? And what should be the question asked? The Political Parties, Elections and Referendums Act 2000 provides that the government should consult the Electoral Commission on the 'intelligibility' of the question, but the final decision is still for ministers. Much of the hostility of the House of Lords to the Commons private member's bill providing for a referendum on the UK's membership of the EU was because the question to be posed did not have Electoral Commission approval.

And, however deftly the question may be phrased, what is to prevent the referendum becoming a vote of confidence on the government of the day? The decisive rejection of the draft EU constitution in French and Dutch referendums in 2005 probably had as much to do with national politics – at least, in France – as with the constitution itself.

Historically, we have not had a habit of referendums in this country; but as interactive technology becomes more sophisticated and widespread, they (and some of these questions and problems) may become more important.

The referendum on Scottish independence, held on 18 September 2014, was a remarkable electoral and constitutional event. It was authorised by legislation but, in this case, legislation of the Scottish Parliament (the Scottish Independence Referendum Act 2013), not of Westminster. The question posed was 'Should Scotland be an independent country?', and the requirement for a positive result was a simple majority of votes cast (not a majority of those eligible to vote, which for the first time included those aged 16 and over). The proposition that Scotland should be independent was defeated by 55.3 per cent to 44.7 per cent – in the circumstances, a decisive majority. The general acceptance of the outcome was buttressed by a very high turnout: 84.59 per cent of an electorate of 4,238,392, which was a good result for democratic engagement. Had the Scots voted for independence, it would have been a serious setback for the Westminster Coalition government; but the promises made in the closing days of the campaign of greater powers for the Scottish Government and Parliament produced an immediate clamour for greater powers for England as part of the United Kingdom, and for the English regions – the West Lothian Question in a new and possibly more intractable form.

So far as the way Parliament itself operates, some of the issues include:

A House Business Committee

A committee 'to assemble a draft agenda to put to the House in a weekly motion' was recommended by the Wright Committee on reform of the House and the proposition was endorsed by the House in March 2010. In the Coalition Agreement, the government undertook to establish a House Business Committee to consider government business (the establishment of a Backbench Business Committee had already been agreed) 'by the end of the third year of the Parliament'. No further progress has been made; the government's stance is that there is insufficient agreement on how such a committee might operate. Certainly, a House Business

Committee means different things to different people. Would it be 'the usual channels' continuing to meet in private but reporting their conclusions formally? Would it be a committee sitting in public, but largely representing the usual channels? Or would it be the full-strength Wright option of a committee with a broad membership proposing a draft agenda to be voted on (and possibly amended) by the House each week? The last option would bring transparency to the way that the House's business is organised, but it is unlikely to be attractive to the government (and, indeed, possibly to the Opposition); and an incoming government may be reluctant to move quickly on the issue – or at all.

A fixed calendar?

The introduction of a calendar of sitting dates a year or so ahead, instead of the notice period being a matter of only a few weeks, made a profound difference to the organisation of Commons business, and to the way in which its members could plan their lives. More radical change is sometimes suggested: that there should be fixed sitting and recess times every year; and that there should be a day a week on which the Chamber did not sit, in order to create a day for committee activity (although further concentrating committee activity would have serious implications for the availability of committee rooms and other resources). Early change seems unlikely; but much more likely is that the House will continue to tinker with its sitting times for each day of the week.

Restoration and renewal: the effect of moving out

As we saw in Chapter 1, one of the biggest challenges for Parliament over the next decade will be securing the Palace of Westminster for future generations, and dealing with the deteriorating services of the building. Two of the three options under consideration, successive 'decants' of each House, and a complete decant of the whole Palace for five or six years, could have a profound effect on Westminster. Churchill's dictum that 'we shape our buildings, and afterwards they shape us' may be very much to the point. If there is a full decant, and the Houses sit in very different surroundings for five or six years, what will be the effect? If the Houses were to get used to sitting in Chambers of a different shape and size, what changes in atmosphere and ways of doing business might follow?

Moreover, there will be a powerful case for taking every advantage of the disruption and massive expenditure, and not merely replacing like with like. The possibility of glassing over all the courtyards, and of using space more innovatively, perhaps also re-thinking access and visitor routes to transform the visitor experience and to make major savings on security expenditure, will be a huge challenge to both Houses and the ways they and their members work. The pressure will be on Parliament not to let slip a once-in-several-generations opportunity.

Legislation: public bills

This is of course a core function of any parliament, and in Chapter 6 we surveyed the Westminster system and some of its strains and inadequacies. A bill needs to be well thought out, properly consulted upon, drafted to a high technical standard, challenged as to principles and scrutinised as to detail. This is easier said than done.

The standard of technical and policy preparation has greatly improved in the 2010 parliament, and there has been much less 'drafting on the hoof' (see page 178). There are many ways in which the legislative process could be improved, but there will always be tensions between the opportunities for scrutiny and challenge, and the pressures of the government's legislative programme. The extent to which MPs (for it is in the Commons that the shoe pinches) are willing to devote time to legislative scrutiny and, if they sit on the government side of the House, to challenge the administration they support, are also factors.

Draft bills can make a real difference. Ministers have less political capital invested in them, and consideration by a select or joint committee offers the possibility of real, evidence-based scrutiny and improvement. However, draft bills place extra demands on scarce expert drafting resources and, because of the lead time involved, are less attractive to governments in the first session of a parliament (especially when there has been a change of government, and the new administration wants to press ahead with its legislation).

More bills could be *committed to select committees after second reading* for the same degree of evidence-based scrutiny, but in this case the opportunity of formal amendments would also arise. These would have to be overturned at report stage if the government did not wish to accept them.

Much has been made of a possible *public reading stage*, where those outside parliament could make representations on bills. But it is difficult to see what more this could provide than is already available through the evidence-taking stage of public bill committees (see page 188).

There is scope for tackling the principle of a bill in a different way. In the nineteenth century, it was routine for a bill to be formally introduced only after approval of a *motion to bring in a bill* (a procedure that survives today with ten-minute rule bills). There might be advantages in seeking approval for the essence of a legislative proposal, and for its aims, before embarking on scrutiny of a major bill. Another approach might be *committal to a select committee as to the principle of a bill*, immediately after a bill had been introduced, in order to inform second reading.

There are many other possibilities for improvement, including: *applying the public bill committee procedure to all bills*, not just those starting in the Commons; *more split committals*, where big issues can be dealt with in Committee of the whole House, and details in public bill committee; *much tougher Speaker's selection* (see page 198) *on report*, to limit debate to the big political issues and genuinely new material, rather than revisiting much of what took place in committee; *use of purposive clauses in the body of a bill*, stating what that particular part of the bill aims to achieve; and universal *use of so-called 'Keeling Schedules'*, so that whenever a bill proposes to amend an existing statute, *the text of that statute as proposed to be amended is set out*, rather than the reader having to navigate amendments to other acts. Some time on the floor of the House might be saved by reverting to the practice that *a debate on third reading would take place only if a motion to that effect were tabled*, on the basis that third reading debates have become formulaic and add little to the scrutiny of legislation.

Perhaps we should be thinking more radically about the scrutiny of legislation. How well are parliamentarians equipped for analysis, as opposed to advocacy? Should they concentrate on principles and aims rather than the detailed provisions? Might an independent commission on the quality of legislation be better equipped to deal with details and report to Parliament on how well a bill implemented the political aims that had been approved?

And Parliament also needs to meet the challenge of 'guidance'. We are used to thinking of legislation as a hierarchy: primary, and then descending categories of secondary legislation (omitting the EU dimension). But, today, people's lives are in practical terms often affected more by guidance that has no statutory basis than they are by what is laid down in Acts of Parliament. To take one example: primary legislation sets out, in broad terms, a health and safety regime. Statutory instruments fill in the detail. But it is guidance, usually at local authority level, that determines how the health and safety regime will impact on the individual. If you are running a restaurant, local authority guidance on how many washbasins you should have, of what sort, and how often they will be inspected, is what affects you, and possibly your profit or loss, too.

Delegated legislation

In Chapter 6, we considered the extraordinary volume of statutory instruments and other delegated legislation, and the difficulty of scrutinising them in any meaningful way. The House of Lords has, through its Secondary Legislation Scrutiny Committee, tackled this more effectively than the Commons. It may be time to take a parliament-wide approach to delegated legislation, pooling expert staff to support a joint committee to scrutinise delegated legislation – if necessary, also working through single-House sub-committees to reflect the different political cultures and approach of each House. The Joint Committee on Statutory Instruments could be subsumed in such a body; it is difficult to defend the current use of that committee's expert resources for the very narrow technical work it carries out (see page 311).

Certainly, longer time needs to be allowed for scrutiny; an increase in 'praying time' from 40 days to 60 has already been recommended (see page 230), as has a rule that no affirmative instrument should be put forward for approval until it has received committee scrutiny and has been reported upon.

Private legislation

Although the number of private bills fell dramatically as a result of the Transport and Works Act 1992, this is still something of a parliamentary backwater, really understood only by a few practitioners. A fundamental review of private legislation is certainly overdue, and would need to be carried out by a joint committee, as the interests of both Houses are equally affected.

Parliamentary Questions

Written PQs

In the right hands, these can be a very effective way of calling ministers to account. Too many are tabled, either because they are an easy way of demonstrating activity, or because they are a short cut through the work that MPs and their staff should be doing. And they are still dogged by the impression that many written PQs are tabled by MPs' staff without the MP concerned knowing much about it. Together with the sheer numbers tabled and, crucially, the reduction in resources in government departments, which reduces their ability to give timely and detailed answers to PQs, these factors have blunted the effectiveness of written PQs. However, there is no readiness among MPs to have this parliamentary opportunity curtailed or more effectively rationed.

Oral PQs

As we saw in Chapter 9, these have largely lost their inquisitorial character; but, in the right hands, they offer the opportunity to put ministers on the spot. Reintroducing the rule against reading supplementaries, or quoting (see page 283) would sharpen Question Time up.

As topical questions (see page 287) have proved effective, now might be the time to turn the whole of Question Time into topicals. MPs would still be able to table substantive oral questions if they wanted to ensure that ministers could not plead lack of notice in giving vague or temporising answers.

Prime Minister's Questions

This is the highest profile event of the parliamentary week, and one which has its passionate supporters and detractors. As we saw in Chapter 9 (page 289), it is not an inquisitorial occasion; no one much expects the Prime Minister to give new information against his will. But this format also means that the House is missing out on the opportunity to question the nation's chief executive for half an hour every week the Commons sits.

In July 2014, the Leader of the Opposition suggested that the Prime Minister should be regularly questioned by a panel of citizens. This would no doubt be an excellent piece of public engagement, but would do little for parliamentary accountability. Indeed, it might be seen as an acknowledgement that Parliament had failed to do the job.

Might another way forward be for every other (or every third, or fourth) PMQs to take place in the relative calm of a select committee room, along the lines of the Liaison Committee sessions with the Prime Minister? The key difference would be that the questioners would be MPs selected by ballot, in exactly the same way that backbenchers are selected to ask questions in the hurly-burly of 'traditional' PMQs. The session would be chaired by the Chairman of Ways and Means, not the Speaker, to mark its distinctive character; it might last for an hour rather than half an hour; and each MP would be able to have several supplementaries.

Reconnecting committees and the Chamber

The Chamber is the forum in which the House takes its decisions; committees are advisory and preparatory. In most cases – the main exception being when bills (as opposed to draft bills) are referred to committees – the result is *advice* rather than something with which the House has to *agree or disagree*.

One option would be to move from a *committee-advised plenary* to a *committee-fuelled plenary*. This would allow the House to play to its acknowledged strength: select committees. Bills would invariably be referred to the relevant departmental select committees after second reading, for scrutiny in the light of expert testimony and public involvement, and in a more flexible format than that provided by public bill committees. (This would, of course, have implications for the resources of departmental select committees – especially the time of their members.)

The same approach could be used for the estimates, with the House being able to approve them only on the basis of a report from the relevant select committee, which would be able to vary individual components up and down if necessary, provided that the overall totals remained the same.

This radical approach would have a number of implications. Committees would be taking serious decisions that the government, if it disagreed, would have to ask the House to reverse. There would be more political pressure on select committees, and it might be difficult to maintain their generally consensual way of working. The process would demand more time and resources; but it would give much greater power to backbenchers.

Qualified majorities

Not all decisions need be taken by a simple majority. The rights of the opposition parties, and of backbenchers on both sides of the House, might be better protected by requiring certain decisions, such as those suspending a normal rule of the House, to be taken by a qualified majority, perhaps two-thirds.

A zero-sum game

Qualified majorities and a mandatory role for select committees in matters of legislation and expenditure are the sorts of things that would cause business managers in governments of either main party to have apoplexy. Most procedural change takes place if there is some balance of advantage and disadvantage to the government of the day. What has become increasingly clear, and especially in the 2010 parliament, is that a greater role for Parliament means a net loss of the power of governments. Whether Parliament takes more power, and how it exercises that power, is in the hands of MPs themselves, just as it is up to MPs how effectively they use the considerable parliamentary opportunities that already exist.

The House of Lords

The background

The changes that have taken place in the Commons in recent years, and the prospects for further change, have been evolutionary in character. The House of Lords, too, has seen evolutionary change and may well see more. But because of a continuing debate about the composition and powers of the House – and, indeed, as to whether the House should exist at all – the Lords has lived with the prospect of fundamental reform of a rather different order for much of the last 100 years. It is useful to see this in historical context.

We saw in Chapter 6 how the powers of the House of Lords over legislation were curtailed by the Parliament Act of 1911 and, again, in 1949 (page 209). Although reform of the composition of the House had been somewhat disingenuously promised by the preamble to the 1911 Act, nothing was to happen for a very long time. Proposals for an indirectly elected House with a continuing hereditary element were developed by the Bryce Commission in 1918, but these proposals and variations of them found little favour at the time, not least because they would not have eliminated the Conservative Party's majority in the House.

1949

Serious discussion of reform did not resume until 1949, when, in the context of the passage of the second Parliament Bill, an all-party conference discussed powers and composition. No agreement was reached on any wider issue, and the 1949 Parliament Act was confined to reducing the period of operation of the so-called 'suspensory veto' from three sessions to two. But a statement of agreed principles on the future of the House was subsequently published. This statement suggested developments such as the admission of women to the House, some form of remuneration, development of a leave of absence scheme and the elimination of the then permanent majority of the Conservative Party – all of which, in time, were to come about. The most interesting idea of all was that, in future, the membership should be partly hereditary and partly for life. This latter concept was given effect by the Life Peerages Act in 1958, which included life peerages for women. In 1963, the Peerage Act allowed women hereditary peers to sit for the first time and any hereditary peer to disclaim his peerage for life on inheritance.

The Wilson proposals

In 1967, the Wilson government made a brave attempt to institute a two-tier House composed of 200 to 250 voting life peers, law lords and some bishops and a remainder of non-voting hereditary peers entitled to sit only for the remainder of their lives. Delaying powers over bills would be reduced to six months, and the government party would have a small majority over opposition parties. Although the proposals were approved in principle by the Lords, a curious alliance of Left and Right in the Commons opposed it, and progress in committee proved to be so slow that the bill was abandoned. The failure of this scheme had the effect of removing Lords reform from the agendas of the two main parties for a generation. The Conservative governments under Margaret Thatcher and John Major showed no interest in the question. Indeed, between 1977 and 1989 Labour Party policy was to abolish the House altogether.

The departure of the hereditary peers and a Royal Commission

Not until the election of Tony Blair's Labour government in 1997 did Lords reform reappear on the political agenda, with proposals to eliminate the hereditary members and set up a Royal Commission to consider long-term proposals. Thus, the House of Lords Act of 1999 disqualified all hereditary peers from sitting, save for the 92 excepted by the Act (see page 35). And, in January 2000, the Royal Commission chaired by Lord Wakeham produced its report *A House for the Future*. The Royal Commission supported the continuation of most of the House's existing powers, including that of the suspensory veto under the Parliament Acts.

On composition, however, the Royal Commission made what were its only really radical recommendations. It suggested a chamber of about 550 members, a 'significant minority' of whom would be elected on a regional basis according to a list system of proportional representation, and the remainder appointed. Although the Commission could not agree on the number to be elected – three alternative figures of 65, 87 and 195 were offered – the genie of election had been let out of the bottle and was to dominate the reform debate thereafter. Both elected and appointed members would serve 15-year terms. Existing life peers would become members for life in the new House. Finally, an Appointments Commission established on a statutory basis would vet nominations for membership of the new second chamber and make its own nominations, chiefly of independent members. The report of the Royal Commission was not particularly well-received by reformers, any more than the government's almost equally conservative response to it published as a White Paper in November 2001. However, a House of Lords Appointments Commission was established in 2000, on a non-statutory basis, to nominate independent members and to vet political nominations for probity. Despite a steady flow of government papers and consultations, votes in both Houses, and backbench and cross-party studies, there would be no further action until after the 2010 general election.

The Constitutional Reform Act and the departure of the Law Lords

In 2005, the Constitutional Reform Act was passed, significantly altering the office of Lord Chancellor, making the Lord Chief Justice the head of the judiciary, setting up a Judicial Appointments Commission, and establishing a Supreme Court to take over the appellate functions of the House of Lords. First announced in June 2003, these proposals were aimed at effecting a separation of powers that had previously existed only imperfectly in the United Kingdom, but they affected the House in three ways. First, they ended the House's judicial role – little missed as it was, in the main, exercised away from the Chamber. Second, they abolished the role of the Lord Chancellor. Although the office was preserved in name as a result of a vote in the Lords at Committee stage, the post-holder is no longer required to be a lawyer or a lord. This led to the election by the House of a Lord Speaker for the first time in July 2006 (see page 68). The Lords, ironically, required no legislation to do this but merely the replacement of Standing Order 18 which dated from 1660 and which provided that the Lord Chancellor should be Speaker of the House of Lords. The third effect was to remove serving Lords of Appeal in Ordinary from the House when, in 2009, the Supreme Court finally opened and to end further appointments to the House under the Appellate Jurisdiction Act 1876 (see page 35). This will eventually have the effect of reducing the number of senior lawyers sitting in the House as there is no reason to suppose that all new members of the Supreme Court will, on retirement, be able to lay claim to a seat in the legislature.

The House of Lords Reform Bill 2012

Despite four White Papers (in 2001, 2003, 2007 and 2008), and reports from backbench and cross-party groups (Mackay of Clashfern 1999, Hunt of Kings Heath 2004 and Tyler *et al.* in 2005), the administrations of Tony Blair and Gordon Brown failed to deliver on further Lords reform. There was no second phase to the 1999 Act. However, all three major parties promised action on Lords reform in their 2010 manifestos, the Conservatives rather less enthusiastically than the other two major parties. Thus, in the coalition agreement we find a commitment 'to bring forward proposals for a wholly or mainly elected upper chamber on the basis of proportional representation'. Cross-party talks were held and a White Paper and draft bill published in May 2011. After exhaustive scrutiny by a joint committee of 26 members of both Houses, a bill was introduced in June 2012. It received a second reading by 462 votes to 124 on 10 July. But there were 91 Conservative rebels and neither they nor the Labour Party would support the necessary programme motion without which progress on the bill would have been impossible. The bill was withdrawn in September 2012.

Ironically, there was very little in the bill that had not been canvassed in the White Papers of the previous government or in the reports of some of the cross-party groups

– in particular, the group chaired by Paul Tyler MP, as he then was, in 2005, *Reforming the House of Lords: Breaking the Deadlock*.

- The bill proposed a hybrid House, part elected and part nominated. First proposed by the Royal Commission, it was a feature of the 2001, 2007 and 2008 White Papers and of *Breaking the Deadlock*.
- The ratio of elected to non-elected members was 80:20, and had been the settled view in the 2008 White Paper.
- Election on a regional basis using a proportional system had been a feature of the 2001, 2001 and 2008 White Papers; and the proposal to elect by thirds had been trailed by the Royal Commission, *Breaking the Deadlock*, and the 2007 and 2008 White Papers.
- The size of the House proposed by the bill was 450, and in the draft bill 300. Neither figure was out of line with earlier proposals.
- Election for non-renewable terms was first recommended by Lord Mackay of Clashfern's *Constitutional Commission* in 1999 and taken up in *Breaking the Deadlock* and in the 2008 White Paper.
- The establishment of a statutory appointments commission as set out in the bill had been proposed consistently since the Royal Commission, except for the 1998 White Paper which proposed the original non-statutory arrangements.
- The bill made no attempt to modify the House's current powers. This was entirely consistent with the papers and studies since 1998, which had neither called them into question nor sought to modify them.

But while the constituent parts had been canvassed before, bringing them together as a whole package of reform awoke old uncertainties. Although in 2007 the Commons had voted for the principle of an 80 per cent or 100 per cent elected second chamber (the Lords, once again, had voted for an appointed House), at the critical moment their will failed them. The chief reason for this was the age-old fear that a mostly elected House would seek to be more assertive, seek to impede Commons bills, and call into question conventions relating to government bills and even Commons financial privilege. A secondary argument was that elected Lords might trespass upon MPs' constituency casework. Furthermore, the assertion relating to Commons primacy over the Lords contained in the draft bill was not convincing (and would have been of no practical effect) and, at the recommendation of the Joint Committee, was removed from the bill itself. But wider political factors also came into play. Should the all-party talks in 2010 have rolled the pitch better, acceding perhaps to demands for a referendum on the issue of reform? In any event, would the Official Opposition – sensing Conservative backbench unrest – ever have surrendered an opportunity to drive a wedge between the coalition partners? Who knows.

House of Lords Reform Act 2014

For all that, the 2010–15 Parliament has actually passed an act to reform the House of Lords, albeit on a very much smaller scale than the 2012 bill. Originally a private member's bill introduced by Dan Byles, the Act allows members of the House of Lords to retire permanently from the service of the House; it compulsorily retires any member – other than those on leave of absence or temporarily disqualified – who failed to attend at all in the previous session; and it permanently disqualifies any member convicted of a serious offence carrying a penalty of over one year's imprisonment, thus bringing the Lords into line with the Commons. These were all the less controversial aspects of a succession of private member's bills introduced in the Lords by Lord Steel of Aikwood in each session since 2006–07 and had been trailed more recently by Baroness Hayman's private member's bill in the 2012–13 session. Given the limited appeal of the voluntary retirement scheme already in place, it is unlikely that the statutory provision will prove more tempting. But the compulsory retirement of non-attenders may well bring about a slight one-off downward adjustment in the notional size of the House.

Future reform of the House of Lords

As this book has illustrated, the House of Lords is a busy place, making an active contribution to the parliamentary process. But, to many writers, the only really interesting characteristic of the House is its membership and the only really interesting question is that of reform of its composition. Some, in the wake of 2012, have spoken of 'incremental' reform and the Dan Byles Act can be seen in that light. But most of the remaining 'incremental' changes that have been suggested are more complicated.

Election. It is not, of course, necessary to elect both Houses of Parliament. A country's democratic credentials do not rest upon whether its second chamber is appointed or elected. But many will continue to argue that a chamber of legislature with the kind of powers that are still vested in the House of Lords should be elected and not appointed under a system of patronage in which the leaders of the political parties have the upper hand. It is conceivable that a bill on the same lines as that introduced in 2012 could be introduced into a future parliament, but its chances of success would be slim without a stronger political will to see it through under a government with a clear and biddable majority in the Commons, or else strong cross-party support. It is possible that a reduction in the proportion of elected to appointed members might allow such a coalition of will to emerge, particularly if supported by a referendum.

Fixing the size. The current House of Lords is not limited by number, save for the Lords Spiritual who number 26. In the past, the size of the House, while reputationally damaging and quite probably inimical to the development of proper support services for members, has not impinged on the practical conduct of business because average attendance was much more modest. If, as daily attendance nudges 500, it is felt that the working House is becoming too big, then it might be possible to set a maximum number beyond which further appointments could not be made. This could be achieved through a voluntary understanding between the parties but only through statute would such a limit prove binding, particularly if the ceiling were set below the current membership and some sort of selection process by the parties were necessary to get the numbers down. Once established, the rate of churn in membership would be low and opportunities for regeneration of the House reduced. A cap on numbers would become a straitjacket without the introduction, at the same time, of an age limit or term appointments.

Age limit. The average age of members of the House of Lords is just over 70 years. 'Grandfathering' as a form of mentoring takes on a different meaning in the House of Lords context! So, if an age limit were imposed it would have to be quite high. At the beginning of the 2014–15 session, an age limit of 75 years would have reduced the members eligible to sit in the House by 33 per cent to 524 and a limit of 80 years would have produced a reduction of 18 per cent to 639. Despite the abolition of formal retirement ages in many walks of life, it would nevertheless be unusual to find many octogenarians still in employment. But the prevailing culture in the House and the contribution made by some older members would make this an unwelcome change and of uneven impact on the political parties.

Term appointments. Appointing members of the House of Lords for a fixed term of, say, 15 years would bring greater flexibility to the present system. It would take some years for the fixed term element to become dominant, but the presence of both life and term appointments in the House would be no different from the experience of the two classes of members – hereditary and life – following the Life Peerages Act in 1958. Such a change would, of course, require legislation, possibly by amendment to the 1958 Act. Life peerages could continue to be awarded if desired though, as with hereditary peerages after 1958, they would probably be given increasingly rarely. The rate of churn eventually might enable the House to be rebalanced in proportion with votes cast at a general election, if that were thought desirable. Some members might have their fixed terms renewed. On the other hand, this would inhibit the very flexibility that fixed term membership would bring, would lead to unseemly talent contests among those seeking reappointment, and would undermine the senatorial spirit that a pretty lengthy non-renewable term is meant to bring.

Phasing out the hereditary members. As we have seen, 90 of the 92 hereditary members excepted under the 1999 Act are refreshed when one of them dies by a by-election procedure, which many now find bizarre. The party and crossbench members are elected by sitting hereditary members of that party or group. Those members originally selected by the House as a whole, supposedly to serve as committee chairs, are elected by the whole House but according to an unwritten presumption that someone of the same party as his or her predecessor will be selected. The candidates are drawn from a list of eligible hereditary peers maintained by the Clerk of the Parliaments and are, by now, often unknown to the electors. The continued presence of the hereditary element was the price of a deal struck between Lord Irvine of Lairg and the Conservative Leader of the Opposition, Lord Cranborne, to facilitate the passage of the original bill, and was meant to last until the elusive second phase of reform was implemented. Thus, when the phasing out of the remaining hereditary element – by ending the by-elections – featured in the 2010–12 version of Lord Steel of Aikwood's private member's bill, it was vigorously opposed by some of those 90 hereditary members although their own positions in the House would not have been affected. A government bill would, of course, fare better and the Constitutional Reform and Governance Bill had, indeed, contained such provisions in 2009–10, which were dropped in the run-up to the general election. But phasing out the hereditary element even by the relatively benign step of ending the by-elections is not quite the standalone quick and easy fix it might appear, because a disproportionate number of the excepted hereditary members are Conservative. Over time, as members died and were not replaced, one political party would be disadvantaged above all others.

House of Lords Appointments Commission. The House of Lords Appointments Commission could be made a statutory body. This would, of course, require legislation, probably on the lines of the clauses and schedules already prepared for this purpose in the House of Lords Reform Bill in 2012. At the same time, it would be possible to widen the Commission's remit. In addition to nominating non-party members, it might also be given authority to nominate party members from lists provided to it by the parties – though, even if party leaders agreed to this diminution in patronage, others would oppose such a development on the grounds that the change merely added some respectability to a deeply flawed system. If the House became fixed in size, the Commission might also police any formula for political proportionality that might be devised to govern new appointments.

Expulsion of members. As we saw in Chapter 4, the House of Lords, unlike the Commons, cannot expel a member permanently, though it may suspend a member for the duration of a Parliament. The Constitutional Reform and Governance Bill in 2009–10 had originally made provision for such a power until it was dropped, as did the House of Lords Reform Bill in 2012. Private members' bills since 2010 avoided the issue but, at the beginning of the 2014–15 session, Baroness Hayman introduced the House of Lords (Expulsion and Suspension) Bill. This private member's bill would enable the House to make standing orders whereby it might expel a member or suspend a member for an unspecified duration.

Senators or nobility. At present, the House of Lords is a house of nobility, though it tries hard not to be. Members, other than bishops, receive a writ of summons to Parliament because they have been given a peerage by letters patent, carrying with it the 'style, dignity, title and honour' of a barony, and the right to sit in Parliament. Now that few peerages are granted solely for 'honour', some feel that the link between members of the House of Lords and the peerage is reputationally damaging and should be ended. Here again, legislation would be required. Instead of sitting in Parliament by virtue of letters patent of nobility, members would receive their writs of summons by virtue of a different entitlement – by simply being entered on a roll maintained by the Clerk of the Crown in Chancery. But this is the kind of change that is far more likely to be effected in conjunction with some other reform.

Where, then, does this leave us? All these possibilities for change would require legislation and, save for a bill on expulsion of members, none is suitable for private members' procedure. If a future administration had the stomach for a further stab at reform, the choice might well lie between a further attempt on the lines of the 2012 bill but with fewer elected members, or a package involving fixing the size of the House, allowing fixed-term appointments and bringing great probity and transparency to appointments through an enhanced role for a statutory Appointments Commission.

Modernisation of practice and procedure in the Lords

As with the Commons, the House of Lords has undergone its own programme of change in working practices in recent years. Many of these changes derive from groups set up by the Leader of the House specifically to review working practices – such as the groups on Sittings of the House in 1995 (the Rippon Group), and on Working Practices in 2001–02 and 2010–11 (chaired by Lord Williams of Mostyn and Lord Goodlad, respectively). And the Procedure Committee continually develops the way in which things are done. All changes are ultimately reported to the House for agreement. By these means, the House has made big changes over the years in the way it does things. Many of these have been recounted elsewhere in this book but it is useful to pull some of them together here, along with a few pointers towards further change.

- Since 1997, the House has developed a far more elaborate system of sessional and *ad hoc* select committees than before, when the focus was almost exclusively on European Union and science and technology issues. And it has increasingly formalised its processes for appointing *ad hoc* select committees, including one post-legislative scrutiny committee per session.
- The Grand Committee procedure has been expanded far beyond the taking of committee stages on bills (see page 207), and in this way more drastic changes to regulate Chamber procedure have been avoided. In the 2013–14 session, the Grand Committee gave the House 31 per cent extra sitting time, enabling it to absorb the effects on Chamber proceedings of higher attendance and rates of participation.
- Great strides have been made recently in trying to make debates more topical, by requiring motions for balloted debates to be renewed each month, and by instituting topical oral questions and topical Questions for Short Debate.

- While the current pattern of sitting hours had become established by 2002–03, in the present Parliament it has now become usual to sit on one Friday a month at 10.00 am, usually for private members' business.
- In Chapter 4, we recounted how, between 2009 and 2010, the House completely overhauled its Code of Conduct, appointed a Commissioner for Standards, re-asserted its right to suspend its members and changed the way in which financial support is given to members.

And how might working practices be developed further? Here are some suggestions.

- The Grand Committee might be developed further. Indeed, the House may have little choice, so as to relieve time pressures in the Chamber. The Goodlad group suggested that the committee stage of all government bills received from the Commons should be taken in the Grand Committee, but the suggestion was rejected by the House by 200 votes on a division in March 2012. Perhaps it is only a matter of time before this is revisited. Under present procedures, this is the only means of making extra sitting hours available to a hard pressed Chamber.
- The scope for a Backbench Business Committee in the Lords is fairly limited. The Goodlad Group thought that such a committee could select topics for debates on those Thursdays used for balloted debates, and for some Questions for Short Debate. The idea has not found favour so far and was also rejected on a division in the House. Many members would prefer the serendipity of a ballot to the involvement – indeed, interference – of a committee. But its time might come, and it would certainly improve topicality and avoid duplication and repetition.
- Committee members are currently selected by the party whips and the Convenor, and committee chairs are appointed following agreement between the parties. While most members are prepared to acquiesce in these arrangements, some find the practice to be opaque and unfair. There is no reason why, if the House wished, the House of Commons practice might be adopted of electing chairs House-wide and of inviting parties and groups to select their nominations for membership through election.
- Finally, just as with the Commons, we might see some unknown – and, indeed, unknowable – developments in working practices that might come about were there to be a decant of the two Houses of Parliament as part of the restoration and renewal of the Palace.

Conclusion

Parliament is an *organism* as much – or more – than it is an *organisation*. It has all the classic attributes of an organism: reactive, unpredictable, sometimes illogical. But in the early years of the twenty-first century, it has much to offer its citizens – and can still play as important a part in the life of the nation as at any time in its history.

After the travails of 2009, Parliament has been revitalised: active, influential, confident, and independent. The citizens of the United Kingdom should feel proud of what their Parliament does for them. There is much still to be done – not least in spreading understanding of Parliament, and in the valuing and sense of ownership that follows. Ultimately, though, Parliament's future is in the hands of parliamentarians themselves.

Glossary of parliamentary terms

In each definition, words in *italics* are further explained elsewhere in the glossary.

Accounting Officer The individual (usually the *Permanent Secretary* of a government department or the chief executive of an executive agency) who is personally responsible for the regularity and propriety of expenditure voted under a particular estimate.

Act paper Laid before Parliament because an Act of Parliament requires it.

Address A formal communication from either House to the Sovereign. The debate on the Queen's Speech takes place on a motion of thanks for the speech (often called the 'Humble Address').

adjournment The end of a *sitting*. In the Commons, an 'adjournment debate' takes place on a motion 'That this House do now adjourn', usually the half-hour adjournment debate at the end of each sitting in the Commons (where MPs may 'raise a subject on the Adjournment'). Major debates formerly on a motion for the adjournment now take place on a motion that the House 'has considered' a specific matter. An adjournment (for example, 'the summer adjournment') is also a more formal name for a *recess*.

Administration Estimate In the Commons, pays for the staff of the House and the services provided by the House departments.

advisory cost limit The estimated cost of answering a parliamentary question (at present £850) above which a minister may decline to answer the question on grounds of 'disproportionate cost'.

affirmation A secular promise of allegiance to the Crown made by MPs or peers who do not wish to take a religious oath.

affirmative instrument A piece of *delegated legislation* that the parent Act requires Parliament to approve explicitly before it can come into effect ('the affirmative procedure').

allocation of time order See *guillotine*.

all-party groups Of greater or lesser formality, these bring together MPs and peers from all parties to discuss matters of common interest. They are established by MPs and peers themselves rather than being creations of either House. The total varies: in 2014, there were some 500 groups. 'Country groups' (about 120) bring together MPs and peers interested in the affairs of particular countries.

ambit of an estimate The formal description of the services to be financed from that *estimate*.

amendment Proposal to change the text of a bill, motion or draft select committee report.

amendment of the law motion Moved by the Chancellor of the Exchequer after his *Budget* statement: 'that it is expedient to amend the law with respect to the National Debt and to make further provision in respect of public finance'. It is the vehicle for the broad Budget debate that follows.

amendment in lieu Amendment proposed by one House to the other as an alternative to one that has been rejected by the former.

Annually Managed Expenditure (AME) A category of government expenditure that is less predictable or controllable than that under *departmental expenditure limits*; for example, social security and Common Agricultural Policy payments.

annulment The act of making a *Statutory Instrument* of no effect. See also *prayer*.

backbencher An MP or peer who is neither a minister, nor (in opposition) a spokesperson for his or her party.

back of the Chair bill See *presentation bill*.

backsheet the last page of a bill, which repeats the *long* and *short title* of the bill, gives the bill number and the session, and lists the MP introducing the bill ('the member in charge') and his or her supporters.

ballot bills In the Commons, the 20 *private members' bills* introduced on the fifth Wednesday of a session following the ballot on the second Thursday of each session.

BBCom Abbreviation for the Backbench Business Committee, a Commons select committee of backbenchers that selects subjects for debate on the (normally) 27 days set aside for backbench business in the Chamber (and additional time in *Westminster Hall*, and which also apportions time for those debates.

bill Draft *primary legislation*.

bill of aids and supplies Old name for a bill granting *Supply* and *Ways and Means*.

Black Rod ('the Gentleman Usher of the Black Rod') An officer of the Lords responsible for aspects of security and ceremonial.

blocking minority The number of votes required to block a proposal in the Council of Ministers of the European Union under *qualified majority voting* (*QMV*) (see Chapter 11).

Boundary Commissions The bodies that keep under review the size, boundaries and numbers of parliamentary *constituencies*, especially to take account of population changes.

Budget Oral statement by the Chancellor of the Exchequer, usually in March, that reviews the nation's finances and makes taxation proposals.

business questions (strictly, 'the Business Question') In the Commons, a type of *urgent question* asked of the *Leader of the House* every Thursday, in response to which he announces the business for the next fortnight and answers questions.

by-election An election in a single *constituency* when a seat becomes vacant because the MP dies or is otherwise no longer eligible to sit.

casting vote In the Commons, the vote cast by the Chair to decide the issue when the numbers voting are equal. How the vote is cast is usually dictated by precedent, except in select committees.

CCLA Commons consideration of *Lords amendments.*

Chairman of Committees (or 'Lord Chairman') The principal Deputy Speaker of the House of Lords and spokesman in the Chamber for the House Committee, which oversees Lords administration. He has special responsibility for *private bills* and chairs the Liaison Committee and the Procedure Committee.

Chairman of Ways and Means The principal Deputy Speaker of the Commons, with special responsibilities for Committees of the whole House, *private bills* and *Westminster Hall.* In the House, he is assisted by First and Second Deputy Chairmen of Ways and Means, who act as Deputy Speakers. He chairs the Speaker's Panel of Chairs, which provides chairmen for *public bill committees.*

Chiltern Hundreds The posts of steward or bailiff of Her Majesty's three Chiltern Hundreds of Stoke, Desborough and Burnham, or of the manor of Northstead, are symbolic 'offices of profit' used to allow an MP to resign his or her seat. If an MP is appointed to one, he or she is disqualified as holding an 'office of profit under the Crown' (an MP cannot simply resign).

clause The basic unit of a *bill*, divided into subsections, then paragraphs, then sub-paragraphs. When a bill becomes an Act, 'clauses' become 'sections' but the names of the other subdivisions stay the same.

Clerk of the House The principal officer of the Commons. Head of the House Service and Corporate Officer, as well as the House's principal adviser on constitutional issues and the procedure, practice, law and privilege of the House.

Clerk of the Parliaments The principal officer of the Lords, with functions similar to those of the Clerk of the House of Commons.

closure In the Commons, a device for curtailing debate, or for securing a decision on a matter that would otherwise be *talked out.* An MP moves a *motion* 'That the Question be now put', which (if allowed by the Chair) is put to a decision immediately, without debate. If a division is forced upon it, not fewer than 100 MPs must vote in the majority for the closure, otherwise the motion is lost. If it is agreed to, the Question originally proposed from the Chair must be put immediately. Rarely moved in the House of Lords until 2011, when it was moved twice in respect of proceedings on the Parliamentary Voting System and Constituencies Bill.

collective responsibility The doctrine under which all members of the government – that is, ministers – support the policies of the government and take responsibility for government action, even if there are elements with which they privately disagree. Open disagreement is normally followed by resignation. However, the doctrine is modified in a coalition government when, on certain matters, it may be agreed that the coalition partners may take differing views.

Command Paper Presented to Parliament by the government, formally 'by Command of Her Majesty'.

commencement The coming into effect of legislation. For Acts of Parliament, this is usually done by an order made by the responsible minister. If there is no commencement provision, the Act comes into force from midnight at the beginning of the day on which *Royal Assent* was given.

Committee of the whole House Used for the committee stage of bills in the House itself rather than in a *public bill committee* in the Commons or, in the Lords, in the Grand Committee. In the Commons, Committee of the whole House is presided over by the *Chairman of Ways and Means* rather than the *Speaker*, and the *Mace* (normally on top of the *Table*) is placed on brackets below the Table to show that the House is in committee. Any MP may take part in proceedings, just as in the House itself.

Commons amendment An amendment made by the Commons to a bill passed by the Lords.

Comptroller and Auditor General A statutorily independent officer of the Commons who heads the National Audit Office (NAO); who approves the release of money from the Consolidated Fund; who audits accounts of government departments and a range of public bodies; and who carries out 'value for money' (VFM) inquiries into the economy, efficiency and effectiveness of public spending. He has a close relationship with the Public Accounts Committee, which considers his reports.

consideration See *report stage*.

Consolidated Fund The government's account at the Bank of England.

consolidation bill One that seeks to set out the law in a particular subject area in a clearer and more up-to-date form without changing its substance.

constituency The area of the country 'returning', or being represented by, each MP.

constituency Friday A non-sitting Friday in a sitting week.

COSAC (known by the French acronym) The Conference of European Affairs Committees that, every six months, brings together representatives of the European Affairs Committees in all the national parliaments of the member states of the EU, and of the Constitutional Affairs Committee of the European Parliament.

Cranborne money Financial assistance to opposition parties in the Lords, named after the then Leader of the House, Viscount Cranborne. The Commons equivalent is *Short money*.

crossbenches Benches in either House facing the Chair rather than on one side or the other of the Chamber. In the Lords, crossbenchers are those peers without party allegiance.

crossing the floor Changing party allegiance (even if the MP's new party, in fact, sits on the same side of the House).

decision Any decision of the EU Council of Ministers is binding upon those to whom it is addressed.

deferred division In the Commons, when on certain types of business an attempt is made to force a vote after the *moment of interruption*, that vote is held in one of the division lobbies between 11.30 a.m. and 2.00 p.m. on the next sitting Wednesday.

delegated legislation sometimes called 'subordinate legislation' or 'secondary legislation' (or 'Statutory Instruments', which most but not all are): Legislation made by a minister, or occasionally by a public body, under powers conferred by an Act of Parliament. Different types of delegated legislation are called variously orders, rules, regulations, schemes or codes, depending on what the 'parent Act' calls them.

departmental annual reports Published in June or July each year, these report on a government department's activities, spending and achievements, especially performance against objectives.

Departmental Expenditure Limit (DEL) Total planned expenditure for a government department, but excluding *annually managed expenditure*.

deposit Sum of £500 forfeited if a candidate receives less than 5 per cent of the votes cast at a parliamentary election.

de-referral In the Commons, a motion to take business (typically, debate on a Statutory Instrument or European Union document) on the floor of the House rather than in the committee to which is has been automatically referred.

despatch boxes At the *Table* of either House, from which *frontbenchers* speak.

dilatory motion A delaying motion, for the adjournment of the debate, committee or House; or to adjourn further consideration of a bill.

directive European legislation binding on member states in terms of the result to be achieved by a certain date.

dissolution The ending of a parliament by royal proclamation, followed by a *general election*.

division A vote 'to divide the House' (or committee) to force a vote. In the Commons, the votes are 'Aye' or 'No'; in the Lords 'Content' or 'Not Content'.

draft bill A bill, not yet formally introduced into either House, that is made available for pre-legislative scrutiny by a select or joint committee.

dummy bill A sheet of paper, with the *short* and *long titles* and list of supporters, presented at the *Table* by a backbench MP introducing a *private member's bill*.

early day motion (EDM) In the Commons, motions set down for 'an early day' and so – apart from *prayers*, which first appear in this form – almost certain not to be debated. EDMs are mainly used to make political points and to test opinion.

elector Someone who has a vote in a parliamentary election.

electoral quota The total number of electors divided by the number of constituencies.

estimate A request from the government to the Commons for the resources required for each main area of public expenditure.

estimates days In the Commons, three days in the course of a session when the *estimates* are approved; select committee reports selected by the Liaison Committee, and linked to particular estimates, provide the subjects for debate on those days.

Excess Votes Seek retrospective authorisation when a government department's spending in a financial year has exceeded what Parliament has authorised, or has been incurred for a purpose that was not authorised.

exempted In the Commons, business that may be taken after the *moment of interruption*, either because it falls into an exempted category, or because it is covered by an order (at the initiative of the government) that specifically exempts it.

explanatory memorandum The government's evidence on each EU document, which is subject to the European scrutiny system of each House.

explanatory notes A document accompanying a government bill that sets out the bill's intention and background in neutral terms, explains the clauses in lay person's language and gives an assessment of the bill's effects on public service manpower and costs, and on private sector business.

Father of the House In the Commons, the MP with the longest continuous service.

first-past-the-post The voting system in which the candidate with the most votes – a relative majority – wins regardless of how many other candidates there are or how close they come to the winning number of votes.

first reading The formal first stage of a bill's passage through Parliament, taken without debate when the bill is introduced. The bill is then ordered to be printed.

floor of the House The Chamber of either House. A matter debated 'on the floor' is discussed in a plenary sitting rather than in a separate committee.

frontbencher A minister or *shadow minister*.

the gallery Originally the collective term for the journalists primarily concerned with reporting proceedings rather than the interpretation of parliamentary and political events, which was more the province of the *lobby*; but, in practice, the distinction has largely disappeared.

general election Following a dissolution of Parliament, an election for every seat in the new House of Commons.

giving way Allowing another member to intervene briefly in a speech to make a point or to ask a question.

Grand Committee In the Lords, for considering the committee stage of bills and certain other forms of business off the floor of the House. In the Commons, the Welsh and Northern Ireland Grand Committees may be used for statements from ministers, oral questions, the consideration of bills and *delegated legislation*, and *adjournment debates*. The Scottish Grand Committee has not sat since 2003.

green card Available in the Central Lobby of the Palace of Westminster and filled in by a constituent seeking a meeting with his or her MP.

Green Paper A document issued by the government for consultation on possible policy options.

grouping The grouping of related *amendments* for debate.

guillotine In the Commons; also known as an 'allocation of time order': at any stage in the passage of a bill, an order that imposes time limits on the remainder of its progress.

hand-out bill A bill that the government wishes to see enacted and that is drafted by *parliamentary counsel*, offered to a backbencher to take forward as a *private member's bill*, usually with the continuing support and briefing of the government department concerned.

Hansard See *Official Report*.

hemicycle A semicircular debating chamber, as in the French *Assemblée nationale*, or the European Parliament.

hereditary peer A member of the House of Lords by virtue of inheriting a title (usually, a son inheriting from a father, although some hereditary peerages can pass to a daughter); 92 hereditary peers elected from among their own number have seats as a result of the House of Lords Act 1999 (which removed the right of other hereditary peers to sit in the Lords).

House of Lords Appointments Commission A non-statutory commission that makes recommendations to the Queen for non-political peers and vets for propriety all nominations for peerages, including those from the political parties.

House of Lords Business The working papers of the House of Lords, published in advance of every sitting day.

hung parliament After a *general election*, when no one party has a majority in the House of Commons.

hybrid bill A bill that combines the characteristics of a public bill (changing the general law) and a private bill (making provision with local or personal effect).

introduction The formal start of a bill's passage through Parliament. The bill is formally given a first reading at the same time and ordered to be printed. Also, used of the formal introduction of a new MP or peer.

IPSA The Independent Parliamentary Standards Authority, established under the Parliamentary Standards Act 2009, which is responsible for determining and paying the pay and allowances of MPs.

joint committee A *select committee* with a membership drawn from both Houses.

Journal The legal record of the proceedings of both Houses (of decisions and events rather than words spoken).

knives The deadlines within a *programme order*. When a knife falls, only specified decisions may be taken, and it may not be possible to debate or decide on certain clauses or amendments.

Law Commission of England and Wales A statutory independent body set up by the Law Commission Act 1965 to keep the law under review and to recommend reform where it is needed. The aim of the Commission is 'to ensure that the law is fair, modern, simple and as cost-effective as possible'. There is an equivalent body for Scotland.

LCCA Lords consideration of *Commons amendments*.

Leader of the House In the Commons, a cabinet minister dealing with House affairs and the organisation of business. The Leader of the House of Lords has a similar role but plays an additional part in guiding the course of business during a sitting.

legislative reform order An order under the Legislative and Regulatory Reform Act 2006 made by a minister to lift burdens on anyone carrying on any activity. An order may be made only after public consultation on a proposal, which is then scrutinised by committees of both Houses, and may be rejected and then submitted in an amended form. The committees also scrutinise the draft order that is brought forward as a result. A legislative reform order is an unusual type of *delegated legislation* in that it may amend *primary legislation*.

life peer A member of the House of Lords for life, having been appointed under the Appellate Jurisdiction Act 1876 (retired law lords) or the Life Peerages Act 1958 (other peers).

lobby (1) A room, as in division lobbies, the Central Lobby, Members' Lobby or Peers' Lobby; (2) to come to Westminster to put a case, either to an individual MP or as part of a demonstration ('mass lobbies'); (3) the group of parliamentary journalists with special access to the Palace of Westminster, reporting parliamentary and political news and opinion.

lobby terms Information given to journalists on the basis that it may be disclosed but not attributed.

locus standi The position of someone directly affected by the provisions of a *private bill*, who therefore has the right to petition against it.

long title The passage at the start of a bill that begins 'a Bill to . . .' and then lists its purposes. The content of the bill must be covered by the long title.

Lord Speaker Presiding officer of the House of Lords.

Lords amendment Made by the Lords to a bill passed by the Commons.

Mace A silver gilt ornamental mace symbolises the authority of each House. It is carried in procession before a sitting and in the Commons remains on the *Table* (under the *Table* when the House is in *Committee of the whole House*) and in the Lords on the Woolsack while the House is sitting.

main estimates The principal request from the government to the Commons for the resources required to run the state in the following financial year. There is one for each government department (and for other bodies such as the Office of Rail Regulation and the NHS Pension Scheme). Published within five weeks of the Budget.

main Question If an *amendment* to a *motion* has been moved, the original motion is known as the main Question.

manifesto Statement of policies and intentions on which a political party fights a *general election*.

measure Legislation of the Church of England, agreed by the General Synod, then considered by the Ecclesiastical Committee (a statutory committee consisting of members of both Houses) and then presented to both Houses for approval.

message Formal communication between one House and the other.

minister of state The second rank of ministers (below secretaries of state).

Ministry of Defence Votes A Published in January or February, these seek the annual authorisation by the Commons of the maximum numbers of personnel in the armed services.

moment of interruption The time at which the main business of the Commons day normally ends (10.00 p.m. on Mondays, 7.00 p.m. on Tuesdays and Wednesdays, 5.00 p.m. on Thursdays and 2.30 p.m. on Fridays).

money bill A bill whose only purpose is to authorise expenditure or taxation, as defined by the Parliament Act 1911.

money resolution A motion (when approved, a resolution) to authorise government expenditure in relation to a bill.

motion A proposal 'moved' by a member. When approved, it becomes a *resolution* or an *order*.

named-day questions In the Commons, written questions for answer on a stated day, with a minimum notice period of three sitting days (but including non-sitting Fridays). An individual MP may ask no more than five such questions per day.

naming (of an MP) A power used by the Chair in the Commons, usually for more serious offences, usually including disregard for the authority of the Chair. Following naming, a motion to suspend the MP concerned (to bar him or her from the precincts and stop payment of salary for a stated period) is moved by the senior minister present and invariably agreed to.

National Audit Office See *Comptroller and Auditor General*.

negative instrument A piece of *delegated legislation* that, under the parent Act, may be made and come into effect unless one or other House decides otherwise ('the negative procedure').

new clause A substantial *amendment* to a bill, usually introducing a separate subject or issue rather than seeking to amend the provisions already in the bill (but to be in order a new clause must be within the *scope* of (or, in the Lords, *relevant* to) the bill).

Next Business Motion In the Lords, see *previous question*.

1922 Committee (sometimes called 'the 22') Body consisting of all Conservative MPs but especially important as a reflection of backbench opinion.

nod To secure agreement to something 'on the nod' is without debate or a vote.

Official Opposition The largest opposition party, sometimes known as 'Her Majesty's Opposition'.

Official Report The essentially verbatim report of debates in both Houses, Westminster Hall, standing committees and grand committees. Also contains written answers to questions. Known as *Hansard*.

Ombudsman See *Parliamentary Commissioner for Administration*.

opposition days In the Commons, twenty days in the course of a session on which the subject of the main debate is chosen by the opposition parties.

order A decision of either House or of a committee on a matter within the power of the body making the order; for example, 'That a select committee be appointed to . . .'. See also *resolution*.

Order in Council A type of *delegated legislation*, made in the name of the Sovereign rather than that of a minister.

orders of reference *Orders* made by either House when setting up a select committee. They set out the committee's task and define its powers.

ordinary written questions in the Commons, written questions that are put down for answer two sitting days after they are received and that, by convention, the government answers within two weeks.

Outlawries Bill An antique bill 'for the more effectual preventing of clandestine outlawries' given a formal first reading in the Commons as a symbol of their right to deal with their own business before proceeding to debate the *Queen's Speech* after the *State Opening* of Parliament. The Lords equivalent is the Select Vestries Bill.

packaging The grouping of Lords amendments together for debate and decision in the Commons. Even though a particular proposition may have been defeated, its appearance as part of a *package* in which *amendments in lieu* are offered may avoid 'double insistence'; that is, when neither House will give way and the bill in question will be lost.

pairing An arrangement between two MPs on opposite sides of the House not to vote in a particular division, so that their absences cancel each other out.

a parliament The main division of parliamentary time: the period between one *general election* and the next.

parliamentary agent A specialist lawyer who represents the *promoter* of a private bill.

Parliamentary Commissioner for Administration (Ombudsman) An independent officer, reporting to Parliament, who investigates maladministration by government departments and other public bodies that has caused injustice that has not been put right. The holder of this office also holds the posts of Health Service Commissioner for England and for Wales (in the latter role, reporting to the National Assembly for Wales). The Parliamentary Commissioner for Administration has a close relationship with the Public Administration Select Committee in the Commons, which considers reports made by the Commissioner.

Parliamentary Commissioner for Standards An independent officer of the Commons who maintains the Register of Members' Interests and other registers of interests, advises MPs and the Committee on Standards on interests and standards issues, monitors the operation of the Code of Conduct, and investigates complaints about MPs' conduct. The House of Lords Commissioner for Standards exercises similar functions in that House.

parliamentary counsel A small group of government lawyers who are expert in legislative drafting and who draft all government bills, including *'hand-out'* bills. *Delegated legislation* is usually drafted not by parliamentary counsel but by the lawyers in the government department concerned.

parliamentary private secretary (PPS) An unpaid MP aide to a secretary of state or a minister of state.

parliamentary secretary *or* **parliamentary under-secretary of state** The third rank of ministers, below *secretaries of state* and *ministers of state*.

Patronage Secretary Formal title for the government Chief Whip in the Commons.

payroll vote Government ministers and *parliamentary private secretaries* – the most reliable supporters of the government in any votes.

PBL The Cabinet Committee on Parliamentary Business and the Legislative Programme, chaired by the *Leader of the House of Commons*. Other members include the *Leader of the House of Lords* and the Chief Whips in both Houses.

Permanent Secretary (in some departments, more formally 'Permanent Under-Secretary of State') The senior civil servant in a government department. Usually also the *Accounting Officer*.

personal statement A statement (in the Commons, made by permission of the Speaker), usually of apology, or explaining the reasons for a ministerial resignation.

petition Either a *public petition* or, in the case of a *private bill*, a case made against it by someone who would be directly affected by its provisions.

ping-pong The to-and-fro of bills and amendments between the two Houses at the end of a bill's passage through both Houses to enable any remaining disagreements to be resolved.

point of order An appeal to the Chair for guidance or a ruling on a matter of order or procedure, but also a means (through 'bogus points of order') of furthering political argument.

polling day The day on which votes are cast in a *general election* or *by-election*.

PLP Parliamentary Labour Party. Consists of all Labour MPs and peers.

PMQs Prime Minister's Questions (in the Commons, for half an hour every sitting Wednesday).

PPC Prospective parliamentary candidate. Someone selected by a party organisation to contest the next election.

PPR A *select committee's* power to send for 'persons, papers and records'.

PPS See *parliamentary private secretary.*

prayer A motion seeking the *annulment* of a *Statutory Instrument.*

praying time The period (usually of forty days, excluding time when both Houses are adjourned for more than four days) during which a motion for the *annulment* of a *Statutory Instrument* must be taken.

pre-legislative scrutiny See *draft bill.*

prerogative sometimes 'the Royal Prerogative' Power of ministers to act in the Queen's name without the approval of Parliament.

presentation bill A bill presented at the *Table*, notice having been given on the Order Paper.

previous Question An old-fashioned *dilatory motion* in the form 'That the Question be not now put'. If it is agreed to, the House moves to the next business; if it is not agreed to, then the matter that was interrupted must be decided immediately, as with a *closure*. The Lords equivalent is now called the *Next Business Motion.*

primary legislation Acts of Parliament.

Prince of Wales's Consent Signification by the Prince of Wales that Parliament may proceed to consider legislation that would affect his interests.

private bill A bill – a draft Act – that, if passed, will have only local or personal, rather than general, effect.

private business Proceedings on *private bills* and related matters. In the Commons, taken immediately after Prayers (the religious prayers at the start of the sitting); if opposed, time for debate is found by the *Chairman of Ways and Means.*

private member's bill A public bill introduced by a 'private member' (not a minister). Not to be confused with *a private bill*. In the Lords, 'private peer's bill'.

private notice question In the Lords, a question of urgent importance asked orally of the government and subject to the discretion of the Lord Speaker. In the Commons, the term has been replaced by *urgent question.*

privilege Parliamentary privilege (a better name would be 'immunity in the public interest') gives the two Houses, their committees and members, the protection from outside interference or legal action necessary to perform their roles. The two main elements are freedom of speech and the right of both Houses to regulate their own affairs. Also (as 'financial privilege') used to describe the pre-eminence of the Commons in financial matters.

privilege amendment A polite fiction to preserve the pre-eminence of the Commons in financial matters; a subsection in a bill starting in the Lords that involves an increase in expenditure or taxation says 'Nothing in this Act shall impose any charge on the people or on public funds'. The subsection is removed when the bill is in committee in the Commons.

Privy Counsellor A member of the Privy Council, consisting of senior politicians past and present, senior judges, some Commonwealth statesmen and certain others of distinction. Members of the Privy Council are styled 'right honourable'.

proclamation A royal proclamation by the Sovereign dissolves Parliament and sets a day for the new parliament to meet after the ensuing *general election*.

programming In the Commons, the imposition of a timetable on the passage of a bill immediately after *second reading*.

programming committee In the Commons, when a programme order applies to proceedings in *Committee of the whole House*, *report stage* or *third reading*, a programming committee (chaired by the *Chairman of Ways and Means* and consisting of up to eight other MPs) may propose how the available time should be allocated; but such committees are, in practice, not used, unlike a programming sub-committee (chaired by the chairman of the *standing committee*, with seven members of the committee), which deals with proceedings in a standing committee.

programme order A timetable for a bill once agreed to by the House.

promoter The body or individual outside Parliament sponsoring a *private bill*.

proposing the Question When the Chair states the proposition on which the House or committee must decide.

prorogation The formal end of a parliamentary *session*, which brings to an end almost all parliamentary business.

public bill A bill – a draft Act – that, if passed, will have general effect in some or all of the constituent parts of the UK.

public bill committee In the Commons, a committee to which most bills are referred for committee stage. If the bill they are considering started in the Commons, they begin in select committee mode with sessions of evidence from witnesses. Public bill committees meet in rooms laid out in the same manner as the Chamber of the House, are chaired by an impartial chair and cease to exist when they have finished considering a bill. A number of public bill committees may be in existence at the same time.

public business Generally, proceedings on the main business of the day (in the Commons, following Question Time and statements).

public petition An application by one or more people outside Parliament to one House or the other (usually the Commons) for some particular action or relief.

qualified majority voting (QMV) A weighted system of voting in the EU Council of Ministers in which larger countries have more votes. See *blocking minority*.

Queen's Consent Signification by the Sovereign that Parliament may proceed to consider legislation that would affect her interests.

Queen's Speech Sometimes called 'the Gracious Speech'; written by the government and delivered by the Queen at the *State Opening* of Parliament, it outlines the government's plans for the new session, especially its legislative programme.

Question (as well as the conventional meaning) A matter for decision.

Question for Short Debate (QSD) In the Lords, a debatable question time limited to one or one-and-a-half hours depending when it is taken. There is no right of reply.

Question rota In the Commons, the order in which ministers answer oral questions.

quorum The number of members required to be present to transact business. In the Lords, the quorum for the Chamber and any committee is three; but on a division on a bill or on *delegated legislation*, at least 30 peers must vote to constitute a quorum. In the Commons there is no quorum except on a division, when at least 40 MPs must be present (35 voting, the 4 tellers and the occupant of the Chair).

reasoned amendment One tabled for the *second* or, rarely, *third reading* of a bill that sets out why the bill should not proceed (or proceed in its current form).

reasons Given by one House to the other for rejecting *amendments* to a bill.

recall The return of Parliament during a recess. In the Commons, it is authorised by the *Speaker* on the request of the government. In the Lords, the power is exercised by the *Lord Speaker*. Also used of a system (not yet introduced) in which an MP would have to face a by-election in certain circumstances (for example, serious misconduct).

recess A longer time of adjournment than over a weekend, usually at Christmas, for a week in February, at Easter, the late spring bank holiday, and from late July to early September, for three weeks or so after the September sitting in the Commons, and briefly in November. Strictly speaking, the word applies to the period of *prorogation* but is rarely used in this sense.

regulation (1) In the UK, a type of *delegated legislation*; (2) in European legislation, regulations have the force of law throughout the EU without member states having to take any action.

remedial order An order made by a minister that amends *primary legislation* when that has been found incompatible with the Human Rights Act 1998. Draft remedial orders are scrutinised by the Joint Committee on Human Rights and are then approved by both Houses. Urgent procedure orders may be made without advance scrutiny but must be confirmed by the approval of both Houses within 120 days.

repeal To make the whole or part of an Act of Parliament have no further effect.

report stage Consideration of a bill in the form in which it left committee, and an opportunity for any member to propose amendments, not just those who were on the committee.

reserved matter One not devolved to Scotland, Wales or Northern Ireland.

resolution A decision of either House, or of a committee that expresses an opinion (for example, 'That this House has no confidence in Her Majesty's Government'). See also *order*.

resource accounting Records the economic cost of the provision of services and the consumption of assets (including depreciation, the cost of using capital assets, and future liabilities such as those for compensation for early retirement). Resource accounts for each government department are laid before Parliament.

revised estimates Change the *ambit of an estimate* if it appears that funds already authorised may have to be spent on something outside the present ambit.

Royal Assent The Sovereign's agreement to a bill passed by both Houses.

Royal Commission Five members of the House of Lords charged with representing the Sovereign in Parliament when she is not herself present, for Prorogation and election of a new Commons Speaker.

ruling A decision by the *Speaker* of the Commons or any other occupant of the Chair (or chairman of a *standing committee*) on a matter of order or procedure.

running whip A requirement for MPs to be available to vote throughout a day or a set period, because the timing of votes is unpredictable (as during a report stage or Committee of the whole House on a Bill)

Salisbury convention (dating from 1945 and named after the fifth Marquess of Salisbury) That the Lords should not reject at second reading any government legislation that has been passed by the Commons and that carries out a *manifesto* commitment.

schedule Schedules appear after the *clauses* of a bill and fill in detail.

scope The ambit of a bill; to be in order, *amendments* must not go beyond the purposes of the bill as summarised in the *long title*. The equivalent rule in the Lords is described as 'relevance'.

scrutiny reserve resolutions Constrain ministers from giving agreement in the EU Council of Ministers to a proposal that has not cleared the European scrutiny systems in both Houses.

second reading Approval, in principle, of a bill. A second reading debate is a discussion of the principle rather than the details of individual *clauses*.

second reading committee In the Commons, a (temporary) committee to which an uncontroversial bill may be referred for a *second reading* debate. There is then no debate when the bill is reported to the House for its second reading. In the Lords, an unselected committee (meaning that any Lord may attend) meeting in the Moses Room to give a second reading debate to Law Commission Bills.

secretary of state One of the top rank of ministers; senior minister in a government department; always a member of the Cabinet.

section The basic unit within an Act of Parliament, divided into subsections, then paragraphs, then sub-paragraphs.

select committee A committee of members of either House charged with investigating a matter and reporting (*ad hoc* select committees), or of monitoring a government department (Commons departmental select committees) or a subject area, or a category of legislative or other proposals and reporting from time to time. Select committees also advise on the administration of both Houses. Select committees that are not *ad hoc* are normally permanent institutions, with their members nominated for the length of a Parliament in the Commons or for a session in the Lords.

selection The decision by the *Speaker*, the *Chairman of Ways and Means* or the chair of a *standing committee* as to which *amendments* (or, in some cases, *motions*) shall be debated or voted upon.

Serjeant at Arms The officer of the Commons with responsibilities for aspects of security and ceremonial matters.

session The main subdivision of time during a parliament: the period from the *State Opening* to *prorogation* (now usually from May or June to October in the following year).

sessional orders Any order of either House that has effect only for the rest of that session of Parliament and, in the Lords, the traditional order passed on the day of the *State Opening* for 'preventing stoppages in the streets' and so ensuring access to the House.

shadow Cabinet Those opposition frontbenchers who 'shadow' members of the Cabinet, presided over by the Leader of the Opposition.

shadow minister An MP who is the spokesperson of an opposition party on a particular subject, mirroring the responsibilities of the 'real' minister in the government.

Short money Financial support for opposition parties in the Commons, named after Edward Short, the Leader of the House when it was introduced. The Lords equivalent is *Cranborne money*.

short title The title by which a bill is known during its passage through Parliament; for example, 'Criminal Justice Bill'. See also *long title*.

sitting A meeting of either House, usually in a single day, at the end of which the House adjourns. Also, a meeting of a committee.

Speaker The presiding officer of the Commons.

special report A report from a *select committee* that is not a substantive report on an inquiry but is used as a vehicle for publishing government replies or informing the House of some difficulty the committee has encountered.

standing orders The rules made by both Houses for the regulation of their proceedings. Standing orders remain in force until they are amended or repealed. 'Temporary standing orders' are typically made for the length of a *session* or *parliament*.

starred questions In the Lords, four oral questions on Mondays to Thursdays taken at the start of business. In the Commons, the term is not used, but a star on the Order Paper against a question indicates that it is for oral answer.

State Opening The ceremonial start to a session of Parliament. The main event is the *Queen's Speech*.

statute An Act of Parliament. 'Statute law' and 'the statute book' are collective terms for all Acts in force.

statute law repeal bill A bill that removes parts of the law that have become redundant.

Statutory Instrument See *delegated legislation*.

strangers The old-fashioned and rather unfriendly description of visitors to Parliament. Now superseded by 'visitors'.

***sub judice* rule** The rule against referring to a current or impending court case (more precisely, when someone has been charged in a criminal case, or, in a civil action, when a case has been set down for trial), to avoid influencing the outcome. The rule may be relaxed at the discretion of the Speakers of each House in certain circumstances, and it need not prevent the consideration of legislation.

subordinate legislation See *delegated legislation*.

subsidiarity In the European context, the principle that a decision should be taken at national level unless the aim could be achieved only by action at EU level.

substantive motion A motion expressing an opinion or taking a decision; not an *adjournment* motion (even though that involves the narrow decision of whether the House or a committee shall adjourn).

sunset clause A provision in legislation that makes it time-limited (and which may also provide for renewal by Parliament after a prescribed period).

supplementary estimates Seek additional resources for a government department.

supplementary question A follow-up oral question.

Supply The granting of money to the Crown for the running of the country.

Supply Bills Give detailed legislative authority for *Supply*: for the total of resources and capital, and cash to be issued from the Consolidated Fund. They set out the *ambit* of each estimate and the amount to be paid ('appropriated') in respect of each, and the numbers of personnel authorised for the armed services. The Lords may not amend Supply Bills.

surgery The time when an MP makes himself or herself available in the constituency for meetings with constituents, usually to discuss their problems.

suspend Informally interrupt the sitting of a House or committee. For suspension of an MP, see *naming*.

table To deposit formally before the House or committee, as 'to table an *amendment*' (or *motion*, question or paper). 'The Table' in both Houses is the table between the frontbenches, and also a collective term for the Clerks at the Table.

talking out In the Commons, debating a *motion* or a proceedings on a bill up to the *moment of interruption*, when the business is lost or postponed.

tellers Two members from each side who count the votes at a *division*.

ten-minute rule bill In the Commons (on Tuesdays and Wednesdays), a bill introduced by leave of the House (with a vote if one is forced) following a speech of not more than ten minutes from the sponsor of the proposal. An opponent may speak for not more than ten minutes in opposition.

test roll A bound parchment book signed by MPs when they take the oath or make *affirmation* after an election (also in the Lords where the parchment is still kept in roll form).

third reading The final stage of the passage of a bill through one House of Parliament; a final review of the contents of the bill, with debate limited to what is actually in the bill rather than, as at *second reading*, what might be included. Substantive *amendments* are allowed at this stage in the Lords but not in the Commons.

unopposed return A motion for an unopposed return seeks the laying of a report or other paper before Parliament, thus giving it the protection of parliamentary *privilege*.

unstarred In the Commons, a question that has been unstarred has been converted from one for oral answer to one for written answer.

'upstairs' In the Commons, means 'in committee' because legislative committees sit in rooms on the first-floor Committee Corridor.

urgent debate In the Commons, an application is made to the Speaker under S.O. No. 24 to debate 'a specific and important matter that should have urgent consideration'. Such debates are rare.

urgent procedure order See *remedial order*.

urgent question (formerly known as a *private notice question* (PNQ)) In the Commons, an oral question to a minister on an urgent matter of public importance, granted by the Speaker.

usual channels The informal and private contacts between the *whips* and business managers on the two sides of each House.

virement Moving funds between the subheads of an *estimate* with Treasury approval but without further parliamentary authority.

the Vote bundle The daily working papers of the Commons.

Votes and Proceedings The legal record of the proceedings of the Commons: decisions taken, papers laid and so on. Later becomes the *Journal*.

Votes on Account Come before the Commons in January or February and cover some 45 per cent of the estimated expenditure of each government department over the coming year; they are to tide the government over until the *main estimates* are approved in July. They must be agreed by the House by 18 March.

ways and means resolution A *motion* (when approved, a *resolution*) to authorise the raising of a tax or imposition of a charge in relation to a bill. 'Ways and Means' is an old name for taxation.

West Lothian question Named after Tam Dalyell MP, then member for that constituency: why should Scottish MPs at Westminster be able to speak, question and vote on matters affecting the rest of the UK when, in Scotland, those matters are devolved to the Scottish Parliament and the Scottish Executive?

Westminster Hall Together with the Great Hall on the west side of the Palace, the parallel Commons debating chamber 'the House sitting in Westminster Hall', which takes place in the Grand Committee Room off the northern end of Westminster Hall. Used mainly for non-controversial debates on subjects put forward by backbenchers, as well as by the government and for debates on select committee reports

whips Members responsible for parliamentary party organisation and discipline. 'The Whip' is circulated weekly by the whips of each party to their own members; it lists the business for the following week, together with the party's expectations as to when its MPs will be required to vote. The 'All-Party' Whip is generally available; it is a sort of Westminster notice-board of forthcoming events, meetings, etc.

White Paper A published statement of government policy (see also *Green Paper*).

wrecking amendment One designed to frustrate the purpose of a bill already approved at *second reading*, or of a *clause* already approved in committee.

writ An order for an election or by-election, issued by the Clerk of the Crown in Chancery upon a warrant from the Speaker. 'Moving the writ', usually by the Chief Whip of the party that had held the seat, initiates the process of a by-election.

Writ of Summons Issued by the Clerk of the Crown in Chancery to every member of the House of Lords at the beginning of a new Parliament, or on first appointment.

written ministerial statements In the Commons, statements by ministers that appear in the next day's *Official Report*, before answers to oral questions. A minister's intention to make a written statement is signalled in the Order Paper at the end of the day's business. In the Lords, such statements may be made by ministers and by the Chairman of Committees. They are printed in the *Official Report*. No notice is required.

Sources of information about Parliament

Books

This is not a bibliography but a highly selective list of publications that may be of further help to readers of this book.

Companion to the Standing Orders and Guide to the Proceedings of the House of Lords, available from Parliament's website and last updated in 2013. Available online at www.publications.parliament.uk/pa/ld/ldcomp/compso.htm
> The chief work of reference on House of Lords practice and procedure. The *Companion* describes every aspect of the House's practice and procedure as established by the standing orders, ancient practice, and decisions of the Procedure Committee and the House itself. It complements *Erskine May* (see below), which for some areas provides more detail and gives precedents.

Dod's Parliamentary Companion, Dods, 2014.
> The annually published reference work with biographies of MPs and peers, detailed results of the last general election, and a great deal of contact and other information on political parties, government departments, public bodies, the devolved institutions and the European Parliament. It also has a useful website directory.

Erskine May's Treatise on the Law, Privileges, Proceedings and Usage of Parliament, twenty-fourth edition, edited by Sir Malcolm Jack, LexisNexis, 2011.
> Usually known simply as *Erskine May*, it is technical and comprehensive rather than highly readable, but it is the pre-eminently authoritative textbook on Parliament and the one most used by practitioners.

Griffith and Ryle on Parliament: Functions, Practice and Procedures, second edition, by Robert Blackburn and Andrew Kennon with Sir Michael Wheeler-Booth, Sweet & Maxwell, 2003.

A detailed survey of the workings of both Houses, with a huge amount of statistical information and examples of every type of event. As well as providing shrewd analysis, it also usefully sets the present operation of Parliament in the context of the institution's development over the last half-century.

Handbook of House of Commons Procedure, eighth edition, 2011, by Paul Evans, and *Handbook of House of Lords Procedure*, second edition, 2006, by Mary Robertson.
Two excellent practical guides to procedure, logically laid out and well cross-referenced. They are written in straightforward language and will be especially useful for those involved at first hand with proceedings in the two Houses.

Members of Parliament 1979–2010, House of Commons Library, edited by Paul Bowers and Oonagh Gay, The Stationery Office, 2011.
Short biographies of every Member of Parliament in the period with some statistical analysis and reflections of 11 members. Also published online without some of the content and available at www.parliament.uk/business/publications/research/briefing-papers/RP10–33/members-19792010

Parliament in British Politics, second edition, Philip Norton, Palgrave Macmillan, 2013.
A clear text covering how Parliament interacts with government, those beyond Westminster (the EU, devolved bodies, courts) and citizens.

The British Constitution in the Twentieth Century, edited by Vernon Bogdanor, Oxford University Press for the British Academy, 2003.
A definitive account of the development of all major British constitutional institutions in the twentieth century, with separate chapters on the House of Commons and the House of Lords. A valuable work of reference for those interested in the recent historical development of Parliament.

The Contemporary House of Lords, Meg Russell, Oxford University Press, 2013.
This comprehensive text concentrates on how the House of Lords has worked since the 1999 reforms. Valuable analysis and insights.

The Standing Orders of the House of Commons: Public Business, The Stationery Office, 2005 (also available on the parliamentary website).

The Standing Orders of the House of Lords relating to Public Business, The Stationery Office, 2005 (also available on the parliamentary website).

Many Peers and MPs have written about their time in the Houses in autobiographies or other texts. Two of the most relevant are *How to be an MP* by Paul Flynn, which provides an entertaining overview of an MP's work, and Chris Mullin's diaries covering 1994 to 2010 which, over three volumes, provide an insight into the role of a backbencher and minister.

Parliament websites

Parliament's website, www.parliament.uk, contains a wealth of information about Parliament. Increasingly, Parliament is making much more available online for both the public and MPs. The website can tell you:

- what's on: current and future business in both Houses and forthcoming meetings of committees (business is normally updated every Thursday);
- the text of Commons *Hansard* from the session 1988–89 onwards and Lords *Hansard* from the session 1994–95, and the *Hansard* of all standing committee debates of bills and other matters from the session 1997–98 onwards. *Hansard* for the two Chambers is available on the website the following day but a rolling version appears on the day with a delay of around three hours;
- progress of legislation in the current and previous sessions, including the text of all bills, both public and private, before Parliament, and their current status, along with related documents, Library papers and proceedings;
- standing orders of both Houses, for both public and private business;
- lists of: MPs by constituency, gender and party; peers; ministers and PPSs; opposition spokespeople; all-party groups and country groups; together with the state of the parties and by-election results;
- find your MP service: www.parliament.uk/mps-lords-and-offices/mps/;
- registers of interests;
- for select committees in both Houses, and joint committees: committee home pages with membership, terms of reference and contact details; press notices; text of reports, all oral and much written evidence (from the session 1997–98 onwards); a guide for witnesses; and weekly bulletins of forthcoming meetings;
- explanatory notes and factsheets on many aspects of the work of Parliament; films about how Parliament works and images from the Palace of Westminster;
- Commons Library research papers on matters of current interest by topic or searchable, together with research notes and longer papers produced by the Parliamentary Office of Science and Technology;
- information about the records stored by Parliament in the Parliamentary Archives;
- current job opportunities in Parliament.

Both Houses have twitter accounts (@UKParliament, @HouseofCommons, @UK HouseofLords) and there are also accounts for individual committees and the Libraries.

You can find passed legislation on legislation.gov.uk, including all passed legislation since 1988 and increasing amounts of pre-1988 legislation (also available at www. parliament.uk).

You can watch proceedings on www.parliamentlive.tv, which gives access to webcast proceedings of both Houses, Westminster Hall, and select committees taking evidence in public, together with a searchable archive.

Parliamentary Outreach (www.parliament.uk/get-involved/outreach-and-training/) provides opportunities for the public to engage with and learn about Parliament, including through free training for individuals and groups. They also manage the Universities Programme, including the Parliamentary Studies module which was taught at thirteen universities in 2013/14.

The Education Service have a wealth of material on their part of the website (www.parliament.uk/education/) which is searchable by key stages/A Level. It has also has details of training opportunities for teachers and education outreach visits.

The government publishes information about Parliament and future business on the website of the Leader of the House of Commons (www.gov.uk/government/organisations/the-office-of-the-leader-of-the-house-of-commons) and the Lords Government Whips' Office (www.lordswhips.org.uk/).

Other parliamentary and political websites

Democracy Live: www.bbc.co.uk/democracylive/ which carries live and recorded clips from both Houses, as well as committees, devolved Parliaments and Assemblies, and the European Parliament.

Details of EU-related legislation and papers are available from the EU website (http://europa.eu/publications/official-documents/index_en.htm) while UK Government Explanatory Memoranda, as well as ministerial letters to Parliament, are available from the Cabinet Office (http://europeanmemoranda.cabinetoffice.gov.uk/). 'Votewatch', is an excellent source of information about how EU legislative decisions are made (www.votewatch.eu/).

The Electoral Commission (www.electoralcommission.org.uk) provides information on the regulation of voting, elections, and political donations.

IPSA – The Independent Parliamentary Standards Authority (http://parliamentarystandards.org.uk/) regulates the pay of MPs; details of claims are published on their website.

www.theyworkforyou.com and www.publicwhip.org.uk are the sites of pressure groups seeking to show constituents MPs' voting records, attitudes to issues, rebelliousness, speed of response to constituents' letters and activity levels. But beware of crude rankings of numbers of questions tabled, speeches made, and so on. Activity is not achievement, and some of the statistics are flawed. For example, www.theyworkforyou.com counts a single sentence asking another member to give way in a debate as a speech!

www.w4mp.org is a site designed for all those working for an MP, including guides for MP's staff, but its material is of general interest, too. It also carries advertisements for jobs as MPs' assistants and researchers.

The Hansard Society (www.hansardsociety.org.uk) describes its mission as 'promoting democracy – strengthening Parliament'. It seeks to explain Parliament and increase involvement in parliamentary politics, and researches and publishes on a wide range of issues, as well as organising a range of lectures, seminars and other events. It also publishes the *Audit of Political Engagement* (www.hansardsociety.org.uk/research/ public-attitudes/audit-of-political-engagement/) which is an annual survey of political engagement with, and views on, the political system.

The Constitution Unit, based in the Department of Political Science at University College London (www.ucl.ac.uk/constitution-unit), is an authoritative academic group that publishes briefings on topical constitutional and political issues, organises seminars and other events, and publishes a regular and very useful newsletter.

The respected Centre for Legislative Studies at Hull University (www.hull.ac.uk/ cls/) provides a great deal of useful information and links, ranging much more widely than legislation.

www.revolts.co.uk is the website of Philip Cowley, an academic who has made the subject of political revolts and parliamentary voting patterns his own. Essential for anyone researching this subject.

There are growing numbers of blogs on politics and parliament, including journalists such as BBC reporters, MPs, political commentators and activists, as well as those related to academia and think tanks. Many of the blogs are also linked to Twitter accounts and other social media.

Television

In addition to normal news coverage, and live broadcasts of Prime Minister's Questions and some other occasions on various channels, BBC Parliament provides a dedicated channel, with real-time coverage of the Commons and 'time-shifted' coverage of the Lords and select committees.

Visiting Parliament

To see proceedings

Both Houses have public galleries, and it is often possible, especially later in the day, to get a seat just by turning up. However, this is difficult on particularly newsworthy occasions (and, in the Commons, for Question Time, and especially Prime Minister's Questions). Then, a public queue forms at the entrance near St Stephen's; but it may not be possible to get in until ticket-holders have left.

To get a ticket for the Gallery of the House of Commons, UK residents should write to their MP (www.parliament.uk/mps-lords-and-offices/mps/find-your-mp). Members have only a small allocation of tickets, so it is a good idea to write well in advance. Overseas visitors should write to their Embassy or High Commission.

It is also possible to attend public sittings of public bill committees, select committees in both Houses (see Chapter 10), and debates in the 'parallel Chamber' in Westminster Hall. You should go to the Central Lobby and seek directions from the reception desk there. Many of the high-profile Commons committee meetings take place in neighbouring Portcullis House which also provides public access to Committee Rooms, so if you want to see a specific committee check the location in advance. It is not possible to reserve seats, and high-profile select committee hearings may be crowded. But if you can get in, some select committee hearings can offer the best theatre in London!

To tour Parliament

People who are resident in the UK should contact their local MP (www.parliament. uk/mps-lords-and-offices/mps/find-your-mp/) or a peer they know. At times when both Houses are sitting, tours are available on Mondays, Tuesdays, Wednesdays and Fridays (on Fridays, all day if the Commons and Lords are not sitting, late afternoon if they are). Timing and access to the Chambers is limited on a Tuesday and Wednesday. Tours are normally conducted in English and are free when booked this way but you generally need to book around six months in advance. Further information is available under 'visiting parliament' on the website.

During recesses, UK residents can continue to arrange tours through their MP, or through a peer they know. During recesses, these tours are generally only available on Fridays. At other times during recess periods, the Palace also arranges guided or audio-guided tours at a charge; this is particularly aimed at overseas visitors (who cannot normally arrange a tour on sitting days) but anyone may book tickets. Tours are available in English and other languages. Details are available through www. parliament.uk/visiting/visiting-and-tours/tours-of-parliament/. Tours are also available of the Elizabeth Tower and Big Ben (for UK residents, via their MP), as well as specialised tours on art and architecture for which there is a charge.

Schools visits

Schools and other educational institutions based in this country may contact their MP to arrange a tour. However, an education programme runs for UK schools covering children aged seven to eighteen which includes a tour of the building. A transport subsidy is also available for schools outside the south-east. Tours are released in term blocks three days each year and slots book up extremely quickly. Over the coming year, Parliament hopes to expand its educational facilities so that many more children can visit. Further information is available from the Education section of the website: www.parliament.uk/education/visit-parliament-with-your-school/palace-of-westminster-tour/

Other useful contact details

Palace of Westminster switchboard: 020 7219 3000.

House of Commons Information Office: House of Commons, London SW1A 2TT; telephone 020 7219 4272; text phone 18001 then 020 7219 4272; hcinfo @parliament.uk; twitter @HouseofCommons

House of Lords Information Office: House of Lords, London SW1A 0PW; telephone 020 7219 3107; text phone 18001 then 7219 3107; hlinfo@parliament.uk; twitter @UKHouseofLords

Parliamentary Archives: London SW1A 0PW; telephone 020 7219 3074; fax 020 7219 2570; archives@parliament.uk

House of Commons and House of Lords Committees: information about forthcoming committee meetings and current inquiries in both Houses can be found on the Parliament website at www.parliament.uk/business/committees

Parliamentary Bookshop (for books, Parliamentary documents and other items): 12 Bridge Street, Parliament Square, London SW1A 2JX; inquiries and telephone orders 020 7219 3890; fax orders 020 7219 3866; or visit the online shop: www.shop.parliament.uk/

TSO: (mail, telephone and fax orders) PO Box 29, Norwich NR3 1GN; general inquiries 0870 600 5522; fax orders 0870 600 5533; online www.tsoshop.co.uk

Devolved parliament and assemblies

Northern Ireland Assembly: Parliament Buildings, Stormont, Belfast BT4 3XX; telephone 028 90 521137; text phone 028 90 521209; website: www.niassembly. gov.uk

Scottish Parliament: Edinburgh EH99 1SP; telephone 0131 348 5000; website: www.scottish.parliament.uk

National Assembly for Wales: Cardiff Bay, Cardiff CF99 1NA; telephone 0845 010 5500; website: www.assemblywales.org.uk

The European Union

European Commission: 1049 Brussels, Belgium; telephone 00 322 299 1111; website www.ec.europa.eu The Commission's Office in the UK: Europe House, 32 Smith Square, London SW1P 3EU; telephone 020 7973 1992; website: www.ec.europa. eu/unitedkingdom (other offices in Scotland, Wales and Northern Ireland).

European Parliament: rue Wiertz, 1047 Brussels, Belgium; telephone 00 322 284 2111; website www.europarl.europa.eu. The European Parliament's Office in the UK: Europe House, 32 Smith Square, London SW1P 3EU; telephone 020 7227 4300; website: www.europarl.org.uk

Political parties

Conservative Party: 4 Matthew Parker Street, London SW1H 9HQ; telephone 020 7222 9000; website: www.conservatives.com

Democratic Unionist Party: 91 Dundela Avenue, Belfast BT4 3BU; telephone 028 90 471155; website: www.mydup.com

Green Party: Development House, 56–64 Leonard Street, London EC2A 4LT; telephone 020 7549 0310; website: www.greenparty.org.uk

Labour Party: Labour Central, Kings Manor, Newcastle upon Tyne NE1 6PA; telephone 0845 092 2299; website: www.labour.org.uk

Liberal Democrats: 8–10 Great George Street, London SW1P 3AE; telephone 020 7222 7999; website: www.libdems.org.uk

Plaid Cymru: 18 Park Grove, Cardiff CF10 3BN; telephone 029 20 646000; website: www.partyofwales.org.uk

Scottish National Party: Gordon Lamb House, 3 Jackson's Entry, Edinburgh EH8 8PJ; telephone 0800 633 5432; website: www.snp.org.uk

Sinn Féin: 44 Parnell Square, Dublin 1; telephone 00 3531 872 6932; website: www.sinnfein.ie

Social Democratic and Labour Party: 121 Ormeau Road, Belfast BT7 1SH; telephone 028 90 247700; website: www.sdlp.ie

Ulster Unionist Party: Strandtown Hall, 2–4 Belmont Road, Belfast BT4 2AN; telephone 028 90 474630; website: www.uup.org.uk

UK Independence Party, UKIP, Lexdrum House, King Charles Business Park, Newton Abbot, Devon, TQ12 6UT; telephone 01626 831290; website: www.ukip.org.uk

Index